Classical Studies

Recent titles in the
Reference Sources in the Humanity Series

American Popular Culture: A Guide to the Reference Literature
Frank W. Hoffman

Philosophy: A Guide to the Reference Literature, Second Edition
Hans E. Bynagle

Journalism: A Guide to the Reference Literature, Second Edition
Jo A. Cates

Children's Literature: A Guide to Information Sources
Margaret W. Denman-West

Reference Works in British and American Literature, Second Edition
James A. Bracken

Reference Guide to Mystery and Detective Fiction
Richard Bleiler

Linguistics: A Guide to the Reference Literature, Second Edition
Anna L. DeMiller

Reference Guide to Science Fiction, Fantasy, and Horror, Second Edition
Michael Burgess and Lisa R. Bartle

Reference and Research Guide to Mystery and Detective Fiction, Second Edition
Richard Bleiler

Journalism: A Guide to the Reference Literature, Third Edition
Jo A. Cates

Film and Television: A Guide to the Reference Literature
Mark Emmons

Classical Studies

A Guide to the Reference Literature
Second Edition

Fred W. Jenkins

Reference Sources in the Humanities
James Rettig, Series Editor

A Member of the Greenwood Publishing Group

Westport, Connecticut • London

Library of Congress Cataloging-in-Publication Data

Jenkins, Fred W.
  Classical studies : a guide to the reference literature / Fred W. Jenkins.— 2nd ed.
    p.   cm. — (Reference sources in the humanities)
  Includes bibliographical references and indexes.
  ISBN 1–59158–119–2
  1. Classical philology—Bibliography.   2. Civilization, Classical—Bibliography.   I. Title.
II. Series: Reference sources in the humanities series.
  Z7016.J4 2006
  [PA91]
  016.48—dc22   2006004705

British Library Cataloguing in Publication Data is available.

Library of Congress Catalog Card Number: 2006004705
ISBN: 1–59158–119–2

First published in 2006

Libraries Unlimited, 88 Post Road West, Westport, CT 06881
A Member of the Greenwood Publishing Group, Inc.
www.lu.com

Printed in the United States of America

The paper used in this book complies with the
Permanent Paper Standard issued by the National
Information Standards Organization (Z39.48–1984).

10   9   8   7   6   5   4   3   2   1

Uxori carissimae
et
in memoriam Caroli Ricardii Trahman et Giraldi Michaelis Browne

Contents

Preface

This book is a guide to the reference literature of classical studies. It focuses on bibliographical and information resources, not on general scholarship in the field. While other works offer introductory surveys of modern classical scholarship (see, for example, entries 15, 16, 26–27), no other English-language work is devoted exclusively to general and specialized reference sources for classics. In general, I have attempted to include the best and most up-to-date reference materials for the study of the Greek and Roman civilization from the Bronze Age through the sixth century A.D. These include works on art and archaeology, history, language and literature, and philosophy. In addition, readers will find a number of works on the history of classical scholarship and on the *Nachleben* (later influence) of the classics. Ancient Near Eastern studies, patristics, Medieval Latin, Neo-Latin, and Byzantine studies receive attention only insofar as they relate to classical studies proper.[1] Because of the relatively early professionalization of classical studies and their international character, this volume contains a larger number of older and foreign-language works than do most in this series. While giving preference to English-language works whenever possible, I have included many important titles in French, German, Italian, and Spanish. Coverage is reasonably complete through the end of 2004; a few works published in 2005 are also noted.

Following the basic principles of the series, I have listed only book-length works in this guide; works appearing in periodicals are generally ignored. A few categories of material, such as catalogs of manuscripts and incunabula and bibliographies of the works of individual classical scholars, have been, for the most part, excluded. Electronic publications, which are of growing importance in classical studies, are fully treated in these pages. A number of Web sites, databases, and electronic journals are noted in the appropriate chapters. These have largely been integrated into the various chapters, although metasites and e-mail discussion lists remain in a separate chapter on Internet resources.

Those familiar with the first edition will find a number of changes. Classical scholarship tends to be agglutinative, so relatively few works have been dropped. An exception is library catalogs (chapter 6 in the first edition): library holdings are now readily available on the Web, either individually or in aggregate (through Worldcat). I have moved from an organizational scheme based primarily on format to one that is more subject oriented. Coverage of individual classical authors has been expanded, with the resulting chapters (15 and 16) modeled on James Bracken's *Reference Works in British and American Literature* (2nd ed., Englewood, CO: Libraries Unlimited, 1998). I have also significantly increased coverage of ancient philosophy, religion (including early Christianity), and art and archaeology. Late antiquity, a major growth area in classical studies, has also received more attention.

In listing individual works, I have normally cited the most complete or best edition in its original printing; the most recent reprint edition, when one exists, is also noted. As for works that appeared simultaneously under multiple imprints, I have usually preferred the American one. Citations are based on the title pages of the works (or its nearest equivalent for electronic publications); I have eschewed mindless consistency in presenting these. However, in the index, authors' names are regularized under the most commonly used form. The annotation accompanying each entry describes the work and frequently offers some evaluation or comparison to similar works. Related works are fully cross-referenced.

Many have contributed to the completion of this work. I should first like to thank James Rettig, my editor, both for offering the opportunity to write the first edition and for his continuing support for the second.

I am grateful for much support and encouragement from my institution and colleagues. The University of Dayton provided release time and other assistance. Many colleagues at Dayton offered help and encouragement; I would particularly like to mention Heidi Gauder for discussing organizational issues relating to the second edition. Thanks are also due to the circulation, document-delivery, and interlibrary loan staff for their many efforts on my behalf, especially Dianne Hoops, Robert Leach, and Robyn Reed.

Many friends and colleagues at other universities also contributed much. Jean Wellington and Michael Braunlin of the University of Cincinnati Burnham Classics Library supplied invaluable assistance in tracking down and obtaining various works through both editions. Michael generously gave me the benefit of his extensive knowledge of ancient numismatics. Gail Hueting (University of Illinois) and Thomas Izbicki (Johns Hopkins University) read chapters and provided references for the first edition. Reviewers of the first edition suggested several improvements; I especially note Paul Naiditch (UCLA), who also discussed aspects of the second edition with me during its early stages. W. Gerald Heverly (New York University) and Linda Jones Hall (St. Mary's College of Maryland) each reviewed numerous chapters of the second edition and provided much good advice.

The Academic Library Association of Ohio awarded me its 1993 Research Award in support of the first edition. I am also grateful to the many libraries whose resources I have used for both editions. The services and resources of OhioLINK have been invaluable, making it possible to do at home much work that previously required extensive travel.

In closing, I thank my wife, Lin Seagren Jenkins, who not only patiently endured the composition of this work but also read the entire manuscript. She has saved my readers from many infelicities of style and lapses of clarity. Needless to say, all remaining defects of this book are due solely to the author, who is, among other faults, stubborn.

NOTE

1. A number of introductory works and guides to the literature are already available for these related fields, although some are in need of updating. Those interested in patristics might consult Berthold Altaner, *Patrology* (New York: Herder, 1961) or Johannes Quasten, *Patrology* (Utrecht, Holland: Spectrum, 1950–1960). For Medieval Latin, see F.A.C. Mantello and A.G. Rigg, *Medieval Latin: An Introduction and Bibliographical Guide* (Washington, DC: Catholic University of America Press, 1996), an indispenable work; broader treatments of medieval studies include James M. Powell, *Medieval Studies: An Introduction* (2nd ed., Syracuse, NY: Syracuse University Press, 1992) and Everett U. Crosby, *Medieval Studies: A Bibliographical Guide* (New York: Garland, 1983). Jozef Ijsewijn's *Companion to Neo-Latin Studies* (1st ed., Amsterdam: North-Holland, 1977; 2nd ed., Louvain: Louven University Press, 1990–1998) covers Latin after the Middle Ages. Unfortunately, there are no general guides or bibliographies for ancient Near Eastern studies or Byzantine studies. However, those with an interest in Byzantine Greek will find Robert Browning's *Medieval and Modern Greek* (London: Hutchinson, 1969) a useful volume.

1
General Bibliographical Resources

This chapter includes guides to study and research, general bibliographies, and bibliographies of two special categories of works: dissertations and translations of the classics. A final section includes compilations of standard abbreviations for classical journals and other works. These works cover classical studies as whole or a major department of it, such as Greek or Roman studies or ancient history. Some of them are reasonably current works, which will serve the needs of both students and scholars. Others are antiquarian works that will chiefly interest bibliographers and historians of scholarship. Coverage of English-language works is relatively complete, while those in other languages are treated more selectively. These self-contained works tend to focus on books, although many include citations of journal articles as well. Their contents can be updated with the aid of the indexes and review journals found in chapters 2 and 3. More-specialized bibliographies may be found in the subject specific chapters.

Students and others seeking an overview of research in classics would do well to begin with the works of Graf (entry 3) for Roman studies and Nesselrath (entry 8) for Greek; those seeking an overview of the literature of classical studies as a whole should consult the works of Poucet and Hannick (entries 26–27), with Halton and O'Leary (entry 16) as a weak second choice. The skeleton outline of standard classical bibliographies in chronological order is: Fabricius (entries 13–14) for pre-eighteenth-century scholarship, Schweiger (entry 29) for late seventeenth- and early eighteenth-century works, Engelmann (entry 12) for 1700–1878, Klussmann (entry 19) for 1878–1896, Lambrino (entry 20) for 1896–1914, and Marouzeau (entry 21) for 1914–1924. The annual volumes of *L'Année philologique* (entry 44) then pick up the thread and provide coverage to the present. While these are the most complete single sources for their periods, none is totally complete and some are more reliable than others. Anyone seeking exhaustive coverage will need to consult the numerous supplementary and specialized bibliographies found throughout this volume.

RESEARCH GUIDES

1.   Bengtson, Hermann. **Introduction to Ancient History.** Translated from the 6th ed. by R.I. Frank and Frank D. Gilliard. Berkeley and Los Angeles: University of California Press, 1970; repr., 1975. 213pp. ISBN 0–520–01723–4. LCCN 78–118685.

This is a translation of *Einführung in die Alte Geschichte* (now in its 8th German edition), the standard introductory work on the subject for German university students. The translators have adapted the work to meet the needs of the English-reading student. In particular, they have revised the general bibliography to include more English-language works. Bengtson discusses the scope of ancient history and briefly outlines the history of the study of antiquity from the Renaissance to the present. He then covers such basics as chronology, geography, anthropology, source materials, archaeology, and subdisciplines of ancient history (epigraphy, papyrology, and numismatics). Each section consists of a short introduction to the topic followed by a bibliographical essay. A final chapter covers reference works and periodicals. A general bibliography (without annotations) follows. Name and subject indexes conclude the work. Although now two decades old, Bengtson is still useful. The only comparable work is Petit's *Guide de l'étudiant en histoire ancienne* (entry 9), which is itself based on earlier editions of Bengtson. Hopwood (entry 18) provides more up-to-date and comprehensive bibliographies.

2.   Defradas, Jean. **Guide de l'étudiant helléniste.** Paris: Presses Universitaires de France, 1968. 156pp. LCCN 75–371371.

A guide for French students of Greek language and literature, this work begins with some discussion of the role and nature of Greek studies in French colleges and universities. An extensive bibliographical survey follows. Defradas first covers research methods and key general works on Greek language, literature, and culture. He then lists the major Greek authors in chronological sequence, with references to important editions and secondary works. Finally, he discusses several ancillary disciplines: palaeography and textual criticism, papyrology, epigraphy, and archaeology. For each he provides an overview of the field and a very selective bibliography. Defradas comments, sometimes extensively, on most of the works cited. There is the expected bias in favor of French-language titles, although many German and English works also appear. Indexes cover subjects, ancient authors, and modern authors. This work is a companion volume to those of Grimal on Latin studies (entry 4) and Petit on ancient history (entry 9).

3.   Graf, Fritz, ed. **Einleitung in die lateinische Philologie.** Einleitung in die Altertumswissenschaft. Stuttgart: Teubner, 1997. 725pp. ISBN 3–519–07434–6. LCCN 97–173619.

This work and its companion volume on Greek philology (entry 8) replace the famous *Einleitung in die Altertumswissenschaft* by Alfred Gercke and Eduard Norden (4. Aufl., Leipzig: Teubner, 1930–1933). Graf has assembled a distinguished team of specialists, mostly German, but with a sprinkling of English, American, and Italian scholars. The contents range much more widely than the title suggests. Nine chapters cover the history of Latin scholarship, the history of Latin texts, the Latin language, Latin literature, Roman history, Roman law, Roman religion, Roman philosophy, and Roman art and archaeology. Many of these are further subdivided by topic or period. For example, the chapter on Latin texts includes sections on textual criticism, palaeography, and epigraphy; that on Latin literature has sections on the republic, the Augustan Age, the empire, the Middle Ages, and Neo-Latin. Each chapter or section gives a narrative overview of its topic, along with brief bibliographies of key works. The well-chosen bibliographies include a mix of classic works and recent scholarship; the contributors have a tendency to cite their own works rather heavily, although the quality of these makes this a forgivable vice. An index of passages cited and a very detailed index of names and subjects facilitate access to this massive volume. Readers also should not miss the pocket inside the back cover that holds a map of ancient Italy and a "Synopse der römischen Literatur." The *Synopse* is a chart listing major Latin authors in chronological sequence and setting them in their broad historical context. Graf provides an excellent resource for anyone seeking an overview and working bibliography for a particular field of Roman studies.

4. Grimal, Pierre. **Guide de l'étudiant latiniste.** Paris: Presses Universitaires de France, 1971. 319pp. LCCN 71–576893.

Written by a distinguished Latinist, this work is intended as a guide for French university students. The first part provides a complete survey of Latin studies in France (ca. 1970), including a discussion of content, approaches, and methods at each level of formal education, and an overview of ancillary and related disciplines, such as numismatics, archaeology, and palaeography. The second part is a bibliographical guide. Its chapters successively cover fundamental reference works, studies of the language, Latin authors (editions and selected secondary works), and Roman history and civilization. Grimal presents the bibliographical chapters in the form of review essays. He provides critical commentary on nearly all the works mentioned. Although geared toward the French reader, Grimal includes many works in English and German. Indexes cover ancient authors, historical persons, subjects, and modern authors. Companion volumes by Defradas (entry 2) and Petit (entry 9) cover Greek studies and ancient history respectively.

5. **Introduzione allo studio della cultura classica.** Milano: Mazorati Editore, 1989–1990. 3v.

This Italian introduction to classical studies consists of many short review essays by individual scholars; the latest edition is essentially an unaltered reprint of the 1977–1982 edition. The volumes treat successively literature, linguistics and philology, and "subsidiary sciences." Coverage of literature is broken down by period, genre, and (less consistently) language. Some attention is given to Byzantine Greek and Medieval Latin literature. The second volume is devoted mainly to traditional philological topics such as grammar, metrics, and textual criticism. The subsidiary sciences of volume 3 include archaeology, numismatics, geography, papyrology, linguistics, and so on. The organization of material is odd; for example, mythology and philosophy are placed in the linguistics and philology volume. While the quality of the essays varies, most provide a serviceable introduction and a good, though now dated, working bibliography for their topics. Indexes to subjects and modern authors appear at the end of the third volume.

6. Irmscher, Johannes, ed. **Einleitung in die klassischen Altertumswissenschaften: Ein Informationsbuch.** Berlin: VEB Deutscher Verlag der Wissenschaften, 1986. 356pp. ISBN 3–326–0005–7.

Designed to meet the needs of East German university students, this work offers a collection of brief introductory sketches on various aspects of classical studies. Most of the topics are predictable (e.g., classical archaeology, lexicography, numismatics), but some, such as Assyriology and classical studies, might not be expected in an introductory survey. There is a strong emphasis on ethnography and comparative studies throughout. Each essay defines its topic, reviews the state of studies (ca. 1980), and provides a short bibliography. Although there are occasional intrusions of Marxist interpretation—which are to be expected of a work published in the former German Democratic Republic—this remains a handy work for readers of German.

7. McGuire, Martin R. P. **Introduction to Classical Scholarship: A Syllabus and Bibliographical Guide.** New and rev. ed. Washington, DC: Catholic University of America, 1961. 257pp. LCCN 61–66521.

Designed for beginning graduate students, McGuire's work takes the form of a syllabus for an introductory course in research methods and bibliography. Its arrangement is topical. Each section provides an overview of a particular area of classical studies and includes a bibliography. The final section is a general bibliography of ancient history and Greek and Latin authors (including early Christian history and literature) arranged by subject and genre. There is an index of modern scholars. The bibliographical portions have been superseded by Halton and O'Leary, *Classical Scholarship* (entry 16).

8.   Nesselrath, Heinz-Günther, ed. **Einleitung in die griechische Philologie.** Einleitung in die Altertumswissenschaft. Stuttgart: Teubner, 1997. 773pp. ISBN 3-519-07435-4. LCCN 98-130741.

This companion volume to Graf's *Einleitung in die lateinische Philologie* (entry 3) supersedes the Greek portions of the famous *Einleitung in die Altertumswissenschaft* by Alfred Gercke and Eduard Norden (4. Aufl., Leipzig: Teubner, 1930-1933). Although the title specifies only philology, the work covers all aspects of the study of ancient Greece and its culture. Eight chapters cover the history of texts, history of scholarship, the Greek language (Mycenaean through Byzantine), Greek literature from Homer through the Byzantine era, Greek history from the Archaic period through late antiquity, Greek religion, Greek philosophy and science, and Greek art. Most chapters are subdivided by topic or period, with each section written by a leading specialist; German scholars predominate, although there is a significant British contingent among the contributors. Each section gives an overview of its topic, with a strong emphasis on the basic facts, and provides a basic working bibliography. Sections on palaeography and Greek art include good-quality black-and-white illustrations. An extensive and detailed index of names and subjects completes the volume. Readers should also not miss the maps and "Synopse der griechischen Literatur," which are located in a pocket inside the back cover. The *Synopse* is a large foldout chart that lists Greek authors chronologically from Homer (the *Iliad*) to Agathias and sets them in their historical contexts. Nesselrath and his collaborators have provided an outstanding resource for students of ancient and medieval Greek literature and culture. The inclusion of the Byzantine era in sections dealing with language and literature is a noteworthy strength. Anyone seeking an orientation to a particular aspect of Hellenic studies is well advised to consult this volume. There is no comparable work in English or French.

9.   Petit, Paul. **Guide de l'étudiant en histoire ancienne.** 3ième éd. Paris: Presses Universitaires de France, 1969. 239pp. LCCN 78-481208.

Petit seeks to provide a guide to the study of ancient history for the French university student. He uses Bengtson (entry 1) as his model. The format of the two works is much the same. Bengtson is somewhat stronger in his coverage of technical aspects of the subject (e.g., chronology) and at least as good, if not better, in other areas as well. English-speaking students will, no doubt, prefer the translation of Bengtson. Thus, Petit is chiefly of use to those interested in a French approach to the subject.

10.   Van Keuren, Frances. **Guide to Research in Classical Art and Mythology.** Chicago: American Library Association, 1991. 307pp. ISBN 0-8389-0564-1. LCCN91-11122.

Van Keuren's work is a guide to library research in classical art and architecture. Mythology is treated primarily as it relates to art, although some attention also is devoted to mythology in literature. The book is divided into three parts. The first part covers general works on Greek, Etruscan, and Roman art in successive chapters. The second part surveys works on mythology in both ancient and later art and literature. The third surveys particular media (e.g., Greek sculpture, Etruscan mirrors, Roman Republican coins) in a series of topical chapters. Van Keuren aims to provide a step-by-step guide to doing research in the field. Each chapter begins with a detailed discussion of a single major reference work on the topic in question. This is followed by a section of "complementary references," which includes brief descriptions of a number of related general and reference works. A third section discusses handbooks on the subject. The final section of each chapter, "supplementary sources," describes a wide range of monographs dealing with more specialized aspects of the subject. The reader is expected to work through each chapter in a linear fashion, although good author-title and subject indexes provide help to the less systematic user. This is an excellent tool for learning and teaching research methods in classical art and archaeology. It also provides a valuable overview of the structure of the literature in the field. Van Keuren's work should not, however, be regarded as a complete bibliographical guide to the field, since she is quite selective and omits a number of significant works.

GENERAL BIBLIOGRAPHIES

11.   Dibdin, Thomas Frognall. **Introduction to the Knowledge of Rare and Valuable Editions of the Greek and Latin Classics. Together with an Account of Polyglot Bibles, Polyglot Psalters, Hebrew Bibles, Greek Bibles and Greek Testaments, the Greek Fathers, and the Latin Fathers.** 4th ed. London: Harding and Lepard, 1827; repr., Hildesheim: Georg Olms, 1977. 2v. LCCN 03–25381.

Itself something of a classic, Dibdin's work is well known to antiquarian book dealers and collectors. Dibdin is primarily useful to those working with early printed editions of the classics, especially bibliographers and historians of scholarship. Bibles appear first and are listed by date of printing. Editions of the Greek fathers, and then the Latin, follow. These are arranged by the author's dates. Finally Dibdin treats the Greek and Latin classics. This section, by far the largest, is arranged alphabetically by author. Dibdin covers nearly all the important early editions, from the beginning of printing to around 1820. His extensive annotations include much information on the editors and printers. He often discusses the history of a particular edition and its relation to earlier and contemporary editions. Dibdin also devotes much space to the aesthetic aspects of the books, such as paper and typography.

12.   Engelmann, Wilhelm, ed. **Bibliotheca Scriptorum Classicorum.** 8. Aufl., umfassend die Literatur von 1700 bis 1878, neu bearb. von E. Preuss. Leipzig: Wilhelm Engelmann, 1880–1882; repr., Hildesheim: Georg Olms, 1959. 2v. LCCN 01–16689.

Engelmann continues the work of Fabricius (entries 13–14) and Schweiger (entry 29). His first volume covers Greek literature, the second Latin. Each is divided into two sections: collected editions (by genre) and individual authors (alphabetically). There are a few cross-references for variant forms; no index is provided. Coverage is mainly philological. The *Bibliotheca* lists editions, translations, commentaries, and critical literature (monographs and articles). Editions and translations far outnumber critical works. Occasionally a brief annotation or contents note accompanies an entry, but these are rare. Although not very satisfactory in either scope or organization, Engelmann remains the primary bibliographical resource for eighteenth- and nineteenth-century classical scholarship. Users should not neglect the additions and corrections at the end of each volume (v. 2 contains additions for both volumes). The *Bibliotheca* is continued by Klussmann (entry 19).

13. Fabricius, Johann Albert. **Ioannis Alberti Fabricii ... Bibliotheca Graeca, sive, Notitia Scriptorum Veterum Graecorum Quorumcumque Monumenta Integra aut Fragmenta Edita Exstant tum Plerorumque e Mss. ac Deperditis ab Auctore Tertium Recognita et Plurimis Locis Aucta.** Editio Quarta variorum curis emendatior atque auctior curante Gottlieb Christophoro Harles; accedunt b. I. A. Fabricii et Christoph. Augusti Heumanni supplementa inedita. Hamburgi: Apud Carolum Ernestum Bohn, 1790–1809; repr., Hildesheim: Georg Olms, 1966–1970. 12v. LCCN 02–6671.

Bibliotheca Graeca has appeared in numerous editions and printings, of which this is the most complete. Most others are serviceable as well. Fabricius's work is part handbook or history of Greek literature and part bibliography. He provides extensive references to ancient literature, early editions of Greek authors, and scholarly works on Greek literature. Fabricius proceeds in roughly chronological order from the beginnings of Greek literature to the fall of Constantinople (A.D. 1453); chapters cover authors or (occasionally) genres. Thus it is necessary to know the approximate date of an author to locate the relevant discussion. Users should also bear in mind that the dating of some authors has changed since the time of Fabricius. There is an index of authors, although the choice of entry and various inaccuracies will sometimes challenge users. While somewhat difficult to consult, the *Bibliotheca* remains a valuable source for early work on the classics. It is particularly useful for those working on later Greek authors.

14. Fabricius, Johann Albert. **Jo. Alberti Fabricii Bibliotheca Latina, sive, Notitia Auctorum Veterum Latinorum, Quorumcumque Scripta ad Nos Pervenerunt, Distributa in Libros IV. Supplementis, Quae Antea Sejunctim Excusa Maximo Lectorum Incommodo Legebantur, Suis Quibusque Locis nunc Primum Insertis.** Venetiis: Apud Sebastium Coleti, 1728. 2v.

Fabricius completed the *Bibliotheca Latina,* which is available in several editions, in 1697. It is a much less ambitious and valuable work than his later *Bibliotheca Graeca* (entry 13). It consists of a chronological listing of Latin authors that is divided into three groupings: the Golden Age (late republic and Augustan Age), the Silver Age (Tiberius through the Antonines), and Bronze/Iron Age (through late antiquity). Fabricius provides a brief biographical note on each author, followed by a list of works with citations of their various editions. A final section covers fragmentary and collected works: early Latin authors; inscriptions; and legal, medical, and technical writers. There is no proper index, although a list of contents appears at the end of the work. The *Bibliotheca Latina* can be helpful to those working with early editions of the Latin authors. Otherwise, it is primarily of antiquarian interest.

15. Gullath, Brigitte, and Frank Heidtmann. **Wie finde ich altertumswissenschaftliche Literatur: Klassische Philologie, Mittel- und Neulatein, Byzantinistik, alte Geschichte und klassische Archäologie.** Orientierungshilfen 23. Berlin: Arno Spitz, 1992. 346pp. ISBN 3–87061–207–X. LCCN 97–106893.

This guide to research covers not only classical studies, but also Medieval Latin, Neo-Latin, and Byzantine studies. The first chapter provides a brief introduction to libraries and bibliographical research from a German perspective; the tenth comprises a glossary of bibliographical terms. The eight chapters in between cover a wide range of reference and general works in all the standard languages of scholarship. Each deals with a broad area: general works on classical studies, classical philology, Medieval Latin and Neo-Latin, Byzantine studies and modern Greek philology, ancient history, classical archaeology, related fields (chiefly Near Eastern studies), and important periodicals. These chapters are extensively subdivided by form (e.g., handbooks, bibliographies). The 1,323 entries, which include articles as well as books, provide an effective general guide to the reference literature and bibliographical apparatus of classical studies and related fields. Coverage of related fields is not always as strong as for classics; the ancient Near East receives particularly cursory coverage. Many entries receive short descriptive annotations. A good general index concludes the work. This work and those of Poucet and Hannick in French (entries 26–27) are the best general bibliographical guides to research in classical studies.

16.   Halton, Thomas P., and Stella O'Leary. **Classical Scholarship: An Annotated Bibliography.** White Plains, NY: Kraus International Publications, 1986. 396pp. ISBN 0–527–37436–9; 0–527–37437–7pa. LCCN 82–48984.

Although originally intended as an update to Martin R. P. McGuire's *Introduction to Classical Scholarship* (entry 7), this book differs substantially from its predecessor. It is strictly a bibliography, covering both reference works and (very selectively) the monographic literature. Most entries include annotations that are generally useful, although content and quality vary greatly. Entries for monographs include references to scholarly reviews. The work is arranged into fifteen major subject chapters, each of which is further subdivided as appropriate. There are author and subject indexes. Few items published after 1980 are included. As a guide to classical scholarship, this work is aimed primarily at advanced undergraduate and graduate students in the field. It is helpful for those seeking a quick orientation to the literature on a specific author or subdiscipline of classical studies as it stood 25 years ago. Readers who want an orientation to the field as a whole (and are able to read French or German) will be served better by Poucet and Hannick (entries 26–27) or Gullath and Heidtmann (entry 15). Poucet and Hannick in particular offer a well-structured guide to the literature of classical studies.

17.   Hoffmann, S.F.W. **Bibliographisches Lexicon der gesammten Literatur der Griechen.** 2. ungearb., durchaus verm., verb., und fortgesetzte Ausgabe. Leipzig: A. F. Böhme, 1838–1845; repr., Amsterdam: A. M. Hakkert, 1961. 3v. LCCN 5–16151.

Primarily of interest to antiquarians and historians of scholarship, Hoffmann provides a bibliographical guide to early work on Greek literature. He covers ancient Greek authors in alphabetical sequence. Under each, Hoffmann lists editions and translations (from the first printed edition), as well as scholarly studies (chiefly from the eighteenth and nineteenth centuries, occasionally as far back as the sixteenth). There are few annotations, and these only remark briefly on the contents or attribution of a work. Hoffman provides a more comprehensive bibliography for Greek studies in the early modern period than either Moss (entry 22) or Dibdin (entry 11) but is much less entertaining to read.

18.   Hopwood, Keith. **Ancient Greece and Rome: A Bibliographical Guide.** History and Related Disciplines Select Bibliographies. Manchester: Manchester University Press, 1995. 450pp. ISBN 0–7190–2401–3. LCCN 95–224070.

"This bibliography is intended to provide a ready entrance for the ever-increasing numbers of people who are turning to ancient history either for serious study or as a leisure pursuit." It will be useful to advanced undergraduate and graduate students researching specific topics; for the laity, Hopwood apparently assumes a Ciceronian *otium* rather than a contemporary approach to leisure activities. Hopwood includes entries for some 8,000 books and articles covering Greek and Roman history between 950 B.C. and A.D. 565. While selective, he misses few important works published between 1930 and 1990; coverage of earlier scholarship is spotty. The first five sections are devoted to general works; maps and atlases; and sources (i.e., secondary works on the nature and use of sources rather than sources themselves); and broad works on society and economy in the ancient world (subarranged by topic). Sections 6 through 21, the heart of the work, cover Greek, Roman, and early Byzantine history period by period, with topical subdivisions. A final section covers *Festschriften,* conference proceedings, and the like. Hopwood does not offer annotations, although he occasionally clarifies obscure titles and provides contents notes for proceedings and collections of essays. There is an index of authors.

19.   Klussmann, Rudolf, ed. **Bibliotheca Scriptorum Classicorum et Graecorum et Latinorum: Die Literatur von 1878 bis 1896 einschliesslich umfassend.** Leipzig: O. R. Reisland, 1909–1913; repr., Hildesheim: Georg Olms, 1976. 2v. in 4. LCCN 10–9097.

Klussmann follows the pattern of Engelmann (entry 12), whose work he continues. His first volume covers Greek authors, his second Latin writers. He cites books and journal articles without annotation. There are fewer editions and translations and far more critical works than in Engelmann. Klussman exhibits a strong literary and philological bias; for example, history is covered only under entries for ancient historical authors. The size of his work also illustrates the vast increase in scholarly activity in the classics during the late nineteenth century: he requires more pages for 18 years than Engelmann needed for 178. As with Engelmann, one should not neglect the addenda published at the end of the work. Klussmann was originally published in *Bursian's Jahresbericht* (entry 70). For subsequent bibliography see Lambrino (entry 20).

20.   Lambrino, Scarlat, ed. **Bibliographie de l'antiquité classique, 1896–1914.** Collection de bibliographie classique. Paris: Les Belles Lettres, 1951. 761pp. LCCN 52–001454.

Undertaken at the suggestion of Jacques Marouzeau, Lambrino's bibliography links Marouzeau's own *Dix années de bibliographie classique* (entry 21) and Klussmann (entry 19). Lambrino planned two volumes: *Auteurs et textes* and *Matières et disciplines.* Only the first was published. It is arranged alphabetically by ancient author, with Greek and Latin authors interfiled. Lambrino includes editions and critical studies. There are no abstracts or annotations, nor an index of modern authors, which was presumably reserved for the second volume. Lambrino also abbreviated or omitted bibliographical details for many items, which were to be supplied in the second volume. Lambrino is the least satisfactory of the major classical bibliographies; those seeking comprehensive coverage should consult other sources as well, such as the *Bibliotheca Philologica Classica,* a supplement to the *Jahresbericht über die Fortschritte der klassischen Altertumswissenschaft* (entry 70).

21. Marouzeau, J. **Dix années de bibliographie classique: Bibliographie critique et analytique de l'antiquité gréco-latine pour la périod 1914–1924.** Collection de bibliographie classique. Paris: Les Belles Lettres, 1927–1928. 2v. LCCN 28–27582.

Marouzeau compiled *Dix années* to remedy the bibliographical chaos brought about by the First World War and subsequent events. His first volume, *Auteurs et textes,* covers editions and studies of individual classical authors in an alphabetical arrangement. The second volume, *Matières et disciplines,* covers general and topical works (e.g., history, archaeology, philology, history of scholarship) in a broad subject arrangement. Marouzeau includes citations of both monographs and articles, for which he provides brief abstracts in French. He also cites scholarly reviews under monographic titles. *Dix années* offers comprehensive coverage of scholarship for the period. For subsequent years, see *L'Année philologique* (entry 44), which Marouzeau also founded. For previous years see Lambrino (entry 20).

22. Moss, Joseph William. **Manual of Classical Bibliography: Comprising a Copious Detail of the Various Editions of the Greek and Latin Classics and of the Critical and Philological Works Published in Illustration of Them, with an Account of the Principal Translations into English, French, Italian, Spanish, German, etc.** 2nd ed. London: Henry G. Bohn, 1837; repr., Port Washington, NY: Kennikat Press, 1969. 2v.

The scope of Moss's work, which covers the classical authors in alphabetical order, is well described by its copious subtitle. His style of citation is abbreviated, sometimes extremely so. His annotations discuss content, publication history, bindings, and typography and often give the price of a copy, as found in a bookseller's catalog of his era. While it can be of use in tracking down old editions and translations, Moss is primarily of antiquarian interest. The miscellaneous and frequently opinionated contents of the annotations will still interest bibliographers and historians of scholarship.

23. Nairn, J.A. **J.A. Nairn's Classical Handlist.** 3rd ed., rev. and enlarged. Oxford: Basil Blackwell, 1953. 164pp. LCCN 54–14555.

First published in 1931 under the title *A Handlist of Books Relating to the Classics and Antiquity,* this book has been updated twice by the staff of B.H. Blackwell. Nairn provides an unannotated list of works in classical studies. The list, which is arranged by subject, includes editions and translations of classical authors, reference works, and selected secondary works. There is an index of authors. Although completely out-of-date, it can still be useful for locating citations of older works.

24. Ooteghem, J. van. **Bibliotheca graeca et latina: À l'usage des professeurs des humanités gréco-latines.** 3ième éd. Namur: Éditions de la Revue "Les études classiques," 1969. 384, 107pp. LCCN 70–851007.

In spite of its Latin title, this work is written in French. It is intended as a guide to classical bibliography for college teachers. Van Ooteghem divides the work into three sections. The first, which he calls "Indications préliminaires," includes general works, bibliographical works, geography, Greek and Roman history, literary history, grammar, lexicography, and metrics. The two remaining parts cover Greek and Latin authors respectively. Van Ooteghem lists the authors alphabetically; under each, he notes editions and studies. These are subarranged by work and topic as needed. There are some annotations, which usually serve to clarify content and, less often, to evaluate. His focus is on major authors who are commonly studied. The bibliography includes nineteenth- and twentieth-century works in English, French, German, and Italian, as well as Greek and Latin. Although van Ooteghem does gather a large amount of basic material, his work is somewhat dated. Gullath and Heidtmann (entry 15), Poucet and Hannick (entries 26–27), and Halton and O'Leary (entry 16) are all better guides to classical bibliography.

25. Platnauer, Maurice, ed. **Fifty Years (and Twelve) of Classical Scholarship: Being Fifty Years of Classical Scholarship, Revised with Appendices.** 2nd ed. New York: Barnes & Noble, 1968. 523pp. LCCN 68–141561.

A reprinting of the 1954 edition, this book consists of the original chapters followed by appendixes that cover the intervening years. In each chapter a distinguished British academic surveys the state of scholarship in a field; whenever possible the same person prepared the appendix to the chapter. Numerous bibliographical references are given. Emphasis is on philological and literary studies; most chapters cover literary genres (e.g., Greek tragedy). The chapters on the Greek and Roman historians provide coverage of historical studies in general, while archaeology is given short shrift. Although now dated, *Fifty Years* remains a good overview of classical scholarship as of 1968. An attractive feature is its narrative treatment of topics. However, its lack of an index is a major drawback.

26. Poucet, Jacques, and Jean-Marie Hannick. **Aux sources de l'antiquité gréco-romaine: Guide bibliographique.** 5ième éd. Bruxelles: Artel, 1997. 313pp. ISBN 2–87374–019–1.

The earliest edition of this work appeared as *Introduction aux études classiques* (1988). A sixth edition appeared in 2000, but no copies of it are currently available in the United States. The work has grown and improved with each edition, while keeping much of its original structure. It was originally designed to serve as a bibliographical introduction to the field for Belgian university students in classical studies. Poucet and Hannick divide their work into three major parts. The first part begins with an overview of literary, epigraphical, papyrological, archaeological, and numismatic source materials. It then provides a sound orientation to the standard series of classical texts, the various collections and corpora of ancient writings, and the frequently arcane publications of the documentary and material remains of antiquity. This part also briefly discusses the literature of such areas as textual criticism, geography, and chronology. For those seeking focused collections of translations, it also lists sourcebooks. The second part covers reference works. These are covered by form: encyclopedias and dictionaries, works on the languages, bibliographies, manuals, reviews, and collections (chiefly the major monographic series and periodicals). Helpful notes and comments often appear at the beginning of sections. Poucet and Hannick also provide annotations for some of the individual works cited. These vary in length from a brief descriptive phrase to several paragraphs outlining the history and contents of a particular work. The third and final part, "Bibliographie d'orientation," lists over 1,200 key works arranged by subject. The compilers intend these to provide an introduction to each area of classical scholarship. It is an excellent list, with few noteworthy omissions and good coverage of both English and European-language works. This well-thought-out volume will furnish undergraduate and graduate students with a solid working knowledge of the literature of classical studies. A detailed table of contents and indexes covering modern authors, ancient authors and subjects, abbreviations, and journal titles provide ready assistance to those interested in a particular subject or work. This work also has an online avatar, the *Bibliotheca Classica Selecta* (entry 27). *BCS* includes nearly all the content of this book, revised and updated on a continuous basis, plus additional material.

27.   Poucet, Jacques, and Jean-Marie Hannick. **Bibliotheca Classica Selecta.** URL: http://bcs.fltr.ucl.ac.be/default.htm.

This Web counterpart to Poucet and Hannick's print work (entry 26) includes nearly all the contents of the printed bibliography, along with significant additional materials. The "Bibliographie d'orientation" corresponds closely to the printed bibliography, although offering updated contents, direct links to Web resources, and keyword searching. *BCS* also provides a mirror site for *TOCS-IN* (entry 60), a guide to other Web sites of classical interest ("Ressources électroniques"), and "Publications électroniques," which consists of an electronic journal, *Folia Electronica Classica;* a mix of articles and course outlines; and a small collection of French translations of classical authors. While *BCS* is in French and much of its content is aimed at Francophone users, it is an extremely useful resource for anyone doing research in classical studies.

28.   Rees, B. R., ed. **Classics: An Outline for the Intending Student.** London: Routledge & Kegan Paul, 1970. 125pp. ISBN 0–7100–6914–6; 0–7100–6915–4pa. LCCN 71–550657.

Although distinctly British in orientation and now a bit old, Rees's introduction to classical studies for beginning undergraduates is still useful as an overview of college studies in classics. Separate chapters cover classical literature, ancient philosophy, history, archaeology, and the influence of the classics on English literature. Each, by a specialist in the field, offers a narrative summary of the then current state of its subject, followed by a short bibliography of major works. Author and subject indexes are included.

29.   Schweiger, F.L.A. **Handbuch der classischen Bibliographie.** Leipzig: Friedrich Fleischer, 1830–1834; repr., Bryn Mawr, PA: Scholasticus Press, 1993. 2v. in 3. LCCN 02–6104.

Schweiger devotes the first volume of his *Handbuch* to Greek authors, and the second to Latin. His arrangement is alphabetical, usually by author, although the occasional topical heading is included also (e.g., "Byzantina," which gathers Byzantine historians and chroniclers). Schweiger includes editions, commentaries, translations, and scholarly studies from the beginning of printing to about 1820. Some entries have brief annotations, which are mainly of a bibliographical nature. Schweiger's coverage overlaps with that of Fabricius (entries 13–14) and of Engelmann (entry 12) and fills the gap between them. Schweiger also lists many useful sources of earlier bibliography in his foreword. Schweiger, along with Fabricius, is a basic source for pre-nineteenth-century classical bibliography.

30.   Whitaker, Graham. **Bibliographical Guide to Classical Studies.** Hildesheim: Olms-Weidmann, 1997. 9v. ISBN 3–487–10465–2 (v. 1) 3–487–10466–0 (v. 2) 3–487–10467–9 (v. 3) 3–487–10468–7 (v. 4). LCCN 98–122331.

Whitaker proposes to cover monographic publications in classical studies for the period 1873–1980 in nine volumes, of which four have appeared to date. The dates of coverage are somewhat fuzzy, as he includes both works begun before 1873 that were completed afterward and works begun before 1980, but continued afterward. He includes most areas of classical studies from prehistory through A.D. 600. Whitaker omits Bronze Age archaeology, biblical and Christian literature, later Greek and later Latin; ironically, most of these have been major growth areas in contemporary scholarship. The omission of periodical literature also reduces the overall value of his work. An exception to this is his inclusion of bibliographies that appeared in periodicals, although this is done inconsistently. However, Whitaker does offer a single source for monographs that must otherwise be sought in many separate bibliographies. He organizes material by subject: the volumes published to date cover general works and literature. General literary works are arranged by type and genre. An A-to-Z listing of individual authors (Greek and Roman intermingled), which covers editions, bibliographies, concordances, and the secondary literature, follows. Future volumes are to cover Greek and Latin language, history and archaeology, natural sciences, history of scholarship, biography, *Festschriften,* and conference proceedings; the final volume will include the index for the entire work. Whitaker provides descriptive annotations, but in many cases these are mere enumerations of contents. He does sometimes give the history of complex works or compare the differences between various editions of a work. This guide is a monument of industry, yet it is of limited value to scholars. The complex and highly fragmented organization of materials make it difficult to use, especially as there are no cross-references and the index has yet to appear. Its collocating function is vitiated by the need to seek journal articles from other sources, and it will be at least a quarter-century out-of-date by the time the final volume appears. Nevertheless, writers of dissertations and compilers of exhaustive bibliographies will need to consult it.

BIBLIOGRAPHIES OF DISSERTATIONS

31. **Catalogus Dissertationum Philologicarum Classicarum: Verzeichnis von etwa 27400 Abhandlungen aus dem Gesamtgebiete de klassischen Philologie und Altertumskunde.** 2. Aufl. Leipzig: Buchhandlung Gustav Fock, 1910; repr. (combined with Editio III), New York: Johnson Reprint, 1963. 652pp.

A bookseller's catalog with a vengeance, the second edition of this compilation issued by the German bookseller Gustav Fock lists over 27,000 dissertations and *Programmschriften* written by German scholars in either Latin or German. Most of the work in this academic genre is obscure and hard to find; some of it is valuable, but much is not worth the effort of finding. Fock's catalog is one of the few comprehensive tools for locating and verifying citations to these writings. Fock's citations tend to be rather Spartan, and information is often abbreviated. The catalog is arranged in broad subject categories: works on Greek authors and Latin authors (both A to Z), and *Altertumswissenschaft* (all other aspects of the study of classical antiquity, with further subdivision into language, history, archaeology, etc.). There is a keyword subject index, but no access by author. The catalog is continued to 1936 by the third edition. This edition contains nearly 6,000 further entries but is more restricted in scope. It supplies only sections on Greek and Latin authors, each arranged alphabetically. There is no index. For later German dissertations see also Drexhage (entry 33), whose work overlaps with this title.

32. **Catalogus Dissertationum Philologicarum Classicarum.** Editio III. Erläuterungschriften zu den griechischen und lateinischen Schriftstellern, enthaltend die Literatur aus den Jahren 1911–1936 und eine Auswahl früher erschiener Schriften. Leipzig: Buchhandlung Gustav Fock, 1937; repr., (2. Aufl.), New York: Johnson Reprint, 1963. 176pp.

33. Drexhage, Hans-Joachim. **Deutschsprachige Dissertationen zur alten Geschichte, 1844–1978.** Wiesbaden: Franz Steiner, 1980. 142pp. ISBN 3–515–03197–9. LCCN 80–507083.

Drexhage lists over 2,200 German-language dissertations on ancient history; he includes works from Austria, the Netherlands, Germany, Switzerland, and parts of central Europe, all of which are arranged in a single alphabetical sequence by author. Drexhage does not provide abstracts, nor does he note subsequent publication of dissertations as books. He does, however, provide good indexes. These cover names of individuals and peoples (as subjects), geographical names, and topical subjects. Many of the earlier dissertations are also listed in the *Catalogus Dissertationum* (entries 31–32); Drexhage has marked these with an asterisk. Drexhage is a much more convenient source; only those seeking very obscure items will need to resort to the *Catalogus*. For German dissertations after 1978, see the lists of "Althistorische Dissertationen" in the annual publication *Chiron* (München: C. H. Beck, 1971–).

34. Lindenlaub, Marie-Luise. **Deutschsprachige Dissertationen zur Archäologie des Mittelmeerraums, 1945–1977.** Berlin: Deutsches Archäologisches Institut, 1979. 288pp. LCCN 80–482439.

Lindenlaub lists some 792 Austrian, German, and Swiss doctoral dissertations on the the art and archaeology of the ancient Mediterranean region. These include works on ancient Near Eastern, Greek, Roman, and early Christian archaeology. Lindenlaub has arranged them by subject. Each entry includes the full citation for the dissertation, information on subsequent publication, the location of any published abstracts, and references to reviews. If the dissertation has been published, Lindenlaub describes the published version; if not, she describes the actual dissertation. Lindenlaub also provides indexes of authors and institutions.

35. MacGregor, Alexander P. **Ten Years of Classicists: Dissertations and Outcomes, 1988–1997.** Wauconda, IL: Bolchazy-Carducci, 1998. 105pp. ISBN 0–86516–405–3. LCCN 97–45995.

This work lists American and Canadian dissertations completed or in progress during the decade covered. It relies mainly on data compiled from *American Philological Association Newsletter* (see entry 1004). MacGregor includes 1,402 dissertations. He provides authors, titles, institutions, and year of completion (if known). There are two separate lists of these, one by author and another by broad subject area. MacGregor is primarily interested in job placement and demographic analysis (hence the outcomes), but the work is useful to bibliographers as well.

36. Thompson, Lawrence S. **Bibliography of American Doctoral Dissertations in Classical Studies and Related Fields.** Hamden, CT: Shoestring Press, 1968. 250pp. LCCN 67–24191.

37.   Thompson, Lawrence S. **Bibliography of Dissertations in Classical Studies: American, 1964–1972; British, 1950–1972.** Hamden, CT: Shoestring Press, 1976. 296pp. ISBN 0–208–01457–8. LCCN 76–41178.

In the first volume above, Thompson attempted to list all American dissertations in classics and related fields from the beginning of graduate study in America to the 1960s. Thompson takes a very broad approach; in addition to works on virtually every aspect of classical studies, he notes many dissertations on early Christian topics. Altogether he lists 2,080 dissertations. Thompson arranges his bibliography alphabetically by author. Each entry includes author, title, university, and date of submission. If a dissertation was subsequently published, Thompson gives the publication information. He generally cites any published abstracts, including those in *Dissertation Abstracts* and in various journals. Indexes cover subjects, titles, topographical names, Greek words, and Latin words.

The second volume follows the pattern of the earlier one, except that it also extends coverage to Great Britain. It adds another 1,917 dissertations. Thompson lists only doctoral dissertations for America but includes British dissertations for all types of degrees. Once again, the indexing is unusually good. Thompson provides cumulative indexes for the period 1861–1972. Together his two volumes form a comprehensive guide to American dissertations in classical studies. More-recent dissertations can, of course, be found in *Dissertation Abstracts International, A: Humanities and Social Science* (Ann Arbor, MI: University Microfilms International, 1969–), or its online avatar, *Digital Dissertations* (www.lib.umi.com/dissertations). The *American Philological Association Newsletter* (see entry 1004) lists both recently completed dissertations and those in progress in North American universities. The *Bulletin of the Institute of Classical Studies* (entry 87) performs a similar service for British dissertations. A substantial online listing of American and British dissertations in classics and ancient history may also be found at www.library.ucla.edu/libraries/url/colls/classics/cldis00b.htm, although it covers only the mid- to late 1990s. A listing of British and Irish dissertations in progress is located at www.tlg.uci.edu/~gabby/directory/ukthesis.html.

BIBLIOGRAPHIES OF TRANSLATIONS

Most of the bibliographies listed below are now badly out-of-date, although they remain useful. There is, alas, no current general bibliography of translations of the Greek and Roman classics. Translations of works by specific authors or in particular genres may often be found in bibliographies noted under the author or genre in chapters 14 through 16. The major series that publish translations of classical authors include the Penguin Classics (http://us.penguinclassics.com), Oxford World Classics (www.oup.co.uk/worldsclassics), and the Loeb Classical Library (www.hup.harvard.edu/loeb). Penguin and Oxford offer the better literary translations of major authors and works; the Loeb Classical Library provides translations (often rather wooden) facing the original Greek or Latin. Loeb also covers a much wider range of authors, including many minor and technical writers.

38.   Brüggemann, Lewis William. **View of the English Editions, Translations and Illustrations of the Ancient Greek and Latin Authors.** Stettin: J. S. Leich, 1797–1801; repr., New York: Burt Franklin, 1971. 2v. LCCN 06–25040.

Brüggemann focuses on works actually published in England, the bulk them being seventeenth- and eighteenth-century imprints. Greek and Latin authors are treated in separate sections, each arranged chronologically. Since the dating of a number of authors has changed sinced Brüggemann's day, some are found in peculiar locations. There are occasional annotations, and reviews are sometimes cited also. Brüggemann provides an index of authors. The main lists are in the first volume; the second volume is a supplement. Primarily of antiquarian interest, Brüggemann can be useful to bibliographers and historians of scholarship.

39.   Palmer, Henrietta R. **List of English Editions and Translations of Greek and Latin Classics Printed Before 1641.** London: Blades, East & Blades for the Bibliographical Society, 1911; repr., Philadelphia: R. West, 1977. 119pp. LCCN 14–9902.

This work is a traditional descriptive bibliography of translations of classical authors that were published in England between 1480 and 1640. These are arranged alphabetically by author. In addition to bibliographical description, each entry includes a brief list of holding libraries (all British). A substantial introduction by Victor Scholderer surveys the activities and interests of translators in the period covered. Palmer is chiefly useful for research in bibliography and in the history of scholarship.

40.   Parks, George B., and Ruth Z. Temple. **Literatures of the World in English Translation: A Bibliography. Vol. 2: The Greek and Latin Literatures.** New York: Frederick Ungar, 1968. 442pp. LCCN 68–31454.

This volume begins with a brief bibliography of reference and general works on classical antiquity. Greek literature is then covered in several chapters. These include both collections and translations of individual authors. Authors are grouped into chronological divisions: early and classical, Hellenistic, Greek Christian, and Byzantine literature. Latin literature is covered in similar fashion, with period subsections for republican, imperial, medieval, and Neo-Latin literature. The work lists a very full selection of translations, ranging from the sixteenth century to the 1960s. There are occasional annotations. The general index is spotty; the names of many translators are omitted. Users should note that many translations that have been published subsequent to 1968 represent substantial improvements over those listed in this work.

41.   Smith, F. Seymour. **Classics in Translation: An Annotated Guide to the Best Translations of the Greek and Latin Classics into English.** London: Scribner's, 1930; repr., New York: Burt Franklin, 1968. 307pp. LCCN 31–5075.

Smith provides separate alphabetical listings of Greek and Latin authors. He includes some Fathers of the Church, medical writers, and Renaissance authors in addition to the strictly classical. Brief annotations accompany most entries. Cross-references are made where appropriate, and an index of translators is provided. Smith's now dated work is still useful for identifying translations of minor authors and for finding translations by well-known figures of English literary history.

BIBLIOGRAPHICAL ABBREVIATIONS IN CLASSICAL STUDIES

42.   Rosumek, Peter. **Index des périodiques dépouillés dans la Collection de bibliographie classique et dans la Revue des comptes rendus des ouvrages relatifs à l'antiquité classique (publiées par J. Marouzeau) et index des leurs sigles.** Paris: Les Belles Lettres, 1982. 76pp. ISBN 2–251–90305–4.

Published as a supplement to volume 51 of *L'Année philologique* (entry 44), this work lists some 1,857 periodicals that have been cited in *L'Année* and its predecessors Lambrino (entry 20) and Marouzeau (entry 21). Rosumek arranges the titles in an alphabetical list. He provides the full title, place of publication, and the abbreviation used by *L'Année*. There is an index of abbreviations that refers back to the numbered entries. While Rosumek's compilation can be useful for identifying periodical abbreviations, it has several drawbacks. He has taken his citations from *L'Année* exactly as they appear, mistakes and all. Places of publication are not always current or accurate. Rosumek's decision to include only those abbreviations used in his source also reduces the value of his index. There are variant forms of abbreviation for many periodicals, and those found in *L'Année* are not always the most common. Wellington (entry 43), whose guide to abbreviations first appeared in 1983 and was updated in 2003, covers far more works and attempts (with considerable success) to note all variant forms of abbreviations.

43.　　Wellington, Jean Susorney. **Dictionary of Bibliographic Abbreviations Found in the Scholarship of Classical Studies and Related Disciplines.** Rev. and expanded ed. Westport, CT: Praeger, 2003. 684pp. ISBN 0–313–32141–8. LCCN 2003–58107.

Classical studies boasts more than its share of abbreviations. In addition to idiosyncrasy and inconsistency for their own sake, one must deal with the varying stylistic conventions of scholars and editors working in many different languages. As a result, a single journal is sometimes represented by a half-dozen different abbreviations, while at times the same abbreviation may refer to three or four different journals. Scholarly organizations and the Internet have added greatly to the classical alphabet soup. Wellington's book provides the means to identify the vast majority of these abbreviations. She includes 16,000 abbreviations for serial titles, corpora, standard works, organizations, and Internet resources. Wellington divides her dictionary into two sections. The first lists abbreviations in alphabetical sequence, with supplementary lists for Greek and Cyrillic (these two are confusingly mislabelled). The second section gives full bibliographical descriptions of the items. Coverage of congresses, *Festschriften,* and papyrological publications is limited. For *Festschriften,* one should consult Rounds (entry 62), and for papyri the *Checklist of Editions of Greek and Latin Papyri, Ostraca, and Tablets* (entries 970–971). Nor are abbreviations for ancient authors included: for these see the preliminaries to Liddell, Scott, and Jones (entry 511) and the *Oxford Latin Dictionary* (entry 508). Overall, Wellington is by far the best source for identifying abbreviations in classical studies. Those whose interests extend beyond the traditional borders of classical studies should also note that Wellington has greatly expanded coverage of titles in Near Eastern and biblical studies and strengthened her already extensive coverage of Byzantine studies in the revised edition.

2
Abstracts and Indexes

This chapter includes indexes to the periodical literature and other regularly updated bibliographical resources. Most appear annually (or are at least intended to), although a few are issued more frequently. Most indexes in classical studies remain in print form at the present, although many now have Web-based versions available. Along with review journals (treated in chapter 3), these represent the most current sources of bibliography. A number of older, now defunct, indexes and abstracts are also listed below because of their important retrospective coverage. The single most important title described in this chapter is *L'Année philologique* (entry 44), which is the standard general bibliographical resource for classical studies.

44. **L'Année philologique: Bibliographie critique et analytique de l'antiquité gréco-latine.** 1925– . Paris: Les Belles Lettres, 1928– . ISSN 0184–6949. URL: www. annee-philologique.com/aph.

45. **Database of Classical Bibliography.** Atlanta, GA: Scholars Press, 1995–1997. 1 CD-ROM. LCCN 95–20503.

L'Année philologique indexes all aspects of classical studies in an annual volume, which usually appears on a two- to three-year delay. Its scope is international. Originally a strictly French venture, it now has editorial offices in the United States and Germany as well as in Paris. Entries cover both books and articles; analytical entries are made for articles in *Festschriften* and other collections. Each entry includes a brief descriptive abstract, which may be in English, French, or German. Book entries also cite scholarly reviews and are repeated with citations of new reviews from year to year (generally up to five years). Organization has remained the same since its inception. The first and longest section is devoted to works on individual ancient authors and texts; it is arranged alphabetically by author (with cross-references when needed). Subsequent sections, with appropriate subdivisions, cover major areas of classical scholarship: literary history, linguistics and philology, history of texts, archaeology, history, law, philosophy, sciences, history of scholarship, pedagogy, bibliography and reference works, and *Festschriften*. A detailed table of contents facilitates subject access. Early volumes had only an index of modern authors. Over the years more indexes have been added: nonliterary ancient authors, collective titles (i.e., title entries in the authors and texts section), humanists (classical scholars as subjects), and geographical names.

The American Philological Association (entry 1004) sponsored a CD-ROM version of *L'Année philologique,* which was edited by Dee L. Clayman. Two versions have appeared, the first covering volumes 47 (1976) through 58 (1987), the second 45 (1974) through 60 (1989). The Web version of *L'Année philologique* became available in 2001; its back files are still being created. As of early 2005, the Web version covers volumes 30 (1959) to 73 (2002) of the printed edition, which itself stands at volume 73. The online version is much more convenient, since it allows one to search across many years at once, rather than volume by volume. In addition to access points found in the print version, it also offers full-text searching. *L'Année philologique* remains the basic and indispensable tool for research in classical studies. For earlier bibliographical coverage, see the headnote to chapter 1.

46.   Archäologische Bibliographie. 1913– . Berlin: G. Reimer, 1914–1918; Berlin: Walter de Gruyter, 1918– . ISSN 0341–8308. LCCN 38–4011.

The Deutsches Archäologisches Institut (entries 1036–1037) produces this annual bibliography, which continues bibliographies previously published in the "Archäologische Anzeiger" section of the *Jahrbuch des Deutschen Archäologischen Instituts* (1889–1912). The volumes for 1913–1972 were issued as supplements to the *Jahrbuch*. The *Bibliographie* provides comprehensive coverage of Greco-Roman archaeology and some coverage of Near Eastern archaeology as well. It includes books, articles, and reviews. Only citations are given; there are no abstracts. Arrangement is topical; a brief table of contents shows the major subject divisions. Recent volumes have included a "Systematische Gliederung," which gives a detailed listing of all subject categories and their subdivisions. There is an index of authors and reviewers in each volume. One of the great virtues of *Archäologische Bibliographie* is its timeliness. The volume for each year is ordinarily published the following year. Those seeking comprehensive retrospective coverage should also consult *Fasti Archaeologici* (entry 54). Users of the *Archäologische Bibliographie* should also note *DYABOLA* (entry 53), another product of the Deutsches Archäologisches Institut. *DYABOLA* is an electronic bibliographical database that covers much of the same material from 1956 on.

47.   Bibliographie internationale de l'Humanisme et de la Renaissance. 1965– . Genève: Librairie Droz, 1966– . ISSN 0067–7000. LCCN 68–2326.

This annual bibliography is produced under the auspices of the Fédération Internationale des Sociétés et Instituts pour l'Étude de la Renaissance. Coverage is best for work on the fifteenth and sixteenth centuries, although there is some attention to the fourteenth and seventeenth centuries as well. The first part of each volume covers individual humanists and their works. The second part offers subject access; it is divided into broad topical categories, which are then further subdivided. An index provides author access; there is also an index of persons treated as subjects (which includes only those who do not receive entries in the first part). There are no abstracts; the *Bibliographie* provides only citations. Early volumes were rather slender efforts, but recent ones offer much fuller coverage of the literature. There is not a Web version, although partial cumulations appear on CD-ROM from time to time; the most recent was published in 2004, covering 1965–1997. While of secondary interest to classicists, this is a very useful source for materials on the history of scholarship and the classical tradition.

48.   Bibliographie papyrologique. 1932– . Bruxelles: Fondation Égyptologique Reine Élisabeth, 1932– . ISSN 0964–7104. URL: www.ulb.ac.be/philo/cpeg/bp.htm.

49.   Electronic Bibliographie papyrologique. Version 1.0. Alpharetta, GA.: Scholars Press, 1993. 3 computer disks.

50. **Subsidia Papyrologica.** Version 2.0. Bruxelles: Fondation Égyptologique Reine Élisabeth, 2004. 1 CD-ROM. URL: www.ulb.ac.be/philo/cpeg/bp.htm.

Unlike most of the indexes in this section, which tend to be issued annually in bound volumes, the *Bibliographie papyrologique* is published on index cards approximately four times yearly. Each "issue" includes about 100 cards (or, more recently, a floppy disk option). It covers papyrological works (both books and articles). While the *Bibliographie* offers the fullest and most current coverage available for papyrological studies, it is difficult to consult. Cards must be arranged by either author or subject (unless two sets are used), and the other form of access is then lost. It is best used as a current-awareness service.

The American Society of Papyrologists (entry 1006), in collaboration with the Fondation Égyptologique Reine Élisabeth, developed an initial electronic version on floppy disks. This covered the years 1976–1990. It was produced with *Pro-Cite* and is intended to be used with that software, although it can be exported to other database programs. This has since been superseded by a new CD-ROM database, *Subsidia Papyrologica,* which is produced by the Fondation Égyptologique Reine Élisabeth and the Association Internationale de Papyrologues (entry 1008). The *Subsidia* offers the full bibliography from 1932 to 2004. It requires Filemaker Pro software. Information about the current state of the bibliography and how to subscribe may be found on the Web site noted above.

51. **Bibliotheca Classica Orientalis: Dokumentation der altertumswissenschaftli chen Literatur der Sowjetunion und der Länder der Volksdemokratie.** Herausgegeben vom Institut für Griechisch-Römische Altertumskunde bei der Deutschen Akademie der Wissenschaft zu Berlin. 1956–1969. Berlin: Akademie-Verlag, 1956–1969. 14 v. ISSN 0523–4697. LCCN 65–8534.

A survey of Eastern European publications in classical and Byzantine studies, this periodical covered publications from the USSR, Albania, Bulgaria, Hungary, Poland, Romania, and Czechoslovakia. East Germany was added with volume 10 (which also included retrospective coverage of East German publications for 1956–1964). Most of the bibliographical citations for Slavic items include a German translation of the title; those for Russian entries also include the Romanized form of the author's name. Many entries are annotated. The annotations are both descriptive and evaluative; all are in German. Arrangement is by subject within 18 broad categories. Often there are only one or two entries per subject in an issue. An index to the first 10 volumes appeared with volume 11 as a *Registerheft;* annual author and subject indexes appeared in each subsequent volume.

52. **Bulletin analytique d'histoire romaine.** 1962– . Strasbourg: Association pour l'Étude de la Civilisation Romaine, 1965– . ISSN 0525–1044. LCCN 93–33397. URL: http://argentoratum.u-strasbg.fr/basesweb/BAHR/html/MENU.htm.

This annual publication abstracts articles on Roman history and archaeology. The first volume covered works published in Belgium, France, and Switzerland. Subsequent volumes have gradually added other countries and now provide reasonably good coverage of Europe. The *Bulletin* is arranged into three broad sections: sources, general history, and regional history. Each of these is further divided into numerous subsections. The detailed table of contents neatly outlines the structure of the whole. Each volume includes an index of names mentioned in the titles of articles; different type faces are used to distinguish authors, other persons, places, and so forth. The abstracts, which are in French, generally give a good description of the original works. The *Bulletin* covers a wide range of materials, not all of which are included in *L'Année philologique* (entry 44). It is particularly useful for ferreting out obscure publications on a particular locality or archaeological site. Unfortunately, the publication schedule is erratic, to say the least. A gap occurs between the volumes for 1974–1975 and 1985 (which was published in 1992), and between 1985 and 1992. Volumes have been published covering 1992–2003 as of early 2005. There is also a searchable database available at the above URL, but only for materials published after 1992.

53.   Deutsches Archäologisches Institute. **DYABOLA.** Ennepetal: Biering & Brinkmann, 1992– . URL: www.dyabola.de/en/indexfrm.htm?page = www.db.dyabola. de/dyabola3/start_en.htm.

     DYABOLA (*Dy*namisch *a*nwachsende Daten*b*ank zu den *O*bjekten und zur *L*iteratur der *A*ltertums- und Kunstwissenschaften) began as a computerized version of the subject catalog of the Deutsches Archäologisches Institut (DAI) in Rome. It has grown considerably over the years and is currently available in CD-ROM and Web versions. The bibliographical components now include the DAI subject catalog (1956–2003), the *Sachkatalog der Römisch-Germanischen Kommission Frankfurt* (1992–1993), the acquisition list of the DAI in Madrid (1991–2002), the *Archäologische Jahresbibliographie* (2003), and the Winckelmann bibliography (works on J.J. Winckelmann from 1755 to 1998). These cover a wide range of books, journal articles, and reviews on classical, early Christian, Byzantine, and Medieval art and archaeology. Some also include works on the ancient Near East. *DYABOLA* offers a number of search capabilities: author, exact title, title keyword, keyword (i.e., any proper name, ancient or modern), and subject (through the built-in hierarchical list of subject terms). While the cumbersome interface sometimes requires an inordinate number of steps and has several peculiarities (e.g., exact title searches must include any initial articles), this database is a valuable tool for research in classical archaeology and related fields. Since the electronic version begins with 1956, the old printed catalog remains useful for its coverage of earlier works: *Kataloge der Bibliothek des Deutschen Archaeologischen Instituts, Rom* [Catalogs from the Library of the German Institute of Archaeology, Rome] (Boston: G. K Hall, 1969).

54.   **Fasti Archaeologici: Annual Bulletin of Classical Archaeology.** 1946–1986. Firenze: Sansone, 1948–1998. LCCN 90–40828.

55.   **Fasti Online.** 2000– . Roma: Associazione Internazionale di Archeologia Classica, 2004– . URL: www.fastionline.org.

     Produced by the International Association for Classical Archaeology, this work attempted to provide full coverage of activities and publications in Greco-Roman archaeology. It was originally an annual publication, but 1969–1970 and subsequent volumes appeared biennially as double volumes. Each volume contains six sections: "Generalia"; "Prehistoric and Classical Greece"; "Italy before the Roman Empire"; "The Hellenistic World and the Provinces of the Eastern Roman Empire"; "The Roman West"; and "Late Antiquity". Each of these is divided into topical and geographical subsections. Contents include brief reports of ongoing excavations and recent discoveries (often accompanied by illustrations and maps), as well as summaries of new publications. There are indexes for authors (ancient and modern), geographical terms, and subjects. *Fasti Archaeologici* ceased publication in 1998 (the last volume to appear only covers publications through 1986). It remains an excellent source of information for older publications. For current coverage in print, it is necessary to consult *Archäologische Bibliographie* (entry 46).

An online successor to *Fasti Archaeologici* has recently appeared. *Fasti Online* offers a searchable GIS database with information on archaeological excavations in Italy from 2000 forward. It includes some preliminary site reports and references to published works. The Web site also includes an online peer-reviewed journal that publishes both preliminary and final excavation reports. *Fasti Online* is less comprehensive than *DYABOLA* (entry 53) but includes material not found in that source.

56.   International Guide to Classical Studies: A Quarterly Index to Periodical Literature. 1961–1973. Darien, CT: American Bibliographic Service, 1961–1973. ISSN 0020–6849. LCCN 83–1176.

Sometimes issued under the title *ABS International Guide to Classical Studies,* this work provides a listing of articles by author. There is no annotation, although occasional clarification is provided for uninformative titles. A fairly detailed subject index follows the listings. There are also indexes of reviews and reviewers. Cumulative indexes appear at the end of each volume. The *International Guide* covers only a selection of the more prominent journals; *L'Année philologique* (entry 44) renders it superfluous. Publication ceased with the death of Stanford Becker, "sole research bibliographer and Director of American Bibliographic Service" (v. 12, no. 1–4, p. 1).

57.   Klassieke Bibliographie: Maandlisten van Tijdsschriftartikeleen met Driemaandelijksche Lijsten van Nieuwe Boekwerken in de Buma-Bibliotheek en in andere Nederlansche Bibliotheken. 1929–1950. Utrecht, 1929–1950. 22v. LCCN 31–2181.

Several Dutch scholars and librarians collaborated in the production of this annual index. They list articles first, then books. The editors' organizational principles are obscure: citations appear in short alphabetical clusters that are arranged in no particular order. No abstracts are provided. Author and keyword indexes are found at the end of each volume. Publication apparently ceased in 1950. *L'Année philologique* (entry 44) provides far superior coverage for the period in question.

58.   Malitz, Jürgen. Gnomon bibliographische Datenbank: Internationales Informationssystem für die klassische Altertumswissenschaft. München: C. H. Beck, 1994– . Annual. 1 CD-ROM.

59.   Gnomon Online. URL: www.gnomon.kueichstaett.de/Gnomon/Gnomon.html.

Produced by Beck (the publisher of *Gnomon* [entry 68]) and the Katholische Universität Eichstätt, this bibliographical database covers all aspects of classical studies. The current release indexes all reviews, personal notes, and obituaries found in volumes 1 (1925) through 75 (2003) of *Gnomon,* as well as the listings found in that journal's *Bibliographische Beilage* from 1990 onward. In addition, for the years 1987 and following, the database indexes reviews from an number of other major journals; these include *Anzeiger für die Altertumswissenschaft* (entry 64), the *American Journal of Archaeology* (entry 74), *Classical Review* (entry 67), *Göttingische Gelehrte Anzeigen,* the *Journal of Hellenic Studies* (entry 109), and the *Journal of Roman Studies* (entry 111). The current

CD-ROM (2004) includes about 312,000 entries. Search options include author, keyword, year, journal, or subject descriptor. The author indexing lacks authority control. The database does contain a German-language thesaurus of 3,000 subject descriptors, which can be viewed in either alphabetical or hierarchical formats. The interface itself is cumbersome and requires some practice to use effectively. There are a number of searching peculiarities, so users are well advised to use the manual to ensure proper retrieval. Manuals and full details are available on the *Gnomon Online* Web site. *Gnomon Online* offers a selection from the full database. This free Web version is relatively complete for 2001 forward but includes very little retrospective coverage, for which the CD-ROM remains necessary. The *Gnomon* database provides more up-to-date bibliographical information than does *L'Année philologique* (entry 44) but is less comprehensive and lacks abstracts.

60.   Matheson, Philippa M. W., and Robert Kallet-Marx. **TOCS-IN: Tables of Contents of Journals of Interest to Classicists.** Toronto, 1992– . URL: www.chass.utoronto. ca/amphoras/tocs.html.

Based at the University of Toronto, *TOCS-IN* is a project to provide online access over the Internet to the tables of contents of journals in all areas of classical studies, including ancient history and archaeology. Material is supplied by volunteer contributors. Currently *TOCS-IN* covers about 185 journals; nearly all major titles are included. Files are divided into broad subject categories: classics, archaeology, religion and Near Eastern studies, and miscellaneous. Within these arrangement is alphabetical by title. It is possible to browse categories or individual journal titles. Keyword searching provides author, article title, and subject access. *TOCS-IN* is best used as a current-awareness service; it is much more up-to-date than such traditional sources as *L'Année philologique* (entry 44). While data is restricted to bibliographical citations, there are links to online full-text articles and abstracts when these are available elsewhere. Those who lack access to libraries with extensive periodical holdings will find this an exceptionally valuable resource.

61.   **Nestor.** Madison: Institute for Research in the Humanities, University of Wisconsin, 1957–1977; Bloomington: Program in Classical Archaeology, Indiana University, 1978–1994; Cincinnati, OH: Department of Classics, University of Cincinnati, 1995– . ISSN 0228–2812. LCCN 84–2227. URL: http://classics.uc.edu/nestor/index.html.

Originally an irregular publication, *Nestor* now appears monthly (September through May); it is also available as a searchable database on the Web. *Nestor* covers current work in Minoan and Mycenaean studies. The bulk of each issue is devoted to a bibliography (unannotated) of current publications in the field. There are also conference notices and summaries and occasionally brief accounts of work in progress. The cumulative *Nestor* bibliography from 1957 to 1999 (more than 30,000 entries) can also be downloaded in machine-readable form as a series of structured ASCII files. The files may also be obtained over the Internet via FTP. *Nestor* is an excellent source for currrent information on developments in Aegean Bronze Age archaeology.

62.   Rounds, Dorothy. **Articles on Antiquity in Festschriften: An Index.** Cambridge, MA: Harvard University Press, 1962. 560pp. LCCN 62–7193.

Rounds's work ranges over the ancient Near East, Greece, Rome, and the Byzantine Empire. She provides an author/title index of articles in *Festschriften* published between 1863 and 1954. All significant words in the titles are indexed. There are also entries for the *Festschriften* themselves (the only full citation made) under the names of institutions and individuals honored. There are many cross-references for topical words and variant forms of proper names. While there is no subject indexing as such, the full indexing of title words and numerous cross-references approximate one. In some ways Rounds is a bit cumbersome to use. Author and title entries require further reference to the actual *Festschrift* entry to find full bibliographic details. The style of the entries tends to be somewhat telegraphic. Although many of these *Festschrift* articles can be found through other sources (such as *L'Année philologique* [entry 44]), Rounds is a valuable tool for tracking down the contents of these difficult works. Her indexing is especially helpful when dealing with a fragmentary citation.

63. **Year's Work in Classical Studies.** 1906–1947. London: John Murray, 1907–1919; Bristol: J. W. Arrowsmith, 1920–1950; repr., Amsterdam: J. Benjamins, 1969–1970. 34v. LCCN 08–12174.

The Classical Association (Great Britain) sponsored this annual collection of review essays. It was intended to help teachers in the field keep up-to-date with scholarly advances. The essays, many written by distinguished scholars, covered recent developments and publications in such areas as Greek literature, Latin literature, Greek history, Roman history, philosophy, religion and mythology, papyrology, Greek archaeology, and Italian archaeology. Various other topics (e.g., Roman law, New Testament, etc.) appeared on a more occasional basis. Publication was suspended after the 1947 volume in deference to *L'Année philologique*'s (entry 44) superior coverage.

3
Review Journals

This chapter notes journals whose primary function is to provide notices and reviews of recent scholarly works. These sources, while not as comprehensive as some of the indexes noted in chapter 2, often provide more current citations. For the works covered, they frequently offer more detailed and critical descriptions as well. The titles below also include several reviews that are published electronically; these are usually the most up-to-date sources for recent publications. Additional general information about electronic publications can be found in the introduction to chapter 15.

64.   Anzeiger für die Altertumswissenschaft. Wien: A. Sexl, 1948–1955; Innsbruck: Universitätsverlag Wagner, 1956– . ISSN 0003–6293. LCCN 53–29776.

This quarterly review edited by the Osterreichischen Humanistischen Gesellschaft offers substantial scholarly reviews of books in classical and Byzantine studies, some brief reviews, and occasional review articles. Most reviews are in German, although a few appear in French, English, or Italian. Unfortunately, despite the quarterly publication schedule, the reviews are rarely timely.

65.   Bolletino di studi latini: Periodico semestrale d'informazione bibliografica. Naples: Loffredo Editore, 1971– . ISSN 0006–6583.

Issued semiannually, this journal is chiefly devoted to reviews and bibliographical surveys, although it does include a few articles as well. A typical number offers several review articles and bibliographical surveys, and around 20 scholarly reviews, all in Italian. These are followed by a survey of recent journal issues, which lists their contents and often supplies brief summaries. This survey provides a convenient way to keep up with a wide range of Italian and other European journals. Each issue concludes with a *Notiziario bibliografico* arranged by subject, which notes recent books and articles. The first *Notiziario* each year lists works about specific ancient authors, while the second covers works on topical subjects. These bibliographies are similar to the *Bibliographische Beilage* in *Gnomon* (entry 68); the listings in *Gnomon* are generally more current and slightly fuller. Along with *Gnomon,* the *Bollettino* is a good place to find items too recent to have appeared in *L'Année philologique* (entry 44).

66.   Bryn Mawr Classical Review. Bryn Mawr, PA: Bryn Mawr College and the University of Pennsylvania, 1990– . ISSN 1055–7660 (print version); 1063–2948 (electronic version). LCCN 92–649894. URL: http://ccat.sas.upenn.edu/bmcr.

This review was published both in electronic and printed versions until 1998, when it became electronic only. The reviews are all of a scholarly nature and often of substantial length; their quality is generally high, although some are rather windy. Occasionally books are reviewed more than once by different reviewers; there are also often responses from authors.

BMCR reviews books in all areas of classical studies; most of the works reviewed are in English, but there is some coverage of Western European scholarship as well. It is one of the most timely sources of substantive reviews. A complete archive of reviews is available at the *BMCR* Web site. It can be searched by keyword or browsed by date, author, or reviewer. One can also sign up for a free subscription through the Web site. Reviews will then appear frequently, but irregularly, via e-mail.

67.   Classical Review. 1887– (n.s., 1951–). Oxford: Oxford University Press, 1887– . ISSN 0009–840X. LCCN 10–32843. URL: http://cr.oupjournals.org.

Originally a monthly, this journal now appears semiannually. It provides reviews and notices of recent books in all areas of classical studies, with special emphasis on literary and historical studies. Works in Western European languages are frequently included. The reviews, which are generally written by highly qualified specialists, tend to be critical and scholarly. This is the best single English-language source for reviews of classical books, although the reviews rarely appear in a timely fashion. A general index of authors and reviewers and an *index locorum* (passages from ancient literature, which are discussed) appears at the end of each volume. Two cumulative indexes have also appeared; one covers the old series (v. 1–64), and the other volumes 1–36 of the new series. *Classical Review* is now available electronically as well, with full-text back issues from 1998 forward on the Web. The full back file from 1887 to 1999 is also available electronically through JSTOR (www.jstor.org).

68.   Gnomon: Kritische Zeitschrift für die Gesamte klassische Altertumswissenschaft. 1925– . Berlin: Weidmann, 1925– . ISSN 0017–1417. LCCN 27–3554.

Gnomon currently appears eight times per year. Each issue includes major reviews of around eight to ten works and short reviews of perhaps a dozen more. Reviews are usually in German, although a few appear in English or French. Odd-numbered issues include the *Bibliographische Beilage,* which is paginated separately. This bibliography, which is arranged by subject, covers books and articles. There are no abstracts. While much less comprehensive than *L'Année philologique* (entry 44), these listings are far more timely. They provide a good tool for current awareness and for locating recent publications. Similar listings also appear in the *Bollettino di studi latini* (entry 65) under the title *Notizario bibliografico.* This *Notizario* is generally not as timely or as extensive as the *Bibliographische Beilage. Gnomon* also includes personal notes (e.g., birthdays and deaths of German classicists) and brief obituaries of major scholars. Annual indexes cover reviewers, authors, and subjects. *Gnomon* now also produces a computerized bibliographical database based on its back files (see entries 58–59).

69.   Ioudaios Review. Lehigh, PA, 1991– . ISSN 1183–9937. URL: http://listserv.lehigh.edu/lists/ioudaios-review.

This review, which is associated with the *Ioudaios* electronic discussion group (entry 183), is published in electronic form over the Internet. It consists entirely of scholarly book reviews. The journal focuses on Hellenistic Judaism; for a time it reviewed nearly every significant new book on Jews in the Greco-Roman world. Since 2000 it has become more selective, offering reviews of no more than 12–15 significant books per year. Both the issue for the current year and the full back file are available at the Web site noted above, although the site is only accessible to those using Internet Explorer. Those who wish to subscribe and receive reviews as published via e-mail may do so by sending the message "sub ioudaios-review Yourfirstname Yourlastname" to listproc@lehigh.edu.

70.   Jahresbericht über die Fortschritte der klassischen Altertumswissenschaft. 1873–1956. Berlin: S. Calvary, 1873–1897; Leipzig: O. R. Reisland, 1898–1956. 285v. LC 28–6999.

Frequently referred to as *Bursian's Jahresbericht,* after its first editor, Conrad Bursian, this periodical provided review essays on major authors or topics. In each of the years 1873 and 1874/75 two volumes were issued; volume 1 of 1874/75 is entitled *Die Fortschritte der Philologie;* volume 2, *Die Fortschritte der Altertumswissenschaft.* From 1876 each year consists of three volumes: *Griechische Klassiker* (later *Griechische Autoren*), *Lateinische Klassiker* (later *Lateinische Autoren*), and *Altertumswissenschaft.* Two supplements offer additional material: *Bibliotheca Philologica Classica* and *Biographisches Jahrbuch für Altertumskunde* (called from 1907 to 1924 *Biographisches Jahrbuch für die Altertumswissenschaft*). The *Bibliotheca* offers a bibliography of books, articles, and dissertations dealing with all aspects of classical antiquity. The unannotated entries are arranged in subject categories. The *Biographisches Jahrbuch* is a useful source of information on modern German classical scholars. It contains lengthy obituaries, which often include full bibliographies, as well as biographies, of the deceased. While the *Jahresbericht* long ago ceased publication, its many review essays and surveys remain a valuable source of retrospective bibliography. Its activities are continued in part by *Lustrum* (entry 71).

71.   Lustrum: Internationale Forschungsberichte aus dem Bereich des klassischen Altertums. Göttingen: Vandenhoeck & Ruprecht, 1957– . ISSN 0024–7421.

Lustrum, which appears irregularly, continues in the vein of *Bursian's Jahresbericht* (entry 70). Issues consist of two or three review articles on particular authors, genres, or topics. These may be in German, French, Italian, or English. Each article is prepared by a specialist in the field and usually surveys scholarship over an extended period of time. Most offer extensive bibliographies with some evaluative comment and discussion of trends. Often the more lengthy individual articles include an index. *Lustrum* is quite useful for keeping abreast of the literature on a wide range of authors and topics.

72.   Scholia Reviews. Durban, South Africa: Dept. of Classics, University of Natal, 1992– . URL: www.classics.und.ac.za/reviews.

Also known as *Scholia E-Reviews,* this is an electronic version of reviews that appear in the printed journal *Scholia.* It offers scholarly reviews of recent works in all aspects of classical studies. While the number of reviews is not large (currently around 15 to 20 per year), they are made available in a timely manner. Subscribers receive each review by electonic mail as soon as it is ready, often long before it appears in printed form. All reviews may also be found on the Web site. Subscription requests may be sent via e-mail to hilton@ukzn.ac.za.

4
Core Periodicals

Several criteria have governed the selection of titles for this chapter. The chief aim has been to provide broad general coverage of the leading journals from all areas of classical studies. Journals with a narrowly specialized focus (e.g., papyrology or epigraphy) have been excluded. Most of the selected journals are well established; a number of them have been published for over a century. In the case of these older titles, the back runs are important resources for research. The journals chosen are, for the most part, widely indexed. Virtually all journals listed here are abstracted in *L'Année philologique* (entry 44); many are indexed in other standard humanities and social science indexes as well. The English-language titles are widely held by American academic libraries; the foreign-language ones are commonly found in American research libraries that collect classical studies. Information about the title changes and publication history, if significant, are to be found in the annotations. For a slightly different mix of classical journals (all in English), see my chapters on "Classical Studies" in *Magazines for Libraries* (9th ed., New Providence, NJ: Bowker, 1997–).

73.   **American Journal of Ancient History.** Cambridge, MA: Harvard University, 1976–2001. New Brunswick, NJ: Dept. of Classics, Rutgers University, 2002– . Semiannual. ISSN 0362–8914. LCCN 76–641269. URL: http://classics.rutgers.edu/ajah.

Launched in 1976 to fill the perceived need for an American journal devoted solely to ancient history, this journal was edited and published by E. Badian with support from the Department of History at Harvard for 15 years. The editorial offices moved to Rutgers University in 2002. The journal publishes articles on Greek and Roman history, and very occasionally items on the ancient Near East. Many distinguished historians may be found among the contributors. The publication schedule tends to be erratic.

74.   **American Journal of Archaeology.** Boston: Archaeological Institute of America, 1885– . Quarterly. ISSN 0002–9114. URL: www.ajaonline.org/index.html.

The *American Journal of Archaeology* covers the "art and archaeology of ancient Europe and the Mediterranean world, including the Near East and Egypt, from prehistoric to late antique times." It publishes field reports, articles, newsletters, necrologies, and a substantial number of scholarly book reviews. Tables of contents with abstracts are available on the journal's Web site from volume 95 (1991) forward; from volume 104 (2000) full text is also available. Volumes 1–103 (1885–1999) are available in electronic format through JSTOR (www.jstor.org). The proceedings of the Archaeological Institute of America's annual conference appear in the April issue each year. This is the single most important English-language journal for classical archaeology and is very widely indexed.

75.   **American Journal of Philology.** Baltimore: Johns Hopkins University Press, 1880– . Quarterly. ISSN 0002–9475 (print); 1086–3168 (electronic). LCCN 05–31891. URL: http://muse.jhu.edu/journals/american_journal_of_philology.

Founded by Basil Lanneau Gildersleeve, *AJP* is one of the oldest and best classical journals published in America. Early issues covered philology in the widest sense of the term, including articles on Germanic, Romance, and Oriental philology as well as classical. In time the journal's focus narrowed to classical studies only. It now publishes articles and scholarly book reviews on Greek and Roman literature and history. Recent issues (v. 117 [1996] and later) are available electronically through Project Muse, and volumes 1–116 (1880–1995) through JSTOR (www.jstor.org).

76. **Ancient Narrative.** Groningen: Barkhuis, 2000– . Annual. ISSN: 1568–3540 (print); 1568–3540 (electronic). LCCN 2003–238922.

This relatively new journal is concerned with ancient prose fiction: classical, Jewish, early Christian, and Byzantine. It covers all aspects of these; articles variously take philological, literary, historical, or theological approaches. *Ancient Narrative* also includes studies of the reception of ancient novels in modern culture. The journal is a continuation of the *Petronian Society Newsletter,* which has a distinct and freely available section on the Web site, and the *Groningen Colloquia on the Ancient Novel.* Most of the content is available only to subscribers. Provisional versions of articles are posted throughout the year, and readers may send comments to the authors. At the end of each year, revised versions of the articles are gathered and published in the annual print volume, and that version is also archived on the Web site.

77. **Ancient Philosophy.** Pittsburg: Mathesis, 1980– . Semiannual. ISSN 0740–2007. LCCN 83–3286. URL: www.ancientphilosophy.com.

Most of the articles in this journal deal with mainstream classical Greek philosophers. Material on ancient science and religion can also be found in its pages. There are contributions by both philosophers and philologists. A typical issue has 8 to 10 articles and notes and 20 or more reviews. It is a good general journal on classical philosophy.

78. **Ancient World.** Chicago: Ares, 1978– . Semiannual. ISSN 0160–9645. LCCN 78–645202. URL: www.arespublishers.com/ANCW.htm.

This journal is "dedicated to original research in antiquity, from the most ancient civilizations to the Byzantine epoch." Overall, it has a strong historical focus, with occasional forays into literature and philosophy. Many of its issues are thematic, some a general miscellany. Quality of content is usually good, although it is not one of the top journals in the field.

79. **Annual of the British School at Athens.** London: British School at Athens, 1895. Annual. ISSN 0068–2454. LCCN 19–19615. URL: www.bsa.gla.ac.uk/pubs/index.htm.

The *Annual* publishes primarily articles on Greek art and archaeology. Topographical and historical studies and, very rarely, literary ones appear as well. It also includes excavation reports on British digs in Greece. A few of the articles deal with medieval Greece. Most of the articles are by members of the school. Abstracts in English and Greek follow the table of contents. A cumulative index covers the first 32 volumes.

80. **Antike Welt: Zeitschrift für Archäologie und Kulturgeschichte.** Mainz am Rhein: Philipp von Zabern, 1970– . Quarterly. ISSN 0003–570X. LCCN 76–641505. URL: www.kunstbuecher-online.de/zabern/antike-welt/index.php.

Most articles in this general archaeology periodical deal with the ancient Mediterranean; many are on classical topics. Other areas (e.g., Mesoamerican archaeology) are covered as well. The approach is a blend of popular and scholarly writing. Many color illustrations supplement the text. *Antike Welt* also provides a calendar of museum exhibits (in Europe) relating to ancient art and archaeology and brief notices of recent books. In many ways it can be considered a German version of *Archaeology* (entry 82), but the content of *Antike Welt* is often more challenging.

81. **Apeiron: A Journal of Ancient Philosophy and Science.** Edmonton, AB: Academic Printing and Publishing, 1966– . Quarterly. ISSN 0003–6390. LCCN 88–30374. URL: www.utexas.edu/cola/depts/philosophy/apeiron.

Apeiron publishes "papers of historical and philosophical interest in the area of ancient history and philosophy." A typical number includes three or four articles, although sometimes it may consist of only one or two long articles. In recent years there have been frequent theme issues. These have had guest editors and are often equipped with indexes. *Apeiron* is one of the few journals that regularly feature articles on ancient science.

82. **Archaeology.** New York: Archaeological Institute of America, 1948– . Bimonthly. ISSN 0003–8113. LCCN 50–37022. URL: www.archaeology.org.

Archaeology is a general archaeological journal with a strong classical component. It is geared toward students and general readers. In addition to classical and Near Eastern archaeology, articles cover Asia and the Americas. Articles are generally well written and accompanied by many illustrations. Each issue lists current museum exhibits (mostly American) of archaeological and historical interest. There are also book reviews. *Archaeology* frequently includes information on travel to archaeological sites as well.

83. **Arethusa.** Baltimore: Johns Hopkins University Press, 1968– . Semiannual. ISSN 0004–0975 (print); 1080–6504 (electronic). LCCN 79–10240. URL: http://muse.jhu.edu/journals/arethusa.

Arethusa focuses on classical literature. A typical issue contains a half-dozen articles. There are no book reviews. *Arethusa* tends to be less traditional than most of the journals included in this chapter. Many articles feature more recent approaches and critical theories. Some issues are theme oriented. Nonspecialists will find *Arethusa* one of the more interesting and approachable journals. From volume 29 (1996) forward, *Arethusa* is available electronically through *Project Muse*.

84. **Arion: A Journal of Humanities and the Classics.** Boston: Boston University, 1962– . 3 times a year. ISSN 0004–1351. URL: www.bu.edu/arion.

This is a nontraditional and occasionally controversial journal. *Arion* is one of the few genuinely interdisciplinary journals in classical studies. Articles tend to be literary. Many are comparative studies. The latest methodological approaches and critical theories (at least for classical studies) are likely to be found here, along with spirited rebuttals of them. In addition to articles, most issues include translations of classical literature, original poetry, and book reviews. An archive of the third series (1990–) is available on the Web site; this provides tables of contents and very selective access to articles.

85. **Athenaeum: studi di letteratura e storia dell'antichità.** Pavia: Università di Pavia, 1913– . Semiannual. ISSN 0004–6574. LCCN 83–645627. URL: http://dobc. unipv.it/dipscant/athenaeum/athenaeum.html.

Athenaeum is the best general Italian journal of classical studies. It publishes articles on both literary and historical topics. It also includes reviews, often lengthy. The journal publishes studies in English, French, and German as well as Italian; book reviews tend to be in Italian. The substantial issues usually contain around 20 articles and notes and as many more reviews. Indexes of authors and book reviews appear in the final issue each year.

86. **Bulletin de correspondance hellénique.** Paris: De Boccard for the École Française d'Athènes, 1877– . Annual (in 2v.). ISSN 0007–4217. LCCN 09–13099.

This venerable French journal is devoted to Greek archaeology and history. It publishes articles and excavation reports. Most are by French scholars connected with the École. It appears in two very substantial volumes, which routinely total 800–1000 pages. The *Bulletin* is a valuable resource for the Hellenist. Two indexes to the *Bulletin* have been published: Vanna Hadjimichali, *Tables du Bulletin de correspondance hellénique, 1892–1946* (Paris: De Boccard, 1969) and Vanna Hadjimichali and Anna Philippa-Touchais, *BCH: Tables, 1947–1970* (Athènes: École Française d'Athènes, 1999).

87. **Bulletin of the Institute of Classical Studies.** London: University of London, Institute of Classical Studies, 1954– . Annual. ISSN 0076–0730. URL: www.sas.ac.uk/icls/institute/publicat.htm.

Many, though not all, of the articles published in this annual are the work of scholars connected to the Institute of Classical Studies (entry 1042) in one way or another. Articles tend to deal chiefly with Greek literature, history, and art; there are occasional contributions on Latin literature and Roman history. Older issues (through 1998) include a review of "Research in Classical Studies for University Degrees in Great Britain and Ireland."

88. **Classical and Modern Literature.** Terre Haute, IN: CML, 1980–2000; Columbia: Dept. of Classical Studies, University of Missouri, 2001– . Quarterly. ISSN 0197–2227. LCCN 81–640263. URL: www.missouri.edu/~classwww/clmjournal.html.

This journal is devoted to studies of the influence of the classics on modern literature (primarily English, European, and American), although it occasionally includes articles on classical influences on medieval and Renaissance literature. It includes articles and occasional book reviews. From 1984 to 1992, one issue per year consisted of an annual "Bibliography of the Classical Tradition," which listed publications on the *Nachleben* of the classics.

89. **Classical Antiquity.** Berkeley and Los Angeles: University of California Press, 1982– . Semiannual. ISSN 0278–6656. LCCN 83–640320. URL: www.ucpress. edu/journals/ca.

This journal really began life in 1968 as *California Studies in Classical Antiquity.* The original journal published primarily the work of University of California faculty and students. The change of title in 1982 reflected a broadening of the contributor pool. *Classical Antiquity* includes a wide range of articles in history, literature, philosophy, art, and archaeology. The content is generally of good quality. The journal is available in both print and electronic versions.

90.   Classical Bulletin. Wauconda, IL: Bolchazy-Carducci, 1925– . Semiannual. ISSN 0009–8337. LCCN 78–648960. URL: www.bolchazy.com/index.php?cat = cb&sub = all.

This journal originally appeared monthly during the academic year (November–April). It was published over the years by several different university classics departments (most notably at St. Louis University) before being acquired by a commercial publisher in 1987. Never one of the more prestigious journals, *Classical Bulletin* traditionally offered short articles and reviews covering the entire field of classical studies. Since then it has undergone an identity crisis, with a shift to a focus on the history of classical scholarship and Eastern European classical scholarship, followed by a return to more mainstream classical topics. It is of primarily historical importance, since at present its quality is mixed and its publication schedule is far from current.

91.   Classical Journal. Charlottesville, VA: Classical Association of the Middle West and South, 1905– . Bimonthly. ISSN 0009–8353. LCCN 08–6753. URL: www.camws. org/CJ/index.html.

A typical number includes several articles on various topics in classical literature and ancient history, one or two notes of pedagogical interest, and a half-dozen substantial book reviews. While somewhat similar in content and format to *Classical World* (entry 95), *Classical Journal* is generally ranked a bit higher. Two cumulative indexes have been issued; the first, compiled by Franklin H. Potter, covers volumes 1–25 (1905–1930), and the second, compiled by Dorrance S. White, covers volumes 26–50 (1930–1955).

92.   Classical Outlook. Oxford, OH: American Classical League, 1923– . Quarterly. ISSN 0009–8361. LCCN 40–2196.

As the official organ of the American Classical League (entry 1003), this journal is aimed at teachers of classics at all levels. It includes short articles concerning pedagogy and reviews of new books in classical studies. Regular columns deal with teaching resources and with computing and the teaching of the classics. Another recurrent feature is *Classica Americana,* which offers biographical sketches of noted American classicists.

93.   Classical Philology. Chicago: University of Chicago Press, 1906– . Quarterly. ISSN 0009–837X. LCCN 07–22643. URL: www.journals.uchicago.edu/CP/home.html.

Edited by the classics department of the University of Chicago since its inception in 1906, this is one of the most distinguished classical journals produced in North America. A typical issue includes a half-dozen articles, a review article, and a half-dozen book reviews. In keeping with the title, articles are primarily on Greek and Latin languages and literature, although there are significant number of articles and reviews that deal with ancient history and philosophy. It is available in both print and electronically from the University of Chicago Press; the back file from volumes 1 through 97 (1906–2002) is available on the Web through JSTOR (www.jstor.org).

94.   Classical Quarterly. Oxford: Oxford University Press for the Classical Association, 1907– . Semiannual. ISSN 0009–8388. LCCN 08–19521. URL: http://cq.oupjournals.org.

Classical Quarterly's scope includes Greek and Roman literature, history, and philosophy. Each issue contains about 20 articles and nearly as many notes. It is characterized by austere, traditional scholarship and is often heavily philological in orientation. Its standards are uniformly high. Author and subject indexes appear in the final issue of each year. There are no reviews; its sister publication, *Classical Review* (entry 67), is devoted entirely to book reviews. Since 2001, Oxford has published the journal in both print and electronic form; the back files are available in electronic form through JSTOR (www.jstor.org).

95.   Classical World. Philadelphia: Classical Association of the Atlantic States, 1907– . Bimonthly. ISSN 0009–8418. LCCN 10–2751. URL: www.caas-cw.org/cwhome.html.

This journal was originally called *Classical Weekly;* the name changed with the frequency of publication. Most issues offer two or three scholarly articles, one or more notes on pedagogy, and a large number of brief book reviews. The journal features studies in Greek and Roman literature and history. *Classical World* is especially valuable for the many topical review essays and bibliographical surveys that it publishes. In the past these have often been reprinted in collections of *Classical World* bibliographies (see entries 599, 609, 614, 840, and 856). Its many news items and announcements concerning matters of scholarly, professional, and pedagogical matters are also quite useful. One quirk of the journal has been its refusal to deal with Greek type; all Greek is printed in transliterated form.

96.   Classics Ireland. Dublin: Classical Association of Ireland, 1994– . Annual. ISSN 0791–9417. LCCN 95–30180. URL: www.ucd.ie/classics/ClassicsIreland.html.

This lively journal is the official journal of the Classical Association of Ireland. In addition to the usual articles on classical literature and history, it includes many essays on the influence of the classics on modern Irish literature and on the history of classical scholarship. The first seven volumes are freely available on the Web. Subsequent issues have appeared only in print.

97.   Electronic Antiquity. Hobart: Dept. of Classics, University of Tasmania, 1993–1998; Blacksburg: Virginia Polytechnic Institute and State University, Digital Library and Archives 1999– . Irregular. ISSN 1320–3606. LCCN 96–31445. URL: http://scholar.lib.vt.edu/ejournals/ElAnt.

Originally based at the University of Tasmania in Australia, this was the first classical journal to be published solely in electronic form. Since 1999 it has been published by Virginia Tech. Its publication is erratic. *Electronic Antiquity* includes short articles, reviews, and conference notices.

98.   Glotta: Zeitschrift für griechische und lateinische Sprache. Göttingen: Vandenhoeck & Ruprecht, 1909– . Two double numbers yearly. ISSN 0017–1298. LCCN 15–21054. URL: www.v-r.de.

Glotta is the only journal devoted entirely to Greek and Latin languages and linguistics. Articles, written chiefly in German and English, deal with etymology, lexicography, phonology, dialects, Indo-European philology, and related topics. The final issue each year includes a keyword index of words discussed; this is subarranged by language. Tables of contents for recent issues may be found on the publisher's Web site.

99.   Greece & Rome. Oxford: Oxford University Press for the Classical Association, 1931– . Semiannual. ISSN 0017–3835. LCCN 34–30109. URL: http://gr.oupjournals.org.

Greece & Rome is aimed at a broad general audience of students, teachers, and scholars within the field of classics. It publishes "scholarly but not technical articles" on all aspects of classical civilization. Each issue contains a half-dozen articles. A particularly valuable feature is the series of review essays which appear in each issue. These survey recent work in the following areas: Greek literature, Roman literature, Greek history, Roman history, archaeology and art, philosophy, and general works. *Greece & Rome* is exceptionally useful for undergraduates because of its readable articles on topics of general interest in classical studies. Since 2001 the journal has appeared in both print and electronic form; back issues from 1931 to 1999 are available through JSTOR (www.jstor.org).

100.   Greek, Roman and Byzantine Studies. Durham, NC: Dept. of Classical Studies, Duke University, 1958– . Quarterly. ISSN 0072–7482. LCCN 64–29901. URL: www.duke. edu/web/classics/grbs.

This journal includes studies of Greek civilization from the beginnings to the fall of the Byzantine Empire. The "Roman" in the title refers to the Greek world under Roman rule; articles on primarily Roman topics and Latin literature are excluded. Early issues tended to focus more on Byzantine subjects, while recent ones have been weighted more toward mainstream classical Greek topics. A typical number consists of five to eight articles. The final issue of each year includes author, subject, and Greek word indexes.

101.   Gymnasium: Zeitschrift für Kultur der Antike und humanistische Bildung. Heidelberg: Carl Winter Univeritätsverlag, 1890– . Bimonthly. ISSN 0017–5943. LCCN 86–12570. URL: www.gymnasium.hu-berlin.de/index.html.

Originally called *Das humanistische Gymnasium,* this began as a general humanities journal aimed at teachers in the humanistic *Gymnasia* (preparatory schools) in Germany. It has always had a considerable classical content, which came eventually to predominate. It now offers articles on Greek and Roman history and literature, classical archaeology, the history of classical scholarship and humanism. *Gymnasium* also carries many book reviews. Most articles are in German.

102.   Harvard Studies in Classical Philology. Cambridge, MA: Harvard University Press, 1890– . Annual. ISSN 0073–0688. LCCN 44–32100. URL: www.fas.harvard.edu/ ~classics/links/hscp.html.

Harvard Studies in Classical Philology, since its inception, has consisted primarily of contributions by faculty and graduates of the Harvard classics department, although works by others also appear in it. Articles tend to be strictly philological, with an occasional foray into ancient history or archaeology. *Harvard Studies* also includes summaries of Harvard dissertations in classics, an especially useful feature since these are not available through *Dissertation Abstracts.* The first 100 volumes (1890–2000) are available electronically through JSTOR (www.jstor.org).

103.   Helios: A Journal Devoted to Critical and Methodological Studies of Classical Culture, Literature and Society. Lubbock: Texas Tech University Press, 1976– . Semiannual. ISSN 0160–0923. LCCN 82–643482. URL: www.ttup.ttu.edu/journals.html#helios.

Previously the journal of the Classical Association of the Southwestern United States, *Helios* has been published by the Department of Classical and Romance Languages at Texas Tech and the Texas Tech University Press since 1981. In its original incarnation, it was a rather undistinguished general journal of classics and comparative literature. With its relatively recent subtitle, *Helios* has found a niche publishing "articles that explore innovative approaches to the study of classical culture, literature, and society." Recent critical methodologies such as anthropological, deconstructive, feminist, reader response, social history, and text theory are featured in its pages, many times under the rubric of a thematic issue.

104.   Hermes: Zeitschrift für klassische Philologie. Wiesbaden: Franz Steiner, 1866– . Quarterly. ISSN 0018–0777. LCCN 10–32853. URL: www.steiner-verlag.de/Hermes.

A typical issue of this venerable journal includes around eight articles and several notes (*Miszellen*). While most articles are in German, a substantial number of English contributions appear as well. Articles tend to be philological, although history and philosophy are by no means excluded. The quality of contributions is generally above average. Indexes of names and subjects, of Greek and Latin words discussed, and of passages discussed appear in the final issue each year.

105.   Hesperia. Princeton, NJ: Institute for Advanced Study for the American School of Classical Studies at Athens, 1932– . Quarterly. ISSN 0018–098X. LCCN 32–17696. URL: www.ascsa.edu.gr/publications/hesperia.htm.

The primary focus of this journal is Greek art and archaeology. It generally includes three to four articles and excavation reports per issue. Articles are often substantially longer than those found in other journals. Epigraphical and literary studies also appear in *Hesperia* on an occasional basis. *Hesperia* is a fundamental journal for the study of classical Greek archaeology. Since 2002, *Hesperia* has been published in electronic as well as print form. Back issues from 1932 to 2001 are available through JSTOR (www.jstor.org).

106.   Historia: Zeitschrift für Alte Geschichte. Wiesbaden: Franz Steiner, 1952– . Quarterly. ISSN 0018–2311. LCCN 53–31306. URL: www.steiner-verlag.de/Historia.

Historia is one of the best journals devoted to ancient history. Its main focus is Greek and Roman history. A typical issue contains a half-dozen articles and two or three notes. Articles are usually in German or English, with a sprinkling of French and Italian contributions. Early issues included book reviews, but these are no longer carried.

107.   Illinois Classical Studies. Urbana: Dept. of the Classics, University of Illinois at Urbana-Champaign, 1976– . Annual. ISSN 0363–1923. LCCN 76–645935. URL: www. classics.uiuc.edu/ics/ICSWebPage.htm.

Founded in 1976, *ICS* has had several publishers, changed frequency several times, and undergone a short hiatus in publishing before recently reemerging. While articles cover the full range of classical studies, the bulk tend to be in literature, philology, and philosophy. Traditional classical scholarship is emphasized. Despite its title, this is perhaps the most international classical journal published in America. It includes articles in all the standard languages of classical scholarship and counts many prominent European scholars among its contributors.

108.   International Journal of the Classical Tradition. New Brunswick, NJ: Transaction, 1994– . Quarterly. ISSN 1073–0508. LCCN 93–4448. URL: www.bu.edu/ict/ijct.

As the official journal of the International Society for the Classical Tradition (entry 1019), this title is "devoted to the scholarly study of the reception of Greco-Roman antiquity in other cultures and later periods." It includes articles on a wide range of topics, although literary studies predominate. The journal also publishes many review articles and book reviews. Tables of contents and abstracts appear on the Web site.

109.   Journal of Hellenic Studies. London: Society for the Promotion of Hellenic Studies, 1880– . Annual. ISSN 0075–4269. LCCN 09–20515. URL: www.hellenicsociety. org.uk.

This journal covers all aspects of ancient Greece: archaeology, art, history, literature, and philosophy. It often publishes longer-than-average articles. The quality tends to be high. The *Journal* also includes a large number of critical book reviews, which together provide a good survey of recent work in the field. Tables of contents for recent volumes are available on the publisher's Web site. The complete back file from 1880 to 1999 is available through JSTOR (www.jstor.org).

110.   Journal of Roman Archaeology. Ann Arbor, MI: Journal of Roman Archaeology, 1988– . Annual. ISSN 1047–7594. LCCN 89–656368. URL: www.journalofromanarch.com.

This journal is "concerned with Italy and all parts of the Roman world from about 700 B.C. to about 700 A.D." It interprets archaeology broadly and includes much material on Roman history in general. While still an annual, the journal now is printed in two fascicles because of its size (typically running over 700 pages). In addition to articles and archaeological reports, each volume includes an extensive array of reviews and review articles that provide an excellent survey of recent work in Roman archaeology. While English predominates, contributions in the standard European languages are fairly common. The *Journal* is a valuable resource for both archaeologists and historians. Tables of contents for all issues are available on the *Journal*'s Web site.

111.   Journal of Roman Studies. London: Society for the Promotion of Roman Studies, 1911– . Annual. ISSN 0075–4358. LCCN 26–2981. URL: www.romansociety.org.

While the *Journal* covers the full range of Roman studies, emphasis tends to be on history and literature. It resembles its sister publication, the *Journal of Hellenic Studies* (entry 109), in format. Many of its articles are of above-average length, and the content is generally of high quality. The many critical book reviews and review essays provide an excellent overview of recent work in Roman studies. Since 2002 the *Journal* has been published in both print and electronic versions; the complete back file from 1911, except for the three most recent years, is available on the Web through JSTOR (www.jstor.org).

112.   Latomus: Revue d'études latines. Tournai: Société d'Études Latines de Bruxelles, 1937– . Quarterly. ISSN 0023–8856. LCCN 41–16538. URL: http://users. belgacom.net/latomus/revue.html.

Latomus publishes articles on Latin language and literature and on Roman history. A typical issue contains a dozen articles and a substantial number of book reviews. Articles are in English and a variety of European languages; reviews are normally in French. The quality of the contents is good, but rarely outstanding. The final issue of each year contains an author index and an index of books reviewed.

113.   Mnemosyne: Bibliotheca Classica Batava. Leiden: Brill, 1852– . Semiannual. ISSN 0026–7074. LCCN 06–31463. URL: www.brill.nl/m_catalogue_sub6_id7366.htm.

This old and distinguished Dutch journal includes work on Greek and Latin literature and philosophy. The journal has a strong philological bent and includes many textual notes. In addition to articles and notes, each volume includes a substantial number of reviews. While early volumes were in Dutch and Latin, currently English and German predominate. Indexes of authors and books reviewed appear in the final number of each volume. *Mnemosyne* is also available electronically from volume 49 (1996) forward at www.ingentaconnect.com/content/brill/mne.

114.   Mouseion. Calgary, AB: University of Calgary Press for the Classical Association of Canada, 2001– . 3 times a year. ISSN 1496–9343. LCCN 2002–252784. URL: www.mun. ca/classics/mouseion.

Along with *Phoenix* (entry 119), *Mouseion* is one of the two official journals of the Classical Association of Canada (entry 1012). It was formerly published under the title *Classical Views/Echos du monde classique* (1957–2000). *Mouseion* primarily publishes the work of Canadian scholars. While the journal publishes in both English and French, most of the contents tend to be in English. One issue per year is devoted to archaeological topics; the other two include work on history, philology, philosophy, and reception studies. Tables of contents and abstracts are available on the Web.

115.   Oxford Journal of Archaeology. Oxford: Basil Blackwell. 3 times a year. 1982– . ISSN 0262–5253. LCCN 0262–5253. URL: www.blackwellpublishing.com/journal. asp?ref = 0262–5253.

This is a general journal of European and Near Eastern archaeology. Chrono-logically, it covers antiquity and the Middle Ages. A large part of its content is devoted to Bronze Age Mediterranean and classical archaeology. It also includes a number of articles concerning technical and theoretical aspects of archaeology. Since 1997 the journal has been available in electronic form as well as print.

116.   Oxford Studies in Ancient Philosophy. New York: Oxford University Press, 1983– . Annual. ISSN 0265–7651. LCCN 84–645022.

Oxford Studies offers papers on a wide variety of topics in ancient philosophy, although primary emphasis is on classical Greek philosophy. It includes both articles and substantial (usually article-length) reviews. Its contributors include many well-known scholars, and the quality is generally high. An *index locorum* appears at the end of each volume.

117.   Papers of the British School at Rome. London: British School at Rome, 1902– . Annual. ISSN 0068–2462. LCCN 10–13288. URL: www.bsr.ac.uk/ENG/sub_pub/BSR_ Pub_Papers01.htm.

This annual publishes articles on the "archaeology, history, and literature of Italy and other parts of the Mediterranean up to early modern times." Articles tend to be substantial. Most are by the staff of the school (entry 1031) and its present and former members. This is a very useful publication for Roman archaeology and history. While it includes articles on medieval and Renaissance Italy, classical topics usually predominate. Tables of contents for recent volumes may be found on the publisher's Web site.

118.   Philologus: Zeitschrift für klassische Philologie. Berlin: Akademie der Wissenschaften der DDR, Zentralinstitut für Alte Geschichte und Archaeologie, 1846– . Semiannual. ISSN 0031–7985. LCCN 05–26859. URL: http://ph.akademie-verlag.de.

Philologus offers articles in the traditional German style on philology, ancient history, and philosophy. Each issue has approximately 10 articles and 5 notes. Articles are mainly in German; a few are in English or other languages. The second issue each year includes indexes of subjects, passages discussed, and Greek and Latin words discussed. The back file is particularly valuable, as its contributors comprise a virtual who's who of nineteenth-century German classical scholars. The publisher's Web site offers tables of contents for recent issues.

119.   Phoenix. Toronto: Classical Association of Canada, 1946– . Quarterly. ISSN 0031–8299. LCCN 52–15373. URL: www.chass.utoronto.ca/~phoenix.

Phoenix, along with its sister journal, *Mouseion* (entry 114), is a journal of the Classical Association of Canada (entry 1012). It publishes articles in English and French (mostly in English) on all aspects of classical studies. While the majority of contributions are by Canadians, Americans frequently publish in it as well. *Phoenix* is a solid general classics journal. An author index appears in the final number of each year. Tables of contents for most issues are available on the Web site; back files from 1946 to 1999 are available on the Web through JSTOR (www.jstor.org).

120.   Phronesis: A Journal for Ancient Philosophy. Leiden: Brill, 1955– . 3 times a year. ISSN 0031–8868. LCCN 59–35648. URL: www.brill.nl/m_catalogue_sub6_id7431.htm.

Phronesis deals primarily with mainstream ancient Greek philosophy. A typical issue runs to four or five articles. Until 1993, a piece called "Editor's Notes," which selectively noted recent work in the field, frequently appeared at the end of an issue. This seems to have been replaced by actual reviews and review articles. Articles are mostly in English, with a sprinkling of German, French, and Italian pieces. Volumes from 36 (1991) forward are available in electronic form at www.ingentaconnect.com/content/brill/phr.

121.   Ramus: Critical Studies in Greek and Latin Literature. Bendigo: Aureal Publications, 1972. Semiannual. ISSN 0048–671X. LCCN 83–642402, URL: www.latrobe.edu.au/arts/ramus.

This Australian journal focuses on literary criticism. Articles tend to be accessible to the nonspecialist. Many issues are thematic. *Ramus* does not include book reviews.

122.   Revue des études anciennes. Bordeaux: Université de Bordeaux III, 1899– . Semiannual. ISSN 0035–2004. LCCN 43–43754. URL: www.montaigne.u-bordeaux.fr/Rea.

The *Revue* publishes articles and reviews on Greek and Roman history, literature, and archaeology. These are chiefly in French. Extensive literature reviews (*chroniques*) covering Roman France, vases of Gaul, and late antiquity appear on a regular basis. Indexes of authors and of works reviewed normally appear in the second issue each year. Sometimes other indexes are printed as well.

123.   Revue des études grecques. Paris: Société des Belles Lettres for the Société des Études Grecques, 1888– . Semiannual. ISSN 0035–2039. LCCN 09–13102. www-reg. montaigne.u-bordeaux.fr.

This journal publishes articles on all aspects of classical Greek culture. It also includes the proceedings of the Société des Études Grecques. A substantial number of brief reviews appear as well. Two substantial bibliographical surveys appear regularly in the *Revue*, the *Bulletin archéologique* and the *Bulletin épigraphique*. The journal's Web site lists the complete tables of contents of all volumes.

124.   Revue des études latines. Paris: Société des Belles Lettres for the Société des Études Latines, 1928– . Annual. ISSN 0373–5737. LCCN 26–7380.

This is roughly the French equivalent of the *Journal of Roman Studies* (entry 111), although not quite as good. It publishes articles and reviews concerning Latin language and literature. All are in French; nearly all are by French scholars. The reviews cover the full range of Roman studies and can be useful, although they are never timely. The *Revue* also includes a list of French doctoral theses in Roman studies each year, which provides author, title, and university.

125.   Rheinisches Museum für Philologie. Frankfurt: J.D. Sauerlaenders, 1827. Quarterly. ISSN 0035–449X. LCCN 05–26861. URL: www.uni-koeln.de/phil-fak/ifa/rhm.

August Boeckh and B. G. Niebuhr were among the founding editors of *Rheinisches Museum;* over the years its contributors have included virtually every German philologist of importance. Its contents are primarily philological, with some attention to ancient history and philosophy. It represents a very traditional Germanic style of scholarship. A typical issue consists of five to eight articles and two to four notes. The majority of contributors are German, although a significant number of Anglo-American scholars publish in it as well. While remaining nominally a quarterly, since 1977 *Rheinisches Museum* has appeared three times per year (with nos. 3–4 combined). Tables of contents for volumes from 1990 and later are available on the Web site.

126.   Transactions of the American Philological Association. Baltimore: Johns Hopkins University Press for the American Philological Association, 1870– . Semiannual. ISSN 0360–5949 (print); 1533–0699 (electronic). LCCN 76–646066. URL: http://muse. jhu.edu/journals/transactions_of_the_american_philological_association.

The official journal of the American Philological Association (entry 1004), this is the oldest classical journal published in North America. Early volumes had a general philo-logical content and included articles on Indo-European-, Germanic-, and Romance-language topics among others. Gradually both the association and the journal shifted to a strictly clas-sical orientation. The journal now publishes articles on all aspects of classical studies. Its reputation has varied over time. In recent years its standing has been greatly improved by a series of vigorous editors. There is an index to the first 100 volumes: J.W. Spaeth, *Index to the Transactions and Proceedings of the American Philological Association, Volumes 1–100, 1870–1969* (Cleveland: Case Western Reserve University for the Association, 1971). *TAPA* was a cloth-bound annual for most of its history; in 2002 it became a paper-bound semiannual publication. An electronic version has been available since 2000 as part of Project Muse, while the full back file is available electronically through JSTOR (www.jstor.org).

127. **Yale Classical Studies.** Cambridge: Cambridge University Press for the Dept. of Classical Studies, Yale University, 1928– . Irregular. ISSN 0084–330X. LCCN 28–23551. URL: www.cambridge.org/uk/series/sSeries.asp?code = YCS.

In its early years this journal contained only articles by Yale faculty and graduates; over time its list of contributors has broadened substantially. *YCS* sometimes publishes considerably longer articles than the typical classical journal. Its contents consist chiefly of literary and philological studies but often include works on ancient history and philosophy as well. Since 1966 volumes have tended to be thematic.

5
General Dictionaries, Encyclopedias, and Handbooks

This chapter includes reference works that cover classical studies as a whole, or multiple areas within the field. The largest and most detailed of these, such as Pauly-Wissowa (entry 152), tend to be in German. All the larger English-language classical dictionaries that are of real value will be found below also; most inquirers will be well served by the *Oxford Classical Dictionary*³ (entry 142). In addition, a selection of the better compact classical dictionaries are noted, although this category is not covered exhaustively. Finally, several handbooks, dictionaries, and books of lists that cover broad aspects of classical civilization appear below. Works devoted to individual areas of study, such as literature or archaeology, or specific topics may be found in the chapters on those topics.

128. Avery, Catherine B., ed. **New Century Classical Handbook.** Editorial consultant, Jotham Johnson. New York: Appleton-Century-Crofts, 1962. 1,162pp. LCCN 62–10069.

Aimed at students and general readers, this encyclopedia of classical civilization is widely available. Chronologically it focuses on the period extending from the beginnings of Greek civilization to the end of the Julio-Claudian dynasty at Rome (A.D. 68). Its more than 6,000 entries treat persons (both historical and mythological), literary works, monuments and works of art, and places. Entries for persons provide biographical and historical information. Articles for literary works consist of summaries, while those for monuments and artworks are largely descriptive. Entries for places give both geographical and historical information. Emphasis is placed on how the material appeared to the ancients rather than on modern interpretations; hence, many of the articles deal more with legend than fact and can mislead those seeking accurate historical information. This problem is exacerbated by errors of fact and interpretation found in some entries. There are no bibliographies, nor is an index provided. The *Oxford Classical Dictionary*³ (entry 142) is a better choice as an all-purpose encyclopedia of classical civilization, since it is more recent, offers reliable historical data, and includes excellent short bibliographies. Around 1972, five smaller works based on material from the *New Century Classical Handbook* were issued. These cover biography, geography, mythology, Greek literature, and Greek art. In some cases these works include new material, in others not. For fuller descriptions see entries 192, 396, 454, 573, and 894.

129. Avi-Yonah, Michael, and Israel Shatzman. **Illustrated Encyclopaedia of the Ancient World.** New York: Harper & Row, 1975. 509pp. ISBN 0–06–010178–4. LCCN 73–14245.

Begun by the Israeli scholar Michael Avi-Yonah, this encyclopedia was completed after his death by his colleague Israel Shatzman. The work is aimed at students and general readers. Its approximately 2,300 articles cover all aspects of Greek and Roman civilization from the Bronze Age to late antiquity. The articles tend to be brief and to focus on factual information: historical and biographical information, descriptions of places and works of art, and summaries of myths and literary works. Most include one or two bibliographical references. There are a number of illustrations, including a few in color. Several maps and a series of chronological listings of ancient kings and emperors follow the main text. Numerous cross-references and a selective index make it relatively easy to navigate the encyclopedia. This is a useful work for students, although it lacks the depth and scholarly detail of the *Oxford Classical Dictionary*[3] (entry 142).

130. Bowersock, G. W., Peter Brown, and Oleg Grabar, eds. **Late Antiquity: A Guide to the Postclassical World.** Cambridge, MA: Belknap Press of Harvard University, 1999. 780pp. ISBN 0–674–51173–5. LCCN 99–25639.

This volume covers the Mediterranean world from A.D. 250 to 800. Its editors and contributors include many of the leading scholars of the period. It begins with a series of essays: "Remaking the Past"; "Sacred Landscapes"; "Philosophical Tradition and Self"; "Religious Communities"; "Barbarians and Ethnicity"; "War and Violence"; "Empire Building"; "Christian Triumph and Controversy"; "Islam"; "The Good Life"; and "Habitat". An A-to-Z encyclopedia follows, offering approximately 500 articles on all aspects of late antiquity. Articles run from a few paragraphs to several pages; each includes a short bibliography. Many illustrations and an index complete the work. This is both an excellent introduction and reference work on the late antique period, useful both for students and scholars. The essays have also been published separately under the title *Interpreting Late Antiquity: Essays on the Postclassical World* (Cambridge, MA: Belknap Press of Harvard University, 2001).

131. Brodersen, Kai, and Bernhard Zimmermann. **Metzler Lexikon der Antike.** Stuttgart: J. B. Metzler, 2000. 703pp. ISBN 3–476–01610–2.

This well-written and attractively illustrated one-volume encyclopedia is suitable for students and general readers; scholars will find it a handy desk reference but lacking the depth of the *Oxford Classical Dictionary*[3] (entry 142). It covers all aspects of classical civilization, with occasional forays into the ancient Near East as well. Articles are brief but provide essential information along with a bibliographical reference or two (not always the most up-to-date). Since entries are often listed under the German rather than the classical term, those with limited German will sometimes find it a challenge. For example *imagines* are listed under the lemma *Ahnenbilder,* without cross-reference (while the *OCD*[3] lists it under the Latin term). Users should not miss the large compilation of helpful materials at the back of the volume: chronological tables, genealogies, ancient weights and measures, and maps. The bibliography includes mostly general works, with a preference for those in German. There is an essay on sources that covers archaeology, epigraphy, papyrology and literary texts; while cursory, it provides an overview and some guidance to further reading.

132. Cancik, Hubert, and Helmuth Schneider, eds. **Der Neue Pauly: Enzyklopädie der Antike.** Stuttgart: J. B. Metzler, 1996– . 16v. in 19. ISBN 3–476–01470–3 (set).

133. Cancik, Hubert, Manfred Landfester, and Helmuth Schneider, eds. **Der Neue Pauly: Supplemente.** Stuttgart: J. B. Metzler, 2004- . 7v. ISBN 3–476–02053–3 (set).

134. Cancik, Hubert, and Helmuth Schneider, eds. **Brill's New Pauly: Encyclopaedia of the Ancient World.** Leiden: Brill, 2002– . v. ISBN 90–04–12259–1 (set). LCCN 2003–275607.

Der Neue Pauly/Brill's New Pauly is *Der Kleine Pauly* (entry 165) updated and enlarged; it is in no way a replacement for the 83 volumes and 15 supplementary volumes of the original *Pauly* (entries 152–153). The first 12 volumes of *Der Neue Pauly* comprise an A-to-Z dictionary of antiquity; volumes 13–15 cover *Rezeptionsgeschichte* and the history of classical scholarship. The sixteenth volume includes a subject index, a concordance of ancient and modern place names, maps, chronologies, and so forth. The product of a large team of editors (23) and contributors (about 700), this work represents a good snapshot of the current state of scholarship. While the primary focus remains on classical antiquity, *Der Neue Pauly* offers much on the ancient Near East as well. Articles are of varying length and quality, as are their accompanying bibliographies. *Der Neue Pauly* reflects many recently discovered texts and archaeological finds not available to its predecessors, as well as new scholarly approaches. Seven supplementary volumes are projected, of which one, which provides lists of ancient kings and other rulers, has appeared that. Future supplements are to include history of texts, mythology, history of scholarship, and an atlas. This is a important reference work for all serious students and scholars, and yet largely accessible to nonspecialists. An English-language edition, *Brill's New Pauly,* is also in progress. As of early 2005, 5 volumes have been published of the projected 20. This edition is a translation of the German text (even articles originally written in English have been retranslated from German!). Bibliographies have been lightly updated and adapted for English readers. When complete, this will be the largest classical dictionary/encyclopedia available in English, with far more depth than the *Oxford Classical Dictionary*[3] (entry 142).

135. Cotterell, Arthur. **From Aristotle to Zoroaster: An A-to-Z Companion to the Classical World.** New York: Free Press, 1998. 483pp. ISBN 0–684–85596–8. LCCN 98–21729.

Cotterell focuses on the classical period but goes well beyond the usual bounds of the classical world to cover Persia, India, and China as well as Greece and Rome. His entries cover persons, places, and topics. Despite the title, he begins with the "Achaean League" and ends with "Zoroastrianism." Articles are short, generally accurate, but superficial. The bibliographies that follow them are likewise brief, but well chosen. The most interesting entries are those that take a comparative approach. For example, "Administration" provides a brief overview of government organization in India, China, Rome, Persia, and Greece, noting significant similarities and differences. Cotterell also provides a chronology and a number of maps. An index provides access to names and subjects that do not occur in the titles of entries. This is a useful work for students and general readers. The more advanced will generally prefer the *Oxford Companion to the Classical World* (entry 143) or the *Oxford Classical Dictionary*[3] (entry 142). Those who want a more extended narrative treatment of the same ground should also see Cotterell's *Penguin Encyclopedia of Classical Civilization* (entry 136).

136. Cotterell, Arthur, ed. **Penguin Encyclopedia of Classical Civilizations.** New York: Viking, 1993. 290pp. ISBN 0–670–82699–5.

Aimed at a popular audience, this work provides overviews of the major civilizations of antiquity. Its chapters, each by a specialist in the field, cover Hellenic civilization (500–338 B.C.), the Hellenistic age (336–31 B.C.), Rome (510 B.C.–A.D. 476), the successive Persian empires (Achaemenid, Parthian, and Sassanian), India (500 B.C.–A.D. 550), and China (481 B.C.–A.D. 316). Cotterell and his collaborators tend to focus on the "classical" periods of the civilizations and give relatively little attention to their early phases. Each chapter includes a chronology, a general historical overview, and sections devoted to social, cultural, and economic history. The work is well written and includes numerous illustrations (some in color). A brief general bibliography and a selective index conclude the volume. The *Encyclopedia* will be most useful to readers and students seeking a concise general overview of one or more of the ancient civilizations represented. It can also be used to compare the various ancient societies, at least in general terms.

137.   Crane, Gregory, ed. **Perseus Digital Library.** www.perseus.tufts.edu.

138.   Crane, Gregory, ed. **Perseus 2.0: Interactive Sources and Studies on Ancient Greece.** Platform Independent version, concise ed. New Haven, CT: Yale University Press, 2000. ISBN 0300080913.

   Perseus began as a general database for classical studies including text and images. It was originally published by Yale University Press on CD-ROM disks, which are still available. The Web version includes much more information, but fewer images, and is more up-to-date. While *Perseus* has expanded beyond classics to include material on the English Renaissance, the history of science, and the history of Tufts University, the bulk of the material remains classical. The classics section currently includes nearly 500 Greek and Latin texts, with both original versions and English translations. It also provides access to over 100 secondary studies, including many important older reference works. It is a good source for Greek and Latin dictionaries and grammars, when printed ones are not handy. *Perseus* also includes maps and images, including a searchable and browsable site catalog with images of ancient Greek sites. The tools menu offers numerous search options, and there are many hotlinks to navigate from one text to another. A separate papyri section includes the online *Duke Databank of Documentary Papryi* (entry 976). *Perseus* is an excellent source of information for the study and teaching of the ancient world.

139.   Daremberg, Ch., and Edm. Saglio, eds. **Dictionnaire des antiquités grecques et romaines d'après les textes et les monuments: Contenant l'explication des termes qui se rapportent aux moeurs, aux institutions, à la religion, aux arts, aux sciences, au costume, au mobilier, à la guerre, à la marine, aux métiers, aux monnaies, poids et mesures, etc., etc., et en general à la vie publique et privée des anciens.** 5 v. in 10. Paris: Hachette, 1877–1919; repr., Graz: Akademische Druck- u. Verlagsanstalt, 1969. LCCN 31–106232.

   This famous work is well known for its unsurpassed coverage of the material culture of antiquity. Though outdated in many respects, it remains the best source of information on *realia* (material remains). A true dictionary of antiquities, it treats objects, institutions, and concepts, not people or places. Articles cover such things as furniture, cooking implements, jewelry, tools, political and religious institutions and offices, and Greek and Latin technical terms relating to government, the military, and to various sciences and trades. Signed articles by a variety of hands offer clear, concise, and adequately detailed information on each topic. Each includes extensive references to the primary sources and to the then-current secondary literature. The work is fully illustrated with black-and-white engravings. Indexes are to be found in the final volume. An analytical table lists the lemmata under 17 broad subject headings. There are also indexes of Greek and Latin words and of ancient authors. In addition, many cross-references link related articles. Written on a far larger scale and superior in quality to Smith's *Dictionary* (entry 160), Daremberg and Saglio continues to be the best single reference work for those interested in the material remains of antiquity. Those who can read only English will find Smith the most helpful general source in this area.

140. **Enciclopedia classica.** Direzione: G. Battista Pighi, Carlo del Grande, Paolo E. Arias. Torino: Società Editrice Internazionale, 1957– . v. LCCN 60–38597.

Fewer than half of the projected 14 volumes of this general handbook on the classical world have been published. Since volumes are issued in fascicles, even some of these have only appeared in part. The work consists of four parts, which cover respectively ancient history, Greek and Latin literature, archaeology, and special topics (e.g., ancient science and mythology). Volumes on Roman history, Greek antiquities, the Latin language, archaeology, Roman art, and Greek art have been published to date. A number of Italian scholars have contributed to the *Enciclopedia;* each is responsible for a whole volume or fascicle. Although on a much larger scale, the *Enciclopedia* is similar in design to the French work of Laurand (entry 146). Despite its incomplete state, it contains much valuable information on Greek and Roman civilization. The numerous illustrations are noteworthy; these include many charts, plans, and aerial photographs that are not readily found elsewhere. Extensive bibliographical notes are supplied throughout the work; indexes appear at the end of each completed volume.

141. Grant, Michael, and Rachel Kitzinger. **Civilization of the Ancient Mediterranean: Greece and Rome.** New York: Scribner's, 1988. 3v. ISBN 0–684–18864–3 (v. 1); 0–684–18865–1 (v. 2); 0–684–18866–X (v. 3). LCCN 87–23465.

Some 88 noted scholars have contributed 97 essays to this handbook on classical civilization. The work begins with a chronological table and summaries of Greek and Roman history from the first millennium B.C. to the late 5th century A.D. A series of topical sections follows: "Land and Sea" (i.e., geography); "Population"; "Agriculture and Food"; "Technology"; "Government and Society"; "Economics"; "Religion"; "Private and Social Life"; "Women and Family Life"; "Literary and Performing Arts"; "Philosophy"; and "Visual Arts." Each of these contains several essays. The writing, while scholarly, is readable and accessible to a general audience. There are many illustrations; a substantial bibliographical note appears at the end of every essay. A detailed general index closes the work. This is an especially useful volume for those seeking extended treatments of broad topics in Greek and Roman civilization.

142. Hornblower, Simon, and Antony Spawforth, eds. **Oxford Classical Dictionary.** 3rd ed., rev. Oxford: Oxford University Press, 2003. 1,640pp. ISBN 0–19–860641–9. LCCN 2003–267385.

The first edition (1949) of the *Oxford Classical Dictionary,* which was edited by Max Cary, aimed to replace Smith's dictionaries of classical antiquities, biography, and geography (entries 160, 232, 413). It immediately became the standard general English-language reference work on the classical world. The second edition, edited by N.G.L. Hammond and H.H. Scullard, appeared in 1970. This edition included some new articles, many revised ones, and many reprinted with minor changes, if any. It focused heavily on literature and on traditional military and political history, giving less attention to economic and social history and to archaeology. The third edition, which first appeared in 1996, vastly expands coverage of previously neglected areas. The revised third edition of 2003 makes largely nugatory changes, correcting minor errors and adding one article on epinician poetry that functions primarily as a cross-reference; it does include some updated bibliographies.

The *OCD*³ covers the period from the beginnings of Greek civilization through late antiquity. Coverage of the later period is considerably stronger than in the second edition, which largely stopped at the death of Constantine (A.D. 337). The *OCD*³ includes articles on ancient authors, historical and mythological figures, places, events, objects, and concepts. It offers coverage of more-recently developed areas of classical studies, particularly through new thematic articles on such topics as "Anthropology and the Classics." Coverage of ancient sexuality, women's studies, the ancient Near East, early Christianity, and Judaism is vastly increased from the second edition. The *OCD*³ remains strongest on people and places, and weakest on *realia* (material culture). Articles range in length from a brief identification consisting of a few lines to several pages. Many articles include bibliographical notes that cite major primary sources and selected secondary works. The absence of maps and illustrations is a significant drawback. Breadth of coverage and the high quality of its content make the *OCD*³ the best work of its kind in English. For more extensive treatment of *realia,* one may consult the older works by Smith (entry 160) or Daremberg and Saglio (entry 139). Readers of German will find the *Lexikon der alten Welt* (entry 149) a valuable work that still offers some coverage beyond that found in *OCD*³ and should not neglect the vastly greater resources of *Der Neue Pauly,* which is slowly becoming available in English as *Brill's New Pauly* (entries 132–134).

143.   Hornblower, Simon, and Antony Spawforth, eds. **Oxford Companion to Classical Civilization.** Oxford: Oxford University Press, 1998. 793pp. ISBN 0–19–860165–4; 0–19–860958–2. LCCN 99–191129.

The first of several derivative works based on the third edition of the *Oxford Classical Dictionary* (entry 142), this volume reprints unaltered a generous selection of entries from the larger work. The editors write for the nonspecialist reader: technical and specialized entries are omitted, and the valuable bibliographies have been stripped away. Unlike the parent work, the *Companion* includes numerous illustrations. A chronology, maps, and an all-too-brief bibliography may be found at the end. The articles are of high quality and the format is more reader friendly than the *OCD*³. Students and general readers will find it attractive and readable, but advanced students and serious scholars will refer to the *OCD*³.

144.   Klauser, Theodor, ed. **Reallexikon für Antike und Christentum: Sachwörterbuch zur Auseinandersetzung des Christentums mit der antiken Welt.** Stuttgart: Hiersemann, 1950– . v. LCCN 54–20747.

145.   Klauser, Theodor, ed. **Reallexikon für Antike und Christentum: Sachwörterbuch zur Auseinandersetzung des Christentums mit der antiken Welt. Supplement.** Stuttgart: Hiersemann, 1985– . v. LCCN 85–182341.

This encyclopedia focuses on the civilization of the ancient Mediterranean world in relation to the early history of Christianity. Thus it offers broad but selective coverage of the ancient Near East and the classical world, combined with detailed coverage of early Christianity through the sixth century A.D. It includes articles on a wide range of topics: individual biographies, literature, philosophy, religion, medicine, and general antiquities. These vary in length; most articles are fairly compact, although some are quite extensive. Many include a substantial bibliography. All entries are signed; while the list of contributors is international, most are German. Issued in fascicles, the *Reallexikon* remains far from complete. As of early 2005, 18 volumes have appeared. Several supplements have also been published. These include both new articles and additions and revisions to existing articles. While the *Reallexikon* does not really provide encyclopedic coverage of the classical world, it is an invaluable resource for anyone seriously interested in ancient philosophy and religion, early Christianity, or late antiquity in general.

146.   Laurand, L., and A. Lauras. **Manuel des études grecques et latines.** Paris: A. et J. Picard, 1955–1970. 2v. LCCN 57–540.

147.   Laurand, L. **Pour mieux comprendre l'antiquité classique: Histoire et méthode historique, pedagogie, linguistique. Supplément au Manuel des études grecques et latines.** Paris: Auguste Picard, 1936. LCCN 38–17459.

After three-quarters of a century, this work has reached the point at which neither of the volumes, nor the supplement, are in the same edition. The first, now in its fourteenth edition, treats Greece. The second, in its fourth edition, covers Rome. Each of these contains a geographical survey, an outline history, discussion of social and political institutions (including coverage of virtually every aspect of daily life), a history of the literature, and a grammar of the language. Each major unit includes its own detailed table of contents and indexes. Many bibliographies are provided throughout the two volumes. The supplement (still in its first edition) offers a summary account of methodology and the transmission of classical texts, followed by an extensive discussion of the influence of the classics in modern times, especially in France. The supplement includes a general index. The work is now dated but remains of interest both for the range of material covered and for the French perspective, which is often quite different from that found in Anglo-Saxon works.

148.   Lemprière, J. **Lemprière's Classical Dictionary of Proper Names Mentioned in Ancient Authors Writ Large.** 3rd ed. London: Routledge & Kegan Paul, 1984. 675pp. ISBN 0–71020–068–4; 0–71020–843–Xpa. LCCN 83–22959.

Originally published in 1788 under the title *Bibliotheca Classica,* Lemprière has been frequently reprinted and widely used ever since. Having been used by such literary figures as Keats, it achieved modest notoriety. F. A. Wright revised this edition. Lemprière has entries only for proper names, including historical and mythological persons, peoples, and geographic names. His articles are usually short, ranging in length from a sentence to (rarely) several columns. He provides basic biographical information for historical individuals, brief summaries of the relevant stories under mythical characters, and identifications of places. Entries for the more important places also include a capsule history. Many of the entries include references to relevant ancient sources. While *Lemprière* is more restricted in scope than the majority of works noted in this chapter, this dictionary is a useful companion for readers of classical literature.

149. **Lexikon der alten Welt.** Zurich: Artemis, 1965. 3,523 cols. LCCN 67–105898.

Often called the *Artemis Lexikon,* this excellent work was compiled by an international (but primarily German) group of contributors. It includes the ancient Near East as well as the classical world. Selective coverage of the Byzantine period is provided also. Entries include people, places, material objects, and topical subjects. The quality of the articles sometimes varies but is generally quite good. Most articles include brief bibliographies. Many photographs, line drawings, and figures illustrate the text. A number of maps (some in color) are also provided. The four appendixes offer much helpful information. These include an alphabetical list of ancients with references to published ancient portraits of them, guidance in identifying and locating manscripts from the Latin names commonly applied to them, a list of abbrevations of papyrological work (now superseded by the *Checklist of Editions of Greek and Latin Papyri, Ostraca, and Tablets* [entries 970–971]), a list of the more important ancient sites and their excavators, a summary treatment of ancient weights and measures, and a small collection of famous sayings from Greek and Latin in both the original and German translation. The *Artemis Lexikon* remains somewhat more expansive than the *Oxford Classical Dictionary*[3] (entry 142) in size and scope. It may still be the best one-volume encyclopedia of the ancient world, although the third edition of the *OCD* is more up-to-date. Those who can read German should use it in addition to the *OCD*[3].

150. Matz, David. **Ancient World Lists and Numbers: Numerical Phrases and Rosters in the Greco-Roman Civilizations.** Jefferson, NC: McFarland, 1995. 254pp. ISBN 0–7864–0039–0. LCCN 95–3197.

This curious work is a list of lists and groups of people and things commonly described by a number. Matz begins with a brief discussion of list making in antiquity (e.g., Homer's catalog of ships, Callimachus). He then gives his lists arranged by number, beginning with threes and extending to the "over five hundreds." One finds the usual suspects: the three fates, the seven sages, the seven hills of Rome, the seven wonders, the nine muses, and so on. Matz also includes many rather artificial items: literary works entered under their number of books, 18 cities founded by Alexander (all called Alexandria!), and so forth. Some include explanatory notes and references to sources, while many do not. Discussion is simplistic and omits useful detail: Matz lists 12 Olympians, the canonical number, without discussion of how this is constructed from the 14 major gods and goddesses. An index provides name and subject access. While Matz does bring together information from many sources, this is an eccentric and not entirely reliable work.

151. Matz, David. **Famous Firsts in the Ancient Greek and Roman World.** Jefferson, NC: McFarland, 2000. 154pp. ISBN 0–7864–0599–6. LCCN 99–52497.

"Famous Firsts" is a well-known genre of reference works; surprisingly Matz's is the first such work to appear concerning the classical world. Matz divides his work into six sections: mythological firsts; politics, oratory, law, and government; military and foreign affairs; innovations and inventions of noted individuals; and miscellaneous. These are generally subdivided into Greek and Roman sections. Anyone seeking a specific event is well advised to consult the index. Matz includes both the significant and the trivial. Nor is he always reliable: some entries (e.g., *devotio*) provide incomplete or misleading information. This is a work to be used with great caution.

152. Pauly, August Friedrich von. **Paulys Realencyclopädie der classischen Alter-tumswissenschaft.** Neue Bearbeitung unter Mitwirkung zahlreicher Fachgenosen herausgegeben von Georg Wissowa. Reihe I, 47v. in 48; Reihe II, 19v. Stuttgart: J.B. Metzler, 1893–1972. LCCN 01–2869.

153. **Paulys Realencyclopädie der classischen Altertumswissenschaft. Supplement.** Stuttgart: J.B. Metzler, 1903–1978. 15v.

154. Erler, Tobias. **Paulys Realencyclopädie der classischen Altertumswissen-schaft: Gesamtregister.** Stuttgart: J.B. Metzler, 1997–2000. 1,158pp. v. 1 + 2 CD-ROms. ISBN 3–476–01195–X.

155. Gartner, Hans, and Albert Wünsch. **Paulys Realencyclopädie der classischen Altertumswissenschaft: Neue Bearbeitung begonnen von Georg Wissowa fortgeführt von Wilhelm Kroll und Karl Mittelhaus ... Register der Nächtrage und Supplemente.** München: Alfred Druckenmüller, 1980. 250pp.

156. Murphy, John P. **Index to the Supplements and Supplementary Volumes of Paul Wissowa's RE: Index to the Nachträge and Berichtigungen in Vols. I–XXIV of the First Series, Vols. I–X of the Second Series, and the Supplementary Vols. I–XIV of Pauly-Wissowa-Kroll's Realenzyklopädie, with an Appendix Containing an Index to Suppl. Vol. XV (Final).** 2nd ed. Chicago: Ares, 1980. 144pp. ISBN 0–89005–174–7.

The massive *Realencyclopädie* is a fundamental reference work for every area of classical studies. It is frequently referred to as Pauly-Wissowa; citations commonly use the abbreviation *RE,* which is followed by the volume and column numbers. The basic encyclopedia appeared in two series, which cover A–Q and R–Z respectively. Corrections and additions are found in the *Nachträge* located in the back of many of these volumes. The *Supplement,* which is itself in 15 volumes, includes both new articles and revisions to existing articles. For a brief history of Pauly-Wissowa, consult Kai Hessling's review of *Der Neue Pauly* in *Reference Reviews Europe Annual* 4 (1998): 150–153.

The product of several generations of German scholars, Pauly-Wissowa covers all aspects of classical studies in great detail. Its entries include people, places, topical subjects, and Greek and Latin terms. Even relatively obscure individuals and places can be found in Pauly-Wissowa. While the articles vary in length, most are substantial. Some articles are actually short monographs. A particularly valuable feature is the exhaustive listing of ancient sources for each subject. Pauly-Wissowa is exceptionally difficult to use. In addition to requiring a solid knowledge of German, its organization is complex and often confusing. Although Pauly-Wissowa's arrangement is alphabetical, one must also consult the *Nachträge* and articles in the *Supplement.* Sometimes even the basic encyclopedia can be challenging. For example, individual Romans are normally listed by the gens (family) name. The result is that dozens, or, in some cases, hundreds, of individuals are gathered under a particular name. While each is marked off and numbered in sequence, it can be a time-consuming process to find the one sought. In general, the best way to consult Pauly-Wissowa is to begin with one of the separately published indexes (Erler, Gartner, or Murphy); this will help both in finding the appropriate article and in locating any relevant *Nachträge* or supplementary articles.

Erler, the best and most complete index, covers the full work, including supplements. His first volume, an alphabetical listing of keywords and article authors, is available in both print and CD-ROM formats; the second (subject) volume is available only on CD-ROM. The CD-ROM, which employs Folio Views software, offers a variety of search options. Gartner and Murphy both provide an alphabetical list of article titles accompanied by references to corrections and supplements. Both also use a coding system to indicate the extent of the new material, which may range from minor additions to complete replacement of the original article. Gartner's entries generally provide more information than do those of Murphy. Gartner also includes an alphabetical index of all contributors to both the original volumes and supplements to Pauly-Wissowa.

There is also an abridged version of Pauly-Wissowa, *Der Kleine Pauly* (entry 165). It is easier to use but includes much less information. Since it frequently includes references to the full articles in the original and its supplements, *Der Kleine Pauly* can also be used as a guide to the larger work. *Der Neue Pauly* (entry 132–133), rather a new and improved version of *Der Kleine Pauly*, updates but in no way supersedes the original work. An English version, *Brill's New Pauly* (entry 134), will at last give those who read only English some access to the riches of these vast reference works.

157.   Peck, Harry Thurston, ed. **Harper's Dictionary of Classical Literature and Antiquities.** New York: American Book, 1896; repr., New York: Cooper Square, 1962. 1,701pp. LCCN 01–20387.

This work is similar to Smith's dictionaries (entries 160, 232, 413), although on a smaller scale. Its many entries deal with virtually every aspect of classical civilization: literature, mythology and religion, history, geography, and archaeology. It is particularly good for *realia* and topics dealing with everyday life in classical antiquity. Articles tend to be brief, although those on broader subjects occasionally run to several pages. Some articles include bibliographies, although these are badly dated. Numerous line drawings and figures accompany the text; many provide handy illustrations of various artifacts. Despite its age, this work remains useful. More recent works, such as the *Oxford Classical Dictionary*[3] (entry 142), should be preferred but do not always include everything in the older works of Smith and Peck.

158.   Richardson, W. F. **Numbering and Measuring in the Classical World: An Introductory Handbook.** Rev. 2nd ed. Bristol: Bristol Phoenix Press, 2004. 82pp. ISBN 1–904675–18–2.

Richardson offers a guide to the often arcane systems used by the ancients for reckoning, weights, and measures. This short book covers only the basics; discussion is limited, although Richardson often refers to the ancient sources. He begins with Roman and Greek numbers and reckoning and then proceeds through symbols, fractions, arithmetic, linear measures, area and volume, weight, capacity, value, financial matters, sizes of pipes and nozzles, and, finally, time. Richardson also provides a short bibliography and indexes of passages quoted and words (English, Greek, and Latin). This is both an excellent handbook for readers of ancient texts and a good starting point for those with a deeper interest in the topic.

159.   Sandys, John Edwin, ed. **Companion to Latin Studies.** 3rd ed. Cambridge: Cambridge University Press, 1935; repr., New York: Hafner, 1968. 891pp. LCCN 26–5843.

Designed as a *vade mecum* for students of Latin, this venerable work represents the combined efforts of 27 notable British scholars of the early twentieth century. Its articles cover every aspect of Roman civilization: the geography and and ethnology of Italy, fauna and flora, an outline of Roman history, religion and mythology, law, finance, population, social organization, industries and commerce, roads and travel, weights and measures, money, the Roman army and navy, art, literature, philosophy, and natural science. Articles are also provided on various specialized fields of study such as epigraphy, palaeography, textual criticism, language, meter, and the history of scholarship. While most of the material is badly dated, much remains of value if used with some care. Sandys remains a handy source of general information on such topics as flora and fauna, weights and measures, and money. The work's four indexes cover ancient peoples and persons, geographical names, scholars and modern writers, and Latin words. There is a companion volume for Greek studies by Whibley (entry 164).

160.   Smith, William, ed. **Dictionary of Greek and Roman Antiquities.** London: John Murray, 1875. 1,293pp. LCCN 16–7351.

Smith's dictionary of antiquities is a companion volume to his similar works on classical biography (entry 232) and geography (413). Like those works, it exists in many editions and printings. The most recent reprint bears the title *A Dictionary of Greek and Roman Culture* (London: I. B. Tauris, 2005). Its contributors include a number of eminent nineteenth-century British classical scholars. Although now badly out-of-date, it remains, along with Daremberg and Saglio (entry 139), one of the few reference sources for information about *realia* (material culture). Its articles cover physical artifacts, Greek and Latin technical terms (legal, military, architectural, etc.), festivals and events, weights, measures, and money. Some illustrations and charts accompany the text. Indexes cover Greek words, Latin words, and subjects. A classified index also lists pertinent entries under broad subject headings. When possible one should use more current dictionaries and handbooks noted elsewhere in this chapter. However, for some material objects, Smith or Daremberg and Saglio still provide the best information available without recourse to highly specialized works. Those who understand French should consult Daremberg and Saglio, which is generally considered the superior work. Smith is now also available on the Web through *Perseus* (entry 137) at www.perseus.tufts.edu/cgi-bin/ptext?doc = Perseus%3Atext%3A1 999.04.0063.

161.   Speake, Graham. **Dictionary of Ancient History.** Oxford: Blackwell, 1994. 758pp. ISBN 0–631–18069–9. LCCN 93–1437.

Intended for students and general readers, this work covers not only Greek and Roman military and political history but also literature, philosophy, religion, art, and society. Its chronological limits range from the first Olympics in 776 B.C. to the fall of the western Roman Empire in A.D. 476. A very few entries, which cover the Greek Bronze Age or the Byzantine Empire, fall outside these boundaries. A team of British historians and classicists prepared the articles; all are signed. The entries include persons, places, events, and topics. Most tend to be brief, often a single paragraph. Occasionally treatment of major topics will extend to a page or more. References for further study appear at the end of most entries. Speake provides an extensive general bibliography, a number of genealogical tables and king lists, and a selection of maps at the end of the volume. The maps are taken from the works of Levi (entry 429) and Cornell and Matthews (entry 420). While there are no indexes, many cross-references are provided throughout the body of the dictionary. This work offers concise articles that supply basic information on a wide range of subjects. Its treatment of these is rarely as full as that found in the *Oxford Classical Dictionary* (entry 142).

162.　　Speake, Graham, ed. **Encyclopedia of Greece and the Hellenic Tradition.** London: Fitzroy Dearborn, 2000. 2v. ISBN 1–57958–141–2.

This work covers the Greek world from the Bronze Age to the modern era. Much of it is devoted to ancient Greece, although Byzantine and modern Greece receive considerable attention. Contributors include many well-known scholars. Articles cover people, places, events, and topics. Most run a page or less; a few run to as many as 14 (for architecture, which is subdivided by type). Some have a brief summary at the end (labelled "Biography" in articles on individuals); all have a useful bibliography. Maps are printed on the endpapers, and many attractive illustrations appear throughout. Alphabetical and thematic lists of entries may be found at the front of the first volume. While the *Oxford Classical Dictionary* (entry 142) offers more extensive coverage of classical Greece, and the *Oxford Dictionary of Byzantium* (Oxford: Oxford University Press, 1991) of Byzantine Greece, no single work offers better coverage of Greek civilization as a whole. (Disclaimer: The author contributed an article to this work.)

163.　　Warrington, John. **Everyman's Classical Dictionary, 800** B.C.–A.D. **337.** 3rd ed. London: J. M. Dent, 1970. 537pp. LCCN 78–110947.

Aimed at students and general readers, this dictionary covers classical civilization from Homer to Constantine. Early Christian matters receive scant attention. Warrington provides an unusually large amount of front matter. This includes a list of modern place names with their ancient equivalents, a list of the principal philosophical schools of antiquity, a genealogical table of the Julio-Claudians, and a select bibliography of general works. A systematic list of the entries follows, which gathers them under a number of broad subject headings, such as geography and topography, Greek literature, and philosophy and science. Only then does one reach the dictionary proper. The relatively short articles emphasize the factual. There are many cross-references to related articles. No bibliographies are provided in the entries. Warrington's dictionary is adequate, although most will be better served by the more comprehensive *Oxford Classical Dictionary*[3] (entry 142). Its compact format makes it somewhat handier as a companion to reading. Because there is little difference between the various editions of this work, those who have access only to earlier ones need not be unduly concerned.

164.　　Whibley, Leonard. **Companion to Greek Studies.** 4th ed. Cambridge: Cambridge University Press, 1931; repr., New York: Hafner, 1968. 790pp. LCCN 33–3397.

Similar in design to Sandys's *Companion to Latin Studies* (entry 159), this work contains articles by some 40 prominent British scholars of the early twentieth century. Every aspect of Greek civilization is covered: geography; ethnology; fauna; flora; history;

literature; philosophy; science; art; mythology and religion; law; finance; population; commerce and industry; weights and measures; money; war; ships; the calendar; family; birth, marriage, and death; education; books and writing; the position of women; dress; daily life; houses and furniture; and medicine. There are also artices on such topics as Greek dialects, epigraphy, palaeography, textual criticism, meter, and the history of scholarship. In its day, this manual provided the basic background material and technical knowledge needed by students of Greek literature. Although much of its content is now badly dated, Whibley is still a good source for some types of information. For example, it is a handy reference for such things as weights and measures, calendars, and flora and fauna of the ancient world. But it should always be used with care. In addition to a very detailed table of contents, the book includes four indexes that cover ancient peoples and persons, geographical names, scholars and modern writers, and Greek words.

165. Ziegler, Konrat, and Walther Sontheimer. **Der Kleine Pauly: Lexikon der Antike auf der Grundlage um Pauly's Realencyclopädie der classischen Altertumswissenschaft.** Stuttgart: Alfred Druckmüller, 1964–1975. 5 v. LCCN 66–780.

This greatly abridged version of *Pauly's Realencyclopädie* (entry 152) is both more current and easier to use than the original, although it covers much less than the original work. The signed articles are compact and informative. All material has been updated and revised. There are entries for people, places, and topical subjects. Articles range in length from a paragraph to several pages. Nearly all include brief bibliographical notes. Corrections and additions appear in the final volume. *Der Kleine Pauly* provides a middle option for those who find the one-volume encyclopedias, such as the *Oxford Classical Dictionary*[3] (entry 142), too limited but who are not inclined to deal with the full-sized *Pauly*. Since it often gives references to the articles in the more complex larger work, *Der Kleine Pauly* also can be used as an index to it. However, *Der Neue Pauly* (entry 132) and its English version, *Brill's New Pauly* (entry 134), now largely supersede *Der Kleine Pauly*.

6
General Internet Resources

The Internet offers access to a variety of new sources of information in classical studies. Most are quite unlike traditional printed sources. Those noted in this chapter include only metasites and electronic discussion groups ("lists"). Many additional Web sites appear in other chapters by form or subject; for example, *Bibliotheca Classica Selecta* (entry 27) is located in chapter 1, *Perseus* (entry 137) in chapter 5. The Web sites of the various classical societies and associations listed in chapter 20 also offer numerous links to online resources. The discussion groups listed below provide news about recent publications, research in progress, and pedagogical matters. They also offer a convenient means of communicating directly with a large body of scholars, students, and others interested in the list's subject area; queries posted to lists often draw helpful responses. Electronic journals may be found in chapters 3 and 4. Do note that Web sites and lists tend to be ephemeral; many of those listed in the first edition of this book no longer exist, and a significant number of links found in the sites listed below are dead. While the Web is often more convenient and timely, it lacks the stability of printed works.

METASITES

166.   Atrium: For Students and Fans of Ancient Greece and Rome. URL: http://web.idirect.com/~atrium.

The *Atrium*, a site maintained by David Meadows, includes both popular and scholarly materials, with a decided emphasis on the popular. Among its features are "This Day in Ancient History" and "The Ancient World on Television." The "Bibliotheca" offers information, a bibliography, and links for a wide range of topics, although not all its subject headings currently lead to content.

167.   Classics Page at Ad Fontes Academy. URL: www.thelatinlibrary.com/classics#texts.

This page, maintained by a private K–12 school in the Washington, D.C., area, offers a wide array of Latin texts as part of its Latin library. These include many standard classical and Medieval Latin works. They are public-domain texts, without critical apparatus. The site also includes links to many other classical sites, including quite a few association pages.

168.   Diotima: Materials for the Study of Women and Gender in the Ancient World. URL: www.stoa.org/diotima.

Diotima covers all aspects of the study of women in antiquity: literary, historical, and archaeological. The site includes a bibliography, articles, primary sources in translation, images, and numerous links to other Web resources. *Diotima* also was originally connected with *Anahita-L,* an electronic discussion group on women and gender in antiquity (entry 176). It still houses some of that list's archives.

169.   Electronic Resources for Classicists: The Second Generation. URL: www.tlg. uci.edu/index/about.html.

Maintained by Maria Pantelia of the University of California, Irvine, and the *Thesaurus Linguae Graecae* (entry 519), this is one of the oldest and best-known metasites for classical studies. It includes links to other metasites, electronic journals, text archives, and other resources. It also offers information about fonts and software, discussion groups, classics departments, and the like. It is an excellent site in range and selection but includes many dead links.

170.   Humbul Humanities Hub: Classics. URL: www.humbul.ac.uk/output/subout. php?subj = classics.

This site, which is hosted by Oxford University, offers both search and browsing features. It divides resources into the following categories: projects and organizations, research-related resources, teaching and learning-related resources, primary sources, secondary sources, and bibliographic sources. There is a fair amount of overlap among these. The site provides links to texts (original and translated), images, museum sites, research projects, and other resources. *Humbul* provides detailed descriptions of the various resources, which is one of its great strengths.

171.   Kirke: Katalog der Internetressourcen für die Klassische Philologie. URL: www.kirke.hu-berlin.de/ressourc/ressourc.html.

This site is in German but does not require much German to navigate. It is well organized and includes many links to resources in English, French, and Italian as well as German. Categories include general resources; bibliographies; electronic discussion groups; ancient authors; Rome; philology and literature; women in antiquity; philosophy, medicine, and science; computers and the ancient world; numismatics; academic institutes and departments; online journals; texts in the original and/or translation; history; palaeography, papyrology, and epigraphy; religion and mythology; late antiquity and Christianity; teaching materials; archaology; and sites and museums. Each includes an extensive array of resources and links. *Kirke* includes many resources not found on other sites, along with the requisite number of dead links.

172.   Library of Congress, Alcove 9: Classical and Medieval History. URL: www. loc.gov/rr/main/alcove9/classics.html.

This rather limited site includes brief descriptions and links for some of the usual suspects such as *Perseus* (entry 137), *Bryn Mawr Classical Review* (entry 66), and *De Imperatoribus Romanis* (entry 204). It also includes links to useful sites on Latin place-names, Roman dates and numerals, and Greek and Latin abbreviations.

173.   Voice of the Shuttle: Classical Studies. URL: http://vos.ucsb.edu/browse.asp? id = 2708.

Along with *Electronic Resources for Classicists* (entry 169), this is one of the older and better-known metasites in the field. *Voice of the Shuttle* also offers a wide array of links, not a few of them dead. Categories include general resources, language resources, archaeology, history and culture, literature (with numerous author listings), philosophy, journals, associations and university departments, and listservs and newsgroups. Among other things this site provides links to texts in the original and in translation, reference works, maps, images, and course sites and syllabi.

174. **VROMA: A Virtual Community for Teaching and Learning Classics.** URL: www.vroma.org.

This NEH-supported Web site encompasses a variety of resources. These include a searchable database of images, numerous resources for teaching Latin and ancient history, and links to many other sites.

ELECTRONIC DISCUSSION GROUPS (LISTSERVS)

These are also called "lists" because many of them run on Listserv software. Some are moderated (i.e., the list owner reviews all postings before forwarding them to the list), while others allow any subscriber to post directly to the list. Many discussion groups allow only subscribers to post messages. In most cases, it is possible to subscribe by sending the following message to the subscription address: subscribe <listname> <first name> <last name>. Some lists also offer the ability to subscribe on their Web pages.

175. **AEGEANET.** URL: http://people.ku.edu/-jyounger/aegeanet.html. Subscription address: listproc@ku.edu.

Based at the University of Kansas, this discussion group focuses on all aspects of Aegean Bronze Age archaeology. Most subscribers are professional archaeologists or ancient historians. To subscribe to this list, just send the message "subscribe aegeanet your name" to the above address. The homepage has additional information about the list. This list has very low traffic.

176. **Anahita-L.** URL: http://groups.yahoo.com/group/Anahita-l. Subscription address: Anahita-l-subscribe@yahoogroups.com.

This list was originally hosted at the University of Kentucky and is closely linked to *Diotima* (entry 168). It focuses on scholarly discussion of women and gender in antiquity, occasionally offering more popular content as well. Subscription information and archives since March 2000 may be found on the list's Web page. Older archives are located at http://lsv.uky.edu/archives/anahita.html.

177. **ANCIEN-L.** Subscription address: listserv@listserv.louisville.edu.

The history of the ancient Mediterranean world is the focus of this list. It covers the ancient Near East as well as the classical world. Content is generally scholarly, with some popular material included. Traffic on the list is usually moderate.

178. **ARCH-L.** URLs: www.lsoft.com/scripts/wl.exe?SL1 = ARCH-L&H = LIST-SERV.TAMU.EDU; http://listserv.tamu.edu/archives/arch-l.html. Subscription address: listserv@tamu.edu.

This is a general discussion group for archaeology. It is especially concerned with current research and excavations. Announcements concerning postions, conferences, and the like frequently appear on it as well. This is normally a low-volume list.

179. **B-Greek.** URL: www.ibiblio.org/bgreek/index.html.

B-Greek is a discussion forum on biblical Greek, including patristic texts as well as the Septuagint and the New Testament. Its participants include both scholars and relative beginners. Postings tend to focus on translation of individual passages, points of grammar, and requests for bibliographies. More information and archives of previous postings are available on the Web site, which also offers instructions for subscribing. The volume tends to be a bit high.

180. **Classicists.** URL: http://listserv.liv.ac.uk/archives/classicists.html.

This listserv is operated by the Classical Association (entry 1011) and is primarily of interest to British classicists. It includes conference announcements and position openings in the United Kingdom. Subscription information and list archives are available on the Web site. There are typically only a few posts per week.

181. **CLASSICS-L.** http://lsv.uky.edu/archives/classics-l.html. Subscription address: listserv@lsv.uky.edu.

The *Classics* list concentrates on the study and teaching of Greek and Latin language and literature, with occasional digressions into history and archaeology. Content is geared toward an academic audience. Traffic on the list runs from moderate to heavy. This list has a decided tendency to get sidetracked on minor or irrelevant issues. It is, however, an excellent news source and a good place to post queries on classical topics. It is possible both to join the list and to browse its archive of previous postings at the list Web site.

182. **ELENCHUS.** Subscription address: listserv@listserv.uottawa.ca.

While primarily of interest to scholars of religion, this discussion group occasionally addresses topics of interest to classicists. Its scope includes the thought and literature of Christianity through the sixth century A.D. The discussion often tends toward technical matters. Volume is usually rather light.

183. **IOUDAIOS-L.** URL: http://listserv.lehigh.edu/lists/ioudaios-l.

This list is devoted to Judaism in the Greco-Roman world. The discussion generally assumes knowledge of Greek and Hebrew. Subscription information and the list archives are available through the list Web site.

184. **LATIN-L.** http://nxport.com/mailman/listinfo/latin. Subscription address: latin@nxport.com.

Intended for those interested in Latin language and literature, this list accepts postings in Latin or English. Many of the active participants are high school Latin teachers. Common topics include pedagogical matters and discussion of how to translate various English expressions into Latin. The volume of postings tends to be light.

185. **LT-ANTIQ.** URL: www.sc.edu/ltantsoc/#ltantiq. Subscription address: listserv@listserv.sc.edu.

This discussion group covers all aspects of late antiquity (defined as ca. A.D. 260–640). Postings on religious and philosophical topics are the most common, although general historical and literary topics also receive attention. Volume on the list is usually moderate.

186. **MEDANT.** URL: www.medicinaantiqua.org.uk/mm_emaildiscussionlist.html.

This discussion list focuses on ancient medicine. It includes the usual announcements of conferences, new publications, and so forth. Subscriptions may be entered through its Web page. An archive of previous postings is available.

187. **MEDTXTL.** URL: http://listserv.uiuc.edu/archives/medtextl.html.

Although aimed primarily at medievalists, this list is useful for anyone interested in palaeography and the transmission of classical literature during the Middle Ages. The list's normal topics include philology, codicology, and the analysis of medieval texts. Information about subscribing and the list's archives may be found on the Web site.

188. **NUMISM-L.** URL: http://listserv.sc.edu/archives/numism-l.html. Subscription address: listserv@univscvm.csd.scarolina.edu.

Aimed at both collectors and scholars, this list offers a discussion forum on ancient and medieval coinage. Chronologically, its scope extends to the fall of Byzantium (A.D. 1454). The list is a good source of current information on this rather specialized field. Previous postings may be found in the list archives at the above URL.

189. **PAPY.** URL: www.listserv.hum.ku.dk/archives/papy.html. Subscription address: listserv@igl.ku.dk.

Based at the University of Copenhagen, this list focuses on papyrology and the study of Greco-Roman Egypt. Postings tend to be sporadic, and their contents are often somewhat technical. It is a good source of information about recent publications and developments in the field. Archives of previous postings are available on the list's Web page.

190. **SOPHIA.** URL: http://listserv.liv.ac.uk/archives/sophia.html. Subscription address: listserv@liverpool.ac.uk.

This list provides a general forum for the discussion of ancient philosophy. Its scope extends from Hesiod to Iamblichus, and from Spain to Palestine. The volume of traffic is normally low and consists mostly of announcements.

7
Biographical Works

A number of different types of works will be found in this chapter. The first section includes dictionaries and other primarily textual works that provide biographical data about ancient Greeks and Romans. The dictionaries tend to deal with famous figures of antiquity: political leaders, generals, artists, writers, and the like. These will accommodate the needs of most people seeking biographical information on the ancients. Prosopographies, on the other hand, include minor officials, soldiers, and ordinary folk, as well as the famous. They are often based on the more esoteric primary sources, such as inscriptions and papyri. For the most part these works will interest specialists. Dictionaries and handbooks treating the lives of classical scholars may be found in chapter 19. The second section is devoted to collections of portraits. These will be of use to anyone who wishes to find a picture of a particular person from classical antiquity. Some of these works also include basic biographical information.

BIOGRAPHICAL DICTIONARIES AND PROSOPOGRAPHIES

191. Alföldy, Géza. **Fasti Hispanienses: Senatorische Reichsbeamte und Offiziere in den spanischen Provinzen des Römischen Reiches von Augustus bis Diokletian.** Wiesbaden: Franz Steiner, 1969. 335pp.

The first part of this work (pp. 1–190) consists of prosopographical lists of imperial officials (governors, *iuridici,* legates, tribunes, etc.) in the Roman provinces of Hispania Citerior, Lusitania, and Baetica. The lists are arranged by office and subarranged chronologically. Entries range from about a half page to several pages. These give the full name of the individual, date of his office in Spain (and date of consulship, if held). Then, literary and epigraphic sources follow. The body of the entry discusses the person's family connections and political and military activities, with emphasis on activities in Spain. Extensive bibliographical references are included. An index of personal names provides alphabetical access. There are also indexes of geographical names, of ancient sources, and of offices and titles. Alföldy is a good supplement to the *Prosopographia Imperii Romani* (entries 228–229) for Romans who served in Spain.

192. Avery, Catherine B., ed. **New Century Handbook of Leaders of the Classical World.** New York: Appleton-Century-Crofts, 1972. 393pp. ISBN 0–390–66948–2. LCCN 71–189007.

Drawn from the larger *New Century Classical Handbook* (entry 128), this work offers short biographies of generals, politicians, kings, queens, and emperors of the Greek and Roman world. Rulers of neighboring states, such as the Persian Empire, are included also. Articles range in length from a paragraph to several pages, depending on the person's relative importance. Most provide an adequate account of the subject's life and activities, although lack of bibliographies is a major weakness. All entries include a guide to pronunciation. While there is no index, Avery supplies plentiful cross-references. Those who seeking a general biographical dictionary that includes cultural as well as military and political figures will find Bowder's two works (entries 194–195) superior. Many of the individuals found in Avery are also discussed in more general handbooks and encyclopedias, such as the *Oxford Classical Dictionary*[3] (entry 142).

193.   Berve, Helmut. **Das Alexanderreich auf prosopographischer Grundlage.** München: C. H. Beck, 1926; repr., Salem, NH: Ayer, 1988. 2v.

The second volume of Berve's work is a prosopography of more than 800 individuals associated with Alexander the Great. They are listed alphabetically (in the Greek alphabet). Entries, which are numbered sequentially, range from a paragraph to several pages. Each provides a brief biography, with bibliographies of primary sources and modern studies. A number of people whom Berve believes to have been incorrectly associated with Alexander are covered in a separate section at the end of the volume. Although somewhat dated, Berve remains a useful resource.

194.   Birley, Anthony R. **Fasti of Roman Britain.** Oxford: Clarendon Press, 1981. 476pp. ISBN 0–19–814821–6. LCCN 80–41709.

Birley, one of the foremost authorities on Roman Britain, covers the higher Roman officials (e.g., governors, military commanders, procurators) in Britain from its subjugation in A.D. 43 to the expulsion of the Roman governor in 409. After a brief general introduction (which provides a good overview of the senatorial career under the empire), Birley presents biographies of individual officials arranged by office and subarranged chronologically. The biographies are compact and readable. Each entry includes information about its subject's career, family, and personality. There are full references to, and often extensive quotations from, the primary sources, and many references to modern studies. Access is facilitated by several indexes. The index of persons highlights in capitals those who are given biographical entries in the text. There are also geographical and general indexes and an index of sources quoted in extenso. Birley is an excellent source for information about any Roman with a British connection.

195.   Bowder, Diana, ed. **Who Was Who in the Greek World, 776 B.C.–30 B.C.** Ithaca, NY: Cornell University Press, 1982. 227pp. ISBN 0–8014–1538–1 LCCN 82–71594.

Bowder offers biographical sketches of the major historical and cultural figures of the Greek world from the traditional date of the first Olympiad (776 B.C.) down to completion of the Roman conquest of the Greek world. Legendary characters of the early period are largely omitted, although the introduction discusses a few of the more important ones. Some Greek notables of the Roman period (30 B.C.–A.D. 476) appear in Bowder's companion volume for the Roman world (entry 196). Entries are brief and factual; nearly all include one or more bibliographical references. The work is also well illustrated with contemporary portraits drawn from coins and works of art. Cross-references lead the reader from variant forms of a name to the proper entry. There is also an index of persons mentioned who do not receive an entry of their own. Bowder also provides glossary of technical terms, several maps, selected genealogical tables, and a short general bibliography.

196. Bowder, Diana, ed. **Who Was Who in the Roman World: 753** B.C.–A.D. **476.** Ithaca, NY: Cornell University Press, 1980. 256pp. ISBN 0–8014–1358–3 LCCN 80–67821.

This companion volume to Bowder's *Who Was Who in the Greek World* (entry 195) provides similar coverage for the ancient Romans. It includes nearly all major historical and cultural figures of the Roman world, which has been broadly defined to include the entire empire and non-Romans who had a significant impact on Roman history. Overlap with the companion work is limited, so that both must be used for full coverage. Entries are brief (one or two paragraphs) and present basic dates and facts. As in the companion volume, nearly every entry has some bibliographical references to works by or about the subject; these are well chosen. Ancient portraits drawn from coins or sculpture illustrate many entries. A chronological table, genealogical tables of the imperial dynasties, numerous maps, and a glossary of frequently used technical terms aid the reader. There is also an index of people mentioned without full entries of their own. Bowder's two volumes and Radice (entry 230) will cover most routine biographical queries.

197. Bradford, Alfred S. **Prosopography of Lacedaemonians from the Death of Alexander the Great, 323** B.C., **to the Sack of Sparta by Alaric,** A.D. **396.** Vestigia 27. München: C. H. Beck, 1977. 499pp. ISBN 3–406–04797–1. LCCN 78–310194.

A continuation of Poralla's *Prosopography of Lacedaimonians* (entry 227), Bradford's work extends coverage down to the destruction of Sparta in A.D. 396. Bradford includes citizens of Sparta and members of the families and households of citizens. He also lists foreigners with honorary Spartan citizenship. Like Poralla, Bradford uses an alphabetical arrangement (names are in the Greek alphabet). Individuals of the same name are distinguished by number; subarrangement varies according to what is known about each person. Cross-references are provided from unused forms, although they do not always make clear the chosen form of entry. Bradford makes no attempt to compose complete biographies for major figures; instead he offers a summary account and refers the reader to published biographies for further information. The standard format of entries is name—sources—biography. The sources consist chiefly of contemporary inscriptions, although literary sources make an occasional appearance. Modern studies are cited in a few entries. The biographies tend to concentrate on family connections and offices held. Most entries are very brief, since most of the subjects are known from a single inscription. Appendixes offer lists that bring together related entries (e.g., eponymous officials) and stemmata of the royal houses. Poralla and Bradford are specialized sources best used for obscure Spartans; Bowder (entry 195), the *Oxford Classical Dictionary*[3] (entry 142), or Pauly-Wissowa (entry 152) are better choices for well-known Spartans.

198. Broughton, T. Robert S. **Magistrates of the Roman Republic.** Philological Monographs 15. 3 v. Chico, CA: Scholars Press, 1984–1986. ISBN 0–89130–706–0 (v. 1); 0–89130–812–1 (v. 2); 0–89130–811–3 (v. 3). LCCN 84–23590.

The first two volumes are reprinted from the original edition (New York: American Philological Association, 1951–1952), while the third is a supplement including additions and corrections. A standard reference work for Roman historians since it first appeared, *MRR* provides information on all known Roman magistrates and officials from 509 B.C. to 31 B.C. Its arrangement is chronological, with offices listed in descending order of importance.

Each entry lists the incumbent(s) for the year, summarizes his activities in office, and provides references to the relevant ancient evidence. There are occasional references to modern studies. The index of careers in the second volume provides alphabetical access to the work; each individual is listed alphabetically, along with offices held and dates. While not primarily a biographical work, *MRR* is extremely useful for finding information about Romans of the Republican period. It is somewhat cumbersome to consult, but apart from Pauly-Wissowa (entry 152), it is the only readily available source on many of its subjects.

199. Bryant, Donald C., ed. **Ancient Greek and Roman Rhetoricians: A Biographical Dictionary.** Columbia, MO: Artcraft Press, 1968. 104pp. LCCN 70–1929.

Compiled for the Speech Association of America, this book was originally intended to be part of a comprehensive biographical dictionary of speech educators. Its contributors include both classicists and communications scholars. It covers theorists, critics, authors of treatises or textbooks, and teachers of speech, but not those who were merely performers or composers. Thus it includes Isocrates and Cicero but omits Demosthenes. Many of those listed are relatively obscure. Entries range from two or three sentences to a maximum of 600 words. Each identifies and dates its subject and then highlights his rhetorical activities. Arrangement is alphabetical. There is a general bibliography at the beginning of the work; individual entries lack bibliographical references. The work is useful for ready reference and is handy for speech and communications specialists with historical interests.

200. Buchwald, Wolfgang, Armin Hohlweg, and Otto Prinz. **Tusculum-Lexikon: Griechischer und lateinischer Autoren des Altertums und des Mittelalters.** 3., neu bearb. und erw. Aufl. München: Artemis, 1982. 862pp. ISBN 3–7608–1641–X.

201. Buchwald, Wolfgang, Armin Hohlweg, and Otto Prinz. **Dictionnaire des auteurs grecs et latines de l'antiquité et du moyen âge.** Traduit et mis à jour par Jean Denis Berger et Jacques Billen. Turnhout: Brepols, 1991. 887pp. ISBN 2–503–50016–1.

This work covers Greek and Latin writers from antiquity through the Renaissance. One or two paragraphs offer essential biographical facts and discuss the scope of each author's work. Entries include references to editions of the author in the original language and sometimes to translations. Occasionally one or two secondary works are cited as well. The French translation essentially reproduces the content of the German original, with the addition of a few (chiefly French-language) items in the bibliographies. While there are equally good or better English-language sources for standard classical authors (e.g., Grant [entry 210] and Luce [entry 556]), the *Tusculum-Lexikon* is useful for later Greek and Latin authors. It also includes articles on many of the more prominent classical scholars of the Middle Ages and Renaissance.

202. Dąbrowa, Edward. **Governors of Roman Syria from Augustus to Septimius Severus.** Antiquitas, Reihe 1: Abhandlungen zur Alten Geschichte 45. Bonn: Rudolf Habelt, 1998. 276pp. ISBN 3–7749–2828–2.

Syria occupied a pivotal position on the Roman frontier with Parthia; as a result it was an exceptionally prestigious and important governorship. Dąbrowa provides a chronological listing of governors from the time of Augustus until A.D. 194, when Septimius Severus divided Syria into two smaller provinces. For each he provides full name, gives dates, cites in full (and in the original language) primary sources relating to the governorship, and gives a brief narrative of the individual's life and career along with his activities in Syria. Dąbrowa provides numerous references to the secondary literature and a bibliography. There are indexes to persons and sources.

203. Davies, J.K. **Athenian Propertied Families: 600–300 B.C.** Oxford: Clarendon Press, 1971. 653pp. ISBN 0–19814–273–0. LCCN 76–857878.

Although a highly specialized book concerning the relation of wealth and politics in classical Athens, Davies can be a valuable source of biographical information. The heart of the work is a prosopography of wealthy Athenians of the archaic and classical periods. This is arranged alphabetically (with the names in Greek alphabet); entries corresponding to names listed in Kirchner's *Prosopographia Attica* (entry 219) have Kirchner's number in the left margin. Davies tends to treat families in a single entry (that for earliest member listed), with cross-references to individual members. He has also provided indexes of names by deme (a political unit), primary sources that are cited, and subjects discussed. Entries tend to focus on the financial affairs and political activities of their subjects. They provide numerous references to source materials and modern studies. There are also many genealogical tables. While primarily of interest to those doing in-depth research on the political and economic history of Athens, Davies provides a partial supplement to Kirchner's very dated work.

204. **De Imperatoribus Romanis: An Online Encyclopedia of Roman Emperors.** URL: www.roman-emperors.org.

This Internet encyclopedia takes a liberal view of the Roman Empire, including its continuation in the East down to the fall of Constantinople in A.D. 1453. Entries cover most emperors from Augustus through Constantine XI; some remain to be written. Most are fairly substantial essays, with extensive documentation and some illustrations. Many are updated more or less regularly. The articles can be accessed chronologically or alphabetically. There are also family trees and an index of imperial battles, which includes brief descriptions and maps. Links to related Web sites of interest also appear on the main page. The editorial board and contributors are mostly academics, including some distinguished scholars, and the site has received numerous awards.

205. Della Corte, Francesco, ed. **Dizionario degli scrittori greci e latini.** Milano: Mazorati Editore, 1987. 3 v. ISBN 88–280–0053–8 (set).

Della Corte's dictionary covers Greek and Latin authors from the beginnings of Greek literature through the sixth century A.D. Major authors receive separate entries, while minor figures are covered in articles devoted to various genres, philosophical schools, and periods. The articles on individual authors include a biography, a discussion of the works, and a substantial bibliography. Those covering a genre or period also provide biographical and critical material on relevant authors, with a general bibliography at the end of the section. The articles tend to be fairly long; all are signed. The content is generally good, although the bibliographies are the most valuable part of the work. Because the *Dizionario* treats so many authors under collective rubrics, it is best approached through the index of names. This also ensures finding all the relevant material, since some authors are discussed in more than one place (e.g., Cicero is covered both in his own chapter and in the chapter on epistolography). Although there is no work on a comparable scale in English, those not fluent in Italian will be well served by Luce (entry 556) and Grant (entry 210).

206. Demougin, Ségolène. **Prosopographie des chevaliers romains julio-claudiens (43 av. J.-C.–70 ap. J.-C.).** Collection de l'École Française de Rome 153. Rome: École Française de Rome, 1992. 715pp. ISBN 2–7283–0248–7. LCCN 93–155994.

Demougin lists all known equestrians of the Julio-Claudian period. Her 770 entries are arranged in chronological order and are numbered consecutively. An alphabetical list of names, accompanied by entry numbers, precedes the actual prosopography. Entries provide citations of primary sources and references to modern studies. These are followed by a brief discussion of the person's public career and family connections. Indexes of names and sources conclude the work. Not all Demougin's subjects can be found in the *Prosopographia Imperii Romani* (entries 228–229) or Pauly-Wissowa (entry 152); her book provides a useful supplement to these works. There is some overlap with Devijver (entry 208).

207. Develin, Robert. **Athenian Officials, 684–321 B.C.** Cambridge: Cambridge University Press, 1989. 556pp. ISBN 0–521–32880–2. LCCN 88–17765.

Develin's work consists of a year-by-year listing of known Athenian officials, subarranged by office. Some are well known; many are obscure. When available, the entry number from Kirchner's *Prosopographia Attica* is provided (see entry 219). Develin cites primary sources (chiefly epigraphical) and occasionally offers discussion of the individual and references to secondary works. The book has a very good index of persons and also an index of tribes and demes (a political unit). It is mainly aimed at political historians. Along with Davies (entry 203) it can be used to supplement and update Kirchner.

208. Devijver, H. **Prosopographia Militarum Equestrium Quae Fuerunt ab Augusto ad Gallienum.** Symbolae Facultatis Litterarum et Philosophiae Lovanensis. Louvain: Universitaire Pers Leuven, 1976– . ISBN 90–6186–046–6 (v. 1); 90–6186–056–3 (v. 2); 90–6186–091–1 (v. 3); 90–6186–234–5 (v. 4); 90–6186–552–2 (v. 5). LCCN 81–478673.

Devijver's ongoing work is an alphabetical listing of equestrian officers in the Roman army from the time of Augustus (27 B.C.) to Gallienus (died A.D. 268). The first three volumes comprise the basic work; the fourth (1987) and the fifth (1993) are supplements. There are approximately 2,000 entries in the basic list. Each includes references to primary sources (usually inscriptions and papyri) and to the modern secondary literature. The individual's *cursus* (sequence of military and civil offices held) and place of origin follow. Entries range from a few lines to a couple of pages. The supplements provide a number of new entries and add new material to many existing ones. Both the basic work and the supplements have very full indexing. In addition to several name indexes and a subject index, there are indexes of geographical names, emperors, gods and goddesses, authors cited, and inscriptions and papyri cited. Although a rather specialized work, Devijver is an excellent source for biographical information on Roman army officers and equestrians in the early empire. Many of these are relatively obscure and do not appear in most other biographical sources. The work is a very useful supplement to the *Prosopographia Imperii Romani* (entries 228–229).

209. Goulet, Richard, ed. **Dictionnaire des philosophes antiques.** Paris: CNRS, 1989– . v. ISBN 2–271–05193–2 (v. 1); 2–271–05195–9 (v. 2); 2–271–05748–5 (v. 3); 2–271–06175–X (suppl. 1). LCCN 91–140105.

The *Dictionnaire*, when complete, will provide an exhaustive listing of all known philosophers of classical antiquity. So far only three volumes covering Abam(m)on to Juvenal have appeared, along with a supplementary volume, which updates and adds new entries to them. Entries begin with the individual's dates and references to Pauly-Wissowa (entry 152) or the *Prosopography of the Later Roman Empire* (entry 217) when available. Apart from this, the content and arrangement of each entry can vary greatly. Normally entries include a summary of all known biographical data, a complete list of relevant ancient *testimonia* and other biographical sources, and a selective bibliography of modern editions and studies. Articles vary considerably in length; most run only a paragraph or two, while some important figures receive many pages (e.g., 10 pages for St. Augustine and 177 pages for Aristotle). However, there are many other sources for major philosophers. Most will find the real value of this dictionary lies in its extensive coverage of minor and obscure figures. Each volume includes an index of proper names and indexes of Greek and Latin keywords from the titles of philosophical works appearing in that volume.

210. Grant, Michael. **Greek and Latin Authors: 800 b.c.–a.d. 1000.** Wilson Authors Series. New York: H. W. Wilson, 1980. 490pp. ISBN 0–8242–0640–1. LCCN 79–27446.

This book includes 376 entries ranging from the beginnings of Greek literature to a.d. 1000. Among them one can find every important classical author and a selection of the better-known Greek and Latin writers of the early Middle Ages. Each entry provides a biographical sketch, which is followed by a description and critical evaluation of the author's works. Entries also include a bibliography of the best editions and translations, along with a few major secondary works. Arrangement is alphabetical. Appendixes provide a list of works of doubtful attribution (with references to the appropriate entry) and a chronological listing of authors by century. There is also a pronunciation guide. An excellent ready-reference tool, this work covers far more authors than Luce's *Ancient Writers* (entry 556), although Luce offers more detailed treatments of major authors.

211. Grant, Michael. **Roman Emperors: A Biographical Guide to the Rulers of Imperial Rome, 31 b.c.–a.d. 476.** New York: Scribner's, 1985; repr., New York: Barnes & Noble, 1997. 367pp. ISBN 0–684–18388–9. LCCN 85–8391.

Grant offers brief sketches of the lives of 92 Roman emperors from Augustus to Romulus Augustulus, arranged in chronological order. Usurpers are covered only in passing and do not receive separate listings. The articles are readable and accurate; most are illustrated with contemporary portraits from ancient coins and busts. The work includes genealogical tables of each dynasty, several maps, and a glossary of Latin terms. No alphabetical access is provided to the emperors, although there is a detailed table of contents. There is an index of Greek and Latin authors cited in the text, and another of maps. *Roman Emperors* is well suited to the needs of students and general readers.

212. Hafner, German. **Prominente der Antike: 337 Portraits in Wort und Bild.** Düsseldorf; Wien: Econ Verlag, 1981. 359pp. ISBN 3–430–13742–X. LCCN 81–152739.

Unlike many of the other biographical dictionaries described here, this one includes both literary and political/historical figures. It also includes both Greeks and Romans. Hafner offers brief biographies of writers, artists, kings and queens, politicians, and generals ranging from Homer to Constantine the Great. Arrangement is alphabetical.

One or more portraits drawn from ancient works of art accompany each entry. These are usually "artistic" portraits rather than real likenesses of the subject. Hafner is a useful reference for those fluent in German. However, most of his subjects can be readily found in English-language reference sources. His chief value is as a source of portraits.

213. Hazel, John. **Who's Who in the Greek World.** Who's Who Series. London: Routledge, 2000. 285pp. ISBN 0–415–12497–2. LCCN 99–46943.

Hazel offers a biographical dictionary for the Greek and Hellenistic world, ranging from Homer (ca. 750 B.C.) through such figures as Philostratus and Plotinus (third century A.D.). He includes historical figures through approximately 100 B.C., when Romans came to dominate military and political affairs in the Greek world; for this period see also his companion volume, *Who's Who in the Roman World* (entry 214). Hazel includes literary authors, philosophers, scientists, and other cultural figures for the whole period. Some non-Greeks who played a significant role are included, for example the two Himilcos (Carthaginian navigator and general respectively) and Judas Maccabaeus. Entries tend to be short, ranging from a line or two to a couple of paragraphs; a few major figures, such as Herodotus, receive a page or more. Each provides significant dates and a summary of the person's career. Many include a few bibliographical references. Hazel also provides a short glossary, a chronological table of major events in Greek history, lists of rulers (Macedonia, Sparta, Persia, the Ptolemies, Seleukids, and Attalids), and several maps. Hazel derives much of his factual data from the *Oxford Classical Dictionary*[3] (entry 142) and Speake's *Dictionary of Ancient History* (entry 161); those who have access to these will find this work superfluous. It is nevertheless a useful and readable compendium for students.

214. Hazel, John. **Who's Who in the Roman World.** Who's Who Series. 2nd ed. London: Routledge, 2002. 367pp. ISBN 0–415–29162–3. LCCN 2002031732.

This companion to *Who's Who in Classical Mythology* (entry 905) and *Who's Who in the Greek World* (entry 213) is a biographical dictionary of the Roman world (not just Romans) from the early days of the republic (ca. 509 B.C.) to the death of Jovian in 364 B.C. Hazel includes over 1,000 entries on political and military leaders, literary authors, philosophers, and scientists. He tries to avoid duplication with his volume on the Greek world, although a few figures appear in both. Hazel is inconsistent in the form of name used for entries but typically prefers the most common English form if there is one. His entries tend to be short, providing important dates, a summary of the subject's career, and occasionally a brief bibliography. Hazel includes a glossary, a chronology of Roman history, a list of emperors, and several maps. Much of his factual content is derived from the *Oxford Classical Dictionary*[3] (entry 142) and Speake's *Dictionary of Ancient History* (entry 161), which are far more extensive works and generally to be preferred. Otherwise, Hazel's work is a useful and readable guide for students.

215. Hofstetter, Josef. **Die Griechen in Persien: Prosopographie der Griechen im Persischen Reich vor Alexander.** Archaeologische Mitteilungen aus Iran. Ergänzungsband 5. Berlin: Dietrich Reimer, 1978. 216pp. LCCN 79–340220.

Hofstetter offers brief biographies of Greeks who were in some way associated with Persia. He covers both Ionian Greeks who lived under Persian rule and those from the Greek mainland who had a significant connection with Persia. He includes both well-known and obscure figures. The arrangement is alphabetical. A bibliographical note, often extensive, concludes each entry. There are several lists at the end of the book that gather together types of individuals (e.g., ambassadors). There is also a chronological listing of those included. While somewhat specialized, Hofstetter is a good supplementary source for Greek biography.

216. Hornblower, Simon, and Antony Spawforth, eds. **Who's Who in the Classical World.** Oxford: Oxford University Press, 2000. 440pp. ISBN 0–19–280107–4.

One of a growing number of derivative works based on the *Oxford Classical Dictionary*³ (entry 142), this volume offers a large selection of the biographical entries from that work. These are restricted to historical persons, and a number of minor figures covered in the *OCD*³ are omitted to save space. Arrangement is alphabetical. The editors have added a chronology of Greco-Roman history from the Bronze Age to Justinian. Several maps appear at the end of the volume. Coverage is wider than Radice (entry 230) but does not include mythological and legendary figures. Hornblower and Spawforth provide a useful, reliable, and inexpensive biographical dictionary for students; scholars and libraries will prefer the *OCD*³.

217. Jones, A.H.M., J. R. Martindale, and J. Morris. **The Prosopography of the Later Roman Empire.** Cambridge: Cambridge University Press, 1971–1992. 3v. in 4. ISBN 521–07233–6 (v. 1); 0–521–201594 (v. 2); 0–521–20160–8 (v. 3). LCCN 77–118859.

A prosopography of the later empire was originally planned and undertaken by Theodor Mommsen as a continuation of the *Prosopographia Imperii Romani* (entries 228–229). This project was a casualty of the two World Wars. A.H.M. Jones launched his effort, now commonly referred to as the *PLRE,* in 1950. Although Jones and, after his death, Martindale have been primarily responsible for the content, an editorial board of distinguished scholars has contributed much to the work. The *PLRE* includes a wide range of Roman aristocrats, public officials, military officers, scholars, and literary figures. There are also entries for their wives and children. Many non-Romans (Franks, Lombards, Visigoths, Persians, etc.) who are significant for the study of the empire are included as well. The first volume covers A.D. 260–395, the second 395–527, and the third (in two parts) 527–641. Individuals whose careers overlap these boundaries are included in both relevant volumes, although the second entry is in summary form, and both must be consulted for a full account. Arrangement of entries within each volume is alphabetical, with cross-references provided from variant forms of names. Entries vary widely in length, ranging from a few lines to several pages; a number of the entries in volume 3 are considerably longer still. They provide whatever information is known about the person's origin, religion, career, and family. There are very full references to primary sources. Relatively few modern studies are cited in the first volume; references to these increase substantially in subsequent volumes. Each volume includes *fasti* (chronological lists of officeholders) and numerous genealogical tables of important families. This is by far the best source of biographical information for the later empire. A further volume of addenda and corrigenda is still in preparation.

218. Kienast, Dietmar. **Römische Kaisertabelle: Grundzüge einer römischen Kaiserchronologie.** 2., durchges. und erw. Aufl. Darmstadt: Wissenschaftliche Buchgesellschaft, 1996. 399pp. ISBN 3–534–13289–0.

This chronology covers Roman emperors from Augustus to Theodosius I. Each entry gives date of birth, parents, full name, offices, and a chronological list of key events in the life of the emperor. Subentries are provided for other prominent members of the imperial household and for failed usurpers. Bibliographies list works on the life, family, and chronology of each emperor. Kienast also provides a listing of births, deaths, and major events by date in a single calendar. A very good source for historians and numismatists, this work can be used even by those with a modest understanding of German.

219.   Kirchner, Johannes. **Prosopographia Attica.** Editio altera lucis ope impressa inscriptionum Graecarum conspectum numerorum addidit Siegfried Lauffer. Berolini: Walter de Gruyter, 1966; repr., Chicago: Ares, 1981. 2v.

220.   Sundwall, J. **Nachträge zur Prosopographia Attica.** Ofversigt af Finska Vetenskaps-Societetens Förhandlingar 52. Helsingfors: Akademiska Bokhandeln, 1910; repr. as **Supplement to J. Kirchner's Prosopographia Attica,** Chicago: Ares, 1981. 77pp.

Kirchner's work, first published in 1901, is an alphabetical listing of all known Athenian citizens. Although this is billed as a second edition, the contents were not updated and remain essentially the same as those of the original 1901 edition. Entries often include some biographical data, and all offer references to primary sources (often inscriptions) and dates whenever available. Most are only a few lines in length, although for better-known Athenians, entries sometimes extend to a page or more. There are also genealogical tables for some families. Two additional lists appear at the end of the main work. One, the *conspectus demotarum,* is essentially an index by demes (a political unit). The second list, the *archontum tabulae,* lists known archons from 683/2 to 30/29 B.C. There is also an index to citations of Greek inscriptions. While information about famous Athenians, such as Cleisthenes or Pericles, can be found readily in many sources, Kirchner provides a valuable resource for biographical material on the more obscure ones.

Sundwall updates some of Kirchner's entries and adds many new names. He mingles both updated and new entries in a single alphabetical sequence; no attempt is made to follow Kirchner's numbering system, although references to Kirchner's numbers appear at the end of updates to existing entries. Many of Sundwall's entries cite then-unpublished inscriptions in various museum collections; since no inventory numbers are provided for these, they can be difficult to identify and track down. Although somewhat different in focus, the more recent works of Davies (entry 203) and Develin (entry 207) can be used to supplement the *Prosopographia Attica.* When completed, Traill's *Persons of Ancient Athens* (entries 234–235) will supersede Kirchner.

221.   Kroh, Paul. **Lexikon der antiken Autoren.** Kröners Taschenausgabe 366. Stuttgart: Alfred Kröner, 1972. 675pp. ISBN 3-520-366-010.

The *Lexikon der antiken Autoren* contains articles on approximately 2,400 Greek and Roman authors from the beginnings to the sixth century A.D. It includes poets, historians, orators, philosophers, and scholarly and technical writers. The articles range from a paragraph to several pages. They tend to be brief and factual. The majority of entries include short bibliographies of editions, translations, and secondary literature. The *Lexikon* is chiefly useful for its coverage of minor and obscure authors who are often omitted from such biographical works.

222. Leunissen, Paul M.M. **Konsuln und Konsulare in der Zeit von Commodus bis Severus Alexander (180–235 n.chr.): Prosopographische Untersuchungen zur senatorischen Elite im römischen Kaiserreich.** Dutch Monographs on Ancient History and Archaeology 6. Amsterdam: J.C. Gieben, 1989. 490pp. ISBN 90–6053–028–6. LCCN 89–177237.

The first part of Leunissen's work consists of studies of the senatorial order from Commodus through the Severans. The second and larger part is a prosopography of consuls and other major magistrates of the period. This is divided into sections listing consuls, provincial governors, and various *praefecti, curatores,* and *iuridici.* Entries provide such information as is known about each individual, with citations of relevant primary sources and secondary literature. Arrangement is generally chronological but somewhat complex, so that those seeking specific individuals should begin with the index of personal names. Those who held multiple offices appear in multiple lists, and all must be consulted for complete information; again recourse to the index is strongly advised. Additional lists look at consuls by their places of origin and their careers. Indexes cover sources, personal names (by gens or family name, with an additional list of cognomina), and subjects. Leunissen provides a rich source of information but is meant primarily for specialists.

223. Lightman, Marjorie, and Benjamin Lightman. **Biographical Dictionary of Ancient Greek and Roman Women: Notable Women from Sappho to Helena.** New York: Checkmark Books, 2000. 298pp. ISBN 0–8160–3112–6; 0–8160–4436–8pa. LCCN 99–20682.

The Lightmans offer biographical information on some 447 Greek and Roman women. Their temporal limits extend from the seventh century B.C. to the fourth century A.D. They include only historical figures, not legendary or mythical ones. Each entry begins with name, dates, geographical association, and a brief charaterization. A short biography follows. Most entries run only a paragraph or two, while a few extend to as many pages. Each concludes with references to relevant ancient sources and one or two secondary sources. A few entries also include portraits (usually images from ancient coins). The Lightmans provide a map, a registry (summary list of entries), a glossary of Greek and Latin terms, and a bibliography. While much of the material is also covered in other sources, no other single source brings together all the material found here. Overall this is a useful and reliable work.

224. Nicolet, Claude. **L'Ordre équestre a l'époque républicaine (312–43 av. J.-C.).** Bibliothèque des Écoles Françaises d'Athènes et de Rome 207. Paris: E. de Boccard, 1966–1974. 2v. LCCN 67–75746.

The second volume of Nicolet's work comprises a prosopography of Roman knights. It lists some 404 equestrians of the republican period. Entries are brief, although some extend to several pages. Each entry begins with the person's dates, place of origin, and rank or offices. A short biography follows; emphasis is on the individual's public career and family connections. There are extensive references to primary and secondary sources. The republican period is not nearly as well served by biographical sources as the empire. Nicolet, Broughton (entry 198), and Pauly-Wissowa (entry 152) are the major resources for Romans of that era.

225. Peremans, W., and E. van't Dack. **Prosopographia Ptolemaica.** Studia Hellenistica. Lovanii: Bibliotheca Universitatis Lovanii, 1950–1981. 9v. LCCN 53–33025.

226. La'da, Csaba A. **Foreign Ethnics in Hellenistic Egypt.** Prosopographia Ptolemaica 10. Leuven: Peeters, 2002. 384pp. ISBN 90–429–1195–6. LCCN 2002–72112.

This highly specialized work attempts to gather information on all known persons who lived in Ptolemaic Egypt (323–30 B.C.). It includes more than 17,000 individuals, many of whom are painfully obscure. Volumes 1–5 comprise the basic list, while volume 6 is a name index. Volumes 8–9 offer addenda and corrigenda. Entries are arranged by occupation; the first volume, for example, covers individuals who were part of the civil or financial administration of Egypt. Each major category is subdivided into specific occupations. Arrangement within each list is alphabetical by name. Entries vary in length; most are brief. They summarize what is known of each person: occupation, family connections, date, and home or place of activity. Primary sources (chiefly papyri) and selected secondary works are cited. A recent tenth volume by La'da gathers ethnic designations from Ptolemaic Egypt and lists all known individuals to whom these apply. Willy Clarysse, with the assistance of other Belgian scholars, has made an online version of the *Prosopographia* available at http://prosptol.arts.kuleuven.ac.be/index.html. This allows one to search by personal name, patronymic, occupation, geographical location, and text. The *Prosopographia* is an indispensible tool for anyone interested in the economic, social, and ethnic history of Egypt for the period.

227. Poralla, Paul. **Prosopography of Lacedaimonians from the Earliest Times to the Death of Alexander the Great (X–323 B.C.) [Prosopographie der Lakedaimonier bis auf die Zeit Alexanders des Grossen].** 2nd ed. with an introduction, addenda, and corrigenda by Alfred S. Bradford. Chicago: Ares, 1985. 202pp. ISBN 0–89005–521–1.

Originally presented as Poralla's doctoral dissertation (Breslau, 1913), this work includes Spartan royalty, Spartiates (full citizens), and *perioeci* (free inhabitants of the Spartan domain without citizenship); *helots* (similar in status to serfs) and resident foreigners are omitted. It records all known individual Lacedaimonians from the archaic and classical periods. Individuals are listed in alphabetical order (names are printed in the Greek alphabet). Individuals with the same name are listed chronologically. Each is assigned a number (1–817); corrupt or false names are printed in smaller characters and not assigned a number. Entries include such biographical data as is known about each and references to primary sources. There are also genealogical tables for the more important Spartan families and lists of *nauarchs* (naval commanders) and ephors (magistrates). Bradford has added two appendixes. The first consists of addenda and corrigenda to individuals already in Poralla. These provide additional citations of primary sources and recent studies, as well as correcting errors in the original work. The second appendix adds 45 new entries. Bradford's additions are in English and Greek; Poralla's text is reprinted in the original German and Greek. The work is continued by Bradford's *Prosopography of Lacedaemonians from the Death of Alexander the Great* (entry 197).

228. **Prosopographia Imperii Romani Saec. I. II. III.** Edita consilio et auctoritate Academiae Scientarum Regiae Borussicae. Berolini: Georgium Reimerum, 1897–1898; repr., Berlin: Walter de Gruyter, 1978. 3v. LCCN 30–30140.

229.   Prosopographia Imperii Romani Saec. I. II. III. Consilio et auctoritate Academiae Litterarum Borussicae iteratis curis ediderunt . . . Editio Altera. Berolini et Lipsiae: Walter de Gruyter, 1933– . v. LCCN 40–106.

One of the many monumental products of nineteenth-century German scholarship, this work was proposed and planned by Theodor Mommsen and sponsored by the Prussian Academy. The first edition was edited by Elimar Klebs, Paul von Rohden, and Hermann Dessau. The *PIR*, as it is commonly abbreviated, covers the Roman Empire from Augustus (31 B.C.) to the accession of Diocletian (A.D. 284). It includes Romans of senatorial and equestrian rank and their families, and many other notable Romans. Romans of plebeian rank who are known only from Christian writers are excluded. Greeks and barbarians who were involved in Roman affairs are included selectively. Entries for emperors only include their activities outside of their reigns. Entries are arranged alphabetically. Each gives an account of the individual's career, lists public offices held, and provides whatever information is known about his family. Primary sources are cited in full. Many entries are brief, sometimes as little as two or three lines, while others are considerably longer. A fourth volume, which was intended to include consular *fasti,* was never published. The *PIR* has long been one of the standard sources for biographical information about Romans of the imperial period.

Edmund Groag and Arthur Stein, both now deceased, were the original editors of the second edition of *PIR*. They were succeeded first by the late Leiva Petersen, then by Werner Eck, the current editor. The criteria and format of entries generally follow those of the first edition. The second edition includes many new entries and augments old ones with new material and greatly expanded citations of primary sources. Cross-references have also been added to the new edition. There are occasional references to modern studies, but no attempt is made to provide a systematic bibliography. Some genealogical tables are provided. This is an excellent biographical source for the period and a great improvement over the first edition. The most recent volume to appear (v. 7, fasc. 1, 1999) reached the letter R; the first edition must still be consulted for the remainder of the alphabet. The Berlin-Brandenburgische Akademie der Wissenschaften maintains a Web site that provides addenda and a searchable index to the *PIR* at www.bbaw.de/forschung/pir/index.html. Those interested in the late empire (from A.D. 260 to 641) should consult *The Prosopography of the Later Roman Empire* (entry 217), which continues the work of the *PIR*.

230.   Radice, Betty. Who's Who in the Ancient World. New York: Stein and Day, 1971. 225pp. ISBN: 0–8128–1338–3 LCCN: 73–127027.

Radice provides a single alphabetical list of Greek and Roman mythological, historical, and cultural figures ranging from the Bronze Age to late antiquity. Entries are brief and informative, with frequent cross-references to related articles. There is also a very complete index. The book is aimed at general readers pursuing classical references in modern art and literature. It has a much wider scope but is less comprehensive than Bowder's two *Who's Who* volumes (entries 195–196). Bowder is superior for those seeking strictly historical information, while Radice is better for those with a more cultural interest. Together they provide good basic biographical coverage of notable Greeks and Romans.

231.   Raepsaet-Charlier, Marie-Thérèse. Prosopographie des femmes de l'ordre sénatorial (Ier –IIe siècles). Fonds René Draguet 4. Lovanii: Peeters, 1987. 2v. ISBN 90–6831–086–0 (v. 1); 90–6831–087–9 (v. 2).

Raepsaet-Charlier's work is intended to remedy, in part, the difficulty in finding information about prominent women of the early empire. In sources such as the *Prosopographia Imperii Romani* (entries 228–229) and Pauly-Wissowa (entry 152) women typically receive only a passing mention in articles concerning their husbands or fathers. Raepsaet-Charlier lists all known women from families of senatorial rank; these include wives, daughters, sisters, and mothers of senators. Each notice includes the woman's complete name, bibliographical references, primary sources, biographical information and discussion, and family connections. Entries are arranged alphabetically; indexes of men, women, and elements of women's names (which serve as cross-references for the more complicated names) facilitate access to the list. An extensive collection of genealogical tables can be found in the second volume. This well-organized work is a mine of information on women in the early empire. While few of the names included are likely to be of general interest, it is a valuable reference tool for those doing historical research on women.

232.   Smith, William, ed. **Dictionary of Greek and Roman Biography and Mythology.** London: John Murray, 1890; repr., London: I. B. Tauris, 2005. 3v. LCCN 11–24983.

Nearly every large library holds one or another edition of this venerable work, which first appeared in 1844. Along with Smith's *Dictionary of Greek and Roman Antiquities* (entry 160) and *Dictionary of Greek and Roman Geography* (entry 413), it is part of his *Encyclopedia of Classical Antiquity*. Smith covers both real people and characters from myth and legend. His work remains the largest and most comprehensive single dictionary of classical biography in English. It includes the names of nearly all noteworthy individuals from the earliest period through late antiquity. Smith also covers the Byzantine Empire, although in less detail. Entries range in length from a few lines to several columns. Their style is clear and readable. They provide references to the pertinent ancient sources, as well as to the secondary literature of the time. While much of the information in Smith remains useful, enough is now outdated or inaccurate that the work should be used with care. When possible, more recent works, such as those of Radice (entry 230), Bowder (entries 195–196), or Hazel (entries 213–214) should be preferred. Smith has particular value for those interested in the history of scholarship during the Victorian era.

233.   Thomasson, Bengt E. **Fasti Africani: Senatorische und ritterliche Amsträger in den römischen Provinzen Nordafrikas von Augustus bis Diokletian.** Skrifter utgivna av Svenska institutet i Rom 4, 53. Stockholm: Paul Åström, 1996. 261pp. ISBN 91–7042–153–6.

Thomasson lists the known senatorial and equestrian magistrates of North Africa. He arranges these by province and office: Africa *proconsularis* (proconsul, *legati,* and quaestors), Mauretania *Caesariensis* (procurators), and Mauretania *Tingitana* (procurators). He also lists commanders of the third legion (Legio III Augusta), which was stationed in North Africa. Under each category incumbents are listed chronologically, followed by those of uncertain date. Entries give the relevant primary sources, a short narrative, and references to Pauly-Wissowa (entry 152), the *Prosopographia Imperii Romani* (entry 228–29), and relevant secondary literature. Indexes cover persons and sources.

234.   Traill, John S. **Persons of Ancient Athens.** Toronto: Athenians, 1994– . 20v. ISBN 0–9692686–2–9 (v. 1); 0–9692686–3–7 (v. 2); 0–9692686–4–5 (v. 3); 0–9692686–5–3 (v. 4); 0–9692686–7–X (v. 5); 0–9692686–8–8 (v. 6); 0–9692686–9–6 (v. 7); 0–

9685232–0–X (v. 8); 0–9685232–1–8 (v. 9); 0–9685232–2–6 (v. 10); 0–9685232–3–4 (v. 11) 0–9685232–4–2 (v. 12); 0–9685232–7–7 (v. 13). LCCN 92–93586.

235. **Website Attica.** URL: www.chass.utoronto.ca/attica.

When this massive work is completed (13 of 20 volumes have been published to date), it will supersede Kirchner's venerable *Prosopographia Attica* (entry 219). Traill goes considerably beyond Kirchner, who included only Athenian citizens and concluded with the Augustan era. *Persons* includes metics (resident aliens), slaves, manumitted persons, and foreigners who were honored by the Athenians or died in Athens. It also extends coverage into the late Roman and early Christian periods. Traill's work is based on the vast card files created by B. D. Merritt at Princeton University over half a century. Traill has added many recently discovered names as well. He enumerates the Athenians in one alpha-to-omega listing. Each entry begins with a six-digit identification number, followed by the name (in Greek alphabet), known information about the individual, and a full listing of the sources, both literary and epigraphical. Users should note that supplements to earlier volumes appear in volumes 4, 8, and 11. The twentieth volume is to be an index. A complementary Web site based at the University of Toronto, Website Attica, provides addenda and corrigenda online and also makes a small part of the full database available for searching. This is strictly a work for specialists: many compressed bibliographical references and much untranslated Greek fill the pages.

236. Traver, Andrew G., ed. **From Polis to Empire—the Ancient World, c. 800 B.C–500 A.D.: A Biographical Dictionary.** Great Cultural Eras of the Western World. Westport, CT: Greenwood Press, 2002. 448pp. ISBN 0–313–30942–6. LCCN 2001016056.

This biographical dictionary of the Greco-Roman world emphasizes cultural figures but does not exclude political and military leaders. The work contains 480 short biographies, which cover most individuals likely to be encountered in a survey of Western civilization or ancient history. One of the strengths of the book is its coverage of the later period, especially of prominent Christians. The quality of the articles varies widely; the level of writing is suitable for high school and undergraduate students. Each biography offers one or two references for further reading; some are odd choices indeed. There are a number of quirks and typographical errors. In addition to the biographies, the book includes a useful chronology of political and cultural events, a short glossary of Greek and Latin terms, a general bibliography and an index. Use with caution.

237. Veh, Otto. **Lexikon der römischen Kaiser: Von Augustus bis Iustinianus I., 27 v. Chr. bis 565 n. Chr.** 3., überarbeitete, ergänzte und mit Bildern versehene Aufl. Zurich: Artemis, 1990. 158pp. ISBN 3–7608–1035–7.

The articles in this biographical dictionary of Roman emperors are generally based on the corresponding entries in the Artemis *Lexikon der alten Welt* (entry 149). Each gives its subject's commonly used name, his full name, dates of his reign or attempted usurpation, and a short biography. Most are a paragraph or two, although some of the more important emperors receive several pages each. When available, references to Pauly-Wissowa (entry 152), *Kleine Pauly* (entry 165), and the *Prosopography of the Later Roman Empire* (entry 217) are provided at the end of each article. Some noteworthy features of the book include its alphabetical arrangement (works on the emperors tend to be arranged chronologically) and its coverage of minor emperors, usurpers, and later emperors. While many English-speaking readers will prefer Grant (entry 211), who offers longer articles on most of the better-known emperors, this is a good alternative. Those working on the later empire especially will find it a handy reference tool.

PORTRAITS

238. Bernoulli, J. J. **Griechische Ikonographie: Mit Ausschluss Alexanders und der Diodochen.** München: F. Bruckmann, 1901; repr., Hildesheim: Georg Olms, 1969. 2v. LCCN 03–6659.

Griechische Ikonographie was long the standard work on Greek portraiture; it is now superseded by Richter's *Portraits of the Greeks* (entry 242). Bernoulli provides a series of articles in chronological sequence that cover notable Greeks of the classical and Hellenistic periods. He includes literary figures, philosophers, statesmen, and generals. Most articles are on individuals, although a few are on collective subjects (e.g., the Seven Sages). Each gives a biographical synopsis and then discusses the person's depiction in art. There are some small illustrations in the body of the text, and a number of plates at the end of each volume. There is both a detailed table of contents and a name and subject index. There is also a geographical index of the sources (i.e., museums) of portraits. Although Bernoulli can still be useful, Richter is both more recent and offers fuller coverage.

239. Bernoulli, J. J. **Römische Ikonographie.** Stuttgart: W. Spemann, 1882–1894; repr., Hildesheim: Georg Olms, 1969. 2v. in 4. LCCN 06–22528.

Bernoulli's monumental work on Roman portraiture consists of two volumes. The first covers prominent Romans (except for emperors and members of their households) from Romulus to the second century A.D. It includes some legendary figures (such as the early kings of Rome), many political and military figures, and the most famous literary authors and philosophers. The second volume covers the emperors. Arrangement is chronological. Each article begins with a biographical summary, followed by a discussion of portraits of the individual. While most articles are brief, some (e.g., Julius Caesar) extend to many pages. Most of the actual portraits are to be found at the end of each volume. There is a detailed table of contents, but no alphabetical access to the work as a whole. There are individual subject indexes in two parts of the second volume, but none for the third part or for the first volume. *Römische Ikonographie* is now badly out-of-date. Toynbee (entry 246) is generally better for historical portraits down to the time of Augustus. For imperial portraiture, there are more options: Calza (entry 240), Felleti Maj (entry 241), and Schindler (entry 245).

240. Calza, Raissa. **Iconografia Romana Imperiale: Da Carausio a Giuliano (287–363 d.C.).** Quaderni e guide di archeologia 3. Roma: "L'Erma" di Bretschneider, 1972. 434, cxxxiii pp. LCCN 72–359178.

Calza continues the work of Felletti Maj (entry 241). Unfortunately, she also follows the organizational pattern of the earlier work. She begins by gathering all the literary evidence for the physical appearance of the emperors from Diocletian to Julian. This is arranged by emperor in a chronological sequence. The passages are quoted in both the original Latin or Greek and in Italian translation. The second part is the actual *iconografia,* which offers discussions of the portraits of emperors from Carausius to Julian. The content of this section mainly deals with art history. The illustrations are in a separate section at the end. These portraits are drawn from coins, statuary, reliefs, paintings, and mosaics. As in Felleti Maj, plates are not captioned and are identified only by number; the key (*indice delle illustrazioni*) or the corresponding sections of text must be used as a guide. There are chronological and alphabetical name indexes and an index of museums that hold the actual portraits used as illustrations. While not intended as a reference tool and somewhat difficult to use, Calza provides a valuable source of information on the physical appearance of Roman emperors for the period covered. Her work is useful as a supplement to the corresponding section of Bernoulli (entry 239).

241. Felleti Maj, Bianca Maria. **Iconografia Romana Imperiale da Severo Alessandro a M. Aurelio Carino (222–285 d.C.).** Quaderni e Guide di Archeologia 2. Roma: "L'Erma" di Bretschneider, 1958. 309, lx pp. LCCN 62–45541.

Felleti Maj's study covers the iconography of Roman emperors and their families for the years A.D. 222 to 285. The organization of her work is cumbersome. She begins with a general bibliography. Next is a compilation of the ancient literary evidence for the physical appearance of the various emperors; Felleti Maj provides the Greek and Latin texts with an Italian translation on the facing page. The third section consists of articles on individual emperors, which are arranged chronologically. Each begins with a brief biographical note. A discussion of the portraits of the individual follows. Illustrations appear in a separate section at the end of the book. Plates are identified only by number; there are no captions. Also, the figure numbers are not entirely sequential. This necessitates constant reference both to the article on a given emperor and the key (*indice delle illustrazioni*) when seeking a portrait. The indexes, which are located between the text and plates, include chronological and alphabetical name indexes and an index of museums that hold the actual portraits. This work is more current and contains more portraits than the corresponding section of Bernoulli's *Römische Ikonographie* (entry 239). It can be useful for finding information on and portraits of the more obscure emperors. The extensive array of source material and the plates are its most valuable features. Felleti Maj's study is continued as far as Julian (A.D. 363) by Calza (entry 240).

242. Richter, Gisela M.A. **The Portraits of the Greeks.** London: Phaidon, 1965. 3v. LCCN 66–4110.

243. Richter, Gisela M.A. **The Portraits of the Greeks. Supplement.** London: Phaidon, 1972. 24pp.

244. Richter, Gisela M.A. **The Portraits of the Greeks.** Abridged and revised by R.R.R. Smith. Ithaca, NY: Cornell University Press, 1984. 254pp. ISBN 0–8014–1683–3. LCCN 83–73222.

Richter wrote this book to replace Bernoulli's *Griechische Ikonographie* (entry 238). It includes "(1) all reliably identified portraits of Greek poets, philosophers, orators, statesmen, generals, and artists; (2) the portraits for which plausible identifications have been proposed; and (3) the portraits merely cited in ancient literature and inscriptions." Unlike Bernoulli, Richter also includes Hellenistic rulers. She follows Bernoulli's chronological arrangement in a modified form, in which she groups her subjects by century and then subdivides them by profession (e.g., poets). Thus, the first volume (after a substantial introduction to the history and study of Greek portraiture) has chapters on the early period and the fifth century B.C.; the second volume covers the fourth, third, and second centuries; and the third treats Hellenistic rulers and Greeks of the Roman period. This arrangement is inconvenient for someone merely seeking the likenesses of an individual, but the detailed table of contents and the index of names provide ready access. Individual entries begin with a short biography, followed by what is known about the person's physical appearance. Then there is a full discussion and listing of both the ancient literary evidence and the extant portraits. The plates are gathered at the end of each volume. These are perhaps the most valuable part of the work: over 2,000 portraits of notable Greeks. The *Supplement* published in 1972 adds newly discovered or identified portraits. Richter covers far more individuals than Bernoulli and provides many more portraits for each. Richter is unlikely to be superseded as the standard work in the field for many years.

Richter herself began the abridgement; after her death, Smith completed it. It includes all notable Greeks from the eighth to the first centuries B.C. of whom a portrait has been identified with more or less certainty. The book covers the same range of material with the exception of Greeks of the Roman period, whom Smith has largely omitted. Each entry includes a brief account of the person's life, portraits recorded in literary sources, evidence for surviving portraits, and the best version(s) of those portraits. However, much of the detailed scholarly apparatus has been omitted, and the reader often is referred back to the unabridged work. Smith has also changed the arrangement of the material. He presents most of the entries in a single alphabetical sequence. An exception is made for the Hellenistic rulers, who still appear in a separate section that is arranged geographically and subarranged chronologically. Also, Smith integrates the illlustrations into the text, which is much more convenient for the user. Smith's abridgement should meet the reference needs of most students and casual readers.

245. Schindler, Wolfgang. **Römische Kaiser: Herrscherbild und Imperium.** Leipzig: Koehler & Amelang, 1985. 219pp.

This study of imperial portraiture covers major emperors from Augustus to Constantine the Great. A preliminary chapter discusses portraits of Roman leaders prior to the principate (27 B.C.). Minor emperors and co-emperors are often omitted (e.g., Lucius Verus, Pertinax, Julius Didianus). While the author's chief concern is the portraiture itself, each entry provides a short biographical sketch of its subject. The many good-quality photographs of contemporary artworks depicting emperors and members of their families are the most valuable feature of Schindler's book. Arrangement is chronological. There is no index, although a fairly detailed table of contents helps in this regard. Grant (entry 211) remains a much better source for imperial biography and provides some portraits as well. Schindler is useful mainly for additional imperial portraits.

246. Toynbee, J.M.C. **Roman Historical Portraits.** Aspects of Greek and Roman Life. Ithaca, NY: Cornell University Press, 1978. 208pp. ISBN 0–8014–1011–8. LCCN 75–38428.

Toynbee aims to provide accurate likenesses of prominent figures in Roman history. She uses only portraits made during the subject's life or based on a contemporary portrait. The first part of the work offers portraits of 52 notable Romans ranging from M. Claudius

Marcellus (consul in 222 B.C.) to C. Asinius Gallus (consul in 8 B.C.). Toynbee includes only those who played an important role in public life during the republican and early Augustan periods; she omits figures of primarily cultural importance. This part is arranged chronologically. For additional coverage, especially of the imperial era, see the older works by Bernoulli (entry 239), Calza (entry 240), and Felleti Maj (entry 241). Schindler (entry 245) also includes many portraits of Roman emperors.

Toynbee's second part consists of portraits of about 205 foreign rulers who had dealings with Rome between the third century B.C. and the fifth century A.D. These rulers are arranged geographically and then subarranged chronologically. Spouses and children are sometimes included under a ruler's entry as well. There are some odd placements. For example, Hamilcar and Hannibal are placed under Spain (there is no heading for Carthage). It is best to consult the general index for the person sought. Entries are mainly concerned with the portrait(s) as such but do include some biographical and historical data. Toynbee is chiefly of value for the illustrations; this is perhaps the only collection that consciously strives to avoid idealized portraits and present real likenesses.

8
Greek and Roman History

This chapter covers works on Greek and Roman history in the broadest sense, including social history, economic history, law, and the history of science and technology, as well as the more traditional political and military history. The first section covers book-length bibliographical works. Readers should be aware that many important bibliographies have appeared in article form as well; some important sources of these include *Classical World* (entry 95), *Lustrum* (entry 71), and, especially, the *Aufstieg und Niedergang der römischen Welt* (entry 315). The second section covers a few general histories of major importance. The third section includes dictionaries, encyclopedias, handbooks, and the rapidly proliferating companions. The study of ancient history cannot be separated from study of the literary and documentary sources; readers should refer to chapter 14 for works on historiography and biography and to chapters 15 and 16 for works on individual historians, such as Herodotus (entries 669–671), Thucydides (entries 736–738), Xenophon (entry 739–743), Caesar (entry 761), Livy (entries 783–784), Sallust (entries 820–821), and Tacitus (entries 827–828). More information on documentary sources may be found in chapter 19 in the sections on epigraphy, numismatics, and papyrology. Those seeking primary source materials in English translation will find collections listed in chapter 9. Finally, works on material remains will be found in chapter 11, "Art and Archaeology." Most works on the Mycenaeans and Etruscans will be found in that chapter, as the bulk of the material is archaeological in nature.

BIBLIOGRAPHIES

247. Beck, Frederick A. G. **Bibliography of Greek Education and Related Topics.** Sydney: F. A. Beck, 1986. 333pp. ISBN 0–9588450–0–X.

Although compiled by a well-known authority on ancient Greek education, this bibliography is disappointing. The work lacks focus; in addition to items specifically about Greek education, it also includes many "related" works on philosophy, rhetoric, literary criticism, the history of writing, and Greek athletics. While not entirely irrelevant, many are peripheral. Also, the book's organization is cumbersome. Beck provides subject access through a classified listing. The citations in this part are usually rather spare; sometimes they are not even sufficient to identify the work clearly. The second part of the book is an alphabetical author list, which offers more-complete citations. Beck also occasionally supplies annotations. In the case of books, these are frequently quotations from or summaries of reviews. Most of these annotations are in the author list, but a few are included with the classified entries. Users will need to check both listings to be sure they have all the relevant information about a given item. Beck does provide some aids for the user; these include an outline of his classification scheme and indexes to the classification, series and serials, and reviewers. While Beck offers very full coverage of Greek education through the 1980s, most will find consulting his bibliography to be a tedious and time-consuming task.

248. Bonser, Wilfrid. **Romano-British Bibliography (55 A.D.–B.C. 449).** Oxford: Basil Blackwell, 1964. 2v. LCCN 65–4078.

Bonser lists works on the period extending from Julius Caesar's first expedition to Britain in 55 B.C. to the arrival of Hengist and Horsa in A.D. 449. The 9,370 unannotated items cited include materials published before 1960. Bonser has arranged these in a classified scheme. The first part covers topics, which are arranged under general headings and their various subdivisions. The second part covers works on specific archaeological sites. The second volume contains indexes to authors, subjects, personal names, and place names. Many of the citations are to relatively obscure works published by local historical and antiquarian societies. These are often overlooked by more general sources of classical bibliography. Bonser is an indispensable work for the study of Roman Britain.

249. Brockmeyer, Norbert, and Ernst Friedrich Schultheiss. **Studienbibliographie: Alte Geschichte.** Wissenschaftliche Paperbacks Studienbibliographien. Wiesbaden: Franz Steiner, 1973. 148pp. LCCN 73–372193.

Intended as a guide for advanced students, this work deals with ancient Near Eastern as well as Greek and Roman history. Books and articles are presented in a topical arrangement. Chapters cover general works, reference works, foundations (chronology, geography, ethnography, sociology, science and technology, the military, law, religion, politics, and historical theory), source materials, ancillary disciplines (epigraphy, numismatics, and papyrology), and secondary sources (editions and studies of the ancient historical writers). Brockmeyer and Schultheiss emphasize basic works and source materials. Their focus is firmly placed on ancient history; literature and archaeology are treated only to the extent that they provide historical sources. Annotations are not supplied. There are author, source, and subject indexes. Bengtson (entry 1), which is available in English, is better as a general guide because of its narrative style and the many annotations in its bibliographical sections. However, Brockmeyer and Schultheiss include a number of works omitted by Bengtson. For those interested primarily in Roman history, Christ (entry 253) offers a more complete bibliography.

250. Burich, Nancy J. **Alexander the Great: A Bibliography.** Kent, Ohio: Kent State University Press, 1970. 153pp. ISBN 0–87338–103–3. LCCN 72–114734.

Burich attempts to include "only those materials which make a real contribution to the knowledge about Alexander and his exploits." She has excluded the medieval Alexander legends, literary works, and most general reference and news items. Burich offers nearly 700 entries under four rubrics: bibliographic aids and general materials, classical sources, pre-nineteenth-century materials, and modern sources. The most useful parts of the book are the chapters on classical and modern sources. Burich supplies an impressive list of ancient sources for the study of Alexander; most entries suggest an edition or translation. In the case of a few items that deal only partly with Alexander, specific references (which are not provided) would have been helpful. The section on modern sources provides a generous selection of scholarly work on Alexander through the early 1960s. Coverage of pre-nineteenth-century works is rather slim; many of those cited were not examined by the compiler. Some entries receive brief descriptive annotations. There are no indexes.

251. Burstein, Stanley M., Nancy Demand, Ian Morris, and Lawrence Tritle. **Current Issues and the Study of Ancient History.** Publications of the Association of Ancient Historians 7. Claremont, CA: Regina Books, 2002. 92pp. ISBN 1–930053–10–X. LCCN 2002–3657.

Continuing the work of *Ancient History: Recent Work and New Directions* (entry 278), this volume surveys the state of scholarship in four areas: ancient history and Afro-centrism; gender studies and ancient history; archaeology and ancient Greek history; and psychology and ancient history. Each essay provides an overview of its topic and a guide to important recent work on it. Bibliography is found only in the footnotes and not in separate listings. There is no index.

252. Calhoun, George M., and Catherine Delamere. **Working Bibliography of Greek Law.** Harvard Series of Legal Bibliographies 1. Cambridge, MA: Harvard University Press, 1927; repr., Buffalo, NY: Hein, 1980. 144pp. LCCN 27–27465.

Calhoun's bibliography focuses on the classical period and is less comprehensive for Hellenistic and later Greek law. He offers limited coverage for works published in the eighteenth century and earlier (Calhoun, in his preface, refers to other bibliographical sources for these). Works are presented in a single alphabetical list, arranged by author. There are neither annotations nor indexes. While dated and generally lacking in bibliographical amenities, Calhoun remains useful for his coverage of nineteenth-and early twentieth-century scholarship.

253. Christ, Karl, ed. **Römische Geschichte: Eine Bibliographie.** Darmstadt: Wissenschaftliche Buchgesellschaft, 1976. 544pp. ISBN 3–534–06074–1.

Intended for German students, this bibliography covers all aspects of Roman history. Its 8,232 unannotated entries are organized by subject. The major sections cover general works, special topics (e.g., law, religion, art), the history of the Roman Republic, the collapse of the republic, the empire (31 B.C. to A.D. 192), the crisis of the third century, and late antiquity. Each is subdivided further by topic and period. Christ includes books, articles, and dissertations in a variety of languages, although German is emphasized. He provides an excellent guide to twentieth-century work on Roman history through 1975. There is a subject index, but not, unfortunately, one for authors.

254. Clark, Gillian. **Women in the Ancient World.** New Surveys in the Classics 21. Oxford: Oxford University Press, 1989. 46pp. LCCN 89–194776.

Since publications on women in antiquity tend to be scattered under many more general rubrics, they can be difficult to find. Clark's survey offers both a good overview of the subject and a working guide to the literature. After a brief introduction, she provides short chapters covering major aspects of the lives of women in antiquity: the nature of women, domesticity, company, fertility, intelligence, power, money, religion, and protection or repression. Each discusses the major primary sources and reviews the current state of scholarship; bibliographical details are given in the notes. Clark covers a wide range of recent publications (through mid-1988). As in other volumes in the series, preference is given to English-language publications. Additional material may be found in Goodwater (entry 261) and in Vérilhac and Vial (entry 279), which offers the most extensive bibliographical coverage of the three.

255.   Corvisier, Jean-Nicolas, and Wiesław Suder. **Polyanthropia—oliganthropia: Bibliographie de la démographie du monde grec.** Wroclaw: Arboretum, 1996. 206pp. ISBN 83–86308–16–8.

Demography has been a hot area of late, as reflected by the large number of important recent works noted by Corvisier and Suder. They gather 1,272 citations for works covering births, deaths, abortion and birth control, population, censuses, burials, and many similar topics for the Greek-speaking eastern Mediterranean world from prehistoric times through late antiquity. Their introduction provides an overview of the field with many references to the bibliography, which is arranged alphabetically by author. An index provides subject access, but only by fairly broad categories. Citations are compressed; users will need to make frequent reference to the list of abbreviations provided. There are no annotations, but reviews of books are noted. Careless editing and typographical errors undermine the reliability of the work, but it remains a useful bibliographical guide for those interested in the demographics of the ancient Greek world. Those seeking demographic studies of the Roman world should also see Suder's earlier work, *Census Populi* (entry 276).

256.   Criniti, Nicola. **Bibliografia catilinaria.** Pubblicazioni dell'Università cattolica del S. Cuore. Saggi e ricerche, ser. 3: Scienze storiche 6. Milano: Editrice Vita e Pensiero, 1971. 84pp. LCCN 72–331657.

Criniti offers a relatively complete bibliography of works on the Catilinarian conspiracy, an event made prominent by the writings of Cicero and Sallust. The first part of the work lists more than 800 historical studies on the conspiracy. These are arranged by author. The second part is devoted to literary and artistic works (including novels, plays, operas, and graphic works) based on the life and conspiracy of Catiline. It includes more than 100 such works, which are arranged by form. Indexes provide subject access to the whole bibliography and also allow for geographical and chronological approaches to the imaginative works in the second part.

257.   Donlan, Walter, ed. **Classical World Bibliography of Greek and Roman History.** Garland Reference Library of the Humanities 94. New York: Garland, 1978. 234pp. ISBN 0–8240–9879–X. LCCN 76–52511.

This volume gathers fourteen bibliographical surveys that originally appeared in *Classical World* (entry 95) between 1954 and 1971. Three each of these are devoted to Herodotus (one general survey and two collectively covering 1954–1969), Thucydides (1942–1967), and Tacitus (1948–1967). The following are each represented by a single survey: Livy (1940–1958), Caesar (1935–1961), Philo and Josephus (1937–1959), Alexander the Great (1948–1967), and Julian the Apostate (1945–1964). The surveys are normally selective, although those on Philo and Josephus and Alexander the Great attempt completeness. All are by well-known specialists on their respective subjects. While style of presentation varies, most of the surveys are arranged topically, and all include descriptive and evaluative comments on the works cited. The compilation reflects a general bias in classical studies toward treating history through historical authors. It is a useful compendium for those seeking retrospective bibliographies on the ancient historians. A general index would have been helpful.

258. Eder, Birgitta. **Staat, Heerschaft, Gesellschaft in frühgriechischer Zeit: Eine Bibliographie 1978–1991/92.** Veröffentlichungen der Mykenischen Kommission 14. Wien: Österreichischen Akademie der Wissenschaften, 1994. 248pp. ISBN 3–7001–2140–7. LCCN 95–106773.

This bibliography of some 2,200 items focuses on society, kingship and the economy in early Greece. A number of works on epigraphy, philology, and archaeology are included, although coverage of these areas is somewhat incidental to the main purpose of the work. Eder limits herself to the Bronze Age. She includes books, articles, conference proceedings, and collected papers in a wide variety of languages. Eder lists works alphabetically by author, then chronologically. She also provides a detailed subject index. This bibliography will be useful to any scholar of early Greece. Students below the doctoral level will find most of the works listed too technical.

259. Flach, Dieter. **Bibliographie zur römischen Agrargeschichte.** Paderborn: Author, 1991. 118pp. LCCN 93–206775.

Flach's bibliography expands on and continues the work of White (entry 284). He includes older work omitted by White as well as extending coverage by another two decades. Arrangement is by broad subject, with subarrangement by author. While Flach is much more complete than his predecessor, he supplies neither introduction nor annotations so that White remains useful. There is no index.

260. Garnsey, Peter, and Richard Saller. **Early Principate: Augustus to Trajan.** New Surveys in the Classics 15. Oxford: Clarendon Press, 1982. 42pp. ISBN 0–903035–12–X LCCN 82–207445.

Garnsey and Saller survey recent work on the early Roman Empire. They do so in a series of brief essays covering major topics, including politics, the empire, administration, society, economy, monarchy, and culture. Bibliographical citations are provided in the notes following each essay. Their overview, which is aimed at undergraduates, provides a good orientation and working bibliography for the period.

261. Goodwater, Leanna. **Women in Antiquity: An Annotated Bibliography.** Metuchen, NJ: Scarecrow Press, 1975. 171pp. ISBN 0–8108–0837–4. LCCN 75–23229.

Goodwater covers both ancient sources and modern studies. The first part of her bibliography is an omnium-gatherum of classical works by or about women. These include, for example, Greek tragedies in which women figure prominently. Some of the sources are cited in Greek or Latin editions, while others are cited in translations of varying quality. The second part lists secondary works under four broad rubrics (general works, Greece, Etruscan women, and Rome). Goodwater's annotations describe the content of each work adequately but generally avoid any evaluation of it. There are indexes of women of antiquity and of authors. While Goodwater supplies some 534 entries (147 in sources, the remainder in modern studies), users should bear in mind that much significant work has been done in this area since 1975. Gillian Clark's recent survey volume (entry 254) provides many more recent references. Vérilhac and Vial (entry 279) is still more extensive, with strong coverage of European-language works as well.

262. Karras, Margret, and Josef Wiesehöfer. **Kindheit und Jugend in der Antike: Eine Bibliographie.** Bonn: Rudolf Habelt, 1981. 123pp. ISBN 3–7749–1852–X. LCCN 81–167551.

Karras and Wiesehöfer list 1,270 works on children and youth in the ancient Near East, Greece, and Rome. They arrange these under broad subject headings such as law, culture, play, and education. Each category is subdivided by culture (general, Greek, Roman, Egyptian, and other). The compilers have included works in a variety of languages, although German and English predominate. Items cited range from scholarly works of general interest to highly technical epigraphical and papyrological publications. Author and subject indexes are provided. The pertinent sections of Krause (entry 264) cover some of the same material and are more up-to-date.

263. Kehne, Peter. **Studienbibliographie zur griechischen Geschichte in klassischer Zeit (500–404 v.Chr.).** Hannover: Witte, 1998. 66pp. ISBN 3–932152–30–1. LCCN 99–176805.

Kehne, whose primary audience is German college students, has compiled a bibliographic survey covering Greek history in the fifth century B.C. He arranges citations partly by form, partly by subject. His selection of material is good and relatively recent; there is a strong German bias (a few English works are cited in German translation), although many works in English and French are listed. Kehne focuses on books, although he does cite a fair number of journal articles. He provides annotations only for a few bibliographical works.

264. Krause, Jens-Uwe. **Die Familie und weitere anthropologische Grundlagen.** Bd. 1: Bibliographie zur römischen Sozialgeschichte. Heidelberger althistorische Beiträge und epigraphische Studien 11. Unter Mitwirkung von Bertram Eisenhauer, Konstanze Szelényi, und Susanne Tschirner. Stuttgart: Franz Steiner, 1992. ISBN 3–515–06044–8. LCCN 93–243284.

This unannotated bibliography lists more than 4,000 works on such topics as demographics, women, marriage, family and relationships, sexuality, childhood, youth, the elderly, death, and burial. It covers Rome, the early Christians, and the early Byzantine Empire. Krause and his fellow compilers have gathered their material from a wide range of sources in classics, history, religious studies, and anthropology. They include books, dissertations, and articles from both journals and *Festschriften*. The material is arranged by subject; author and subject indexes provide additional access. Krause's bibliography is an invaluable resource for research on Roman social history.

265. Krause, Jens-Uwe, Jannis Mylonopoulos, and Raffaella Cengia. **Schichten, Konflikte, religiöse Gruppen, materielle Kultur.** Bd. 2: Bibliographie zur römischen Sozialgeschichte. Stuttgart: Franz Steiner, 1998. 876pp. ISBN 3–515–07269–1.

This massive bibliography of Roman social history covers classes, conflicts, religions, and material culture from the beginnings of Rome to the time of Justinian (A.D. 565). The editors employ a complex subject arrangement. The first section covers general works. The next is arranged chronologically by period. The third, which comprises the bulk of the work, is arranged by topic; broad subdivisions include demography, social structures, the various social/political classes, land ownership and use, mining and quarrying, cities and urbanization, crafts, trade, banking, associations, intellectual life, slavery, the emperor, food, clothing, housing, entertainment, education, patron-client relationships, social mobility, romanization, social conflicts, crime and law, regional mobility, Rome and foreigners, pagan religions, magic, Jews, Christianity, public administration, administration of justice, taxation, and the army. All are further subdivided. A fourth and final section covers regional studies, arranged by region. In spite of its size (approximately 16,000 entries spanning the twentieth century), this remains a selective bibliography. The editors provide no annotations. While extensive lists of cross-references appear at the end of each section, there is no index. In spite of these drawbacks, this is an excellent starting point for anyone doing research in Roman social history.

266. Oleson, John Peter. **Bronze Age, Greek, and Roman Technology: A Selected, Annotated Bibliography.** Bibliographies of the History of Science and Technology 13. Garland Reference Library of the Humanities 646. New York: Garland, 1986. 515pp. ISBN 0–8240–8677–5. LCCN 85–45143.

Oleson covers primarily Greco-Roman technology but also includes some material on the ancient Near East. His chronological limits extend from the Bronze Age to the sixth century A.D. He includes books and articles in English, French, German, Italian, and Spanish. Topical chapters cover all major aspects of technology: mining, food production, energy, engineering, manufacturing, transportation, record keeping and standards, military technology, and cultural aspects of technology. In addition, two introductory chapters cover sources and general surveys. An index provides access by author. Oleson, who has himself done significant research in the field, provides strong annotations that describe and assess each entry. This wide-ranging bibliography includes works from many disciplines, including classical and Near Eastern studies, anthropology, and the history of science. It is an excellent guide to a rapidly developing aspect of ancient studies.

267. Oster, Richard E. **Bibliography of Ancient Ephesus.** ATLA Bibliography Series 19. Metuchen, NJ: American Theological Library Association and Scarecrow Press, 1987. 155pp. ISBN 0–8108–1996–1. LCCN 87–12617.

While intended primarily for New Testament scholars, this work is of value to anyone interested in this important Greco-Roman city in Asia Minor. Oster's scope covers "the ancient history, culture, and archaeological evidence of Ephesus." Works on archaeological excavations, inscriptions, and numismatics comprise the majority of his citations. The 1,535 numbered entries, which range in date from the eighteenth century to the 1980s, include books, dissertations, and journal articles. Oster arranges these by author; a subject index is also provided. Although the individual entries do not include annotations, Oster's introduction supplies a good overview of scholarly work on Ephesus.

268. **Les provinces hellénophones de l'empire romain de Pompée au milieu du IIIe siècle ap. J.-C.: Recueil bibliographique à partir des analyses du BAHR (1962 à 1974).** Strasbourg: AECR, 1986. 515pp. ISBN 2–904–337–16–4.

This bibliography is compiled from 13 volumes of the *Bulletin analytique d'histoire romaine* (entry 52), which cover the years 1962–1974. All entries concerning the Greek-speaking provinces of the Roman Empire through the third century A.D. are gathered here in a geographical arrangement. Each province receives a separate chapter, while general works and those dealing with several provinces are found in an initial general chapter. Chapters are divided into two general sections, sources and historical studies. These are further subdivided by topic as the material in each chapter requires. The scheme is neatly laid out in the table of contents. Lack of indexes is a major drawback; there is, for example, no author access. The strength of the work is in its abstracts, which are often lengthy and provide good descriptions of the items.

269. Rhodes, P. J. **Athenian Empire.** New Surveys in the Classics 17. Oxford: Clarendon Press, 1985. 47pp. ISBN 0–90–303514–6. LCCN 85–220204.

Rhodes, a well-known specialist in Greek history, offers a succinct review of scholarly work on the Athenian empire. He concentrates on the period following 1924, when the first studies of the Athenian tribute lists began to appear. After a general introduction, brief essays summarize scholarship on various aspects of the development and fall of the empire; bibliographical details are relegated to the notes following each.

270. Rollins, Alden M. **Fall of Rome: A Reference Guide.** Jefferson, NC: McFarland, 1983. 130pp. ISBN 0–89950–034–X. LCCN 82–23918.

This bibliography suffers from lack of a clear sense of its intended audience and purpose. The preface describes it as a "select and selectively annotated guide to twentieth-century literature in English on the fall of Rome," although a few French- and German-language items and some nineteenth-century publications are found in it. Rollins presents a farrago of popular and scholarly works; scholars will find it too general and incomplete to be of real use, while more general inquirers will find much that is unlikely to be accessible to them, such as doctoral dissertations. The 260 entries include standard historical treatises, popularizing books, articles from both learned and general periodicals, published lectures, reviews, and dissertations. Rollins arranges these alphabetically by author. He provides extensive annotations for most entries. These supply good summaries, which are sometimes accompanied by useful commentary and references to related works. A brief index includes authors and subjects.

271. Rollins, Alden. **Rome in the Fourth Century** A.D.: **An Annotated Bibliography with Historical Overview.** Jefferson, NC: McFarland, 1991. 324pp. ISBN 0–89950–624–0. LCCN 91–52762.

The Roman Empire of the fourth century A.D. is of interest to Byzantinists and medievalists as well as classicists. As a result, relevant publications are found in the literature of several disciplines. Rollins has gathered twentieth-century English-language materials through 1988. His more than 1,400 entries include books, dissertations, and articles. He arranges these into 11 broad subject categories, such as politics and government, military matters, literature and education, and so forth. Together they cover virtually every aspect of fourth-century history and life. Rollins annotates most entries. His annotations vary in quality. Some are merely one- or two-line summaries, while others are more detailed and offer evaluative remarks as well. Some book annotations also include citations for selected reviews. There is an index of subjects, but not one for authors. Rollins is a handy guide to English-language work in this extremely active area of research. Students especially will find this book useful.

272. Sargenti, Manlius, ed. **Operum ad Ius Romanum Pertinentium Quae ab Anno MCMXL ad Annum MCMLXX Edita Sunt Index Modo et Ratione Ordinatus.** Ticini: Alma Ticinensis Universitas, Institutum Romani et Historiae Iuris, 1978. 3 v.

273. Sargenti, Manlius. **Operum ad Ius Romanum Pertinentium Quae inde ab Anno MCMLXXI usque ad Annum MCMLXXX Edita Sunt Index Modo et Ratione Ordinatus.** Mediolani: Cisalpino-Goliardico, 1988–1990. 3 v. ISBN 88–205–0614–9 (v. 1); 88–205–0646–7 (v. 2); 88–205–0683–1 (v. 3).

The volume of publication on Roman law is well illustrated by Sargenti's massive bibliography for the years 1940–1970; a mere thirty years' work requires more than 2,000 pages. This is an exceptionally wide-ranging bibliography and includes many works whose relation to the study of Roman law is somewhat tangential. Sargenti arranges the citations by subject. His single alphabetical sequence includes both general topics and technical terms of Roman law as headings. Sargenti lists books and articles; book reviews are sometimes cited under the entry for the work reviewed. There are no annotations. Sargenti provides indexes of subject headings and of authors. The author index is particularly helpful: it gives both the subject heading and the page reference. The second work follows the pattern of Sargenti's earlier bibliography and extends coverage to 1980.

274. Scanlon, Thomas F. **Greek and Roman Athletics: A Bibliography.** Chicago: Ares, 1984. 142pp. ISBN 0–89005–522–X. LCCN 91–187821.

Scanlon's bibliography lists more than 1,600 works on sports in the ancient world. It includes works published in a variety of languages between 1573 and 1983. Work on ancient sports is interdisciplinary, so relevant material is often found in sources unfamiliar to classicists. Therefore, Scanlon gathers publications from such fields as physical education, sociology, and anthropology, as well as from classical studies. He arranges these in broad subject categories, which he further subdivides as necessary. Scanlon does not provide annotations, although he does cite reviews in entries for books. His substantial introduction discusses overall trends in the study of ancient sports and comments on a few specific works. An index of authors concludes the work.

275. Seibert, Jakob. **Das Zeitalter der Diadochen.** Erträge der Forschung 185. Darmstadt: Wissenschaftliche Buchgesellschaft, 1983. 272pp. ISBN 3–534–04657–9.

This extended bibliographical essay covers Alexander's successors. Its various sections deal with literary, epigraphic, and numismatic sources; chronology; dynasties and individual kings; major problems in the history of the successors; prosopography; and various topical studies of the period. Each section is extensively subdivided. The bulk of the works cited are in English, French, and German; they range in date from the nineteenth century to late 1970s. An author index and a name and subject index conclude the work. Seibert provides a good overview of older work on the Diadochoi.

276. Suder, Wiesław. **Census Populi: Bibliographie de la démographie de l'antiquité romaine.** Bonn: Rudolf Habelt, 1988. 127pp. ISBN 3–7749–2294–2. LCCN 88–200879.

Suder gathers 1,007 demographic studies of the ancient Roman world in a single A-to-Z listing. He includes works ranging in date from the nineteenth century through the mid-1980s and covers all the standard languages of classical scholarship. In addition to works specifically on censuses and population, Suder includes many works on such topics as abortion, childhood, colonization, disease, families, old age, and urbanization. Entries are compressed; users must frequently consult the lengthy table of abbreviations. There are no annotations. Suder does provide a subject index (headings are in French, but also translated into English). For works on ancient Greek demography see Corvisier and Suder (entry 255).

277. Suder, Wiesław. **Geras: Old Age in Greco-Roman Antiquity. A Classified Bibliography.** Wroclaw: Profil, 1991. 169pp. ISBN 83–900102–2-4.

An interdisciplinary work, this bibliography covers publications in classics, medicine, sociology, and anthropology through 1989. Its 1,040 numbered citations include books, articles, and dissertations. While many of these are in English, works in French, German, Italian, and Spanish are also well represented. Suder arranges the entries alphabetically by author; an index provides subject access. There are no annotations.

278. Thomas, Carol G., ed. **Ancient History: Recent Work and New Directions.** Publications of the Association of Ancient Historians 5. Claremont, CA: Regina Books, 1997. 107pp. ISBN 0–941690–79–2; 0–941690–78–4pa. LCCN 97–35440.

Taking Chester Starr's *Past and Future in Ancient History* (Lanham, MD: University Press of America, 1987) as its point of departure, this volume surveys the state of the field as of 1997. It consists of four bibliographical essays covering Greece (Kurt Raaflaub), the Hellenistic age (Stanley Burstein), the Roman Republic (Allen Ward), and the Roman Empire (Ramsay MacMullen). The discussions and extensive bibliographical notes provide a good overview of major works on ancient history at the end of the twentieth century. A later collection, *Current Issues and the Study of Ancient History* (entry 251), looks at some contemporary approaches to ancient history.

279. Vérilhac, A. M., and C. Vial. **La Femme grecque et romaine: Bibliographie.** La Femme dans le monde méditerranéen 2. Travaux de la Maison de l'Orient. Lyon: Maison de l'Orient, 1990. 209pp. ISBN 2–903264–48–1.

In this bibliography Vérilhac and Vial list some 3,300 works relating to women in classical antiquity. These include books, articles, selected dissertations, and editions of primary sources. Most are in English, French, German, or Italian. While a few nineteenth-century publications are noted, most works cited are more recent. The bibliography provides good coverage through the mid-1980s; the latest work cited is from 1986. Entries consist of citations, alphanumeric subject classifications, and subject keywords. A few also include brief critical comments. Arrangement is alphabetical by author. Cross-references are supplied for works with multiple authors. Two indexes provide subject access. One is based on the broad alphanumeric subject classes assigned by the editors; the other is a keyword index. This bibliography is much more detailed than the works of Clark (entry 254) and Goodwater (entry 261). It also provides better coverage of works in languages other than English.

280. Vogt, Joseph, and Heinz Bellen, eds. **Bibliographie zur antiken Sklaverei.** Neubearbeiten von Elisabeth Hermann. Bochum: Studienverlag Dr. N. Brockmeyer, 1983. 2v. ISBN 3–88339–363–0. LCCN 84–181935.

Vogt and Bellen have compiled a wide-ranging bibliography that covers slavery in the ancient Near East and the classical world. There is token coverage on the ancient Far East as well. The bulk of the material concerns the classical world. The bibliography deals with all aspects of slavery in antiquity, including works on the role of slaves in literature as well as more strictly historical studies. Many general works touching on ancient slavery are also noted. These include works on such topics as ancient agriculture, manufacturing, and social organization. While not exhaustive, the *Bibliographie zur antiken Sklaverei* is a major resource: this greatly expanded second edition includes 5,162 entries. There are no annotations. The citations are arranged in subject categories, with numerous cross-references provided. An extensive array of indexes appears in the second volume: Greek words, Latin words, personal names (as subjects), geographical names, subjects, and authors. This bibliography is best suited to those doing advanced research; Wiedemann (entry 285) offers a good survey of recent and important work on ancient slavery for undergraduates and graduate students. Those seeking exhaustive coverage should also consult Heinz Schulz-Falkenthal, ed., *Sklaverei in der griechisch-römischen Antike: Eine Bibliographie wissenschaftlicher Literatur vom ausgehenden 15. Jahrhundert bis zur Mittel des 19. Jahrhundert* (Halle: Universitäts- und Landesbibliothek Sachsent-Anhalt, 1985).

281. Vollmer, Dankward. **Alte Geschichte in Studium und Unterricht: Eine Einfuhrung mit kommentiert Literaturverzeichnis.** Mit Markus Merl, Markus Sehlmeyer, und Uwe Walter. Stuttgart: Franz Steiner, 1994. 205pp. ISBN 3–515–06468–0.

282. Sehlmeyer, Markus. **Ergänzung zur 1. Auflage.** October 2001. URL: http://sehlmeyer.bei.t-online.de/vollmer.htm.

This classified bibliography of ancient history is intended for German undergraduates and their teachers. It offers a good, if idiosyncratic, overview of the literature. Vollmer arranges his material both by form (e.g., handbooks, lexica, bibliographies) and subject (e.g., papyrology, military history). He provides primarily descriptive annotations, which are generally helpful although not always reliable. Those seeking a quick orientation to the basic works in a particular area, such as prosopography, will find Vollmer useful. A detailed table of contents and an index of authors aid the user in navigating the work, although a title index is lacking. Sehlmeyer, who assisted Vollmer in compiling this work, provides an online supplement to update its contents.

283. Weiler, Ingomar. **Griechische Geschichte: Einführung, Quellenkunde, Bibliographie.** 2. durchges. und erw. Aufl. Darmstadt: Wissenschaftliche Buchgesellschaft, 1988. 314pp. ISBN 3–534–06358–9. LCCN 91–123839.

Weiler provides a good, although now dated, bibliographical manual for the study of Greek history. The first section includes general works, bibliographies, journals, geography, chronology, and a brief history of scholarship prior to the twentieth century. The second section is devoted to early Greece through the Doric invasions. The third and longest section covers Greek history from the time of Homer through the Roman conquest of Greece. This section has numerous subdivisions covering topics, major city-states, and periods (all neatly laid out in the table of contents). The fourth and final section covers sources: literary, epigraphical, numismatic, and papyrological. Each section/subsection typically begins with a short narrative overview, which often outlines major issues; a dense and lengthy bibliography follows. Indexes cover subjects, places, ancient persons, and modern authors. As a book, Weiler is unreadable but a great source to mine for bibliography.

284. White, K. D. **Bibliography of Roman Agriculture.** Bibliographies in Agricultural History 1. Reading: University of Reading, 1970. 63pp. ISBN 0–900724–03–X. LCCN 73–852088.

Compiled by one of the leading authorities on Roman agriculture, this working bibliography provides an excellent guide to the subject through 1970. A substantial introduction provides an overview of the field and a reliable guide to the most important literary and archaeological source material. The actual bibliography brings together some 918 items from a wide range of publications in classical studies, history, and agriculture. These are arranged by subject; an outline of the classification scheme appears at the beginning of the bibliography. White supplies descriptive and evaluative annotations for many entries. There is no index. For more recent work and earlier works omitted by White, see Flach (entry 259).

285. Wiedemann, T.E.J. **Slavery.** New Surveys in the Classics 19. Oxford: Clarendon Press, 1987. 51pp. ISBN 0–903035–48–0. LCCN 88–157411.

Wiedemann supplies a selective survey of work on slavery in antiquity. His emphasis is on recent studies, although he also includes significant earlier works. Wiedemann divides his material into six topical chapters: "Historiographical Issues," "Interpreting the Evidence," "Slavery as a Social Institution," "Slaves as Producers and Servants," "Slaves in Public Service," and "Discontent and Rebellion." These follow the normal format of the series: a brief critical survey of scholarly work on each topic, followed by bibliographical endnotes. Wiedemann provides a good overview of the field for students of ancient history. The 1992 and 1997 reprints of this work include addenda. Those who need more extensive bibliographical coverage should consult Vogt and Bellen (entry 280).

GENERAL HISTORIES

286. Boardman, John, Jasper Griffin, and Oswyn Murray, eds. **Oxford History of the Classical World.** Oxford: Oxford University Press, 1986. 882pp. ISBN 0–19–872112–9. LCCN 85–21774.

287. Boardman, John, Jasper Griffin, and Oswyn Murray, eds. **Oxford History of Greece and the Hellenistic World.** Oxford: Oxford University Press, 1991. 520pp. ISBN 0–19–285247–7. LCCN 91–11926.

288. Boardman, John, Jasper Griffin, and Oswyn Murray, eds. **Oxford History of the Roman World.** Oxford: Oxford University Press, 1991. 518pp. ISBN 0–18–285248–5. LCCN 91–11763.

The first item listed above is an excellent one-volume history of Greece and Rome that is designed for the student and general reader. It is also available in the two paperback volumes noted. The three major sections cover Greece (from Homer to the rise of Alexander),

Greece and Rome (essentially the Hellenistic period), and Rome (from Augustus to the fall of the empire in the west). In addition to political history, the work covers cultural and social history. Various chapters within each section include such topics as literature, philosophy, art and architecture, and religion as well as historical overviews. Each chapter is by a well-known scholar in the area and includes notes for further reading. The book is richly illustrated and includes a number of maps. A lengthy "table of events" at the end of the text provides a convenient chronology of the classical world. A general index concludes the volume. This is a good choice for the layperson. Those who require more detailed and scholarly treatment should consult the *Cambridge Ancient History* (entry 289).

289.   Cambridge Ancient History. 1st–3rd eds. Cambridge: Cambridge University Press, 1923– . Details for individual volumes:

V. 1, pt. 1: **Prolegomena and Prehistory.** 3rd ed. 1971. 758pp. ISBN 0–521–07051–1. LCCN 75–85719.

V. 1, pt. 2: **Early History of the Middle East.** 3rd ed. 1971. 1,058pp. ISBN 0–521–07791–5. LCCN 73–116845.

V. 2, pt. 1: **History of the Middle East and Aegean Region, 1800–1300** B.C. 3rd ed. 1973. 891pp. ISBN 0–521–08230–7. LCCN 75–85719.

V. 2, pt. 2: **The Assyrian and Babylonian Empires, the Eastern Mediterranean and the Black Sea, 1380–1000** B.C. 3rd ed. 1975. 1,128pp. 0–521–08691–4. LCCN 75–85719.

Plates to Volumes I and II. New ed. 1977. 181pp. ISBN 0–521–20571–9. LCCN 75–85719.

V. 3, pt. 1: **The Prehistory of the Balkans, the Middle East and the Aegean World, Tenth to Eighth Centuries** B.C. 2nd ed. 1982. 1,088pp. ISBN 0–521–22496–9. LCCN 75–85719.

V. 3, pt. 2: **The Assyrian and Babylonian Empires and Other States of the Near East, from the Eighth to the Sixth Centuries** B.C. 2nd ed. 1992. 962pp. ISBN 0–521–22717–8. LCCN 75–85719.

V. 3, pt. 3: **The Expansion of the Greek World, Eighth to Sixth Centuries** B.C. 2nd ed. 1982. 554pp. ISBN 0–521–23447–6. LCCN 75–85719.

Plates to Volume III. New ed. 1984. 313pp. ISBN 0–521–24289–4. LCCN 75–85719.

V. 4: **Persia, Greece, and the Western Mediterranean, c. 525–479** B.C. 2nd ed. 1988. 960pp. ISBN 0–521–22804–2. LCCN 75–85719.

Plates to Volume IV. New ed. 1988. 264pp. ISBN 0–521–30580–2. LCCN 77–378456.

V. 5: **The Fifth Century** B.C. 2nd ed. 1992. 619pp. ISBN 0–521–23347–X. LCCN 75–85719.

V. 6: **The Fourth Century** B.C. 2nd ed. 1994. 1,077pp. ISBN 0–521–23348–8. LCCN 75–85719.

Plates to Volumes V and VI. 2nd ed. 1995. 220pp. ISBN 0–521–23349–6

V. 7, pt. 1: **The Hellenistic World.** 2nd ed. 1984. 641pp. ISBN 0–521–23445–X. LCCN 75–85719.

Plates to Volume VII, Part. 1. New ed. 1984. 224pp. ISBN 0–521–24354–8. LCCN 83–5186.

V. 7, pt. 2: The Rise of Rome to 220 B.C. 2nd ed. 1990. 600pp. ISBN 0–521–23446–8. LCCN 75–85719.

V. 8: Rome and the Mediterranean to 133 B.C. 2nd ed. 1989. 650pp. ISBN 0–521–23448–4. LCCN 75–85719.

V. 9: The Last Age of the Roman Republic, 146–43 B.C. 2nd ed. 1994. 929pp. ISBN 0–521–25603–8. LCCN 75–85719.

V. 10: The Augustan Empire, 43 B.C.–A.D. 69. 2nd ed. 1996. 1,193pp. ISBN 0–521–26430–8.

V. 11: The High Empire, A.D. 70–192. 2nd ed. 2000. 1,222pp. ISBN 0–521–26335–2. LCCN 75–85719.

V. 12: The Crisis of Empire, A.D. 193–337. 2nd ed. 2005. 878pp. ISBN 0–521–30199–8. LCCN 75–85719.

V.13: The Late Empire, A.D. 337–425. 1998. 889pp. ISBN 0–521–30200–5. LCCN 75–85719.

V.14: Late Antiquity: Empire and Successors, A.D. 425–600. 2000. 1,166pp. ISBN 0–521–32591–9. LCCN 75–85719.

The first edition of the *Cambridge Ancient History* appeared in 12 volumes with five volumes of plates (1923–1939); it has been under continuous revision, and as a result its parts are now in various editions. Two additional volumes have been added to the original set, extending coverage through the age of Justinian. The above listing will serve as a guide both to the most current manifestation and to the contents of each volume. Since the appearance of the second edition of volume 12, the entire work is at last in either the second or third edition. The *CAH* counts among its contributors the leading British classical and Near Eastern scholars of several generations, along with a number of notable American and European scholars. It moves in a broad chronological procession through the history of the ancient Mediterranean world from the prehistoric era to A.D. 600. The work covers political, social, economic, and cultural history. Volumes cover particular eras and sometimes regions. Within each volume, long chapters by various hands treat different regions, periods, and topics. Many maps and genealogical tables are provided. Each volume includes an extensive bibliography and a substantial index. Plates appear in separate volumes. Designed for the use of scholars and advanced students, the *CAH* is the most substantial and all-inclusive survey of ancient history available. The more casual inquirer may also find it of use. Its text is generally reliable and often authoritative.

DICTIONARIES, ENCYCLOPEDIAS, AND HANDBOOKS

290. Adkins, Lesley, and Roy A. Adkins. **Handbook to Life in Ancient Greece.** New York: Facts on File, 1997; repr., Oxford: Oxford University Press, 1998. 472pp. ISBN 0–19–512491–X. LCCN 98–11568.

This handbook covers the Greek world from the Bronze Age to the Roman conquest of Egypt (30 B.C.). The Adkinses arrange their material in 10 topical chapters. The first, "Civilizations, City-States, and Empires," provides an overview of political and military history, including a chronology of events. The second, "Rulers and Leaders," gives brief biographies of notable kings, generals, and politicians. Remaining chapters cover military matters, geography; the economy; urban and rural life; language and literature; religion and mythology; art, science, and philosophy; and everyday life. Many illustrations, maps, and lists accompany the text. Each chapter includes a guide to further reading. There is also a general bibliography and a detailed index. Students, especially beginners, will find this a useful aid, with a strong emphasis on social, economic, and cultural history.

291. Adkins, Lesley, and Roy A. Adkins. **Handbook to Life in Ancient Rome.** Updated ed. New York: Facts on File, 2004. 450pp. ISBN 0–8160–5026–0. LCCN 2003049255.

The Adkinses provide a very useful handbook for high school and college students. They begin with general historical information: a chronology of major events from the founding of Rome in 753 B.C. to the death of Justinian in A.D. 565. Thumbnail sketches of prominent Romans (in alphabetical order) and emperors (in chronological order) follow. An overview of social structures, government, and the legal system round out this section. Subsequent chapters cover military affairs, geography, towns and countryside, travel and trade, written evidence, religion, the economy, and everyday life. The work focuses on everyday life and material culture rather than political history. Those interested, for example, in the structure of a Roman ship or what the Romans ate will find basic information and hints for further study. The Adkinses sometimes miss the mark, as in the section on the Latin language, where they give either too much or too little information: many readers will be left disappointed or confused. But for the most part, they offer a handy guide to beginning and intermediate students. Their guides to further reading and bibliography tend to be up-to-date and on target, although sometimes omitting important earlier works. They also include many maps, illustrations, and a detailed subject index.

292. Berger, Adolf. **Encyclopedic Dictionary of Roman Law.** Transactions of the American Philosophical Society, n.s., 43, pt. 2. Philadelphia: American Philosophical Society, 1953. pp. 333–809. LCCN 53–7641.

Of interest to legal historians as well as classicists, this work is a guide to the technical terminology of Roman law. Berger defines and discusses each term. Many articles include references to the scholarly literature. Berger provides numerous cross-references for related entries. There is an English-Latin glossary, which facilitates access for those who are interested in a particular legal concept but lack the Latin term.

293. Bickermann, E. J. **Chronology of the Ancient World.** Aspects of Greek and Roman Life. Ithaca, NY: Cornell University Press, 1980. 2nd ed. 223pp. ISBN 0–8014–1282–X. LCCN 78–58899.

Bickermann first published his handbook more than fifty years ago under the title *Chronologie* (Leipzig: Teubner, 1933). It has since undergone extensive revision and expansion and has been translated into several languages. The first part of the work provides a general overview of the chronology of the ancient world, with particular emphasis on Greece, Rome, and Greco-Roman Egypt. Among other things, Bickermann discusses the astronomical basis and history of the various ancient calendars and the types of chronographic systems (regnal years, eponymous magistrates, etc.) used by the ancients. The second part is a collection of tables. These include lists of astronomical data, kings, emperors, and magistrates. A synchronistic table brings together the most common systems of the classical world (Olympian years, the Varronian years *ab urbe condita,* and Egyptian mobile years) with modern equivalents. Bickermann also provides a chronological table of Greek and Roman history, which gives a year-by-year listing of major historical events from 776 B.C. to A.D. 476. There is a short general index. Bickermann is the most accessible general treatment of ancient chronology and is particularly good for students. Samuel (entry 311) covers much of the same ground but is geared more toward the working scholar.

294.   Bunson, Matthew. **Encyclopedia of the Roman Empire.** Rev. ed. New York: Facts on File, 2002. 636pp. ISBN 0–8160–4562–3. LCCN 2001–53253.

Bunson covers the Roman world from approximately 59 B.C. to A.D. 476. The front matter of his book includes a discussion of Roman names and a chronology of major military, political, and cultural events. The encyclopedia proper consists of roughly 2,000 entries. Compact articles cover people, places, important Latin terms (especially those relating to politics and the military), topics, and events. Some broader topics such as literature, medicine, and Christianity receive more extended treatment. The revised edition is substantially larger than its predecessor and includes more topical entries, although biographical entries remain the largest category. The clear and readable articles are well suited to the needs of students and general readers, Bunson's intended audience. Reading lists accompany some articles in the revised edition; this is a notable improvement, yet numerous others still lack them. Many attractive illustrations and maps appear throughout the volume. Appendixes provide a list of Roman emperors, genealogical tables of the major imperial houses, and a glossary. The general bibliography is a disaster: works in Latin only are included in what purports to be a list of primary sources in translation, the works of Sallust and Seneca are conflated, primary and secondary sources are confused, and several works are cited in older editions. A detailed index and many cross-references facilitate access. Suitable for those not up to the *Oxford Classical Dictionary*[3] (entry 142) or other more scholarly works, but to be used with caution.

295.   Cristofani, Mauro, ed. **Dizionario della civiltà etrusca.** Archeologia. Firenze: Giunti Martello, 1985. 340pp. LCCN 85–198607.

The only dictionary of Etruscan civilization available, Cristofani directs his work toward the student and the interested layperson rather than the scholar. Its compact and informative articles cover every aspect of Etruscan culture. There are entries for people, places, objects, and topics. Cristofani has also included entries on major museum collections of Etruscan artifacts and on modern pioneers of Etruscan studies, such as George Dennis. A number of authors, mostly Italian, have contributed to the dictionary; all articles are signed. Many well-chosen illustrations accompany the text. A time line at the back of the volume offers a comparative overview of Etruscan and other Mediterranean cultures from the fifteenth century B.C. to 200 B.C. Lack of bibliographies and an index is the chief defect of this work. Otherwise it provides an attractive reference work on this mysterious culture.

296.   Dalby, Andrew. **Food in the Ancient World from A to Z.** Ancient World from A to Z. London: Routledge, 2003. 408pp. ISBN 0–415–23259–7. LCCN 2002–31942.

Dalby has produced an interesting compendium of all things related to food in the ancient world. Obviously this includes foodstuffs, wines, writers on food, and so on. But Dalby often goes much further afield, including entries for people and places only tangentially connected to food (e.g., sites where depictions of food or inscriptions about it have been found). In addition to Greece and Rome, he covers Egypt and the ancient Near East. Entries are quirky: those for countries and regions survey the regional cuisine as known from ancient sources. An article on cooking utensils lists known Greek and Latin terms for such, with references to the sources, but there are no separate entries for these or cross-references from them to the article. The entry on recipes is less an entry than a bibliography of modern books that translate or adapt ancient recipes. Dalby's articles draw heavily on ancient sources; nearly every entry includes numerous references to these, and many include references to modern scholarship. His writing is unusually lively for such a work. A few maps and line drawings are scattered through the work; more illustrations are needed. The selective bibliography covers reference works, ancient culinary writers, and secondary works on food, drink, plants, animals, and agriculture. Dalby provides indexes to scientific names of plants and animals, to Latin terms, and to Greek terms.

297. Erskine, Andrew, ed. **Companion to the Hellenistic World.** Blackwell Companions to the Ancient World. Malden, MA: Blackwell, 2003. 588pp. ISBN 0–631–22537–4. LCCN 2002015293.

Both students and scholars will find this an excellent source of information on Hellenistic civilization. Erskine and his outstanding team of contributors cover the Greek world from the death of Alexander (323 B.C.) to the Roman conquest of Egypt (31 B.C.). Erskine begins with an overview of Hellenistic history and the primary sources. Seven sections cover narrative history (five essays on major chronological divisions); the successor dynasties (four essays on the Ptolemies, Seleukids, Antigonids, and Attalids); change and continuity (four essays); Greeks and others (four essays); society and economy (five essays); religion (two essays); and science, philosophy, literature, and art (four essays). Each essay offers a readable overview of its topic and a guide to further reading. Frequent cross-references and an excellent index help readers to pursue topics throughout the volume. The bibliography focuses on recent work while not neglecting important older contributions.

298. Flower, Harriet I., ed. **Cambridge Companion to the Roman Republic.** Cambridge: Cambridge University Press, 2004. 405pp. ISBN 0–521–80794–8; 0–521–00390–3pa. LCCN 2003048572.

This handbook covers the Roman Republic from its traditional beginning in 509 B.C. to approximately 49 B.C. While far from comprehensive, it treats most major topics. The first section covers political and military history, albeit selectively, with essays on the early republic, the Roman constitution, the military, and the crisis of the late republic. The second section, on social history, includes studies of households, women, law, and religion. Rome's growing empire is the focus of the third section, which covers her growth in Italy, the war with Carthage, and her relations with the Greek world. The fourth section covers Roman culture: literature, art, and the games. A final essay on "The Roman Republic and the French and American Revolutions" is somewhat out of keeping with the rest of the work. Flower's contributors are all leading scholars in their areas. Each provides a solid overview of his or her topic with good coverage of both ancient sources and current scholarship. Flower has provided a very good bibliography, arranged by topic. The work also includes maps, illustrations, and a time line of events. A detailed index concludes the volume.

299.   Golden, Mark. **Sport in the Ancient World from A to Z.** Ancient World from A to Z. London: Routledge, 2004. 184pp. ISBN 0–415–24881–7. LCCN 2003–46671.

Golden's dictionary, like the earlier work of Matz (entry 306), is selective. He covers both Greek and Roman sport, including gladiatorial combat. His introduction provides a brief overview of the nature of ancient sport and how it differs from its modern offspring. A chronology sets in context key events in the history of ancient sport. Golden's entries cover the sites of ancient competitions, events, individuals associated with sports (sponsors, officials, and athletes), and technical terms. They are clear and informative, if somewhat dry. While they tend to be brief, some, such as that for the *Panathenaea,* run to several pages. Golden offers a higher standard of scholarship than Matz, both in level of detail and in his citation of primary and secondary sources for most articles. Lack of illustrations is a major weakness, although Golden does provide a map and a few charts. There are numerous cross-references and an index.

300.   Hansen, Mogens Herman, and Thomas Heine Neilsen. **Inventory of Archaic and Classical Greek Poleis.** Oxford: Oxford University Press, 2004. 1,396pp. ISBN 0–19–814099–1.

This work is the product of 49 scholars working under the auspices of the Copenhagen Polis Centre. Hansen, the leading contemporary scholar of Greek poleis (city-states), has directed the work of the CPC and the creation of this volume. The book is essentially a reference guide to all known poleis of archaic and classical Greece (ca. 650 to 325 B.C.). Hansen's extensive introduction provides a guide to the definition, nature, and classification of poleis; it also includes much useful general information on Greek political and religious history. The heart of the book consists of entries for some 1,035 individual poleis, arranged by region and then alphabetically by toponym. Each entry offers information on the type of polis, territory, ethnic character, history, political institutions, local divinities and cults, coinage, colonies, and more. Secondary settlements are treated in passing. Map references for each polis refer to the *Barrington Atlas* (entry 439). Some 27 indexes conclude the volume. The first is essentially a table of contents listing the 1,035 poleis in order of appearance. The second and third cover toponyms and ethnics for poleis, and the fourth for secondary settlements; these are essential for those seeking a specific polis or other settlement. The remaining indexes provide various types of subject access. This massive volume has something for everyone interested in the history of archaic and classical Greece.

301.   Jacobs, Philip Walker. **Guide to the Study of Greco-Roman and Jewish and Christian History and Literature.** Lanham, MD: University Press of America, 1994. 118pp. ISBN 0–8191–9517–0. LCCN 94–9218.

The title of this work is misleading. It is really a chronology of historical and literary events in antiquity. Jacobs begins in 200 B.C. and ends with A.D. 259. These are odd choices; certainly Constantine (d. A.D. 337) would have made a more appropriate terminus. Jewish and Christian events and Greco-Roman events appear on facing pages. Walker notes major historical events by date. He enters authors under their year of birth and provides brief biographical notes and selective lists of their works. His general bibliography includes a number of standard works but is dated and heavily weighted toward textbooks. Walker's bibliography of translations of ancient literary works features mainly series (Loeb Classical Library, Anti-Nicene Fathers, etc.) and shows little awareness that the best translations are often found elsewhere. There are indexes of literary works (by title) and of persons. Walker will be of use to those wishing to see Jewish and Christian history in their Greco-Roman context (and vice versa) but remains an unsophisticated work at best.

302.   Kirby, John T., ed. **Classical Greek Civilization, 800–323** B.C.E. World Eras 6. Detroit: Gale, 2001. 395pp. ISBN 0–7876–1707–5. LCCN 00–047648.

The World Eras series offers a broad interdisciplinary approach to history, with a strong focus on everyday life. The target audience is high school students, although the work is suitable for beginning undergraduates as well. This volume covers Greece from the dark ages through the death of Alexander in a series of thematic chapters: "World Events"; "Geography"; "The Arts"; "Communication, Transportation, and Exploration"; "Social Class System and the Economy"; "Politics, Law, and the Military"; "Leisure, Recreation, and Daily Life"; "The Family and Social trends"; "Religion and Philosophy"; and "Science, Technology, and Health." "World Events" is a chronology of what was happening elsewhere in the ancient world during this period. Each subsequent chapter follows a set pattern: chronology, overview, topics, significant people, and documentary sources. Coverage is very selective and concise but provides a good overview for its intended audiences. There are numerous excerpts from primary sources and many black-and-white illustrations. Most sections offer a few bibliographical citations. There is a glossary, a selective general bibliography, and an index. Users should note that in addition to the detailed general table of contents, an even more specific one may be found at the head of each section.

303.   Kirby, John T., ed. **Roman Republic and Empire, 264** B.C.E.**–476** C.E. World Eras 3. Detroit: Gale, 2001. 454pp. ISBN 0–7876–4504–4. LCCN 00–050386.

This work follows the pattern of the series and its sister volume on classical Greece (entry 302). It begins with a brief overview of early Rome (origins to 264 B.C.) and a chronology of world events. Subsequent chapters cover "Geography"; "The Arts"; "Communication, Transportation, and Exploration"; "Social Class System and the Economy"; "Politics, Law, and the Military"; "Leisure, Recreation, and Daily Life"; "The Family and Social Trends"; "Religion and Philosophy"; and "Science, Technology, and Health." Each contains the same subdivisions: chronology, overview, topics, significant people, and documentary sources. Kirby has provided a useful compendium of historical, cultural, and biographical information for ancient Rome. His text is readable, concise, and highly selective; there are many quotations from primary sources and many black-and-white illustrations. A glossary, brief bibliography, and general index conclude the volume. The book is appropriate for high school students and beginning undergraduates.

304.   Matyszak, Philip. **Chronicle of the Roman Republic: The Rulers of Rome from Romulus to Augustus.** London: Thames & Hudson, 2003. 240pp. ISBN 0–500–05121–6. LCCN 2002111074.

A companion volume to Scarre's *Chronicle of the Roman Emperors* (entry 312), this richly illustrated work surveys Roman history from the founding of the city in 753 B.C.

to Octavian's victory at Actium in 31 B.C. Matyszak divides his book into four sections: the age of kings, the founding of the republic, the mid-republic, and the last republicans. The readable and accurate text is aimed at general readers and beginning students. Many maps, time lines, and charts accompany the text. Matyszak offers a good overview of Roman Republican history and covers key figures and events. He gives a good flavor of Roman culture and society as well. The bibliography is excellent, although somewhat ambitious for the intended audience. There is also a detailed index.

305.   Matz, David. **Ancient Rome Chronology, 264–27** B.C. Jefferson, NC: McFarland, 1997. 227pp. ISBN 0–7864–0161–3. LCCN 96–46861.

Matz provides chronologies of events from the beginning of the First Punic War to end of the republic and Augustus's final consolidation of power in 27 B.C. It is a curious and cumbersome work. Rather than a single year-by-year listing, Matz provides several topical chronologies: politics; laws, decrees, and speeches; military events; literary milestones; art and architecture; and miscellaneous. Many events do not clearly fall into one category, so the reader must make constant reference to the index to find specific events. The appendixes focus on more specific topics: the Second Punic War, Cicero's speeches, the career of Julius Caesar, omens, birth and death dates of notable individuals, and Roman consuls from 264 to 44 B.C. Matz relies on standard reference works, such as the *Oxford Classical Dictionary* (entry 142), for his information. Students may find it helpful in sorting out sequences of events, while scholars will find it useful only as a teaching aid.

306.   Matz, David. **Greek and Roman Sport: A Dictionary of Athletes and Events from the Eighth Century** B.C. **to the Third Century** A.D. Jefferson, NC: McFarland, 1991. 169pp. ISBN 0–89950–558–9. LCCN 90–53509.

This work is handy for ready reference, although less detailed and scholarly than the more recent work of Golden (entry 299). Matz's introductory material includes an outline history of the subject and a brief survey of ancient sources and modern works. His bibliography has some curious omissions. The dictionary proper, which is arranged alphabetically, includes entries for athletes, events, various Greek and Latin technical terms relating to athletics, and specific athletic games and festivals. The length of entries varies. Biographical articles range from a line or two to several pages; these often cite primary sources. Other entries tend to offer a brief identification of a place, event, or term. Several "special essays" are appended to the dictionary. These expand on some individual entries or pull together materials from related entries. Matz also provides a number of lists (drawn from the ancient sources) of athletes and horses. A glossary of places identifies ancient places by type (city, island, etc.) and locates them. A subject index concludes the volume.

307.   Montagu, John Drogo. **Battles of the Greek and Roman Worlds: A Chronological Compendium of 667 Battles to 31 BC, from the Historians of the Ancient World.** Mechanicsburg, PA: Stackpole, 2000. 256pp. ISBN 1–85367–389–7. LCCN 00–23945.

This guide covers significant ancient battles for which the approximate date and location are known; these range from the battle of Ithome in ca. 724 B.C. down to the battle of Actium in 31 B.C. The book, like Gaul, is divided into three parts. The first part offers a short introduction to Greek and Roman warfare. The second and third parts cover Greek and Roman battles respectively. Each opens with a chronological table of battles.

A short account of each battle follows, again in chronological sequence. These accounts rely largely on the ancient sources, which are cited at the end of each entry. Charts and diagrams accompany a few entries. Montagu rarely cites modern scholarship, although he does offer a brief general bibliography. Cross-references are provided for battles that might be classed as both Greek and Roman. Indexes cover persons and places.

308.   Nicholas, Barry. **Introduction to Roman Law.** Oxford: Clarendon Press, 1962. 282pp. ISBN 0–19–876003–5. LCCN 62–4467.

For more than 40 years Nicholas's frequently reprinted work has been the standard introduction to the subject for students in the English-speaking world. An introductory section covers the history and sources of Roman law. Subsequent sections cover various types of law: of persons, of property, of obligations, and of succession. Nicholas's focus is on private law, although he occasionally touches on constitutional and other public aspects of the law. The book is well organized and as clear and readable as a work on this complex subject can be. The selective bibliography, though now dated, will direct the reader to the most important fundamental works on Roman law. Nicholas also provides a good subject index.

309.   Roisman, Joseph, ed. **Brill's Companion to Alexander the Great.** Leiden: Brill, 2003. 400pp. ISBN 90–04–12463–2.

"Intended as an informative and scholarly companion for advanced students, scholars, and nonspecialists who are interested in Alexander the Great, this book aims to acquaint the reader with central issues in Alexander studies, with scholarly trends in the discussion and interpretation of these issues." In general, Roisman has achieved this aim. Contributors include a number of established ancient historians, many of whom have done extensive prior work on Alexander. Thirteen essays are grouped in five sections covering the ancient evidence, Alexander's Macedonian and Greek backgrounds, Alexander's conquests, political and cultural perspectives, and Alexander's legacy. Readers will find a good survey of the literary evidence and an outstanding survey of Alexander in Greek and Roman art by Andrew Stewart, with excellent black-and-white plates. Major political and cultural aspects of Alexander studies are well covered. The section on Alexander's legacy is both one of the strongest and weakest of the book. Both essays are of high quality: Richard Stoneman provides a fine discussion of Alexander as a moral exemplum in the ancient philosophers, and Loring Danforth (an anthropologist) an interesting study of Alexander's role in contemporary Balkan politics and nationalism. However, readers will look in vain for information about much of Alexander's *Nachleben* during the Middle Ages and modern era. The *Companion's* substantial bibliography provides a good guide to recent scholarship. An adequate index concludes the volume.

310.   Sacks, David. **Encyclopedia of the Ancient Greek World.** New York: Facts on File, 1995. 306pp. ISBN 0–8160–2323–9. LCCN 94–33229.

"Aimed at high-school and college students and general readers, the book tries to convey the achievements of the Greek world, while also showing its warts." Sacks does a good job of this. His style is colloquial, and he does not assume any previous knowledge of ancient Greece. Articles cover people, places, events, mythical figures, and various other topics. Sacks emphasizes history, although literature and art receive due attention. Articles do not include bibliographical references; there is an adequate general bibliography. There are many cross-references and a detailed index. The book is suitable for its intended audience, although college students would be better advised to consult the *Oxford Classical Dictionary*[3] (entry 142). This work has also appeared as *A Dictionary of the Ancient Greek World* (New York: Oxford University Press, 1995).

311. Samuel, Alan E. **Greek and Roman Chronology: Calendars and Years in Classical Antiquity.** Handbuch der Altertumswissenschaft, Abt. 1, t. 7. München: C. H. Beck, 1972. 307pp. ISBN 3–406–03348–2. LCCN 72–185353.

Samuel covers the same ground as Bickermann (entry 293) but does so in much more detail. After a chapter on the astronomical background, he covers virtually all known Greek and Roman calendars in a series of chapters arranged by region and period. These include Greek astronomical calendars, Greek civil calendars, calendars of the Hellenistic kingdoms, the Roman calendar, and calendars of the eastern Roman provinces. The final two chapters cover Greek and Roman chronography. Indexes of subjects, months, and sources conclude the volume. In most cases, Samuel offers fuller and more detailed information than does Bickermann. His lists of Athenian archons and Roman consuls are more complete and include many notes and references to the scholarly literature. He also provides coverage of many local calendars, while Bickermann concentrates on the better-known and more widespread calendars. However, Bickermann offers a more accessible guide for the layperson and student.

312. Scarre, Chris. **Chronicle of the Roman Emperors: The Reign by Reign Record of the Rulers of Imperial Rome.** London: Thames & Hudson, 1995. 240pp. ISBN 0–500–05077–5. LCCN 95–60277.

In this richly illustrated book, Scarre treats the Roman emperors from Augustus to Romulus Augustulus (deposed A.D. 476) in chronological order. Scarre supplies the basic biographical and historical facts about each, along with the ever-popular stories and anecdotes. He also provides time lines, genealogical charts, and numerous excerpts from ancient authors. Scarre is strongest on the Julio-Claudians and Flavians; coverage of the late emperors is somewhat thin: Constantius and Julian surely deserve more than two pages between them. Scarre has produced an attractive and readable account of the emperors, suitable for beginning students and general readers. While there are no bibliographical references as such, the select bibliography is surprisingly strong and includes a number of works that will challenge his audience. For the Roman Republic, see the companion volume by Matyszak (entry 304).

313. Scarre, Chris, ed. **Smithsonian Timelines of the Ancient World.** New York: Dorling Kindersley, 1991. 256pp. ISBN 1–56458–305–8. LCCN 93–18480.

The editor of this profusely illustrated work has adopted a liberal definition for "ancient world" and includes everything from prehistory through A.D. 1500. While the book is not primarily about the classical world, it does provide extensive coverage of Greek and Roman civilization. Each of the 18 chapters covers a span of years that can range from millenia for prehistoric eras to a few centuries for more recent periods. Chapters include a brief introduction, maps, time lines, and a short feature article on some topic from the period. The time lines cover four broad subject areas (food and environment, shelter and architecture, technology and innovation, art and ritual) in five geographical regions (Americas, East Asia and Australasia, the Middle East and South Asia, Europe, and Africa). Coverage of the classical world can be found under the relevant time periods in the sections on Europe, the Middle East, and Africa. The time lines present selected highlights rather than a comprehensive chronology of the various civilizations. They are chiefly useful for setting developments within particular cultures in a broader context. A selective index and a brief general bibliography conclude the volume. This visually appealing work is designed for the student or casual inquirer rather than the scholar.

314. Spence, Iain G. **Historical Dictionary of Ancient Greek Warfare.** Historical Dictionaries of War, Revolution, and Civil Unrest 16. Lanham, MD: Scarecrow Press, 2002. 390pp. ISBN 0–8108–4099–5. LCCN 2002021103.

Spence begins with a lengthy chronology of Greek military history from the possible date of the Trojan War (1270 B.C.) to the fall of Ptolemaic Egypt in 30 B.C. Then the introduction sets the context and provides an overview of Greek weapons and tactics. The dictionary proper, which follows, includes articles on people, places, wars and battles, weapons, and other military topics. The articles are densely written and full of detail; there are many cross-references. A glossary of Greek military terms and a substantial bibliography conclude the book. The bibliography is relatively up-to-date and misses few significant works (one noteworthy omission being Peter Green's *Greco-Persian Wars*). Spence includes maps and illustrations. The illustrations are cartoonish drawings but generally depict arms and armor effectively. Overall, students of military history will find this a useful and reliable tool.

315. Temporini, Hildegard, and Wolfgang Haase, eds. **Aufstieg und Niedergang der römischen Welt: Geschichte und Kultur Roms im Spiegel der neueren Forschung.** Berlin: Walter de Gruyter, 1972– . LCCN 77–83058.

The *ANRW* began life as a *Festschrift* honoring the seventy-fifth birthday of German historian Joseph Vogt but has since mushroomed into a publishing venture rivaling Pauly-Wissowa (entry 152) in size, if not scope. Approximately 70 volumes have appeared to date, with many more in preparation. This ongoing project, which surveys virtually all aspects of the Roman world, will include contributions by more than 1,000 scholars from around the world when completed. The *ANRW* consists of three parts. The first of these, which covers Rome from its origins to the end of the republic, is complete in four volumes. The part that deals with the principate (the early empire) is still in progress, with more than 60 volumes now in print. The third part, which is concerned with late antiquity, remains in preparation. Each part of the *ANRW* includes six sections: political history, law, religion, language and literature, philosophy and the sciences, and the arts. Within each area, numerous articles, variously written in English, French, German, or Italian, cover both major and minor topics. These include mainly surveys and review articles, although many include the results of original research as well. All the articles are long and scholarly; some are nearly book length. Many include their own tables of contents. Quality varies from item to item but is generally good. While the *ANRW* is an extremely valuable resource for all areas of Roman studies, it has several significant drawbacks. Its sheer size makes it difficult to use; a guide volume with tables of contents for the whole work and some form of index are badly needed. This problem is exacerbated by lack of a coherent overall plan, which results in some volumes being a collection of loosely related articles rather than part of a well-designed handbook. Another major problem is the time lag from writing to publication. Because of the slow pace of production, some articles languish in press for more than a decade and are already dated when they appear in print, although this is often not made clear to users. A list of volumes published and a searchable index are available at www.uky.edu/ArtsSciences/Classics/biblio/anrw.html. Another list of published and forthcoming volumes, with tables of contents, may be found at www.bu.edu/ict/anrw/index.html.

316.   Todd, Malcolm, ed. **Companion to Roman Britain.** Blackwell Companions to British History. Malden, MA: Blackwell, 2004. 508pp. ISBN 0–631–21823–8. LCCN 2003051821.

A volume in a series cosponsored by the Historical Association, this is the work (not surprisingly) of British academics from a variety of fields: history, classics, and archaeology. Todd and company survey many aspects of Roman Britain. The first nine essays provide a rough chronological overview of Britain from the pre-Roman background to the fifth century A.D. The following 14 essays cover specific topics, such as cities and urban life, religion, health and disease, family life, material culture, the economy, agriculture, and the army. The introduction and the final essay, "The Rediscovery of Roman Britain," together provide an overview and history of the study of Roman Britain. Each essay is accompanied by a focused bibliography, and a very substantial general bibliography concludes the book. There is a short general index. Todd provides an up-to-date and reasonably comprehensive guide to Roman Britain; this is an excellent starting point and reference work for both student and scholar.

317.   Weeber, Karl-Wilhelm. **Alltag im alten Rom.** Zurich: Artemis, 1995– . ISBN 3–7608–1091–8 (v. 1); 3–7608–1963–X (v. 2).

Weeber is writing an encyclopedia of everyday life in ancient Rome. His first volume is general in scope, covering a wide range of topics in alphabetical sequence. Some examples include waste removal, work, birth, money, and school holidays. The second volume, subtitled *Das Landleben,* deals with aspects of country life. At least one more volume is projected: *Das Leben beim Militär* will cover army life. Articles run from a paragraph to a dozen pages. Two sets of bibliographical references accompany each article: one for primary sources, another for secondary works. These are usually well chosen and frequently include works in English as well as German. Many illustrations enhance the work. Each volume concludes with a bibliography and both Latin and German indexes.

318.   Wiltshire, Katharine. **British Museum Timeline of the Ancient World: Mesopotamia, Egypt, Greece, Rome.** New York: Palgrave MacMillan, 2004. 32pp. + foldout chart. ISBN 1–4039–6609–5.

This is strictly a work for beginning students, although the actual timeline may be of use to others. Wiltshire covers the four ancient Mediterranean civilizations from prehistoric times to A.D. 395. She provides a brief overview of ancient chronological systems and of the four civilizations. The bibliography is geared largely to high school students. The large foldout time line is divided into five horizontal sections, one for each of the four civilizations, plus a fifth for major events elsewhere in the world (China, South America, etc.). The time line gives brief descriptions of the events and includes many illustrations. Even more sophisticated students and their teachers may find it useful in providing a synchronic view of ancient civilizations. For most, Scarre (entry 313), who offers more detail and a wider context, will be a better choice.

319. Younger, John G. **Sex in the Ancient World from A to Z.** Ancient World A to Z. London: Routledge, 2005. 217pp. ISBN 0–415–24252–5. LCCN 2004–9365.

Younger focuses on "the sexual practices, expressions, and attitudes of the Greeks and Romans in the lands around the Mediterranean in the period between 1000 B.C.E. and 300 C.E." He covers gender but gives more attention to sex. His articles cover people, topics, literary works, artifacts, places, and terminology. Since sexuality abounds in mythology, Younger includes many myths and mythical figures. Articles range from a paragraph to a couple of pages. These are based primarily on the ancient sources, although Younger gives some attention to modern theory and interpretation. He cites ancient sources and modern scholarly works in most articles. As an archaeologist, Younger also emphasizes material remains. Two sections of plates offer black-and-white images of ancient artworks. Younger provides a substantial bibliography and lists of ancient sources and works of art cited. A general index concludes the work. Overall, Younger offers a balanced, scholarly guide to ancient sexuality, written so circumspectly that many undergraduates will be disappointed.

9
Primary Sources in Translation

While translations of the works of both major and minor classical authors are readily available in the Loeb Classical Library series, the Penguin Classics, Oxford World Classics, and other editions, English versions of documentary sources can be difficult to find. Tracking down primary sources on a given topic can also present formidable challenges. Fortunately, in recent years many anthologies of source material in English translation have appeared. Most of these cover a particular place and period, such as Greece in the fourth century B.C., or a particular subject, such as women in antiquity. The works described below include both general and specialized collections of primary sources. Most of these works are intended to be used in conjunction with other books (e.g., textbooks) or in the framework of a course, although they can be used independently. Those unfamiliar with the nature of the ancient sources and the problems involved in using them might also wish to consult Michael Crawford's *Sources for Ancient History* (Cambridge: Cambridge University Press, 1983), which discusses some, but not all, types of primary sources used by classicists and ancient historians. Those interested in more background on the nature and use of primary sources should also consult chapter 19, "Ancillary Disciplines," as well as the section on historiography in chapter 14.

320.   Adkins, Arthur W. H., and Peter White. **Greek Polis.** University of Chicago Readings in Western Civilization 1. Chicago: University of Chicago Press, 1986. 351pp. ISBN 0–226–06934–6; 0–226–06935–4pa. LCCN 85–16328.

This was developed as one of a series of volumes to support the introductory course in Western Civilization at the University of Chicago. Rather than covering Greek civilization as a whole, Adkins and White focus on the idea and development of the Greek polis (city-state) from the seventh to fourth centuries B.C. They include substantial excerpts from Homer, Tyrtaeus, Solon, Theognis, Pindar, Herodotus, the Old Oligarch, Aristophanes, Lysias, Demosthenes, Plato, Aristotle, Epicurus, and Epictetus. A brief introduction describes each author and the context of his work. The very occasional notes mostly translate Greek terms or provide other clarifications. There is a general index. Adkins and White cover important literary texts but do not include documentary evidence such as inscriptions. Rhodes (entry 376) also covers the Greek city-state, with fewer literary texts but many more documentary ones. In addition, Stanton covers many relevant texts in his sourcebook on Greek politics (entry 385). Those seeking broader coverage of Greek history in this period should consult such works as Crawford and Whitehead (entry 333) or Dillon and Garland (entry 335).

321.   Arnaoutoglou, Ilias. **Ancient Greek Laws: A Sourcebook.** London: Routledge, 1998. 164pp. ISBN 0–415–14984–3; 0–415–14985–1pa. LCCN 97–25557.

Arnaoutoglou has compiled a collection of ancient Greek laws, as found in literary and epigraphical sources. His selections range from the sixth century B.C. to the

Roman era and span the entire Greek world. While Arnaoutoglou includes a number of Athenian texts, he gives priority to laws from the broader Greek world and covers many city-states. Arnaoutoglou focuses on the laws of cities but also includes some promulgated by federations. He arranges the texts in three broad categories: the household (*oikos*), marketplace (agora), and city (polis). The first covers laws concerning persons, families, and their relationships; the second, laws on trade; and the third, such areas as religion and interstate relations as well as criminal and constitutional law. This method is generally effective, although it leads users to assume there existed a monolithic Greek law across independent city-states and to ignore significant local differences. Those preferring a place-based approach will need to use the index. Arnaoutoglou provides an introduction and bibliographies of related texts and secondary studies for each text. He also supplies a glossary, general bibliography, and indexes of sources and subjects. Arnaoutoglou indicates his intended audience is undergraduate and graduate students. Most undergraduates are likely to find it daunting; graduate students and scholars of legal history will find it of interest.

322.   Austin, M. M. **The Hellenistic World from Alexander to the Roman Conquest: A Selection of Ancient Sources in Translation.** Cambridge: Cambridge University Press, 1981. 488pp. ISBN 0–521–22829–8; 0–521–29666–8pa. LCCN 81–6136.

The most comprehensive of the three general source books for the Hellenistic period (see also entries 323 and 327), Austin offers some 279 selections from literary, epigraphical, and papyrological sources. Austin is much better than his rivals in presenting the literary sources, both major and minor, and nearly their equal in documentary texts. His arrangement combines chronological and geographical approaches. Austin begins chronologically with two chapters covering Alexander and his successors. Then he shifts to a geographical division with chapters on Macedon and the Greek mainland, the Greek cities (social and economic conditions), the Seleukids and Asia, the Attalids of Pergamum, and the Ptolemies and Egypt. The individual selections range from a few lines to several pages in length. Some have brief introductions; all include short bibliographies and explanatory notes. With a few exceptions, all translations are by Austin; these are clear and generally reliable. Austin also provides a number of maps, chronological tables, a general bibliography, an index of ancient sources, and a general index. Austin offers a better-balanced selection than Bagnall and Derow (entry 323), and a substantially larger one than Burstein (entry 327). However, these other works include much material not found in Austin, and sometimes provide better explanatory matter. Those interested primarily in Ptolemaic Egypt will find stronger coverage in Bagnall and Derow.

323.   Bagnall, Roger S., and Peter Derow. **Hellenistic Period: Historical Sources in Translation.** Blackwell Sourcebooks in Ancient History. Malden, MA: Blackwell, 2004. 319pp. ISBN 1–4051–0132–6; 1–4051–0133–4pa. LCCN 2002–153416.

The first edition of this work appeared in 1981 under the title *Greek Historical Documents: The Hellenistic Period.* Bagnall and Derow provide translations of documentary sources for the history of the Greek world from 336 B.C. to 30 B.C. They include only epigraphical and papyrological texts; literary materials are excluded. Bagnall and Derow originally designed the book to serve as a companion volume to C. B. Welles's *Alexander and the Hellenistic World* (Toronto: A. M. Hakkert, 1970) and have generally followed his organization. The first and longest section deals with political history for the whole period; the documents in it are arranged chronologically. Subsequent chapters cover various broad topics in social, economic, and cultural history. While their scope extends to the entire Hellenistic world, Bagnall and Derow devote more than half of their space to Ptolemaic Egypt. This bias accurately reflects the distribution of the surviving documents but also means that the volume is most useful to those interested in Ptolemaic history. Bagnall and Derow have equipped each selection with an informative introduction that supplies background material. They also provide some explanatory notes and a glossary of Greek terms. Concordances of papyri, inscriptions, and entry numbers for the first and second editions, along with a general index, conclude the volume. Burstein (entry 327), whose work treats the same period, offers better coverage of the other Hellenistic kingdoms. Austin (entry 322) also covers the same ground; his work offers both a combination of literary and documentary sources and a more balanced treatment of the various Hellenistic kingdoms.

324.   Barker, Andrew, ed. **Greek Musical Writings.** Cambridge Readings in the Literature of Music. Cambridge: Cambridge University Press, 1984–1989. 2v. ISBN 0–521–23593–6 (v. 1); 0–521–30220–X (v. 2). LCCN 83–20924.

Ancient music is widely considered to be a complex and difficult subject. Barker's work provides translations of relevant ancient works. His first volume, *The Musician and His Art,* is reasonably accessible to the nonspecialist. It includes 196 selections concerning music from Greek writers ranging from Homer to Athenaeus. Barker presents these in chronological sequence, with introductions and extensive notes. The volume concludes with a bibliography and a general index.

The second volume, *Harmonic and Acoustic Theory,* is highly technical and much more challenging than the first. In it, Barker translates and comments on some 12 texts, which are chiefly by philosophers. For the most part, these are complete works rather than excerpts or selections. Barker again employs a chronological arrangement. He also provides a bibliography, an index of words and topics, and an index of proper names. Those interested in the survival of actual Greek musical works should consult Egert Pöhlmann and Martin L. West, *Documents of Ancient Greek Music: The Extant Melodies and Fragments* (Oxford: Clarendon Press, 2001), which offers Greek texts, modern transcriptions of surviving Greek music, and commentary.

325.   Beard, Mary, John North, and Simon Price. **Religions of Rome: A Source-book.** Cambridge: Cambridge University Press, 1998. 416pp. ISBN 0–521–45015–2; 0–521–45646–0pa. LCCN 97–21302.

The second of a two-volume set (for the first, see entry 896), this volume is an extensive sourcebook for the history of religion in Rome. The various sections cover earliest Rome, deities of Rome, the calendar, religious places, festivals and ceremonies, sacrifices, divination and diviners, priests and priestesses, individuals and the gods, Rome outside Rome, threats to the Roman order, religious groups, and perspectives. It is sometimes difficult to find materials under these rubrics. For example, magic is under "Threats to the Roman Order," and Christianity and Judaism under "Religious Groups"; users are well advised to consult the index. Beard, North, and Price include a wide range of literary texts, legal texts, inscriptions, papyri, and coin legends. They provide useful introductions and notes. Other features include many illustrations, a glossary, a list of deities and their epithets, a very substantial bibliography, index of texts cited, and a general index. This is the largest and best collection of translated texts on the subject, although Ferguson (entry 337) and Warrior (entry 391) are both useful and include some material not found in *Religions of Rome.*

326. Braund, David C. **Augustus to Nero: A Sourcebook on Roman History,** 31 B.C.–A.D. **68.** Totowa, N.J.: Barnes & Noble, 1985. 334pp. ISBN 0–3892–0536–2. LCCN 84–20368.

Intended as a supplementary text for students, this work covers one of the best-known and most frequently studied periods of Roman history. Braund gathers 849 texts from inscriptions, papyri, coin legends, and the lesser-known literary sources; he deliberately excludes the major literary sources (i.e., Tacitus, Suetonius, and Cassius Dio). He organizes these into eight topical chapters, which cover social and economic matters as well as political and military affairs. In addition to the translations, entries include references to published versions of the Greek or Latin original and to related primary sources, date and place (for documentary texts), and occasional notes that provide background or explanatory information. Since Braund assumes that his collection will be used in conjunction with a good narrative history (several are suggested in his bibliographical note), the notes tend to be rather sketchy. He does provide a substantial introduction that offers an excellent discussion of the different types of primary sources and how to use them properly. Indexes of personal names and of sources conclude the volume.

327. Burstein, Stanley M., ed. and trans. **The Hellenistic Age from the Battle of Ipsos to the Death of Kleopatra VII.** Translated Documents of Greece and Rome 3. Cambridge: Cambridge University Press, 1985. 173pp. ISBN 0–521–23691–6; 0–521–28158–Xpa. LCCN 84–29251.

Burstein has gathered and translated a selection of primary sources for the history of the Hellenistic period from 300 B.C. to 30 B.C. His intended audience includes both students and scholars. He covers social and cultural as well as political history. Although Burstein includes some passages from literary authors, the bulk of the volume consists of documentary texts drawn from inscriptions and papyri. Because the Hellenistic states spread over such a wide area and were so diverse in character, Burstein has departed from the chronological arrangement customarily used in this series in favor of a geographical arrangement. Each chapter is devoted to the history of a specific region. Within the chapters, a brief description, date, and short bibliography precede each selection. The explanatory notes that follow the texts supply the necessary background information to enable students to understand the text. Burstein also provides a glossary of Greek terms, several lists of Hellenistic kings, and a short discussion of chronology. There are indexes for personal and geographical names, subjects, and sources. While Burstein covers essentially the same period as Bagnall and Derow (entry 323), there is remarkably little overlap in the texts selected for each. Burstein offers somewhat better coverage of the Hellenistic kingdoms other than Egypt, while Bagnall and Derow cover Ptolemaic Egypt in much greater detail. Austin's similar work (entry 322) offers perhaps the most balanced treatment of the period as a whole and also includes a good selection of literary sources as well as documentary texts.

328. Campbell, Brian. **Roman Army, 31** B.C.–A.D. **337: A Sourcebook.** London: Routledge, 1994. 272pp. ISBN 0–415–07172–0; 0–415–07173–9pa. LCCN 93–9032.

Designed for students of ancient and military history, this work gathers and translates a wide array of materials about the Roman army from the rise of Augustus to the death of Constantine the Great. While Campbell makes use of literary sources when appropriate, he draws most heavily on inscriptions and papyri. He groups the texts under nine rubrics: the soldiers; the officers; the emperor as commander-in-chief; the army in the field; the army in peacetime; the army, the local community, and the law; the army in politics; veterans; and the army in the later empire. Campbell further subdivides most of these into several topical sections. He provides an introduction for each section and, occasionally, commentary on individual selections. His selections are well chosen to illustrate the various aspects of Roman military history, including the social, political, and economic impact of the army on the empire. The translations are clear and generally readable, although the content is sometimes dry. A number of maps, charts, and illustrations supplement the text. A good working bibliography and indexes of translated passages and of names and subjects conclude the volume.

329. Cherry, David, ed. **Roman World: A Sourcebook.** Malden, MA: Blackwell, 2001. 268pp. ISBN 0–631–21783–5; 0–631–21784–3pa. LCCN 00–049428.

Cherry's collection is a general one, designed to accompany a Roman history course. He offers 57 selected texts arranged under nine broad rubrics: "The Social Order"; "Women, Marriage, and Family"; "Economy"; "Science and Medicine"; "Politics and Government"; "Rome and the Provinces"; "The Army"; "Beyond the Frontier"; and "Pagans and Christians." The majority are from standard literary sources, although he includes some lesser-known authors, papyri, and inscriptions as well. Most are derived from widely available translations, including other sourcebooks. The selections are often of some length; Cherry provides introductions and reading guides for each section. Explanatory notes are provided at the back of the book, along with maps, diagrams, a list of emperors, a chronological table, and a brief guide to Roman coins, weights, and measures. Cherry is a useful work for students and general readers but offers far less range and depth than many of the other sourcebooks listed here. Lewis and Reinhold (entry 357) are more comprehensive; numerous specialized sourcebooks offer better coverage of law, the military, religion, women, and other topics.

330. Chisholm, Kitty, and John Ferguson, eds. **Rome, the Augustan Age: A Source Book.** Oxford: Oxford University Press in association with the Open University Press, 1981. 708pp. ISBN 0–19–872108–0; 0–19–872109–9pa. LCCN 82–126744.

Originally compiled as a textbook for an Open University course on Rome in the Augustan Age, this work's temporal limits actually go well beyond the title's implications. While the book does indeed focus on the era of Augustus, it also provides much material concerning the last years of the Roman Republic and the early empire in general. It is the most complete collection of source material in English on the Augustan period. The editors have arranged their material by subject, under such rubrics as politics, administration, art and architecture, and the provinces. In addition to generous selections from well-known literary sources, the editors have included a number of passages from minor authors and many important inscriptions and papyri. Brief introductions to each chapter and selection supply the necessary background material. The translations, which are by a variety of hands, are generally accurate and readable. There is an index of sources, which is helpful for users who need a translation of a particular document. One of the few drawbacks to this work is the lack of a good subject index.

331. Cohen, Morris R., and I. E. Drabkin. **Source Book in Greek Science.** Source Books in the History of the Sciences. New York: McGraw-Hill, 1948; repr., Cambridge, MA: Harvard University Press, 1966. 579pp. LCCN 48–009579.

Compiled by two distinguished philosophy professors who had a strong interest in ancient science, this volume gathers some of the most significant passages from the surviving scienctific writings of the ancient Greeks. It also includes Latin writings that reflect Greek thought and methods. The time period represented ranges from the sixth century B.C. through the second century A.D. The material is organized into nine broad subject categories: mathematics, astronomy, mathematical geography, physics, chemistry and chemical technology, geology and meteorology, biology, medicine, and physiological psychology. Each of these is subdivided into a number of topical sections. Extensive notes accompany each selection. The compilers have generally employed existing translations. Although long out of print and now partly superseded by the more recent work of Irby-Massie and Keyser (entry 346), Cohen and Drabkin remains a valuable resource. In particular, the authors cover a wider chronological span, including Aristotle, and offer more explanatory notes than do Irby-Massie and Keyser.

332. Condos, Theony. **Star Myths of the Greeks and Romans: A Sourcebook.** Grand Rapids, MI: Phanes Press, 1997. 287pp. ISBN 1–890482–92–7; 1–890482–93–5pa. LCCN 97–29207.

This work presents translations of two major ancient works on myth and astronomy: the *Katasterismi* of Pseudo-Eratosthenes (first/second century B.C.) and the second book of Hyginus's *De Astronomia*. Condos provides a brief introduction to these works, followed by an A-to-Z listing of constellations with mythic associations. Under each she provides translations of the relevant passages of the two works, with commentary. Appendixes include a list of Greek and Latin equivalents for mythical names, standard abbreviations for constellations, and star charts. Condos also supplies extensive notes, a lengthy bibliography, and indexes of authors and subjects. She has created an excellent resource for students both of astronomy and mythology.

333. Crawford, Michael H., and David Whitehead. **Archaic and Classical Greece: A Selection of Ancient Sources in Translation.** Cambridge: Cambridge University Press, 1983. 634pp. ISBN 0–521–22775–5; 0–521–29638–2pa. LCCN 82–4355.

Crawford and Whitehead have compiled a comprehensive sourcebook for Greek history from the eighth through fourth centuries B.C. They draw their selections from both major (e.g., Herodotus and Thucydides) and minor literary authors and from the surviving inscriptions. Their overall arrangement is chronological; the four major divisions of the book cover the archaic period, the fifth century, the Peloponnesian War, and the fourth century. Within each of these, Crawford and Whitehead group sources under several broad topics. The general introduction provides a useful discussion of the nature of the surviving sources, while introductions to the various sections supply historical overviews and bibliographies. The actual selections are furnished with explanatory notes as necessary. There are also many maps and illustrations. Supplementary materials include a glossary of Greek terms, chronological tables, and a full set of indexes. Crawford and Whitehead remains the best one-volume collection of primary sources for Greek history, although Dillon and Garland (entry 335) provide stiff competition and better coverage of social and economic history. Fornara (entry 338), Lewis (entry 354), and Wickersham and Verbrugghe (entry 392) all cover shorter periods and are more restricted in scope. However, these all do include valuable materials that are not in Crawford and Whitehead. For Greek history after the fourth century, see Austin (entry 322), Bagnall and Derow (entry 323), and Burstein (entry 327).

334. Croke, Brian, and Jill Harries. **Religious Conflict in Fourth Century Rome: A Documentary Study.** Sources in Ancient History. Sydney: Sydney University Press, 1982. 139pp. ISBN 0–424–00091–1. LCCN 82–100681.

Croke and Harries assemble and translate some 94 documents that are key sources for the conflict between Christians and pagans during the fourth century A.D. These documents include primarily selections from literary and legal texts, along with a few inscriptions. Many were not previously readily available in English versions. They are well chosen to illuminate the religious conflicts of the era; most focus on two events: the Altar of Victory debate and the short reign of the pagan usurper Eugenius. Croke and Harries employ a thematic arrangement. Their introductory comments place each document in context and supply necessary background. Relevant scholarly studies are discussed in the notes, while the general bibliography lists translations and important general studies. A glossary, an index of documents, and a general index complete the work.

335. Dillon, Matthew, and Lynda Garland. **Ancient Greece: Social and Historical Documents from Archaic Times to the Death of Socrates (c.800–399 B.C.).** 2nd ed. London: Routledge, 2000. 543pp. ISBN 0–415–21754–7; 0–415–21755–5pa. LCCN 99–32499.

This work began as a teaching aid for the authors' Greek history courses in Australia and developed into a general sourcebook on Greek history through the fifth century B.C. Their work is comparable in scope to Crawford and Whitehead (entry 333), although there are significant differences. Crawford and Whitehead focus more on traditional political and military history and extend coverage through the fourth century B.C. Dillon and Garland, reflecting current emphases, include much on social history as well. They gather their material under 14 broad chronological and topical headings: colonization; tyrants; law givers; Peisistratos and his sons; Kleisthenes; Sparta; the Persian Wars; the Delian League and Pentekontaetia; the Peloponnesian War; the polis (city-state); labor; religion; women, sexuality, and the family; and the ancient sources (how the ancient Greeks viewed their own literary genres). Dillon and Garland draw heavily on the standard authors, such as Herodotus, Thucydides, and Aristophanes, but also include many minor writers and inscriptions. Each section has a brief introduction; each selection has an introductory headnote that sets the context and often includes bibliographical references. The translations are notable for following the originals as closely as possible (sometimes to the point of being stilted). Maps, a glossary, genealogical tables, and a substantial bibliography enhance the work. The indexes are adequate, but not generous. Overall, a work with much to commend it.

336. Dudley, Donald R. **Urbs Roma: A Source Book of Classical Texts on the City and Its Monuments.** London: Phaidon, 1967. 339pp. LCCN 67–100815.

In this book, Dudley collects literary *testimonia* on notable places and structures of the city of Rome from its founding to the death of Constantine (A.D. 337). The excerpts offered here come from numerous classical authors, both famous and obscure, and from ancient inscriptions. Dudley translated all the selections himself. In a number of cases, where the original is exceptionally important or not readily accessible, he provides the Latin text as well. Dudley divides his collection into three sections: the site of Rome, buildings and monuments, and praises of Rome. The section on buildings and monuments is extensively subdivided and includes passages on virtually every monument of consequence. Dudley's introductions and notes provide useful background material and bibliography. He has also included a large number of black-and-white plates to illustrate the sites and monuments discussed in the *testimonia*. There are indexes of ancient authors, inscriptions, names, and places.

337.   Ferguson, John. **Greek and Roman Religion: A Source Book.** Park Ridge, NJ: Noyes Press, 1980. 208pp. ISBN 0–8155–5055–3. LCCN 79–23009.

Designed for students and general readers, this work contains more than 150 translated passages concerning religion in the classical world. Ferguson organizes these into eight chapters by subject: the Olympians, the religion of the countryside, ritual and observance, political religion, philosophical religion, fears and needs, beliefs about death, and the mystery religions. He presents the translations within a loose narrative framework that provides both context and continuity for the reader. Brief explanatory notes and comments, set in smaller type, sometimes follow the selections. Ferguson draws most of his material from literary sources, particularly poets and philosophers. He also includes some documentary texts from inscriptions and papyri. The passages are well chosen to illustrate the various aspects of Greek and Roman religion. The translations, which are Ferguson's own, are generally accurate, although occasionally stilted. An index of passages cited and a general index round out the volume. Beard, North, and Price (entry 325) offer more extensive coverage of Roman religion; Warrior's less extensive treatment (entry 391) still includes some texts not found in either of the other works.

338.   Fornara, Charles W., ed. and trans. **Archaic Times to the End of the Peloponnesian War.** Translated Documents of Greece and Rome 1. 2nd ed. Cambridge: Cambridge University Press, 1983. 241pp. ISBN 0–521–25019–6; 0–521–29946–2pa. LCCN 79–054018.

Fornara's compilation was originally published by Johns Hopkins University Press in 1977; this edition includes some additions and corrections. It is aimed at college and graduate-level students of ancient history. Fornara intends to supplement standard and readily available sources for the period covered (roughly 776 B.C. to 403 B.C.). Hence, he does not include selections from the major literary sources (e.g., Herodotus and Thucydides) but rather draws his material from less-well-known authors and from inscriptions. Fornara includes such texts as city foundation stories, laws, official and private letters, accounts, and dedications. Although fifth-century Athenian documents predominate (reflecting the nature of the surviving evidence), Fornara has made an effort to provide a selection of the more important non-Athenian documents. Presentation follows the pattern of the series. The selections are arranged in chronological sequence. Each is supplied with a descriptive title, date, and selected bibliography. Notes furnish background information to assist in understanding passages. The appendixes include a useful glossary of Greek terms, as well as information about Athenian political organization. Full indexes provide access by name and subject. Crawford and Whitehead (entry 333) cover the same period plus the fourth century. Unlike Fornara, they also include excerpts from the major literary sources. However, their coverage of documentary sources is considerably weaker than Fornara's.

339.   Gagarin, Michael, and Paul Woodruff, eds. **Early Greek Political Thought from Homer to the Sophists.** Cambridge Texts in the History of Political Thought. Cambridge: Cambridge University Press, 1995. 324pp. ISBN 0–521–43192–1; 0–521–43768–7. LCCN 94–36323.

Gagarin and Woodruff provide selective excerpts from a variety of texts to illustrate the development of Greek political thinking down to the Sophists in the fifth century B.C. They include a somewhat different set of texts than does Kagan (entry 350), although there is considerable overlap. Gagarin and Woodruff include more fragments from those whose work is largely lost, but less of some major surviving works than Kagan does. Some of the selections in this collection would take some effort to find in translation elsewhere. The editors have made fresh translations, which are both readable and accurate, for this volume. They also supply helpful introductions and notes, along with a chronology, bibliography, and glossary. The subject index facilitates finding passages on specific events or topics. Overall, this is a more useful work for students than Kagan, but they should also remember that Kagan provides coverage down to the second century B.C.

340. Gardner, Jane F., and Thomas Wiedemann. **Roman Household: A Sourcebook.** London: Routledge, 1991. 210pp. ISBN 0–415–04421–9; 0–415–04422–7pa. LCCN 90–8691.

Compiled by two well-known scholars of Roman social history, this book focuses on "the activities and the often conflicting aspirations of individuals within the household (Latin *domus*)." Since the Roman household was often a large one that included extended family, slaves, servants, and various other dependents, it is somewhat different from its modern counterpart in size and scope. Gardner and Wiedemann cover all the social, economic, and legal aspects of the Roman household. Their 217 selections, which are arranged topically, are drawn from both literary and documentary sources. These selections span a wide range of dates (from the second century B.C. to the sixth century A.D.) and represent all parts of the Roman world except Egypt. The brief introductions that accompany most entries provide useful background information and set the passages in context. A good bibliography and a general index round out the volume.

341. Grubbs, Judith Evans. **Women and the Law in the Roman Empire: A Sourcebook on Marriage, Divorce, and Widowhood.** London: Routledge, 2002. 349pp. ISBN 0–415–15240–2; 0–415–15241–0pa; 0–203–44252–0 (e-book).

Grubbs collects primary materials relating to women and the law from the time of Augustus (ca. 31 B.C.) to the end of the western empire in A.D. 476. While she draws principally on the major compilations of Roman law (the *Digest,* the Institutes of Gaius, and the codes of Justinian and Theodosius), Grubbs also includes many epigraphical and papyrological texts, along with a few literary texts. Her introduction orients the reader to these texts and discusses the Roman legal system. The selections are arranged by topic into five sections covering the legal status of women, marriage, prohibited and nonlegal unions, divorce, and widows. Grubbs provides helpful introductions and notes; her translations are as clear as is possible in view of the technical nature of her material. She also provides a glossary of legal terms. Grubbs has done an excellent job of gathering and explaining highly technical texts from recondite sources. A substantial bibliography, index of sources, and general index complete the work.

342. Harding, Phillip, ed. **From the End of the Peloponnesian War to the Battle of Ipsus.** Translated Documents of Greece and Rome 2. Cambridge: Cambridge University Press, 1985. 210pp. ISBN 0–521–23435–2; 0–521–29949–7pa. LCCN 83–15444.

In this volume Harding gathers more than 140 selections from the lesser-known literary and documentary sources for fourth-century B.C. Greek history. The majority are drawn from inscriptions. In keeping with the nature of the surviving evidence, Athens receives proportionally more coverage than do other parts of the Greek world. Harding arranges his numbered selections (some of which include two or more related texts) in chronological sequence. Each has a descriptive title and date; some have additional introductory material as well. Harding also equips each with a short bibliography and explanatory notes. All translations are Harding's own. These are reliable and generally readable, although the series' requirement that translations of inscriptions be line by line has resulted in some rather strained versions. The end matter includes a glossary of technical terms and offices, short appendixes covering chronological matters and money, and a full array of indexes (names, subjects, and translated passages). Harding largely supersedes the earlier collection of Wickersham and Verbrugghe (entry 392). Those who need broader chronological coverage that includes the fourth century should consult Crawford and Whitehead (entry 333).

343.　　Heckel, Waldemar, and J. C. Yardley. **Alexander the Great: Historical Texts in Translation.** Blackwell Sourcebooks in Ancient History. Malden, MA: Blackwell, 2004. 342pp. ISBN 0–631–22820–9; 0–631–22821–7pa. LCCN 2002153417.

This collection includes only literary sources, although Heckel and Yardley weave together many minor, fragementary, and late sources along with the usual suspects. Both are established scholars in the field, which they clearly command. Their introduction provides a thumbnail sketch of Alexander's career together with an overview of the major sources, both lost and extant. The various chapters cover Alexander's Macedonian background, Philip II, Alexander's early life and family, the Persians, Alexander and the Greeks, the army, Alexander and the barbarians, Alexander and women, the cult of Alexander, his relations with the Macedonians, his death and successors, Roman views of Alexander, and the cities founded by him. Extensive notes and sidebars provide explanatory, critical, and bibliographical information. Heckel and Yardley supply maps, family trees, a chronology, and a glossary. A selective but excellent bibliography and an unusually detailed index complete the volume.

344.　　Hubbard, Thomas K., ed. **Homosexuality in Greece and Rome: A Sourcebook of Basic Documents.** Berkeley and Los Angeles: University of California Press, 2003. 558pp. ISBN 0–520–22381–0; 0–520–23430–8pa. LCCN 2002–13904.

Hubbard gathers a massive array of ancient literary texts to illustrate gay and lesbian identities and practices in Greco-Roman antiquity and the response of the broader society to them. He arranges his material (447 passages, including some whole works) into 10 chapters following a roughly chronological sequence, with Greek texts by genre (lyric, historical texts, comedy, oratory, philosophy, Hellenistic poetry), and Roman more strictly by period (republic, Augustan Rome, early empire, later antiquity). His general introduction provides a survey of current scholarship in the area, defines Hubbard's own take on it, and discusses the nature of the evidence. Hubbard carefully takes a diachronic rather than synchronic approach to his topic; each chapter has an introduction that provides background for the period and, when appropriate, the genre. The selection of texts is good and in many cases comprehensive. In general, the Greek sections are much stronger than the Roman. Hubbard focuses heavily on literary texts; although he includes a few inscriptions and papyri, he omits many relevant texts from documentary sources. Hubbard also includes a very small amount of artistic evidence, largely photographs of vase paintings. Translations, which are drawn from a variety of sources, are usually reliable. The bibliographical notes to each chapter and the general bibliography are extensive but have surprising omissions. Hubbard supplies a detailed table of contents and a brief general index to assist the reader; more could have been done. In spite of some flaws, Hubbard has produced an invaluable resource for anyone working on gender or sexuality in the Greco-Roman world.

345. Humphrey, John W., John P. Oleson, and Andrew N. Sherwood. **Greek and Roman Technology: A Sourcebook.** London: Routledge, 1998. 623pp. ISBN 0–415–06136–9; 0–415–06137–7pa. LCCN 97–008327.

The compilers of this work have great experience teaching ancient technology and have published extensively on the topic. Their massive sourcebook covers a wide range of material, with chapters covering the rise of human technology; sources of energy and basic mechanical devices; agriculture; food processing; mining and quarrying; metallurgy; construction engineering; hydraulic engineering; household crafts; transport and trade; record keeping; military technology; and attitudes toward labor, innovation, and technology. While they include such standard literary authors as Hesiod and Homer, they draw most passages from the well-known but seldom-read, such as Pliny the Elder; the technical, such as Columella, Vitruvius, and Galen; and the obscure, such as Dioscorides and Pappus. If you are seeking ancient sources on roads, bridges, baths, dye making, tanning, or a myriad of other everyday technologies, this is the book for you. There is a brief bibliography, although those seeking more should refer also to Oleson's separately published bibliography (entry 266). There are indexes of passages cited and subjects.

346. Irby-Massie, Georgia L., and Paul T. Keyser. **Greek Science of the Hellenistic Era: A Sourcebook.** London: Routledge, 2002. 392pp. ISBN 0–415–23847–1; 0–415–23848–Xpa. LCCN 2001–41999.

A large number of scientific texts survive from antiquity. However, these are highly technical in nature and remain largely the preserve of a small subset of specialists among classical scholars. Irby-Massie and Keyser, who both have backgrounds in science (mathematics and physics respectively) as well as classics, attempt to make these recondite texts more accessible to students and teachers. Their work is intended to replace the older volume by Cohen and Drabkin (entry 331), although they cover a more limited time span (most notably omitting Aristotle and Hippocrates). Irby-Massie and Keyser employ a topical arrangement: mathematics, astronomy, astrology, geography, mechanics, optics, hydrostatics and pneumatics, alchemy, biology (botany and zoology), medicine, and psychology. They arrange texts chronologically under each rubric. While they use existing translations when possible, Irby-Massie and Keyser have translated some texts specifically for this volume. They include a time line of authors, maps, a substantial bibliography, and a variety of indexes. Overall strengths include the range of texts, quality of translations, useful illustrations, and up-to-date scholarship. The major weakness is the paucity of explanatory notes to help students deal with such difficult texts. Irby-Massie and Keyser have also made other choices, such as the use of exact transliterations of Greek names (often in preference to more commonly used English forms) and the use of the peculiar dating style affected by historians of astronomy. Whatever the scholarly justification, these practices make the work less accessible to its intended audience. Those interested in Greek medicine should also consult Longrigg (entry 359), who covers earlier material as well.

347.   Ireland, S. **Roman Britain: A Sourcebook.** 2nd ed. London: Routledge, 1996. 280pp. ISBN 0–415–13134–0.

Prepared by a scholar with impeccable credentials, this work offers an extensive selection of primary sources for the study of Roman Britain. Ireland draws on the full range of literary, epigraphical, and numismatic sources. Because of the bulk of material available, he has been extremely selective. His translations are readable and accurate; the brief comments that accompany them serve to set them in context. Ireland marshals his material into three sections: the geography and people of Britain; political and military history; and religion, commerce, and society. The second part is by far the longest. It is arranged chronologically, while the other two parts are arranged thematically. Ireland also provides a bibliography, separate indexes for literary sources and inscriptions, and a general index. He provides illustrations of Roman coins to accompany their legends. The main difference between the first and second editions is that the second incorporates new epigraphic evidence and interpretations. Although an extremely useful tool for students of Roman Britain, this work may present some difficulties for the uninitiated, since Ireland's commentary is fairly abbreviated.

348.   Jones, A.H.M., ed. **History of Rome Through the Fifth Century.** Documentary History of Western Civilization. New York: Walker, 1968–1970. 2v. LCCN 68–13332.

The title of this volume misleadingly suggests a narrative history of Rome, however, it is really a collection of primary sources in translation. The first volume, which contains 150 selections, covers the Roman Republic. The bulk of the volume consists of four chapters that cover Roman military and political history from the origins of the city to 44 B.C. The remaining chapters cover major topics— the constitution, politics, Italy, and the provinces—in greater detail. Most of the selections are from fairly well-known literary and legal texts; there are relatively few documents and no surprises. Jones's introductions do an adequate job of setting the scene for each text. The volume includes a short general bibliography and a subject index. It is a serviceable work but lacks the breadth and balance of the corresponding volume of Lewis and Reinhold (entry 357).

The second volume, which covers the empire, is a far superior work. This is not surprising, since Jones was one of foremost twentieth-century historians of the Roman Empire. His approach in this volume is strictly topical; the chapters cover all aspects of Roman imperial history rather than merely political and military matters. While not neglecting the literary sources, Jones makes much greater use of documentary texts, such as inscriptions and papyri, in this part of this work. He presents 184 texts with brief but informative introductions. Again the volume includes its own bibliography and index. While Lewis and Reinhold is the better overall collection of sources for Roman history, those interested primarily in the empire will find Jones well worth consulting.

349.   Kaegi, Walter Emil, Jr., and Peter White. **Rome: Late Republic and Principate.** University of Chicago Readings in Western Civilization 2. Chicago: University of Chicago Press, 1986. 308pp. ISBN 0–226–06936–2; 0–226–06937–0pa. LC 85–16328.

Part of the same series as Adkins and White (entry 320), this work offers a selection of literary texts concerning Roman history from the third century B.C. through the fifth century A.D. The various chapters cover political ideas and practices from the republic to the principate; Rome and its subjects; legal foundations of Roman society; public and private life; and problems of the late Roman Empire. These consist of large excerpts from well-known authors, such as Polybius, Cicero, Sallust, Tacitus, and Quintilian, along with a few lesser-known authors; legal texts; and documentary texts. Each is equipped with a brief introduction providing information about the author and the context. The relatively few notes explain Latin terms or provide other clarifications. There is a brief general index. It is a useful work, but rather thin on documentary content, and certainly not as comprehensive as Lewis and Reinhold (entry 357).

350. Kagan, Donald, ed. **Sources in Greek Political Thought: From Homer to Polybius.** Sources in Western Political Thought. New York: Free Press, 1965. 305pp. LCCN 65–12728.

Although Kagan intended this collection as a companion to his *The Great Dialogue: A History of Greek Political Thought from Homer to Polybius* (New York: Free Press, 1965), it can also serve as a general sourcebook. Kagan has used, for the most part, existing translations of varying quality. He arranges texts in a roughly chronological sequence. Chapters include "The World of Homer," "The Emergence of the Polis," "The Aristocratic Response," "The Search for Freedom and Responsible Government (Aeschylus and Herodotus)," "Democratic Political Theory," "Thucydides," "The Sophists and Socrates," "Xenophon and Isocrates," "The Hellenistic Period," and "Polybius." Kagan offers many and sometimes extensive excerpts from the major literary authors; he includes relatively few minor works and no documentary sources such as inscriptions. He includes one excerpt from the Code of Hammurabi to show contemporary thinking from the Near East that influenced Greek thought; more could have been done in this regard. Kagan supplies brief introductions but no explanatory notes. There is no index to aid those seeking discussion of a particular idea. Overall, he provides a useful compendium of the major Greek political thinkers. Gagarin and Woodruff (entry 339) include a similar range of authors, although they cover only Homer through the Sophists. They do offer a number of texts not found in Kagan and more help to the reader in the form of introductions and notes.

351. Kraemer, Ross Shepard. **Women's Religions in the Greco-Roman World.** Oxford: Oxford University Press, 2004. 487pp. ISBN 0–19–517065–2; 0–19–514278–0pa. LCCN 2003–69777.

The first edition of this work appeared as *Maenads, Martyrs, Matrons, Monastics: A Sourcebook on Women's Religions in the Greco-Roman World* (Philadelphia: Fortress Press, 1988). Kraemer pulls together a generous selection of well-chosen texts concerning women's religious activities in classical antiquity. She draws more than 200 passages from a variety of literary and documentary sources and includes, for example, excerpts from Euripides, ancient novels, the letters of St. Jerome, the Talmud, and funerary inscriptions. Religions represented include the traditional cults of the Olympians, various pagan mystery religions, Judaism, and Christianity. Kraemer arranges her material in broad subject categories: observances, rituals, and festivals; documents to, from, and by women; religious office; new religious affiliation and conversion; holy, pious, and exemplary women; and the feminine divine. A source reference and date are given at the beginning of each entry; Kraemer also provides biographical notes about the authors and brief characterizations of the works. Some entries include substantial bibliographical notes. Indexes of female names and sources conclude the work. A general subject index would have been an excellent addition! Ferguson (entry 337) also offers relevant material, although he focuses more broadly on Greek and Roman religions.

352. Lefkowitz, Mary R., and Maureen B. Fant. **Women's Life in Greece & Rome: A Source Book in Translation.** 2nd ed. Baltimore: Johns Hopkins University Press, 1992. 387pp. ISBN 0–8018–4474–6; 0–8018–4475–4pa. LCCN 92–6845.

Now in its second edition, this well-received compendium gathers a wide array of ancient writings and documents concerning women. These include excerpts from literary, philosophical, legal, and medical works; private letters and legal documents; and funerary inscriptions. Many are drawn from relatively obscure sources, and a number of the texts were not previously available in English translation. Lefkowitz and Fant arrange the texts in broad subject categories: women's voices, men's opinions, philosophers on the role of women, legal status, public life, private life, occupations, medicine, and religion. Subarrangement within each category is chronological. Each selection begins with a brief descriptive title and a reference to the Greek or Latin original. Many also have introductory notes that supply useful background material. The compilers have provided a concordance of sources, an index of women and goddesses, and a general index. This remains a good general sourcebook on women in the Greco-Roman world, but many more-specialized works have appeared since. Those concerned with women and religion should also consult Kraemer (entry 351); with women and law, Grubbs (entry 341); with Egypt, Rowlandson (entry 379).

353. Levick, Barbara. **Government of the Roman Empire: A Sourcebook.** 2nd ed. London: Routledge, 2000. 278pp. ISBN 0–415–23236–8; 0–415–23237–6pa. LCCN 2000–25440.

In this book Levick presents 236 selections concerning the governing of the Roman Empire from 27 B.C. to A.D. 285. She draws these from both literary and documentary sources. Less-readily accessible sources, such as legal texts, inscriptions, papyri, and coin legends, are especially well represented. Levick organizes the selections into a series of topical chapters. She supplies a brief introduction for each chapter and background notes for many of the individual passages. Levick also provides much supplementary material: maps, a chronological list of emperors, and a table of weights, measures, and currencies. The bibliography, which is arranged to correspond to the various chapters, offers reliable guidance for further study. Two indexes close the work. The first, an index of passages cited, includes bio-bibliographical notes about the various authors and works. The second is a geographical index.

354. Lewis, Naphtali. **The Fifth Century B.C.** Greek Historical Documents. Toronto: A. M. Hakkert, 1971. 124pp. ISBN 88866–503–2; 88866–504–0pa. LCCN 75–148096.

This slim volume deals primarily with Athens during the fifth century B.C. In fact, it is divided into two parts: Athens (which consumes more than half Lewis's space) and "elsewhere." Within each of these sections Lewis arranges his material chronologically by the event described. Most of the selections are documents (chiefly inscriptions), although excerpts from a few minor literary authors are included. Lewis omits standard authors, such as Herodotus and Thucydides, since they are readily available. Most of the passages selected focus on politics, war, and diplomacy; there is not much in the way of social history. The brief introductions to each selection supply background material needed to understand the document and sometimes refer to important studies. Lewis also provides a glossary of Greek terms, a short general bibliography, a general index, and a concordance of texts translated. This work offers a good general collection of materials for the study of fifth-century B.C. Greek political history. Those with broader interests would do well to consult one of the more general source books on Greek history, such as Fornara (entry 338), Crawford and Whitehead (entry 333), or Dillon and Garland (entry 335).

355. Lewis, Naphtali. **Ides of March.** Sanibel, FL: Samuel Stevens, 1984. 164pp. ISBN 0–89522–026–1; 0–89522–027–Xpa. LCCN 84–24118.

Despite its ominous title, this work covers the entire career of Julius Caesar, not just his assassination. Lewis collects and translates the most important primary sources for Caesar's life. These cover the years 60 B.C. (the First Triumvirate) to 42 B.C. (the Battle of Philippi). The excerpts are all from literary authors: Caesar himself, Cicero, Suetonius, Velleius Paterculus, Appian, Dio Cassius, Plutarch, and Nicolaus of Damascus. Since most of these are readily available in translated editions, Lewis's chief service is in gathering all the relevant passages in one place. He also provides an introduction, a glossary, and a short bibliography. There is no index.

356. Lewis, Naphtali. **Roman Principate, 27 B.C.–285 A.D.** Greek Historical Documents. Toronto: A. M. Hakkert, 1974. 149pp. ISBN 0–88866–574–4; 0–88866–548–2pa. LCCN 73–94074.

In this volume Lewis collects primary source material for the Greek-speaking portion of the Roman Empire from the Augustan era to the accession of Diocletian. Although he includes excerpts from a few minor authors, Lewis chiefly focuses on documentary sources, such as inscriptions and papyri. He marshalls these into four groups: government, economy, society, and religion. Each of these is further subdivided by topic. Lewis is particularly good for material on economic and social history, since he includes many documents on such topics as imperial cult, taxes, prices and inflation, trade, professions, entertainment, and slaves. His selection of documents is interesting and includes many not found in other sourcebooks. The translations are readable. Some have introductions, while others do not. In general, the editorial material is minimal. Indexes provide access by Roman emperors, proper names (very selectively), and subject. There is no concordance of sources.

357. Lewis, Naphtali, and Meyer Reinhold, eds. **Roman Civilization: Selected Readings.** 3rd ed. New York: Columbia University Press, 1990. 2v. ISBN 0–231–07054–3; 0–231–07055–1pa. LCCN 90–33405.

This venerable work, now in its third edition, first appeared as part of the famous Columbia Records of Civilization series in 1951. It is a massive gathering of primary sources for the study of Roman history and culture from the founding of the city through the fourth century A.D. Lewis and Reinhold include excerpts from both major and minor classical authors (which form the bulk of the collection), legal writings, inscriptions, papyri, and coin legends. They generally use a chronological approach in arranging the selections, although occasionally, as in the chapter on Roman women, they adopt a topical approach instead. The first volume covers the republic and the Augustan era, while the second is devoted to the empire. The introduction provides an excellent description both of the different types of sources and of many of the individual authors and works excerpted in *Roman Civilization*. While Lewis and Reinhold tend to draw heavily on well-known authors, they also offer strong coverage of minor and technical works. Their selection of documentary sources is adequate, but not as extensive as that found in the various collections by Sherk (entries 382–383). They supply a glossary, bibliographies, and a brief subject index in each volume. Unfortunately, there is no index of sources. This lack creates difficulties for those seeking a particular passage or document.

Roman Civilization is the best single collection of sources for Roman history. It offers more up-to-date scholarship and a stronger, better-balanced selection of materials than Jones (entry 348), the only work of comparable scale. However, Jones's volume on the empire is still worth consulting because of his exeptional knowledge of the period. Some of the more narrowly focused works, such as those of Sherk, offer better coverage of documentary materials and better indexing, but none equal Lewis and Reinhold in scope and comprehensiveness.

358.　　Lomas, Kathyrn. **Roman Italy, 338 B.C.—A.D. 200: A Sourcebook.** London: UCL Press, 1996. 274pp. ISBN 1–85728–180–2; 1–85728–181–0pa. LCCN 96–24878.

Rome's relations with and eventual domination of her Italian neighbors is a complex and important topic. Lomas gathers a wide range of primary material including both inscriptions and selections from literary authors such as Livy, Cicero, and Polybius. She arranges these into nine topical units. The first four cover the rise of Rome and her political relations with the other Italians through the civil wars of the first century A.D. in a chronological framework. The fifth covers Italy and the emperor. The remaining four cover the economy, religion, urbanization, and municipal government. The selections are well chosen. Lomas also supplies an introductory overview to the work as a whole and each unit. A bibliography and general index conclude the work. Lomas has provided a valuable resource on the growth of Roman power in Italy, Roman politics and diplomacy, and urban development in ancient Italy.

359.　　Longrigg, James. **Greek Medicine from the Heroic to the Hellenistic Age: A Source Book.** London: Duckworth, 1998. 244pp. ISBN 0–7156–2771–6. LCCN 98–015593.

Greek medical texts are among the most challenging: highly technical works often available only in forbidding scholarly editions. Longrigg, who has published extensively on Greek medicine, gathers a generous selection of key passages for the use of students. He focuses on texts that illustrate the rational and theoretical apects of ancient Greek medicine. In addition to medical writers such as Hippocrates and Celsus, he includes relevant passages from Egyptian and Mesopotamian sources, literary texts such as Homer, and philosophical writers such as Plato. Longrigg begins with a chronological approach, offering chapters on the general development of medical thinking from the earliest period through the Hellenistic era, and then shifts to a topical approach, covering Hippocratic deontology, disease and physiology, epidemis, prognosis and diagnosis, dietetics, pharmacology, anatomy, surgery, and gynecology. He supplies introductions and notes for many passages. Longrigg also provides a glossary of technical terms, a substantial bibliography, an index of passages cited, and a general index. Additional relevant materials may be found in Irby-Massie and Keyser's chapter on medicine (entry 346).

360. Luck, Georg. **Arcana Mundi: Magic and the Occult in the Greek and Roman Worlds.** Baltimore: Johns Hopkins University Press, 1985. 395pp. ISBN 0–8018–2523–7; 0–8018–2548–2pa. LCCN 84–28852.

The study of magic and the occult in classical antiquity has become fashionable in recent years. Luck's volume, one of the early products of this trend, gathers 122 selections under six rubrics: magic, miracles, demonology, divination, astrology, and alchemy. His sources include both well-known authors, such as Homer and Vergil, and those who are seldom read, such as Iamblichus and Artemidorus. He also incorporates a number of inscriptions and papyri in his collection. Luck provides a substantial introduction to each chapter. Individual selections also have introductory notes that give historical background and discuss content. A general bibliography, an index of ancient sources, and a general index conclude the volume. This is a very useful selection of primary source materials for students and for general readers with an interest in the area. Many of the texts are otherwise rather inaccessible. A more recent work by Ogden (entry 371) includes far more texts, especially documentary texts, and is based on more up-to-date scholarship (including texts published since Luck, as well as more recent interpretations). Those interested in alchemy and astrology should also consult the relevant sections of Irby-Massie and Keyser (entry 346).

361. Maas, Michael. **Readings in Late Antiquity: A Sourcebook.** London: Routledge, 2000. 375pp. ISBN 0–415–15987–3; 0–415–15988–1pa. LCCN 99–21404.

Maas provides a selection of sources for the period stretching from the reign of Diocletian (late third century A.D.) to the rise of Islam (seventh century). He divides the book into 13 major sections: the Roman Empire, the Roman army, Christianity, polytheism, Jews, women, law, medicine, philosophy, Persia, Germanic invaders and successor states, steppe peoples and Slavs, and Islam. Many of these are further subdivided; the detailed table of contents, along with source and subject indexes, offer ready access. The passages are well chosen to illustrate political, military, and social history. Maas provides good coverage of Germanic, Slavic, and Islamic peoples in the late antique period, as well as of the Roman Empire. While many of his excerpts are from the usual suspects, such as Ammianus Marcellinus, Julian, and Eusebius, others are from less-well-known writers and inscriptions. Maas supplies a brief introduction and bibliographical references for each selection. This is an excellent work for students and teachers alike.

362. MacMullen, Ramsay, and Eugene N. Lane, eds. **Paganism and Christianity, 125–425 c.e.: A Sourcebook.** Minneapolis, MN: Fortress Press, 1992. 296pp. ISBN 0–8006–2647–8. LCCN 92–3069.

MacMullen and Lane offer about 175 translated texts from the period between A.D. 125 and 425. These include primarily literary works along with a selection of papyri and inscriptions. Many of the texts illustrate the popular religions and philosophical beliefs prevalent in the Roman Empire. They cover such topics as magic, healing shrines, cults, hymns, imperial cult, and holy men. Later chapters focus more on Christianity, covering perceptions of Jews and Christians, apologists, conversion, and persecutions. The introductions to chapters and individual selections are quite helpful. The inclusion of a number of longer texts is also a strength. A more comprehensive index and more-durable binding would have enhanced the book. It does not offer as much on late antiquity as Maas (entry 361), nor does it compete with Stevenson (entries 387–388) on early Christianity, but overall it is a useful compendium for anyone interested in religion in the later empire. Those seeking additional texts should also see Valantasis (entry 390).

363. Mahoney, Anne. **Roman Sports and Spectacles: A Sourcebook.** Focus Classical Sources. Newburyport, MA: Focus, 2001. 119pp. ISBN 0–58510–009–9.

Mahoney focuses on a narrow but important topic. Gladiatorial combat, the chariot races, and similar public entertainments are among the most widely known features of Roman civilization. Mahoney provides a brief historical overview of these in her introduction. She arranges her material into seven thematic chapters: origins and foundations, gladiators, chariots and circus *ludi,* theater and Greek athletics, women and sports, politics and sports, and attitudes about sports and spectacles. Each has its own introduction and is subdivided by topic. Mahoney draws on a wide range of sources. Her chapter on gladiators includes selections from Lucilius, the *Epitomes* of the lost books of Livy, Plutarch, Horace, Juvenal, Petronius, the younger Pliny, and a number of inscriptions. She emphasizes the pagan religious origins of many of the games and includes early Christian texts (Tertullian and Augustine) criticizing them. Mahoney supplies some explanatory notes, a glossary, maps, a very cursory chronology, a bibliography, and indexes of sources and subjects. She offers much more information on Roman sports and spectacles than any other sourcebook. Those interested in a broader perspective on Roman society should consult Shelton (entry 381), who also covers sports, although in less detail. Miller (entry 367), Robinson (entry 377), and Sweet (entry 389) also focus on Greek sports.

364. Meijer, Fik, and Onno van Nijf. **Trade, Transport, and Society in the Ancient World: A Sourcebook.** London: Routledge, 1992. 201pp. ISBN 0–415–00344–X; 0–415–00345–8pa. LCCN 91–46010.

Intended for both college students and general readers with a serious interest in ancient history, this work deals primarily with ancient trade. Meijer and Van Nijf draw their material from both literary and documentary sources. Their 238 selections are organized into thematic sections. These sections, with numerous subdivisions, cover the ideology and practice of trade, commodities traded, and means of transport. Brief introductions to each section and passage provide background information. The compilers have used existing English translations whenever possible and have provided new translations for the remaining selections. The introductory matter includes discussion of Greek and Roman measures, weights, and coins (with modern equivalents). A general bibliography, an index of passages cited (which also dates and identifies the authors of literary texts), and a very selective general index conclude the volume. This is a very useful work for anyone seeking primary source material on ancient economic activity.

365. Melville Jones, John R. **Testimonia Numaria: Greek and Latin Texts concerning Ancient Greek Coinage.** London: Spink, 1993. 544pp. ISBN 0–907605–40–0 (v. 1).

Aimed primarily at scholars, this work gathers the majority of extant documents relevant to the study of ancient Greek coinage. Melville Jones draws these from a wide range of sources, which include literary texts, inscriptions, and papyri. The first volume contains the texts, with the Latin or Greek originals and English translations on facing pages. Melville Jones arranges these by topic. Chapters cover, for example, particular

Greek cities, mints, forgeries, hoards and treasures, money changers, and weights and denominations. An *index locorum* is provided at the end of the volume. The second volume, which has not yet been published, will contain commentary and essays.

366. Meyer, Marvin W., ed. **Ancient Mysteries: A Sourcebook.** San Francisco: Harper & Row, 1987. 267pp. ISBN 0–06–065571; 0–06–065576–3pa. LCCN 86–45022.

Compiled by an established scholar in the field, this volume gathers a generous selection of texts concerning the Greco-Roman mystery religions. Meyer draws his materials from a variety of literary and documentary sources; some of these were not previously accessible to students or general readers. The selections are presented in topical chapters that cover respectively the Eleusinian mysteries, the Andanian mysteries, Dionysus, the Magna Mater, Isis and Osiris, Mithras, and "mysteries within Judaism and Christianity." Many of the texts are of substantial length. Although no notes are provided, Meyer prefaces each text with a brief introduction. The translations, which are by a variety of hands, are quite readable. Meyer has also equipped the book with a good general introduction and a glossary. There is no index.

367. Miller, Stephen G. **Arete: Greek Sports from Ancient Sources.** 3rd ed. Berkeley and Los Angeles: University of California Press, 2004. 235pp. ISBN 0–520–24154–1pa. LCCN 2003019000.

Designed as a supplementary textbook for college courses on Greek athletics, *Arete* is a collection of translations from literary texts, papyri, and inscriptions. Miller has arranged these thematically. The passages are well chosen and illustrate all major aspects of ancient Greek athletics. Miller has made his own translations, which are not only accurate but readable and idiomatic as well. He has also equipped each selection with introductory notes to set the context and provide needed historical information. A short general bibliography and a combination index and glossary conclude the volume. Miller, who has become the leading authority on Greek athletics, offers a collection far more up-to-date and accurate than his rivals, Robinson (entry 377) and Sweet (entry 389). Those who strongly prefer a chronological arrangement might wish to use Robinson. Sweet's work has two major virtues: he covers a much wider range of sports and recreation than the other books, and his work is heavily illustrated. For Greek athletics in Rome, as well as Roman sports and spectacles, see also Mahoney (entry 363).

368. Monroe, Paul. **Source Book of the History of Education for the Greek and Roman Period.** New York: Macmillan, 1901. 515pp. LCCN 01–25603.

This rather old volume is still the only general collection of primary sources on education in the classical world. It is available in a number of unaltered reprint editions (the last appearing in 1932). Separate sections cover Greek and Roman education. Within these, Monroe combines chronological and topical approaches to organizing his material. Each chapter begins with a substantial introductory note that sets the stage and supplies background information. Monroe then presents translated selections from one or more classical authors. He draws chiefly on philosophical and rhetorical authors, although he also includes selections from the poets as well. Monroe's excerpts are much longer on average than those found in most sourcebooks. A general index is provided. While Monroe's translations have not always aged well, and his scholarship is now dated, the book is still usable. Some more-recent volumes, such as Shelton (entry 381), include primary materials on education in the ancient world, but these are much less extensive than Monroe.

369. Morrison, Karl F. **Church in the Roman Empire.** University of Chicago Readings in Western Civilization 3. Chicago: University of Chicago Press, 1986. 248pp. ISBN 0–226–06938–9; 0–226–06939–7pa. LCCN 85–16328.

This anthology is part of a series prepared to support the University of Chicago's introductory course on Western civilization (see also entries 320 and 349). Morrison covers the history of Christianity from the third to the sixth centuries. He gathers selections from works by apologists, Fathers of the Church, historians, as well as law codes. Morrison arranges these under six headings: "The Call to Conversion in a Hostile Environment"; "From Persecuted to Persecutor"; "Relations between the Church and the Imperial Administration"; "Christianity and Paganism"; "Asceticism"; and "Church Order." He provides a brief introduction and bibliography, minimal notes, and an index of names.

370. Nagle, D. Brendan, and Stanley M. Burstein. **Ancient World: Readings in Social and Cultural History.** 2nd ed. Upper Saddle River, NJ: Prentice-Hall, 2002. 354pp. ISBN 0–13–091250–6. LCCN 2001–21996.

Nagle and Burstein aim "to provide students in ancient history and civilization courses with a selection of texts illustrating the social and cultural life of the peoples of Western Asia and the Mediterranean in antiquity." Their book largely accomplishes this. The 17 chapters proceed in a roughly chronological fashion from the ancient Near East (Mesopotamia, Egypt, Persia) through Greece, to the Roman Empire. Within each large segment, chapters have topical themes, such as warfare and the polis or society and culture in the Roman Empire. Nagle and Burstein draw texts from inscriptions, papyri, and literary works; many are substantial. They provide introductory notes that give background and context. A detailed table of contents makes it easy to locate topics, but lack of an index will frustrate those seeking translations of specific texts. Many of the other works in this chapter offer greater depth, but few cover as wide a scope. There is some overlap with Burstein (entry 327).

371. Ogden, Daniel. **Magic, Witchcraft, and Ghosts in the Greek and Roman Worlds.** Oxford: Oxford University Press, 2002. 353pp. ISBN 0–19–513575–X; 0–19–515123–2pa. LCCN 2001036667.

Ogden, who has done extensive research on ancient magic, intends this work to replace the older compilation by Georg Luck (entry 360). He only partially succeeds. Ogden includes far more texts (300 numbered items), some of substantial length. These include both famous and obscure literary texts, along with a generous selection of documentary texts (papyri, curse tablets, inscriptions from amulets, etc.) He arranges the texts into 13 chapters covering Greek sorcerers, alien sorcerers, rivals of Jesus, Medea and Circe, witches in Greek literature, witches in Latin literature, ghosts, necromancy, curses, erotic magic, voodoo dolls and magical images, amulets, and magic and the law. His translations are readable and reliable, with extensive notes to provide background and context. Ogden, unlike Luck, includes texts on ancient magic and Christianity. He also offers far more nonliterary texts such as curse tablets. However, Ogden includes far less on such topics as alchemy and divination. While Ogden is the best overall general source collection on ancient magic, Luck must still be consulted. Irby-Massie and Keyser (entry 346) also offer useful collections of alchemical and astrological texts not found in either Luck or Ogden. Those seeking additional magical texts in translation will also want to consult Hans Dieter Betz, *Greek Magical Papyri* (2nd rev. ed., Chicago: University of Chicago Press, 1996); John G. Gager, *Curse Tablets and Binding Spells from the Ancient World* (Oxford: Oxford University Press, 1992), and Roy Kotansky, *Greek Magical Amulets* (Opladen: Westdeutscher, 1994–).

372. Platthy, Jenö. **Sources on the Earliest Greek Libraries: With the Testimonia.** Amsterdam: A. M. Hakkert, 1968. 203pp. LCCN 67–16334.

Unlike most of the works found in this chapter, Platthy's volume is aimed at scholars rather than students. In it he gathers passages from literary, epigraphical, and papyrological sources to illustrate the early history of book collecting and libraries in classical Greece. Platthy restricts himself to Greece and Asia Minor; he does not cover the Alexandrian library or libraries of the Roman era. After a lengthy introduction, Platthy presents the primary sources in a geographical arrangement. Each of the 182 passages is presented both in the original Greek or Latin and in English. A selective bibliography and an index of sources close the volume.

373. Pollitt, J. J. **Art of Ancient Greece: Sources and Documents.** 2nd ed. Cambridge: Cambridge University Press, 1990. 298pp. ISBN 0–521–25368–3; 0–521–27366–8pa. LCCN 90–1494.

Originally published as *The Art of Greece, 1400–31* B.C. (Englewood Cliffs, NJ: Prentice-Hall, 1965), this volume presents a comprehensive collection of the ancient literary evidence for the study of Greek art. After a brief introductory chapter that treats the earliest period as a whole, Pollitt arranges his translated passages by media: sculpture, painting, architecture, and decorative arts. Each of these is subarranged chronologically. A final chapter covers art history, aesthetics, and comparative criticism. Pollitt draws his material from a wide range of sources, including both famous and obscure authors. His running commentary sets the passages in context and provides background information and references for further study. Additional explanatory material and bibliography appear in the footnotes. Pollitt also provides an extensive, well-organized bibliography (arranged by subject) and indexes covering artists, places, and general subjects.

374. Pollitt, J. J. **Art of Rome, c. 753** B.C.–**337** A.D.: **Sources and Documents.** Sources and Documents in the History of Art. Englewood Cliffs, NJ: Prentice-Hall, 1966; repr., Cambridge: Cambridge University Press, 1983. 252pp. LCCN 66–18490.

In this companion volume to *The Art of Ancient Greece* (entry 373), Pollitt gathers and translates the literary *testimonia* for Roman art. His selections come from a wide range of authors, many of them seldom read except by specialists. These passages show the Romans' views on art and describe both extant and lost works of art. Pollitt employs a chronological arrangement. When the material under a given period warrants it, he subdivides it by artist, work, or medium. His introductions and notes supply much historical and biographical information. Special indexes provide access by artist and geographical location. Pollitt also provides a good general index. This work covers Roman art as a whole. Those interested specifically in the monuments of city of Rome should also consult Dudley (entry 336).

375.   Reinhold, Meyer. **Diaspora: The Jews among the Greeks and Romans.** Sarasota, FL: Samuel Stevens, 1983. 182pp. ISBN 0–89522–020–2; 0–89522–021–0pa. LCCN 81–9361.

Reinhold has collected a wide array of source materials concerning the Jews in the Greco-Roman world. He presents a good balance of literary and documentary texts. His literary sources include the Bible, Philo, Josephus, Tacitus, Suetonius, and others. He draws documentary material from inscriptions, papyri, and coin legends. The overall framework is chronological; the major divisions include Jews in the Greek world, Jewish statehood, Jews in the Roman world, and Christians and Jews. A number of topical subdivisions appear under each of these rubrics. His annotation is light: brief introductions to each section set the context, while individual selections rarely receive more than a sentence or two of comment or background information. Most selections are unannotated. There are many maps and illustrations. A glossary, a bibliography, and a selective general index conclude the volume. Williams (entry 394) now offers a larger selection of texts on the Jewish Diaspora. Stern (entry 386) is the most comprehensive collection of literary texts but does not cover documents. Kraemer (entry 351), although her focus is somewhat different, also has relevant primary source materials on Jews in the ancient world.

376.   Rhodes, P. J. **Greek City State: A Source Book.** Norman: University of Oklahoma Press, 1986. 266pp. ISBN 0–8061–2010–X; 0–8061–2013–4pa. LCCN 86–3375.

The purpose of Rhodes's book is to gather primary sources that illustrate the workings of the Greek city-state. His intended audience includes college-level students of ancient history and political science. Rhodes presents a good mix of both well-known and obscure materials drawn from literary texts, inscriptions, and papyri. His overall arrangement is chronological. Sparta and Athens, each of which receives its own chapter, get considerably more attention than the other cities. Rhodes prepared his own translations for this collection. His introductory notes to the sections and to individual passages supply much useful background information. Rhodes provides an index of passages cited and a rather selective index of names and subjects. The indexes double as glossaries, and a number of their entries include explanatory notes.

377.   Robinson, Rachel Sargent. **Sources for the History of Greek Athletics in English Translation: With Introductions, Notes, Bibliography, and Indices.** Cincinnati: Author, 1955; repr., Chicago: Ares, 1984. 289pp. ISBN 0–8900–5297–2.

Robinson gathers a large number of texts, chiefly from literary sources, concerning Greek sports. She arranges these chronologically; chapters consist of passages concerning a single period. Although this format gives an overview of the development of Greek athletics as a whole, it creates obvious difficulties for anyone seeking material on a single athletic event or activity. Long the only work of its type, Robinson has now been largely superseded by the more recent works of Sweet (entry 389) and Miller (entry 367). Both of these offer more up-to-date scholarship in their editorial and bibliographical matter. Miller, in particular, is stronger in coverage of documentary material, much of which has come to light only in recent years.

378.   Rodewald, Cosmo. **Democracy: Ideas and Realities.** The Ancient World. London: J. M. Dent, 1974. 138pp. ISBN 0–460–10302–4; 0–460–11302–Xpa. LCCN 76–364816.

Suitable for students of both ancient history and political science, this volume brings together approximately 60 translated passages concerning democracy in the classical world. Not surprisingly, most of these concern Athens. Rodewald takes his selections mainly from literary works; excerpts from the Greek philosophers, orators, and historians predominate. He arranges them under several broad topics: Athens in the fifth and fourth centuries, the origins of Greek democracy, democracy and society, attitudes to democracy in Greece, democracy and empire (the period of Alexander), and democracy in the Roman Empire. Brief introductions set each selection in context; Rodewald also provides occasional explanatory notes that supply background information and define technical terms. A general index concludes the volume. Readers primarily interested in early Athenian politics should consult Stanton (entry 385), whose work offers both more primary materials and much better notes.

379. Rowlandson, Jane, ed. **Women and Society in Greek and Roman Egypt: A Sourcebook.** Cambridge: Cambridge University Press, 1998. 406pp. ISBN 0–521–58212–1; 0–521–58815–4pa. LCCN 97–32001.

A number of distinguished papyrologists and historians have contributed to this work, which is intended for the nonspecialist reader. They draw texts mostly from papyri, although some inscriptions and literary texts appear as well. The papyrological texts include many personal documents (letters, and business and legal documents) of the sort that have rarely survived from antiquity outside Egypt and are even more rarely presented for the laity. The selections cover the period from 332 B.C. to A.D. 641. Rowlandson gathers the material into broad categories: royalty and religion (not easily separated in ancient Egypt!), family matters, status and law, economic activities, and being female. Subarrangement is by topic, then chronological. She often groups together in "archives" related documents that have survived. Rowlandson and company provide many aids for readers trying to comprehend these documents (which often remain difficult even in translation): a substantial historical introduction, detailed introductions and notes to individual chapters and texts; notes on dating systems, money, weights, and measures; and a glossary. They also include many maps, genealogical charts, and illustrations. An excellent bibliography and index conclude the work. While this book is aimed at nonspecialists, the detailed notes and references make it equally valuable to scholars. Those seeking further information on the background and interpretation of papyri should consult the works in the papyrology section of chapter 19, particularly Bagnall's *Reading Papyri, Writing Ancient History* (entry 975).

380. Sage, Michael M. **Warfare in Ancient Greece: A Sourcebook.** London: Routledge, 1996. 252pp. ISBN 0–415–14354–3; 0–415–14355–1pa. LCCN 95–39155.

Sage offers some 300 selections from ancient writers and inscriptions illustrating the various aspects of warfare in Greece from the time of Homer to the Hellenistic era. After providing an overview of the subject, Sage arranges his material into chapters by broad historical period: Homer and the dark ages, the age of the hoplite (fifth century B.C.), the fourth century, Philip and Alexander, and Hellenistic warfare. Each is subdivided by topic; while these vary, each typically includes weapons, tactics, sieges, and the like. In addition to troops, weapons, and tactics, Sage covers the social and political aspects of war, such as causes, codes of conduct, treaties and alliances, and the treatment of the vanquished. The one major omission is naval warfare. Sage supplies useful introductions to each chapter and to many of the individual passages. The classified bibliography is most helpful. Indexes provide access by passage cited and by subject.

381. Shelton, Jo-Ann. **As the Romans Did: A Sourcebook in Roman Social History.** 2nd ed. New York: Oxford University Press, 1998. 483pp. ISBN 0–19–508973–1; 0–19–508974–Xpa. LCCN 95–35257.

Those interested in everyday life in the ancient world will find this anthology quite useful. Shelton covers a wide range of topics, such as families, marriage, housing, domestic and personal concerns, education, work, slaves, government and politics, the army, provinces, women, leisure, and religion. She gathers 473 selections from many sources: letters, legal documents, graffiti, agricultural handbooks, medical texts, contracts, and funerary inscriptions. Her well-chosen texts are presented in accurate and readable translations. Arrangement is by subject; numerous cross-references and an index facilitate access. Shelton generally provides brief introductory comments under each heading and explanatory notes throughout the work. Several genealogical tables and diagrams accompany the text. Appendixes supply background information about the ancient authors and documentary sources used in the book, a brief discussion of Roman money, and a chronological table that covers 753 B.C. to A.D. 565. Shelton provides the best overall collection of source materials on Roman social history; those interested in specific topics may find other collections listed in this chapter helpful as well.

382. Sherk, Robert K., ed. and trans. **Roman Empire: Augustus to Hadrian.** Translated Documents of Greece and Rome 6. Cambridge: Cambridge University Press, 1988. 302pp. ISBN 0–521–33025–4; 0–521–33887–5pa. LCCN 87–24204.

This volume, like others in its series, is intended for university students in ancient history. In it, Sherk gathers some 200 readings drawn from lesser-known classical authors, inscriptions, and papyri. He deliberately omits the works of major literary authors such as Tacitus, since these are readily available elsewhere. Sherk divides his material into two parts. The first, which deals with the imperial government, is arranged into sections by emperor. The second part covers various aspects of Roman society during the period. Sherk provides short bibliographies and notes for many of the texts. The indexes cover personal, divine, and geographic names; subjects; and translated passages. There is some overlap with Chisholm and Ferguson (entry 330), although Sherk extends coverage considerably later. Sherk also concentrates much more on less accessible source materials than do either Chisholm and Ferguson or Lewis and Reinhold (entry 357).

383. Sherk, Robert K., ed. and trans. **Rome and the Greek East to the Death of Augustus.** Translated Documents of Greece and Rome 4. Cambridge: Cambridge University Press, 1984. 181pp. ISBN 0–521–24995–3; 0–521–27123–1pa. LCCN 83–1833.

Aimed at college and graduate-level students of ancient history, this volume offers a selection of translated source materials on Roman relations with the Greek-speaking East from the end of the third century B.C. to the death of Augustus in A.D. 14. The selections cover political, diplomatic, and military matters. Sherk omits commonly available authors, such as Livy and Polybius, in order to concentrate on less accessible sources such as inscriptions, papyri, coin legends, and excerpts from minor authors. He arranges the material chronologically. For each selection Sherk provides a brief description, date, a short bibliography, and helpful explanatory notes. The translations are sometimes rather stilted, since they are designed to reflect the originals as closely as possible. Supplementary materials include a glossary of Greek and Latin technical terms and appendixes covering Roman names, consuls (200 B.C. to A.D. 14), and Greek and Roman chronology. Indexes provide access by name, subject, and source. Sherk includes a number of documents that are not available in English elsewhere.

384. Spyridakis, Stylianos V., and Bradley P. Nystrom, eds. **Ancient Greece: Documentary Perspectives.** Dubuque, IA: Kendall-Hunt, 1985. 287pp. ISBN 0–8403–3546–6. LCCN 84–52799.

This collection offers just over 100 selections from ancient Greek sources. It consists primarily of literary texts, with little in the way of inscriptions. Spyridakis and Nystrom group these into seven sections: "Politics and Society," "Philosophy," "Religion," "The Greeks at War," "Women in Greece," "The Greek Outlook: Theater and Epigram," and "Science." A brief introduction accompanies each selection, providing background information and context. The collection offers a nice balance of sources both for political and military history and for social and intellectual history. While useful for students, it is not nearly as extensive or well done as the larger works of Crawford and Whitehead (entry 333) or Dillon and Garland (entry 335).

385. Stanton, G. R. **Athenian Politics, c. 800–500 B.C.: A Sourcebook.** London: Routledge, 1990. 226pp. ISBN 0–415–04060–4; 0–415–04061–2pa. LCCN 89–71345.

In this volume Stanton collects in translation nearly all the relevant primary sources for early Athenian politics. These include a large number of epigraphical texts as well as selections from literary authors. Stanton organizes the material by period, with topical subdivisions. His introductory comments to the various sections provide the context for the selections. The extensive notes that accompany each selection go far beyond providing explanatory material and will interest scholars as well as students. This exemplary volume also includes maps, genealogical tables, and a good working bibliography. Stanton has provided indexes both of sources translated and of names and subjects.

386. Stern, Menahem,ed. **Greek and Latin Authors on Jews and Judaism.** Fontes ad res Judaicas spectantes. Jerusalem: Israel Academy of Sciences and Humanities, 1974–1984. 3v. LCCN 75–316869.

This monumental collection builds on the work of Theodore Reinach, *Textes d'auteurs grecs et latins relatifs au Juifs et Judaïsme* (Paris: E. Leroux, 1895; repr. Hildesheim: Georg Olms, 1963). Stern systematically gathers Greek and Latin texts pertaining to Jews and Judaism. He proceeds author by author, in chronological sequence, offering a brief introduction to each followed by the relevant passages in the original and in English translation. Stern provides copious notes, with many bibliographical references. The first volume covers Herodotus to Plutarch, the second Tacitus through Simplicius (sixth century A.D.). It also contains addenda and corrigenda to the first volume. The third volume includes an appendix treating problematical texts and those that did not strictly meet the criteria to be included in the main work. It also includes legal writers, addenda and corrigenda to volume 2, and an array of indexes. Stern gives us an exhaustive collection of literary texts; he does not, however, cover inscriptions or papyri. For a selection of documentary texts see Williams (entry 394).

387. Stevenson, J., ed. **New Eusebius: Documents Illustrating the History of the Church to** A.D. **337.** Rev. with additional documents by W.H.C. Frend. London: SPCK, 1987. 404pp. ISBN 0–281–04268–3. LCCN 87–148784.

388. Stevenson, J., ed. **Creeds, Councils, and Controversies: Documents Illustrating the History of the Church, AD 337–461.** Rev. with additional documents by W.H.C. Frend. London: SPCK, 1989. 410pp. ISBN 0–281–04327–2.

James Stevenson first prepared these books in 1957 and 1966 as successors to the first two volumes of B. J. Kidd, *Documents Illustrative of the History of the Church* (London: SPCK, 1920–1923). They have become standard resources on the history of the early Church and have gone through many printings and revisions, most recently by W.H.C. Frend. Stevenson includes selections from both pagan and Christian texts: historians, controversial and apologetic writings, letters, theological treatises, and conciliar documents. Frend has added recently discovered documents, such as gnostic texts from Nag Hammadi, for a total of 571 texts. Coverage extends from the beginnings to the Council of Chalcedon (A.D. 451). While of primary value to students of patristics and the early Church, Stevenson is also extremely useful to students of Greek and Roman history, especially those concerned with the later empire. Relatively few of his documents will be found in other sourcebooks. Brief explanatory notes accompany each passage. Each volume includes a detailed chronological table, a short bibliography, and an index.

389. Sweet, Waldo E. **Sport and Recreation in Ancient Greece: A Sourcebook with Translations.** New York: Oxford University Press, 1987. 281pp. ISBN 0–19–504126–7; 0–19–504127–5pa. LCCN 86–18209.

Sweet's compilation, like those of Robinson (entry 377) and Miller (entry 367), is aimed at college students. Sweet, however, covers a much wider range of activities than do his rivals. He goes beyond the traditional focus on competitive athletics to include chapters on such topics as walking and mountaineering, swimming and boating, hunting, dance, and the like. His 33 topical chapters cover virtually every aspect of Greek sport and recreation. Introductions and notes provide historical background and possible interpretations. An index of *testimonia* and a combined general index and glossary conclude this heavily illustrated work. While Miller is somewhat better for coverage of the traditional Greek athletic events and competitions, Sweet is really the only source of translated primary materials for the study of most other sports and recreational activities.

390. Valantasis, Richard, ed. **Religions of Late Antiquity in Practice.** Princeton Readings in Religion. Princeton: Princeton University Press, 2000. 511pp. ISBN 0–691–05750–8; 0–691–05751–6pa. LCCN 99–049325.

This collection offers 44 translated texts gathered under nine rubrics: biography, asceticism, organizations, community, law, ritual, hymnody, martyrology, and philosophy and theology. While Christianity (Latin, Greek, and Coptic) receives the most attention, many other religions of late antiquity—Judaism, Manichaeism, Mithraism, and the worship of Isis—are represented as well. Neoplatonism and magic also appear. Valantasis selected texts not readily available in translation, with a decided emphasis on the practice of the religions rather than philosophical/theological aspects; he also recruited a strong cadre of translators. Each text is accompanied by a substantial introduction and a bibliography. An adequate subject index concludes the volume.

391. Warrior, Valerie M. **Roman Religion: A Sourcebook.** Focus Classical Sources. Newburyport, MA: Focus, 2002. 215pp. ISBN 1–58510–030–7.

Warrior offers a generous selection of texts illustrating Roman religious beliefs and practices. She draws these from literary, epigraphic, papyrological, and legal sources. Warrior groups texts under a variety of topical headings: early Roman religion and divination; religion of the family; ritual; priests and religious authority; war and religion; acceptance of new gods, cults and religions; control of non-Roman cults; games, religion, and politics; becoming a god; magic, the occult, and astronomy; skepticism of traditional religion; Jews in the Roman world; and Christianity. While Warrior makes heavy use of the standard sources, such as Livy, Cicero, and Ovid, she also includes those less commonly encountered, such as Aulus Gellius and Festus. In addition, Warrior includes excerpts from major Christian sources: Augustine, Tertullian, and the New Testament. Her translations are readable and accurate; she is careful to indicate how she has interpreted difficult and ambiguous Latin terms. Warrior's running commentary, which frequently verges on a narrative account, provides much helpful information. Useful materials at the back of the book include a list of major gods, a glossary, a chronology, maps, notes on the ancient authors and sources, and a select bibliography. There is an index of passages cited and a general index. There is some overlap with Ferguson (entry 337), who also covers Greek religion; however, Warrior is somewhat stronger on Roman religion. Beard, North, and Price (entry 325) offers a more extensive selection of texts on Roman religion and is the strongest of the three, although Warrior includes some texts they do not.

392. Wickersham, John, and Gerald Verbrugghe. **The Fourth Century B.C.** Greek Historical Documents. Toronto: A.M. Hakkert, 1973. 129pp. ISBN 88866–527–X; 888–66–528–8pa. LCCN 73–83517.

A companion volume to Naphtali Lewis's *The Fifth Century* B.C. (entry 354), this work presents primary sources for Greek history from the end of the Peloponnesian War (403 B.C.) to the rise of Alexander the Great (336 B.C.). Although Wickersham and Verbrugghe include a few excerpts from the literary sources, the bulk of the 76 texts are epigraphical. Their emphasis is on political, military, and diplomatic history. They have equipped each text with a short commentary that provides background material. Supplementary materials include a glossary of Greek terms and a number of tables providing information on chronological and monetary matters. A concordance of sources and indexes of personal and geographic names close the work. Harding (entry 342) covers roughly the same period; he offers more material, and his notes and bibliography are somewhat more current. Those in need of material covering a wider temporal span might consult Crawford and Whitehead (entry 333), who provide sources for the whole of the archaic and classical period; they also tend to emphasize literary authors more, while, for this period, both Harding and Wickersham and Verbrugghe are stronger for documentary sources.

393. Wiedemann, Thomas. **Greek and Roman Slavery.** London: Croom Helm, 1981; repr., London: Routledge, 2004. 284pp. ISBN 0–415–02972–4.

The primary sources concerning slavery in the ancient world are exceptionally diverse and scattered. Wiedemann's collection makes a generous selection of these accessible to students and general readers. He presents some 243 selections under the following topics: the slave as property, debt-bondage and serfdom, manumission, slaves as moral inferiors, the slave as status symbol or economic investment, sources of slaves, slaves owned by the state, treatment of slaves, resistance, rebellion, and Stoics and Christians. Because of space limitations, Wiedemann focuses on Athens in the fifth and fourth centuries B.C. and Rome in the first centuries B.C. and A.D. He draws his texts primarily from literary sources, although he does include some inscriptions and papyri. Roman legal writings are well represented in his compilation. Brief introductory notes supply context and background for each selection. Wiedemann also provides a bibliography, an excellent index of passages cited (which includes notes on the authors and texts), and a general index.

394.   Williams, Margaret. **Jews among the Greeks and Romans: A Diasporan Sourcebook.** Baltimore: Johns Hopkins University Press, 1998. 236pp. ISBN 0–8018–5937–9; 0–8018–5938–7pa. LCCN 97–32880.

Jews were one of the few groups to retain a distinctive and independent identity under Greco-Roman rule. Williams concerns herself primarily with Jews living outside Palestine, scattered throughout the Greco-Roman *oikumene.* She covers the period from the death of Alexander (323 B.C.) to the end of the Jewish Patriachate (ca. A.D. 420). She includes some literary texts but focuses on inscriptions and papyri, since literary texts have already been covered exhaustively by Stern (entry 386). Williams arranges her material under seven rubrics: the Jewish Diaspora in the Hellenistic and early Roman imperial periods, life inside the Jewish Diaspora community, Jews of the Diaspora and the Jewish homeland, Jewish interaction with Greek and Roman authorities, the Jews among the Greeks, the Jews among the Romans, and pagans and Judaism. Each of these is further subdivided by topic. Appendixes include lists of major rulers and a few additional aids. A modest bibliography and a subject index conclude the book. Williams has gathered and translated many valuable texts otherwise accessible only to specialists. Yet her compendium is of limited value to students, who are presumably the intended audience. Introductory material and notes are spartan and inadequate; students will all too often find themselves at sea with inscriptions that they are not prepared to interpret or use. Reinhold (entry 375) covers much the same ground but offers fewer texts and little more in the way of help to the uninitiated.

10
Geographical Works

All manner of resources pertaining to classical geography will be found in this chapter. The first part includes essentially textual works such as dictionaries, manuals, and the like. The second covers maps and atlases. Readers should consult the headnote to the second section for a brief discussion of cartographic resources for the ancient world and pertinent bibliography on the topic. An excellent general resource available through the Internet is the *Ancient World Mapping Center* (entry 395), which provides both maps and updates on recent developments in ancient geography and cartography.

DICTIONARIES, HANDBOOKS, AND GAZETTEERS

395.   Ancient World Mapping Center. URL: www.unc.edu/awmc.

This center's Web site is an excellent general resource for both students and scholars. News of recent developments and scholarly publications appears regularly. Many maps are available for viewing or downloading. The center is connected with the *Barrington Atlas* (entry 439) and maintains a list of corrections and additions to it online. Navigation of the site is surprisingly easy, with quick links to items of major interest, a detailed table of contents, indexes to place-names and topics, and a Google search engine.

396.   Avery, Catherine B., ed. New Century Handbook of Classical Geography. New York: Appleton-Century-Crofts, 1972. 362pp. ISBN 0–390–66930–X. LCCN 78–189006.

This work is based on *The New Century Classical Handbook* (entry 128); the material has been updated, and a number of new entries included. Its intended audience consists of travelers and students. Arrangement is alphabetical; there is no index, although occasional cross-references are provided. Entries cover cities, mountains, rivers, and islands of the Mediterranean region. Articles tend to be brief, with a few notable exceptions (e.g., the Acropolis receives six pages). Each gives the pronunciation of the place-name, ancient variants, and the modern name (if different). Then it locates the place and describes it concisely. A summary of any legends or historical events associated with the site concludes the entry. There are no bibliographical references. Maps of Italy and Greece are bound in the center of the volume; these are not very detailed and do not include most of the entries. Avery will serve for ready-reference purposes, although Grant (entry 401) is preferable: his work is more up-to-date, a bit more comprehensive, and it has better maps.

397.   Bell, Robert E. Place-Names in Classical Mythology: Greece. Santa Barbara, CA: ABC-Clio, 1989. 350pp. ISBN 0–87436–507–4.

Bell's intention is to put the myths and legends of Greece into their geographical contexts. He limits his coverage to the boundaries of modern Greece. This excludes many important sites in Ionia and Asia Minor, which Bell proposes to treat in a future volume. There are entries for approximately 1,000 place-names. These are arranged alphabetically by the ancient name, with the modern name (when different) given in parentheses. Cross-references are made from variant names. Each entry identifies and locates the place, be it a town, district, river, mountain, or other geographical feature. A brief discussion of its mythological associations follows. Bell cites relevant ancient literary sources in the course of each article. The length of entries ranges from a few lines to several pages, depending both upon the importance of the site and the amount of information available. In lieu of indexes, Bell provides two lists, one of modern place-names and another of personal names mentioned in the various entries. This readable and accurate book is the only work of its kind.

398. Cary, M. **Geographic Background of Greek and Roman History.** Oxford: Clarendon Press, 1949; repr., Westport, CT: Greenwood Press, 1981. 331pp. LCCN 49–3013.

Cary provides a geographical survey of the entire Greco-Roman world. He begins with a general overview of the Mediterranean region, followed by separate chapters on each of the major regions of the ancient world. Greece and Italy receive two chapters apiece (a general and a regional one); other areas, such as North Africa or Western Europe, receive only one. Cary covers many topics such as climate, topography, natural resources, plant life, agriculture, and the cultural and social aspects of the geographical environment. It is a useful handbook on the subject, though now rather dated. One of its major drawbacks is that its coverage is heavily biased in favor of Greece and Italy; other parts of the ancient world receive less-detailed, sometimes cursory, attention. The number of maps is adequate, although some lack adequate detail. The bibliography of both ancient and modern works is good, but outdated. The index of place-names and geographical features includes both ancient and modern names.

399. Fry, Eileen, and Maryly Snow, eds. **Concordance of Ancient Site Names.** Topical Paper 2. Raleigh, NC: Art Libraries Society of North America, 1995. 1 v. + 1 computer disk. ISBN 0–942740–13–0.

This is a collection of ancient place-names based on the catalogs of three slide library/photo collections from Indiana University, the University of California at Berkeley, and the Getty Museum. The index attempts to bring together all the common variants of ancient place-names from Western Europe, North Africa, and the Near East. The index provides an A-to-Z list of names and variants, with cross-references. After finding the preferred form in the index, one can look up the place in the tables, which provide the modern equivalent, the language/culture of the area, the modern country, and variant forms in parallel columns. While by no means a complete list, this concordance is a useful guide to classical and ancient Near Eastern place-names. It is available both as a printed booklet and as a Macintosh or DOS disk.

400. Graesse, J.G.T., Friedrich Benedict, und Helmut Plechl. **Orbis Latinus: Lexikon lateinischer geographischer Namen.** Handausgabe. Lateinisch-Deutsch, Deutsch-Lateinisch. Vierte revidierte und erweiterte Aufl. Braunschweig: Klinkhardt & Biermann, 1971. 579pp. LCCN 76–886535.

This is the latest incarnation of a work that has been a standby for more than a century. *Orbis Latinus* is the best guide to Latin place-names employed in antiquity, the Middle Ages, and the Renaissance. It consists of two lists, the first of Latin place-names, followed by modern equivalents, and the second of modern place-names, followed by Latin equivalents. Many cross-references are provided. The modern names, although in German, are generally recognizable to the English reader. There are many different editions and printings of *Orbis Latinus;* most are serviceable. An online version of the 1909 edition can be found at www.columbia.edu/acis/ets/Graesse/contents.html.

401. Grant, Michael. **Guide to the Ancient World: A Dictionary of Classical Place Names.** New York: H. W. Wilson, 1986. 728pp. ISBN 0–8242–0742–4. LCCN 86–15785.

Grant provides an alphabetical listing of approximately 900 places in the ancient world. He includes primarily towns, cities, provinces, and the like, although rivers, mountains, and lakes are included when appropriate. Grant's chronological limits extend from the first millennium B.C. to the later fifth century A.D. Ancient variant forms of names and modern equivalents are noted by cross-references. Entries begin with the geographical facts and then offer historical and archaeological information. Material on art and mythology is included when relevant. Entries range in length from a few sentences to several pages. The series of maps, gathered at the front of the book, includes all places listed in the dictionary. A general bibliography of both ancient and modern sources concludes the work. This quite readable book is a good all-purpose reference work for students, travelers, and general readers.

402. Haselberger, Lothar, dir., in collaboration with David Gilman Romano. **Mapping Augustan Rome.** Journal of Roman Archaeology Supplementary Series 50. Ed. Elisha Ann Dumser. Portsmouth, RI: Journal of Roman Archaeology, 2002. 277pp. + 2 folded maps. ISBN 1–887829–50–4.

Previous works on the topography and monuments of Rome, notably Platner and Ashby (entry 408), Richardson (entry 409), and Steinby (entry 415), take a diachronic approach to their subject. Haselberger and his team take a synchronic approach, attempting to present the topography and monuments as they existed in A.D. 14, at the height of Augustan Rome. The core of their work consists of two large maps: one of the entire city on a scale of 1:6000, and a second of the central part of Rome on a scale of 1:3000. The book itself includes an extensive introduction on the project and the maps, along with a gazetteer of places and monuments. Each entry includes relevant historical and archaeological information, a bibliography, and map references. This is an invaluable resource for historians and archaeologists.

403. Higgins, Michael Denis, and Reynold Higgins. **Geological Companion to Greece and the Aegean.** Ithaca, NY: Cornell University Press, 1996. 240pp. ISBN 0–8014–3337–1. LCCN 96–18855.

The work of a distinguished archaeologist (the late Reynold Higgins) and his son, a geologist, this book intends to provide geological background information for archaeologists. It does a good deal more, including information on the history, legends, and topography of cities and regions throughout Greece. The first two chapters provide geological background information and a geological history of the Mediterranean. Then the Higginses proceed through Greece region by region, beginning with Attica and ending with Crete. They include ancient Greek lands now part of Turkey. Each section begins with a cultural and historical orientation to the place, followed by a geological description and history. A final chapter covers "future geological hazards." Many maps, drawings, and photographs accompany the text. An appendix lists important marbles and other stones in Greece and the Aegean. A glossary of geological terms, a substantial bibliography, and an index complete the volume. Readers should be wary of the large number of typographical errors, particularly in some of the charts and maps.

404. Lauffer, Siegfried, ed. **Griechenland: Lexikon der historischen Stätten von den Anfängen bis zur Gegenwart.** München: C. H. Beck, 1989. 775pp. ISBN 3–406–33302–8. LCCN 89–211323.

The scope of this work is limited to places of human habitation or activity, mainly cities and towns. Natural geographical features, such as rivers, are omitted. A substantial introduction gives an overview of ancient, Byzantine, and modern Greek history. The lexicon itself is arranged alphabetically. Headings include the place-name in transliterated form, followed by the Greek form and a map reference. The body of each entry begins with the geographical location (usually fairly exact; for smaller sites the direction and distance from a larger place are often given). Historical and cultural material on the site follows. This includes information on prehistoric, ancient, Byzantine, and modern periods. Each entry concludes with extensive bibliographical references. Entries range from a paragraph to several pages. A list of headings, which precedes the lexicon proper, gives an overview of the contents. An index and a set of detailed sectional maps of Greece are provided as well. The *Lexikon* is particularly valuable for locating information about small and obscure places.

405 **Lexicon of the Greek and Roman Cities and Place Names in Antiquity, ca. 1500 B.C.–ca. A.D. 500.** Amsterdam: A. M. Hakkert, 1992– . ISBN 90–256–0985–6 (fasc. 1); 90–256–1033–1 (fasc. 2); 90–256–0985–6 (fasc. 3).

This new lexicon is being issued in fascicles, of which six covering A to Artnada are currently available (only three have ISBNs!). It covers chiefly cities and towns, although other types of places are included as well (e.g., military posts, road stations). Articles are usually brief, ranging from a couple of lines up to (rarely) several columns. Each entry locates and describes the place then provides an historical summary, if appropriate. All articles include a bibliography of both ancient and modern sources; some of these are quite extensive. Many entries are accompanied by small maps, which are useful but sometimes hard to read. All articles are signed by the contributor. This is a good source of information, particularly for small and obscure places. It will be a valuable reference work when (or if) completed.

406. Lugli, Giuseppe, ed. **Fontes ad Topographiam Veteris Urbis Romae Pertinentes.** Roma: Università di Roma, Istituto di Topografia Antica, 1952– . LCCN 56–36611.

Lugli gathers the ancient literary sources, inscriptions, and other documentary sources pertaining to the topography and monuments of ancient Rome. The arrangement of material is complex. Lugli begins with references to the city as a whole then proceeds to large general features of the city (the various city walls, the Tiber, bridges, and so forth).

He then goes through the city by *regiones* (the ancient districts of the city), covering topographical features in each by type (e.g., streets, fountains, and so on). Each volume has its own *index topographicus* and a few illustrations and plans. Lugli provides an exhaustive compilation of source material for most of the city (not all volumes have published).

407.   Nash, Ernest. **Pictorial Dictionary of Ancient Rome.** Rev. ed. London: Thames & Hudson, 1968; repr., New York: Hacker, 1981. 2v. LCCN 72–355732.

The original publication of this work was sponsored by the German Archaeological Institute. Nash provides excellent black-and-white photographs of the archaeological remains and topographical features. He generally follows Platner and Ashby (entry 408) in the "arrangement and denomination" of entries. His bibliographical references are designed to complement and update those of Platner and Ashby. Nash's entries, which are arranged alphabetically, offer a brief description of each site or monument and a bibliography (often extensive), followed by illustrations. Most of the illustrations are modern photographs, although a few reproduce old engravings that provide views or details no longer available. An excellent general index provides access by a number of approaches, including the names of modern streets and squares in which monuments are located. This outstanding contribution to the study of Roman topography is best used in conjunction with Platner and Ashby or with Richardson's more recent work (entry 409).

408.   Platner, Samuel Ball. **A Topographical Dictionary of Ancient Rome.** Completed and revised by Thomas Ashby. London: Oxford University Press, 1929; repr., Rome: "L'Erma" di Bretschneider, 1965. 608pp. LCCN 30–10804.

This classic work covers the buildings, places, and natural features of ancient Rome. It includes both those surviving and those known only from ancient literary and documentary sources. Entries, which are arranged alphabetically, range from a line or two to several pages. Platner and Ashby cite the ancient sources extensively. Selective bibliographies of secondary literature appear at the end of some entries. The small number of illustrations is a major drawback in a work of this type. There is a single map, which is small and crowded. The only index is a chronological one to dated monuments. Platner and Ashby are now largely superseded by Richardson (entry 409). For extensive illustrations of the sites covered by both of these see Nash (entry 407). Platner is now also available online through *Perseus* (entry 137) at www.perseus.tufts.edu.

409.   Richardson, L., Jr. **New Topographical Dictionary of Ancient Rome.** Baltimore: Johns Hopkins University Press, 1992. 458pp. ISBN 0–8018–4300–6. LCCN 91–45406.

This recent work covers all significant sites, monuments, and buildings from the earliest settlements at Rome to the sixth century A.D., with the exception of most Christian churches and tombs. The entries are arranged alphabetically, with cross-references where appropriate. The clearly written articles identify and describe the sites and monuments and concisely provide what is known of their histories. Many include references to ancient sources and to the modern secondary literature. The introduction includes a wide-ranging survey of source materials and the history of the study of Roman topography. Richardson provides a substantial bibliography, although he refers readers to Platner and Ashby (entry 408) for earlier works and to Lugli (entry 406) for a full conspectus of the ancient sources. The work includes a fair number of maps and plans, but for illustrations of most sites it is necessary to refer to Nash (entry 407). Richardson, who has devoted a lifetime of study to his subject, has a close personal knowledge of the remains of ancient Rome. This is now the best single source and the starting point for further studies on Roman monuments and topography.

410. Rivet, A.L.F., and Colin Smith. **Place-Names of Roman Britain.** Princeton, NJ: Princeton University Press, 1979. 526pp. ISBN 0–691–03953–4. LCCN 79–21616.

This unusual work lists alphabetically all known place-names of Roman Britain. Each entry gives sources for the name, its derivation, and an identification (type of place and location). An index of modern names in England, Scotland, and Wales is provided. There is also a massive introduction that discusses the source material employed by the editors. The work serves as an exhaustive gazetteer for Roman Britain.

411. Schoder, Raymond V. **Ancient Greece from the Air.** London: Thames & Hudson, 1974. 256pp. ISBN 0–500–05016–3; 0–500–27045–7pa. LCCN 74–196316.

Father Schoder's well-known work, which was also published under the title *Wings over Hellas,* is of both geographical and archaeological interest. He provides spectacular aerial views (all in color) of the principal Greek archaeological sites. The work is arranged alphabetically by the sites' modern Greek names. Each section offers a brief description of the site, which includes historical, geographical, and archaeological information. This is followed by one or more photos and often by plans of the site and its buildings. A brief chronology, bibliographies for each site, and an index conclude the work. This is an excellent source of pictures of Greek archaeological sites. There is one curious omission: the book lacks a map locating all the sites.

412. Simpson, R. Hope, and O.T.P.K. Dickinson. **Gazetteer of Aegean Civilisation in the Bronze Age: The Mainland and the Islands.** Studies in Mediterranean Archaeology 52. Göteborg: Paul Åström, 1979. 430pp. ISBN 91–85058–81–5. LCCN 80–151552.

This gazetteer has much useful information but is not particularly easy to consult. It is arranged by region, first covering the mainland and nearby islands, then the Aegean Islands. Sites are keyed to maps of each region. Those looking for a particular site should begin with the site index. Simpson and Dickinson limit themselves to Mycenaean sites; they do not cover Macedonia and Thrace. Each entry in the gazetteer includes a description of the site itself and the archaeological remains, along with extensive bibliography. A chronological chart and maps may be found at the end of the volume. This work is primarily of use to professional scholars.

413. Smith, William, ed. **Dictionary of Greek and Roman Geography.** London: Walton and Maberly; London: John Murray, 1854–1857; repr., London: I. B. Tauris, 2005. 2v. LCCN 2001–21133.

Part of Smith's *Encyclopedia of Antiquity* (see also entries 160 and 232), these two massive volumes cover Greek, Roman, and biblical geography. Names of cities, towns, rivers, and mountains are included. Each entry locates and briefly describes its subject, gives relevant historical and mythological data about it, discusses its name, and lists any known variant names. Smith does a good job of citing ancient sources, although most of the secondary literature cited is now outdated. There are many small illustrations. This work is now antiquated and contains much obsolete and erroneous information. It remains, however, one of most comprehensive works on ancient geography, and one of the most widely available. It may be used with caution. The text is now also available online through *Perseus* (entry 137) at www.perseus.tufts.edu/cgi-bin/ptext?doc = Perseus%3Atext%3A1 999.04.0064.

414. Sonnabend, Holger, ed. **Mensch und Landwirtschaft in der Antike: Lexikon der Historischen Geographie.** Stuttgart: J. B. Metzler, 1999. 660pp. ISBN 3–476–01285–9.

Sonnabend has produced a pioneering dictionary of historical geography for students of antiquity. He includes 214 signed articles by more than 50 scholars (mostly European). The lexicon covers many topics in such areas as demography, ethnography, and topography. There is surprisingly strong coverage of religion in its various historical and geographical aspects. Sonnabend provides alphabetical and thematic lists of all the articles at the front of the book and indexes of sources, persons, places, and subjects at the back. The quality of the work overall is mixed, but Sonnabend gathers much useful material for anyone interested in ancient historical and cultural geography.

415. Steinby, Eva Margareta, ed. **Lexicon Topographicum Urbis Romae.** Roma: Edizioni Quasar, 1993–2000. 6v. ISBN 88–7097–019–1 (v. 1, A–C); 88–7140–073–9 (v. 2, D–G); 88–7140–096–8 (v. 3, H–O); 88–7140–135–2 (v. 4, P–S); 88–7140–162–X (v. 5, T–Z); 88–7140–172–7 (v. 6, index). LCCN 94–117766.

This work is intended to replace the venerable dictionaries of Platner and Ashby (entry 408) and Nash (entry 407). It covers the places and monuments of the city of Rome from its beginnings through the seventh century A.D. The contributors include many well-known archaeologists; all have first-hand knowledge of the sites and monuments that they discuss. Most of the articles are written in Italian, although some are in English or French. Entries attempt to present the present state of research in a concise manner. Each includes the ancient and medieval names of the site or monument, its history (drawn from literary sources), archaeological data, and brief bibliographies. Many cross-references are provided. Plates and figures appear at the end of each volume; these consist of photographs of the actual remains, plans, sketches, and reconstructions. Addenda and corrigenda may be found in both volumes 5 and 6; users of earlier volumes should be sure to consult these also. Volume 6 consists of extensive indexes covering topography, prosopography, and the popes. This is the most comprehensive reference work available on the topography of Rome. While the *Lexicon* is indispensable for scholars, students and casual inquirers will find Richardson (entry 409) more suited to their needs.

416. Stillwell, Richard, ed. **Princeton Encyclopedia of Classical Sites.** Princeton, NJ: Princeton University Press, 1976. 1019pp. LCCN 75–30210.

This aim of this work is "to provide a one-volume source of information on sites that show remains from the classical period." The encyclopedia covers the entire classical Mediterranean world. Its chronological limits run from the mid-eighth century B.C. to the sixth century A.D.; early Christian sites of the fourth and fifth centuries A.D. are generally omitted. There are entries by nearly 400 authors on about 3,000 sites. Entries normally represent sites with actual remains and are arranged alphabetically under the ancient name. Each includes description and location (with a map reference), followed by a brief history with references to the ancient sources. Each also has a bibliography. There are no site maps or illustrations. A series of general maps is supplied at the end of the book for locating the sites. This work is extremely useful for the study of geography, history, and archaeology. The text is now also available online through *Perseus* (entry 137) at www.perseus.tufts.edu.

417. Travlos, John. **Bildlexikon zur Topographie des antiken Attika.** Tübingen: Ernst Wasmuth, 1988. 486pp. ISBN 3–803–01036–5. LCCN 89–160506.

A companion to Travlos's earlier work on Athens (entry 418), this also was sponsored by the German Archaeological Institute (entry 1036). It covers the whole of ancient Attica. The format and features resemble those of the earlier volume. Travlos covers the districts of Attica in alphabetical sequence. In each section a brief introduction provides an historical and archaeological overview of the district. This is followed by a bibliography and plates. The illustrations are the heart of the work; Travlos provides numerous maps, plans, and photos of the archaeological remains. Unfortunately, it has not yet been translated into English.

418. Travlos, John. **Pictorial Dictionary of Ancient Athens.** New York: Praeger, 1971; repr., New York: Hacker, 1980. 590pp. LCCN 70–89608.

This dictionary was sponsored by the German Archaeological Institute (entry 1036) and was published simultaneously in German and English. It is the Athenian equivalent of Nash's work on Rome (entry 407). Travlos arranged his material alphabetically by name of site or monument (e.g., agora, Parthenon). Each entry includes location, description, history, and a detailed bibliography. These are followed by many plans, sketches, and black-and-white photographs. The illustrations are of high quality. There is a very full general index and an index of inscriptions. The author had a close personal knowledge of the monuments. His work is a valuable resource for students of ancient topography, archaeology, and history. His *Bildlexikon zur Topographie des antiken Attika* (entry 417) extends coverage to all of Attika.

ATLASES

The complex history of modern attempts to map the ancient world is ably covered by R.J.A. Talbert in his article "Mapping the Classical World: Major Atlases and Map Series, 1872–1990," *Journal of Roman Archaeology* 5 (1992): 5–38. Interested readers might also consult the comparative study by Clive Foss, "Classical Atlases," *Classical World* 80 (1987): 337–65, and the recent review article by Kai Brodersen, "Mapping (in) the Ancient World," *Journal of Roman Studies* 94 (2004): 183–190. While many atlases suitable for the varying needs of students, scholars, and the merely curious can be found below, the best and now standard atlas is Talbert's *Barrington Atlas of the Greek and Roman World* (entry 439).

419. Bengtson, Hermann, and Vladimir Milojcic, eds. **Grosser historischer Weltatlas. Teil 1: Vorgeschichte und Altertum.** 5. überarbeitete und erweiterte Aufl. München: Bayerischer Schulbuch, 1972. 56, 19pp. LCCN 71–650154.

This excellent atlas offers a wide range of color maps for the study of the ancient world. It begins with a series of maps of prehistoric Europe. Next are several maps of the world as conceived by ancient geographers, followed by a series of maps covering the ancient Near East and the world of the Old Testament. The classical world then receives full coverage. There are separate maps for nearly every major period of Greco-Roman civilization. These often include insets of city and battle plans. The maps are both designed and arranged to show historical development. For example, maps of the same region or province at different times are often grouped together to show changes. The maps offer much topographical, as well as historical, information. *GHW* extends to ca. A.D. 600 and includes maps of India and China also. The extremely detailed index will assist in locating a large number of places. This is the best all-around choice for those willing to deal with German, although it does not really require that much German, since the place-names are the same as or very similar to those used in English.

420.   Cornell, Tim, and John Matthews. **Atlas of the Roman World.** New York: Facts on File, 1982. 240pp. ISBN 0–87196–652–2. LCCN 81–19591.

"The purpose of this atlas is to give a comprehensive general view of the Roman world in its physical and cultural setting." It follows the recent trend in thematic atlases and offers much more text and illustration while relegating maps to more of a supporting role. Cornell and Matthews cover the topograpy and climate of Italy well but do little for the rest of the empire. They focus on historical and cultural developments. The actual maps are attractively designed and make effective use of color. As a whole they show the development and expansion of the Roman world throughout the Mediterranean. There are good basic maps of the city of Rome during both the republican and imperial eras. Maps are also provided for other major cities and archaeological sites. Coverage of the provinces is better than average. The text and illustrations are excellent. A gazetteer and an index conclude the book. This is a good atlas for the student of Roman history. It is somewhat weak for those interested primarily in topographical information, which is provided only in one map (of Italy), and the total number of places shown on the maps is insufficient for effectively locating any but the best-known sites. This work is a companion to Levi's *Atlas of the Greek World* (entry 429).

421.   Finley, M. I. **Atlas of Classical Archaeology.** New York: McGraw-Hill, 1977. 256pp. ISBN 0–07–021025–X. LCCN 76–16761.

Finley covers Greek and Roman civilization from roughly 1000 B.C. to A.D. 500. He surveys major sites throughout the Greco-Roman world, moving west to east, from Britain to the Euphrates. Finley supplies a brief textual description of each site and provides some bibliographical references. This is accompanied by illustrations and maps. There are many regional maps (based on provinces of the Roman Empire) and numerous city maps and plans of archaeological sites. A general index concludes the work. This is a useful supplement to the broader historical atlases, and particularly useful when information about a specific site is needed.

422.   Grant, Michael. **Atlas of Classical History.** 5th ed. New York: Oxford University Press, 1994. 116pp. ISBN 0–19–521074–3; 0–19–521078–6 (paper). LCCN 93–48331.

Previously published under the titles *Ancient History Atlas* and *Atlas of Ancient History,* this work covers the ancient Near East, the classical world, and biblical history. Its chronological span reaches from 1700 B.C. to A.D. 565. Maps are arranged in chronological sequence. These tend to be simple and lacking in detail; all are black and white (mostly white). The focus of the maps is historical rather than geographical. There are, for example, maps of the various kingdoms and empires at particular times, of the expansion of Rome, and of trade and agricultural products. The atlas is useful for the study of political and economic history, although even then it must be used with care. There are a number of inaccuracies in the information provided. Grant's atlas is exceptionally poor for locating places or forming any idea of the actual topography. The short index of place-names highlights the work's lack of detail.

423. Grundy, G. B., ed. **Murray's Small Classical Atlas.** 2nd ed. London: John Murray, 1917. 23pp. 14 maps. LCCN 21–949.

This compact atlas is easy to use, but somewhat deficient in the range of information provided. It provides maps of the ancient Near Eastern empires, two general maps of the Roman Empire, maps of the provinces, city plans (several each of Rome and Athens), and plans of the principal battles in Greek and Roman history. A number of these maps, which are actually insets in larger ones, are rather small. Grundy is not very useful for historical study, since there are too few maps and he does not give a good picture of different periods. There is an index. Grundy will serve for locating places, although Kiepert (entry 426), the *Grosser historischer Weltatlas* (entry 419), and Hammond (entry 424) all offer a larger number of toponyms.

424. Hammond, Nicholas G. L., ed. **Atlas of the Greek and Roman World in Antiquity.** Park Ridge, NJ: Noyes Press, 1981. 56pp. ISBN 0–8155–5060–X. LCCN 81–675203.

This atlas, which includes a number of distinguished historians and archaeologists among its contributors, covers the Greco-Roman world from the neolithic period to the sixth century A.D. Its large format provides for maps of generous size and detail. Both topographical and historical information are provided. The atlas does have a number of drawbacks. The heart of the work, a series of topographical maps of the entire region at the same scale (1:1,500,00), has been rendered difficult to use by the procrustean manner in which they have been chopped up to fit the pages. The labelling and symbols on some of the historical maps are confusing and hard to follow. The maps are all in black and white. However, the atlas is generally serviceable and is one of the best all-around choices available at the present time.

425. Jones, Barri, and David Mattingly. **Atlas of Roman Britain.** Oxford: Blackwell, 1990. 341pp. ISBN 0–631–13791–2. LCCN 90–675155.

Britain is the best known archaeologically of all the provinces of the Roman Empire. Jones and Mattingly have taken advantage of this to provide an extremely detailed atlas. Separate chapters cover such topics as the topography and climate, Britain as viewed by the ancient geographers, Britain before the conquest (A.D. 43), the conquest and garrisoning of Britain, the economy, and religion. The many maps present all sorts of both general and specialized information. In addition, numerous site plans, aerial photographs of sites, and reproductions of antique maps and plans enrich the work. A large bibliography and detailed general index complete the work. This atlas is an indispensable aid for the study of Roman Britain.

426. Kiepert, Heinrich. **Atlas Antiquus: Zwolf Karten zur Alten.** 12. berichtige Aufl. Berlin: Dietrich Reimer, 1902. LCCN 3–14223.

Although outdated in some ways, this old standard work is still useful. The atlas covers the ancient Near East as well as the classical world. It has a limited number of maps, but these are very detailed and show more than 9,000 place-names, all of which are fully indexed. Kiepert also does a fairly good job of showing relief. Thus, his maps remain a good source of topographical information. However, they are not very good for historical study, since they do not show changes over time in the political boundaries of antiquity. *Atlas Antiquus* has appeared in numerous editions and printings and is widely available.

427. Kiepert, Heinrich, and Ch. Huelsen. **Formae Urbis Romae Antiquae. Accedit Nomenclator Topographicus.** Editio altera auctior et emendate. Berolini: Dietrich Reimer, 1912. 162pp. 4 folded maps in pocket. LCCN 14–14626.

Kiepert and Huelsen has long been a fundamental work. It was intended for those who found Lanciani (entry 428) too detailed. Although now badly out-of-date, its maps are still useful. The first three maps, which are clear and readable, cover Rome in the time of the republic, the early empire, and the late empire. The fourth map is a more detailed plan of the heart of the city as it was in the imperial era. Due to the acidic paper on which they were printed, the maps now are generally in delicate condition and must be handled with care.

428. Lanciani, Rodolfo. **Formae Urbis Romae.** Mediolani: Ulricum Hoepli, 1893–1901; repr., Roma: Edizioni Quasar, 1989. 12pp. 46 double maps.

Lanciani provides a series of extremely valuable detailed maps of Rome. These show the entire city at a scale of 1:1,000. The known remains of the ancient city are superimposed on the modern city streets and buildings. The maps are quite readable, although sections cover such small areas that it is easy to lose a sense of perspective. There are two indexes. One covers the monuments and places of the ancient city, the other the buildings and places of the modern city. The reprint edition has maps at a scale of 1:2,000.

429. Levi, Peter. **Atlas of the Greek World.** New York: Facts on File, 1980. 239pp. ISBN 0–87196–448–1. LCCN 81–122477.

Like its companion volume, *Atlas of the Roman World* (entry 420), this work is more of a cultural than a geographical atlas. While there are a significant number of maps, the accompanying text and illustrations comprise a history of ancient Greek civilization. The illustrations are quite good, but the text is quirky and not always reliable. The maps, especially the historical ones, are usually acceptable. However, there are occasional inaccuracies. There is also insufficient topographical detail. Those interested in basic geographical information would do better to consult Kiepert (entry 426), *Grosser historischer Welt* (entry 419), Hammond (entry 424), or Talbert (entry 438).

430. Morkot, Robert. **Penguin Historical Atlas of Ancient Greece.** London: Penguin, 1996. 143pp. ISBN 0–14–0–5133353. LCCN 97–675026.

Continuing the recent trend in atlases designed for student use, Morkot provides much besides maps. He begins with color-coded historical time lines that range from 7000 B.C. to 30 B.C. These include major events from Greece, the Near East, and Europe, along with a running chronology of developments in culture and technology. Five chapters cover the major eras of Greek history from the Bronze Age through Alexander and his successors. The text (reliable and readable, albeit superficial) offers an overview of Greek history and culture. There are numerous color illustrations. Approximately 60 maps cover the atlas aspect of the work. In addition to locating cities and regions, these show the distribution of dialects, patterns of migration, trade, and colonization, military campaigns, and the like. There are also floor plans (e.g., the Palace at Knossos) and maps of cities. There is a brief bibliography, generally up-to-date and adequate for beginning students, and a general index. What is lacking are lists of maps and plans. Most similar to Levi (entry 429) of the atlases discussed here, Morkot is a newer and in some ways better choice. Scarre's *Penguin Historical Atlas of Ancient Rome* (entry 434) provides a comparable treatment of Rome.

431. Muir, Ramsay. **Muir's Atlas of Ancient and Classical History.** Ed. R. F. Treharne and Harold Fullard. 6th ed. London: George Philip, 1963. ISBN 0–540–05433–X.

This is a very useful basic atlas for students. It begins by presenting various ancient conceptions of the world (i.e., those of Herodotus, Erastosthenes, Strabo, and Ptolemy). Then there is a chronological sequence of maps of the ancient Near East and the classical world. The attractive color maps provide adequate but not overwhelming detail. Many of the larger maps have useful insets; for example, the general map of Greece includes insets of the Acropolis, Athens, the Propontis, and Crete. While the overall number of maps is modest (47 on 20 plates), they provide a good overall picture of the ancient world and manage to cover key places and periods.

432. Myers, J. Wilson, Eleanor Emlyn Myers, and Gerald Cadogan, eds. **Aerial Atlas of Ancient Crete.** Berkeley and Los Angeles: University of California Press, 1992. 318pp. ISBN 0–520–07382–7. LCCN 91–20649.

This atlas covers one of the most important centers of early Greek civilization. The substantial introduction includes essays on the geomorphology and history of Crete. The atlas proper surveys some 44 archaeological sites in Crete. These are arranged alphabetically. Each article includes a general discussion of the site and its history, the history of the excavation and location of finds, and a bibliography. Plans of the sites and spectacular color aerial photographs follow. The text of each entry has been prepared by the current director of research at each site. A very full index concludes the work. The atlas is a valuable geographical and archaeological resource.

433. Oliphant, Margaret. **Atlas of the Ancient World: Charting the Great Civilizations of the Past.** New York: Simon and Schuster, 1992. 220pp. ISBN 0–671–75103–4. LCCN 91–38075.

Oliphant covers the entire ancient world: the Near East, prehistoric Europe, Greece, Rome, India, China, and the Americas. She follows the recent trend of combining relatively few maps with a general cultural and historical text and many illustrations. Greece and the Aegean receive six small maps and several plans of individual sites and buildings. A general map of Greece presents topographical information but is not very detailed. Other maps are historical in character, covering topics or periods. The maps of the Roman world are similar in number and type. The work is colorful and offers a readable, if sketchy and basic, text. Its focus is cultural rather than geographical. This work might be suitable for high school students or the less-demanding general reader but is not recommended as an atlas.

434. Scarre, Chris. **Penguin Historical Atlas of Ancient Rome.** London: Penguin, 1995. 144pp. ISBN 0–14–051329–9. LCCN 95–220804.

A companion volume to the *Penguin Historical Atlas of Ancient Greece* (entry 430), this work "is an introduction to the Roman Empire based on maps." Scarre provides a highly selective time line of historical and cultural events from 800 B.C. to A.D. 540. The five chapters of the book provide a narrative overview of Roman history for this period. Scarre also provides many color illustrations. Approximately 60 maps provide the atlas portion of the work. These cover the city of Rome, Italy, and the empire and its neighbors at various periods. In addition to places, maps focus on wars and battles, burial customs, trade routes, and the spread of Christianity. There are also maps of various cities around the empire. A list of emperors, a short bibliography, and a general index may be found at the end of the volume. As in the companion work, there is no list of maps. While students will find this a reliable guide, the similar atlas by Cornell and Matthews (entry 420) is a more detailed and superior work.

435.   Shepherd, William R. **Shepherd's Historical Atlas.** 9th ed., rev. and updated. New York: Barnes & Noble, 1964. 226, 115pp. ISBN 06–013846–7. LCCN Map 64–26.

Shepherd, a general historical atlas, has long been a standard reference work. It has a reasonably strong section of maps covering the ancient Near East and the classical world. Shepherd is more than adequate for historical study. It includes a variety of maps covering the major periods of ancient history. For example, the development of the Roman Empire is covered by a series of maps, and the provinces are shown at several different times in the history of the empire. There are a number of plans of major cities (Athens, Rome, Alexandria, Jerusalem, and others). Sufficient topographical information is given: many maps show relief, and a fairly large number of places are shown. Unfortunately, many of the maps are too small and crowded for easy consultation. There is a substantial general index to aid in locating places. This is a serviceable atlas, although *Grosser historischer Weltatlas* (entry 419) is better as a general historical atlas. Hammond (entry 424) and Talbert (entry 438) offer far more specific help to students of Greek and Roman history.

436.   Stier, Hans-Erich, and Ernst Kirsten, eds. **Westermanns Atlas zur Weltgeschichte. Teil I: Vorzeit und Altertum.** Berlin: Georg Westermann, 1963. 44pp. LCCN 66–220.

This atlas includes the ancient Near East and prehistoric Europe as well as the classical world. The many attractive color maps offer a wealth of detail. There are numerous maps of cities and parts of cities and of individual provinces of the Roman Empire at various periods. The sequence of maps is roughly chronological. Overview maps are inserted at appropriate points. *Westermann's Atlas* will serve well those engaged in historical studies. However, this otherwise admirable work lacks an index.

437.   **Tabula Imperii Romani.** 1930– .

The *Tabula Imperii Romani* is an international project under the sponsorship of the Union Académique Internationale. Its aim is to produce, in sections, a complete map of the Roman Empire at a scale of 1:1,000,000. There are a number of problems in finding and using such parts as are available. Because it is an international project, the mapping and publication of each part of the empire is the responsibility of its modern successor state. The result has been chaotic. Not all sections (usually called sheets) have been completed or published; many have appeared only in provisional form. Each has a different publisher and place of publication. Those that have appeared in definitive form consist of a gazetteer and bibliography in book form, with the map in a folded pocket. In general the maps are attractively printed and convey a great deal of information. For a list of sheets available in some form, provisional or definitive, see R.J.A. Talbert, "Mapping the Classical World 1872–1990," *Journal of Roman Archaeology* 5 (1992): 35–37. No library is known to have a complete set, and it is difficult to locate or obtain copies of many sheets.

438. Talbert, Richard J.A., ed. **Atlas of Classical History.** New York: MacMillan, 1985; repr., London: Routledge, 1988. 217pp. ISBN 0–0293–3110–2. LCCN 85–675113.

This atlas, which focuses almost entirely on the Greco-Roman world, is aimed at college students. There is a good range of maps, which cover key places and periods. Unfortunately, these are all in black and white. An extensive amount of text accompanies the maps; this provides an historical summary for the period or events covered by each map. The maps are presented in chronological sequence. A strong point of the atlas is the use of many smaller maps and insets to present towns, archaeological sites, and battle plans, although these are sometimes too small and crowded. The larger maps include enough detail to be really useful but are rarely crowded. The bibliography at the end, which is arranged by period to correspond with sections of maps and text, rounds up the usual suspects to provide a good basic reading list. A gazetteer concludes the work. Talbert's atlas is somewhat weak in the topographical department; few of the maps show relief, and it shows only half as many places as Hammond (entry 424) and the *Grosser historischer Weltatlas* (entry 419). It is, however, useful and up-to-date for historical purposes.

439. Talbert, Richard J.A., ed. **Barrington Atlas of the Greek and Roman World.** Princeton, NJ: Princeton University Press, 2000. 1v. + 1 CD-ROM. ISBN 0–691–03169–X. LCCN 00–030044.

440. Talbert, Richard J.A., ed. **Barrington Atlas of the Greek and Roman World: Map-by-Map Directory.** Princeton, NJ: Princeton University Press, 2000. 2v. ISBN 0–691–04945–9.

The product of an international team working under the auspices of the American Philological Association (entry 1004), this atlas is now the standard work on this subject. It is the result of more than a decade of collaboration between classical scholars and professional cartographers. The maps include physical and cultural features. The atlas begins with six overview maps at a 1:5,000,000 scale and then proceeds region by region with more-detailed maps. The table of contents, along with the endpapers (maps of the entire Mediterranean *oikumene,* with numbered sections corresponding to individual maps), will assist users in finding the right map. The maps are clear, readable, and accurate. A map-by-map directory on CD-ROM accompanies the atlas; this is also available in a two-volume printed edition. These include separate directories for each map that supply an introduction, a list of place-names (ancient, with modern equivalents) and features, and a bibliography. While a monumental achievement, the *Barrington Atlas* is not without drawbacks. The use of ancient, primarily Latin names, will hinder novices. The editor's laudable goal of simplicity has necessitated the omission of many minor sites; nor do maps readily avail themselves to diachronic representation: each site is presented in its primary role. Many of these drawbacks can be overcome through the directories, which all users should view as essential. Those seeking historical information of other sorts, such as trade patterns, burial customs, and the like, will need to consult other smaller atlases listed here, such as Talbert (entry 438), Scarre (entry 434), or Morkot (entry 430). Those interested in a more detailed discussion of the *Barrington Atlas* should see Brodersen's review article (cited in the introduction to this section) or the review by Susan E. Alcock, Hendrik W. Dey, and Grant Parker in the *Journal of Roman Archaeology* 14 (2001): 454–461. Updates to the *Barrington Atlas* appear on the Web site of the Ancient World Mapping Center (entry 395).

441. Van der Heyden, A.A.M., and H. H. Scullard, eds. **Atlas of the Classical World.** London: Nelson, 1959. 221pp. LCCN 61–1130.

This work was the first classical atlas to include extensive text and illustrations. The text is rather pedestrian and often irrelevant to the needs of those consulting an atlas. The atlas is weak in topography: its maps include relatively few place-names and almost never show relief. On the other hand, there is a wide range of maps for historical study. These cover the major periods and events of Greco-Roman history adequately. There are also some unusual topical maps, such as "Greek Buildings and Monuments in the Mediterranean Area" and a map of the birthplaces of important Greek authors and scholars. This atlas is an adequate work for students of history and is widely available. However, the *Grosser historischer Weltatlas* (entry 419), Hammond (entry 424), and Talbert (entry 438) are all more recent and offer equal or better coverage.

442. Warrington, J. **Everyman's Atlas of Ancient and Classical Geography.** Rev. ed. New York: E. P. Dutton, 1952. 256pp. LCCN 53–270.

This atlas includes 43 color and 20 line maps. The maps are small in size and weak in showing relief. A set of maps at the beginning shows various ancient conceptions of the world. Then follows a series of maps of the ancient Near Eastern empires, Greece, Rome, and the Roman Empire. There are some detailed maps of cities (Rome and Athens). The atlas also includes maps to assist students (the voyage of the Argo, the voyages of Aeneas, and plans of famous battles). A gazetteer covers major sites only but does so in considerable detail. It locates the places and gives extended topographical descriptions of them. There is also a good index of place-names. While it has its faults as a geographical tool, *Everyman's Atlas* provides a serviceable companion to students and general readers.

11
Art and Archaeology

This chapter covers classical art and archaeology, with the exception of a few areas noted below. One of the peculiarities of classical as opposed to other archaeologies is the inseparability of art history and archaeology, so the two are normally treated as a unit (as here). The majority of works below deal predominantly with art history, and Greece receives the most attention. Bronze Age (Mycenaean) and Etruscan civilizations, known chiefly through their material remains, are primarily covered in this chapter. Relevant works covering geology and topography (including monuments) will be found among geographical works in chapter 10. For numismatics see chapter 19.

BIBLIOGRAPHIES

443. Carpenter, Thomas H. **Summary Guide to Corpus Vasorum Antiquorum.** 2nd ed. Updated by Thomas Mannack. Oxford: Oxford University Press for the British Academy, 2000. 100pp. ISBN 0–19–726203–1.

444. **CVA Project.** URL: www.cvaonline.org/cva/ProjectPages/CVA1.htm.

The *Corpus Vasorum Antiquorum* is an international project to publish all known ancient vases. It began in 1919; over 300 fascicles have appeared, and more are in preparation. Volumes are by country, city, and collection. Each includes plates of every vase in that collection (large ones have multiple fascicles), along with descriptive information and bibliography. Due to its size and complexity, the *CVA* is a difficult work to consult. Carpenter provides indexes of fascicles by country and by city, of shapes (Attic vases only), and other wares (earlier Attic and non-Attic). The CVA Project now offers an online version of the index that can be browsed or searched; the full text of out-of-print *CVA* volumes is also available on the Web site.

445. Coulson, William D. E., and Patricia N. Freiert. **Greek and Roman Art, Architecture, and Archaeology: An Annotated Bibliography.** Garland Reference Library of the Humanities 580. 2nd ed., rev. New York: Garland, 1987. 203pp. ISBN 0–8240–8756–9. LCCN 84–48860.

Coulson and Freiert, both established archaeologists, aim their bibliography at four types of users: general readers, teachers, undergraduates, and graduate students. Their first seven chapters cover all major aspects of the subject: general works, the methodology and history of archaeology, Aegean prehistory, the Greeks, the Etruscans, the Romans, and sites of multiple periods. In these, Coulson and Freiert list a wide array of both scholarly books and the better sort of popular books. The bibliography does not include articles. The vast majority of works noted are in English. Coulson and Freiert have supplied substantial annotations for each entry; these provide clear descriptions and assessments. They have also added an eighth chapter called "Additional Resources" to the second edition. This covers bibliographical resources (including a very useful digression on publishers and distributors of archaeological works), monographic series, museum collections and publications, the classical tradition and its influence, and novels set in the ancient world. There is also an index of authors. This is an exceptionally well-done bibliography.

446.   Fay, George E. **Bibliography of Etruscan Culture and Archaeology, 1498–1981.** Occasional Publications in Classical Studies 1. Greeley: Museum of Anthropology, University of Northern Colorado, 1981. 2v. LCCN 84–620585.

Fay, an anthropologist with no special expertise in Etruscan studies, compiled his bibliography chiefly from secondary sources and rarely examined the actual works. He covers all aspects of Etruscan history and culture; not surprisingly, most of the items deal with archaeology or epigraphy. Fay arranged materials alphabetically by author; subarrangement is by date of publication. The majority of the items listed are in Italian, although all pertinent languages are included. Fay provides no annotations, nor does he supply an index. However, his two volumes contain more than 5,500 citations, including virtually everything found in Lopes Pegna's earlier bibliography (entry 449). While a number of libraries possess the first volume (A–J) of Fay's bibliography, far fewer hold the comparatively scarce second volume (K–Z).

447.   Feuer, Bryan. **Mycenaean Civilization: An Annotated Bibliography through 2002.** Rev. ed. Jefferson, NC: McFarland, 2004. 381 pp. ISBN 0–7864–1748–X. LCCN 2003–27001.

Originally published as *Mycenaean Civilization: A Research Guide* (New York: Garland, 1996), Feuer's bibliography includes 2,046 items covering the Bronze Age Greek people commonly referred to as the Mycenaeans and their civilization. These range in date from the late nineteenth century (Schliemann's publications) to 2002. While Feuer explicitly addresses himself to the nonspecialist reader, such readers will find most of the works he lists challenging. His introduction provides an overview of Mycenaean civilization and its chronology. It also offers an orientation to the major resources for the field: museums, journals, monograph series, congresses and colloquia, and Internet resources (some already vanished, such as *Argos*). Feuer divides the bibliography into six sections: general works; cultural history and society; material culture; intellectual life; new directions (recent theoretical and methodological approaches); and regional syntheses and site reports. Most of these are extensively subdivided; the headnotes to many of the subsections are quite useful. Descriptive annotations accompany each entry. Feuer supplies many cross-references; these, along with indexes of authors, place-names, and subjects, make it relatively easy to navigate the work. This is an excellent resource for students and scholars, although the latter will regret Feuer's decision to omit most foreign-language publications. Moon's earlier bibliographies (entries 450–451) remain useful supplements for 1935–1960.

448.   Hitzl, Konrad. **Bibliographie zur archäologischen Denkmälerkunde.** Subsidia Classica 2. St. Katharinen: Scripta Mercaturae, 1999. 272pp. ISBN 3–89590–084–2. LCCN 2000–393297.

Hitzl intends this bibliography for students of classical archaeology. He gathers books and articles under the following rubrics: general and reference works, topography (subdivided by place), architecture, sculpture, pottery, painting, mosaics, and minor arts (*Kleinkunst*). Two special bibliographies, one on early Greece and a second on Roman metalwork conclude the volume. Hitzl's focus appears to be on relatively recent works: most of those listed are after 1960, and many dated from the 1980s and 1990s. Although there is no index, the detailed table of contents will help in navigating the book. Nor are there annotations. This may be useful for graduate students but will not meet the needs of beginners.

449. Lopes Pegna, Mario. **Saggio di bibliografia etrusca.** Biblioteca di bibliografia italiana. Firenze: Olschki, 1953. 89pp. LCCN 53–37853.

This bibliography covers all aspects of Etruscan studies from 1498 through 1952. Lopes Pegna uses broad subject divisions to organize the citations: history, archaeology and topography; linguistics and epigraphy; art; religion; technology and science; numismatics and metrology; and cartography. Within each of these, entries are presented chronologically by date of publication. The works cited are in a variety of languages, with Italian being the most common. There are no annotations. Lopes Pegna has provided an index of personal and geographic names. Fay's much larger bibliography (entry 446) includes everything listed in this work plus many additional citations. However, Lopes Pegna offers certain advantages, such as access by subject.

450. Moon, Brenda E. **Mycenaean Civilization, Publications Since 1935: A Bibliography.** Bulletin of the Institute of Classical Studies. Supplement 3. London: University of London, Institute of Classical Studies, 1957. 77pp.

451. Moon, Brenda E. **Mycenaean Civilization, Publications 1956–60: A Second Bibliography.** Bulletin of the Institute of Classical Studies. Supplement 12. London: University of London, Institute of Classical Studies, 1961. 130pp. LCCN 67–8205.

Moon's first volume covered Mycenaean civilization in a rather strict sense: "the Late Helladic culture centered in Greece c. 1600–1100 B.C." She further excluded works on Mycenaean language, literacy, and epigraphy. In her second compilation, Moon decided to include works on language and epigraphy (from 1953) and to expand the scope of the bibliography to include Minoan civilization during the same period (with retrospective coverage to 1936). No attempt was made to cover related areas such as Homeric or Near Eastern studies. Moon included books and periodical articles, but not reviews or items in the popular press. She arranged entries alphabetically by author. Her "subject list" functions essentially as an index to the author listings. There is also a topographical index. Moon's two volumes provide a useful guide to an important period in Mycenaean studies. For both earlier and late coverage, see also Feuer (entry 447).

452. Sparkes, Brian A. **Greek Art.** New Surveys in the Classics 22. Oxford: Oxford University Press, 1991. 77pp. ISBN 019–922071–9. LCCN 92–183877.

Sparkes surveys scholarly work on ancient Greek art, with emphasis on the 1970s and 1980s. He cites primarily English-language studies. Sparkes discusses general works on Greek art in his introduction. The remaining chapters concentrate on sculpture and vase painting; other art forms receive scant attention. Each chapter takes the form of a review essay, with the bibliographical citations relegated to the endnotes. While it does not cover all aspects of Greek art, Sparkes's work is readable and nicely illustrated. It is well suited to the needs of both undergraduates and graduate students.

453. Stewart, Peter. **Roman Art.** New Surveys in the Classics 34. Oxford: Oxford University Press for the Classical Association, 2004. 155pp. ISBN 0–19–852081–6. LCCN 20043–1312.

Stewart offers a selective survey of the state of scholarship on Roman art. His introduction provides an overview of changing scholarly approaches and notes the recent shift among scholars from viewing Roman art as largely derivative to accepting it on its own terms. The various chapters cover portraits, public monuments, funerary art, painting, mosaics and sculptures, and later Roman art. Each provides a narrative overview, with numerous references. The book is nicely illustrated and includes a substantial bibliography. Stewart emphasizes recent English-language works in his survey but also includes key works in the standard European languages of scholarship.

DICTIONARIES, ENCYCLOPEDIAS, AND HANDBOOKS

454. Avery, Catherine B., ed. **New Century Handbook of Greek Art and Architecture.** New York: Appleton-Century-Crofts, 1972. 213pp. LCCN 72–187738.

Most of the articles in this volume are derived from the larger *New Century Classical Handbook* (entry 128), although a number of additions and revisions have been made. The work takes the form of a dictionary. Its articles provide basic factual information on artists, individual works of art, sites, and various technical terms. These are clearly written and aimed at a general audience. Numerous black and white illustrations accompany the text. Lack of bibliographies is the chief drawback. This handbook is most useful as a ready reference work. Those who want an extended discussion of a particular artistic medium should use Richter's handbook (entry 474) instead.

455. Beazley Archive. URL: www.beazley.ox.ac.uk/BeazleyAdmin/Script2/default.htm.

This important site is the Internet presence of the Beazley Archive at Oxford University. The actual archive, with its collections and workrooms, is located on the lower level of the Ashmolean Museum. The nucleus of the collection was the personal library and archive of Sir John Beazley, the great scholar of Attic vase painting. The site includes a number of resources. There is a dictionary of names and terms relating to Greek history, myth, geography, art, and architecture. Online catalogs of gems, pottery, and sculture are available; these include images, descriptions, and bibliography. A number of bibliographies, which are based on Oxford undergraduate reading lists in art and archaeology, are also posted on the site.

456. Biers, William R. **Archaeology of Greece: An Introduction.** 2nd ed. Ithaca, NY: Cornell University Press, 1996. 350pp. ISBN 0–8014–3173–5; 0–8014–8280–1. LCCN 95–48905.

Biers covers Greek archaeology from the Minoans through the Hellenistic era. After a brief orientation to the subject, he covers each historical era chapter by chapter.

He supplies historical background, chronology, and a discussion of major excavations and remains. Biers presents technical matters clearly. He includes many illustrations, maps, floorplans, and reconstructions. Those seeking illustrations of typical shapes and styles of pottery, the architectural orders, or plans of famous temples will find them here. The notes and guide to further reading provide a suitable orientation for beginning students. A glossary and general index conclude the work. Overall, this is an excellent handbook for beginning students and general readers.

457. Biers, William R. **Art, Artefacts, and Chronology in Classical Archaeology.** London: Routledge, 1992. 105pp. ISBN 0–415–06318–3; 0–415–06319–1pa. LCCN 91–45632.

This little handbook grew out of a seminar on chronology at the American School of Classical Studies in Athens (entry 1029) during 1989–1990. Biers offers a clear and readable introduction to how ancient art and artifacts are dated. He covers such topics as how time was recorded in antiquity, relative dating, absolute dating, and interpretation of evidence. Anyone looking for a brief and lucid account of stratigraphy or the dating of art objects by style will find Biers helpful. Soda addicts will even find photos of Coca-Cola bottles from 1894 to 1956 illustrating variations over time. While there is no bibliography, the notes offer excellent guidance for further reading. There is a short but adequate index.

458. Boardman, John, ed. **Oxford History of Classical Art.** Oxford: Oxford University Press, 1993. 406pp. ISBN 0–19–814386–9. LCCN 93–6825.

Designed as a companion volume to the *Oxford History of the Classical World* (entry 286), this work is aimed at a wide audience. Its various chapters, each by an expert in the field, cover broad chronological periods: pre-classical Greece, the classical period, the Hellenistic period, Rome (republic and early empire), and the later Roman Empire. Boardman also provides an introduction and a concluding chapter on the diffusion of classical art through the ancient Mediterranean world. No coverage is given to Bronze Age Greece or the Etruscans, and Christian art of the later empire receives little attention. Many illustrations (some in color) accompany the well-written text. A brief bibliography provides a good guide to the more important and accessible recent work on classical art. There is a general index. Although excellent as a single-volume survey of the field, Boardman does not offer the depth of coverage that some of the more specialized surveys do. Those interested primarily in Greek art will find more in Richter (entry 474), Robertson (entry 476), and Pedley (entry 472); for Roman art, Henig (entry 470) offers more detailed treatment.

459. Brendel, Otto J. **Etruscan Art.** Pelikan History of Art. New Haven, CT: Yale University Press, 1995. 535pp. ISBN 0–300–06446–2pa. LCCN 95–15894.

Brendel's *Etruscan Art* was originally published in 1978. For this edition Francesca R. Serra Ridgeway updated the bibliography; the content remains unchanged. Brendel proceeds chronologically, covering the major periods: the Villanovan and orientalizing periods, the early and middle archaic periods, the late archaic period, the fifth century B.C., the fourth century B.C., and the Hellenistic period. Each of these chapters is subdivided by medium: sculpture, painting, metalwork, stonework, and so on. Brendel provides many excellent black-and-white illustrations. His notes and bibliography are extensive; Serra Ridgeway's bibliographical supplement follows these. Overall, Brendel is an excellent guide to Etruscan art, with more detail and bibliography than Spivey (entry 480), although not as up-to-date.

460. Claridge, Amanda. **Rome: An Oxford Archaeological Guide.** Oxford: Oxford University Press, 1998. 455pp. ISBN 0–19–288003–9. LCCN 97–39072.

This high-end guide for tourists also serves as a useful reference handbook on the monuments of Rome. Claridge, an archaeologist who was long associated with the British School at Rome (entry 1031), has produced a concise but scholarly guide to the archaeology of Rome from the beginnings through the eighth century A.D. She begins with a short historical overview that focuses on the physical development of the city and its monuments. A guide to documentary sources and a glossary of building materials and architectural terms follow. Then Claridge surveys the remains by region of the city: the Roman forum, the upper Via Sacra, the Palatine, the imperial fora, the Campus Martius, the Capitoline Hill, the Circus Flaminius to the Circus Maximus, the Colosseum and the Esquiline Hill, and the Caelian Hill and Via Appis. Lastly she treats miscellaneous other sites, museums, and the catacombs. Claridge describes the remains, supplies some historical background, and very occasionally gives information about the excavation of a site. She provides numerous maps, plans, and illustrations. A superficial chronology appears toward the end. The general bibliography is very selective; more detailed references to both primary and secondary sources are given for major monuments. The book includes a good subject index.

461. De Grummond, Nancy Thomson. **Encyclopedia of the History of Classical Archaeology.** Westport, CT: Greenwood Press, 1996. 2v. ISBN 0–313–22066–2 (set); 0–313–30204–9 (v. 1); 0–313–30205–7 (v. 2). LCCN 94–29838.

This work is useful both for the study of classical archaeology and of the history of scholarship. It includes 1,125 entries by 171 scholars. De Grummond and company cover the study of Greco-Roman physical remains, including Aegean Bronze Age and Etruscan remains, throughout the Mediterranean. Articles cover prominent sites, notable monuments and works of art, topics, organizations, and individuals (scholars, artists, and travelers). Most are brief, usually running less than a page; each includes a short bibliography. While all focus on the history of classical archaeology, they provide much of value for current students and archaeologists engaged in interpreting sites and monuments. The *Encyclopedia* offers much to students of art history and intellectual history as well.

462. Dickinson, Oliver. **Aegean Bronze Age.** Cambridge World Archaeology. Cambridge: Cambridge University Press, 1994. 342pp. ISBN 0–521–24280–0; 0–521–45664–9pa. LCCN 93–2666.

Dickinson covers the archaeology of the Aegean Bronze Age, including the Minoans and Mycenaeans, from roughly 3300 to 1000 B.C. The introduction briefly sketches the history of Aegean Bronze Age archaeology from Schliemann to the present. The first chapter orients the beginner to the somewhat complex chronological systems used by Bronze Age archaeologists. Subsequent thematic chapters include natural environment and resources, first human populations, settlement and economy, arts and crafts, burial customs, trade, and religion. Dickinson provides numerous maps, plans, and illustrations.

His handbook provides a convenient and accessible overview with bibliography for further exploration. Those seeking a more popular treatment of this period should see Runnels and Murray (entry 479).

463.   Enciclopedia dell'arte antica classica e orientale. Roma: Istituto della Enciclopedia italiana, 1958–1966. 7v. LCCN 58–37080.

464.   Supplemento. Roma: Istituto della Enciclopedia italiana, 1973. 951pp.

465.   Atlante dei complessi figurati e degli ordini architettonici. Roma: Istituto della Enciclopedia italiana, 1973. 384, 40pp.

466.   Atlante delle forme ceramiche. Roma: Istituto della Enciclopedia italiana, 1981–1985. 2v.

467.   Indici dei nomi e delle cose notevoli dei volumi I–VIII e del primo supplemento. Roma: Istituto della Enciclopedia italiana, 1984. 629pp.

Produced under the general direction of the eminent art historian Ranuccio Bianchi Bandinelli, this encyclopedia covers art in the ancient Mediterranean world from prehistory to ca. A.D. 500. Covering artists, artistic subjects (including historical and mythological figures), places, and topics (e.g., amphitheatres, arches, types of pottery), its articles are both compact and informative; a short bibliographical note appears at the end of each. Many entries are also accompanied by illustrations (black and white for the most part). The *Enciclopedia* will serve both the casual inquirer and the specialist. Unfortunately, there is no comparable work in English.

Several supplementary volumes have appeared since the completion of the *Enciclopedia*. These include the *Supplemento,* which includes addenda to many existing articles and a number of totally new entries. The *Atlante dei complessi figurati* offers section-by-section illustrations of large works (e.g., Trajan's Column, which alone occupies 31 pages of plates) and extensive illustrations of the architectural orders. The *Atlante delle forme ceramiche* is a technical typological work on the shapes of ancient pottery. The separate index volume provides an exhaustive index to people, places, and topics discussed in the *Enciclopedia* and the *Supplemento.*

468.   Ginouvès, René, and Roland Martin. Dictionnaire méthodique de l'architecture grecque et romaine. Collection de l'École Française de Rome 84. Paris: De Boccard, 1985–1998. 3v. ISBN 2–7238–0105–0 (v. 1); 2–7283–0239–8 (v. 2); 2–7283–0529–3 (v. 3). LCCN 86–179913.

Ginouvès and Martin have written a guide to the terminology of Greek and Roman architecture. The first volume covers materials, construction techniques, and decorative techniques. The second deals with structural elements, and the third with architectural spaces. A classified subject arrangement is employed within each volume. Entries, which are listed under the French term, give a brief definition and the equivalent terms in German, English, Italian, modern Greek, ancient Greek, and Latin. The extensive footnotes contain many references to the scholarly literature on classical architecture. Numerous illustrations are provided in separate sections at the end of each volume. Each volume also includes its own bibliography and separate indexes of architectural terms for each language. This work is exceptionally useful for those working with scholarly publications in foreign languages, since relatively few bilingual dictionaries cover such technical terms.

469. Goette, Hans Rupprecht. **Athens, Attica, and the Megarid: An Archaeological Guide.** London: Routledge, 2001. 400pp. ISBN 0–415–24370–X. LCCN 2000–06281.

This is a revised and expanded version of the German original (1993). It is a guide-book for travelers and students, but a scholarly one. Goette covers Athens and its environs: Attica, Megara and the Megarid, and the major islands of the Saronic Gulf (Salamis, Aigina, and Poros). He describes the monuments in considerable detail, with some historical background. While he focuses on Bronze Age and classical remains, Goette includes Byzantine and later monuments as well. The many drawings, plans, and photos are one of the strongest features of the book. Appendixes offer much useful information on the geography of Attica, the modern government and economy, and flora and fauna. Goette also provides an illustrated glossary of ancient architecture, a chronological guide to Byzantine churches, and a list of major monuments in chronological order. He closes with an index of sites and monuments and a bibliography.

470. Henig, Martin, ed. **Handbook of Roman Art: A Comprehensive Survey of All the Arts of the Roman World.** Ithaca, NY: Cornell University Press, 1983. 288pp. ISBN 0–8014–1539–X; 0–8014–9242–4pa. LCCN 82–071591.

Henig and his contributors cover all aspects of Roman art. Early Roman art and that of the late empire are treated in separate chapters at either end of the book. Otherwise, chapters deal with the various artistic forms and media: architecture, sculpture, wall painting, mosaics, decorative metalwork and jewelry, coins, pottery, terra-cottas, glass, and epigraphy. Useful supplementary material includes a guide to the major pottery forms, a glossary, an excellent bibliography arranged by topic, and a general index. Well written and illlustrated, Henig serves as a handy reference work as well as a readable survey of Roman art.

471. Mee, Christopher, and Antony Spawforth. **Greece: An Oxford Archaeological Guide.** Oxford: Oxford University Press, 2001. 464pp. ISBN 0–19–288058–6.

This handbook for travelers covers Greece from the prehistoric period to the seventh century A.D. A substantial introduction covers the geography, geology, and climate, as well as giving an historical and cultural overview. Mee and Spawforth then survey the archaeological sites by region: Attika, Corinth, the Argolid, Lakonia, Messenia, Arkadia, Achaia and Elis, central Greece and Euboia, Akarnania and Aitolia, Thessaly, Epeiros, and Macedonia. The detailed table of contents notes the sites treated under each. They cover nearly all major sites, supplying descriptions and historical background. Mee and Spawforth draw frequently upon the ancient authors, especially the Pausanias's second-century A.D. description of Greece. They provide numerous maps, plans, and illustrations. A chronology, glossary, highly selective bibliography, and index may be found at the end of the volume. Mee and Spawforth have produced a readable and accurate guide to the monuments that includes a rich trove of historical and cultural detail.

472. Pedley, John Griffiths. **Greek Art and Archaeology.** 3rd ed. London: Laurence King, 2002. 400pp. ISBN 1–85–669286–8.

Intended as an introduction to Greek art and archaeology, this work is an excellent general source of information on the subject. The readable and up-to-date text is accompanied by numerous well-chosen illustrations (chiefly black and white). Pedley covers architecture, sculpture, pottery, and wall painting from the Bronze Age through the Hellenistic period. He also provides some historical background material on each period. The overall arrangement of the book is chronological, with subarrangement by categories of artwork. Pedley also includes a short chronology, a glossary, and a selective bibliography. A general index concludes the volume. For the categories of art not covered by Pedley, one should consult Richter's *Handbook of Greek Art* (entry 474).

473. Preston, Percy. **Dictionary of Pictorial Subjects from Classical Literature: A Guide to Their Identification in Works of Art.** New York: Scribner's, 1983. 311pp. ISBN 0–684–17913–X. LCCN 83–4470.

Preston has compiled a dictionary of objects, creatures, activities, and distinguishing features found in representations of individuals and themes drawn from classical literature and mythology. His purpose is not to provide a catalog of paintings, drawings, and the like with classical themes or allusions, but rather a tool for identifying such themes and allusions. Entries include, for example, "castaway," "drinking," "falling," and "monster" (variously subdivided). Each notes what mythical or literary figure is associated with it and provides references to literary treatments in the ancient authors. There are a few illustrations. Preston is by no means exhaustive. He concentrates on the more important Greek and Roman literary works. His work is useful both for identifying classical themes in later works of art and for bringing together material on particular topics. Preston makes liberal use of cross-references but does not provide an index. Those seeking works of art based on specific myths or historical events should consult Reid (entry 921) or Rochelle (entry 478).

474. Richter, Gisela M.A. Richter. **Handbook of Greek Art.** 9th ed. New York: Da Capo, 1987. 431pp. ISBN 0–306–80298–8. LCCN 87–6810.

Since it first appeared in 1959, Richter's *Handbook* has become a standard work. The seventh edition (1974) was the last to be revised by the author, who died in 1972. Subsequent editions have incorporated corrections and updated bibliographies but are otherwise unchanged. Richter covers all aspects of Greek art from about 1100 B.C. to 100 B.C. She organizes her material into chapters by form and material: architecture, larger works of sculpture, statuettes, decorative metalwork, terra-cottas, engraved gems, coins, jewelry, paintings and mosaics, pottery, furniture, textiles, glass, ornament, and epigraphy. The text is readable and profusely illustrated (although all illustrations are black and white). Supplementary materials include maps, a substantial bibliography, a chronology of Greek sculptural works, and indexes of places and names. Richter covers a much wider range of materials than Pedley (entry 472) but is not as current. Pedley also covers Bronze Age Greece, which Richter does not.

475. Robertson, D.S. **Greek and Roman Architecture.** 2nd ed. Cambridge: Cambridge University Press, 1969. 407pp. ISBN 0–521–06104–0; 0–521–09452–6pa. LCCN 76–407810.

Originally published in 1929 as a *Handbook of Greek and Roman Architecture,* this highly regarded work covers all aspects of classical architecture. Chapters proceed in roughly chronological order from Minoan Crete, Troy, and pre-Mycenaean Greece to the fourth century A.D. There are a few departures from the chronological scheme, such as the chapter on Greek and Roman houses. Many figures and illustrations are provided. Particularly useful appendixes supply a selective chronological table of Greek, Etruscan, and Roman buidings from 1000 B.C. to A.D. 330 and a glossary of architectural terms. While the book is now rather old, Robertson's focus on the essential and well-established facts has kept the work from becoming obsolete except in a few details. It remains an excellent source of general information on Greek and Roman architecture, although the bibliography (which has remained unaltered since the first edition) must be supplemented from other sources.

476.   Robertson, Martin. **History of Greek Art.** Cambridge: Cambridge University Press, 1975. 2v. ISNB 0–521–20277–9. LCCN 73–79317.

477.   Robertson, Martin. **Shorter History of Greek Art.** Cambridge: Cambridge University Press, 1981. 240pp. ISBN 0–521–23629–0; 0–521–28084–2pa. LCCN 80–41026.

Robertson's massive work, the largest and most comprehensive treatment of the subject by an individual writer in English, covers all Greek art (except for architecture) from the archaic period through the Hellenistic age. He intends the work for both scholars and general readers and so translates all Greek and Latin. The text, which comprises the first volume, proceeds chronologically and is intended to be read rather than consulted. The second volume contains the extensive bibliographical apparatus, illustrations, and indexes. The selection of illustrations has been faulted by some, since it does not include all the important works discussed in the text. Those seeking information on a specific topic would do best to approach this work through the indexes. Since their organization is more suited to the casual inquirer, Richter (entry 474) and Pedley (entry 472) are better choices for most reference purposes. Their works also cover architecture. However, Robertson frequently offers better coverage of a particular topic or information not found in the other works.

The abridged version, which is intended for use as a textbook, retains the same chapter divisions, although the content is considerably reduced. Illustrations are integrated into the text. While Robertson generally refers readers to his larger work for more information, there is a brief bibliography. There is also a detailed general index.

478.   Rochelle, Mercedes. **Mythological and Classical World Art Index: A Locator of Paintings, Sculptures, Frescoes, Manuscript Illuminations, Sketches, Woodcuts, and Engravings Executed 1200 B.C. TO A.D. 1900, with a Directory of the Institutions Holding Them.** Jefferson, NC: McFarland, 1991. 279pp. ISBN 0–89950–566–X. LCCN 91–52503.

Rochelle provides a useful resource for anyone seeking artworks depicting classical myth and history. Persons, gods, goddesses, and events appear as subjects. Under each, Rochelle lists a selection of artworks. She arranges these chronologically by date of creation, "beginning with contemporaneous works and continuing through the Romantic movement." For each work Rochelle gives the title or a description, the artist's name (if known), the date, the museum holding the original, and references to published reproductions. A directory of museums (with addresses) and an index of artists follow the text. Although Reid (entry 921) supplies better and more complete information on classical myths in modern art, Rochelle covers a much wider range of material by including artworks created before 1300 and historical subjects.

479.   Runnels, Curtis, and Priscilla Murray. **Greece Before History: An Archaeological Companion and Guide.** Stanford, CA: Stanford University Press, 2001. 202pp. ISBN 0–8047–4036–4; 0–8047–4050–Xpa. LCCN 00–058835.

Runnels and Murray intend this guide for students, general readers, and travelers. They proceed by period: the Old Stone Age, the New Stone Age, the Bronze Age, and the end of the Bronze Age world. The section for each of these provides an overview of the period and its culture, with brief discussions of key sites. The last three chapters cover Santorini and the legend of Atlantis, principal monuments of prehistoric Greece (aimed at travelers), and the authors' final reflections. Appendixes cover chronology, Schliemann's travels and excavations, and advice on planning an archaeological tour. Many maps and line drawings accompany the text. There is also a bibliographical essay, with sections keyed to the chapters, that provides a good selection of general and scholarly works. This is a good introduction for beginning students and travelers. Those seeking a more scholarly text might also consult Dickinson (entry 462).

480.   Spivey, Nigel. **Etruscan Art.** World of Art. London: Thames & Hudson, 1997. 216pp. ISBN 0–500–20304–0pa. LCCN 97–60250.

Spivey surveys what we know about Etruria and Etruscan art. After an overview of Etruscan culture, he examines the emergence of the Etruscan cities and their relations with others (the Near East, Greece, Rome). A final chapter examines the legacy of the Etruscans. While Spivey always keeps his focus on art, the fact that we know the Etruscans chiefly from material remains also makes this a survey of their civilization as a whole. He includes many excellent illustrations (some in color). A time line, chronology, and selective bibliography appear at the end of the volume. There is a subject index. Spivey is a useful handbook of Etruscan art and civilization, a bit more up-to-date than Brendel (entry 459) but far less detailed and with less scholarly apparatus.

481.   Whitley, James. **Archaeology of Ancient Greece.** Cambridge World Archaeology. Cambridge: Cambridge University Press, 2001. 484pp. ISBN 0–521–62205–0; 0–521–62733–8pa. LCCN 2001018438.

Whitley covers Greek archaeology from 1000 to 300 B.C., essentially covering archaic and classical Greece. The first part of his book provides an introduction to classical archaeology and its aims, a brief survey of the history of classical archaeology, a discussion of modern archaeological practice (since 1977) in Greece, and an overview of chronology and terminology. The bulk of the book falls into two parts, the first covering the archaic Greece (1000–479 B.C.). This includes chapters on the early Iron Age and Greece's interactions with her neighbors in the following (orientalizing) period. Whitley then turns to a topical approach, covering sacred places, the city, art, and regionalism. The second part looks at classical Greece (479–300 B.C.), beginning with a discussion of what is classical. Whitley then devotes chapters to cities and sanctuaries, Athens, and the countryside, followed by a brief look forward to the Hellenistic era. He presents technical material clearly and supplies many charts, diagrams, floor plans, and illustrations. Whitley provides a good synthesis of recent research. He also gives much attention to the use of archaeology and material remains for historical research. Notes for further reading, an extensive bibliography, and an index round out the work. Whitley has produces an excellent and up-to-date handbook for students of Greek archaeology, which focuses on archaeology rather than art. Those primarily interest in art should consult the works of Richter (entry 474), Robertson (entry 476), and Pedley (entry 472).

12
Greek and Latin Languages

This chapter lists a selection of basic works on the Greek and Latin languages. These include general works on the history of the languages and the standard dictionaries and reference grammars. Smaller dictionaries and grammars designed for the use of students are, for the most part, excluded. Many valuable specialized lexica and grammatical works have also been omitted because of their narrow focus. A few popular phrase books that list and gloss Latin phrases commonly used in English are also noted below.

GENERAL WORKS

482.   Allen, W. Sidney. **Vox Graeca: A Guide to the Pronunciation of Clasical Greek.** 3rd ed. Cambridge: Cambridge University Press, 1987. 179pp. ISBN 0–521–33367–9; 0–521–33555–8pa. LCCN 86–31063.

Vox Graeca is the standard work in English on the pronunciation of ancient Greek. While he focuses on Attic Greek, he does not neglect other dialects and periods. Chapters include consonants, vowels, vowel length, vowel junction, quantity, and accent. Appendixes cover the pronunciation of Greek in England, oral accentuation of Greek, evidence from the ancient grammarians, and the Greek alphabet. Allen also provides an index of Greek technical terms and a very select bibliography. A summary of recommended pronunciations concludes the book.

483.   Allen, W. Sidney. **Vox Latina: A Guide to the Pronunciation of Classical Latin.** 2nd ed., rev. Cambridge: Cambridge University Press, 1989. 133pp. ISBN 0–521–37936–9.

Allen is the standard work in English on the pronunciation of Latin. His chapters cover consonants, vowels, vowel length, vowel junction, accent, and quantity. Appendixes discuss evidence from the Latin grammarians, the pronunciation of Latin in England, and the letters of the Latin alphabet. Supplementary notes and a short bibliography are also provided. Allen also includes a summary list of recommended pronunciations.

484.   Baldi, Philip. **Foundations of Latin.** Trends in Linguistics: Studies and Monographs 117. Berlin: Mouton de Gruyter, 1999. 534pp. ISBN 3–11–016294–6. LCCN 98–51324.

Baldi has written a historical and comparative handbook of Latin. He begins with an extensive discussion of method in historical and comparative linguistics before proceeding into an overview of the Indo-European family of languages and Proto-Indo-European. Baldi then turns to the languages of ancient Italy, primarily the Indo-European Italic languages but also non Indo-European languages such as Etruscan. In each case Baldi discusses their relationship with Latin. After nearly 200 pages of background, Baldi finally turns to the Latin language proper with a collection of materials for the study of Latin. These include inscriptions, literary texts, and papyri arranged in chronological order, with discussion and commentary. Subsequent chapters cover the development of Latin phonology and morphology from Proto-Indo-European. Among the strengths of the book are its relatively approachable (if still challenging) introduction to the methods and principles of historical and comparative philology and the excellent collection of historical Latin texts. A major weakness is the deliberate omission of Latin syntax. Baldi provides a substantial bibliography and indexes of forms (by language), authors, classical references, and subjects. Many classical students will still find the older work of Palmer (entry 488) a more congenial starting point. Palmer also covers syntax.

485. Hammond, Mason. **Latin: A Historical and Linguistic Handbook.** Cambridge, MA: Harvard University Press, 1976. 292pp. ISBN 0–674–51290–1. LCCN 75–33359.

Hammond intends "to present a historical and linguistic introduction to Latin." His work is aimed at teachers of Latin, particularly at the secondary level, and students. It assumes relatively little knowledge, beyond a basic grasp of Latin. The first four chapters supply some background material in linguistics and show the relation of Latin to the Indo-European language family and to the other languages of ancient Italy. Subsequent chapters focus on specific aspects of the Latin language: alphabet, pronunciation, morphology, formation of compounds, syntax, and versification. The concluding chapters cover postclassical Latin and its relation to the romance languages, and Latin and English. There is an adequate bibliography and a general index. Hammond is sometimes superficial and does not do as much as his introduction claims; Palmer (entry 488) is a much better book overall. Still, Hammond covers a few topics that Palmer does not—for example, the alphabet, versification, and the relation of Latin and English. The work is an adequate source of general information on the Latin language.

486. Janson, Tore. **Natural History of Latin.** Oxford: Oxford University Press, 2004. 305pp. ISBN 0–19–926309–4. LCCN 2004276203.

Janson has written a cultural history of Latin for the general reader. The first part of the book covers Latin from its origins through St. Augustine. Janson discusses the nature of the language, the literature, politics, and so forth. In the second part he discusses the Latin in Europe from the Middle Ages to modern times, surveying its role in the Church, learning, and science. The remaining three parts of the book cover grammar, basic vocabulary, and common phrases and expressions. Janson is accurate and scholarly but aims at a popular audience, and his treatment is relatively superficial. He provides a brief guide to further reading and an index. This is a useful guide to the history of the language for nonspecialists.

487. Palmer, L. R. **The Greek Language.** The Great Languages. Atlantic Highlands, NJ: Humanities Press, 1980; repr., Norman: University of Oklahoma Press, 1996. 355pp. ISBN 0–391–01203–7. LCCN 79–26758.

This forms a companion work to Palmer's earlier volume on the Latin language (entry 488). "Like its predecessor, the book is divided into two parts: the first concentrates on tracing the development and ramifications of the language as a vehicle and instrument of a great culture . . . The second part is a condensed Comparative-Historical Grammar."

Part 1 covers the prehistory of the Greek language, Linear B, dialects, the development of the literary language, and postclassical Greek. Part 2 offers chapters on writing and pronunciation, phonology, and morphology; syntax was omitted for reasons of space. A brief bibliography points the way for those who wish to pursue a topic further. There are indexes to subjects, Greek words, and Linear B words. Palmer summarizes a vast amount of research on the Greek language in a manageable and readable volume, which has become the standard work on the subject in English.

488. Palmer, L. R. **The Latin Language.** The Great Languages. London: Faber and Faber, 1954; repr., Norman: University of Oklahoma Press, 1988. 372pp. LCCN 54–3075.

Considered a standard work since its publication in 1954, *The Latin Language* is the best general work on the Latin language available in English. Palmer's intention is "to summarize for classical students, for fellow scholars working in other fields, and for the interested laity the results reached by research into the history of Latin from the Bronze Age down to the break up of the Roman Empire." The book consists of two parts. The first is an outline history of the language; this covers Latin in relation to other Indo-European languages and to other Italic languages, Latin dialects and early texts, spoken Latin, the development of the literary language, Vulgar Latin, and Christian Latin. Palmer's discussions of spoken Latin and of the literary language in particular are highly regarded. The second part is a brief comparative-historical grammar, with chapters on phonology, morphology, and syntax. Palmer then provides a good, if short, bibliography with some useful annotations. There are also indexes of subjects and Latin words. Baldi's more recent work (entry 484) reflects more up-to-date linguistic scholarship. Baldi focuses more on comparative grammar and is more technical than Palmer. Many students will still prefer to begin with Palmer.

BIBLIOGRAPHIES

489. Boned Colera, Pilar, and Juan Rodríguez Somolinos. **Repertorio bibliográfico de la lexicografía griega.** Diccionario Griego Español 3. Madrid: Consejo Superior de Investigaciones Científicas, 1998. 540pp. ISBN 84–00–07722–9.

Boned Colera and Rodríguez Somolinos prepared this bibliography of Greek lexicography in conjunction with the Diccionario Griego Español project. The first part of the work, an extensive update of Riesenfeld (entry 562), lists indexes, lexica, and concordances of Greek authors; these are arranged by author and title. The second part lists over 3,300 studies and general works on Greek lexicography by author. A thematic index at the end of the volume also provides limited subject access to these. The third and largest section is a bibliography of studies of individual Greek words; these are arranged alphabetically by word. While more than 6,000 works on about 34,000 Greek words are cited, these include a mix of additional works and cross-references to those in the second part. No annotations are provided. This is the most complete enumeration of Greek lexicographical works available, covering publications in a variety of languages from the late nineteenth century to the 1990s.

490. Cousin, Jean. **Bibliographie de la langue latine, 1880–1948.** Collection de bibliographie classique. Paris: Les Belles Lettres, 1951. 375pp. LCCN 51–8399.

Cousin's bibliography covers all aspects of the study of the Latin language. It is arranged by subject; major headings cover such topics as general linguistic works, the relation of Latin to other languages, the history of the language, writing and pronunciation, phonology, morphology, syntax, word order, stylistics, and lexicography. Since Cousin worked closely with Jules Marouzeau, his coverage of works published in 1914 and later largely duplicates that of the corresponding sections of *Dix années* (entry 21) and *L'Année philologique* (entry 44). There are no annotations. Cousin does provide indexes to Latin words and to names (chiefly of Latin authors). His work is comprehensive for the years covered; for later bibliography, see Cupaiuolo (entry 491).

491.   Cupaiuolo, Fabio. **Bibliografia della lingua latina (1949–1991).** Studi latini 11. Napoli: Loffredo Editore, 1993. 592pp.

Continuing the work of Cousin (entry 490), Cupaiuolo's bibliography closely follows his predecessor in scope and form. Cupaiuolo gathers a vast number of citations covering every aspect of the Latin language. He also includes many linguistic works that, while not directly concerned with Latin, are useful to students of the language. Arrangement is by subject, with chapters covering such topics as linguistics, origins of the Latin language, orthography and pronunciation, phonetics, morphology, syntax, stylistics, and lexicography. For those concerned primarily with a single author, Cupaiuolo has provided a chapter on the language and style of individual authors, which is subarranged alphabetically by ancient author. Many entries include brief descriptive annotations, and entries for books also list reviews. Lack of an index is a major drawback. There are occasional typographical errors and inaccuracies of citation as well, although not enough to seriously reduce the value of the work. Together, Cousin and Cupaiuolo provide an excellent guide to works on the Latin language.

492.   Householder, Fred W., and Gregory Nagy. **Greek: A Survey of Recent Work.** Janua Linguarum, Series Practica 211. The Hague: Mouton, 1972. 105pp. LCCN 73–161227.

No longer recent, but still useful, this volume provides a wide-ranging survey of much of the most significant work done on the Greek language in the twentieth century. Particular emphasis is given to studies published in the 1950s and 1960s, a time of exceptional activity in the field due to the decipherment of Linear B by Michael Ventris in 1952. Householder and Nagy review their material in narrative chapters covering generalities, phonology, morphology, syntax, etymology and vocabulary, and dialectology. Two bibliographies (the second being a supplemental listing for works published in the years 1968–1972) provide full citations for all works discussed. Both authors are distinguished experts on the Greek language; their commentary is no less valuable than the bibliography.

POPULAR PHRASE BOOKS AND GLOSSARIES

See also the section "Quotations and Proverbs" in chapter 14.

493.   Branyon, Richard A. **Latin Phrases and Quotations.** Rev. ed. New York: Hippocrene Books, 1997. 256pp. ISBN 0–7818–0260–1. LCCN 96–38585.

Intended as an aid to readers of English literature, this collection lists more than 4,200 Latin phrases along with their English equivalents. These include both quotations from literary works and common Latin expressions that are sometimes used in English. Quotations are generally identified by author, although Branyon does not provide full references. Branyon arranges the phrases alphabetically. His translations leave a good deal to be desired. They generally provide the gist of the original but often fail to communicate its tone and force. Ehrlich's similar works (entries 494–495) offer far superior translations. Appendixes list major Latin and Greek authors, the Latin mottos of selected states, and the Latin phrases and quotations most frequently found in English. Branyon does not indicate how he determined frequency. No index of any sort is provided.

494. Ehrlich, Eugene. **Amo, Amas, Amat and More: How to Use Latin to Your Own Advantage and to the Astonishment of Others.** New York: Harper & Row, 1985. 328pp. ISBN 0–06–181249–8. LCCN 84–48594.

495. Erhlich, Eugene. **Veni, Vidi, Vici: Conquer Your Friends, Impress Your Enemies with Everyday Latin.** New York: HarperPerennial, 1995. 297pp. ISBN 0–06–273365–6. LCCN 94–42354.

Amo, Amas, Amat is a dictionary of Latin expressions and tags used in English. In addition to those expressions that used to be common among the literate, it includes scholarly abbreviations, mottos, proverbs, and technical terms from various fields such as law. Each entry includes the Latin word or phrase, a guide to pronunciation, and an idiomatic translation. The translations generally reflect the spirit rather than the letter of the original. A descriptive passage concludes many of the entries. This gives the literal meaning (if not covered by the translation) and explains when and how English speakers might use the expression. Ehrlich also provides the source, if it is from a well-known work of Latin literature. An index gives English phrases and refers to the Latin equivalent; a subject index would have been more useful. *Veni, Vidi, Vici* follows the pattern of the earlier work, adding many new Latin phrases and mottos with very little overlap. Ehrlich's books are a great help both in translating Latin phrases found in reading English and for discovering how to "say something in Latin." Stone's two collections (entries 499–500) include more Latin expressions and sayings but offer less context and commentary.

496. Gray, John. **Lawyer's Latin: A Vade-Mecum.** London: Robert Hale, 2002. 143pp. ISBN 0–7090–7066–7.

Roman law, along with English common law, had great influence on modern law. Not surprisingly, legal writings include many Latin phrases. This handbook by a British barrister covers Latin terms commonly used in British legal writings and documents. While some are peculiar to Britain, others will be found in legal usage elsewhere, and others still are of broader application. Gray lists terms alphabetically. He gives a translation for each and provides many notes on their historical and current legal use. Many cross-references are provided. For those interested specifically in Latin legal terms, this is by far the best book.

497. Morwood, James. **Dictionary of Latin Words and Phrases.** Oxford: Oxford University Press, 1998. 224pp. ISBN 0–19–860229–4; 0–19–860109–3pa. LCCN 98–182742.

Morwood is by far the most scholarly of the phrase books noted here. His collection is not as large as those of Ehrlich (entries 494–495) and Stone (entries 499–500) but offers a well-chosen collection of expressions, bon mots, and proverbs accompanied by translations and notes on their origins and use. Morwood provides full citations to the ancient authors, which is a signal virtue of the work. His notes often give the original context, first usage in English, and other interesting bits of information. The quality of these is so good that it is a shock when Morwood fails to cite Chaucer's general prologue to the *Canterbury Tales* (line 162) as a parody of *labor omnia vincit,* especially as he discusses Chaucer's use of Latin in the introduction. He also provides biographical notes on Latin authors. His main index is sensibly arranged by topic, with separate indexes on Christianity and the Church, law, and proverbs.

498.   Neal, Bill. **Gardener's Latin.** Chapel Hill, NC: Algonquin Books, 1992. ISBN 0–945575–94–7; 1–56512–384–0pa. LCCN 92–2652.

Botanical Latin, based on the eighteenth-century classification system of Carl Linnaeus, is a peculiar species of Latin quite different from that learned in the typical language class. Neal has compiled a popular guide to botanical Latin for gardeners. The introduction (by Barbara Damrosch, a well-known author of gardening books) extols the benefits of knowing the Latin terms, since they often provide information about the plant (e.g., its soil or water preferences, whether it is low lying, etc.). Neal then offers an A-to-Z listing of Latin plant names and Latin adjectives applied to plants. Running sidebars in each margin provide historical and literary notes on selected terms.

499.   Stone, Jon R. **Latin for the Illiterati: Exorcising the Ghosts of a Dead Language.** New York: Routledge, 1996. 201pp. ISBN 0–415–91774–3; 0–415–91775–1pa. LCCN 95–47985.

500.   Stone, Jon R. **More Latin for the Illiterati: A Guide to Everyday Medical, Legal, and Religious Latin.** New York: Routledge, 1999. 208pp. ISBN 0–415–92210–0; 0–415–92211–9pa. LCCN 98–43820.

Stone is the most recent contender in the Latin phrase book category, following Ehrlich's two volumes (entries 494–495) with his own; surprisingly, Stone does not mention Ehrlich in his introduction or bibliography. Stone describes his first book, *Latin for the Illiterati,* as "nearly 6,000 Latin words, phrases, and standard abbreviations taken from the world of art, music, law, philosophy, theology, medicine, and the theater as well as miscellaneous remarks and sagely advice from ancient writers." This is a fair description. Stone marshals his material into three alphabetical listings: *verba* (common words and expressions), *dicta* (common phrases and familiar sayings), and abbreviations. These are mostly bare listings of the Latin expressions with an English translation. Stone rarely provides much comment either on the ancient phrase or its modern application; Ehrlich covers far fewer words and phrases but does a better job of providing background and explanatory material. Morwood (entry 497) also supplies better citations, examples, and background information. Stone's organizational scheme also breaks up related phrases: *ab ovo* (from the egg) appears in *verba; ab ovo usque ad mala* ("from egg to fruit," the usual sequence of a Roman banquet) in *dicta,* with no cross-referencing. Stone provides attributions (but not full citations) for many of the phrases among the *dicta.* He misses many, a case in point being *ab ovo usque ad mala* (Horace, *Satires* 1.3.6), a famous tag that goes without attribution. A final miscellaneous section lists Latin names for months and days, colors, the seven hills of Rome, various countries, and numbers.

More Latin for the Illiterati is patterned on its predecessor but is categorized by subject. Its various sections cover medical Latin, legal Latin, religious Latin, abbreviations, and miscellaneous information. A final section offers excerpts from the Roman Catholic liturgy in Latin and English. Both volumes have English to Latin indexes; a topical index is sorely missed. Stone is more comprehensive than the other works listed in this section but offers much less of the cultural context.

DICTIONARIES AND THESAURI

501. Bauer, Walter. **Greek-English Lexicon of the New Testament and Other Early Christian Literature.** 3rd ed. Rev. and ed. Frederick W. Danker based on Walter Bauer's *Griechisch-deutsches Wörterbuch zu den Schriften des Neuen Testaments und der frühchristlichen Literatur,* 6th ed., ed. Kurt Aland and Barbara Aland, with Viktor Reichmann and on previous English editions by W. F. Arndt, F. W. Gingrich, and F. W. Danker. Chicago: University of Chicago Press, 2000. 1,108pp. ISBN 0–226–03933–1. LCCN 00–026844.

Bauer is the standard lexicon for New Testament Greek. In addition to the New Testament and early Christian writers, it frequently cites the Septuagint, Hellenistic Jewish authors such as Philo and Josephus, a wide range of papyri, and some Byzantine authors. Articles provide definitions and discussions of forms; many also cite pertinent secondary works. The most recent (third) edition not only takes account of recent scholarship and discoveries, but it also offers expanded coverage of early Christian writers beyond the New Testament. The various editions are often cited by editor of abbreviation: Bauer-Arndt-Gingrich, or BAG (first); Bauer-Arndt-Gingrich-Danker, or BADG (second); and Bauer-Danker-Arndt-Gingrich, or BDAG (third). A useful tool for all who deal with Hellenistic and later Greek, this lexicon forms a valuable supplement to Liddell-Scott-Jones (entry 511) and other Greek-English dictionaries.

502. Boisacq, Emile. **Dictionnaire étymologique de la langue grecque: Étudiée dans ses rapports avec les autres langues indo-européenes.** 4ième éd., augmentée d'un index par Helmut Rix. Heidelberg: Carl Winter Universitätsverlag, 1950. 1,256pp. LCCN 51–2358.

A respected, if now dated, work on Greek etymology, Boisacq is primarily concerned with the relation of Greek to other Indo-European languages. The history of words within the Greek language receives less attention; for this, one should consult Chantraine (entry 503). Boisacq's entries provide extensive bibliographical references. There are frequent cross-references from words and forms, which are treated as part of a larger article. Boisacq also provides indexes to non-Greek words by language; these are arranged by language family. Although Boisacq remains useful, Frisk (entry 507) is more up-to-date and should be preferred.

503. Chantraine, Pierre. **Dictionnaire étymologique de la langue grecque: Histoire des mots.** Paris: Klincksieck, 1968–1980. 2v. ISBN 2–252–02210–8. LCCN 68–136031.

Chantraine's work is modelled on Ernout-Meillet's Latin etymological dictionary (entry 504); its relation to Frisk's etymological dictionary (entry 507) is similar to that of Ernout-Meillet's to Walde-Hofmann (entry 521). Chantraine is more concerned with the histories of the words than with their origins and linguistic affiliations. He provides much information on the forms and meanings of words at various periods in the history of the Greek language. His etymologies draw heavily on Frisk, although he occasionally offers an alternative etymology. Also, since Chantraine's dictionary was written later, he is able to take into account extensive recent work on the early history of Greek as revealed by the Linear B tablets. Indexes to Mycenaean Greek words and non-Greek words conclude the work.

504.   Ernout, A., and A. Meillet. **Dictionnaire étymologique de la langue latine: Histoire des mots.** 4ième éd., deuxième tirage augmentée de corrections nouvelles. Paris: Klincksieck, 1967. 827pp. LCCN 68–68022.

This work is generally considered to be the standard Latin etymological dictionary. Ernout, one of the foremost French Latinists of the twentieth century, is responsible for providing the history of each word from early Latin through late antiquity. Meillet discusses the Indo-European roots of each word. Many of the entries include references to modern studies. Less problematic word histories are often treated in less detail and equipped with a smaller bibliographical apparatus; for further information on these, one can consult Walde-Hofmann (entry 521). Many cross-references are provided from forms treated under another entry. There are also word indexes for non-Latin words; these are divided by language.

505.   Estienne, Henri. **Thesaurus Graecae Linguae.** Post editionem Anglicam novis additamentis auctum, ordineque alphabetico digestum tertium ediderunt Carolus Benedictus Hase, Gulielmus Dindorfius, et Ludovicus Dindorfius. Parisiis: Excudebat Ambrosius Firmin Didot, 1831–1865. 8v. in 9. LCCN 06–39594.

Long the basic compendium for the study of classical and Byzantine Greek lexicography, the *Thesaurus Graecae Linguae* is based on obsolete texts and methods. The work of a Renaissance Hellenist, it was revised and expanded in the nineteenth century by a trio of distinguished German classical scholars. It is much larger than Liddell-Scott-Jones (entry 511) and is only partly superseded by it. For exhaustive citations of all known uses of a particular word or form, the computerized *Thesaurus Linguae Graecae* (entry 519) is a far better tool. However, the *TLG* database does not offer definitions or other lexicographical information at the present time. Specialists will still find Estienne's venerable work of use on occasion.

506.   Forcellini, Egidio. **Totius Latinitatis Lexicon.** In hac editione post tertiam auctam et emendatum a Josepho Furlanetto . . . amplissime auctum atque emendatum cura et studio Doct. Vincentii De-Vit. Prati: Typis Aldinianis, 1858–1875. 6v. LCCN 09–25614–5.

Forcellini's large Latin dictionary was his life's work. He completed it in 1753; it was published posthumously in 1771. A number of scholars have reworked it. Vincenzo De-Vit's edition is both the most commonly cited and the most readily available. Long the fullest and most complete Latin dictionary, Forcellini is gradually being superseded by the *Thesaurus Linguae Latinae* (entry 520). Even the *Oxford Latin Dictionary* (entry 508), which in terms of currency and lexicographical method is far superior, generally offers fewer examples and citations. For those parts of the alphabet not yet covered by the *TLL*, Forcellini remains a valuable resource.

507. Frisk, Hjalmar. **Griechisches Etymologisches Wörterbuch.** Indogermanische Bibliothek. 2. unveränderte Aufl. Heidelberg: Carl Winter Universitätsverlag, 1973–1979. 3v. ISBN 3–533–00652–2 (v. 1–2); 3–533–02203–X (v. 3).

Frisk is the standard etymological dictionary for the Greek language. His compact entries provide a wealth of information on the forms and meanings of Greek words, although his chief concern is to present their linguistic connections and etymologies. Frisk also supplies numerous references to the scholarly literature. Corrigenda and addenda are found in the third volume, which also includes a number of indexes to non-Greek words. The indexes are arranged by language. Frisk is complemented by Chantraine's somewhat later work (entry 503), which concentrates primarily on word histories.

508. Glare, P.G.W., ed. **Oxford Latin Dictionary.** Oxford: Clarendon Press, 1982. 2,126pp. ISBN 0–19–864224–5. LCCN 82–8162.

This is the first and only entirely new comprehensive dictionary of classical Latin to appear since the nineteenth century. Based on a fresh reading of the Latin sources, it is completely independent from its predecessor, Lewis and Short (entry 510), and from the *Thesaurus Linguae Latinae* (entry 520). Editorial work began in 1933. The dictionary was issued in fascicles as the work progressed; the final fascicle and the single volume edition were published in 1982. The dictionary treats "classical Latin from its beginnings to the end of the second century A.D." The lower limit is somewhat fuzzy: coverage occasionally extends to the third century, while patristic authors of the late second century are generally omitted. Christian Latin is out of scope; for both this and late antique pagan authors one must consult Souter's glossary (entry 518). Within its chronological limits the dictionary treats all known words thoroughly; a sizeable number of proper names (place-names, Roman family names, and mythological characters) are covered as well. In general, the *OLD* follows the same lexicographical principles and imitates the formal layout of the *Oxford English Dictionary*. One of the *OLD*'s strengths is the large number of examples cited in the entries. Brief etymological notes are supplied also. This is now the standard Latin-English dictionary. It is considerably larger and much more up-to-date than Lewis and Short. However, those working in late Latin or requiring detailed etymological information or exhaustive citations of examples of a particular usage still will have to consult other works.

509. Lampe, G.W.H., ed. **Patristic Greek Lexicon.** Oxford: Clarendon Press, 1961. 1,568pp. ISBN 0–19–864213–X. LCCN 77–372171.

The *Patristic Greek Lexicon* serves as a companion volume to the ninth edition of Liddell-Scott-Jones (enty 511), which excluded all post-biblical Christian writers. It covers Christian authors from Clement of Rome (first century A.D.) to Theodore of Studium (d. A.D. 826). The focus of the lexicon is on theological and ecclesiastical vocabulary. Words found in *LSJ* are not generally repeated unless they are of particular interest to the reader of the Fathers of the Church. Nor are common meanings of words covered by *LSJ* repeated, so that a Greek word may be listed with a single uncommon meaning, although its usual meanings also appear in patristic literature. Since the scope of the dictionary is restricted to patristic usage, it also does not cover the usage of the Septuagint or New Testament. Lampe covers many Greek words not found in other dictionaries and is of use to the general student of later Greek as well as to patristic scholars.

510.   Lewis, Charlton T., and Charles Short. **Latin Dictionary.** Founded on Andrew's edition of Freund's *Latin Dictionary,* revised, enlarged, and in great part rewritten. Oxford: Clarendon Press, 1879. 2,019pp. ISBN 0–19–864201–6.

This work, popularly called Lewis and Short, has a long history. It is based on E.A. Andrews's 1850 translation of Wilhelm Freund's *Wörterbuch der lateinischen Sprache* (Leipzig: Hahn, 1834–1840). Freund's own work was, in turn, based largely on Forcellini. Lewis and Short extensively reworked the earlier dictionary. Their dictionary, which has been reprinted frequently, remained the standard Latin-English dictionary until the completion of the *Oxford Latin Dictionary* (entry 508) in 1982. Lewis and Short cover the entire classical period, from the beginnings of Latin literature to the fourth century A.D. The dictionary is based on antiquated principles and obsolete editions; it also contains many errors. In general, the *Oxford Latin Dictionary* should be preferred to Lewis and Short. However, Lewis and Short is widely available and remains a serviceable dictionary, if used with some care. It is also available on the Web through *Perseus* (entry 137) at www.perseus.tufts.edu/cgi-bin/ptext?doc = Perseus%3Atext%3A1999.04.0059.

511.   Liddell, Henry George, and Robert Scott. **Greek-English Lexicon.** 9th ed. Revised and augmented throughout by Sir Henry Stuart Jones, with the assistance of Roderick McKenzie and with the cooperation of many scholars. With a supplement. Oxford: Clarendon Press, 1996. 2,042, 320pp. ISBN 0–19–864214–8. LCCN 71–2271.

512.   Liddell, Henry George, and Robert Scott. **Lexicon Abridged from Liddell and Scott's Greek-English Lexicon.** Oxford: Clarendon Press, 1871. 804pp. ISBN 0–19–910207–4.

513.   Liddell, Henry George, and Robert Scott. **Intermediate Greek-English Lexicon.** Founded upon the 7th edition of Liddell and Scott's *Greek-English Lexicon.* Oxford: Clarendon Press, 1889. 910pp. ISBN 0–19–910206–6.

This dictionary, which is commonly referred to as *LSJ,* is the standard Greek-English lexicon. The most recent edition is the ninth (1940). Printings from 1968 onward include a supplement edited by E.A. Barber and others, which was also published separately. The 1996 reprinting contains a revised and greatly enlarged supplement. The lexicon covers the Greek language from Homer to approximately A.D. 600. It addresses itself primarily to meanings of words; discussion of etymology is largely omitted. The editors have supplied many citations and examples in the entries. Their coverage of the classical authors is quite strong. While *LSJ* does include many words and citations from epigraphical and papyrological texts (especially in the supplement), those with interests in these areas will need the assistance of more specialized works. Mycenaean Greek (i.e., linear B texts) is not covered at all and also requires consultation of specialized publications. *LSJ* is also available in the two frequently reprinted abridged versions intended for students. These are both based on earlier editions of the larger work. While these smaller works are suitable for everyday use, those requiring the fullest and most accurate information should consult the large ninth edition.

514.   Lust, J., E. Eynikel, and K. Hauspie. **Greek-English Lexicon of the Septuagint.** Stuttgart: Deutsche Bibelgesellschaft, 1992–1996. 2v. ISBN 3–438–05125–7 (v. 1); 3–438–05126–7 (v. 2).

This lexicon of the Septuagint, the first in well over a century, is designed to accompany the edition of A. Rahlfs (Stuttgart: Würtemburgische Bibelanstatt, 1935). The editors provide citations from the Septuagint and translations for each word. They also often include the Hebrew, when it helps clarify the intended meaning of the Greek. Many entries include references to relevant secondary works. While many of the other lexica listed in this chapter can help in reading the Septuagint, given the many peculiarities of its Greek, a specialized work such as this is the best choice.

515.   Smith, William and Theophilus D. Hall. **Copious and Critical English-Latin Dictionary.** To which is added a dictionary of proper names. New York: American Book, 1871; repr., Nashville, TN: Wimbledon, 2000. 964, 709–754pp.

516.   Smith, William. **Smaller English-Latin Dictionary.** London: John Murray, 1870. 719pp.

This frequently reprinted work is the most complete English-Latin dictionary available. Its original audience (which, to a large extent, no longer exists) consisted of students of Latin prose composition. Entries generally cite authorities and often provide examples of usage. A dictionary of proper names, which gives the correct Latin forms of these, is appended. There is also an abridged version, which will serve the needs of most students.

517.   Sophocles, E.A. **Greek Lexicon of the Roman and Byzantine Periods (from B.C. 146 to A.D. 1100).** Memorial edition. Cambridge, MA: Harvard University Press, 1914; repr., Hildesheim: Georg Olms, 1992. 1,188pp.

Sophocles first published his lexicon in 1870. Subsequent editions include a few corrections, but no additions or revisions of any substance. It remains the only Greek-English lexicon for the Byzantine period; as such it is a useful supplement to Liddell-Scott-Jones (entry 511) and Lampe (entry 509). It is also sometimes helpful for Greek authors who flourished under the Roman Empire, although these are, for the most part, covered by *LSJ.* A new Byzantine Greek lexicon remains a desideratum.

518.   Souter, Alexander. **Glossary of Later Latin to 600 A.D.** Oxford: Clarendon Press, 1949. 459pp. LCCN 50–7994.

Souter, one of the editors of the *Oxford Latin Dictionary,* compiled this glossary to cover the gap between the *OLD*'s coverage and the beginning of the medieval period. "The glossary is intended to include all known 'common' words that, according to the witness of surviving writings and documents, do not occur in the period before A.D. 180 and yet may be certainly or reasonably assigned to a date earlier than A.D. 600." Souter's work is truly a glossary rather than a dictionary. He gives only the basic form of the word and its definition and does not discuss forms or quote examples. Citations of specific works are given only for those words for which Souter found no more than three or four occurrences. This is a handy tool for those working in late Latin and the Church Fathers.

519.   **Thesaurus Linguae Graecae.** Irvine: Thesaurus Linguae Graecae Project, University of California, Irvine, 1985– .

The *Thesaurus Linguae Graecae* (*TLG*) is a computerized database of ancient Greek literature. It now contains virtually all extant Greek literary texts from Homer (eighth century B.C.) to A.D. 600, and the texts of many Byzantine historiographical, lexicographical, and scholiastic writers as well. Documentary texts, such as most inscriptions and papyri, are not included in the database; these are included in other databases, such as those produced by the Packard Humanities Institute (see entries 581–582) and the *Duke Databank of Documentary Papyri* (entry 976). At the present time, *TLG* functions strictly as a gigantic concordance to Greek literature. Through it one can find all occurrences of a particular word, form of a word, or phrase. However, definitions and other lexicographical information are not provided. *TLG* is available for lease both as a CD-ROM and (since 2001) on the Web. The most recent disk, *TLG-E*, was released in 2000 and will not be updated (all future updates will be on the Web only). *TLG* does not supply search software for CD-ROMs, although the Web version includes a search engine. Several third-party vendors offer software to run *TLG* on DOS and Macintosh computers. The *Thesaurus Linguae Graecae Canon of Greek Authors and Works* (entry 544) lists all authors and works included in the database; it also specifies which editions were used. The most recent information on *TLG* can be found at www.tlg.uci.edu.

520.   Thesaurus Linguae Latinae. Editus auctoritate et consilio Academiarum Quinque Germanicarum Berolinensis, Gottingensis, Lipsiensis, Monacensis, Vindobonensis. Lipsiae: Teubner, 1900– . LCCN 77–11275.

This project began in 1893, at the instigation of Theodor Mommsen. The first fascicle of *TLL* appeared in 1900; subsequent fascicles have been appeared at irregular intervals. The volumes for A through O are now complete, and parts of P have appeared as well. Several supplementary volumes covering proper names have also been published. Work continues on the remaining fascicles at the *TLL* offices in Munich. The *Thesaurus* is intended to cover Latin in full from the beginnings to the Antonine age, with selective coverage extending up to the seventh century A.D. Individual scholars prepare the entry for each word; all articles are signed. Entries discuss forms, gender, and, when appropriate, vowel quantities. They then give the full history of the word. The treatment is exhaustive; each entry includes a massive number of examples and citations. The *TLL* is the best and fullest source available for the study of Latin lexicography. The latest information on the *TLL* can be found on its Web site: www.thesaurus.badw.de. For the parts of the alphabet not yet covered by the *Thesaurus* one must rely the *Oxford Latin Dictionary* (entry 508) supplemented by Forcellini (entry 506). The Packard Humanities Institute CD-ROMs (entries 581–582) are also useful for locating occurrences of particular Latin words.

521.   Walde, A. Lateinisches Etymologisches Wörterbuch. Indogermanische Bibliothek. 4. Aufl. von J. B. Hofmann. Heidelberg: Carl Winter Universitätsverlag, 1965. 3v. LCCN 68–83380.

This edition is essentially a reproduction of the third edition (1938–1956). It is the German counterpart of Ernout-Meillet (entry 504); since both works have gone through a number of editions, they cite each other frequently. Walde-Hofmann generally offers a much more detailed treatment, with longer entries and more citations of texts and secondary literature. Occasionally, Ernout-Meillet offers fuller treatment of a particular word. Walde-Hofmann tends to offer more hard-core Indo-European etymology and pays less attention to the history of words within the Latin language. Although a denser, less readable work, Walde-Hofmann is a valuable and informative dictionary. Those who are concerned with the Latin language proper rather than Indo-European linguistics will prefer Ernout-Meillet in most instances. The third volume of Walde-Hofmann consists of extensive indexes of non-Latin words grouped by language family and language.

522. Woodhouse, S. C. **English-Greek Dictionary: A Vocabulary of the Attic Language.** 2nd impression with a supplement. London: Routledge & Kegan Paul, 1932. 1,029pp. LCCN 39–8394.

Woodhouse compiled his dictionary as an aid to writers of Greek prose compositions in schools and universities. Although this use is now rare, the work is still useful for those seeking the Greek equivalent for an English expression. The supplement noted in the edition statement is a list of proper names, many of them famous Romans of antiquity, which provides the correct Greek equivalent. Woodhouse has been reprinted a number of times and is both more readily available and more up-to-date than Yonge's slightly larger dictionary (entry 523).

523. Yonge, C. D. **English-Greek Lexicon: With Many New Articles, an Appendix of Proper Names, and Pillon's Greek Synonyms.** Ed. Henry Drisler. New York: American Book, 1870. 663, 115pp.

Yonge's lexicon, which first appeared in 1849, was aimed at the student writer of Greek prose and verse. It is based strictly on classical authors, chiefly those of the fifth and fourth centuries B.C. His goal was to provide "a complete English vocabulary, so far, at least, as there are words in the Greek language by which the English words can be literally or adequately rendered, and where this cannot be done, to supply, wherever practicable, the deficiency by phrases." Yonge's *Lexicon,* with its small type and densely packed columns, is actually a bit larger than Woodhouse's *Dictionary* (entry 522). It is, however, based on older scholarship and is less readily available. Yonge exists in a number of nineteenth-century editions and reprints; there are relatively few differences among them.

DICTIONARIES OF PERSONAL NAMES

524. Fraser, P. M., and E. Matthews, eds. **Lexicon of Greek Personal Names.** Oxford: Clarendon Press, 1987– . LCCN 87–12344. Details for individual volumes:

V. 1. **Aegean Islands, Cyprus, and Cyrenaica.** 1988. 528pp. ISBN 0–19–864222–9

V. 2. **Attica.** 1994. 536pp. ISBN 0–19–814990–5.

V. 3A. **Peloponnese, Western Greece, Sicily, and Magna Graecia.** 1998. 552pp. ISBN 0–19–815229–9.

V. 3B. **Central Greece from the Megarid to Thessaly.** 2001. 504pp. ISBN 0–19–815293–0.

V. 4. **Macedonia, Thrace, and the Northern Regions of the Black Sea.** 2005. 450pp. ISBN 0–19–927333–2.

Intended as a replacement for the nineteenth-century compilation of Wilhelm Pape (entry 525), this work is being produced by an international team of scholars under the sponsorship of the British Academy. When completed, it will include all attested Greek personal names, with the exception of most names from mythology and Greek epic poetry. Most, though not all, foreign names in Greek are also excluded; a supplementary work by

M. J. Osborne and Sean G. Byrne, *Foreign Residents of Athens: An Annex to the Lexicon of Greek Personal Names* (Leuven: Peeters, 1996), covers these for Athens. The overall arrangement of the lexicon is geographical; each volume is devoted to a particular region of the Greek world. Within each volume, entries are arranged alphabetically. The same names will often be found in more than one volume. Entries cite the ancient attestations and give approximate dates for each occurrence. Further information about the project and an online index to the published volumes may be found at www.lgpn.ox.ac.uk. Since this work is highly technical and presents the names in Greek characters, it is chiefly of use to graduate students and professional scholars.

525.   Pape, W. **Wörterbuch der griechischen Eigennamen.** Handwörterbuch der griechischen Sprache 3. Aufl. Neu bearb. von Gustav Eduard Benseler. Braunschweig: Friedrich Vieweg, 1863–1870; repr., Graz: Akademische Druck- u. Verlagsanstalt, 1959. 2v. LCCN 61–33368.

Often referred to as Pape-Benseler, this work is a dictionary of Greek proper names. It is compiled chiefly from literary sources, unlike the Oxford *Lexicon of Greek Personal Names* (entry 524), which emphasizes documentary sources over literary ones. Pape-Benseler also includes geographical names. Each entry includes the name and citations of occurrences. Although dated, Pape-Benseler remains useful and will not be entirely superseded even when the Oxford *Lexicon* is completed.

GRAMMARS

526.   Allen, Joseph H., and J. B. Greenough. **Allen and Greenough's New Latin Grammar for Schools and Colleges: Founded on Comparative Grammar.** Ed. J. B. Greenough, G. L. Kittredge, A. A. Howard, and Benj. L. D'Ooge. Boston: Ginn, 1903; repr., Newburypoint, MA: Focus, 2001. 490pp. LCCN 03–23416.

The original edition of this old standby appeared in 1872. It reached its final form in the 1903 revision and has since been reprinted regularly. Allen and Greenough remains a quite reliable descriptive grammar of Latin, possibly the best available in English. It covers the morphology, syntax, and prosody of Latin more than adequately, although it lacks the massive thoroughness of Kühner-Stegmann (entry 534). Its manner of presentation is clearer and less quirky than that of Hale and Buck (entry 531). A detailed table of contents and ample word and subject indexes make the book easy to consult. A Web version (from the 1903 edition) is now available through *Perseus* (entry 137) at www.perseus.tufts.edu/cgi-bin/ ptext?doc = Perseus%3Atext%3A1999.04.0001. The most recent reprinting (Newburyport, MA: Focus, 2001) includes new material on Latin meter by Anne Mahoney.

527.   Blass, F., and A. Debrunner. **Greek Grammar of the New Testament and other Early Christian Literature.** A translation and revision of the 9th–10th German edition incorporating supplementary notes of A. Debrunner by Robert Funk. Chicago: University of Chicago Press, 1961. 325pp. ISBN 0–226–27110–2. LCCN 61–8077.

Blass-Debrunner-Funk, as it is frequently called, is the standard grammar of New Testament Greek and serves as a companion volume to Bauer-Danker-Arndt-Gingrich, *A Greek English Lexicon of the New Testament* (entry 501). Blass's *Grammatik des neutestamentlichen Griechisch* first appeared in 1896 and has been frequently revised (from 1913 to 1954 by Albert Debrunner, currently by Friedrich Rehkopf). The English edition also includes new material added by Funk. Blass-Debrunner-Funk does not treat the New Testament in isolation; it also covers a wide range of Hellenistic Greek writings, including the Septuagint, early Christian authors, papyri, and some Byzantine authors. The work deals with all standard aspects of grammar: phonology, accidence and word formation, and syntax. The grammar includes many illustrative examples from Greek texts and frequently cites pertinent scholarly literature. It is a valuable tool for the study of Hellenistic Greek. There are indexes of subjects, Greek words and forms, and passages cited. The sixteenth German edition of the grammar revised by Rehkopf (Göttingen: Vandenhoeck & Ruprecht, 1984) contains much new material; those who read German should consult it in preference to the English edition.

528. Buck, Carl Darling. **Comparative Grammar of Greek and Latin.** Chicago: University of Chicago Press, 1933. 405pp. LCCN 33–11254.

Although there is no compelling linguistic reason for the comparative study of Greek and Latin, the subject has become a traditional one because of the cultural affinities of the Greeks and Romans. Buck has long been the standard comparative grammar for Greek and Latin. Buck's introduction covers the Indo-European languages and various features of linguistic history in general and provides outline histories of Greek and Latin languages. The major sections of the grammar proper cover phonology, inflection, and word formation. Syntax was deliberately omitted. There is still much useful information in Buck, although the book is now badly dated and should be used with caution. Andrew Sihler's recent *New Comparative Grammar of Greek and Latin* (entry 540) replaces Buck as the standard work on this topic.

529. Goodwin, William Watson. **Greek Grammar.** Rev. Charles Burton Gulick. Boston: Ginn, 1930; repr., New Rochelle, NY: Caratzas, 1992. 457pp. LCCN 30–21632.

Goodwin's *Greek Grammar* has been a standby of students since the nineteenth century. It was last revised by Gulick in 1930; this revision is often called Goodwin and Gulick. It covers the usual departments of phonology, morphology (inflection), word formation, syntax, and versification. Goodwin's explication is clear and concise, although with much less linguistic background than Smyth (entry 541). Goodwin is particularly strong in its treatment of verbs, particularly moods and tenses, upon which Goodwin was a notable expert. He includes a catalog of "all verbs in ordinary use in classic Greek which have any such peculiarities as to present difficulties to a student." Entries in it often give principal parts, note oddities, and supply references to all relevant passages in the *Grammar.*

530. Goodwin, William Watson. **Syntax of the Moods and Tenses of the Greek Verb.** Rewritten and enlarged. Boston: Ginn, 1890; repr., New York: St. Martin's, 1965. 464pp.

First published in 1860, Goodwin revised this classic work a number of times. The 1890 edition, frequently reprinted, represents his final version. In spite of its age, Goodwin's work remains the most comprehensive and reliable handbook in English on Greek verbs. He covers moods, tenses, various particles used with verbs, the use of moods in both independent and subordinate clauses, infinitives, and participles. His detailed discussion of such topics as conditional sentences and indirect discourse goes far beyond that found in the standard grammars. In addition to lucid discussion of sometimes murky topics, Goodwin supplies numerous examples from Greek literature for virtually every construction. The work is also available on the Web through *Perseus* (entry 137) at www. perseus.tufts.edu/cgi-bin/ptext?doc = Perseus%3Atext%3A1999.04.0065.

531.   Hale, William Gardner, and Carl Darling Buck. **Latin Grammar.** Boston: Ginn, 1903; repr., University: University of Alabama Press, 1966. 388pp. LCCN 03–17596.

Hale and Buck is a reliable and readily available descriptive grammar of Latin. It is considerably less detailed than Kühner-Stegmann's large work (entry 534) but will generally serve the needs of English-speaking students. Hale and Buck occasionally arrange or present their material in an unusual manner, so that many prefer their chief English-language competitor, *Allen and Greenough's New Latin Grammar* (entry 526). Allen and Greenough also has superior indexing.

532.   Kühner, Raphael, Friedrich Blass, and Bernhard Gerth. **Ausführliche Grammatik der griechischen Sprache.** 3. Aufl. Hannover: Hahnsche Buchhandlung, 1890–1904. 4v. LCCN 01–2623.

533.   Calder, William M., III. **Index Locorum zu Kühner-Gerth.** Darmstadt: Wissenschaftliche Buchgesellschaft, 1965. 164pp. LCCN 67–74716.

Kühner's nineteenth-century work remains the fundamental descriptive grammar of Greek. The first part (in two volumes) covers phonology and morphology. This was revised by Friedrich Blass and is usually referred to as Kühner-Blass. This part, while still useful, is somewhat dated; Schwyzer (entry 539) is generally superior for such information. The second part (also in two volumes) deals with syntax. It is routinely called Kühner-Gerth, since it was revised by Bernhard Gerth. This is a sound and detailed treatment of Greek syntax, which is still frequently cited. Both parts of the grammar have very full indexes to subjects and Greek words. While they do not include indexes to Greek and Latin passages cited, an *index locorum* to Kühner-Gerth has been published by W. M. Calder. There have been several reprintings of Kühner's Greek grammar, some of which advertise themselves as a fourth edition. These are, however, merely reprints and not a new edition. A Web version is also available through *Perseus* (entry 137). There is no work of comparable scope in English; those who read only English will have to make do with Smyth's much smaller *Greek Grammar* (entry 541).

534.   Kühner, Raphael, Friedrich Holzweissig, and Carl Stegmann. **Ausführliche Grammatik der lateinischen Sprache.** 2. Aufl. (T. 1) and 5. Aufl. (T. 2). Hannover: Hahnsche Buchhandlung, 1976–1982. 2v. in 3. ISBN 3–7752–5189–8 (T. 1); 3–7752–5284–3 (T. 2, Bd. 1); 3–7752–5284–3 (T. 2, Bd. 2).

535.   Schwartz, Gary S., and Richard L. Wertis. **Index Locorum zu Kühner-Stegmann "Satzlehre."** Darmstadt: Wissenchaftliche Buchgesellschaft, 1980. 254pp. ISBN 3–5340–4341–3. LCCN 86–672472.

Like his companion work on Greek grammar (entry 532), Kühner's massive nineteenth-century Latin grammar remains a standard work. The first volume, which covers phonology and morphology, was revised by Holzweissig in 1912. Holzweissig's revision was never very satisfactory and has largely fallen into disuse. The second volume, as revised by Carl Stegmann, is a different matter. Kühner-Stegmann covers Latin syntax in great detail and offers a vast array of examples drawn from the ancient authors. It has been revised several times since Stegmann's original reworking in 1914. Kühner-Stegmann is the best descriptive Latin grammar available. A separately published index to Latin and Greek authors cited in Kühner-Stegmann now makes up one of the few deficiencies of this important work. For comparative and historical grammar one should consult Leumann-Hofmann-Szantyr (entry 536). There is no satisfactory English equivalent; the school grammars of Allen and Greenough (entry 526) and of Hale and Buck (entry 531) are serviceable but offer far less.

536. Leumann, Manu, J.B. Hofmann, and Anton Szantyr. **Lateinische Grammmatik.** Handbuch der Altertumswissenschaft, Abt. 2, 2. München: C.H. Beck, 1972–1979. 3v. ISBN 3–406–01426–7 (v. 1); 3–406–01347–3 (v. 2); 3–406–06072–2 (v. 3). LCCN 72–374136.

This is the best available comprehensive Latin grammar. While Kühner-Stegmann (entry 534) remains the better descriptive grammar, Leumann-Hofmann-Szantyr is the standard reference work for all other aspects of Latin grammar, especially comparative and historical grammar. The first volume covers phonology and morphology; it is much superior to the corresponding volume of Kühner. The second volume, which is the work of Anton Szantyr, offers a valuable treatment of syntax and stylistics. Appended to this is a brief history of the Latin language and a general introduction to the grammar as a whole. Indexes of subjects and words appear at the end of each volume. Fritz Radt and Abel Westerbrink compiled the *index locorum* and the index of non-Latin words, which comprise the third volume.

537. Morwood, James. **Latin Grammar.** Oxford: Oxford University Press, 1999. 194pp. ISBN 0–19–860277–4.

Morwood designed this relatively abbreviated grammar for the needs of students. It covers the essentials of phonology, morphology, and syntax but lacks the detail of such larger works as Allen and Greenough (entry 526). It is, however, easy to navigate and more comprehensible to contemporary students. Morwood provides a handy glossary of grammatical terms at the beginning; the appendixes cover Roman dates, money, weights and measures, names, and literary terms. He also supplies a Latin-English vocabulary. Morwood's *Latin Grammar* is an excellent basic reference, although the more advanced will need to refer to more extensive works.

538. Morwood, James. **Oxford Grammar of Classical Greek.** Oxford: Oxford University Press, 2001. 270pp. ISBN0–19–521851–5. LCCN 2001–275344.

As with his *Latin Grammar,* Morwood intends this work for students. It is compact and focuses on Attic Greek (ca. 500–300 B.C.), although some basic information about Homeric, Ionic, and New Testament Greek may be found in the appendixes. Morwood provides the essentials in a style suited for beginning students; this grammar is much less detailed than Goodwin (entry 529) or Smyth (entry 541). He supplies a glossary of grammatical terms, and his appendixes also cover accents, the dual, and common literary terms. A Greek-English vocabulary, an unusual feature in such grammars, makes this a more self-contained work for beginners. There are indexes of Greek works and of subjects. Overall, this is an excellent reference for students; the more advanced should use Smyth.

539. Schwyzer, Eduard. **Griechische Grammatik: Auf der Grundlage von Karl Brugmanns Griechischer Grammatik.** Handbuch der Altertumswissenschaft, Abt. 2, 1. München: C. H. Beck, 1966–1971. 4v. ISBN 3–406–01339–2 (v. 1); 3–406–01341–4 (v. 2); 3–406–01343–0 (v. 3); 3–406–03397–0 (v. 4).

Along with Kühner-Blass (entry 532), this is one of the two standard reference grammars for ancient Greek. The first volume, now in its fourth edition, covers phonology, word formation, and morphology. It is far better than the corresponding volume of Kühner. This is also the only part that Schwyzer himself completed before his death in 1943. Albert Debrunner is responsible for the second volume, which deals with syntax and stylistics. It offers extensive illustrative examples from Greek literature and a generous array of citations from the secondary literature. However, Kühner-Gerth is often more helpful for purely descriptive grammar. The remaining two volumes consist of indexes. The third contains the word indexes, which were compiled by Demetrius J. Georgacas. The final volume is an *index locorum* by Fritz and Stephen Radt. Both index volumes include corrections and additions to the grammar.

540. Sihler, Andrew L. **New Comparative Grammar of Greek and Latin.** New York: Oxford University Press, 1995. 686pp. ISBN 0–19–508345–6. LCCN 93–38929.

Originally begun as a revision of Buck's *Comparative Grammar of Greek and Latin* (entry 528), Sihler's grammar ended as an entirely new work. It is nearly twice as long as Buck and includes the results of much new work in the field. Sihler's introduction provides a brief overview of the Indo-European family of languages and of the history of the Greek and Latin languages. The various parts of the book then cover phonology, declension, pronouns, numerals, and conjugation. To make room for new material, Sihler omitted several topics covered by Buck, such as the fundamentals of historical linguistics and word formation. Like Buck, Sihler also does not cover syntax. This valuable book supersedes Buck as the standard work in the field.

541. Smyth, Herbert Weir. **Greek Grammar.** Rev. Gordon M. Messing. Cambridge, MA: Harvard University Press, 1956. 784pp. ISBN 0–674–36250–0. LCCN 57–2203.

542. Schumann, Walter A. **Index of Passages Cited in Herbert Weir Smyth, Greek Grammar.** Scholarly Aids 1. Cambridge, MA: Greek, Roman, and Byzantine Studies, 1961. 28pp.

Originally published as *A Greek Grammar for Colleges,* this work has been for over 70 years the standard reference grammar of ancient Greek for English-speaking students. In the 1956 edition Messing has revised the historical and comparative sections to reflect more recent linguistic scholarship. Otherwise, the work remains much as when it first appeared. It is, for the most part, a descriptive grammar. Smyth provides a clear guide to the complexities of Greek morphology and syntax. This venerable work serves well the needs of students; scholars will need to supplement it with the larger German grammars of Kühner-Blass (entry 532) and Schwyzer (entry 539). Smyth includes English and Greek indexes; Walter Schumann published a separate *index locorum.*

543.   Woodcock, E. C. **New Latin Syntax.** Cambridge, MA: Harvard University Press, 1959; repr., Chicago: Bolchazy-Carducci, 1985. 267pp. LCCN 60–1729.

The classic English-language work on Latin syntax, Woodcock goes well beyond most grammars in detail. He presents syntax historically, from Plautus and Terence through Tacitus. His explanations of constructions are clear, and he provides many examples from classical texts. The very detailed table of contents, along with indexes covering subjects, Latin words, and passages discussed, makes it easy to find the needed section.

13
Greek and Latin Literature: General Works

This chapter includes works covering Greek and Latin literature, together or separately, from a broad perspective. A few more-specialized works, such as those on metrics, that do not fit conveniently elsewhere also appear below. Under each category, works are subdivided into bibliographies, literary histories, and handbooks/dictionaries. Bibliographies of translations of the classics, as well as bibliographies of secondary works appear below. A generous selection of older literary histories will be found, in addition to more current works. As a rule, the older works tend to focus more on biographical, historical, and bibliographical aspects, while more recent works often focus more on literary criticism or approach the literatures from various theoretical standpoints. For works on literary genres, see chapter 14; for individual authors, see chapters 15–16. Relevant titles also appear in chapter 7, "Biographical Works."

GREEK AND LATIN LITERATURE

BIBLIOGRAPHIES

544.   Berkowitz, Luci, and Karl A. Squittier. **Thesaurus Linguae Graecae Canon of Greek Authors and Works.** 3rd ed. New York: Oxford University Press, 1990. 471pp. ISBN 0–19–506037–7. LCCN 89–49454.

Originally designed as a working tool for the *TLG* project (see entry 519), the *Canon* has now grown to be an extremely useful bibliographical reference source. It lists the source editions for each Greek author and work included in the *TLG* database. The *Canon* now covers more than 3,000 Greek authors and over 9,000 individual works. It includes virtually all extant Greek authors and texts from Homer to A.D. 600 and a considerable number of later Byzantine works as well. Entries are arranged alphabetically by author (or title for anonymous works). The *TLG* number, and century and place of origin, if known, is provided for each author. Individual works are then listed along with the selected edition for each. In most cases, the best available critical edition is cited. The *Canon,* which is indispensable to users of the *TLG* database, is also of great value to anyone seeking editions of particular Greek authors and works. A list of addenda and corrigenda to the printed addition, along with an updated, searchable electronic version, can be found at www.tlg.uci.edu.

545.   Cuypers, Martin. **Hellenistic Bibliography.** URL: www.gltc.leidenuniv.nl/index. php3?m = 57&c = 86.

This Web-based bibliography covers Hellenistic Greek poetry and its influence (including many works on Latin poetry). As of late 2004, the bibliographies include over 14,000 citations, most from 2000 or later. A few of the component bibliographies, such as Apollonius Rhodius, include significant retrospective coverage. Arrangement is by author, followed by a few topical bibliographies. There are also comprehensive listings by year for 2000–2004 (alphabetical by author within each year). The bibliographies are updated on a regular basis. *A Hellenistic Bibliography* is a good source for recent work in this area.

546. Gwinup, Thomas, and Fidelia Dickinson. **Greek and Roman Authors: A Checklist of Criticism.** 2nd ed. Metuchen, NJ: Scarecrow Press, 1982. 280pp. ISBN 0–8108–1528–1. LCCN 82–690.

"The purpose of this bibliography is to provide a comprehensive list of recent criticism of the authors of *belles-lettres* of ancient Greece and Rome." It is aimed at students in comparative and world literature and general humanities courses. The compilers include only items in English and claim to place emphasis on newer works. Nearly 4,000 works are listed on authors ranging from Homer to St. Augustine. The bibliography begins with a list of general works covering Greek and Roman literary history, criticism, history, and art history. This somewhat strange list includes many first-rate titles intermingled with outdated items and a number of rather technical works unlikely to be of use to the intended audience. For example, students who read only English are rarely interested in metrical analyses of Greek tragic choruses. Many old works are cited in reprint editions without any indication of their true dates. The second section, which covers individual classical authors in alphabetical sequence, is little better. It mingles the excellent, the good, the mediocre, and the highly technical without discrimination; no annotations are provided to guide the unwary. There are no indexes. While students can find much of use here, they will also find much that is ill suited to their needs. The compilers display confusion and a lack of judgment.

547. Pöschl, Viktor, Helga Gärtner, and Waltrout Heyke. **Bibliographie zur Antiken Bilderspache.** Bibliothek der klassischen Altertumswissenschaften. Heidelberg: Carl Winter Universitätsverlag, 1964. 674pp. LCCN 66–55568.

Pöschl and his assistants have compiled a somewhat unusual bibliography dealing with studies of metaphorical language in classical literature. The bibliography comprises two parts. The general section, *Allgemeine Literatur,* is arranged by topic (e.g., linguistics, mythology, literary history). The second part covers works on individual Greek and Latin authors and is arranged alphabetically by ancient author. Entries occasionally include a brief annotation, usually to clarify the content or to indicate what metaphor is discussed. A very detailed index of metaphors follows, so that one can find discussions of a particular metaphor in ancient literature. There is also an index of modern authors.

LITERARY HISTORIES

548. Dihle, Albrecht. **Greek and Latin Literature of the Roman Empire: From Augustus to Justinian.** Trans. Manfred Malzahn. London: Routledge, 1994. 647pp. ISBN 0–415–06367–1. LC 93–45284.

Dihle treats both Latin and Greek literature in this sequel to his earlier history of Greek literature (entry 563). His temporal limits extend from the late first century B.C. to the early sixth century A.D. Dihle's chapters are based on historical periods: the Julio-Claudian era, the Flavian era, the second century, the Severan era, the third century, the era of Diocletian and Constantine, and the Christian empire. Each contains a number of sections, which cover genres or major authors. Dihle's work has many virtues. It offers much more extensive coverage of late antique authors than do Lesky (entry 566) and the two volumes of the *Cambridge History of Classical Literature* (entries 564 and 593). Lesser-known authors receive considerable attention. The book is also very readable; Dihle writes effectively for the general reader and the student. While the focus is on the actual literary works, Dihle provides ample historical and biographical background. His bibliography, which is keyed to chapters and pages, is very brief but usually provides adequate starting points for further research. A general index concludes the volume.

549. Rutherford, Richard. **Classical Literature: A Concise History.** Blackwell Introductions to the Classical World. Malden, MA: Blackwell, 2005. 350pp. ISBN: 0–631–23132–3; 0–631–233–1. LCCN 2003–024528.

Rutherford covers both Greek and Latin literature from Homer to St. Augustine (roughly from 750 B.C. to A.D. 400). He intends his work for the general reader but provides sufficient notes and references to serve both undergraduate and graduate students. Arrangement is by genre rather than chronological order. Chapters cover epic; drama; rhetoric; history, biography, and fiction; erotic literature; literature and power; aspects of wit; thinkers; and believers. The focus is on literature as such, so Plato receives considerable coverage, while Aristotle is scanted. Some chapters, such as that on literature and power, view works thematically rather than by genre. In most chapters, Rutherford provides an overview of the genre and then discusses major works. He provides some biographical and historical information but focuses on the works as literature. Rutherford does include a fair amount of direct quotation from the works discussed. Appendixes provide a time line, a list of Roman emperors, and a list of the major Greek and Roman gods (although only a bare list). The notes and "Further Reading" are highly selective but will give the reader good leads to explore. Rutherford provides a readable and up-to-date overview, well suited to the needs of nonclassicists. Those who want detailed treatment should turn to the more comprehensive works of Easterling and Knox (entry 564), Lesky (entry 566), Dihle (entries 563 and 548), and Schmid-Stählin (entry 571) for Greek literature, and Kenney and Clausen (entry 593), Conte (entry 586), and Schanz-Hosius (entry 595) for Latin literature.

DICTIONARIES, ENCYCLOPEDIAS, AND HANDBOOKS

550. Feder, Lillian. **Crowell's Handbook of Classical Literature.** New York: Crowell, 1964. 448pp. LCCN 64–18162. Reprinted as **Meridian Handbook of Classical Literature,** New York: New American Library, 1986.

Designed as a guide for students and general readers interested in classical literature and its influence, this handbook summarizes many of the best-known classical writings and provides useful background information. Feder supplies entries for authors (chiefly biographical), works (summaries and criticism), places, and historical and mythical figures. Except for those that summarize major works (e.g., *The Odyssey*), entries tend to be brief; emphasis is on the factual and descriptive. They are all gathered in a single alphabetical sequence. Although there is no index, there are numerous cross-references. Feder is generally a reliable guide to the major authors and works but provides little coverage for minor figures. She is particularly weak for the Hellenistic period of Greek literature, Silver Latin literature, and the literature of late antiquity. Howatson (entry 552) is more current than Feder and also supplies much more of the historical and cultural background material required for a proper understanding of classical literature.

551. Halporn, James W., Martin Ostwald, and Thomas G. Rosenmeyer. **Meters of Greek and Latin Poetry.** Rev. ed. Norman: University of Oklahoma Press, 1980; repr., Indianapolis: Hackett, 1994. 137pp. ISBN 0–8061–1558–0. LCCN 79–6718.

Since it first appeared in 1963, this has been the standard handbook on metrics for English-speaking students of Greek and Latin poetry. The book is divided into two independent sections, one on Greek, the other on Latin meters. Material is repeated as necessary, so that those interested in only one language need refer only to that half. Each unit begins with introductory chapters that discuss the basic terms and concepts of the meters of quantitative verse. Each then proceeds through the basic meters of epic, elegiac, dramatic, and lyric poetry. The presentation is reasonably clear, with many examples given. A glossary of technical terms and a table of meters appear at the end of the volume. There are also indexes of Greek and Latin authors cited in the text. This is a good introductory work on a sometimes complex subject.

552. Howatson, M. C. **Oxford Companion to Classical Literature.** 2nd ed. Oxford: Oxford University Press, 1989. 615pp. ISBN 0–19–866121–5. LCCN 88–27330.

553. Howatson, M. C., and Ian Chilvers. **Concise Oxford Companion to Classical Literature.** Oxford: Oxford University Press, 1993. 575pp. ISBN 0–19–211687–8; 0–19–282708–1pa. LCCN 92–018585.

Sir Paul Harvey's original *Companion,* which appeared in 1937, enjoyed a long life as a standard reference in the field. It has now been replaced by Howatson's revision, which takes into account both recent scholarship and changes in our approaches to the study of classical literature. The work takes the form of a dictionary. Entries, which vary in length from a single line to several columns, cover persons (both authors and historical figures), literary and mythological characters, individual literary works (background material and summaries), and a wide range of topics. While the focus always remains on literature, the *Companion* contains much general information on the ancient world. Its articles are clearly written and provide ample information to assist students and readers in gaining a basic understanding of works of classical literature. A chronological table of historical and literary events and a number of maps appear at the end of the work. Howatson has provided cross-references, but not an index. Bibliographical references are also lacking. The abridged version contains about one-third less material than the full edition. This was achieved largely by reducing in length or dropping the long general entries of a historical nature.

Howatson is the best of the general literary handbooks. Feder (entry 550) is adequate but consists mainly of author biographies and plot summaries. She provides much less on the general cultural background than does Howatson. Lang and Dudley (entry 555) also tend to offer author biographies and summaries of literary works, along with a modicum of historical background material. Many of their articles do include bibliographical notes and suggestions for further reading.

554. Kennedy, George A., ed. **Classical Criticism.** Cambridge History of Literary Criticism 1. Cambridge: Cambridge University Press, 1989. 378pp. ISBN 0–521–30006–1. LCCN 89–901.

Kennedy has assembled several leading classicists to provide a history of classical literary criticism. The work proceeds chronologically from early Greece through the later Roman Empire; chapters include "Early Greek Views of Poetry," "Language and Meaning in Archaic and Classical Greece," "Plato and poetry," "Aristotle's *Poetics*," "The Evolution of a Theory of Artistic Prose," "Hellenistic Literary and Philosophical Scholarship," "The Growth of Literature and Criticism at Rome," "Augustan Critics," "Latin Criticism of the Early Empire," "Greek Criticism of the Empire," and "Christianity and Criticism." Each is subdivided into sections on specific topics and authors. The contributors as a whole focus on ancient criticism in its context and do not anachronistically intrude modern theory. They provide substantial bibliographies of primary texts and secondary studies. The subject index is adequate, although an *index locorum* is sorely missed.

555.   Lang, D. M., and D. R. Dudley, eds. **Penguin Companion to Classical, Oriental, and African Literature.** New York: McGraw-Hill, 1969. 359 pp. ISBN 0–07–04281–6. LCCN 78–158064.

Despite its wide-ranging title, more than half of this book is devoted to classical literature. There is a separate section for each literature (classical, Byzantine, Oriental, and African). The classical section covers Greek and Latin literature from the beginnings to the fifth century A.D.; the Byzantine section extends coverage of Greek literature through the fall of Constantinople (A.D. 1453). Dudley, a Latin scholar, edited the classical and Byzantine portions. A number of British scholars contributed entries on the classics, while the Byzantine section is largely the work of Robert Browning, a notable authority on later Greek. These articles, which are arranged alphabetically, cover authors and genres. Author entries provide basic biographical information and brief descriptions of their works. Entries for genres give their characteristics and provide a summary history of their development. Brief bibliographies accompany most entries. Although there is no index, numerous cross-references are provided. This is a good guide for those concerned primarily with literature, although it does not provide as much historical and cultural background material as Howatson (entry 552).

556.   Luce, T. James, ed. **Ancient Writers: Greece and Rome.** New York: Scribner's, 1982. 2v. ISBN 0–684–16595–3 LCCN 82–50612.

This work consists of 47 articles covering the major classical authors. Each has been written by a leading specialist. While the approach and emphasis vary, all offer biographical information, a description of the author's works, and an orientation to the major aspects of criticism and research. Bibliographies list major editions, translations, and commentaries, and the more important scholarly literature (primarily recent studies and standard works). Articles are arranged chronologically. There is an index of names and titles. This is a very good introduction to the major figures of classical literature and a convenient point of departure for more detailed study of the authors.

557.   Nickel, Rainer. **Lexikon der antiken Literatur.** Düsseldorf: Artemis & Winkler, 1999. 904pp. ISBN 3–538–07089–X. LCCN 2001–349452.

Most dictionaries of ancient literature have author-based entries. Nickel's *Lexikon* has entries alphabetically by title for about 2,300 individual works. Nickel defines literature broadly, including philosophy, scientific and technical writings, and the like. His chronological span is equally broad, extending from the earliest Greek writings through late antiquity, encompassing early Christian as well as pagan authors. The form of entry is the commonly accepted version of the original Latin or Greek title. Thus, Livy's history appears first, under *Ab urbe condita*. A few exceptions are under the German title, such as *Zauberpapyri* (Magical Papyri), a corpus of papyri by various authors. The author index will help the uncertain. Each entry provides a German translation of the title, the author (with dates), genre, and a brief characterization of the work. Many also include a discussion of the author's sources and the historical background. Each concludes with a short bibliography of editions, German translations, and key secondary works. Nickel has also supplied indexes of genres and of German titles. Handy for major works, and invaluable for the more obscure, this is an extremely useful reference work for those who read German.

558.   Schütze, Oliver, ed. **Metzler Lexikon antiker Autoren.** Stuttgart: J. B. Metzler, 1977. 791pp. ISBN 3–476–01547–5. LCCN 98–111160.

This lexicon covers Greek and Latin authors from the beginnings through the sixth century A.D., including Christian as well as pagan authors. A large number of German scholars have contributed signed articles, which are arranged alphabetically. Articles provide basic biographical information and some discussion of the works. Each ends with a brief bibliographical note citing editions and a few key secondary works. Most entries are relatively brief; those on major authors run 5 to 10 pages. An index of names concludes the volume. Schütze is valuable for the wide range of authors covered, especially minor and late authors.

559.   Sharrock, Alison, and Rhiannon Ash. **Fifty Key Classical Authors.** Routledge Key Guides. New York: Routledge, 2002. 421pp. ISBN 0–415–16510–5; 0–415–16511–3pa. LCCN 2001–48305.

This handbook for students covers 50 Greek and Latin authors from Homer through the second century A.D. Arrangement is chronological, with authors grouped by historical period. While there are surprising inclusions and omissions, Sharrock and Ash cover most authors likely to be read by undergraduates. Each essay supplies biographical and historical background, along with critical discussion of the author's works. Each is accompanied by a brief bibliography noting editions, commentaries, translations, and a selection of notable secondary works. In addition, the general introduction discusses the major series of texts and translations, as well as listing major literary histories. A detailed time line at the end of the volume correlates literary with historical and political events. Sharrock and Ash provide a competent and current guide for beginning and intermediate students.

GREEK LITERATURE

BIBLIOGRAPHIES

560.   Fantuzzi, Marco. **Letterature greca antica, bizantina e neoellenica.** Strumenti di studio: Guide bibliografiche 1. Milano: Garzanti, 1989. 471pp. ISBN 88–11–47506–6. LCCN 89–174152.

Despite the all-encompassing title, more than three-quarters of this work is devoted to ancient Greek literature. Coverage of this extends from the beginnings through the Greco-Roman era. The first chapter includes general works, periodicals, grammars and lexica, metrics, palaeography, papyrology, and mythology. Subsequent chapters cover periods and genres: archaic epic, lyric poetry (seventh through fifth centuries B.C.), archaic and classical prose and historiography, classical drama, artistic prose of the fourth century B.C., Plato and Aristotle, Hellenistic literature, and literature of the Greco-Roman era. All these are further subdivided; the table of contents lays out the entire scheme. Each section lists standard editions and translations for the author(s), along with a generous selection of the scholarly literature. Although the bibliography includes works in a variety of languages (including many items in English), it emphasizes those in Italian. For example, a number of well-known books that originally appeared in English are listed only in their Italian translations. Fantuzzi occasionally provides descriptive comments about the works cited. There is also an index of names. This bibliography is relatively current, and its use requires little knowledge of Italian. While very selective, it offers a good range of citations for most Greek authors.

561. Kessels, A.H.M., and W.J. Verdenius. **Concise Bibliography of Ancient Greek Literature.** 2nd ed., rev. and enl. Apeldoorn: Administratief Centrum, 1982. 145pp.

This bibliography is "intended to be used primarily by students and teachers of classics." Kessels and Verdenius first list bibliographical, reference, and general works. Then they cover individual authors and genres in a roughly chronological sequence. They tend to include only major authors. Often authors are treated in groups; thus all the tragedians are gathered under the heading "Tragedy." Kessels and Verdenius note editions, commentaries, indexes, and a selection of the scholarly literature (books only; no articles are included). There is a list of the major classical periodicals. The index covers mainly authors, although a few titles and subjects are found there also. This bibliography is not very detailed but will serve as an adequate general guide for students.

562. Riesenfeld, Harald, and Blenda Riesenfeld. **Repertorium Lexicographicum Graecum [Catalogue of Indexes and Dictionaries to Greek Authors].** Stockholm: Almqvist & Wiksell, 1954. 95pp. LCCN 54–5571.

In spite of the Latin title, the introduction and commentary in this book are in English. In it the Riesenfelds gather "lexicographical material bearing upon Greek literature from its beginning to the end of the Byzantine epoch." They restrict themselves to literary material; papyri, inscriptions, and ostraca are generally ignored. The Riesenfelds arrange their material alphabetically by Greek author. Their listings include indexes in editions as well as separately published indexes, concordances, and dictionaries. They are selective in the inclusion of earlier indexes, especially if a modern glossary or index is available. Coverage is strongest for classical and Hellenistic Greek authors, and weakest for the Byzantines. The recent but not widely available *Repertorio bibliográfico de la lexicografía griega* (entry 489) offers an updated and vastly expanded list of such works, with significantly better coverage of Byzantine authors. The *Thesaurus Linguae Graecae* (entry 519) has replaced printed indexes to a large extent, although the dictionaries still remain useful.

LITERARY HISTORIES

563. Dihle, Albrecht. **History of Greek Literature: From Homer to the Hellenistic Period.** Trans. Clare Krojzl. London: Routledge, 1994. 332pp. ISBN 0–415–08620–5. LCCN 93–45284.

Aimed at the student and general reader, this work covers Greek literature from Homer through the time of Augustus (for the later period see entry 548). Dihle divides the volume into four chronological sections: archaic literature, classical literature of the fifth century B.C., classical literature of the fourth century B.C., and Hellenistic literature. Chapters within each section cover major authors and genres. While Dihle focuses on the more prominent authors, he also takes note of a number of minor figures as well. He provides both the requisite biographical and historical information and a critical discussion of the literary works themselves. His bibliography is relatively brief but provides a good basis for further study. An index closes the volume. This is a good choice for the casual reader or a beginning student; the more advanced may prefer Lesky (entry 566) or the appropriate volume of the *Cambridge History of Classical Literature* (entry 564).

564.   Easterling, P. E., and B.M.W. Knox. **Cambridge History of Classical Literature 1:Greek Literature.** Cambridge: Cambridge University Press, 1985. 936 pp. ISBN 0–521–21042–9. LCCN 82–22048.

The product of a team of distinguished British and American scholars, this work is the best and most current scholarly history of classical Greek literature available in English. The substantial general introduction discusses books and readers in the Greek world. The work then proceeds in chronological sequence through the major authors and genres of ancient Greek literature. Coverage is fairly thorough from Homer through the second century A.D. but then becomes spotty. Nonnus of Panopolis, an epic poet of the fifth century A.D., is the latest writer discussed (in the epilogue). In a departure from the traditional approach of biography and summary, the primary focus of this work is genuinely literary. The reader will find much more actual discussion and appreciation of the works themselves than is typical in histories of Greek or Latin literature. Biographical details and bibliographies are relegated to an "Appendix of Authors and Works." The bibliographies note major editions, commentaries, and translations and recommend a few studies for further reading. In the case of a few authors, they supply a more substantial list of scholarly works. A second appendix provides a concise introduction to Greek meters. The volume concludes with an extensive general bibliography and a detailed index. Those who want a more traditional approach to literary history (with more emphasis on biography and the historical background) will prefer Lesky (entry 566) or Rose (entry 568). Dihle's two volumes (entries 563 and 548) occupy something of a middle ground in approach but are addressed more to the student and general reader than the scholar. Schmid and Stählin's massive work (entry 571) offers much more detail than either Lesky or *Cambridge* but is available only in German.

565.   Hadas, Moses. **History of Greek Literature.** New York: Columbia University Press, 1950. 327pp. LCCN 50–07015.

Hadas offers a solid, readable, old-fashioned history of Greek literature for students and general readers. After short chapters on the nature of Greek literature and its origins and transmission, Hadas proceeds in a loosely chronological framework from Homer to Lucian. To the extent possible within this framework, he uses genre as a subprinciple of organization. Hadas covers the major surviving authors and some minor ones. He provides biographical information, historical context, summaries, and appreciations of the various works. The bibliographical notes, good in their day, are now far out-of-date. The index is good. While 50 years of scholarship and changing tastes render Hadas's work less useful, it remains, for the most part, a reliable overview of Greek literature.

566. Lesky, Albin. **History of Greek Literature.** Trans. James Willis and Cornelis de Heer. New York: Crowell, 1966; repr., Indianapolis: Hackett, 1996. 921 pp. LCCN 65–25033.

This English version is based on the second edition of Lesky's *Geschichte der griechischen Literatur* (Bern: Francke, 1963). Lesky intended "to give a broad outline for the student, initial guidance to the researcher, and to the interested public a speedy but not superficial approach to the literature of Greece." He accomplished this sufficiently well that for many years his work was the standard history of Greek literature. Although now supplanted in this role by the Greek volume of the more recent *Cambridge History of Classical Literature* (entry 564), Lesky is still a valuable guide to Greek literature. He approaches his subject chronologically, assigning a chapter to each major period. He discusses major authors and genres within each chapter. To keep the size of his book manageable, Lesky omits a number of minor authors, gives somewhat short shrift to the writers of the Roman period, and does not discuss Christian Greek writings at all; for the later period, see Dihle (entry 548). Lesky is strongest in his coverage of the early period and the fifth and fourth centuries B.C. He writes traditional literary history with a healthy dose of biography and historical background but does not neglect literary criticism either. He provides such facts as we have and discusses significant problems. Lesky's notes and bibliographies are a good guide to further study; although not as current as those in the *Cambridge History,* they are sometimes more extensive. A detailed table of contents and very full indexing make the work easy to consult.

567. Levi, Peter. **History of Greek Literature.** New York: Viking, 1985. 511pp. ISBN 0–670–80100–3. LCCN 84–51892.

Although far from comprehensive, Levi is a lively guide to the high points of Greek literature. He covers major authors and works from Homer to Plutarch, with a few exceptions. Minor and technical writers are largely ignored. Levi gives the basic facts, describes and interprets the works, includes copious quotations from them, and provides brief but well-chosen bibliographies. A comprehensive index rounds out the volume. Levi is an excellent resource for students and general readers. Scholars may find him entertaining but will turn to Lesky (entry 566), Easterling and Knox (entry 564), or Schmid-Stählin (entry 571) for the details.

568. Rose, H. J. **Handbook of Greek Literature: From Homer to the Age of Lucian.** 4th ed. London: Methuen, 1951. 458pp.

Often reprinted, this work is a very traditional literary history, with heavy emphasis on biography and history. Many summaries and descriptions of literary works are provided, but there is little in the way of criticism or interpretation. Rose proceeds in roughly chronological fashion, with his chapters organized around major authors or genres. Discussion of minor authors and works is set in smaller type, and technical matters (such as details of chronology) are generally relegated to the footnotes. There is a bibliography (now rather dated) and an index. Rose is generally dry but informative. Lesky (entry 566), who takes a similar approach, although giving somewhat more attention to literary criticism, is fuller and more current. The Greek volume of the *Cambridge History of Classical Literature* (entry 564), which is also more recent, has a more literary and less historical orientation.

569. Saïd, Suzanne, and Monique Trédé. **Short History of Greek Literature.** Trans. Trista Selous and others. New York: Routledge, 1999. 213 pp. ISBN 0–415–12271–6; 0–415–12272–4pa. LCCN 99–19803.

In spite of its brevity, this work offers many advantages. It is relatively up-to-date and notes recent discoveries and advances. Saïd and Trédé provide a balanced survey of Greek literature from Homer through the Greek Fathers of the fifth century A.D. Their overall organization is chronological; within this framework they often subgroup writers and works by genre. They focus on major figures but also cover many lesser authors in passing. Saïd and Trédé do a marvelous job of presenting historical context, biographical information, synopses of works, and critical comment in a very compact format. Their highly selective bibliography, which is arranged by period and author, also reflects favorably on the authors' taste and judgment. Readers with an understanding of French should also consult their larger work (entry 570).

570. Saïd, Suzanne, Monique Trédé, and Alain le Bolluec. **Histoire de la littérature grecque.** Collection premier cycle. Paris: Presses Universitaires de France, 1997. 720pp. ISBN 2–13–048233–3.

This substantial one-volume history of Greek literature is both up-to-date and reasonably comprehensive in its coverage. Its six major sections cover the archaic period, the classical era, the Hellenistic period, the early empire, late antiquity, and Greek Christian literature. Each of these is subdivided by genre. The detailed table of contents (found at the front of the volume, contrary to usual French practice) and the index provide ready access for those seeking a particular author or topic. Readers will find historical and biographical information as well as critical discussion. The authors often quote extensively from works discussed. The lengthy bibliography follows the divisions of the overall work, so that everything on a specific author or period is conveniently grouped; commentaries, key critical works, and the like, are listed for each author. Francophone readers will find this the best of recent histories of Greek literature.

571. Schmid, Wilhelm, and Otto Stählin. **Geschichte der griechischen Literatur.** Handbuch der Altertumswissenschaft 7. München: C. H. Beck, 1929–1948. 2v. in 7. ISBN 3–406–01376–7 (1, 1); 3–406–01378–3 (1, 2); 3–406–01380–5 (1, 3); 3–406–01382–1 (1, 4); 3–406–01384–8 (1, 5); 3–406–01386–4 (2, 1); 3–406–01388–0 (2, 2). LCCN 35–14442.

The Greek equivalent of Schanz-Hosius (entry 595), Schmid-Stählin is the most complete and detailed history of Greek literature available. The first volume, in five parts, covers Greek literature from the beginnings to ca. 400 B.C. A sixth part covering the fourth century B.C. was to have been written by Hans Herter; this has never appeared and leaves a major gap in the work. The second volume, which is in two parts, covers 320 B.C. to A.D. 530. Schmid-Stählin is organized by period, with subarrangment by genre. It covers both major and minor authors and works. Sections on individual authors provide biographical information, summaries and discussions of their works, and extensive bibliographies. For major authors Schmid-Stählin also includes extended essays on various aspects of their work. Indexes are provided at the end of each part (except the fourth) of the first volume. The index for the second volume appears at the end of the final part. While no English language work is comparable in size and scope to Schmid-Stählin, Lesky (entry 566) and the Greek volume of the *Cambridge History of Classical Literature* (entry 564) will serve the needs of most English readers quite well.

572. Whitmarsh, Tim. **Ancient Greek Literature.** Cultural History of Literature. Malden, MA: Polity, 2004. 284pp. ISBN: 0–7456–2791–9; 0–7456–2729–7pa. LCCN 2003–20332.

Whitmarsh offers a rather different take on Greek literature. He abandons the traditional chronological format and arranges his work by three broad categories: concepts, contexts, and conflicts. "Concepts" provides an overview of Greek literature and cultural history. "Contexts" looks at the literature according to where it was performed or read: festival, symposium, theater, political speeches, and the archive (chiefly prose and didactic works). "Conflicts" examines Greek literature in relation to ethnicity, gender, and slavery. This book is designed to be read rather than consulted; those seeking information on a particular author or work will need to resort to the index first. Whitmarsh provides a complete index of Greek authors discussed and an adequate general index. His bibliography is a very good guide to recent work in English. Readers seeking to approach Greek literature through contemporary critical theories will find Whitmarsh a valuable resource. Those who need the kind of information provided by traditional literary histories will prefer Easterling and Knox (entry 564) or the venerable work of Albin Lesky (entry 566).

DICTIONARIES, ENCYCLOPEDIAS, AND HANDBOOKS

573. Avery, Catherine B., ed. **New Century Handbook of Greek Literature.** New York: Appleton-Century-Crofts, 1972. 213pp. LCCN 79–183797.

Drawn from the larger *New Century Classical Handbook* (entry 128), this work focuses specifically on Greek literature. Entries, which are all signed, cover authors, genres, and individual works. These include nearly all major authors and a good many minor ones. The articles are arranged alphabetically. Their content consists largely of basic biographical information on the authors and summaries of literary works. A guide to pronunciation is provided, but there are neither bibliographical references nor an index. This work aims low and will satisfy the needs of only the most basic user. Howatson's *Oxford Companion to Classical Literature* (entry 552), which also covers Latin literature, is a far superior work and should be preferred.

574. Briggs, Ward W., ed. **Ancient Greek Authors.** Dictionary of Literary Biography 176. Detroit: Gale, 1997. 472pp. ISBN 0–8103–9939–3. LCCN 97–435.

This handbook targets an audience of students and general readers. Briggs provides A-to-Z coverage of major and some minor Greek authors from the eighth century B.C. to the third century A.D. He omits few authors commonly studied and includes representative authors from nearly every genre and period, although the Greek romances receive short shrift. Articles typically begin with lists of major works and citations of the editio princeps, standard editions, English translations, and commentaries. The body of each article offers biographical details and a survey of the works. Each concludes with a selective bibliography of secondary literature; as a rule these are quite strong. Most articles are by leading experts on the author in question. Attractive illustrations are sprinkled throughout the work. Overall, this is an excellent work for students and anyone seeking an orientation to one of the authors covered. Briggs has also edited a companion volume on Latin authors (entry 596).

LATIN LITERATURE

BIBLIOGRAPHIES

575.   Cupaiolo, Fabio. **Bibliografia della metrica latina.** Studi latini 15. Napoli: Loffredo, 1995. 222pp. ISBN 88–8096411–3.

Cupaiolo covers more than a century of work on Latin prosody and metrics ranging from the late nineteenth century to the early 1990s. He arranged citations by topic: bibliographies, general works on prosody, particular problems (ictus and accent, caesura, etc.), general principles of metrics, individual meters (arranged by meter), metrical studies of individual poets (alphabetical by poet), works in mixed verse, and prose and rhythmic prose. Occasional annotations clarify contents or list reviews. There is no index.

576.   Faider, Paul. **Répertoire des éditions de scolies et commentaires d'auteurs latins.** Collections d'études, série scientifique 8. Paris: Les Belles Lettres, 1931. 48pp. LCCN 41–36.

Faider deals with the relatively obscure area of ancient commentators on the Latin classics. These include both separate commentaries (e.g., Servius on Vergil) and marginalia (often called *scholia*) found in ancient and medieval manuscripts. Faider lists Latin authors alphabetically and cites editions of the relevant ancient commentators and scholiasts under each. Faider's headnotes often provide historical information and bibliography on individual commentators. The work is now badly dated; for example, new editions of Servius (on Vergil) and Asconius (on Cicero) have subsequently appeared. Faider does remain useful for tracking down the less prominent scholiasts, for whom we still often depend on nineteenth-century editions.

577.   Guidobaldi, Maria Paola, and Fabrizio Pesando, eds. **Scripta latina: Index editionum quae ad usum historicorum maxime asdunt.** Bibliotheca ad Apollinis. Rome: Quasar, 1993. 662pp. ISBN 88–7097–023–X.

This bibliography covers editions of Latin writings from the beginnings to the time of Charlemagne (A.D. 768–814). The editors offer a single A-to-Z listing of authors and works. They take a curiously broad notion of work, including such things as *Chartae Latinae Antiquiores* and the *Corpus Inscriptionum Latinorum.* Under each they enumerate editions, translations, and concordances and indexes. There are lapses: for example, under Catullus they omit the useful critical edition by D.F.S. Thomson (1978; they could not have known about his 1997 edition). Citations are compressed, and the editors rely heavily on abbreviations, which will confound the uninitiated (who probably should not use this book unassisted). The primary value of this rather eccentric work is in locating editions of the minor, the obscure, and the late.

578.   Herescu, N. I. **Bibliographie de la littérature latine.** Collection de bibliographie. Paris: Les Belles Lettres, 1943. 426pp. LCCN 46–3765.

Herescu's work is a general bibliography for the study of Latin literature. His introduction lists bibliographical resources and selected reference works. The body of the work is arranged in chapters corresponding to the standard period divisions in Latin literature. Each begins with a section on general works and then lists individual authors.

Under each author, Herescu lists extant manuscripts and gives references to facsimiles and studies of them. He then lists editions, translations, indexes, and secondary works. Herescu includes both articles and books under secondary works and often subarranges these by topic. He also provides an index of Latin authors. Herescu's bibliography is a good working guide for pre-1940 publications on Latin literature. It is more comprehensive than Leeman's *Bibliographia Latina Selecta* (entry 579), but less up-to-date.

579. Leeman, A. D. **Bibliographia Latina Selecta.** Operam praebentibus G. Bouma, H. Pinkster. Amsterdam: A. M. Hakkert, 1966. 173pp. LCCN 68–98448.

Leeman's compilation is a selective general bibliography on Latin language and literature. It is aimed primarily at European university students. The first part, which is arranged by topic, covers bibliography, reference works, linguistics, metrics, literary history, Roman law, palaeography and textual criticism, history of scholarship, the influence of the classics, and collected editions. The second part is devoted to individual Latin authors. Leeman arranges these chronologically. He lists a selection of editions, translations, indexes, commentaries, and critical studies for each author. Leeman includes only book-length works. There is an index of Latin authors. Leeman shows a strong European bias in his selection of works and is now rather dated. For the most part, English-speaking students will be better served by consulting the bibliographies found at the end of the Latin volume of the *Cambridge History of Classical Literature* (entry 593).

580. Quellet, Henri. **Bibliographia Indicum, Lexicorum, et Concordantium Auctorum Latinorum [Répertoire bibliographique des index, lexiques, et concordances des auteurs latines].** Hildesheim: Georg Olms, 1980. 262pp. ISBN 3–487–070146. LCCN 81–182390.

Despite the author's modest claims that he makes no pretence of being exhaustive, his work may be considered so for all practical purposes. He gathers some 1,097 works in his main list and addenda. Quellet includes indexes at the end of editions of texts, as well as separately published indexes, concordances, and lexica to the various Latin authors. He arranges his material alphabetically by Latin author. Symbols in the margin by each citation indicate the degree of completeness of the particular index. An appendix lists a number of related works—studies and compilations of Latin names of stars, animals, and so forth. There is also an index to the names of the compilers of the indexes and lexica. A number of indexes and concordances have appeared since 1980; these must be sought in *L'Année philologique* (entry 44). Until computerized databases of Latin literature render printed indexes totally obsolete, Quellet will remain a useful tool for those interested in Latin language and lexicography.

ELECTRONIC TEXT COLLECTIONS

See also *Perseus* (entry 137).

581. Packard Humanities Institute. **PHI CD-ROM #5.3.** Los Altos, CA: Packard Humanities Institute, 1991. 1 disk.

582. Packard Humanities Institute. **PHI CD-ROM #7.** Los Altos, CA: Packard Humanities Institute, 1996. 1 disk.

These two CD-ROM products allow one to do word searches of a large body of Latin and Greek texts. PHI CD-ROM #5.3 includes the full text of more than 350 Latin authors; virtually all Latin literature through the end of the second century A.D. is covered, along with a few later texts. This disk also contains a number of versions of the Bible, including the Hebrew text, the Septuagint, the Greek New Testament, the Latin Vulgate, the Coptic New Testament, and the authorized and revised standard versions. PHI CD-ROM #7 is a database of Greek and Latin inscriptions and papyri. A selection of Coptic texts is also provided on this disk. These CD-ROMS can be used with either DOS or Macintosh computers. Search software is not supplied by the institute and must be obtained through various third-party vendors. Usually the same software can be used for both PHI disks and *Thesaurus Linguae Graecae* disks (entry 519).

583. Tombeur, Paul, ed. **Bibliotheca Teubneriana Latina on CD-ROM.** 2nd ed. Turnhout: Brepols; Stuttgart: Teubner, 2002. ISBN 2503512631 (Brepols); 3598405030 (Teubner).

This CD-ROM contains all the Latin texts found in the famous series Bibliotheca Scriptorum Romanorum Teubneriana. It does not, however, include the important prefaces or critical apparatus. The first release comprised editions of about 800 Latin works written between 300 B.C. and A.D. 800. The second added to these the *Grammatici Latini* and a few other texts. Future releases are expected to include older, out-of-print editions that still have scholarly value. The disk is useful for searching texts, or for texts not otherwise available; it is not a substitute for the printed editions with *apparatus criticus.*

LITERARY HISTORIES

584. Albrecht, Michael von. **History of Roman Literature from Livius Andronicus to Boethius.** Mnemosyne, bibliotheca classica Batava. Supplementum 165. Rev. Gareth Schmeling and the author. Leiden: Brill, 1997. 2v. ISBN 90–04–10712–6 (set); 90–04–10709–6 (v. 1); 90–04–10711–8 (v. 2). LCCN 96–38926.

This massive work, originally published in German as *Geschichte der römischen Literatur* (München: K. G. Saur, 1994), is learned, invaluable, and infuriating. It offers frequent lapses in English style and usage, treats subjects in a fragmented way at disparate points, and is unwieldy in more than size. Von Albrecht covers Latin literature more comprehensively than any other work in English and is especially valuable for extending coverage to Christian Latin authors through Boethius. His first chapter covers background material. Subsequent chapters cover periods in chronological order: the republic, the Augustan period, the early empire, and the middle and late empire. Each of these is divided into three main sections: a survey, poetry, and prose. Von Albrecht further subdivides these by genre and author. He discusses the nature of the various genres; for authors he covers life, works, style, transmission, and influence. A final chapter covers the transmission of Latin literature. The work contains a vast amount of information and many acute observations. It is uneven in quality, as single-author works of this type tend to be. The bibliographies are extensive and somewhat idiosyncratic, as is the general index. Graduate students and scholars will consult it frequently, undergraduates probably avoid it, and nobody will actually read it.

585.   Bardon, Henry. **La littérature latin inconnue.** Paris: Klincksieck, 1952–1956. 2v. LCCN 52–6573.

Most histories of Latin literature focus on the writers whose works have survived. Bardon's unique volume deals with those authors whose works are either totally lost or now exist only in fragments. He covers authors chronologically by period; periods are subdivided by literary genres. Bardon reconstructs what he can about each author from *testimonia* in other authors and from any surviving fragments of their works. His notes provide full references to the ancient sources and to relevant secondary works. Some of the information found in Bardon is rather speculative. However, most of these authors receive short shrift from the standard literary histories, and many are omitted altogether. The only other readily available work that covers such authors in any detail is the large German history of Latin literature by Schanz and Hosius (entry 595). Each of Bardon's two volumes includes an index of ancient authors.

586.   Conte, Gian Biagio. **Latin Literature: A History.** Trans. Joseph B. Solodow. Rev. Don Fowler and Glenn W. Most. Baltimore: Johns Hopkins University Press, 1994. 827pp. ISBN 0–8018–4638–2. LCCN 93–20985.

Based on the Italian original, which appeared in 1987, this history of Latin literature has been adapted somewhat to meet the needs of English-speaking students better. It provides an excellent survey of the major Latin authors and genres from the beginnings to the sixth century A.D. Conte divides his work into five parts: the early and middle republic, the late republic, the age of Augustus, the early empire, and the late empire. Within each of these parts, chapters cover authors and genres. The unit on the late empire, which is first arranged chronologically and then by genre, is an exception to this pattern. Conte offers perhaps the best-balanced treatment of Latin literature available. He provides ample historical background and biographical information about the authors, lists of their works (including dates and brief descriptions) and of ancient sources of information concerning them, and critical discussion of the works. Conte also supplies substantial annotated bibliographies throughout the volume. The appendixes include chronological tables of Roman and Greek history and culture, an alphabetical listing of Greek authors and texts, a glossary of Latin political and social terminology, and a glossary of terms concerning rhetoric, metrics, and literary criticism. An index of names rounds out the volume. The physical design of the book is also exceptional: clear typefaces, wide margins, and the use of marginal lemmata make the work easy to consult.

Conte is now clearly the leading rival to the Latin volume of the *Cambridge History of Classical Literature* (entry 593), a work that focuses on the critical aspects of literary history and sometimes neglects to provide adequate background material. Those whose needs go beyond these two histories must refer to Von Albrecht (entry 584) or the much larger German work of Schanz-Hosius (entry 595).

587.   Copley, Frank O. **Latin Literature: From the Beginnings to the Close of the Second Century** A.D. Ann Arbor: University of Michigan Press, 1969. 372pp. LCCN 76–90760.

Written by a distinguished Latinist of the former generation, this work draws heavily on the works of J. Wight Duff (entries 588–589) for its factual content. Copley covers Latin literature from its beginnings through Apuleius (second century A.D.). Though dated, it is readable and generally reliable. Copley's critical discussion of the literature and his translations from works discussed are its strongest features. The bibliography must be supplemented from more recent works; there is an adequate index. Copley may be recommended to beginning and intermediate students. Those in need of more detailed and current treatment should look rather to the Cambridge volume of Kenney and Clausen (entry 593) or the recent work of Conte (entry 586).

588.   Duff, J. Wight. **Literary History of Rome: From the Origins to the Close of the Golden Age.** 3rd ed. Ed. A. M. Duff. New York: Barnes & Noble, 1959. 543pp. LCCN 60–1962.

589.   Duff, J. Wight. **Literary History of Rome in the Silver Age: From Tiberius to Hadrian.** 3rd ed. Ed. A. M. Duff. New York: Barnes & Noble, 1964; repr., Westport, CT: Greenwood Press, 1979. 599pp. LCCN 65–775.

The several editions of this old standby have endured nearly a century (the first appeared in 1909). While Duff is somewhat dated and represents the traditional approach of an earlier generation of scholars, his book remains a mine of useful basic information on Latin literature. In the first volume Duff covers Latin literature from the earliest fragments to the close of the Augustan era; he continues the history to the mid-second century A.D. in the second. He provides historical background and biographical information for each author before briefly describing and commenting on his works. Duff aimed his work at those with some training in the classics. Although not inaccessible to the general reader, it does include much untranslated Latin. Each volume contains a bibliography (now very out-of-date) and a good general index. Conte (entry 586) and the second volume of the *Cambridge History of Classical Literature* (entry 593) are much more current works and are to be preferred as scholarly histories. They also go far beyond Duff's temporal limits to treat Latin literature as late as the sixth and fourth centuries A.D. respectively.

590.   Hadas, Moses. **History of Latin Literature.** New York: Columbia University Press, 1952. 474pp. ISBN 0–231–01848–7. LCCN 52–07637.

Like his *History of Greek Literature* (entry 565), this volume is addressed to beginning students and general readers. Hadas covers Latin literature from its beginnings through late antiquity. He employs a chronological framework overall but groups authors by genre when possible. Hadas goes much later than most similar good popular histories of Latin literature: he covers such writers as Symmachus, Ammianus, Claudian, Ambrose, Augustine, and Jerome. His approach is the traditional blend of biography, history, summary, and criticism. Bibliographical notes, a chronological table of authors, and an index conclude the work. While dated, Hadas remains an attractive work for general readers.

591.   Herzog, Reinhart, and Peter Lebrecht Schmidt, eds. **Handbuch der lateinischen Literatur der Antike.** Handbuch der Altertumswissenschaft 8. München: C. H. Beck, 1989– . 8v. LCCN 90–137623. Details for individual volumes:

v. 1: Suerbaum, Werner, ed. **Die archaische Literatur von den Anfängen bis Sullas Tod: Die vorliterarische Periode und die Zeit von 240 bis 78 v.Chr.** 2002. 611pp. ISBN 3–406–48134–5.

v. 4: Sallmann, Klaus, ed. **Die Literatur des Umbruchs von der römischen zur christlichen Literatur, 117 bis 284 n.Chr.** 1997. 651pp. ISBN 3–406–39020–X.

v. 5: Herzog, Reinhart, ed. **Restauration und Erneuerung: Die lateinische Literatur von 284 bis 374 n.Chr.** 1989. 559pp. ISBN 3–40631863–0.

592. Herzog, Reinhart, and Peter Lebrecht Schmidt, eds. **Nouvelle histoire de la littérature latine.** Paris: Brepols, 1993– . 8v. Details for individual volumes:

v. 4: Sallman, Klaus, ed. **L'Âge de transition : De la littérature romaine à la littérature chrétienne de 117 à 284 apres J.-C.** 2000. 758pp. ISBN 2–503–51013–2.

v. 5: Herzog, Reinhart, ed. **Restauration et renouveau: Littérature latine de 284 à 374 après J.-C.** 1993. 646pp. ISBN 2–503–50069–2.

Herzog and Schmidt are preparing a new major history of Latin literature, which will replace that of Schanz-Hosius (entry 595) in the Handbuch der Altertumswissenschaft series. It is being published in both German and French editions. Eight volumes are projected; to date three have appeared in German, and only two of these in French. The published volumes are the most detailed treatments of their periods available. They cover all known authors and works, both major and minor. These are arranged by genre within an overall chronological framework. Sections on major authors are often extensively subdivided. This handbook provides biographical information about the authors, pertinent historical background, summaries and discussions of the literary works, and substantial bibliographies. Each volume includes a detailed index. When completed, this will be the standard history of Latin literature. Schanz-Hosius remains useful for its coverage of older scholarship. Anglophone readers will generally prefer the less comprehensive works by Kenney and Clausen (entry 593) and Conte (entry 586) or the barely English edition of Von Albrecht (entry 584).

593. Kenney, E. J., and W. V. Clausen, eds. **Cambridge History of Classical Literature 1: Latin Literature.** Cambridge: Cambridge University Press, 1982. 973 pp. ISBN 0–521–21043–7. LCCN 79–121.

A product of collaboration, this volume counts among its contributors a number of distinguished British and American classical scholars. The work begins with a substantial introduction on "Readers and Critics," which provides an overview of the business end of ancient literature: writing as a profession, publication, the physical production of books, and the reading public. It then proceeds in broadly chronological order from the beginnings of Latin literature through the fourth century A.D. Chapters cover individual authors or genres. The primary focus of the history is on the literary works themselves. The main text is entirely critical, with biographical and bibliographical material relegated to an "Appendix of Authors and Works." The bibliographies found there generally provide a good selection of editions, commentaries, translations, and basic studies. There is also a brief appendix on Latin metrics. This is a solid, reasonably current treatment of Latin literature and is now widely regarded to be the standard work in English. Von Albrecht (entry 584) is more comprehensive and more recent, but less accessible. Some, especially students, may prefer Conte's recent work (entry 586), which combines a healthy amount of biographical and historical background with a critical appreciation of the literature. The older, more traditional works of Duff (entries 588–589) and Rose (entry 594), now rather dated but still useful, tend to offer biographies of the authors and summaries of their works.

594.   Rose, H. J. **Handbook of Latin Literature: From the Earliest Times to the Death of St. Augustine.** 3rd ed., repr. with a supplementary bibliography by E. Courtney. London: Methuen, 1967; repr., Wauconda, IL: Bolchazy-Carduccci, 1996. 582pp. LCCN 67–76490.

This frequently reprinted history of Latin literature was long the chief rival to Duff (entries 588–589) as the standard English-language history of Latin literature. Rose is more compact and offers somewhat less detail, but, unlike Duff, he extends his coverage through the fourth century A.D. He uses a chronological framework in which each major period receives one or more chapters. The only exception to this is his treatment of technical writers and scholars, whom he places in a separate chapter. Rose follows the traditional approach: his work includes historical background, biography, and summaries of the various works. It is a readable, if sometimes plodding, book. There is a good index. Those who want a more critical approach to the literature should use the Latin volume of the *Cambridge History of Classical Literature* (entry 593), which is also more current. This and Conte's recent work (entry 586) largely supersede Rose.

595.   Schanz, Martin. **Geschichte der römischen Literatur bis zum Gesetzgebungswerk des Kaisers Justinian.** Handbuch der Altertumswissenschaft 8. 2.–4. Aufl. München: C. H. Beck, 1914–1935. 4v. ISBN 3–406–01390–2 (v. 1); 3–406–01392–9 (v. 2); 3–406–01394–5 (v. 3); 3–406–01396–1 (v. 4). LCCN 28–4494.

This massive work is the standard scholarly history of Latin literature. It is often referred to as Schanz-Hosius because the later editions were revised by Carl Hosius. Only the first two volumes appeared in a fourth edition; the third volume is in its third edition, and the fourth is in its second edition. These four volumes cover respectively the Roman Republic, the empire from Augustus to Hadrian, Hadrian to Constantine the Great, and the fourth to sixth centuries A.D.

Within each volume material is organized by period and genre. Schanz-Hosius covers virtually every known author and work from the beginnings of Latin literature through the sixth century. Sections for individual authors include biographical information, summaries and discussions of the individual works, and extensive bibliographies. For major authors Schanz-Hosius also provides general critical discussion and essays on particular aspects of their works. Each volume has its own detailed index; a more sketchy index to the whole work appears at the end of the final volume. Herzog and Schmidt (entry 591) are preparing a wholly new history of Latin literature to replace Schanz-Hosius; at this time only three volumes have appeared. Pending the completion of this new work, Schanz-Hosius remains the most complete and detailed treatment of Latin literature available. Those who read only English will be best served by Conte (entry 586) or the Latin volume of the *Cambridge History of Classical Literature* (entry 593), although neither is remotely comparable in either size or scope.

DICTIONARIES, ENCYCLOPEDIAS, AND HANDBOOKS

596.   Briggs, Ward W., ed. **Ancient Roman Writers.** Dictionary of Literary Biography 211. Detroit: Gale, 1999. 438pp. ISBN 0–7876–3105–1. LCCN 99–33325.

A survey of major and some minor Roman authors, this attractively illustrated work is aimed at the student and general reader. The introduction provides an outline of Roman history and some general comments on the nature and history of Latin literature. A general discussion of the "Uniqueness of Latin Literature" by Brooks Otis and a note on the transmission of Latin literature follow the introduction. The core of the book is an A-to-Z treatment of Roman authors. Each article begins with a list of major works then cites the editio princeps, standard editions, English translations, and commentaries. Each provides basic biographical information about the author and a discussion of his works. Many quote fairly extensively from the works in translation. A brief bibliography concludes every article. Most are written by noted authorities on the respective author. There are few omissions of note, though it is surprising to include Ammianus but omit Claudian. In fact, coverage of fourth-century authors is spotty at best. Briggs and his contributors provide good orientations to the various authors for their intended audience. This work complements Briggs's earlier volume on Greek authors (entry 574).

597. Harrison, Stephen, ed. **Companion to Latin Literature.** Malden, MA: Blackwell, 2005. 450pp. ISBN 0–631–23529–9. LCCN 2004–5855.

"This volume is aimed at university students of Latin literature and their teachers, and at scholarly colleagues in other subjects who need orientation in Latin literature." To accomplish this, Harrison has gathered a group of distinguished British and American Latinists. They cover Latin literature from its beginnings until about A.D. 200. Harrison chose to employ multiple approaches. The first section offers five essays covering Latin literature by period: early republic, late republic, Augustan Age, early empire, and high empire. These provide useful overviews. The second section covers genres: narrative epic, didactic epic, tragedy, comedy, pastoral, love elegy, satire, lyric and iambic poetry, epigram, the novel, dialogues and treatises, historiography and biography, oratory, and epistolography. The third and final section treats themes in Latin literature: decline and nostalgia; art and text; the passions; sex and gender; friendship and patronage; marriage and family; slavery and class; and center and periphery. There is considerable overlap among the sections; cross-references help link treatments, although more are needed. Essays are of necessity very selective, since they run only 10 to 20 pages. Each does include a brief note on further reading. Harrison also provides a chronological table, which covers both literary and historical events. His general introduction includes short bibliographies (including Web resources) for the 20 most important Latin authors. A substantial general bibliography and an index complete the volume. This should not be taken as a substitute for a history of Latin literature but is a very useful reference for those seeking a quick orientation to a period or genre in Roman literature.

14
Greek and Latin Literature: Genres

This chapter includes works that specifically deal with literary genres. Poetric genres appear first, followed by prose. Each is subdivided into two sections: (1) bibliographies and (2) dictionaries, encyclopedias, and handbooks. Additional relevant material can be found in chapters 13 ("Greek and Latin Literature: General Works"), 15 ("Greek Authors"), and 16 ("Latin Authors"). A final section covers quotations and proverbs, which might loosely be defined as a genre; such collections were found in antiquity and have certainly flourished since the Renaissance (witness the *Adagia* of Eramus).

DRAMA

BIBLIOGRAPHIES

See also Donlan (entry 609).

598. Arnott, W. Geoffrey. **Menander, Plautus, and Terence.** New Surveys in the Classics 9. Oxford: Clarendon Press, 1975. 62pp. LCCN 77–367418.

Arnott's survey covers the three surviving writers of New Comedy. He treats Menander in the first chapter, and Plautus and Terence together in the second. Each section begins with a brief general bibliography, which lists the chief editions, commentaries, translations, and general works. Arnott then reviews the major areas of scholarly research in a series of sections. The notes to these provide many additional citations. In general, Arnott provides a good overview of research in the area and a sound working bibliography of pre-1975 publications.

599. Donlan, Walter, ed. **Classical World Bibliography of Greek Drama and Poetry.** Garland Reference Library of the Humanities 93. New York: Garland, 1978. 339pp. ISBN 0–8240–9880–3. LCCN 76–52510.

Donlan here gathers 13 surveys that were published in *Classical World* (entry 95) between 1953 and 1976. There are two review articles on Homeric studies, one covering major trends in scholarship during the years 1939–1955, the other focusing on Homeric originality (listing studies published between 1928 and 1971). Greek tragedy is covered well with two surveys each on Aeschylus (collectively covering 1947–1964) and Euripides (1940–1965), and one on Sophocles (1945–1956). Two articles cover work on Aristophanes and Old Comedy for the years 1946–1967. A complete bibliography of publications on Menander's *Dyskolos* (which was rediscovered and published in 1958) for the years 1959–1960 rounds out the drama section. Three essays surveying work on Greek lyric poetry for the years 1946–1975 conclude the volume. These are much more comprehensive than the other surveys and take up nearly half the book. All the surveys employ some form of subject arrangement, and all include descriptive and evaluative discussion of the works cited. Unless otherwise noted, they are selective bibliographies. Although they are not up-to-date, the surveys are a useful source of bibliography on important authors and genres in Greek literature. Lack of an index, however, is a major drawback.

600. Forman, Robert J. **Classical Greek and Roman Drama: An Annotated Bibliography.** Magill Bibliographies. Pasadena, CA: Salem Press, 1989. 239pp. ISBN 0–89336–659–4. LCCN 89–10805.

Forman, an English professor, intends his work for "high school students, college undergraduates, and general readers as a guide to reading and research." He includes translations, commentaries, and critical works, which are chosen both for basic importance and for their wide availability in libraries. Forman begins with a unit called "General Studies" in which he gathers general works on classical drama. Few significant English-language works are omitted. Then Forman proceeds to cover individual dramatists: Aeschylus, Aristophanes, Ennius, Euripides, Menander, Plautus, Seneca, Sophocles, and Terence. Forman offers a good selection of the available translations and scholarly literature. Occasionally he includes dated items or somewhat difficult technical works, but most of his choices are on target for his audience. He also provides annotations, which clearly indicate the content and value of each work. An author index concludes the volume.

DICTIONARIES, ENCYCLOPEDIAS, AND HANDBOOKS

601. Bieber, Margarete. **History of Greek and Roman Theatre.** 2nd ed. Princeton, NJ: Princeton University Press, 1961. 343pp. LCCN 60–9367.

While now rather dated, this venerable and highly regarded book remains valuable. Bieber covers ancient theater in chronological sequence from the origin of Greek drama through the younger Seneca. Her work is noteworthy for its balanced attention to literary, epigraphical, and archaeological evidence. She discusses the plays, the related religious festivals, staging, and the development of the theater buildings. Many excellent illustrations accompany the text: Bieber is the first place to look for depictions of ancient drama or photos and plans of ancient theaters. An historical chronology of Greco-Roman theater and a glossary of technical terms appear near the beginning of the volume. The substantial notes and bibliography are an excellent guide to older work but now must be supplemented from more recent sources. The index provides ready access to illustrations as well as the text.

602. Duckworth, George. **Nature of Roman Comedy: A Study in Popular Entertainment.** 2nd ed. With a foreword and bibliographical appendix by Richard Hunter. Norman: University of Oklahoma Press, 1994. 509pp. ISBN 0–8061–2620–5. LCCN 93–27544.

Since it was first published in 1952 by Princeton University Press, Duckworth has remained the standard handbook on Roman comedy. While focusing on the surviving works of Plautus and Terence, Duckworth also covers their Greek and Italian predecessors. His 15 chapters include early Italian comedy, Greek comedy, the Golden Age of drama at Rome, presentation and staging, stage conventions, theme and treatment, composition, foreshadowing and suspense, characters and characterization, thought and moral tone, comic spirit in charac-ter and situation, language and style, meter and song, originality of Roman comedy, and the subsequent literary influence of Roman comedy. Although dated in some areas, especially the treatment of Greek comedy where new discoveries have greatly enhanced our knowledge, Duckworth continues to be a sound guide to his subject. The second edition (1994) includes a bibliographical appendix that updates Duckworth's substantial original bibliography; this is the only notable difference between the editions. A detailed index concludes the work.

603.   Easterling, P.E., ed. **Cambridge Companion to Greek Tragedy.** Cambridge: Cambridge University Press, 1997. 392pp. ISBN 0–521–41245–5; 0–521–42351–1pa. LCCN 96–37392.

Easterling, the Regius Professor of Greek at Cambridge, brings together a distin-guished group of contributors for this volume. They approach tragedy as a genre throughout, although there is much discussion of individual plays and playwrights. The first section offers four essays on tragedy in its historical contexts: their role in civic and religious life, the audience, and the depiction of tragedy in ancient art. The second focuses on the plays: sociology, language, performance, and myth. The final section covers reception: the forma-tion of the canon, modern adaptations and performances, and modern critical approaches. A glossary of Greek terms and a chronology may be found following the essays. Easterling also provides a guide to important editions, commentaries, and translations of the tragedians, along with a substantial bibliography of secondary literature. A detailed index concludes the work. Anyone seeking an orientation to recent scholarly work will find this most helpful.

604.   Ferguson, John. **Companion to Greek Tragedy.** Austin: University of Texas Press, 1972. 623pp. ISBN 0–292–71000–3. LCCN 74–38380.

This handbook begins with a general overview of the origins of Greek tragedy, the audience, and the theater. Ferguson then covers successively Aeschylus, Sophocles, and Euripides. He provides a short biography of each. Chapters on individual plays provide background, a synopsis, and critical discussion. The *Rhesus* (often attributed to Euripides) is listed separately as an anonymous work. Ferguson then includes a section on satyr and pro-satyric plays, with an introduction to this subgenre of tragedy and discussions of sev-eral surviving plays by Sophocles and Euripides. Frequent and extensive quotation from the plays is a notable strength. A glossary of Greek terms, a substantial bibliography, and an index complete the work. This is a useful guide for students that is both more detailed and more sophisticated than McLeish (entry 607) although not as up-to-date, nor offering coverage of comedy.

605.   Harsh, Philip Whaley. **Handbook of Classical Drama.** Stanford, CA: Stanford University Press, 1944. 526pp. LCCN 44–4205.

Intended as an aid to modern readers who lack a background in classical studies, this work covers the major dramatic genres of antiquity: Greek tragedy, Old Comedy, New Comedy, Roman comedy, and Roman tragedy. For each, Harsh provides an introduction describing its character, origins, subject matter, meters, and typical structure. His treatment of the surviving authors and their works follows. This includes a biography and general critical appreciation of each dramatist and individual discussions of his surviving plays. Harsh supplies both background information and critical commentary on the plays. The work includes extensive notes and bibliography and an index. Although still useful for readers studying ancient drama at a basic level, 50 years of scholarship have left Harsh's book badly dated, especially in its critical approaches. Even some of the factual material is now incorrect (e.g., the early dating of Aeschylus's *Suppliants* is no longer widely accepted). Hathorn (entry 606) is more current, though not entirely up-to-date himself. Hathorn's handbook is also rather different in character, since it is organized as a dictionary and focuses more on plot summaries and background information.

606. Hathorn, Richmond Y. **Crowell's Handbook of Classical Drama.** New York: Crowell, 1967. 350pp. LCCN 67–12403.

Hathorn's work is a dictionary of ancient drama. His entries cover the playwrights, their individual works, characters from the plays, places, ancient technical terms relating to drama, and historical and cultural background material. The entries range from a sentence to several pages. Major dramatists receive extensive entries, while the articles on their individual works include both detailed summaries and some (often not very inspired) critical commentary. Hathorn also includes brief entries on many minor dramatists and their works. He does not provide either a bibliography or an index. His handbook is a useful ready-reference tool for those reading classical drama in translation.

607. McLeish, Kenneth. **Guide to Greek Theatre and Drama.** London: Methuen, 2003. 310pp. ISBN 0–413–72030–6.

McLeish died before this book was finished. Trevor R. Griffiths completed it and saw it through the press. Its purpose is "to provide a general survey of the place and purpose of theatre in ancient Greece, of the conditions and styles of performance, of all the extant plays and their authors." An initial chapter covers the origins of drama at Athens, the dramatic festivals, the physical theater, scenery, props, actors and the chorus, comedy and tragedy. McLeish then proceeds through the surviving plays of Aeschylus, Sophocles, Euripides, Aristophanes, and Menander. He provides an overview of the life and works of each dramatist, followed by entries for the surviving plays. These offer a list of characters, a synopsis, and a brief discussion. A final chapter discusses Aristotle's *Poetics* and Greek tragedy. Supplementary material includes summaries of key myths, a glossary of terms from Greek drama, a chronology, and a very selective bibliography. There is a general index. This is a useful work for students and others approaching Greek drama for the first time, or for those who merely want a plot summary of a play. The more ambitious will find Ferguson (entry 604) a more sophisticated and informative work for tragedy.

EPIC POETRY

BIBLIOGRAPHIES

See also Donlan (entry 599).

608. Sienkewicz, Thomas J. **Classical Epic: An Annotated Bibliography.** Magill Bibliographies. Pasadena, CA: Salem Press, 1991. 265pp. ISBN 0–89356–663–2. LCCN 90–48884.

Despite its broad title, this work deals only with Homer and Vergil. Sienkewicz designed the bibliography for students and general readers approaching Homer or Vergil for the first time; for the most part, he serves this audience well. His introduction offers a general appreciation of the two poets and some guidance for their readers, along with a short list of general works on epic poetry. The bibliography consists of two parts, which cover Homer and Vergil respectively. Within each Sienkiewicz arranges entries by subject. The Homeric part covers general studies, historical background, biography, the authorship question, and broader literary studies of the Homeric poems, the *Iliad,* the *Odyssey,* and Homer's influence. The sections on the individual poems note editions and translations, as well as critical works. The Vergilian section is similarly arranged, including both general works on Vergil and works specifically on the *Aeneid.* Sienkewicz restricts himself to English-language works that are readily available. His entries include books, chapters in books, and journal articles. The accompanying annotations provide good descriptions of each item. There is an index of authors. This work is particularly useful for the study and teaching of Homer and Vergil at the secondary and college levels.

LYRIC AND ELEGIAC POETRY

BIBLIOGRAPHIES

See also Donlan (entry 599).

609. Donlan, Walter, ed. **Classical World Bibliography of Roman Drama and Poetry and Ancient Fiction.** Garland Reference Library of the Humanities 97. New York: Garland, 1978. 387pp. ISBN 0–8240–9876–5. LC 76–52516.

This gathering of bibliographies, which originally appeared in *Classical World* (entry 95) between 1953 and 1975, is something of a hodgepodge. Roman drama and poetry are represented by literature surveys on Plautus (1950–1964), Terence (1934–1958), Catullus (two items together covering 1934–1969), Horace (1945–1957), Propertius (1960–1972), Ovid (1958–1968), and Roman satire (three surveys covering 1937–1968). Under the rubric of ancient fiction are two general surveys (1937–1970), two review essays covering work on Petronius (1940–1968), and one on Apuleius (1938–1970). Two additional surveys deal with psychoanalytical studies of classical authors (1911–1960) and teaching the classics in translation (1924–1975). The surveys all generally conform to the pattern of *CW* surveys: they are arranged by subject and include descriptive and evaluative comments. A few attempt relative completeness; most are selective. They remain useful, especially for those seeking retrospective bibliography on particular authors. No index is provided.

610. Tarrant, Richard. **Greek and Latin Lyric Poetry in Translation.** Urbana, IL: American Philological Association, 1972. 62pp.

Tarrant reviews in considerable detail English translations of Greek and Latin lyric poetry. He intends the book to serve as a guide to those teaching or studying ancient literature in translation. His definition of lyric poetry is somewhat elastic and extends to pastoral (Theocritus and Vergil) and elegiac verse (Tibullus, Propertius, and Ovid) as well. Tarrant includes both anthologies and translations of individual poets. He has selected mainly translations from the 1950s and 1960s, although a few earlier ones are included as well. His discussion touches on both the accuracy and the literary quality of each translation. There are indexes of pubishers and translators.

DICTIONARIES, ENCYCLOPEDIAS, AND HANDBOOKS

611.   Gerber, Douglas E., ed. **Companion to the Greek Lyric Poets.** Mnemosyne Supplements 173. Leiden: Brill, 1997. 287pp. ISBN 90–04–09944–1. LCCN 97–28625.

"The primary aim of this book . . . is to make the reader aware of the main problems and controversies associated with the Greek lyric poets and to provide the necessary bibliography for further study." Gerber's general introduction defines what is generally included in Greek lyric poetry (which will surprise the uninitiated): virtually all Greek poetry written from the seventh to mid-fifth centuries B.C. except epic and dramatic verse. Gerber also very briefly addresses transmission, occasion, poet's voice, and classification in the introduction. The bulk of the work consists of four chapters covering iambic, elegiac, personal, and public poetry. Each has a short introduction and sections on the individual poets who fall within the category. All the contributors are capable specialists. They provide a solid overview of the subject that will benefit both students and teachers of Greek lyric. Those studying Greek poetry in translation will find the *Companion* difficult going, due to the large amounts of untranslated Latin and Greek and the highly technical nature of some of the material. The notes and bibliographies are a strong point and will guide readers to standard editions and the more important scholarly literature through the mid-1990s. Indexing is minimal: Greek words, passages discussed, and a very short subject index.

SATIRE

BIBLIOGRAPHIES

See also Donlan (entry 609).

612.   Braund, Susan H. **Roman Verse Satire.** New Surveys in the Classics 23. Oxford: Oxford University Press, 1992. 65pp. ISBN 019–922072–7. LCCN 92–221767.

This survey, like others in its series, is aimed primarily at undergraduates. Braund covers both general topics (e.g., the origins and characteristics of satire) and chief exponents of genre (Lucilius, Horace, Persius, and Juvenal) in a series of brief essays. She reviews recent scholarship both in the text and in the detailed notes. Braund is highly selective and concentrates on recent English-language work.

613.   Kirk, Eugene P. **Menippean Satire: An Annotated Catalogue of Texts and Criticism.** Garland Reference Library of the Humanities 191. New York: Garland, 1980. 313pp. ISBN 0–8240–9533–2. LCCN 79–7921.

For those interested in the history of the genre of Menippean satire, this work provides a comprehensive bibliographical resource. It attempts "to list exhaustively all Menippean satires written before 1660 in the languages of Western Europe, and all the criticism published in those same languages about Menippean satire, up to the present time." Kirk's introduction gives a good overview of the genre and its history in the course of explaining the scope and organization of his catalogue. He then lists the authors of Menippean satire in roughly chronological sequence from Menippus of Gadara, the inventor of the form, to Abraham Cowley (1618–1667). Under each he notes all their works that might be characterized as Menippean satire and cites modern editions and translations. The texts cited, as in the case of Petronius, do not always include the best critical editions. Kirk's annotations in the author listings include much biographical, bibliographical, and critical information. Kirk also provides, in a separate chapter, a selective bibliography of important Renaissance editions of the classical Menippean satires. The final chapter includes entries for more than 200 critical works on the genre, arranged alphabetically by author. Most of these are acompanied by brief summaries. An index of authors and subjects concludes the volume. This work is useful for the study of medieval and Renaissance literature as well as that of classical literature and its influence.

HISTORY AND BIOGRAPHY

BIBLIOGRAPHIES

614.   Donlan, Walter, ed. **Classical World Bibliography of Greek and Roman History.** Garland Reference Library of the Humanities 94. New York: Garland, 1978. 234pp. ISBN 0–8240–9879–X. LC 76–52511.

This volume gathers 14 bibliographical surveys that originally appeared in *Classical World* (entry 95) between 1954 and 1971. Three of these are devoted each to Herodotus (one general survey and two collectively covering 1954–1969), Thucydides (1942–1967), and Tacitus (1948–1967). The following are each covered by a single survey: Livy (1940–1958), Caesar (1935–1961), Philo and Josephus (1937–1959), Alexander the Great (1948–1967), and Julian the Apostate (1945–1964). These surveys are normally selective, although those on Philo and Josephus and Alexander the Great attempt completeness. All are by well-known specialists on the respective subjects. There is some variation in presentation, but most of the surveys are arranged topically, and all include descriptive and evaluative comments on the works cited. The compilation reflects a general bias in classical studies toward treating history through historical authors. It is a useful compendium for those seeking retrospective bibliographies on the ancient historians. A general index would have been helpful.

615.   Kraus, C. S., and A. J. Woodman. **Latin Historians.** New Surveys in the Classics 27. Oxford: Oxford University Press, 1997. 132pp. ISBN 0–19–922293–2.

This slim volume surveys the major historians of the late republic and early empire: Sallust, Livy, and Tacitus. Kraus and Woodman also give brief attention to the minor historians of the first century A.D., Velleius Paterculus and Curtius. They take a decidedly literary position on the interpretation of the ancient historians, following the lead of T. P. Wiseman's *Clio's Cosmetics* (Totowa, NJ: Rowman and Littlefield, 1979) and Woodman's own *Rhetoric in Classical Historiography* (London: Croon Helm, 1988). Kraus and Woodman discuss the characteristics of each of their subjects' work and survey (almost incidentally) the salient scholarship, both recent and classic works. A bibliographical appendix notes major editions, bibliographies, and general works for each of the historians. The select bibliography is an excellent starting point for further research.

616. Marincola, John. **Greek Historians.** New Surveys in the Classics 31. Oxford: Oxford University Press, 2001. 162pp. ISBN 019–922501–X.

In a highly selective fashion Marincola surveys approximately 30 years' work on Greek historiography and historians. He occasionally notes important earlier publications and, while emphasizing English-language publications, also includes exceptionally important titles in other languages. His introduction discusses the predominant modern schools of thought on ancient historiography. The next chapter covers the antecedents of Greek history: Homer, praise poetry, and the Ionians. Marincola gives the most space to major figures, with chapters on Herodotus, Thucydides, and Polybius. Each is subdivided to cover such topics as life and times, structure and subject matter, narrative manner, themes, and *Nachleben*. Other historians are relegated to a short chapter on Hellenistic historians or remarks in passing elsewhere in the book. A bibliographical note indicates important editions, translations, commentaries, lexica, and bibliographies for Herodotus, Thucydides, and Polybius. The select bibliography lists most of the works discussed or cited. The index is useful for uncovering discussion of minor figures. Overall, Marincola has produced a valuable guide to recent work on the Greek historians.

DICTIONARIES, ENCYCLOPEDIAS, AND HANDBOOKS

617. Flach, Dieter. **Römische Geschichtsschreibung.** 3., neubearb. Aufl. Darmstadt: Wissenschaftliche Buchgesellschaft, 1998. 337pp. ISBN 3–534–13709–4.

Earlier editions of this appeared with the title *Einführung in die römische Geschichtsschreibung*. Flach provides a systematic handbook on Roman historical writing. He begins with a brief discussion of the ancient Greek historians who influenced the writing of Roman history. Then he proceeds in chronological order from the earliest works (*Annales Maximi, Fabius Pictor*) through Ammianus Marcellinus in the fourth century A.D. Flach focuses on the historiography and only covers the lives of the authors incidentally. He lists key works on each author, although his bibliography is not as up-to-date as it should be, omitting, for example, key works of the 1980s and 1990s on Ammianus. The chronology (*Zeittafel*) and enumeration of editions, translations, and commentaries found at the end of the work are useful.

618. Sonnabend, Holger. **Geschichte der antiken Biographie: Von Isokrates bis Isokrates zur Historia Augusta.** Stuttgart: J. B. Metzler, 2002. 246pp. ISBN 3–476–01914–4.

While not intended as a reference work per se, Sonnabend's history of ancient biography essentially provides us with a handbook of biography from the third century B.C. through the third century A.D. It is arguable that Isocrates and Xenophon mark the beginnings of biography in the classical world, and this is where Sonnabend starts; for earlier proto-biographies see A. Momigliano, *Development of Greek Biography* (Cambridge, MA: Harvard University Press, 1971; expanded ed., 1993). Sonnabend opens with a general overview of ancient biography, and its relation to historiography and to modern biography. He then covers Greek biographies and autobiographies down to the Roman era, covering authors and works one by one. A brief chapter on the origins of Roman biographical writing provides the transition to Rome; Sonnabend then goes through biographical and autobiographical writers and works of the Roman world (including Greek authors of the period, such as Plutarch Diogenes Laertius). He follows a loosely chronological sequence, providing background information for each author and a discussion of his biographical works. His bibliographies enumerate editions and translations of each, as well as listing key secondary works. Indexes cover personal names and passages discussed.

MEDICAL AND TECHNICAL WRITERS

BIBLIOGRAPHIES

619.   Leitner, Helmut. **Bibliography to the Ancient Medical Authors.** Bern: Hans Huber, 1973. 61pp. ISBN 3–456–00322–6. LCCN 72–86911.

Leitner's general bibliography of editions and translations of the ancient medical writers arranges the authors alphabetically. Under each he lists individual works by title, followed by collected editions and collected translations. Leitner includes mostly twentieth-century editions; occasionally nineteenth-century ones are noted, if they are the only or best edition of a given author. He covers the whole of antiquity from Hippocrates to Paulos of Aigina (seventh century A.D.). A couple of later authors are also included. Writers on veterinary medicine are excluded. Leitner is somewhat stronger on Greek than Latin writers. Additional material on Latin medical writers can be found in Sabbah's *Bibliographie des textes médicaux latins* (entry 620).

620.   Sabbah, Guy, Pierre-Paul Corsetti, and Klaus-Dietrich Fischer. **Bibliographie des textes médicaux latins: Antiquité et haut moyen âge.** Centre Jean-Palerne. Mémoires 6. Saint-Étienne: Publications de l'Université, 1987. 174pp. LCCN 92–234605.

This bibliography covers the Latin medical writers of antiquity and the Middle Ages. All the authors are listed in a single alphabetical sequence. Editions, commentaries, translations, indexes, concordances, and lexica are noted under each. The occasional annotations are primarily of a bibliographical nature. Sabbah and his collaborators cover many authors, including those on veterinary medicine, omitted by Leitner (entry 619). There are indexes of manuscripts and of modern authors.

DICTIONARIES, ENCYCLOPEDIAS, AND HANDBOOKS

621.   **Medicina Antiqua.** URL: www.medicinaantiqua.org.uk/index.html.

This Web site is based at the Wellcome Trust Center for the History of Medicine at the University of London. It offers a variety of resources for the study of ancient medicine. These include short essays on a variety of topics in ancient medicine, ancient medical texts in English translation, and links to other relevant Web sites. It also provides conference announcements, as well as information about the Society for Ancient Medicine (entry 1023) and the *Medant* discussion list (entry 186).

ORATORY AND RHETORIC

BIBLIOGRAPHIES

See Donlan (entry 856).

DICTIONARIES, ENCYCLOPEDIAS, AND HANDBOOKS

622. Anderson, R. Dean. **Glossary of Greek Rhetorical Terms Connected to Methods of Argumentation, Figures, and Tropes from Anaximenes to Quintilian.** Contributions to Biblical Exegesis and Theology 24. Leuven: Peeters, 2000. 130pp. ISBN 90–429–0846–7. LCCN 00–400573.

This glossary is an outgrowth of Anderson's *Ancient Rhetorical Theory and Paul* (Leuven: Peeters, 1998). In it Anderson selectively treats rhetorical terms through the first century A.D., although he goes beyond this period to include Alexander's *On Figures* (second century A.D.). This is not a book for the Greekless: lemmata are in Greek, and much untranslated Greek and Latin appear in the entries. It is valuable for its discussion of the meanings of rhetorical terms and enumeration of ancient sources. Modern secondary literature is noted, although not extensively. Indexes of Latin rhetorical terms and biblical passages conclude the volume.

623. Kennedy, George. **Art of Persuasion in Greece.** History of Rhetoric 1. Princeton, NJ: Princeton University Press, 1963. 350pp. ISBN 0–691–06008–8. LCCN 63–7070.

This treatment of Greek rhetoric is the first of Kennedy's standard works on the history of classical rhetoric (see also entries 624–625). Kennedy begins with a general discussion of rhetoric, followed by an examination of rhetorical techniques from Homer through the fifth century B.C. He then covers successively the early rhetorical theorists, the Attic orators, and Hellenistic rhetoric through Dionysius of Halicarnassus. Kennedy is both learned and readable. While he does not provide a bibliography, the footnotes provide thorough coverage of the relevant literature. A detailed table of contents and index make it easy to consult the book on specific points and individuals. *Art of Persuasion* is also the most dated of Kennedy's works and must now be supplemented by his later abridgement, *A New History of Classical Rhetoric* (entry 626). It remains among the best general sources for English-speaking students.

624. Kennedy, George. **Art of Rhetoric in the Roman World, 300 B.C.–A.D. 300.** History of Rhetoric 2. Princeton, NJ: Princeton University Press, 1972. 658pp. ISBN 0–691–03505–9. LCCN 72–166380.

The central and largest volume of Kennedy's *History of Rhetoric* (see also entries 623 and 625) covers rhetoric at Rome from the early days of the republic through the end of the classical period. Kennedy traces the development of the rhetorical art, demonstrating the Roman emphasis on style and prose artistry over persuasion. He follows a chronological arrangement, with chapters covering early Roman rhetoric; Cicero's *De inventione* and the *Rhetorica ad Herennium;* Cicero and his younger contemporaries, oratory and rhetorical criticism in Augustan Rome, Augustan rhetoric and Augustan literature, eloquence in the early empire, Quintilian and his younger contemporaries, the second Sophistic, and

Greek rhetoricians of the empire. This remains the best and most detailed survey of the Roman rhetoric available. While Kennedy does not include a bibliography, his notes lead to an extensive selection of major scholarly studies. There is a detailed index. For later bibliography and other updates, see Kennedy's *New History of Classical Rhetoric* (entry 626).

625. Kennedy, George A. **Greek Rhetoric under the Christian Emperors.** History of Rhetoric 3. Princeton, NJ: Princeton University Press, 1983. 333pp. ISBN 0–691–03565–2; 0–691–10145–0pa. LCCN 82–51044.

The final volume of Kennedy's trilogy on Greek and Roman rhetoric (see also entries 623–624) begins with the fourth century A.D. and extends into the Byzantine Empire, ending around 1300. In it he deals with the continuity and change inherent in the transition of pagan antiquity to the Christian era. He covers secular speech in late antiquity, later Greek rhetorical theory, the schools of late antiquity, Christianity and rhetoric, and Byzantine rhetoric. Kennedy discusses many notable theorists and practitioners of the period, along with particular topics. As with the other volumes in this series, no bibliography is provided, although there are extensive footnotes. A detailed index concludes the book. While primarily of value to those interested in the history of rhetoric, this book also has much for those studying early Christianity and the history of education. Bibliographical and other updates may be found in Kennedy's *New History of Classical Rhetoric* (entry 626).

626. Kennedy, George. **New History of Classical Rhetoric.** Princeton, NJ: Princeton University Press, 1994. ISBN 0–691–03443–5; 0–691–00059–Xpa. LCCN 94–11249.

In this volume, Kennedy offers an abridgement of and update to his earlier three-volume history of rhetoric in the classical world (entries 623–625). He surveys rhetoric from its origins in Greece through the Roman Empire. He supplies much less detail here than in the original work, and much less bibliographical apparatus. The *New History* is aimed primarily at students; scholars will still value it for the its coverage of more recent research and for its extension of coverage into late antiquity. A good but very selective bibliography and a modest index conclude the volume. This supplements rather than replaces the earlier work.

627. Lausberg, Heinrich. **Handbook of Literary Rhetoric: A Foundation for Literary Study.** Trans. Matthew T. Bliss, Annemiek Jansen, and David E. Orton. Ed. David E. Orton and R. Dean Anderson. Leiden: Brill, 1998. 921pp. ISBN 90–04–10705–3. LCCN 97–51646.

Lausberg's *Handbuch der literarischen Rhetorik* first appeared in in 1960; this version is translated from the second edition (München: Max Heuber, 1973). In his preface, Lausberg states that "he seeks to smooth the beginner's way;" what he does not say is that he expects the beginner to have a substantial background in Latin and Greek. His preliminary remarks cover the definitions of *ars, artes liberales,* and grammar. Then he turns to rhetoric proper, which consumes nearly 500 pages. This is divided into two sections: definition and place of rhetoric, and the organization and description of rhetoric, which is extensively subdivided. Finally Lausberg turns to poetics. He provides a large bibliography (through 1973) and extensive indexes of Latin, Greek, and French terms. This is an excellent systematic handbook of classical rhetoric, firmly rooted in the ancient sources. It is not, despite its author's assertion to the contrary, a book for beginners.

628. Martin, Josef. **Antike Rhetorik: Technik und Methode.** Handbuch der Altertumwissenschaft 2, T. 3. München: C. H. Beck, 1974. 420pp. ISBN 3–406–04770–X.

Reviewers have not been kind to Martin's handbook, and with some reason. He offers a very short introduction on the definition and history of rhetoric. The bulk of the work consists of five parts, following the well-worn pattern of the ancients: *inventio, dispositio, elocutio, memoria,* and *pronuntiatio.* He is useful as a compendium of ancient rhetorical theorists, with full references to the primary sources. He largely ignores ancient oratory as a practical art. Martin is also weak on the secondary literature. Indexes cover names, words and subjects, and sources. Most seeking discussions of ancient rhetorical terms and theories will find Lausberg's (entry 627) arrangement more congenial. Those wanting a readable treatment should consult the various works of George Kennedy (entries 623–626).

629. Porter, Stanley E., ed. **Handbook of Classical Rhetoric in the Hellenistic Period, 330 B.C.–A.D. 400.** Leiden: Brill, 1997. 901pp. ISBN 90–04–09963–4. LCCN 96–47335.

Porter seeks to provide a thorough overview of rhetoric and its uses from the time of Alexander through late antiquity. He divides the volume into three parts. The first, "Rhetoric Defined," offers a short history of classical rhetoric, a survey of the genres of rhetoric, and discussions of such topics as arrangement, invention, style, and delivery. The second part, "Rhetoric in Practice," looks at the use of rhetoric in the various genres, such as epistles, philosophy, history, poetry, drama, and romance. The chapters in part 3, "Individual Writers and the Rhetorical Tradition," focus on the use of rhetoric by an individual writer. In addition to the usual classical suspects, there is strong coverage of early Christian literature. Each chapter includes extensive references and a working bibliography. Porter and his distinguished team of contributors offer an excellent reference work for any student of rhetoric. The only major deficiencies are lack of a glossary of rhetorical terms and a subject index. The work does include indexes of ancient and modern writers.

QUOTATIONS AND PROVERBS

DICTIONARIES, ENCYCLOPEDIAS, AND HANDBOOKS

See also the section "Popular Phrase Books and Glossaries" in chapter 12.

630. Bartels, Klaus, and Ludwig Huber. **Veni, Vidi, Vici: Geflügelte Worte aus dem Griechischen und Lateinischen.** 9. Aufl. Darmstadt: Wissenshaftliche Gesellschaft, 1992. 216pp. ISBN 3–534–11920–7.

For those comfortable in German, this attractive volume provides an excellent selection of quotations and notable phrases from the Greek and Latin classics. Greek and Latin quotations are gathered into separate lists, each alphabetized by keyword. The phrase is given in the original, followed by a German translation and a citation for the ancient source. Occasionally an extended note provides some history of the quotation, such as its adoption by subsequent writers. The excellent selection of material is a tribute to the taste and scholarship of the editors. The latest edition, unlike some of the earlier ones, includes an index, although an index of sources is still needed.

631.   Bayer, Karl. **Nota bene! Das lateinische Zitatenlexikon.** 3. erw. und überarb. Aufl. Düsseldorf: Artemis & Winkler, 1999. 676pp. ISBN 3–7608–1161–2.

Bayer, a retired German schoolteacher, gathers 3,000 Latin quotations and presents them alphabetically. Bayer provides the Latin, along with a German translation. He frequently provides citations and parallels from classical and medieval sources. Bayer provides four indexes: German keywords, names, subjects, and sources. Those without passable German will find navigation difficult. The level of scholarship is considerably below Bartels and Huber (entry 630) and Tosi (entry 639). *Nota bene* is noteworthy chiefly for the number of quotations provided, which exceeds many other collections.

632.   Guterman, Norbert. **Anchor Book of Latin Quotations with English Translations.** New York: Doubleday, 1990. 433pp. ISBN 0–385–41391–2. LC 90–237.

Originally published as *A Book of Latin Quotations* in 1966, this compilation includes more than 1,500 quotations from Latin literature. Guterman arranges the quotations chronologically by author (the least useful choice for such a dictionary). The Latin original and the English translation appear on facing pages. While most of the better-known phrases appear in these pages, there are also many surprises. Occasionally Guterman lapses into being an anthologist rather than a compiler of quotations. The majority of the translations are by Guterman, although some are by well-known literary figures. There are indexes of ancient authors, subjects (in English), and Latin keywords. Aside from browsers, most will need to turn to these first. Sweet (entry 638) offers comparable coverage, while Stone (entry 637) provides far more quotations with less information and inferior indexing.

633.   Harbottle, Thomas Benfield. **Dictionary of Quotations (Classical).** 3rd ed. New York: MacMillan, 1906. 684pp. Reprinted as *Anthology of Classical Quotations,* San Antonio, TX: Scylax Press, 1984.

This work is divided into two parts, one for Latin quotations, the other for Greek. Within each the quotations are arranged alphabetically by the first word. Harbottle supplies the original Latin or Greek, its source, and an English translation. In addition to famous phrases, he includes many less-well-known quotations. Harbottle provides an author index and subject indexes in Latin, Greek, and English. His dictionary remains useful both for finding and identifying classical quotations. The more recent work of Guterman (entry 632) includes only Latin quotations. Bartels (entry 630), a collection containing both Greek and Latin quotations, is a good alternative but requires at least some knowledge of German. Tosi (entry 639) also offers an excellent dictionary of both Latin and Greek quotations but is in Italian.

634.   Kudla, Hubertus, ed. **Lexikon der lateinischen Zitate: 3500 Originale mit Übersetzungen und Belegstellen.** München: C. H. Beck, 1999. 603pp. ISBN 3–406–42124–5. LCCN 00–316339.

Kudla, another retired German schoolteacher, gathers 3,524 Latin quotations, proverbs, and bons mots. While he draws the majority of these from classical Latin literature, Kudla also includes Greek authors in Latin translation, the Vulgate, and medieval and Renaissance authors. Kudla marshals them under several hundred subject headings (in German). Each entry provides the Latin original, references to the source used and similar expressions elsewhere, a German translation, and often a brief commentary. Not all quotations have attributions; those without atttibution are largely drawn from other collections. Kudla offers far more quotations than most of his competitors and includes many not readily found elsewhere. He also includes short biographical notes on major Latin and Greek authors, bibliographies of other collections of quotations and of his sources, and an alphabetical index of quotation incipits. This index is an invaluable feature in a work arranged by subject and should be included in more such works; however, a Latin keyword index would be even more effective. Lack of an index of sources is a major drawback.

635.   Otto, A. **Die Sprichwörter und sprichwörterlichen Redensarten der Römer.** Leipzig: Teubner, 1890; repr., Hildesheim: Georg Olms, 1971. 436pp. LCCN 31–20573.

636.   Häussler, Reinhard, ed. **Nachträge zu A. Otto, Sprichwörter und sprich-wörterlichen Redensarten der Römer.** Hildesheim: Georg Olms, 1968. 324pp. LCCN 31–20573.

Otto's work is the classic compilation of Latin proverbs and bons mots. He culled these from the whole corpus of Latin literature. The proverbs are arranged alphabetically by keyword. Under each term the selected sayings are quoted in full in the original Latin. Otto also cites the source and sometimes provides a German translation. Very occasionally there is some discussion of the proverb. Numerous cross-references are provided. Häussler gathers a number of reviews and articles by various hands, which supplement Otto. He also supplies an index, which correlates the additions with the appropriate entry in Otto.

637.   Stone, Jon R. **Routledge Dictionary of Latin Quotations: The Illiterati's Guide to Latin Maxims, Mottoes, Proverbs, and Sayings.** New York: Routledge, 2005. ISBN 0–415–96908–5; 0–415–96909–3pa. LCCN 2004–2081.

With nearly 8,000 quotations and proverbs, this is one of the largest collections available. Stone divides it into three sections: Latin proverbs and maxims, Latin mottoes and phrases, and familiar Latin quotation. As Stone notes, these are not mutually exclusive, so the division is sometimes ambiguous and artificial. Within each category quotations and phrase are listed alphabetically. Stone gives the Latin original followed by an English translation. He attributes many to ancient authors but does not provide citations. Tables of abbreviations and of authors cited appear after the main text. Stone provides a rather ineffective English-Latin index: pages of phrases indexed under direct and indirect articles are next to useless. Keyword indexes, both Latin and English, would be far more helpful. Sweet (entry 638) and Guterman (632) offer far fewer quotations but better source citations and indexes.

638.   Sweet, Waldo E. **Latin Proverbs: Wisdom from Ancient to Modern Times.** Wauconda, IL: Bolchazy-Carducci, 2002. 278pp. ISBN 0–86516–544–0. LCCN 2002–12846.

Sweet offers 1,188 quotations and phrases (not all can be described as proverbs) drawn from ancient literature, the Bible, mottos, and the law. The order of presentation can only be described as random. All are given in Latin followed by an idiomatic English translation. Sweet does provide sources, often specific, for many. He does ascribe some to Greek sources, such as Lucian and Plutarch, without citing the Latin intermediary. Indexes provide access by English keyword and author. Sweet also includes biographical notes on the ancient authors. Stone (entry 637) is more comprehensive, but Sweet and Guterman (entry 632) offer more effective indexing.

639. Tosi, Renzo. **Dizionario delle sentenze latine e greche: 10.000 citazioni dall'antichità al rinascimento nell'originale e in traduzione con commento storico letterario e filologico. 13. ed.** Milano: Rizzoli, 2000. 885pp. ISBN 88–17–14636–6.

For those who can manage Italian, this is among the best general dictionaries of classical quotations and sayings. It lists some 1,841 notable quotations and proverbial expressions from ancient and medieval sources. Each is given in the original Latin or Greek, followed by an Italian translation. The commentary to each expression notes its first known use and discusses its meaning. Many entries include citations of the quotation's subsequent appearances in Western literature as well. The quotations are well chosen; the commentary provides many interesting historical sidelights on Western literature and culture. Tosi sensibly employs a thematic arrangement, which is clearly laid out by his table of contents. Latin and Greek indexes also provide alphabetical access for those who need it. There is little difference among the varying editions (really printings) of this work; one may consult whichever happens to be most readily available. Readers who prefer an English-language work might consult Guterman (entry 632), Harbottle (entry 633), Stone (entry 637), or Sweet (entry 638).

15
Greek Authors and Works

Here are found works that deal with an individual Greek author. These include several categories: book-length bibliographies; dictionaries, encyclopedias, and handbooks; indexes and concordances; and journals. Readers should be aware that there are also many article-length bibliographies that are not included here. *Lustrum* (entry 71) and *Classical World* (entry 95) are good places to check for these. In order to supplement the bibliographies listed below with more current material, one should also consult the appropriate author entry in the annual volumes of *L'Année philologique* (entry 44) or its online avatar. Handbooks include the many companions to various authors, a major growth industry in classical publishing of late; see the remarks of Andrew Dyck on this subject in his review of *Brill's Companion to Cicero* (entry 766), *Bryn Mawr Classical Review* (2003.01.17) at http://ccat.sas.upenn.edu/bmcr/2003/2003–01–17.html. While many will automatically turn to such online resources as the *Thesaurus Linguae Graecae* (entry 519), printed indexes and concordances remain widely available and still serve many purposes well. Listings of such works here are selective: the focus is on the best and/or most recent concordances of major authors. See Reisenfeld (entry 562) and the recent work of Boned Colera and Rodríguez Somolinos (entry 489) for additional references to such works.

AESCHYLUS

BIBLIOGRAPHIES

See Donlan (entry 599) and Forman (entry 600).

640.   Ireland, S. **Aeschylus.** New Surveys in the Classics 18. Oxford: Clarendon Press, 1986. 41pp. ISBN 0–903035–154. LCCN 86–198700.

Ireland's survey aims "to provide an introductory guide to the main areas of Aeschylean scholarship in recent times." While focusing on recent English-language studies of Aeschylus, he also includes important older and foreign-language works. Ireland follows the general pattern of the New Surveys series and organizes his material into several topical bibliographical essays that cover both general concerns and the individual plays of Aeschylus. He provides a readable and knowledgeable overview of Aeschylean studies, which is suitable for both undergraduate and graduate students. Those who require exhaustive bibliographical coverage will also need to consult Wartelle's large retrospective bibliography (entry 641).

641.   Wartelle, André. **Bibliographie historique et critique d'Eschyle et de la tragédie grecque, 1518–1974.** Collection d'études anciennes. Paris: Les Belles Lettres, 1978. 685pp. LCCN 79–346983.

This massive compilation begins with the 1518 editio princeps of Aeschylus and proceeds to list in chronological order editions, commentaries, translations, and studies through 1974. Arrangement within each year is alphabetical by author. Earlier works generally lack annotations; those provided tend to be bibliographical in nature. Many of the later works (especially those of the twentieth century) receive brief descriptive summaries and, occasionally, critical comment. Book reviews are listed under the book entry. In addition to works specifically on Aeschylus, many more general studies of Greek tragedy are included as well. Separate indexes provide name and title access to authors, editions, and translations. There is also a subject index and an "index," which is a list of periodicals surveyed for the bibliography.

INDEXES AND CONCORDANCES

642.   Italie, G. **Index Aeschyleus.** Editio altera, corr. et aucta. Ed. S. L. Radt. Leiden: Brill, 1964. 345pp. LCCN 68–129528.

Gabriel Italie's indexes to the Greek tragedians are highly regarded for their care and accuracy. The presentation is traditional, with each entry listing the basic form of the word, its meaning in Latin, and an enumeration of its instances in the surviving works of Aeschylus. Italie gives the forms and citations, noting variants and emendations. Radt's corrections and additions are presented in an appendix. These take into account Gilbert Murray's Oxford Classical Text edition (1955) and H. J. Mette's *Die Fragemente der Tragödien des Aischylos* (Berlin: Akademie-Verlag, 1959). Radt provides a supplement to the concordance in his *Tragicorum Graecorum Fragmenta,* volume 3: *Aeschylus* (Göttingen: Vandenhoeck & Rupprecht, 1985).

APOLLONIUS OF RHODES

DICTIONARIES, ENCYCLOPEDIAS, AND HANDBOOKS

643.   Papanghelis, Theodore D., and Antonios Rengakos, eds. **Companion to Apollonius Rhodius.** Mnemosyne Supplements 217. Leiden: Brill, 2001. 362pp. ISBN 90–04–11752–0. LCCN 2001–025887.

Apollonius, after a long period of neglect as a second-rater, has undergone a renaissance in the last few decades. This *Companion* seeks to cover major trends in recent Apollonian scholarship; its contributors include leading scholars from Europe and America. The first four essays are typical of such companions: a bibliographic survey (1955–1999), the textual tradition of the *Argonautica,* the life of Apollonius, and the chronology of various Hellenistic poets. The bibliographic survey is highly selective but, used in combination with the general bibliography at the end of the volume, will provide a good working introduction to Apollonian studies. The remaining 10 essays address poetics, influences on Apollonius, and his *Nachleben.* They cover such topics as narrative, interior monologues, similes, epic formulae, Apollonius's influence on Vergil and later Greek epic, and the cultural afterlife of the myth of the Golden Fleece. There is a brief and totally inadequate index. The work as a whole is a useful reference for Apollonian studies, though parts will be helpful only to professional scholars.

INDEXES AND CONCORDANCES

644. Campbell, Malcolm. **Index Verborum in Apollonium Rhodium.** Alpha-Omega, Reihe A, 62. Hildesheim: Georg Olms, 1983. 292pp. ISBN 3–487–07342–0. LCCN 83–222908.

Campbell provides a complete word index to the *Argonautica* and to most of the fragments ascribed to Apollonius in J. U. Powell, *Collectanea Alexandrina* (Oxford: Oxford University Press, 1925). Campbell uses the highly regarded edition of F. Vian and E. Delage (Paris: Les Belles Lettres, 1974–1981) for the *Argonautica*. All instances of a word are gathered under the normal lexical form, with the various conjugated and declined forms clearly indicated. Campbell notes all manuscript variants from Vian's apparatus, but only conjectures that have been adopted in the text.

645. Papathomopoulos, Manolis. **Apollonii Rhodii Argonauticorum Concordantia.** Alpha-Omega, Reihe A, 170. Hildesheim: Olms-Weidmann, 1996. 410pp. ISBN 3–487–10237–4. LC 97–116579.

Like Campbell (entry 644), Papathomopoulos bases his work on Vian's edition. He restricts his concordance to the *Argonautica* and does not include the fragments of other works attributed to Apollonius. Papathomopoulos provides a fully lemmatized concordance, with a metrical line of context for each instance of a word. The various inflected forms of a word are listed separately. While Papathomopoulos does provide an immediate context, in most other respects users will find Campbell of more help: all forms of a word are gathered in one place, and Campbell takes account of textual variants.

646. Pompella, Giuseppe. **Apollonii Rhodii Lexicon.** Alpha-Omega, Reihe A, 194. Hildesheim: Olms-Weidmann, 2001. 674pp. ISBN 3–487–11301–5.

Pompella's work is a lexicon rather than a concordance, although he lists most instances of each word. He does provide a Latin meaning for each word and translates many individual passages into Latin. Pompella relies most heavily on Vian's text. This work is a useful companion to the concordances of Campbell (entry 644) and Papthomopoulos (entry 645).

ARISTOPHANES

BIBLIOGRAPHIES

See also Donlan (entry 599) and Forman (entry 600).

647. Ussher, R. G. **Aristophanes.** New Surveys in the Classics 13. Oxford: Clarendon Press, 1979. 44pp. ISBN 0–9030–35–10–3. LCCN 80–492020.

Ussher surveys the state of Aristophanic studies, ca. 1979, in a series of short topical essays. Some of these will present a challenge to the Greekless reader, since they deal with relatively technical aspects of Aristophanes' work and contain a considerable amount of untranslated Greek. Ussher covers a wide range of works, mostly published since 1950, in his extensive notes. He includes somewhat more foreign-language works than is typical for volumes in this series. Ussher is a good source of bibliography for advanced Greek students; he is of less use to those studying Aristophanes in translation.

INDEXES AND CONCORDANCES

648.   Dunbar, Henry. **Complete Concordance to the Comedies and Fragments of Aristophanes.** New edition completely rev. and enl. by Benedetto Marzullo. Hildesheim: Georg Olms, 1973. 372pp. ISBN 3–487–05017–X.

Marzullo offers an updated version of Dunbar's 1883 concordance to Aristophanes. Dunbar founded his concordance on the edition of Wilhelm Dindorf (Oxford: University Press, 1835–1838) and August Meineke's edition of the fragments (Berlin: Reimer, 1840), with some cognizance of other and later editions. Marzullo has brought the lemmata, though not the body of the entries, into conformity with F.W. Hall and William Geldart's edition (Oxford: Clarendon Press, 1906). His corrections and additions, which are indicated by various sigla in the margins of the original concordance, appear in an appendix. Marzullo also supplies a long and petulant preface, chiefly addressed to critics of his other ventures in concordance updating. The principal benefit of this work is setting words in context (one metrical line provided for each); otherwise, Todd (entry 649) is much more convenient.

649.   Todd, O. J. **Index Aristophaneus.** Cambridge, MA: Harvard University Press, 1932. 275pp. LCCN 32–003739

The Oxford Classical Text edition of Hall and Geldart forms the basis of the index; deviances from this are noted immediately following the preface. Each word has an entry under its normal lexical form, with all inflected forms marshaled within. Todd is very much an index, with a straightforward enumeration of instances and very little additional matter.

ARISTOTLE

BIBLIOGRAPHIES

See also Barnes (entry 656) and Donlan (entry 856).

650.   Cooper, Lane, and Alfred Gudeman. **Bibliography of the Poetics of Aristotle.** Cornell Studies in English 11. New Haven, CT: Yale University Press, 1928. 193pp. LCCN 28–12280.

Compiled by two noted scholars, this is a helpful guide to the earlier literature on one of Aristotle's most influential works. It provides citations for approximately 1,500 items and offers good coverage through the mid-1920s. Material is arranged by form (Greek editions, translations, commentaries, and articles) and date of publication. All types of publication are included with the exception of book reviews. The compilers have provided an author index and occasional cross-references; however, lack of subject access is a major drawback. While now superseded by Schrier (entry 654), it remains far more widely available than that work.

651.   Erickson, Keith V. **Aristotle's Rhetoric: Five Centuries of Philological Research.** Metuchen, NJ: Scarecrow Press, 1975. 187pp. ISBN 0–8108–0809–9 LCCN 75–5639.

Erickson's "five centuries" refer to the years 1475–1975. The almost 1,600 entries cover books, dissertations, and articles. Some reviews appear as entries, although no systematic effort is made to list them. Entries do not include annotations. Erickson arranges works alphabetically by author; the only index is a chronological one. Lack of subject access requires the user to browse the entire bibliography to locate works of interest. A work of the literary and historical significance of the *Rhetoric* really deserves better.

652.   Ingardia, Richard. **Aristotle Bibliography.** URL: www.aristotlebibliography.com.

This online bibliography, which is available by subscription, is based at St. John's University. Ingardia, a philosopher, had accumulated more than 45,000 entries as of 2004. These include books, dissertations, articles, and reviews published in 1900 or later. The database can be searched by author or by keyword. The search form suggests that one can search authors only by last name, but it is possible to do a more precise search by entering "last name, first name." There is no controlled subject access, nor can the bibliography be browsed. It is possible to limit searches by date. There are currently no abstracts, although Ingardia hopes to add these in the future. While still under development and far from complete, the *Aristotle Bibliography* is a powerful tool. For older material one must still consult the venerable work of Schwab (entry 655).

653.   Radice, Roberto, and Richard Davies. **Aristotle's Metaphysics: Annotated Bibliography of the Twentieth-Century Literature.** Brill's Annotated Bibliographies 1. Leiden: Brill, 1997. 904pp. ISBN 90–04–10895–5. LCCN 97–22097.

Radice, supported by nearly 50 contributors in various countries, has gathered approximately 3,500 works (plus about 1,000 book reviews) dealing with the *Metaphysics* of Aristotle. He brings together work in classics, philosophy, theology, and history of science. Coverage includes Latin America and Eastern Europe as well as the more readily available work from North America and Western Europe. Entries are arranged in several categories: editions, translations, commentaries, bibliographical works, and secondary works. Generally these are grouped by year, then author. Translations, an exception, are arranged by language and then year. Most entries include descriptive annotations. Book reviews are noted under the title reviewed. There are also numerous cross-references to subsequent editions, related works, and the like. Coverage is exhaustive from 1900 through 1996. Reprints of earlier works are often included, and there are a few citations for works published in 1997. Detailed indexes provide access by subject, Greek term, author, and passage discussed. This is an indispensable resource for serious study of the *Metaphysics*.

654.   Schrier, Omert J. **Poetics of Aristotle and the Tractatus Coislinianus: A Bibliography from about 900 till 1996.** Mnemosyne Supplements 184. Leiden: Brill, 1998. 350pp. ISBN 90–04–11132–8. LCCN 98–6542.

Schrier supersedes the old standard bibliography by Cooper and Gudeman (entry 650). He attempts to cover all editions, commentaries, translations, and secondary works relating to the *Poetics* from the beginning of printing (and some older manuscript material) through 1996. Schrier also covers the *Tractatus Coislinianus,* a work thought by some to include fragments of and allusions to the lost second part of the *Poetics* (on comedy). A brief preliminary list notes translations and commentaries antedating 1481, with cross-references to later editions and studies of them. Most of these early works are in Arabic, Syriac, or Latin. The main list covers all types of works, except translations, year by year from 1481 to 1996. Entries sometimes include very brief annotations that serve to clarify the nature or subject of the work. Reviews are listed under the relevant book titles. Translations of the *Poetics* appear in a separate list, arranged by language and date. Schrier provides numerous cross-references and indexes to editions, Latin translations, commentaries, passages, subjects, Greek words, and names. His labor has not always resulted in good access. The subject index is complex and problematic. Many of the entries consist of transliterated Greek words, sometimes translated, sometimes not. Cross-referencing between Greek and English terms is incomplete and inconsistent. The index of Greek words refers the user back to the transliterated form in the subject index. In spite of these difficulties, Schrier provides a wealth of literature on the *Poetics* for those with the time and energy to rummage his work.

655. Schwab, Moise. **Bibliographie d'Aristote.** Paris: H. Welter, 1896; repr., New York: Burt Franklin, 1967. 380pp. LCCN 01–8386.

Useful for those seeking older works on Aristotle, Schwab's compilation is the last large-scale general bibliography of Aristotle. It lists some 3,742 items, which include both editions and secondary works. These range in date from the 1490s to the late nineteenth century. The initial chapters deal with biographical works, general studies, manuscripts, and complete editions of Aristotle's works. The remaining chapters cover Aristotle's individual works, grouped by topic (e.g., logic, metaphysics, rhetoric). Schwab's rare annotations are mostly of a bibliographical nature. An index of authors is provided.

DICTIONARIES, ENCYCLOPEDIAS, AND HANDBOOKS

656. Barnes, Jonathan, ed. **Cambridge Companion to Aristotle.** Cambridge: Cambridge University Press, 1995. 404pp. ISBN 0–521–41133–5; 0–521–42294–9pa. LCCN 94–516.

This work is a philosophical companion to Aristotle, written by philosophers (mainly Oxonians) of the analytic tradition. It targets students, undergraduate and graduate, approaching Aristotle for the first time. Barnes begins the work with a lively and iconoclastic introduction. A guide to Aristotle's writings follows: it lists all the works (with standard abbreviations) and explains the Bekker numbers by which individual passages are customarily cited. The nine chapters cover Aristotle's life and work, logic, metaphysics, philosophy of science, science, psychology, ethics, politics, and rhetoric and poetics. "Suggestions for Reading" recommends both translations and the best Greek editions. It also outlines some approaches to reading Aristotle and lists basic secondary works on him. The bibliography, a revised and updated version of the editor's *Aristotle: A Selective Bibliography* (new ed., Oxford: Subfaculty of Philosophy, 1988) runs to 89 pages. It offers a generous selection of the most important works on Aristotle, arranged by subject. Three indexes round out the volume: passages cited, names, and subjects. Barnes and his contributors provide an excellent aid to the study of Aristotle.

INDEXES AND CONCORDANCES

657. Bonitz, H. **Index Aristotelicus.** Berlin: G. Reimer, 1870; repr. Berlin: Akademie-Verlag, 1870. 878pp. LCCN 07–22716.

Bonitz remains the only index to Aristotle's works as a whole. He founded it upon the great edition that Immanuel Bekker prepared for the Royal Prussian Academy. Unfortunately, Bekker represents the state of the text ca. 1831. Bonitz lists nouns and adjectives under the nominative form, and verbs under the infinitive. The type is small, and a magnifying glass recommended.

658.   Organ, Troy Wilson. **Index to Aristotle in English Translation.** Princeton, NJ: Princeton University Press, 1949. 181pp. LCCN 49–007450.

Organ provides an English topical index to the works of Aristotle. He bases it upon the translation of W. D. Ross and J. A. Smith (Oxford: Clarendon Press, 1908–1931); references are by the standard Bekker numbers, so that the index can be used with almost any modern edition of Aristotle and many translations. Even those using the Greek text will find it useful in providing subject access to the whole corpus, rather than merely indexing Greek words as does Bonitz (entry 657). Greek terms are noted for many of the entries, and there are many cross-references. Organ does not index the *Constitution of Athens* (*Athenaion Politeia*) although it was available to him at the time, nor the fragments, which appeared as a twelfth volume of the Ross translation in 1952.

CALLIMACHUS

BIBLIOGRAPHIES

659.   Lehnus, Luigi. **Nuova Bibliografia Callimachea, 1489–1998.** Hellenica 3. Alessandria: Edizioni dell'Orso, 2000. 509pp. ISBN 88–7694–416–8.

Lehnus covers five centuries of Callimachean scholarship. The new edition adds a very active decade of work, plus other modest improvements. His bibliography is comprehensive and relatively recent, although not always easy to use. Lehnus divides his material into two major sections. The first, which is somewhat confusingly called "Opere" (Works), includes not only editions and translations but also studies of specific works. After noting complete editions and translations, Lehnus proceeds one by one through the individual works of Callimachus. Subarrangement is chronological. The second part ("Studi") deals with topical studies: manuscripts, metrics, biography, and so on. In this section Lehnus provides extensive coverage of Callimachus's influence on later authors, which is perhaps the most important aspect of Callimachean studies for the majority of classicists. There are no annotations. Lehnus does provide an author index. The detailed table of contents also provides some help in navigating the work, but not enough.

DEMOSTHENES

INDEXES AND CONCORDANCES

660.   Preuss, Sigmund. **Index Demosthenicus.** Leipzig: Teubner, 1892; repr. Hildesheim: Georg Olms, 1963. 330pp. LCCN 10–019871.

This venerable work remains the only printed index to Demosthenes. It is based on Friedrich Blass's edition of the orations (4th ed., Leipzig: Teubner, 1887). Preuss indicates the various inflections under each entry, but otherwise it consists entirely of textual references, with no context or discussion.

EPICTETUS

BIBLIOGRAPHIES

661.   Oldfather, W. A. **Contributions toward a Bibliography of Epictetus.** Urbana: University of Illinois, 1927. 201pp. LCCN 28–2296.

662.   Oldfather, W. A. **Contributions toward a Bibliography of Epictetus. A Supplement.** Ed. Marian Harman, with a preliminary list of Epictetus manuscripts by W. H. Friedrich and C. U. Faye. Urbana: University of Illinois Press, 1952. 177pp. LCCN 28–2296//r.

This selective, yet extensive, bibliography is a product of one of the foremost American classicists of the twentieth century. Oldfather arranged his material by form; chapters cover editions, translations, ancient commentaries, and modern criticism. He gives fairly full coverage of editions and translations. Subarrangement is by date for editions and by language for translations. For the earlier works, Oldfather often supplies reasonably complete title-page transcriptions and notes libraries known to hold copies. Many entries are equipped with learned, critical annotations that deal both with content and publishing history. Oldfather is most selective in his coverage of critical works, which are arranged alphabetically by author. His annotations of these entries range from brief summary to scholarly discussion.

Oldfather had nearly finished the supplement before his death in a canoeing accident in 1945. His former student Marian Harman prepared the manuscript for publication. The supplement, which includes works published through 1946, follows the pattern of the original bibliography. In addition to some new items, it contains many updated, corrected, and expanded versions of entries from the original volume. A handlist of manuscripts of the *Encheiridion* of Epictetus has been appended. The supplement also includes indexes for both volumes; these cover editors, translators, and authors; printers and publishers; and places of publication.

EUCLID

BIBLIOGRAPHIES

663.   Steck, Max. **Bibliographia Euclideana.** Arbor Scientarum: Beiträge zur Wissenschaftsgeschichte, Reihe C: Bibliographien 1. Hildesheim: Gerstenberg, 1981. 444pp. ISBN 3–8067–0848–7. LCCN 82–183576.

Steck lists manuscripts and printed editions of Euclid. He arranged printed editions by century: incunabula followed by the sixteenth through twentieth centuries. Steck provides basic bibliographical information and notes some libraries that hold copies. Indexes cover languages, translators and editors, publishers and printers, and places. Many early title pages are reproduced at the back of the volume.

EURIPIDES

BIBLIOGRAPHIES

See also Donlan (entry 599) and Forman (entry 600).

INDEXES AND CONCORDANCES

664. Allen, James T., and Gabriel Italie. **Concordance to Euripides.** Berkeley and Los Angeles: University of California Press, 1954; London: Cambridge University Press, 1954; repr. Groningen: Bouma, 1970. 686pp. LCCN 55–008636.

665. Collard, Christopher. **Supplement to the Allen and Italie Concordance to Euripides.** Groningen: Bouma, 1971. 52pp. LCCN 72–183872.

Allen and Italie's concordance to Euripides has long been regarded as an exceptionally accurate and careful work. They cover all the complete surviving works of Euripides (including the *Rhesus*) and many of the more substantial fragments. For fragments they rely heavily on the *Tragicorum Graecorum Fragmenta* of August Nauck (2nd ed., Leipzig: Teubner, 1926); texts surviving on papyrus are largely derived from Denys Page's *Greek Literary Papyri* (Cambridge, MA: Harvard University Press, 1942). The concordance is based upon a variety of editions (from that of Adolf Kirchhoff to the Oxford Classical Text edition of Gilbert Murray). While the compilers specifically state that "conjectures as a rule are omitted," they do, in fact, included many conjectures and alternate readings. All forms of each word are gathered under a single lemma, with each inflected form presented as a subgrouping. For most words, all instances are cited. A few common words are only partially indexed (as indicated by the use of *passim, etc.,* or *ktl* in the entry). Collard's *Supplement* adds much new material that came to light in the papyri subsequent to Allen and Italie. He also includes numerous corrections and new readings. A noteworthy feature is the inclusion of many references to lexical discussions of various words and passages.

GALEN

BIBLIOGRAPHIES

666. Fichtner, Gerhard. **Corpus Galenicum: Verzeichnis der galenischen und pseudogalenischen Schriften.** Tübingen: Institut für Geschichte der Medizin, 1989. 192pp.

Fichtner's bibliography covers editions, translations, and studies of the individual works of the *Corpus Galenicum*. Works are listed in the order in which they appear in Karl Gottlob Kuhn's edition (Leipzig, 1821–1833); works not appearing in Kuhn follow in alphabetical sequence based on their Latin titles. Fichtner relies heavily on previously published bibliographies. Citations tend to be minimalist at best. There is an extensive array of indexes, covering titles and incipits in several languages, and translators. It is a pity that Fichtner did not expend this zeal and energy on the actual bibliography.

HERACLITUS

BIBLIOGRAPHIES

667. De Martino, Francesco, Livio Rossetti, and Pierpaolo Rosati. **Eraclito: Bibliografia, 1970–1984, e complementi, 1621–1969.** Perugia: Edizioni Scientifiche Italiane, 1986. 176pp. LCCN 87–158563.

De Martino and his collaborators pick up where Roussos (entry 668) leaves off, extending coverage for another 14 years. They also note some titles missed by Roussos. After a narrative overview of Heraclitean scholarship from 1970 to 1984, they provide a bibliography for that period, arranged by author. A separate bibliography includes the earlier titles omitted by Roussos. A series of listings (one hesitates to call them indexes) supply access by date of publication, subject, and passage discussed. While the content is valuable, the design and execution of this work leave much to be desired. The compilers would have done well to follow Roussos's model.

668. Roussos, Evangelos N. **Heraklit-Bibliographie.** Darmstadt: Wissenschaftliche Buchgesellschaft, 1971. 164pp. ISBN 3–534–05585–3. LCCN 72–317298.

In addition to works specifically about Heraclitus, this wide-ranging bibliography includes many general works on Greek literature and philosophy that touch on him. Both the philological and philosophical aspects of Heraclitean studies receive good coverage. Roussos arranges his material under three general headings: text, the teachings of Heraclitus, and influence. The text chapter includes sections on bibliography, texts (editions, translations, and commentaries), the life of Heraclitus, and technical studies (transmission, language, and style). The second chapter, which is divided into a number of topical sections, covers all major aspects of Heraclitus's thought. The third and final chapter covers the influence of Heraclitus on later philosophers from antiquity through Martin Heidegger. It is arranged into several chronological units. There are no annotations. Roussos provides chronological and author indexes. Researchers will find Roussos an excellent source for earlier work (1491–1970) on Heraclitus. De Martino (entry 667) extends coverage to 1984 and adds some titles that Roussos missed.

HERODOTUS

BIBLIOGRAPHIES

See also Donlan (entry 614).

669. Bubel, Frank. **Herodot-Bibliographie, 1980–1988.** Altertumswissenschaftliche Texte und Studien 20. Hildesheim: Olms-Weidmann, 1991. 63pp. ISBN 3–487–09507–6.

Bubel's compilation, which is based on *L'Année philologique* (entry 44), contains roughly 600 works. It is arranged in 19 broad subject categories. In addition to works published within the designated years, Bubel includes a few earlier books that were reviewed during that time. There are no annotations. Reviews are listed under the works reviewed. Bubel provides indexes to authors, names and subjects, and passages discussed. Although essentially a derivative work, Bubel is more convenient to use than the individual volumes of *L'Année philologique* and offers somewhat better access.

DICTIONARIES, ENCYCLOPEDIAS, AND HANDBOOKS

670. Bakker, Egbert J., Irene J. F. De Jong, and Hans van Wees, eds. **Brill's Companion to Herodotus.** Leiden: Brill, 2002. 652pp. ISBN 90–04–12060–2. LCCN 2002–284099.

This *Companion* offers 25 papers gathered into five sections: "Herodotus and His Work," "Herodotus and His World," "The *Histories* as Narrative," "Historical Method," and "History and Ethnography." In them, leading scholars examine all major facets of Herodotean studies and provide a solid introduction and guide for advanced students and scholars. The essays provide a good balance of literary, historical, and ethnographic approaches; many supply original insights in addition to overview and analysis of the topic at hand. A substantial bibliography, general index, and an index of passages cited round out the volume.

INDEXES AND CONCORDANCES

671. Powell, J. Enoch. **Lexicon to Herodotus.** 2nd ed. Hildesheim: Georg Olms, 1977. 391pp. ISBN 3–487–01149–2. LCCN 68–100081.

Although described as a second edition, this is essentially an unaltered reprint of the 1938 Cambridge University Press edition. Powell's famous and highly regarded lexicon is based on Karl Hude's text of Herodotus (Oxford: Clarendon Press, 1926). It combines features of a lexicon and index. All instances of every word except *kai* are noted. Under each entry, Powell gives the English meaning(s), and references are gathered by meaning. Anyone studying Herodotus in Greek will find this an indispensable tool.

HESIOD

INDEXES AND CONCORDANCES

672. Minton, William W. **Concordance to the Hesiodic Corpus.** Leiden: Brill, 1976. 313pp. ISBN 90–04–04381–0.

Minton intends his concordance as "a tool for the study of style in the Hesiodic poems, including its relation to oral composition." Like Tebben's concordance (entry 673), Minton uses the editions of Rzach and of Merkelbach and West. He includes the *Theogony,* the *Works and Days,* and the *Shield,* along with a rather eccentric selection of the fragments. Words appear in alphabetical sequence, with each inflected form appearing separately. Each word appears in its full metrical line. One useful feature of Minton is the inclusion of all words, even the most common, such as definite articles. Minton is more attractively printed and easier to read than the Tebben concordance; otherwise the differences between the two are nugatory.

673. Tebben, Joseph R. **Hesiod-Konkordanz: A Computer Concordance to Hesiod.** Alpha-Omega, Reihe A, 34. Hildesheim: Georg Olms, 1977. 326pp. ISBN 3–487–06268–2. LCCN 77–398020.

Tebben, who has published computer-generated concordances for much of early Greek poetry, here offers an unlemmatized, keyword-in-context concordance to the works of Hesiod. It contains "every whole word in the *Theogony, Works and Days, Shield, and fragments.*" Approximately two metrical lines of context are provided for each instance of a keyword, which is useful for identifying formulae as well as individual words. Tebben used the editions of A. Rzach (Stuttgart: Teubner, 1958) and Reinhold Merkelbach and M. L. West (Oxford: Oxford University Press, 1967).

HIPPOCRATES

BIBLIOGRAPHIES

674. Bruni Celli, Blas. **Bibliografía Hipocrática.** Caracas: Universidad Central de Venezuela, 1984. 500pp. LCCN 85–121395.

Completed just as the bibliography of Maloney and Savoie (entry 676) appeared, this work includes over 1,000 more entries (4,496 in all). Bruni Celli includes editions, translations, and secondary works from the earliest printed editions through works from the early 1980s. He arranges these alphabetically by author or editor. Although Bruni Celli does not annotate his entries, he provides biographical notes for some early authors, occasional content notes (especially for partial editions of the *Corpus Hippocraticum*), and references to other bibliographies as applicable. The work is illustrated with small reproductions of title pages from early editions of the Hippocratic writings. In addition to name and subject indexes, Bruni Celli provides an index to editions of individual Hippocratic works and an index of cities and printers for the major editions. Bruni Celli seems to have been unable to decide whether he wanted to compile a bibliographical guide to the early editions or a guide to the Hippocratic literature in general. What he has produced is a useful, if not entirely satisfactory, combination of the two.

675. Fichtner, Gerhard. **Corpus Hippocraticum: Verzeichnis der hippokratischen und pseudohippokratischen Schriften.** Tübingen: Institut für Geschichte der Medizin, 1989. 148pp.

Fichtner covers editions, translations, commentaries, and studies of the individual components of the *Corpus Hippocraticum*. He does not include studies of the *Corpus* as a whole. Fichtner presents each Hippocratic writing separately, in the order found in Emile Littré's edition of the corpus (Paris: J. B. Baillière, 1839–1861). His bibliography is largely derived from the works of Leitner (entry 619) and Maloney and Savoie (entry 676). He does include a few items subsequent to the works of Bruni Celli (entry 674) and Maloney and Savoie. Otherwise, it is a much less complete and informative work than either of its predecessors. Those seeking a quick bibliography on a particular Hippocratic writing may find it convenient. Fichtner provides a large array of indexes (consuming more than a third of the volume), which cover titles, incipits, early translations into a variety of languages, and editors and authors.

676. Maloney, G., and R. Savoie. **Cinq cents ans de bibliographique hippocratique.** Québec: Les Éditions du Sphinx, 1982. 291pp. ISBN 2–920123–01–7. LCCN 82–210317.

Of interest to historians of medicine as well as classicists, this bibliography gathers five centuries of work on Hippocrates and the *Corpus Hippocraticum*. It lists some 3,332 works, including editions, commentaries, translations, and scholarly studies. The compilers have covered all aspects—historical, medical, and philological—of Hippocratic studies. Their coverage is relatively complete for works published in Western Europe and North America; publications from other regions are included, but no effort was made to do so comprehensively. They have arranged the citations chronologically, with the entries for each year subarranged alphabetically. The entries do not include any annotations or summaries. There is an index of authors, but no provision for subject access. Bruni Celli's slightly later work (entry 674) provides both many additional citations and better subject access.

HOMER

BIBLIOGRAPHIES

See also Donlan (entry 599).

677. Hainsworth, J. B. **Homer.** New Surveys in the Classics 3. Oxford: Clarendon Press, 1969. 44pp. LCCN 77–469334.

Hainsworth, a distinguished Homerist, reviews selected aspects of recent Homeric scholarship. He organizes these under the rubrics of text, comparison, craft, and art. The chapter on text discusses not only the history of the text, but also the performance of the poem and the Homeric Question. Hainsworth's discussion of comparative studies of epic is a good introduction to the topic. Craft includes both formulaic composition and versification. The chapter on art covers several aspects of the interpretation and appreciation of Homer. A brief appendix lists the principal editions, commentaries, lexica, grammars, and translations. Hainsworth covers roughly the same span as Packard and Meyers (entry 679). Although he cites far fewer works, his review essays make for a more coherent introduction to the scholarly literature. The 1979 reprint of this work includes a bibliographical appendix. Rutherford's newer volume in the same series (entry 680) extends and updates it.

678. Heubeck, Alfred. **Die Homerische Frage: Ein Bericht über die Forschung der letzten Jahrzehnte.** Erträge der Forschung 27. Darmstadt: Wissenschaftliche Buchgesellschaft, 1974. 326pp. ISBN 3–534–03864–9.

Heubeck offers an extended bibliographic essay on the Homeric Question, covering most significant twentieth-century work through the 1960s. The first section, "Higher Criticism," introduces the reader to the long-running Analyst-Unitarian controversy in Homeric criticism and then reviews studies of oral poetry theory that supplanted it. The second section covers a variety of topics: elements of the epic, gods and men, language and style, Homer's world, and the history of the text. A lengthy bibliography provides full details on all works discussed and is the most useful feature for those without German. Indexes cover names and subjects, passages, modern authors, Greek words, and Homeric characters. The Germanless should also avail themselves of Heubeck's "Homeric Studies Today: Results and Prospects," pp. 1–17 in *Homer: Tradition and Invention,* edited by Bernard C. Fenik (Leiden: Brill, 1978), which summarizes the high points of this work in English but lacks the extensive bibliographical apparatus.

679.   Packard, David W., and Tania Meyers. **Bibliography of Homeric Scholarship. Preliminary edition, 1930–1970.** Malibu, CA: Undena, 1974. 183pp. ISBN 0–8900–3005–7. LCCN 74–18918.

This bibliography is based on the yearly listings found in *L'Année philologique* (entry 44), with some expansions and corrections. Only citations are provided; there are no abstracts (although these can be found in the various volumes of *L'Année*). Packard and Meyers have arranged the entries in a single alphabetical list by author. They have also provided a classified subject index and an index to Homeric passages discussed in the various works. This derivative work offers both more and less than the corresponding sections of *L'Année*. Everything is gathered in a single volume with better access tools, but without the abstracts.

680.   Rutherford, R. B. **Homer.** New Surveys in the Classics 26. Oxford: Oxford University Press, 1996. 116pp. ISBN 0–19–922209–6.

Rutherford justly views his work as complementing and updating, rather than superseding, Hainsworth's earlier contribution to this series (entry 677). His survey emphasizes the poems as works of literature. Chapters cover background (history, myth, composition and transmission, influence and reception), the *Iliad,* the *Odyssey,* and some specific scenes from the two epics. The "Bibliographic Note" provides an overview of editions, translations, commentaries, and bibliographies, as well as a concise listing of important work on Homer. Much additional bibliography can be found in the notes to individual chapters. This is an excellent overview of Homeric scholarship for students reading Homer, whether in Greek or translation. However, those primarily interested in historical or archaeological aspects will need to look elsewhere.

681.   Young, Philip H. **Printed Homer: A 3,000 Year Publishing and Translation History of the Iliad and the Odyssey.** Jefferson, NC: McFarland, 2003. 481pp. ISBN 0–7864–1550–9. LCCN 2003–13979.

The first part of this book is a brief narrative history of Homer and his works. Chapters address the identity of Homer and the transmission of his text through the ages. The longest chapter, which covers modern (1470–2000) editions and translations of Homer, focuses predominantly on translations. Young writes for nonspecialists; Homerists will find little new, although they may recommend it to their students as an overview. The second part attempts to list all editions, translations, and adaptations of Homer, including all works once ascribed to Homer, such as the *Batrachomyomachia* and the *Hymns,* in addition to the *Iliad* and *Odyssey.* Young lists everything in a single sequence by date. He provides titles as they appear on the title page, editor and/or translator, imprint, series, and, for translations, the language. Unfortunately, Young does not supply collations, references to standard bibliographies, or holdings information for works published before 1800. Most of the so-called appendixes are actually indexes to editors and translators, printers and publishers, and places of publication. Another appendix lists first printing in each vernacular language. In spite of some quirks and a failure to recognize that the natural audience for such a work consists of scholars, book collectors, and librarians, Young has created a valuable bibliographic tool, which lists over 5,000 publications.

DICTIONARIES, ENCYCLOPEDIAS, AND HANDBOOKS

682. Fowler, Robert. **Cambridge Companion to Homer.** Cambridge: Cambridge University Press, 2004. 419pp. ISBN 0–521–81302–6; 0–521–01246–5pa.

Fowler has gathered an outstanding group of contributors for this recent handbook on Homer. The general charge for the Cambridge Companions is to provide the essentials for students and also to indicate new lines of inquiry for scholars; Fowler and his collaborators generally achieve this. After a general introduction, the book offers 21 essays in five sections. These cover the poems and their narrator, the characters, the poet's craft, text and context, and reception. The first four cover the usual topics: overviews of the poems, gods and men, formulas, similes, speeches, genre, and the Homeric Question, along with a few more recent perspectives, such as gender. By far the largest section deals with *Rezeptionsgeschichte,* variously discussing Homer and Greek literature, Homer and Roman literature, the Romantics, Joyce, images of Homer throughout Western history, contemporary receptions (surprisingly omitting films such as *Cold Mountain* and *O Brother, Where Art Thou?*), and translations. For the most part the essays provide an excellent overview of Homeric studies and ample bibliographical clues to follow. The book concludes with a highly selective time line, a good bibliography, and a very wimpy index.

683. Morris, Ian, and Barry Powell. **New Companion to Homer.** Mnemosyne Supplements 163. Leiden: Brill, 1997. 755pp. ISBN 90–04–09989–1. LCCN 96–38925.

Intended as a contemporary version of Wace and Stubbings (entry 685), the *New Companion* presents a very different view of the Homeric epics. It not only takes account of the two generations of scholarship since the inception of its predecessor but also offers a fundamentally different emphasis with much more attention paid to literary issues and somewhat less to Bronze Age archaeology. Another major shift is in audience: much of the volume is intended to assist the student of Homer in translation, as well as Greek students. The *New Companion* consists of four sections. The first, "Transmission and History of Interpretation," includes chapters on Homer and writing, Homer in antiquity, Homeric papyri, the scholia, the Homeric Question, oral tradition, and neoanalysis. The second, on "Homer's Language," offers essays on such matters as dialect, meter, and formulae. "Homer as Literature," the third part, includes chapters on structure, theoretical approaches, genre, myth, folktale, Homer and Hesiod, and the Homeric hymns. The final section, "Homer's Worlds," addresses such topics as the Bronze Age, Homer and Greek art, relations with the Near East, and the social and cultural milieu of the poems. The contributors are a distinguished lot, primarily Americans, with a sprinkling of British scholars. A substantial bibliography and adequate, but not generous, subject index round out the volume. This volume is an excellent guide to contemporary Homeric scholarship.

684. Morrison, James. **Companion to Homer's Odyssey.** Westport, CT: Greenwood Press, 2003. 210pp. ISBN 0–313–31854–9. LCCN 2002075311.

Designed for students and general readers, Morrison's *Companion* seeks to elucidate the historical, mythological, and literary background of the *Odyssey.* He begins with a note on translations, which will help the undecided select one. Three introductory chapters lay out general background information. The core of the book is a book-by-book discussion of the *Odyssey*, which includes mostly plot summaries and basic interpretation. A series of appendixes offers a character index with pronunciation guide, later works based on or influenced by the *Odyssey*, a highly selective and idiosyncratic bibliography, an annotated list of movies inspired by the *Odyssey*, and a cursory but valuable guide to relevant Web resources. Morrison's index lacks detail but will direct readers to key topics. The *Companion* also includes maps and attractive black-and-white illustrations. This work will provide suitable help for beginners reading the *Odyssey* in translation; advanced students and scholars will prefer Morris and Powell (entry 683).

685. Wace, Alan J.B., and Frank H. Stubbings. **Companion to Homer.** London: MacMillan; New York: St. Martin's, 1962. 595pp. LCCN 62–6433.

Long the only broad general survey of Homeric scholarship in English, this work was begun in the 1930s, interrupted by the Second World War, completed in the late 1950s, and published only in 1962. While contributors were able to take some account of later developments, it remains in many ways a work of the prewar generation. For example, Milman Parry's work on oral composition and formulae receives short shrift (witness Stubbings's remarks in the preface) and Ventris's decipherment of Linear B remained too recent to receive full value. There is also a very heavy emphasis on Aegean Bronze Age archaeology to the detriment of more purely literary issues. The editors intended this volume to meet the needs of school and university students reading Homer in Greek for the first time. Its age alone would preclude such an audience today; in looking at its scope and complexity, one must assume that their students were made of stern stuff indeed. The *Companion* remains a valuable guide to earlier work on Homer and will well serve graduate students and scholars in this capacity. Its various sections cover such topics as the poems themselves (meter, style, composition, language, and comparison with other epic poetry), the transmission of the text, the Homeric Question, the geography of Greece and the Aegean, Aegean Bronze Age archaeology, and Homeric society and material culture. The contributors comprise a veritable who's who of the day: Maurice Bowra, L.R. Palmer, A.B. Lord, J.A. Davison, N.G.L. Hammond, H.J. Rose, and Carl Blegen, among others. There are three indexes: passages of Homer cited, general, and Greek words. Morris and Powell's *New Companion* (entry 683) will better suit most inquirers.

INDEXES AND CONCORDANCES

686. Tebben, Joseph R. **Concordantia Homerica. Pars I, Odyssea: A Computer Concordance to the van Thiel Edition of Homer's Odyssey.** Alpha-Omega, Reihe A, 141.1. Hildesheim: Olms-Wiedmann, 1994. 2v. ISBN 3–487–09784–2 (v. 1); 3–487–09785–0 (v. 2).

687. Tebben, Joseph R. **Concordantia Homerica. Pars II, Ilias: A Computer Concordance to the van Thiel Edition of Homer's Iliad.** Alpha-Omega, Reihe A, 141.2. Hildesheim: Olms-Wiedmann, 1998. 3v. ISBN 3–487–10669–8 (set).

These concordances cover all occurrences of every word in H. van Thiel's editions of the *Odyssey* (Hildesheim: Georg Olms, 1991) and *Iliad* (Hildesheim: George Olms, 1996). As with most computer-generated concordances, this one uses the keyword-in-context format, supplying a bit more than two lines of Homeric verse with each word. Tebben includes, but marks with a bullet, lines widely believed to be later interpolations. He also includes significant variant readings, marked with an equal sign. Both interpolations and variants are enumerated in the appendixes to the respective parts.

688.   Tebben, Joseph R. **Homer-Konkordanz: A Computer Concordance to the Homeric Hymns.** Alpha-Omega, Reihe A, 35. Hildesheim: Georg Olms, 1977. 226pp. ISBN 3–487–06270–4.

Tebben's concordance of the Homeric Hymns follows the format of his other concordances: unlemmatized, keyword-in-context (with approximately two metrical lines of context in each case). The keyword-in-context format is particularly useful for identifying formulae in early Greek verse. Tebben used the edition of the *Hymns* by T. W. Allen, which is found in volume 5 of the Oxford Classical Text edition of *Homeri Opera* (1965).

JOSEPHUS

BIBLIOGRAPHIES

689.   Feldman, Louis H. **Josephus: A Supplementary Bibliography.** Garland Reference Library of the Humanities 645. New York: Garland, 1986. 696pp. ISBN 0–8240–8792–5. LCCN 84–48399.

Feldman intended this work as a supplement to Schreckenberg's bibliography (entries 691–692). Roughly half of Feldman's 3,500 entries are pre-1976 items missed by Schreckenberg. Another quarter are items listed by Schreckenberg for which Feldman provides additional information and/or corrections. The remaining entries provide coverage for the years 1976–1984. Feldman departs from Schreckenberg's chronological scheme and arranges his entries alphabetically by author; however, he does continue to use Schreckenberg's numerical classification scheme and provides an index to it in order to facilitate subject access. Feldman's entries also include useful summaries and occasional critical remarks. He provides indexes to citations of Josephus and to Greek words discussed both for this volume and for Schreckenberg's *Supplementband*, which lacked them. Feldman also provides corrigenda for his *Josephus and Modern Scholarship* (entry 690). Together, the works of Schreckenberg and Feldman provide exhaustive coverage of work on Josephus and a valuable resource for the study of Hellenistic Judaism in general.

690.   Feldman, Louis H. **Josephus and Modern Scholarship (1937–1980).** Berlin: Walter de Gruyter, 1984. 1,055pp. ISBN 3–11–008138–5.

This work updates and expands the Josephus portion of Feldman's *Scholarship on Philo and Josephus (1937–1962)* (entry 697). Feldman uses a very detailed subject classification scheme (neatly laid out by his table of contents) to organize about 3,500 entries. Bibliographical citations are listed at the beginning of each subject section. In the discussion that follows, Feldman summarizes and critically reviews the items. Feldman covers the literature exhaustively for his period; he also includes some works published prior to 1937. There is a very full *index locorum*. Feldman also provides indexes of Greek, Latin, Hebrew, and other words discussed and of modern scholars. Most readers will prefer Feldman to Schreckenberg (entries 691–692) for the years covered, since the discussion of works is in English. Also, only Feldman's work provides suitable subject access. However, Schreckenberg remains indispensable for his coverage of Josephan scholarship before 1937.

691. Schreckenberg, Heinz. **Bibliographie zu Flavius Josephus.** Arbeiten zur Literatur und Geschichte des hellenistischen Judentums 1. Leiden: Brill, 1968. 336pp. LCCN 76–395269.

692. Schreckenberg, Heinz. **Bibliographie zu Flavius Josephus: Supplementband mit Gesamtregister.** Arbeiten zur Literatur und Geschicht des hellenistischen Judentums 14. Leiden: Brill, 1979. 242pp. ISBN 90–04–05968–7.

Schreckenberg's original bibliography lists about 2,200 items, which include editions, commentaries, translations, and secondary works. He also cites many works on Judaism and ancient history in general, as well as works specifically on Josephus. Schreckenberg arranges his entries chronologically by date of publication, beginning with the editio princeps and extending to 1968. His coverage is reasonably complete through 1965. Annotations (in German), some quite extensive, accompany many entries. Schreckenberg provides indexes of persons, passages of Josephus's works, and Greek works. He also employs a curious form of subject classification: the numbers 1–25 are assigned to various form and subject headings; Schreckenberg then places the appropriate number(s) in the margin beside each enty. Their value is limited, however, since no index to these is provided.

Schreckenberg includes in the supplement all additional works on Jospehus that came to his attention by March 1979. Together with the earlier volume, it can be considered reasonably complete through 1975. Schreckenberg follows a quite different plan of organization in the supplement. He places all secondary materials in a single alphabetical list, arranged by author. A second section includes editions (arranged chronologically) and translations (by language). Schreckenberg again annotates some but not all entries. He also provides alphabetical and chronological indexes of authors, and a separate index of editors and translators of Josephus. Feldman's bibliographies (entries 689–690) should be consulted for additional material.

INDEXES AND CONCORDANCES

693. Rengstorf, Karl Heinrich, ed. **Complete Concordance to Flavius Josephus.** Study edition. Leiden: Brill, 2002. 2v. ISBN 90–04–12829–8 (set).

This two-volume reissue of the first edition (Leiden: Brill, 1973–1983) includes Abraham Schalit's *Namenwörterbuch zu Flavius Josephus,* which originally appeared separately as a supplement to the first edition. The concordance draws upon four different editions as its basis: B. Niese and J. von Destinon's *editio maior* (1885–1895), Niese's *editio minor* (1888–1895), S. A. Naber (1888–1896), and the Loeb Classical Library edition (1926–1965). Lemmata appear in their standard dictionary form. English and German definitions are provided; all occurrences of the word appear in context with a citation. The *Namenwörterbuch,* which follows the main concordance, lists all occurrences of proper names with variant readings, Hebrew forms where appropriate, and additional information about their identities.

LONGINUS

BIBLIOGRAPHIES

694. Marin, Demetrios St., comp. **Bibliography on the "Essay on the Sublime."** Printed privately for the author, 1967. 101pp. LCCN 68–118876.

Marin's bibliography, complete through 1956, covers work on the "Essay on the Sublime," which traditionally has been ascribed to Longinus. He also includes a number of items concerning other rhetoricians, such as Dionysius of Halicarnassus, for purposes of comparative study. Marin arranges his material by form and subject. The first section lists and briefly discusses the known manuscripts of the "Essay." The second includes general and specialized bibliographies. Editions, commentaries, and translations are found in the third chapter. The final section covers scholarly studies and is divided into several broad subject categories. Many of the entries include annotations, which variously offer summaries, bibliographical information, or critical comment. Indexes of ancient and modern authors conclude the work. Marin is a useful, if dated, source of material on this problematic and important work.

MENANDER

BIBLIOGRAPHIES

See also Arnott (entry 598), Donlan (entry 599), and Forman (entry 600).

695.   Katsouris, Andreas G. **Menander Bibliography.** Thessalonike: University Studio Press, 1995. 159pp. ISBN 960–12–0504–7.

Katsouris's bibliography covers work on Menander from the sixteenth century through the early 1990s. Coverage is relatively full through 1992; some works published in 1991 or 1992 appear in an addendum at the end of the bibliography. In all, Katsouris lists 2,628 publications. His organizational scheme is subject based, but somewhat vague and ill thought out. He begins with editions of Menander, both complete and partial. Then he lists general studies ("commentaries"), followed by those dealing with specific plays. Other subject groupings follow: comparative studies of Menander and other ancient authors, language, meter, characterization, and so on. The concluding sections cover bibliographies and translations. Citations are adequate, if somewhat spartan. Katsouris uses many standard abbreviations for journal titles but does not provide a key; the uninitiated must consult the table of abbreviations from a recent volume of *L'Année philologique* (entry 44) or Wellington's compendium (entry 43). There are no annotations, although book reviews are listed under the work reviewed. Supplemental material includes several useful lists at the front of the book: papyri of Menander, titles of all known plays by him, and adaptations by Plautus and Terence. An index of names and a general index conclude the book. Serious researchers will find this an invaluable resource; casual students will find it confusing.

INDEXES AND CONCORDANCES

696.   Pompella, Giuseppe. **Lexicon Menandreum.** Alpha-Omega, Reihe A, 142. Hildesheim: Olms-Weidmann, 1996. 289pp. ISBN 3–487–10255–2.

Pompella bases his *Lexicon* upon the editions of F. H. Sandbach (Oxford: Clarendon Press, 1972) and Alfred Koerte (Leipzig: Teubner, 1959) for the plays, and the edition of Siegfried Jaeckel (Leipzig: Teubner, 1964) for the *Sententiae*. Readings from different editions are clearly marked, as are words supplied by editors. Lemmata appear in bold, with all occurrences of each word marshaled beneath in their various inflected forms. Pompella notes the metrical position in its verse for each instance. He also provides a Latin translation for every entry.

PHILO

BIBLIOGRAPHIES

697.   Feldman, Louis H. **Scholarship on Philo and Josephus (1937–1962).** Studies in Judaica. New York: Yeshiva University, n.d. 62pp.

The original version of this survey was printed in *Classical World* (entry 95) and was subsequently reprinted in one of collected volumes of *Classical World* bibliographies (entry 614). This separate edition adds supplementary items and several indexes. Feldman attempts complete coverage for the specified years. He arranges the material by subject. Feldman also provides descriptive and evaluative comments. There are indexes to ancient passages discussed; to Hebrew, Greek, and Latin words; and to names of modern scholars. For Josephus, this work is superseded by Schreckenberg (entries 691–692) and Feldman's other bibliographies (entries 689–690). For Philo, Radice and Runia (entry 699) is a much more complete bibliography. Its annotations remain useful.

698.   Goodhart, Howard L., and Goodenough, Erwin R. **Politics of Philo Judaeus . . . with a General Bibliography of Philo.** New Haven, CT: Yale University Press, 1938. 348pp. (Bibliography: pp. 125–348) LCCN 38–015333.

It is no accident that both Feldman (entry 697) and Radice and Runia (entry 699) take 1937 as a starting date for their bibliographies of Philo. This magisterial bibliography by Goodhart and Goodenough provides exemplary coverage of Philonic studies through 1936. While bound with their study of Philo's politics, the bibliography constitutes the bulk of the work and has its own title page and table of contents. They begin with a detailed listing of manuscripts of Philo arranged by language (Greek, Latin, Armenian, and miscellaneous), followed by an enumeration of editions both in Greek and in translation (again by language). Bibliographies and general studies appear next, to be followed by some 26 chapters of works arranged by subject. A final three chapters cover mentions of Philo in printed books of the fifteenth century, miscellaneous references to Philo, and pseudo-Philonic writings. Goodhart and Goodenough miss little of significance; they amply cover Philo's *Nachleben* as well as scholarship on him. There are numerous cross-references and occasional annotations. Separate indexes cover the manuscripts (personal and geographic names) and the rest of the bibliography (personal names).

699.   Radice, Roberto, and David T. Runia. **Philo of Alexandria: An Annotated Bibliography, 1937–1986.** Supplements to *Vigiliae Christianae* 8. Leiden: Brill, 1988; repr. 1992. 469pp. ISBN 90–04–08986–1. LCCN 88–26242.

Based on Radice's earlier effort in Italian, *Filone di Alessandria: Bibliografia generale 1937–1982* (Naples: Bibliopolis, 1983), this work continues Goodhart and Goodenough (entry 698). Radice and Runia cover 50 years of scholarship, with some 1,666 entries. They include works in English, French, German, Italian, Hebrew, Spanish, Dutch, and Latin. The only major exclusions are works of less than three pages (with a few exceptions), works pertaining to the *Liber Antiquitatum Biblicarum,* which is generally considered spurious, and unaltered reprints of works first published before 1937. The first part covers bibliographies, critical editions, translations into modern languages, anthologies, commentaries, indexes, and lexicographical studies, and the single journal devoted to Philonic studies. The second part, which comprises the bulk of the work, lists critical studies by year of publication and author. Most entries include a summary, some extensive. Reviews are listed at the end of the summaries. There are indexes for authors, reviewers, biblical passages, Philonic passages, subjects, and Greek words. Coverage for the last few years is, of course, less than complete. Radice and Runia, along with various collaborators, have published bibliographical updates each year in *Studia Philonica Annual.* Those for 1987 to 1996 have been gathered, with additions, in Runia (entry 700).

700.   Runia, David T., with the assistance of H. M. Keizer. **Philo of Alexandria: An Annotated Bibliography, 1987–1996.** Supplements to *Vigiliae Christianae* 57. Leiden: Brill, 2000. 412pp. ISBN 90–04–11682–6.

This work continues the earlier bibliography by Radice and Runia (entry 699) and follows the same format. Runia has extended its scope to all languages, so that works in Scandinavian and Central and Eastern European languages are now included. However, coverage remains most complete for Western European-language works and much less so for others. Runia lists some 953 items for the decade covered and adds 160 items from 1937 through 1986 to those in the previous volume. He also includes a list of corrigenda to the entries in the earlier work. Updates to this bibliography appear each year in *Studia Philonica Annual.*

INDEXES AND CONCORDANCES

701.   Borgen, Peder, Kåre Fuglseth, and Roald Skarsten. **Philo Index: A Complete Greek Word Index to the Writings of Philo of Alexandria.** Grand Rapids, MI: Eerdmans; Leiden: Brill, 2000. 371pp. ISBN 0–8028–3883–9 (Eerdmans); 90–04–11477–7 (Brill). LCCN 99–46459.

This is a product of those whose enthusiasm for computer technology outstrips their desire to be useful. The index is based on four editions: L. Cohn and P. Wendland, *Philonis Alexandrini opera quae supersunt* (Berlin: Reimer, 1896–1915); F. H. Colson, *Hypothetica* and *De Providentia* from the ninth volume of the Loeb edition (Cambridge, MA: Harvard University Press, 1941); F. Petit, *Quaestiones in Genesim et in Exodum, Fragmenta Graeca* (Paris: Éditions du Cerf, 1978); and J. Paramelle, *Philon d'Alexandrie Quaestiones in Genesim, Liber 2, 1–7* (Geneva: Cramer, 1984). The index uses the standard dictionary form as lemmata, with all instances in a single entry and no distinction made for declined or conjugated forms. Nor are the compilers concerned with textual variants. The work is useful for finding the instances and frequency of words in Philo but is rather unsophisticated. Alas, it is the only index to Philo.

PINDAR

BIBLIOGRAPHIES

702. Gerber, Douglas E. **Bibliography of Pindar, 1513–1966.** Philological Monographs 28. Cleveland: Published for the American Philological Association by the Press of Case Western Reserve University, 1969. 160pp. LCCN 68–8750.

Gerber lists editions, commentaries, translations, and studies of Pindar; he begins with the first printed edition in 1513 and attempts to cover all materials that had appeared by March 1967. The citations are arranged into 30 sections by form and subject; many of these sections are further subdivided. When appropriate, items are included under more than one heading. Reviews are listed with the work reviewed. There are no abstracts, although Gerber sometimes reproduces the table of contents for books. Lack of an index is a major defect of the work. It is otherwise a useful tool and appears to be reasonably complete for the years covered.

INDEXES AND CONCORDANCES

703. Slater, William J. **Lexicon to Pindar.** Berlin: Walter de Gruyter, 1969. 563pp. LCCN 75–478561.

Modelled on Powell's *Lexicon to Herodotus* (entry 671) and Italie's *Index Aeschyleus* (entry 642), this is a genuine work of learning rather than a mere compilation. Slater uses Bruno Snell's edition (Leipzig: Teubner, 1964) as his basis, although departing from it in a few places as noted in the introduction. Entries are in alphabetical sequence, with lemmata in bold. Each includes the English meaning and an enumeration of occurrences with brief contexts. Slater notes variant readings and cites pertinent literature on the meanings and forms of words. Proper nouns (persons and places) are included, with short explanations.

PLATO

BIBLIOGRAPHIES

704. Brisson, Luc, and Frédéric Plin. **Platon: 1990–1995 bibliographie.** Tradition de la Pensée Classique. Paris: J. Vrin, 1999. 415pp. ISBN 2–7116–1412–3.

In this volume Brisson continues the earlier Plato bibliographies that he published in *Lustrum* (entry 71). He divides the bibliography into two parts: Plato's works, and interpretive studies. In both cases Brisson picks up the numbering of entries from his previous efforts. The first section lists some 70 editions and translations. Brisson groups these by collected works, selected works, individual works (alphabetical by title), and anthologies. In each subsection he first lists editions in ancient Greek and then translations by language. The enumeration of interpretive studies runs to some 1,780 entries, arranged alphabetically by author. Most, but not all, include brief summaries, which are variously in French, German, or English. Many of the summaries are derived from *L'Année philologique* (entry 44).

Brisson also cites reviews under book-length works. Subject access is provided through a detailed analytical index with its own lengthy table of contents. Addenda provide links back to Brisson's earlier bibliographies: one list enumerates entry numbers from the 1980–1985 and 1985–1990 lists for which new editions or translations appeared in 1990–1995, and a second lists additional book reviews for items in them. In the preface, Brisson indicates that he will cover 1995–2000 in a future volume and also hopes to provide coverage for 1950–2000 on CD-ROM. In the interval, Brisson has made his *Bibliographie platonicienne* available on the Web in two- to three-year increments (1994–1996, 1996–1998, 1997–1999, 1999–2000, 2000–2001) at http://upr_76.vjf.cnrs.fr/Instruments_travail/Bibliogr_spec/ Bibl_plat/BPFrontFrench.html.

705. Deschoux, Marcel. **Comprendre Platon: Un siècle de bibliographie platonicienne de langue française, 1880–1980.** Collection d'études anciennes. Paris: Les Belles Lettres, 1981. 206pp. ISBN 2–251–32606–5. LCCN 82–131192.

Deschoux's bibliography will primarily interest serious researchers. He offers extensive retrospective coverage of French-language work on Plato. His first section covers general works on fifth-century Greece and ancient Greek philosophy. Subsequent sections cover Socrates, works on Plato in French (translations, books, philosophical articles, historical and literary articles), and works not in French that were the subject of French reviews or studies. The final section includes many English or German works, but mainly as a vehicle for listing French reviews or responses. Subarrangement is various and eccentric; for example, articles are listed by journal title, then date. Users should be sure to consult the "Table analytique des matières," which appears at the end of the volume. Several indexes cover authors and subjects, although their design is not helpful. Bibliographical information is minimalist and not always sufficient. Deschoux does not provide annotations or comments. In spite of its many deficiencies, Deschoux's book covers much older French work on Socrates and Plato.

706. McKirahan, Richard D., Jr. **Plato and Socrates: A Comprehensive Bibliography, 1958–1973.** Garland Reference Library of the Humanities 78. New York: Garland, 1978. 592pp. ISBN 0–8240–9895–1. LCCN 76–52670.

This bibliography is a continuation of H. F. Cherniss's bibliographies for 1950–1957, which appeared in the journal *Lustrum* (entry 71). McKirahan's more than 4,600 entries for only 15 years well illustrate the difficulty of keeping abreast of scholarship on Plato and Socrates. He has arranged the entries by subject; his table of contents effectively lays out the scheme. Within each category, works are subarranged chronologically. There are no annotations. Reviews are listed under the entry for the book reviewed. An author index concludes the volume. For additional coverage of Socrates see Navia and Katz (entry 730).

707. Ritter, Constantin. **Bibliographies on Plato, 1912–1930.** Ancient Philosophy. New York: Garland, 1980. 909pp. ISBN 0–8240–9590–1. LCCN 78–66617.

This volume consists of reprints of six bibliographical surveys that originally appeared in *Bursian's Jahresbericht* (entry 70) between 1912 and 1930. All are in German. Together, they provide a fairly complete report of scholarly work on Plato during the first three decades of this century. The publisher has merely reprinted the original texts; no table of contents or index is provided (there is not even continuous pagination). As a result, the work is rather difficult to use. For this reason, and because of the language and date, Ritter is of use chiefly to professional scholars.

708. Saunders, Trevor J., and Luc Brisson. **Bibliography on Plato's Laws, Revised and Completed with an additional Bibliography on the Epinomis.** International Plato Studies 12. 3rd ed. Sankt Augustin: Academia-Verlag, 2000. 141pp. ISBN 3–89665–172–2. LCCN 2001–422340.

Saunders includes only material that deals primarily with the *Laws;* more general works on Plato are excluded. He does admit a very few works antedating 1920. Within his chronological limits, Saunders covers all aspects of work, both philological and philosophical, on the *Laws.* His material is divided into three sections: texts and translations, books and articles (subarranged into thirteen categories by subject), and discussions of individual passages. The rare annotation serves chiefly to clarify content when titles are ambiguous. There are no indexes. Luc Brisson, who prepared the third edition from Saunders's notes, has extended coverage to 2000 and added a bibliography on the *Epinomis* that follows the same format. Saunders provides a useful working guide, although most will want to use his work as a supplement to more general bibliographies of Platonic studies.

709. Skemp, J. B. **Plato.** New Surveys in the Classics 10. Oxford: Clarendon Press, 1976. 63pp. LCCN 77–367770.

Skemp selectively reviews work on Plato from 1945 to 1975 in a series of brief bibliographical essays. These cover all the major aspects of scholarship on Plato. While he emphasizes English-language studies, Skemp also includes major works in French and German. His summaries and valuations of the items discussed are generally helpful and reliable. Skemp, although far from comprehensive and now rather dated, remains a useful aid in grappling with the vast bibliography on Plato.

710. Zimbrich, Ulrike. **Bibliographie zu Platons Staat: Die Rezeption der Politeia im deutschsprachigen Raum von 1800 bis 1970.** Frankfurt am Main: V. Klostermann, 1994. 312pp. ISBN 3–465–02632–7.

Zimbrich's bibliography covers editions and studies of Plato's *Republic* published in Germany between 1800 and 1970. Editions are listed first, subdivided into complete works, selected dialogues, the *Republic,* and selections. Translations follow with a similar breakdown; then come secondary studies. Within each category, works are listed in chronological order. A final section lists bibliographies. There are occasional annotations, although most merely clarify the contents or provide cross-references, as well as indexes of authors and subjects.

DICTIONARIES, ENCYCLOPEDIAS, AND HANDBOOKS

711. Kraut, Richard, ed.. **Cambridge Companion to Plato.** Cambridge Companions to Philosophy. Cambridge: Cambridge University Press, 1992.) 560pp. ISBN 0–521–43018; 0–521–43610–9pa. LCCN 92–4991.

Kraut has assembled a distinguised team of British, German, and North American scholars for this work. Students will find it a helpful adjunct to the study of Plato, while for the more advanced it offers a useful survey of Platonic studies ca. 1992. The first three essays provide the basics: an introduction to the study of Plato, the intellectual background (Presocratics, Sophists, and the general culture of fifth-century Athens), and style and chronology. The 12 subsequent chapters addresses specific topics, dialogues, or groups of dialogues. These cover such issues as Plato's relation to Socrates, his views on poetry and religion, his epistemology, and his political thought. The extensive bibliography, which is classified by subject, will guide users to most of the essential works on Plato in English and a select few in other languages. There is an index of names and subjects, and another of passages cited from Greek authors.

712.   Nails, Deborah. **People of Plato: A Prosopography of Plato and Other Socratics.** Indianapolis: Hackett, 2002. 414pp. ISBN 0–87220–564–9. LCCN 2002068496.

Nails reminds us that the people of Plato's dialogues were real, living Athenians. Her work is a guide to them and their relationships. She also includes people who appear in the Socratic writings of Antisthenes, Aeschines, and Xenophon. They are listed alphabetically. Each entry includes references to other works on Athenian prosopography and personal names, references to works of Plato in which they occur, lists of known relatives, and short biographies. Appendixes cover the dramatic dates, characters, and settings of the dialogues, peripheral persons, Athenian clan and tribal units, and a general chronology of the period. Nails also provides a glossary, a bibliography, maps, and a subject index. This is an invaluable work for any student of Plato.

INDEXES AND CONCORDANCES

713.   Abott, Evelyn. **Subject-Index to the Dialogues of Plato.** Oxford: Clarendon Press, 1875; repr., New York: Burt Franklin, 1971. LCCN 78–146345.

A name and subject index to the dialogues, this work is old but still useful. Abbott uses Stephanus pages, the standard system of reference to Plato's text, so that his index may be used with any edition or translation. It includes things not found in Stockhammer (entry 716) and is the work of a much better scholar. One interesting entry is "Etymology," which offers a list of all Greek words whose etymology is discussed in Plato, with full references. Anyone pursuing a specific subject or person in Plato's works will find this a valuable resource.

714.   Brandwood, Leonard. **Word Index to Plato.** Compendia 8. Leeds: W. S. Maney, 1976. 1,003pp. LCCN 76–380277.

This index is based on the Oxford Classical Text edition of John Burnet (Oxford: Clarendon Press, 1900–1907); Brandwood uses the traditional Stephanus numbers for textual references. He indexes all words except the definite article and *kai*. Lemmata are typically the nominative singular for nouns and adjectives, the present infinitive for verbs; Brandwood explains variances in great detail in the introduction. Variant readings are noted. Corrigenda and additional variant readings are listed at the head of the index.

715.   Siviero, Mauro. **Concordantiae in Platonis Opera Omnia.** Alpha-Omega, Reihe A, 110. Hildesheim: Olms-Weidmann, 1994 ISBN 3–487–09360–X (pt. 1); ISBN 3–487–10225–0 (pt. 2); ISBN 3–487–10483–0 (pt. 3); ISBN 3–487–1084–9 (pt. 4). LCCN 95–154608.

Siviero's concordance is a work in progress. Each part covers a single work of Plato. The four that have appeared to date cover the *Euthyphro, Apologia, Crito,* and *Phaedo* respectively. Several more volumes are in preparation, and numerous others projected. This is a lemmatized, keyword-in-context concordance. Like Brandwood's index (entry 714), it is based on Burnet's Oxford Classical Text edition. Each part includes information on word frequencies and the distribution of different parts of speech. Those interested in individual works of Plato or working on stylistic analyses will find this concordance of great value. Brandwood will be much more convenient for those seeking instances of a word throughout the Platonic corpus. For most of Plato's works, Brandwood will be the only resource for many years to come, given the slow pace of publication for this concordance.

716. Stockhammer, Morris. **Plato Dictionary.** New York: Philosophical Library, 1963. 287pp. LCCN 63–11488.

This curious work has both a preface and an introduction; neither addresses method or purpose. It is essentially a selective name and subject index to the Benjamin Jowett translation of Plato. Under each lemma the user will find one or more relevant passages of Plato in English. Stockhammer will aid the Greekless student or casual reader in tracking specific people or topics in the *Dialogues.* Serious students will prefer Abbott (entry 713).

JOURNALS

717. **Journal of the International Plato Society.** Notre Dame, IN: University of Notre Dame, 2001– . Annual. URL: www.nd.edu/~plato.

This journal is freely available on the Web. Sponsored by the International Plato Society (see www.platon.org), it publishes articles on all aspects of Platonic studies. Articles may be in English, French, German, Italian, or Spanish. While relatively new, the journal's contributors include many prominent scholars.

PLOTINUS

BIBLIOGRAPHIES

718. Dufour, Richard. **Plotinus: A Bibliography 1950–2000.** Rev. ed. Leiden: Brill, 2002. 174pp. ISBN 90–04–12780–1.

The first edition of this work appeared in *Phronesis* 46 (August 2000). It is surprising that Dufour makes no reference to Mariën (entry 719), since his bibliography picks up approximately where Mariën ends. Dufour divides his work into two major sections: "Greek Text and Translations" and "Studies." In the first section, he lists Greek editions, followed by works dealing with textual criticism, manuscripts, and linguistic issues. These are followed by translations and commentaries. "Studies" comprises the bulk of Dufour's bibliography, covering all other aspects of Plotinian studies. It includes 1,542 numbered entries ranged alphabetically by author. Subject access is provided by four indexes covering themes (in Plotinus), authors (other than Plotinus) and their themes, Plotinian treatises, and Greek words. Dufour's coverage is comprehensive through the end of 1995, and somewhat spotty thereafter.

719. Mariën, Bert. **Bibliografia critica degli studi Plotiniani: Con rassegna delle loro recensioni.** Riveduta e curata da V. Cilento. Bari: Laterza, 1949. 273 pp.

Mariën offers extensive coverage of Platonism and Neoplatonism in general, as well as all aspects of Plotinus's life, work, and influence. The earliest work cited is Ficino's Latin translation of the works of Plotinus (1492), and many other early works are included, although most items cited date from the nineteenth and first half of the twentieth century. Mariën arranges his material by subject categories. Many entries include brief descriptive annotations. Reviews are listed under the appropriate book entries. The work is well indexed and includes supplementary subject indexes in addition to an author index. Mariën is useful for the study both of late antique philosophy and of Neoplatonism during the Renaissance. Because of its date, Mariën's compilation will be of interest chiefly to specialized scholars. For subsequent bibliography see Dufour (entry 718).

DICTIONARIES, ENCYCLOPEDIAS, AND HANDBOOKS

720. Gerson, Lloyd P., ed. **Cambridge Companion to Plotinus.** Cambridge: Cambridge University Press, 1996. 462pp. ISBN 0–521–47093–5; 0–521–47676–3pa. LCCN 95–45305.

Plotinus, a notoriously difficult philosopher, is well served by this handbook. Gerson has gathered a strong international cast of contributors, including such leading scholars in the field as John Dillon and Dominic O'Meara. Gerson's introduction surveys what is known of Plotinus's life and provides a brief overview of Plotinian studies. Sixteen essays cover major topics, such as the Platonic tradition and the foundations of Neoplatonism, metaphysics, soul and intellect, the nature of physical reality, evil, time, cognition, self-knowledge, body and soul, human freedom, ethics, language, and Plotinus and Christian philosophy. The *Companion* includes a substantial general bibliography, an index of passages, and another of names and subjects. This volume is a useful resource for those seeking information on a particular aspect of Plotinus's work, as well as an excellent guide both for students and scholars.

INDEXES AND CONCORDANCES

721. Sleeman, J. H., and Gilbert Pollet. **Lexicon Plotinianum.** Ancient and Medieval Philosophy, ser. 1, 2. Leiden: Brill; Leuven: Leuven University Press, 1980. 1164 cols. ISBN 90–6186–083–0. LCCN 80–505958.

Sleeman began this *Lexicon* in 1946. After his death in 1963, the project fell to Gilbert Pollet. It is based on the edition of P. Henry and H.-J. Schwyzer (Paris: Desclée de Brouwer; Leiden: Brill, 1951–1973). As is everything involving Plotinus, the *Lexicon* is complex. Pollet arranges the citations under each lemma or sublemma according to the topological order of the *Enneads*. The full context is provided only for what Pollet considers the "key-word to the philosophical or grammatical context"; cross-references lead to this from the other words. Pollet provides source references for Plotinus's quotations from other Greek authors, such as Plato, Aristotle, and Homer. Word meanings are in English.

PLUTARCH

BIBLIOGRAPHIES

722. Scardigli, Barbara. **Die Römerbiographien Plutarchs.** München: C.H. Beck, 1979. 230pp. ISBN 3-406-07400-6. LCCN 80-493511.

Scardigli surveys the scholarly literature on Plutarch's *Lives* from 1935 through 1978; she covers only the Roman biographies. The introduction notes and discusses general works on Plutarch, biography as a genre in antiquity, and the *Lives*. Scardigli then devotes a separate chapter to each of the lives, from Romulus through Galba and Otho. For each, Scardigli provides a brief narrative overview of recent work followed by the bibliographical citations. These are divided into studies of particular passages and textual studies. Many additional relevant works are cited in the notes to the narrative passages. This is a useful source, but it does not lend itself to quick consultation since so much information is buried in the notes. The indexes of passages from ancient literature and of personal names are thorough and fully cover the notes as well as the text.

723. Titchener, Frances, ed. **Plutarch Bibliography.** URL: www.usu.edu/history/ploutarchos/plutbib.htm.

The International Plutarch Society (entry 725) sponsors this extensive online bibliography, which is frequently updated. The bibliography covers all types of scholarly work on Plutarch, from textual and literary criticism to studies of his influence in the Renaissance. Works listed are in a variety of languages, with English, French, German, and Spanish among the most common. The bibliography is alphabetical by author, with no subject access provided. Citations are adequate but minimal; there are no abstracts or annotations.

JOURNALS

724. **Ploutarchos.** International Plutarch Society, 1985– . Semiannual. ISSN 0258-655X. LCCN 86-13983. URL: www.usu.edu/history/ploutarchos.

Published by the International Plutarch Society (entry 725), this journal deals with all aspects of Plutarch's life and works. In includes articles in English, French, German, Greek, Italian, Portuguese, and Spanish. The journal also includes a substantial number of book reviews. Information about recent issues is available on the society's Web site.

ASSOCIATIONS

725. **International Plutarch Society (North American Branch).** *Ploutarchos,* Dept. of History, 0710 Old Main Hill, Utah State University, Logan, UT 84322-0710. URL: www.usu.edu/history/ploutarchos.

This society is devoted to the study of the life, writings, and influence of Plutarch. It publishes a journal, *Ploutarchos* (entry 724), and frequently sponsors sessions at the annual meetings of the American Philological Association (entry 1004) and other larger associations.

PORPHYRY

BIBLIOGRAPHIES

726. Girgenti, Giuseppe. **Porfirio negli ultimi cinquant'anni: Bibliografia sistematica e ragionata della letteratura primaria e secondaria riguardante il pensiero porfiriano e i suoi influssi storici.** Milano: Vita e Pensiero, 1994. 376pp. ISBN 88–343–0807–7; 88–343–0813–1pa.

Girgenti begins with an overview of Porphyry's life, works, and influence, followed by a brief discussion of Porphyrian studies through 1939. The bibliography starts with 1940; material is presented by decade with subarrangement by year. There is no discernible pattern of arrangement within each year. Coverage is relatively full through 1993, and thin for 1994. Girgenti draws primarily from scholarship in classics and religion. North American and Western European work is well represented, with some coverage of Eastern Europe. Most entries have extensive annotations (in Italian). Indexes provide access by the individual works of Porphyry, Scriptural passages discussed, subjects, ancient medieval and modern authors in relation to Porphyry, and authors of works cited in the bibliography. While those interested in Porphyry will find much of use in Girgenti, his erratic organization will frustrate them.

PROCLUS

BIBLIOGRAPHIES

727. Scotti Muth, Nicoletta. **Proclo negli ultimi quarant'anni: Bibliografia ragionata della letteratura primaria e secondaria riguardante il pensiero procliano e i suoi influssi storici (anni 1949–1992).** Milano: Vita e Pensiero, 1993. 416pp. ISBN 88–343–0548–5 (brossura); 88–343–0549–3 (rilegato). LCCN 94–166721.

An important but often neglected figure in Neoplatonism, Proclus is largely the province of specialists. Scotti Muth surveys 44 years of scholarship, including both works specifically about Proclus and more general works that have significant content relating to him. She employs a chronological arrangement, with works listed alphabetically by author under each year. The modest number of entries under most years reflects a general lack of scholarly attention rather then a lack of diligence on the part of the compiler. Generous descriptive annotations accompany most entries. An array of indexes provides subject and author access.

PTOLEMY

BIBLIOGRAPHIES

728. Stahl, William Harris. **Ptolemy's Geography: A Select Bibliography.** New York: New York Public Library, 1953. 86pp. LCCN 54–10090.

Stahl gathers a generous selection from the vast literature on Ptolemy's *Geography.* His bibliography runs to 1,464 entries, although the actual number of works is somewhat less, since some items are cited more than once. It includes both books and articles. Stahl covers works published through 1948; he includes many important eighteenth- and nineteenth-century items as well as more recent studies. He arranges his material by subject and form. The major divisions include regional geography, Ptolemaic studies, mathematical geography, and maps. The appendixes include bibliographies of editions, translations, and works on such topics as the history of the text and Ptolemy's sources. While there are no annotations, entries for books also list reviews. Stahl cites works under more than one heading when appropriate. An index of authors concludes the work.

PYTHAGORAS

BIBLIOGRAPHIES

729.   Navia, Luis E. **Pythagoras: An Annotated Bibliography.** Garland Reference Library of the Humanities 1128. New York: Garland, 1990. 381pp. ISBN 0–8240–4380–4. LCCN 90–33296.

Navia's selective bibliography presents over 1,000 works about Pythagoras and Pythagoreanism. He covers works in English, French, German, Italian, and Spanish. His eclectic assortment includes primarily philosophical and philological works but also extends to Neoplatonic and theological works, and to the history of such fields as science and music. In addition, there is much on Pythagoras's considerable influence on later generations. Navia has conveniently arranged his material by form and subject. He also supplies annotations, often extensive, which give good descriptions of the works cited. Navia provides indexes of authors and of names of subjects. His book is a necessary guide to the diverse and far-flung publications relating to Pythagoras.

SOCRATES

BIBLIOGRAPHIES

730.   Navia, Luis E., and Ellen L. Katz. **Socrates: An Annotated Bibliography.** Garland Reference Library of the Humanities 844. New York: Garland, 1988. 536pp. ISBN 0–8240–5740–6. LCCN 88–10264.

Since Socrates' life and thought are known only through the works of his contemporaries, a bibliography on Socrates inevitably becomes a bibliography on numerous other ancients as well. While their focus always stays on Socrates, Navia and Katz cite many works concerning Aristophanes, Xenophon, and Plato (who are our major sources of information about Socrates) as well. Their scope is comprehensive in terms of forms and subjects, but coverage is selective within each category. They include works in English and in the standard Western European languages. No attempt is made to be exhaustive, which the compilers note would result in "an unrealizable project." They do, however, cover a wide range of materials, including fiction, poetry, and drama about Socrates. Navia and Katz arrange their nearly 2,000 entries by form and subject; cross-references are made for works that fit in more than one category. Their annotations, which are strictly descriptive, do a good job of summarizing the works. There is an index of authors. This is an excellent working bibliography for the study of Socrates. One can also consult McKirahan's *Plato and Socrates* (entry 706), which lists far more citations covering a much shorter period of time. Patzer (entry 731) also provides more extensive coverage, but no annotations.

731. Patzer, Andreas. **Bibliographia Socratica: Die wissenschaftliche Literatur über Sokrates von den Anfängen bis auf die neueste Zeit in systematisch-chronologischer Anordnung.** Freiburg: Karl Alber, 1985. 365pp. ISBN 3–495–47585–0. LCCN 86–100918.

Patzer's bibliography, with over 2,300 entries, includes quite a few more items than Navia and Katz (entry 730). However, he provides no annotations. Patzer arranges his material by form and subject. There are four main sections: *Hilfsmittel* (bibliographies, surveys, and other auxiliary works), *Quellentexte* (editions and commentaries for all authors who are sources for the life and thought of Socrates), *Wissenschaftliche Literatur* (scholarly studies), and *Varia* (miscellaneous works on Socrates). Each includes numerous subdivisions; the overall scheme is made clear in the lengthy table of contents. *Wissenschaftliche Literatur,* which comprises nearly two-thirds of the book, is by far the largest part. Patzer provides cross-references as well as an index of names and subjects. He covers a wide range of works in a variety of languages. Although Navia will be the first choice for most readers of English, Patzer includes many additional citations and should also be consulted by anyone needing exhaustive coverage.

SOPHOCLES

BIBLIOGRAPHIES

See also Donlan (entry 599) and Forman (600).

732. Buxton, R.G.A. **Sophocles.** New Surveys in the Classics 16. Oxford: Clarendon Press, 1984. 38pp. ISBN 0–903035–138. LCCN 85–205399.

Buxton's survey is aimed chiefly at university students. He follows the standard approach of the series: brief topical essays present a synthesis of recent scholarship in the area, with bibliographical details supplied in the notes. Buxton cites English-language works as much as possible but also includes important work in other languages. While touching on all major aspects of Sophoclean studies, Buxton gives emphasis to literary and dramatic criticism. He provides a good working introduction to the study of Sophocles and his plays.

733. Moreau, Alain. **Bibliographie de l'Ajax de Sophocle.** Supplément aux Cahiers du Gita 10. Montpellier: Université Paul-Valéry, 1997. 45pp.

Moreau offers a highly selective bibliography of the *Ajax* that focuses on the "problèmes essentiels posés par la pièce." He arranges his material by topic. Brief sections cover bibliography, editions, translations, the history of the text, commentaries, scholia, indexes, style, and meter. Two larger sections cover general works on Sophocles that include discussions of the *Ajax* and works specifically on the *Ajax*. Moreau ranges through twentieth-century scholarship and misses little of major significance. He provides summaries for some items; he has taken many summaries directly from *L'Année philologique* (entry 44), while others are his own. Moreau is a useful guide to any student of this play.

INDEXES AND CONCORDANCES

734. Ellendt, Friedrich. **Lexicon Sophocleum.** Ed. alt. Cur. Hermann Genthe. Berolini: Borntraeger, 1872; repr. Hildesheim: Georg Olms, 1986. 812pp. ISBN 3–487–00038–5. LCCN 59–007376.

Ellendt's venerable work remains the primary tool of its type for Sophocles. Many have noted its accuracy and learning, although much progress has been made over the past century in the study of Sophocles' text and language. For each word, Ellendt provides Latin translations and an enumeration of passages, with discussion of usages and variant readings. There is no concordance to Sophocles as such, aside from the *Thesaurus Linguae Graecae* (entry 519), and Ellendt provides a useful substitute for those without access to the *TLG.*

STRABO

BIBLIOGRAPHIES

735. Biraschi, A.M., P. Maribelli, G.D. Massaro, and M.A. Pagnotta. **Strabone: Saggio di bibliografia, 1469–1978.** Pubblicazioni degli Istituti di Storia Antica e di Storia Medioevale e Moderna della Facoltà di Lettere e Filosofia. Perugia: Università degli Studi, 1981. 137pp. LCCN 88–176341.

This bibliography covers works by and about Strabo from the publication of the earliest printed version (a Latin translation) in 1469 through 1978. The compilers have grouped their material in three sections: editions, translations, and studies. They have arranged entries within each of these chronologically. While the section devoted to secondary studies includes a number of items of historical and geographical interest, philological works predominate. There are no annotations. Indexes provide access by subject (only very broad terms) and author. There is also a brief and not very satisfactory *index locorum,* which covers only those passages expressly mentioned in the titles of works cited.

THUCYDIDES

BIBLIOGRAPIES

See also Donlan (entry 614) and Marincola (616).

736. Dover, K.J. **Thucydides.** New Surveys in the Classics 7. Oxford: Clarendon Press, 1973. 44pp. LCCN 74–171533.

Written by one of the leading Greek scholars of the twentieth century, this slender volume surveys the state of Thucydidean studies as of 1973. The first chapter lists and comments upon most important editions, commentaries, translations, and general works.

Subsequent chapters deal with specific aspects of Thucydides' *History:* its authority, the text, style, composition, the speeches, acts and intentions, and judgment and generalization. Each cites and discusses relevant studies. While in some ways this work is more a collection of brief essays than a bibliographical survey, it does provide a good overview of work on Thucydides during the first three-quarters of the twentieth century.

737. Ramón Palerm, Vicente. **Estudios sobre Tucídides: Ensayo de un Repertorio Bibliográfico (1973–1995).** Zaragoza: Departamento de Ciencias de la Antigüedad, Universidad de Zaragoza, 1996. 139pp. ISBN 84–920431–2-1.

While Ramón Palerm consciously continues the work of O. Luschnat's bibliography of Thucydides in the *Nachträge* to *Supplementband* XII of *Pauly's Realencyclopädie* (entry 153), he also picks up where Dover (entry 736) leaves off. His work covers 32 years of Thucydidean studies compiled from the usual bibliographical sources, such as *L'Année philologique* (entry 44). Ramón Palerm begins with a narrative survey of trends in Thucydidean scholarship during his period. The actual bibliography follows. Ramón Palerm organizes it into broad subject categories. Indexes provide access by author, subject, and passage of Thucydides discussed.

INDEXES AND CONCORDANCES

738. Schrader, Carlos. **Concordantia Thucydidea.** Alpha-Omega, Reihe A, 99. Hildesheim: Olms-Weidmann, 1998. 4v. ISBN 3–487–10697–3 (v. 1); 3–487–10698–1 (v. 2); 3–487–10699–X (v. 3); 3–487–10700–7 (v. 4).

Schrader bases his concordance on the Oxford Classical Texts edition of Sir Henry Stuart Jones and J. Enoch Powell (Oxford: Clarendon Press, 1942). He follows a lemmatized, keyword-in-context format.

XENOPHON

BIBLIOGRAPHIES

739. Morrison, Donald R. **Bibliography of Editions, Translations, and Commentary on Xenophon's Socratic Writings, 1600–Present.** Pittsburgh: Mathesis, 1988. 103pp. ISBN 0–935225–02–1. LCCN 88–1063.

Morrison began this bibliography as an aid to his own researches rather than a project for publication, which explains a few of its idiosyncracies. He covers the actual Socratic works (the *Memorabilia,* the *Apology,* the *Symposium,* and the *Oeconomicus*) plus *Hiero* and *Agesilaus.* He attempts to cover editions and translations of these exhaustively within his time frame. Morrison also attempts to cover completely the secondary literature pertaining specifically to these works but is less comprehensive in his treatment of general works on Xenophon. His rather misleading use of the term "commentary" means secondary studies, not just actual commentaries. He does exclude editions and translations of excerpts from Xenophon, as well as book reviews. Altogether Morrison lists 1,382 items. His first chapter covers "Special Topics": general works, biography, political thought, religious thought, and so forth. Following chapters cover collected works, selected works, and each of the individual works. He subdivides each into editions and translations (by language). The chapters on individual works also include sections on textual criticism and commentary. While a treasure trove for the student of Xenophon, the bibliography is not without problems. It was mostly compiled from other bibliographies with the result that bibliographic information is sometimes incomplete or even incorrect. Although Morrison does not give a firm terminus, coverage trails off in the 1980s. There are no indexes.

740. Vela Tejada, José. **Post H. R. Breitenbach: Tres Décadas de Estudios sobre Jenofonte (1967–1997): Actualizacion Cientifica Bibliográfica.** Zaragoza: Ediciones del Departamento de Ciencias de la Antigüedad, Area de Filología Griega, Universidad de Zaragoza, 1998. 221pp. ISBN 84–920431–7-2.

This bibliographic survey picks up where that in H. R. Breitenbach's article in *Pauly's Realencyclopädie* (entry 152) ends. In the first part Vela Tejada offers a narrative survey of the literature from 1967 through 1997. This covers Xenophon's works by broad category (historical, philosophical, etc.). The second, and much longer, part comprises the bibliography proper. Vela Tejada arranges this by subject: general works (including editions), archaeology, bibliography, biography, textual studies, sciences and technology (which deceptively includes hunting and military science), law, philosophy, geography, history, language, literature, religion, and influence. Works are listed by author within each category. He includes books, dissertations, articles, and book reviews (listed under the book title). There are no annotations in the bibliography, although a number of the works are discussed briefly in the narrative section. Indexes provide access by author, passage of Xenophon discussed, and passage of other ancient authors discussed.

INDEXES AND CONCORDANCES

741. Róspide López, Alfredo, and Francisco Martín García. **Index Socraticorum Xenophontis Operum.** Alpha-Omega, Reihe A, 156. Hildesheim: Olms-Weidmann, 1995. 236pp. ISBN 3–487–10018–5.

This work covers Xenophon's *Memorabilia, Oeconomicus, Symposium,* and *Apology of Socrates.* The compilers have based the index on the edition of E. C. Marchant (Oxford: Clarendon Press, 1901). They include all words except *kai* and the definite article (except dual forms, which are noted). All occurrences of each word are listed together, with various inflections noted in sequence.

742. Róspide López, Alfredo, and Francisco Martín García. **Index Xenophontis Opusculorum.** Alpha-Omega, Reihe A, 147. Hildesheim: Olms-Weidmann, 1994. 218pp. ISBN 3–487–09794–X.

In this work, Róspide and Martín García index the minor works of Xenophon, as found in the fifth volume of E. C. Marchant's edition of the works of Xenophon (Oxford: Clarendon Press, 1920). For the epistles, they employ the edition of R. Hercher, *Epistolographi Graeci* (Paris: Firmin Didot, 1873). Among the works covered are *Agesilaus, Atheniensium respublica, Cynegeticus, Epistulae, De equitandi ratione, De equitum magistro, Hiero, De republica Lacedaimoniorum,* and *De vectigalibus.* Scholia are also indexed. All instances of each word are listed in sequence (by case or tense and mood, as appropriate).

743. Schrader, Carlos, José Vela, and Vicente Ramón. **Xenophontis Operum Concordantiae.** . Alpha-Omega, Reihe A, 200. Hildesheim, Germany: Olms-Weidmann, 2002–. 5v. in 8. ISBN 3-487-11716-9 (v. 1, pt. 1); 3-487-11717-7 (v. 1, pt. 2); 3-487-11718-5 (v. 2, pt. 1); 3-487-11719-3 (v. 2, pt. 2).

Only the first two volumes of this work have appeared to date; these cover the *Hellenica* and the *Anabasis* respectively. Future volumes will cover the *Cyropaedia,* the Socratic works, and the *opuscula* (minor works). This lemmatized concordance is based on the edition of E.C. Marchant (Oxford: Clarendon Press, 1901–1920). Each instance of a word appears centered in a line of context. As with many computer-generated concordances, the typeface is small and unattractive.

16
Latin Authors and Works

This chapter covers individual Latin authors and works. These include several categories: book-length bibliographies; dictionaries, encyclopedias, and handbooks; concordances and indexes; and journals. Internet resources are included very selectively under these headings as appropriate. Readers should be aware that there are also many article-length bibliographies that are not included here. *Lustrum* (entry 71), *Classical World* (entry 95), and the *Aufstieg und Niedergang der römischen Welt* (entry 315) are good places to check for these. In order to supplement the bibliographies listed below with more current material, one should also consult the appropriate author entry in the annual volumes of *L'Année philologique* (entry 44). Handbooks include the many companions to various authors, a major growth industry in classical publishing of late; see the remarks of Andrew Dyck on this subject in his review of *Brill's Companion to Cicero* (entry 766), *Bryn Mawr Classical Review* (2003.01.17), http://ccat.sas. upenn.edu/bmcr/2003/2003–01–17.html. Concordances and indexes are covered somewhat selectively, with a focus on the best and most recent works. Additional concordances may be found in Quellet (entry 580). Since the *Thesaurus Linguae Latinae* (entry 520) has yet to be made available online (or completed, for that matter), the best equivalent to an electronic concordance for Latin literature remains the Packard Humanities database (entry 581).

AMMIANUS MARCELLINUS

BIBLIOGRAPHIES

744.   Rosen, Klaus. **Ammianus Marcellinus.** Erträge der Forschung 183. Darmstadt: Wissenschaftliche Buchgesellschaft, 1982. 237pp. ISBN 3–534–06373–2. LCCN 83–127709.

Rosen's overview of Ammianus Marcellinus is essentially an extended bibliographic essay, which ranges from the sixteenth century through 1979. His introduction covers editions and general works on Ammianus, as well as broader works on his era. Subsequent chapters cover Ammianus's life and times, his *Res Gestae* as a literary work, his worldview, his reliability, and his relations with contemporaries. Indexes provide additional access by passage of the *Res Gestae,* ancient author, ancient names, and subject. Rosen's bibliography lists 384 works arranged by topic. He misses little of significance within his time frame. Since Ammianean studies have expanded rapidly in recent years, it is exceptionally important to update Rosen through the relevant sections of *L'Année philologique* (entry 44).

INDEXES AND CONCORDANCES

745.   Chiabò, Maria. **Index Verborum Ammiani Marcellini.** Alpha-Omega, Reihe A, 44. Hildesheim: Georg Olms, 1983. 2v. ISBN 3–487–07354–4 (v. 1); 3–487–07355–2 (v. 2). LCCN 83–227672.

Chiabò uses the edition of Charles Upson Clark (Berlin: Weidmann, 1910–1915) for her index. Her work is a typical index, which presents the text without information about textual variants or emendations. Corrupt passages and Greek words are gathered into separate lists at the end of the main index. Chiabò is a serviceable work, but Viansino (entry 746) often provides more information and is based on a more recent edition.

746.   Viansino, Ioannes. **Ammiani Marcellini Rerum Gestarum Lexicon.** Alpha-Omega, Reihe A, 79. Hildesheim: Olms-Weidmann, 1985. 2v. ISBN 3–487–07711–6 (v. 1); 3–487–07712–4 (v. 2). LCCN 86–217566.

Viansino combines elements of a lexicon and index. Entries gather all instances of a word under its normal dictionary form, with subarrangement by its various meainigs and senses. Viansino gives brief definitions in Latin but is generally unsatisfactory as a lexicon. He does provide a fairly full conspectus of the words used by Ammianus; those using the work as an index will be more satisfied. Viansino sometimes quotes a phrase in full but more often gives a bare citation. He uses the more recent edition of W. Seyfarth (Leipzig: Teubner, 1978), which, though founded on the work of Clark, covers 70 years of additional work on the text.

APULEIUS

BIBLIOGRAPHIES

See Donlan (entry 609).

INDEXES AND CONCORDANCES

747.   Oldfather, William Abbott, Howard Vernon Canter, and Ben Edwin Perry. **Index Apuleianus.** Philological Monographs 3. Middletown, CT: American Philological Association, 1934; repr. Hildesheim: Georg Olms, 1979. 490pp. LCCN 35–9910.

A product of the Oldfather index assembly line, this volume is the work of many contributors. It relies upon the editions of Rudolf Helm for the *Metamorphoses* (2nd ed., Leipzig: Teubner, 1913), the *Apologia* (2nd ed., Leipzig: Teubner, 1912), and the *Florida* (Leipzig: Teubner, 1910) and that of Paul Thomas for the philosophical writings (Leipzig: Teubner, 1908). Oldfather takes full account of variant readings. Entries are typical for an index, with all instances gathered under the dictionary entry. Inflected forms and their occurrences are listed, without comment or context. Overall, this is a reliable and useful work.

AUGUSTINE OF HIPPO

BIBLIOGRAPHIES

748.   Andresen, Carl, ed. **Bibliographia Augustiniana.** 2. völlig neubearb. Aufl. Darmstadt: Wissenschaftliche Buchgesellschaft, 1973. 317pp. ISBN 3–534–01145–7.

Andresen covers work on St. Augustine from as far back as the eighteenth century but focuses primarily on publications of the 1950s and 1960s. He arranges the bibliography by form and subject. Andresen lists editions, translations, and commentaries first; he also gathers textual studies, concordances, and the like in these sections. Then he turns to secondary works, which comprise the bulk of the bibliography. These are arranged by topic: general works, life, Augustine as a philosopher, Augustine as a theologian, and his influence. Each of these is extensively subdivided; the table of contents lays out the organization nicely. He is strongest in coverage of European publications, somewhat weaker on English and American work. Indexes cover passages from Augustine, the Bible, other ancient authors, Latin terms, names in titles of works, and modern authors. Andresen has provided a useful work, although he does not annotate entries. Van Bavel (entry 754) offers more detailed coverage of the 1950s. For more recent work, see Miethe (entry 751) and Geerlings (entry 750).

749.   Donnelly, Dorothy F., and Mark A. Sherman. **Augustine's De civitate Dei: An Annotated Bibliography of Modern Criticism, 1960–1990.** New York: Peter Lang, 1991. 109pp. ISBN 0–8204–1607–X. LCCN 91–26511.

The main part of this bibliography lists 64 American and Canadian studies primarily or in large part concerned with *De civitate Dei*. These are listed alphabetically by author. Supplementary sections list 13 significant earlier works in English (one wonders how these were selected from the vast bibliography on this work) and 18 English-language works published abroad between 1960 and 1990. Annotations are generous but largely descriptive. A chronological list of writings by Augustine and a selective bibliography of works about Augustine not included in the annotated bibliography complete the volume. This bibliography offers a very limited perspective on *De civitate Dei* and is at best a starting point.

750.   Geerlings, Wilhelm. **Augustinus—Leben und Werk: Eine bibliographisches Einführung.** Paderborn: Ferdinand Schöningh, 2002. 212pp. ISBN 3–506–71020–6.

Geerlings's bibliography best serves as a bibliographical orientation to particular works of St. Augustine. He begins with a brief section on Augustine's life: a narrative based on primary sources (all documented in the notes), followed by a short bibliography of biographies. Geerlings then turns to the works of Augustine, grouping them by theme and form: autobiographical, philosophical and anti-pagan, anti-Manichaean, anti-Donatist, anti-Pelagian, anti-Arian, hermeneutic and exegetical, doctrinal and dogmatic, and pastoral works; sermons; letters; doubtful works; and lost works. The "Systematische Werkübersicht" provides a guide to the placement of individual works in this scheme. Under each work Geerlings gives the standard abbreviation, the date, and a brief description. He then provides a list of editions followed by a list of secondary works. His bibliographies are very selective and focus primarily upon recent works. They do include works in a variety of languages and from various perspectives. Geerlings offers a good starting place but is far from comprehensive. For earlier work see the other bibliographies listed in this section.

751.   Miethe, Terry L. **Augustinian Bibliography, 1970–1980.** Westport, CT: Greenwood, 1982. 218pp. ISBN 0–313–22629–6. LCCN 82–6173.

Miethe offers 1,400 numbered citations, most for works published between 1970 and 1980. He does include some earlier works missed by other bibliographies. Miethe also makes a special effort to cover American and Canadian doctoral dissertations that have been neglected by other Augustinian bibliographers. He includes 218 dissertations ranging in date from the 1890s to the 1980s. He provides a chronological list of Augustine's works, with both Latin and English titles. The bibliography proper is arranged by subject in six sections: bibliographies, life, writings, philosophical issues, theological issues, and historical and doctrinal relations. Each of these has numerous subdivisions, which are detailed in the table of contents. Miethe does not provide annotations but does occasionally translate foreign-language titles and note reviews under books. There is a name index. Miethe also includes several essays on St. Augustine. For earlier work see Nebreda (752), Van Bavel (entry 754), and Andresen (entry 748); for later work see Geerlings (entry 750).

752. Nebreda, Eulogius. **Bibliographia Augustiniana, seu, Operum collectio, quae divi Augustini vitam et doctrinam quadantenus exponunt.** Bibliotheca Commentarii pro religiosis. Sectio bibliographica 1. Roma: Typ. Pol. "Cuore di Maria," 1928. 272pp. LCCN 56–54211.

Nebreda is a useful source of older editions of and works on St. Augustine. He describes some 934 works. His first section lists the works of Augustine by title in chronological order. The second section covers editions, textual studies, commentaries, and translations into various languages. Subsequent sections cover works about his life; his works about the liberal arts, philosophy, doctrine and scripture, and ascetic and mystical theology; and apologetic and controversial works. Bibliographical information tends to be sketchy, and the occasional annotations are in Latin. Nebreda is far from complete and very weak in his coverage of English-language works. He provides chronological and author indexes.

753. Severson, Richard. **Confessions of Saint Augustine: An Annotated Bibliography of Modern Criticism, 1888–1995.** Bibliographies and Indexes in Religious Studies 40. Westport, CT: Greenwood Press, 1996. 149pp. ISBN 0–313–29995–1. LCCN 96–9465.

Unlike most other Augustinian bibliographies noted here, Severson limits himself to a single work, the *Confessions,* and to English-language scholarship. He lists 468 works (books, articles, and dissertations) published between 1888 and 1995. Severson arranged these under nine broad rubrics: modern criticism of the *Confessions,* autobiographical studies, classical and literary scholarship, conversion experience, time and other philosophical issues, psychological criticism, spirituality and reader guidance, structural unity of the text, and theological interpretation. Severson lays out the subdivisions of these in the table of contents and gives an overview of each major section in his introduction. Each entry includes a brief descriptive annotation. Indexes cover authors, titles, and subjects; Severson also provides many cross-references throughout the bibliography. This is a useful survey, although students will find many of the works too demanding, and scholars will regret the absence of works in French and German.

754. Van Bavel, Tarsicius. **Répertoire bibliographique de Saint Augustin, 1950–1960.** Instrumenta Patristica 3. Steenbrugis: In Abbatia Sancti Petri; The Hague: Martinus Nijhoff, 1963. 991pp. LCCN 64–33473.

Van Bavel gives a good idea of the vast amount of work published on Augustine: he lists 5,502 works for a single decade. While most of the works are variously in English, Dutch, French, German, Italian, or Spanish, Van Bavel also covers some titles in Eastern European languages. He does include a number of background works that touch upon Augustine only in part. Van Bavel arranges the bibliography by subject; major divisions are biography, works, doctrine, and influence. Van Bavel subdivides each into numerous chapters and subsections, as laid out in the "Plan de la bibliographie." His principles of arrangement within any given section are opaque. In addition to citations, Van Bavel notes reviews under book titles and often supplies brief descriptive annotations. An array of indexes provide access by name, subject, and author. Van Bavel is a mine of valuable bibliography but often not easy to navigate. For later work see Andresen (entry 748), Miethe (entry 751), and Geerlings (entry 750).

DICTIONARIES, ENCYCLOPEDIAS, AND HANDBOOKS

755.   Fitzgerald, Allan D., ed. **Augustine through the Ages: An Encyclopedia.** Grand Rapids, MI: Eerdmans, 1999. 902pp. ISBN 0–8028–3843-X. LCCN 99–12518.

Nearly 150 distinguished scholars have contributed articles to this encyclopedia covering all aspects of St. Augustine: his life, works, and times; influences on him; and his influence on others. Fitzgerald has included articles on people, places, topics, and individual works of Augustine. Little of significance has been missed. Many of the articles are fairly substantial, and all include excellent bibliographies. Two useful tables appear at the head of the work. Both list Augustine's works alphabetically (by Latin title); the first table notes abbreviations, English titles, Latin editions, and English translations. The second gives the dates and circumstances of their composition. An excellent index concludes the volume. While the encyclopedia exhibits a high level of scholarship, it also remains useful to students and general readers.

756.   Stump, Eleonore, and Norman Kretzmann. **Cambridge Companion to Augustine.** Cambridge: Cambridge University Press, 2001. 307pp. ISBN 0–521–65018–6; 0–521–65985–X. LCCN 00–31173.

This important introduction to the life and work of Augustine includes 18 essays by 16 leading scholars. These cover his life and times; faith and reason; evil and original sin; predestination, Pelagianism, and foreknowledge; biblical interpretation; the divine nature; *De trinitate;* time and creation; Augustine's theory of the soul; free will; his philosophy of memory; his response to skepticism; knowledge and illumination; Augustine's philosophy of language; his ethics; his political philosophy; Augustine and medieval philosophy; and post-medieval Augustinianism. Each article provides a scholarly but accessible discussion of its topic, with references to the primary sources and salient secondary literature. Stump has also supplied an excellent working bibliography and a detailed index. While Fitzgerald (entry 755) is the best resource for those seeking information on a specific topic or work of Augustine, Stump is the best for those seeking an overall introduction or an orientation to a major aspect of Augustine's work and thought.

INDEXES AND CONCORDANCES

757.   Cooper, Rodney H., Leo C. Ferrari, Peter M. Ruddock, J. Robert Smith. **Concordantia in libros XIII Confessionum S. Aurelii Augustini.** Alpha-Omega, Reihe A, 124. Hildesheim: Olms-Weidmann, 1991. 2v. ISBN 3–487–09490–8 (v. 1); 3–487–09491–6 (v. 2).

This concordance to the *Confessiones* is based on the well-known edition of M. Skutella, as revised by H. Juergens and W. Schaub (Stuttgart: Teubner, 1969). The authors have chosen the keyword-in-context format. All inflected forms are sensibly gathered under a single lemma, usually the normal dictionary form (see their introduction for exceptions). The authors unfortunately chose to provide page and line number references to Skutella rather than the more normal book and section number references, so that those working from a different text will find the concordance useless. Two appendixes provide word frequency information.

JOURNALS

758. **Augustinian Studies.** Villanova, PA: Villanova University, 1970– . Semiannual. ISSN 0094–5323. LCCN79–141613.

This journal publishes articles on St. Augustine from historical, philosophical, and theological perspectives. It also includes works on his influence. Each issue contains several substantial book reviews. All articles are normally in English.

759. **Revue des études augustiniennes.** Paris: Institut d'études augustiniennes, 1955–2003. Quarterly. ISSN 0035–2012. LCCN 62–66823.

760. **Revue des études augustiniennes et patristiques.** Paris: Institut d'études augustiniennes, 2004– . Semiannual. LCCN 2004–252089.

This journal focuses on research on St. Augustine and his influence, although the recent title change indicates some broader coverage of patristics as well. It has long published important studies in English, French, German, Italian, and Spanish. Since 1958 it has included an annual bibliographical review of work on Augustine, under the title *Recherches augustiniennes.*

CAESAR

BIBLIOGRAPHIES

See Donlan (entry 614).

INDEXES AND CONCORDANCES

761. Birch, Cordelia Margaret. **Concordantia et Index Caesaris [Concordance and Index to Caesar].** Alpha-Omega, Reihe A, 100. Hildesheim: Olms-Weidmann, 1989. 2v. ISBN 3–487–07992–5 (v. 1); 3–487–07993–3 (v. 2).

Birch used the Oxford Classical Text edition of R. DuPontet (Oxford: Clarendon Press, 1900–1908) as the basis for the concordance. She provides a list of variant readings found in other editions in the preliminaries. Birch covers not only the genuine works of Caesar but also the eighth book of *De Bello Gallico,* written by Aulus Hirtius, and the three works of disputed authorship: *Bellum Alexandrinum, Bellum Africum,* and *Bellum Hispaniense.*

The concordance lists every word in alphabetical sequence, in a keyword-in-context format. The index, a separate listing, likewise follows a strictly alphabetical pattern: Birch makes no effort to gather the inflected forms into a single entry under the normal lexical form. The concordance is serviceable, while the index fails to achieve the normal end of such a work: gathering all occurrences of a word in one place.

CATULLUS

BIBLIOGRAPHIES

See also Donlan (entry 609).

762.   Ferguson, John. **Catullus.** New Surveys in the Classics 20. Oxford: Clarendon Press, 1988. 50pp. LCCN 88–190314.

For those who do not require the fullness of Harrauer (entry 763) or Holoka (entry 764), Ferguson's survey provides a convenient and highly readable guide to the high points of Catullan scholarship. His brief chapters cover the history of the text, Catullus's life, his literary influences, the poems, and modern translations and Catullus's impact on subsequent literature. In each Ferguson provides an overview of his subject and discusses the most important scholarly works on it. A good working bibliography appears at the end of the volume.

763.   Harrauer, Hermann. **Bibliography to Catullus.** Bibliography to the Augustan Poetry 3. Hildesheim: Gerstenberg, 1979. 206pp. ISBN 3–8067–0787–1. LCCN 80–450064.

Harrauer's *Catullus* contains 2,931 numbered entries (actually somewhat more items are listed, because of supplementary entries). It covers works published between 1500 and 1976, with a few entries for 1977 as well. Coverage through the eighteenth century is less than complete, owing to the defective bibliographical apparatus available for the period. Harrauer includes editions, translations, commentaries, books, and articles. Reviews are listed under the work reviewed. There are no annotations. The citations are arranged in 17 topical chapters; several of these are further subdivided. Works within a given category are subarranged chronologically. As in earlier volumes in this series (entries 817 and 832), Harrauer provides outstanding indexing. The *index locorum* provides access to discussions of individual poems and even specific lines. The subject index offers access to additional subjects not brought out by the chapter arrangement and to discussions of particular Latin words. There is also an author index. Harrauer is generally superior to Holoka's bibliography of Catullus (entry 764), both because of the wider span of years covered and the superior access afforded. However, both must be used to obtain reasonably exhaustive coverage.

764.   Holoka, James P. **Gaius Valerius Catullus: A Systematic Bibliography.** Garland Reference Library of the Humanities 513. New York: Garland, 1985. 324pp. ISBN 0–8240–8897–2. LCCN 84–45404.

It is not clear why this work was published just six years after Harrauer's major bibliography of Catullus (entry 763). Holoka offers roughly the same number of entries (3,111) and covers the years 1878 to 1981 (a few items published in 1982 and 1983 are included also). The citations are arranged in nine broad topical chapters; most of these are subdivided into a number of additional categories. Subarrangement within a category is chronological. Holoka includes editions, translations, books, and articles. Reviews are listed under the work reviewed. Some entries include very brief descriptive annotations; most do not. Holoka also includes tables of contents for many of the books listed. There are some cross-references to related entries. There is only an author index, which leaves one totally dependent on the chapter and section headings for other access. Holoka picks up a few items that Harrauer missed and carries the work five years later. Harrauer is generally better in breadth of coverage and provides far better access.

INDEXES AND CONCORDANCES

765. McCarren, V. P. **Critical Concordance to Catullus.** Leiden: Brill, 1977. 210pp. ISBN 90–04–05224–0. LCCN 77–574567.

McCarren based his concordance on the standard edition of R.A.B. Mynors (Oxford: Clarendon Press, 1958) but includes variant readings both from other commonly consulted editions and the manuscripts. Two to three metrical lines of context are provided for each instance of a word. Users will find his method of citing references to the text annoying but should prefer this work to M. N. Wetmore's badly dated *Index Verborum Catullianus* (New Haven, CT: Yale University Press, 1912), which is based on inferior editions.

CICERO

BIBLIOGRAPHIES

See Donlan (entry 856).

DICTIONARIES, ENCYCLOPEDIAS, AND HANDBOOKS

766. May, James M., ed. **Brill's Companion to Cicero: Oratory and Rhetoric.** Leiden: Brill, 2002. 632pp. ISBN 90–04–12147–1. LCCN 2002–066555.

May provides an excellent resource for the study of Cicero's orations and rhetorical works; the epistles and *philosophica* appear only when they are relevant to oratory. The contributors include many leading Ciceronian scholars, such as May himself, Harold Gotoff, Emanuele Narducci, George Kennedy, and Christopher Craig. The opening essays cover Cicero's life and works (with a strong focus on the speeches and *Rhetorica*), rhetorical education in Cicero's time, and the historical and cultural context of Ciceronian oratory. The next seven essays deal with Cicero's orations, primarily in five major chronological groupings: early speeches, consular speeches, the *post reditum* speeches, the Caesarians, and the *Philippics*. The two exceptions address "Ciceronian Invective," and the lost and fragmentary speeches. The *Rhetorica* are covered in five essays, one on their intellectual background and four on individual works in roughly chronological order. Two concluding essays offer an overview of Cicero's influence from antiquity through the nineteenth century and a bibliographic survey of recent studies (1975–1998) on Cicero's speeches and rhetorical works. A substantial bibliography of more than 50 pages complements the survey. A general index and an *index locorum* complete the volume.

INDEXES AND CONCORDANCES

767. Abbott, Kenneth Morgan, William Abbott Oldfather, and Howard Vernon Canter. **Index Verborum in Ciceronis Rhetorica Necnon Incerti Auctoris Libros ad Herennium.** Urbana: University of Illinois Press, 1964. 1160pp. LCCN 64–19115.

Three editors began this work in the 1930s; one, K.M. Abbott, survived to see it published in 1964. Abbott used the text of A.S. Wilkins (Oxford: Clarendon Press, 1903) for all but one of Cicero's rhetorical works. For *De Inventione,* he used the edition of Eduard Stroebel (Leipzig: Teubner, 1915). Abbott also included the *Rhetorica ad Herennium,* once ascribed to Cicero; for this he used Friedrich Marx's second edition (Leipzig: Teubner, 1923). Abbott followed the principles used for the other indexes produced by Oldfather and his various collaborators. He indexed all words in the *Rhetorica* except proper nouns and Greek words. Abbott also includes manuscript variants and emendations from the *apparatus criticus* of the editions used; he notes significant later emendations in the *additamentum* that precedes the index. This is a useful resource for anyone studying the text or style of the *Rhetorica.* For proper nouns, see Shackleton Bailey's *Onomasticon to Cicero's Treatises* (entry 772).

768. Kinapenne, Catherine. **M. Tulli Ciceronis Orationes: Index Verborum, Liste de fréquence.** Alpha-Omega, Reihe A, 213. Hildesheim: Olms-Weidmann, 2001. 4v. ISBN 3–487–11287–6 (v.1); 3–487–11288–4 (v.2); 3–487–11289–2 (v.3); 3–487–11290–6 (v.4).

Kinapenne has produced the first and only concordance to Cicero's speeches, supplementing but not replacing H. Merguet, *Lexikon zu den Reden des Cicero* (Jena: H. Dufft, 1877–1884). She relies upon the Oxford Classical Text edition of A.C. Clark and G. Peterson (Oxford: Clarendon Press, 1905–1918) and, for the fragments, the edition of Friedrich Schoell (Leipzig: Teubner, 1918). She does not index a number of common prepositions and conjunctions. Kinapenne does include proper nouns. The total number of occurrences for each word follows the lemma, with the various inflected forms marshalled below. Several word frequency tables follow the index.

769. Oldfather, William Abbott, Howard Vernon Canter, and Kenneth Morgan Abbott. **Index Verborum Ciceronis Epistularum.** Urbana: University of Illinois Press, 1938; repr. Hildesheim: Georg Olms, 1965. 583pp. LCCN 39–12693.

This well-conceived and beautifully printed index is, alas, based upon the old and faulty edition of L.C. Purser (Oxford: Clarendon Press, 1901–1903). It omits proper nouns and Greek words but otherwise includes all words found in Cicero's *Letters.* For proper nouns, see Shackleton Bailey's onomasticon to the letters (entry 770). As with other indexes by Oldfather, this work takes full account of variant readings and conjectures. The *additamentum* preceding the index proper enumerates emendations published subsequent to Purser's edition.

770. Shackleton Bailey, D.R. **Onomasticon to Cicero's Letters.** Stuttgart: Teubner, 1995. 161pp. ISBN 3–519–07426–5.

Shackleton Bailey here indexes the proper names in Cicero's letters. He gathers these into several lists: persons and deities, places, laws, the 35 Roman tribes, and miscellaneous. Romans are normally listed under the nomen or gens name; a list of cognomina with associated *gentilicia* follows the list of persons and will provide some access from that form of name as well. In addition to enumerating occurrences, Shackleton Bailey offers some information on the identity of people and places, along with notes on forms of names and references to the *Realencyclopädie* (entry 152) and other works. Shackleton Bailey also includes a list of headings found in the letters, and author indexes to the Greek and Latin quotations found in them.

771. Shackleton Bailey, D.R. **Onomasticon to Cicero's Speeches.** 2nd rev. ed. Stuttgart: Teubner, 1992. 140pp. ISBN 3–519–17416–2.

Shackleton Bailey indexes all the proper names in Cicero's speeches. As in his other onomastica, he follows the conventions of the Pauly-Wissowa *Realencyclopädie* (entry 152) and provides references to the listings in that work. Separate listings cover persons and deities, cognomina, places, laws, and the 35 Roman tribes. A final miscellaneous list gathers those names that do not fit elsewhere, such as religious festivals and philosophical schools. Many entries include useful notes on textual matters, form of name, and the identity of particular individuals.

772. Shackleton Bailey, D. R. **Onomasticon to Cicero's Treatises.** Stuttgart: Teubner, 1996. 142pp. ISBN 3–519–07432–X.

In this work, Shackleton Bailey indexes all the proper names found in the surviving philosophical and rhetorical writings of Cicero. Separate alphabetical lists cover Roman and Italian persons, non-Italian persons, philosophers and philosophies, mythological names, places and peoples, laws, and miscellaneous. Romans are entered under the nomen or gens name (a list of cognomina with associated *gentilicia* provides access from that form of address). In addition to enumerating instances, Shackleton Bailey includes notes on the identities of individuals and normal usage of their names. He often gives references to the *Realencyclopädie* (entry 152) articles and other secondary works. As a final service Shackleton Bailey provides an index of quotations found in Cicero's treatises; this is alphabetical by author.

773. Spaeth, John William, Jr. **Index Verborum Ciceronis Poeticorum Fragmentorum.** Urbana: University of Illinois Press, 1955. 130pp. LCCN 55–8836.

Yet another product of the Oldfather indexing atelier, Spaeth covers the important but often neglected poetry of Cicero. Spaeth lists all forms of each work under a single lemma, with declined and conjugated forms in the usual order; words found only in the *apparatus criticus* are presented in square brackets. He bases the index on the texts of Emil Baehrens, *Poetae Latini Minores* (Leipzig: Teubner, 1879–1883) and *Fragmenta Poetarum Romanorum* (Leipzig: Teubner, 1886); these rather badly dated editions have been superseded: see now Edward Courtney, *The Fragmentary Latin Poets* (Oxford: Oxford University Press, 1993).

CLAUDIAN

INDEXES AND CONCORDANCES

774. Christiansen, Peder G. **Concordantia in Claudianum [A Concordance to Claudianus].** Alpha-Omega, Reihe A, 47. Hildesheim: Olms-Weidmann, 1988. 432pp. ISBN 3–487–07848–1.

This first and only concordance to Claudian's works is based upon Theodor Birt's 1892 edition in the *Monumenta Germaniae Historica*. It is fully lemmatized and gathers inflected forms under the normal dictionary entry. One metrical line of context is provided. Since neither lemmata nor keywords are highlighted in any way, this work is rather difficult to navigate.

ENNIUS

BIBLIOGRAPHIES

775. Suerbaum, Werner. **Ennius in der Forschung des 20. Jahrhunderts: Eine kommentierte Bibliographie für 1900–1999, mit systematischen Hinweisen nebst einer Kurzdarstellung des Q. Ennius (239–169 v. Chr.).** Bibliographien zur Klassischen Philologie 1. Hildesheim: Georg Olms, 2003. 280pp. ISBN 3–487–11866–1.

Suerbaum provides a comprehensive listing of twentieth-century work on Ennius, along with a small selection of key nineteenth-century works. Entries are arranged by year of original publication, with cross-references from reprints and translations. Many entries include brief descriptive annotations; reviews are cited under book-length publications. In addition to works specifically on Ennius, Suerbaum notes many more general works that contain significant material on him. The "Systematische Hinweise," which follows the bibliography proper, provides subject access and additional comment on some of the works. An author index and a reprint of Suerbaum's article on Ennius in the *Neue Pauly* (entry 132) conclude the volume. This is an indispensable resource for anyone doing serious research on Ennius.

HORACE

BIBLIOGRAPHIES

See also Donlan (entry 609) and Braund (entry 612).

776. Doblhofer, Ernst. **Horaz in der Forschung nach 1957.** Erträge der Forschung 279. Darmstadt: Wissenschaftliche Buchgesellschaft, 1992. 205pp. ISBN 3–534–04505–X. LCCN 93–156228.

Doblhofer reviews publications on Horace for the period 1957 to 1987. He also discusses a number of important works that appeared before 1957. His work takes the form of a series of topical review essays that cover all aspects of Horatian studies. These progress from general aspects (textual history, editions, biography, literary history, and criticism) to studies of specific works and poems. Doblhofer gives a good overview of the scholarship in each area. He indicates the scope of each item, sets it in the context of other work on the topic, and occasionally provides his own assessment of its value. The actual bibliography, which is arranged in sections corresponding to the review essays, includes 1,157 numbered items. There are indexes of persons and subjects. Doblhofer covers far more works than Williams (entry 777) and is much more current. However, some knowledge of German is required to make effective use of Doblhofer.

777.   Williams, Gordon. **Horace.** New Surveys in the Classics 6. Oxford: Clarendon Press, 1972. 49pp. LCCN 73–163573.

In this survey, a noted scholar of Augustan poetry covers the works of Horace in chronological order. Williams's introduction discusses general treatments of Horace. Subsequent chapters review scholarly work on the individual books of poetry. In each, Williams first notes the principal editions, commentaries, and major studies of the work and then proceeds to studies of particular aspects of the poems. The majority of the publications cited are relatively recent, and many are in English, although Williams includes a generous selection of the most important older and foreign-language works as well.

DICTIONARIES, ENCYCLOPEDIAS, AND HANDBOOKS

778.   **Orazio: Enciclopedia Oraziana.** Roma: Istituto della Enciclopedia Italiana, 1996–1998. 3v.

This is not a traditional A-to-Z encyclopedia. The first section of this work serves up the writings of Horace in Latin and Italian. A detailed account of his life and times is found in the second section. Subsequent sections cover the composition of his works, the manuscript tradition, editions and translations, places and people related to his life and works, his literary and philosophical influences, anthropology and society, religion and mythology, concepts, literary forms and motives, language and style, *Fortuna* in antiquity and after, Horace in various countries, twentieth-century celebrations of Horace (bimillenia of his birth and death), music and art, and ancient scholia. The list of contributors includes many distinguished scholars. The work as a whole is beautifully illustrated and includes many topical bibliographies. Indexes cover names and subjects, passages cited (both Horace and other ancient authors), illustrations, and contributors.

INDEXES AND CONCORDANCES

779.   Cooper, Lane. **Concordance to the Works of Horace.** Washington, DC: Carnegie Institute, 1916; repr. New York: Barnes & Noble, 1961. 593pp. LCCN 16–20920.

Cooper based his concordance on Friedrich Vollmer's *editio minor* of 1910, noting also variant readings from this, Vollmer's 1912 *editio maior,* and E. C. Wickham's editions (Oxford: Clarendon Press, 1903–1904). Cooper provides lemmata, the full metrical line for each instance of the word, and citations. Variant readings are marked as such. Although based on older editions, the concordance is accurate and attractively printed. In many ways, Cooper remains the best concordance to Horace.

780.   Iso Echegoyen, José-Javier. **Concordantia Horatiana [A Concordance to Horace].** Alpha-Omega. Hildesheim: Olms-Weidmann, 1990. 594pp. ISBN 3–487–09362–6.

Iso Echegoyen offers a typical computer-generated concordance, unlemmatized with keyword–in-context. It is based on the now standard edition of Horace by D. R. Shackleton Bailey (Stuttgart: Teubner, 1985), although Iso Echegoyen occasionally departs from Shackleton Bailey's readings without explanation. This is disturbing, since Iso does not list variants in his concordance. There are numerous typographical errors and mistakes, including a number of keywords misspelled. Cooper (entry 779) is both more accurate and a more attractive work typographically. Those who choose to refer to Iso Echegoyen, whether for the benefits of Shackleton Bailey's text or because it is the only Horatian concordance at hand, should do so with great care.

JUVENAL

BIBLIOGRAPHIES

See Braund (entry 612).

INDEXES AND CONCORDANCES

781.   Dubrocard, Michel. **Juvenal-Satires: Index Verborum, Relevés Statistiques.** Alpha-Omega 28. Hildesheim: Georg Olms, 1976. 248, 27pp. ISBN 3–487–06011–6. LCCN 76–487307.

Dubrocard's index is based on the edition of W. V. Clausen (Oxford: Clarendon Press, 1959). Under each lemma, he enumerates the various inflectional forms and their occurrences. The total number of occurrences is given at the head of each entry. His reference system is somewhat unusual. In addition to the number of the particular *Satire* and the line number, Dubrocard gives a number representing the word's position in the line. Dubrocard also provides a sizeable amount of statistical data on the use of different forms and parts of speech, as well as a table of words in descending order of frequency. While a useful work, overall it shows more concern with computational gymnastics than the study of Juvenal.

782.   Kelling, Lucile, and Albert Suskin. **Index Verborum Iuvenalis.** Chapel Hill: University of North Carolina Press, 1951. 139pp. LCCN 51–8087.

This work remains particularly useful to those studying the text of Juvenal. It is based on four editions: N. Vianello (Turin: Paravia, 1935), S. G. Owen (2nd ed., Oxford: Clarendon Press, 1908), A. E. Housman (Cambridge: Cambridge University Press, 1938), and Otto Jahn (4th ed., Berlin: Weidmann, 1910). A number of other texts were consulted as well. Kelling and Suskin include the full range of manuscript readings and editorial emendations, each identified through a system of parentheses and brackets. Under each lemma, they indicate the various forms and their occurrences. The work is nicely printed and easier on the eye than Dubrocard (entry 781). Dubrocard is based on a more recent and highly regarded edition, but Kelling and Suskin provide a better picture of the textual history and variants.

LIVY

BIBLIOGRAPHIES

See also Donlan (614) and Kraus (615).

783.   Walsh, P. G. **Livy.** New Surveys in the Classics 8. Oxford: Clarendon Press, 1974. 38pp. LCCN 75–324622.

Walsh, who has himself done notable work on Livy, offers a "general assessment" of recent scholarship on Livy in selected areas. In a series of brief review essays he covers Livy as an Augustan historian, as an historian of Rome, and as a literary artist. Walsh also provides a brief treatment of Livy's *Nachleben* and studies of it. He provides fuller coverage of foreign-language scholarship, especially German works, than is typically found in volumes of this series. In fact, this attractive survey pulls together most of the significant work done on Livy in this century. An appendix lists the principal editions, commentaries, translations, and lexica.

INDEXES AND CONCORDANCES

784. Packard, David. **Concordance to Livy.** Cambridge, MA: Harvard University Press, 1968. 4v. LCCN 68–29181.

Packard was a pioneer in using computers to generate concordances to classical authors. His massive concordance to Livy includes every word, even *et.* Packard lists each word in alphabetical sequence and makes no attempt to gather all the inflected forms under the normal dictionary entry. Repeated instances of word are subalphabetized by the words that follow, so that identical phrases appear together. Keywords are centered in a generous amount of context (roughly two lines from a standard printed text), with citations running down the margin of the page. He uses the Oxford Classical Text edition through book 35, and the Teubner edition of Livy for later books. Users should be wary of the resulting orthographic inconsistencies.

LUCAN

BIBLIOGRAPHIES

785. Walde, Christine. **Lucan-Projekt.** URL: http://pages.unibas.ch/klaphil/fs/lucan.html.

This Web-based bibliography covers work on Lucan from the late nineteenth century to the present. Earlier coverage is somewhat spotty, while most of the twentieth century is well covered. Walde includes many works only partially concerned with Lucan, such as those on Pompey and the civil war. She also includes works on his later influence. Two main listings are offered: one alphabetical by author, the other chronological by year. These currently cover nearly 2,000 items. Separate lists include recent publications and works on the reception of Lucan (these are also in the main lists). Walde provides basic bibliographical information for each entry, but no annotations. The bibliography is regularly updated.

INDEXES AND CONCORDANCES

786. Deferrari, Roy J., Maria Walburg Fanning, and Anne Stanislaus Sullivan. **Concordance to Lucan.** Washington, DC: Catholic University of America Press, 1940; repr. Hildesheim: Georg Olms, 1965. 602pp. LCCN 40–31224.

This concordance is based on the edition of A. E. Housman (Oxford: Blackwell, 1927), which remains the best available. Deferrari and his collaborators include many variants from the *apparatus criticus* in the concordance. All inflected forms are gathered under the usual dictionary entry. Most words are presented in context, usually in a complete phrase. For some common words, such as prepositions and conjunctions, Deferarri gives only a list of citations. Wacht (entry 787) covers all words fully and provides more context.

787. Wacht, Manfred. **Concordantia in Lucanum.** Alpha-Omega, Reihe A, 125. Hildesheim: Olms-Weidmann, 1992. 891pp. ISBN 3–487–09494–0.

Wacht bases his concordance on the edition of D. R. Shackleton Bailey (Stuttgart: Teubner, 1988). He uses the keyword-in-context format, with two lines of context provided. Wacht marshals all inflected forms under the normal dictionary heading. He also provides word frequency tables. While there are the usual minor inconsistencies, it is a serviceable concordance and should be preferred to Deferrari (entry 786) when available.

LUCRETIUS

BIBLIOGRAPHIES

See also Donlan (entry 856).

788. Gordon, Cosmo Alexander. **A Bibliography of Lucretius.** 2nd ed. Introduction and notes by E. J. Kenney. London: St. Paul's Bibliographies, 1985. 323pp. ISBN 0–90675–06–0.

Gordon first published his bibliography in 1962; this reissue includes additional material by Kenney. This work is a traditional descriptive bibliography of editions and translations of Lucretius, extending from the editio princeps of 1473 to Konrad Müller's 1975 edition of *De Rerum Natura*. It includes much of interest to bibliographers, textual critics, and historians of scholarship. The well-designed index provides ready access by names of editors, illustrators, printers, and the like.

INDEXES AND CONCORDANCES

789. Roberts, Louis. **Concordance of Lucretius.** Garland Library of Latin Poetry. New York: Garland, 1977. 359pp. ISBN 0–8240–2978–X. LCCN 77–70759.

This work appeared earlier as a supplement to the journal *Agon* (Berkeley, CA: Agon, 1968). Roberts uses the text of Cyril Bailey's three-volume edition (Oxford: Clarendon Press, 1947, rev. 1950; there is no 1963 edition corresponding to Roberts's citation in the introduction). He has produced a typical computer-generated concordance. Inflected forms appear as separate entries rather than being gathered into one under their dictionary form. There are also the usual inconsistencies (e.g., different words and forms distinguished only by vowel quantity are intermingled). A line of context is provided for each occurrence. Roberts notes major variant readings and emendations in an appendix.

790. Wacht, Manfred. **Concordantia in Lucretium.** Alpha-Omega, Reihe A, 122. Hildesheim: Olms-Weidmann, 1991. 845pp. ISBN 3–487–09404–5.

Like Roberts (entry 789), Wacht employs the 1950 edition of Cyril Bailey. His work is somewhat more useful: he groups all inflected forms under a single dictionary entry and provides two lines of context rather than one. Wacht employs the keyword-in-context format. He also provides word frequency tables at the end of the volume.

MARTIAL

INDEXES AND CONCORDANCES

791. Siedschlag, Edgar. **Martial-Konkordanz.** Alpha-Omega, Reihe A, 38. Hildesheim: Georg Olms, 1979. ISBN 3–487–06821–4. LCCN 80–454698.

Siedslag uses W. M. Lindsay's Oxford Classical Text edition of Martial (2nd ed., Oxford: Clarendon Press, 1929) as the basis for his concordance. He does not give a single A-to-Z listing. *Cruces* (insoluble textual problems) come first, followed by transliterated Greek words, proper names, and finally all other words. The main listing provides standard dictionary lemmata, which gather all inflected forms in one place, although it orders them alphabetically rather than in a rational sequence by form. Siedschlag provides about two lines of context for each word. Several lengthy tables at the end of the volume supply information about word frequency in Martial.

OVID

BIBLIOGRAPHIES

See also Donlan (entry 609).

792. Barsby, John. **Ovid.** New Surveys in the Classics 12. Oxford: Clarendon Press, 1978. 49pp. LCCN 79–310588.

Barsby surveys work on Ovid since 1955, although he also includes a few significant older items. He focuses chiefly on readily available studies in English. Barsby notes general works in his introduction; subsequent chapters cover Ovid's various books of poetry. Each chapter provides a synthesis of recent scholarship, with bibliographical particulars relegated to the notes. While no longer really current, Barsby's survey is well suited to the needs of students.

793. Paratore, Ettore. **Bibliografia Ovidiana.** Sulmona: Comitato per le Celebrazioni de Bimillenario, 1958. 169pp. LCCN 59–4252.

Paratore compiled this bibliography for the bimillenary of Ovid's birth. He arranged his material by form into six chapters: *incunabula* (editions, complete and partial, to 1700, rather than the term's more normal meaning of pre-1501 imprints); editions (from 1700); translations; dissertations, books, and chapters in books; journal articles; and lexica. All are subarranged chronologically. Citations of early publications are very abbreviated. There are no annotations of any sort. Paratore also failed to provide indexes. As a result, this work is difficult to consult and of limited value.

DICTIONARIES, ENCYCLOPEDIAS, AND HANDBOOKS

794.   Boyd, Barbara Weiden, ed. **Brill's Companion to Ovid.** Leiden: Brill, 2002. 533pp. ISBN 90–04–12156–0. LCCN 2002–282461.

This very traditional handbook includes essays by 14 leading Ovid scholars, most of whom are American or British. The first essay, "Ovid and His Milieu" by Peter White, surveys what we know of Ovid's life and discusses his literary and historical context. The second, by E. J. Kenney, covers Ovid's language and style, with pride of place given to the *Metamorphoses.* Subsequent essays cover individual works in chronological order: the *Amores,* the *Heroides,* the didactic works (*Ars Amatoria,* etc.), the *Fasti* (two essays), *Metamorphoses* (three essays), and the exilic poetry. Three final essays cover Ovid's influence in the first five centuries A.D., Ovid in the Middle Ages, and the manuscript tradition and transmission of Ovid's works. While occasionally breaking new ground, most are content to present the current state of scholarship. The work includes a substantial bibliography, general index, and *index locorum.* Boyd and her contributors have produced a solid and informative reference volume for anyone studying the works of Ovid. Readers whose primary interest lies in Ovid's influence and reception in later periods likely will find Hardie's compilation (entry 795) superior.

795.   Hardie, Philip. **Cambridge Companion to Ovid.** Cambridge: Cambridge University Press, 2002. 408pp. ISBN 0–521–77281–8; 0–521–77528–0pa. LCCN 2001–037923.

"Ovid is arguably the single most important author from classical antiquity for the post-classical western tradition. This *Companion* aims to locate Ovid's dazzling *oeuvre* within the history of ancient Roman culture and literature, and also to illustrate some of the many ways his texts have been used by later writers and artists. It is designed both as an introduction to basic aspects of Ovid's works and their reception, and as a sample of the range of approaches that have emerged." Hardie's prefatory comments well describe his work and mark its principal differences from Boyd (entry 794). Like Boyd, Hardie has gathered a distinguished set of contributors, and a much more international one. His *Companion* falls into three parts. The first, "Contexts and History," offers four essays on Ovid in his ancient literary and historical setting. The second, "Themes and Works," comprises 10 essays. Most discuss individual works by Ovid, although several deal with broader themes—genre, gender, and myth. The final section, "Reception," includes essays on English translations of Ovid, Ovid in the Middle Ages, Ovid in the English Renaissance (two), Ovid in recent literature, and Ovid in art. The work concludes with a "Dateline," which supplies a chronology of Ovid's life and times and a (very) selective list of dates relating to Ovid's *Rezeptionsgeschichte.* There is a general index, but those seeking discussions of specific passages in Ovid will be hampered by the lack of an *index locorum.* Readers primarily concerned with Ovid's life and works should turn first to Boyd, although they will find much of use in Hardie as well. Those with theoretical tastes or an interest in Ovid's *Nachleben* will find Hardie the stronger work.

796.   **Ovid im WWW.** URL: www.kirke.hu-berlin.de/ovid/start.html.

Part of the excellent *Kirke* site (see entry 171), this page covers all aspects of Ovidian studies. It begins with a short biography (in German). The site then provides many links to full-text works, abstracts, reviews, and bibliographies. These are arrranged under *Leben und Werk* (life and work), *Texte und Übersetzungen* (texts and translations), *online verfügbare Publikationen* (online full-text publications), *weitere WWW Projekte* (other Web sites on Ovid and related topics), *Rezeptionsgeschichte* (reception history, influence), and *Bibliographisches*. Some of the links lead to sites restricted to subscribers. Some of the better features of the site include links to all reviews of books about Ovid in the *Bryn Mawr Classical Review* (entry 66) and to some substantial online bibliographies. While the site is in German, many links lead to English-language resources, and the site can be navigated with minimal German.

INDEXES AND CONCORDANCES

797. Deferrari, Roy J., M. Inviolata Barry, and Martin R. P. McGuire. **Concordance of Ovid.** Washington, DC: Catholic University Press of America, 1939; repr., Hildesheim: Georg Olms, 1968. 2220pp. LCCN 39–21894.

This massive work covers the entire corpus of Ovid. It combines features of a concordance and an index, since some common words are indexed without context to save space. It is based upon the now somewhat antiquated Teubner editions produced by Rudolf Ehwald and Friedrich Vollmer in the early twentieth century. All words are listed in one A-to-Z sequence, with inflected forms grouped under normal dictionary lemmata. This remains the only complete concordance of Ovid, and the only one for some of his works.

798. Purnelle, Gérald. **Ovide, Amores: Index verborum, listes de fréquences, relevés grammaticaux.** Série du Laboratoire d'analyse statistique des langues anciennes 18. Liège: Centre Informatique de Philosophie et Lettres, 1990. 240pp. LCCN 91–194805.

Purnelle has created a fairly typical index of Ovid's love elegies, the *Amores*. He bases his work on the text of F. W. Lenz (Berlin: Akademie-Verlag, 1965). Purnelle uses standard dictionary forms as his lemmata, with inflected forms grouped beneath them. As is usual with indexes, no context is provided, only lists of citations. Each entry indicates the number of times the word occurs. Purnelle also indicates textual problems and variants through various typographical conventions, which are explained in his introduction. An extensive array of tables of word frequencies and grammatical preferences follows the index.

799. Purnelle, Gérald. **Ovide, Epistulae Heroidum: Index Verborum, listes de fréquences, relevés grammaticaux.** Série du Laboratoire d'analyse statistique des langues anciennes 19. Liège: Centre Informatique de Philosophie et Lettres, 1990. 328pp. LCCN 91–157103.

This work closely follows the pattern of Purnelle's index of the *Amores* (entry 798). He uses the edition of H. Dörrie (Berlin: Walter de Gruyter, 1971) as the basis for his index of the *Heroides*. Purnelle gathers all occurrences of inflected forms under their dictionary lemmata, notes variant readings and textual problems, and indicates word frequency. He also provides numerous tables describing word frequency and grammatical choices.

800. Purnelle-Simart, Cl., and G. Purnelle. **Ovide, Ars amatoria, Remedia amoris, De medicamine: Index Verborum, listes de fréquences, relevés grammaticaux.** Série du Laboratoire d'analyse statistique des langues anciennes 12. Liège: Centre Informatique de Philosophie et Lettres, 1987. 298pp. LCCN 89–127850.

This index covers Ovid's three poetic handbooks on love. The authors use the editions of F. W. Lenz (Berlin: Akademie-Verlag, 1968 and 1969) as a basis. Lemmata appear in their standard dictionary forms, with the various inflected forms grouped beneath them. Citations from the three works are listed, along with numerical codes in parentheses, which indicate variant readings and conjectures. Extensive word frequency tables follow the index, along with tables on grammatical preferences.

PERSIUS

BIBLIOGRAPHIES

See also Braund (entry 612).

801. Morgan, Morris H. **Bibliography of Persius.** Bibliographical Contributions of the Library of Harvard University 58. Cambridge, MA: Harvard University Library, 1909. 90pp. LCCN 10–009827.

Morgan is a valuable resource for those interested in early editions of Persius and pre-twentieth-century scholarship on him. Morgan's own extensive collection formed the basis for this bibliography, although he also used various libraries and consulted the standard printed bibliographies. He lists 1,029 works, including 486 editions, 292 translations, and 252 secondary works. Morgan arranges editions by date, translations by language and then date, and writings on Persius by author. The list of editions is especially noteworthy. It includes a wealth of title-page transcriptions, collations, notes on the history of printing and editing, and selective information about library holdings. There are also a number of reproductions of pages and illustrations from the earlier editions. Similar information is provided for many of the translations. For the secondary works, Morgan occasionally provides brief notes on contents, but mostly bare citations. Indexes cover printers, editors, and translators.

INDEXES AND CONCORDANCES

802. Berkowitz, Luci, and Theodore F. Brunner. **Index Verborum Quae in Saturis Auli Persi Flacci Reperiuntur.** Alpha-Omega, Reihe A, 7. Hildesheim: Georg Olms, 1967, 160pp. LCCN 68–106551.

Berkowitz and Brunner use the text of Wendell Clausen (Oxford: Clarendon Press, 1959). They also record variants and emendations in his apparatus and gather those published subsequently in the *additamentum,* which appears before the index proper. There are numerous cross-references from variant spellings (especially those resulting from assimilation in compound words). Their bibliography, although now dated, remains a useful guide to editions and textual studies.

PETRONIUS

BIBLIOGRAPHIES

See also Donlan (entry 609).

803. Schmeling, Gareth L., and Johanna H. Stuckey. **Bibliography of Petronius.** Mnemosyne Supplements 39. Leiden: Brill, 1977. 239pp. ISBN 90–04–04753–0. LCCN 77–550459.

This work, which the authors describe as a handlist, is something of a hybrid between a traditional descriptive author bibliography and an annotated bibliography of secondary works. The substantial introduction surveys the manuscript tradition and printing history of Petronius and provides brief historical overviews of translations and of Petronian scholarship from the Renaissance to the 1960s. The actual bibliography is arranged into four sections. The first and shortest is devoted to manuscripts of Petronius; these are arranged alphabetically by sigla and by location. The second section covers printed books, by which the authors mean editions and translations of Petronius. They present these in chronological order. The third and longest section deals with scholarly works on Petronius; these are arranged alphabetically by author. The final section covers "Petroniana," works based on or influenced by Petronius (e.g., Fellini's *Satyricon*). Many entries include annotations providing bibliographical information or a summary of the content. This is a comprehensive bibliography with over 2,000 entries, but it is not always easy to use. Subject access, which is provided through the short general index, is rather weak. Nor is there an index of particular passages discussed in the secondary works. However, it is an indispensable tool for the study of Petronius. It is also nicely illustrated with reproductions of title pages of early editions and of manuscript leaves. Those seeking more current publications should refer to the excellent bibliographies published in the *Petronian Society Newsletter* (entry 806).

DICTIONARIES, ENCYCLOPEDIAS, AND HANDBOOKS

804. Courtney, Edward. **Companion to Petronius.** Oxford: Oxford University Press, 2001. 238pp. ISBN 0–19–924552–5; 0–19–924594–0pa. LCCN 2002–280390.

Courtney intends his *Companion* for graduate students in classics but has tried to make it accessible to the Latinless as well. The first two chapters provide necessary background for the reader: the much-vexed question of authorship and various literary issues (the novel genre in antiquity, employment of verse, first-person narrative, identity of the protagonists, the lost books, and characterization). The next five chapters cover the major surviving sections of the *Satyricon* in sequence. The final chapter, "Overall Aspects," briefly addresses literary allusions and influences, sex, and symbolism. A short but carefully selected bibliography stands at the head of the work; this will introduce the novice to the highpoints of Petronian scholarship. A useful general index concludes the volume. Courtney is a first-class Latinist who has done a real service for all readers of the *Satyricon*.

INDEXES AND CONCORDANCES

805. Korn, Matthias, and Stefan, Reitzer. **Concordantia Petroniana: Computerkonkordanz zu den Satyrica des Petron.** Alpha-Omega, Reihe A, 71. Hildesheim: Olms-Weidmann, 1986. ISBN 3–487–07695–0.

Korn and Reitzer follow the now standard text of Konrad Müller, using his German-Latin edition (Munich: Artemis, 1983). Some of the fragments (31–53) are from the eighth edition of F. Buecheler (Berlin: Weidmann, 1963). They use a key-word-in-context format. Small type and poor legibility are a major problem.

JOURNALS

806. **Petronian Society Newsletter.** Gainesville: Dept. of Classics, University of Florida, 1970– . Annual. LCCN 91–22743; 2001–229205 (online). URL: www.ancientnarrative.com/PSN/index.htm.

This journal was published semiannually in paper format from 1970 through 2000; since then it has appeared only on the Web, with new issues released annually. The full back files are available online. The *Newsletter* is noteworthy for its bibliographies, which cover all aspects of the ancient novel. It also includes conference announcements, book reviews, and occasional articles. For more information on the society see entry 807.

ASSOCIATIONS

807. **Petronian Society.** c/o Prof. Gareth Schmeling, Dept. of Classics, University of Florida, Gainesville, Florida 32611. Tel.: (904) 392–2075. Fax: (904) 846–0297. E-mail: schmelin@classics.ufl.edu. URLs: www.ancientnarrative.com/PSN; www.chss.montclair.edu/classics/petron/PSNNOVEL.HTML.

The Petronian Society, which was established in 1970, has a somewhat broader scope than is implied in its name. Its international membership comprises scholars interested in all aspects of the ancient novel. The society long published a newsletter, which included scholarly notes, book reviews, an annotated bibliography of recent publications on the ancient novel, and reports on relevant conferences (see entry 806). This was recently incorporated into a new journal, *Ancient Narrative* (entry 76), although it maintains a quasi-separate identity. The society sometimes sponsors sessions at the annual meeting of the American Philological Association (entry 1004).

PLAUTUS

BIBLIOGRAPHIES

See also Arnott (entry 598), Donlan (entry 609), and Forman (entry 600).

808. Bubel, Frank, ed. **Bibliographie zu Plautus, 1976–1989.** Bonn: Rudolf Habelt, 1992. 53pp. ISBN 3–7749–2576–3.

Beginning where Hughes (entry 809) left off, Bubel gathers 14 years of work on Plautus. His 576 citations, which are drawn entirely from *L'Année philologique* (entry 44), include books, dissertations, and articles. He presents these in a topical arrangement. Reviews are cited under book titles, but no summaries or annotations are provided. Thus readers who want abstracts will still need to consult the individual volumes of *L'Année philologique*. Bubel has done a good job of indexing the bibliography. Separate indexes cover specific passages of Plautus, names and subjects, linguistic topics, metrics, Latin words, and authors.

809.   Hughes, J. David. **Bibliography of Scholarship on Plautus.** Amsterdam: A.M. Hakkert, 1975. 154 pp. ISBN 90–256–0769–1. LCCN 76–353120.

Hughes concentrates on works published since the mid-nineteenth century. He includes books, articles, and published theses; editions of Plautus's works and reviews are omitted. His 2,328 citations are arranged by subject. A detailed table of contents neatly lays out the headings. There are cross-references for works that fall into more than one category. Hughes does not provide annotations. An index of authors concludes the work. Hughes covers most of the significant work done on Plautus and a number of more general works on Roman comedy as well. Those who prefer a selective overview of Plautine studies might consult the nearly contemporary survey by Arnott (entry 598). For more recent materials see Bubel (entry 808).

INDEXES AND CONCORDANCES

810.   Lodge, Gonzalez. **Lexicon Plautinianum.** Leipzig: Teubner, 1924; repr. Hildesheim: Georg Olms, 2002. 2v.

Lodge's preface, though less than two pages, offers an amusing and chastening discussion of the major nineteenth-century editions of Plautus by such scholars as Friedrich Leo and Friedrich Ritschl. Lodge uses all these, plus the excellent edition by Wallace Lindsay (Oxford: Clarendon Press, 1903), which appeared rather late during Lodge's 30 years of labor on this *Lexicon.* As a result some of Lindsay's variant readings appear in the addenda located in the front matter of the first volume. Lodge provides an index, a dictionary, and a fount of information on Plautine textual criticism. Despite its age, this is still a valuable work. The entire text is in Latin.

PLINY THE ELDER

BIBLIOGRAPHIES

811.   Le Bonniec, H. **Bibliographie de l'Histoire naturelle de Pline l'Ancien.** Collection d'études latines, série scientifique 21. Paris: Les Belles Lettres, 1946. 58pp. LCCN 48–2102.

Le Bonniec focuses on items appearing after 1800, although he includes a selection of important earlier works as well. Despite the publication date of 1946, coverage drops off after 1939; the latest publication listed in the bibliography is from 1941. Le Bonniec uses a subject arrangment. He begins with biographical works on the elder Pliny. Then he covers general works on the *Natural History* under such rubrics as sources, influence, manuscripts, and language and style. The bulk of the bibliography covers studies of individual books and passages of the *Natural History.* Many of these are also useful for the more general study of ancient science and technology. Le Bonniec occasionally supplies descriptive notes to clarify the content of a book or article. There are no indexes. Although sadly out-of-date, Le Bonniec remains a useful aid for the study of a comparatively neglected author.

INDEXES AND CONCORDANCES

812. Rosumek, Peter, and Dietmar Najock. **Concordantia in C. Plinii Secundi Naturalem Historiam.** Hildesheim: Olms-Weidmann, 1996. 7v. ISBN 3–487–09949–7 (set).

Rosumek and Najock base their concordance on the edition of L. Jan and C. Mayhoff (Leipzig: Teubner, 1892–1909). They offer a typical keyword-in-context format, with standard dictionary forms as lemmata. They gather inflected forms under each in a logical manner by case, tense, and so on. Rosumek and Najock list proper names first, followed by other Latin words, with Greek words bringing up the rear. The seventh (supplementary) volume covers numbers, textual gaps, and variant readings. It also contains word and form frequency lists.

PLINY THE YOUNGER

INDEXES AND CONCORDANCES

813. Birley, Anthony R. **Onomasticon to the Younger Pliny: Letters and Panegyric.** Munich: Saur, 2000. 110pp. ISBN 3–598–73001–2. LCCN 2001–405614.

This guide to the proper names in Pliny the Younger is a mine of information about people and places mentioned in his works. Birley offers three alphabetical sequences: persons and deities, geographical names, and miscellaneous. For persons, by far the largest category, he supplies dates, offices, relationships, and citations to standard reference works, such as the *Prosopographia Imperii Romani* (entries 228–229). Places are generally matched with their modern equivalent. The substantial introduction covers Pliny's life and career, his correspondents, and his naming practices. Birley is an excellent reference source both for Pliny and the history of his period.

814. Heberlein, Friedrich, and Wolfgang Slaby, eds. **Concordantiae in C. Plinii Caecilii Secundi opera.** Alpha-Omega, Reihe A, 114. Hildesheim: Olms-Weidmann, 1991–1994. 5v. ISBN 3–487–09468–1 (pars 1, v. 1); 3–487–09469–X (pars 1, v. 2); 3–487–09470–3 (pars 1, v. 3); 3–487–09471–1 (pars 1, v. 4); 3–487–09000–7 (pars 2).

The first four volumes of this concordance cover Pliny's *Epistles.* For these the editors employ the texts of R.A.B. Mynors (Oxford: Clarendon Press, 1966), M. Schuster (3rd ed., rev. R. Hanslik, Leipzig: Teubner, 1958), and H. Kasten (München: Heimeran, 1968). The fifth volume (*pars* 2) is devoted to the Panegyricus; it is based on the texts of R.A.B. Mynors (Oxford: Clarendon Press, 1964), H. Kasten (München: Heimeran, 1968), and W. Kühn (Darmstadt: Wissenschaftliche Buchgesellschaft, 1985). The format is keyword-in-context, with running lemmata down the left margin of each page. Lemmata are in dictionary form, with the various inflections grouped under each. The volumes for the *Epistles* include proper names in a single sequence with other words; that for the *Panegyricus* has a separate listing of proper names at the end. There is also a list of corrigenda at the end of the final volume.

815. Jacques, Xavier, and J. van Ooteghem. **Index de Pline le Jeune.** Classe des Lettres: Memoires, ser. 2, 58.3. Brussels: Académie royal de Belgique, 1968. 981pp. LCCN 66–294.

This work is a complete index to both the *Epistles* and the *Panegyricus*. It includes proper names (listed under the *gentilicium*, with cross-references from cognomina). The index is based upon the text of M. Schuster (3rd ed., rev. R. Hanslik, Leipzig: Teubner, 1958). Entries appear under the normal dictionary form, with inflected forms and their occurrences noted. The editors clearly mark words belonging to letters of Trajan found in *Epistles* X, They also list variant readings in this well-designed and useful index.

PROPERTIUS

BIBLIOGRAPHIES

See also Donlan (entry 609).

816.   Fedeli, P., and P. Pinotti. **Bibliografia properziana (1946–1983).** Atti Accademia properziana del Subasio, ser. 6, 9. Assisi: Tipografia Porziuncola, 1985. 111pp. LCCN 86–157091.

Published on the occasion of the bimillenary of Propertius's death, this work is a continuation of the bibliography in P. J. Enk's *Sex. Propertii Elegiarum Liber I (Monobiblos)* (Leiden: Brill, 1946). Fedeli and Pinotti organize their entries by form and subject. Entries for books include citations of reviews; otherwise there are no annotations. Items that fit under multiple headings are cross-referenced. There is an author index. The chief value of Fedeli and Pinotti is for coverage of works published since Harrauer compiled his bibliography (entry 817). Harrauer offers more comprehensive coverage of the literature before 1973 and better indexing.

817.   Harrauer, Hermann. **Bibliography to Propertius.** Bibliography to the Augustan Poetry 2. Hildesheim: Gerstenberg, 1973. 219pp. ISBN 3–8067–0352–3. LCCN 73–178623.

This work generally follows the plan of Harrauer's *Bibliography of the Corpus Tibullianum* (entry 832). It aims at complete coverage of work published after 1900; earlier work is covered selectively. Harrauer lists, without annotations, 1,833 items in 15 topical chapters. Subarrangement is chronological. Reviews are cited under the entry for the work reviewed. Occasionally, a major review receives an additional independent entry. A full set of indexes concludes the work. The *index locorum* clearly differentiates works on whole poems and on single lines and groups of lines. There are also subject and author indexes.

INDEXES AND CONCORDANCES

818.   Purnelle, Gerald. **Properce, Elegiae: Index Verborum, Listes de fréquence.** Alpha-Omega, Reihe A, 187. Hildesheim: Olms-Weidmann, 1997. 377pp. ISBN 3–487–10323–0.

Purnelle's index is based on the edition of E. A. Barber (2nd ed, Oxford: Clarendon Press, 1960). All words appear under their normal dictionary entry, with the various forms and their instances enumerated. Extensive analysis follows the index, with word frequency tables and lists of subordinating conjunctions used by Propertius, along with verbs used. This is a useful work, especially for those doing stylistic analyses. However, Schmeisser (entry 819) gives much more information on variant readings, an important feature in view of the many difficulties in the transmission of Propertius. In any case, both Purnelle and Schmeisser are far superior to J. S. Phillimore, *Index Verborum Propertianus* (Oxford: Clarendon Press, 1905).

819. Schmeisser, Brigitte. **Concordance to the Elegies of Propertius.** Hildesheim: Gerstenberg, 1972. 950pp. ISBN 3–8067–0193–8.

Schmeisser prepared this concordance as a doctoral dissertation under the direction of Rudolf Hanslik. Not surprisingly, it is based on Hanslik's edition of Propertius (Leipzig: Teubner, 1979), to which she had access in manuscript form. She also consulted the editions of Barber, Camps, Luck, Enk, and others. As the transmission of Propertius is very problematic, Schmeisser rightly includes many variants from these editions in her work. These are fully cross-referenced. All entries are under the normal dictionary form. Schmeisser provides a brief context for each word, usually only its immediate phrase. Given the slender size of the *Elegiae,* this is an amazingly bulky work.

SALLUST

BIBLIOGRAPHIES

See also Kraus and Woodman (entry 615).

820. Leeman, A. D. **Systematical Bibliography of Sallust (1879–1964).** Mnemosyne Supplements 4. Rev. and aug. ed. Leiden: Brill, 1965. 109pp.

Leeman lists about 1,000 items (his 1,252 numbered entries include a good many cross-references). He covers works in English, French, German and the Scandinavian languages, Italian, Spanish, Russian, Greek, and Latin. Leeman omits many school editions and limits his coverage of translations to the most important English, French, and German ones. Otherwise he aims for completeness within the specified dates; a number of important earlier editions and studies are also included. He arranges his entries into seven broad categories by form and subject. Each of these has numerous subdivisions. Leeman tends to give rather summary bibliographic citations, although the information provided is usually sufficient to identify works. Many entries include brief descriptive annotations. Entries for books often provide the table of contents. Reviews are also cited under book entries. An author index concludes the volume. Although now badly in need of a supplement, Leeman remains an excellent resource.

INDEXES AND CONCORDANCES

821. Rapsch, Jürgen, Dietmar Najock, and Adam Nowosad. **Concordantia in Corpus Sallustianum.** Alpha-Omega, Reihe A, 9. Hildesheim: Olms-Wiedmann, 1991. 2v. ISBN 3–487–09385–5 (v. 1); 3–487–09386–3 (v. 2).

This concordance covers not only the *Coniuratio Catalinae* and the *Bellum Iugurthinum,* but also the fragments of the *Historiae* and the various works sometimes wrongly attributed to Sallust, such as the invective against Cicero. It is based upon the

Teubner editions of A. Kurfess (Leipzig: Teubner, 1968 and 1970) and B. Maurenbrecher's edition of the fragments of the *Historiae* (Leipzig: Teubner, 1893). All instances of a word are gathered under its normal dictionary form, with a full sentence of context for each. Word frequency tables (alphabetical and in descending order of occurrence) appear at the end of the volume, with counts for each separate work.

SENECA THE YOUNGER

BIBLIOGRAPHIES

See also Forman (entry 600).

822.   Motto, Anna Lydia, and John R. Clark. **Seneca, A Critical Bibliography, 1900–1980: Scholarship on his Life, Thought, Prose, and Influence.** Amsterdam: A. M. Hakkert, 1989. 372pp. ISBN 90–256–0959–7. LCCN 90–147965.

Motto and Clark, who are the leading American authorities on the younger Seneca, here cover both general works on him and studies of his prose works and their influence; works dealing with his tragedies are generally excluded. They arrange their 1,759 entries into broad categories by form and subject. They also provide annotations for most items (except dissertations), which summarize and evaluate the work. An author index concludes the volume. Because of Seneca's lasting influence on Western literature and thought, even nonclassicists will find much of interest in this bibliography.

INDEXES AND CONCORDANCES

823.   Busa, R., and A. Zampolli. **Concordantiae Senecanae.** Alpha-Omega, Reihe A, 21. Hildesheim: Georg Olms, 1971. 2v. ISBN 3–487–05672–0 (v. 1); 3–487–05673–9.

Busa and Zampolli cover all Seneca's writings, using the various Teubner editions as their working text. Their computer-generated concordance illustrates most of the faults of its genre. Each inflected form appears on its own, so that it is difficult to gather all instances of a single word. The concordance is arranged in two columns per page, with lemmata and citations running along the right side of each column. The type is small and ugly. Word frequency tables appear in the second volume. Those primarily concerned with the tragedies may turn, with relief, to the far superior work of Oldfather (entry 824).

824.   Oldfather, William Abbott, Arthur Stanley Pease, and Howard Vernon Canter. **Index Verborum Quae in Senecae Fabulis necnon in Octavia Praetexta Reperiuntur.** University of Illinois Studies in Language and Literature 4, nos. 2–4. Urbana: University of Illinois Press, 1918; repr. Hildesheim: Georg Olms, 1983. 332pp. LCCN 18–15253.

This work indexes the tragedies of Seneca. Oldfather uses the second edition of Rudolf Peiper and Gustav Richter (Leipzig: Teubner, 1902) as a basis, although he includes many variant readings from other sources as well. In addition to being an accurate and very full index, it is an excellent resource for those engaged in textual criticism. Much of the preface consists of a lengthy bibliography of editions and textual studies.

STATIUS

INDEXES AND CONCORDANCES

825. Deferrari, Roy J., and M. Clement Eagan. **Concordance of Statius.** Brookland, DC: Author, 1943; repr., Hildesheim: Olms, 1966. 926pp. LCCN 43–13902.

This concordance employs the now badly dated Oxford Classical Text editions of J. S. Phillimore and H. W. Garrod, published in 1905 and 1906 respectively. A few common prepositions and conjunctions are merely indexed; other words receive a full metrical line of context. Under each entry instances are listed in order of occurrence rather than grouped by inflection. It is adequate, but Wacht (entry 826) is to be preferred, if available. Joseph Klecka's *Concordantia in Publium Papinium Statium* (Hildesheim: Georg Olms, 1983) is, like Wacht, based upon better editions; however, it is virtually unreadable due to small type size and poor production quality.

826. Wacht, Manfred. **Concordantia in Statium.** Alpha-Omega, Reihe A, 126. Hildesheim: Olms-Weidmann, 2000. 2v. ISBN 3–487–11048–2 (v. 1); 3–487–11049–0 (v. 2); 3–487–11050–4 (v. 3).

Wacht employs the editions of Alfred Klotz (Leipzig: Teubner, 1973) and Aldo Marastoni (Leipzig: Teubner, 1974) for the epics, and the Oxford Classical Text edition of E. Courtney (Oxford: Clarendon Press, 1990) for the *Silvae.* His concordance is lemmatized and follows the standard keyword-in-context format. Wacht provides just over two metrical lines of context for each word. He also notes the number of occurrences for each word. Word frequency tables appear at the end of the third volume. This is the best of the available concordances to Statius.

TACITUS

BIBLIOGRAPHIES

See also Donlan (entry 614) and Kraus and Woodman (615).

827. Goodyear, F.R.D. **Tacitus.** New Surveys in the Classics 4. Oxford: Clarendon Press, 1970. 44pp. LCCN 79–570213.

Goodyear, who has himself done extensive work on Tacitus, offers us a "personal synthesis" of the scholarly literature on his subject. His brief introduction notes many of the most significant general works on Tacitus and on the history of the early empire. The various chapters cover the minor works, the *Histories* and the *Annals,* Tacitus as a historian, and his language and style. Goodyear provides a good overview of twentieth-century Tacitean studies through the 1960s. He also notes, as the publication patterns require, more German language works than is the norm for volumes in this series.

INDEXES AND CONCORDANCES

828. Blackman, D.R., and G.G. Betts. **Concordantia Tacitea [A Concordance to Tacitus].** Alpha-Omega. Reihe A, 74. Hildesheim: Olms-Weidmann, 1986. 2v. ISBN 3–487–07749–3 (v. 1); 3–487–07750–7 (v. 2).

Blackman and Betts state that they base this concordance to the surviving works of Tacitus upon the Teubner edition. There are several such editions; as they do not specify, it is presumably that of Erich Koestermann (3rd ed., 1969–1971). The concordance is a typical computer-generated product. All words are listed alphabetically, in the keyword-in-context format.

TERENCE

BIBLIOGRAPHIES

See also Arnott (entry 598), Donlan (entry 609), and Forman (entry 600).

829. Cupaiuolo, Giovanni, ed. **Bibliografia terenziana (1470–1983).** Studi e testi dell'antichità 16. Napoli: Società Editrice Napoletana, 1984. 551 pp.

Cupaiuolo lists some 5,190 items beginning with the first printed edition of Terence (1470). He devotes the first part of the bibliography to editions, commentaries, and translations. This is arranged into sections for complete editions, partial editions, and editions of individual plays. In each case, translations, which are arranged by language, follow the list of editions. Cupaiuolo's coverage is exhaustive (2,794 editions and translations are noted). He also provides references to standard bibliographies and library catalogs under entries for earlier editions (primarily those of the fifteenth and sixteenth centuries) and to reviews for modern editions. In the second part, Cupaiuolo lists an extensive array of scholarly studies of Terence; these date mostly from the nineteenth and twentieth centuries. He arranges these by subject. Virtually every aspect of Terentian studies is covered in detail. In addition to items dealing specifically with Terence, Cupaiuolo also includes many general works that contain significant discussion of him. An index of names concludes the volume.

INDEXES AND CONCORDANCES

830. Jenkins, Edgar B. **Index Verborum Terentianus.** Chapel Hill: University of North Carolina Press, 1932; repr. Hildesheim: Georg Olms, 1962. 187pp. LCCN 32-029754.

This index is based on the text of R. Kauer and W. M. Lindsay (Oxford: Clarendon Press, 1926). It includes variant readings from a number of editions published between 1870 and 1902. The introduction provides a very full explanation of the system of presentation. Generally, words are listed under their common dictionary form as found in *Harpers' Latin Dictionary* (a predecessor of Lewis and Short [entry 510]), and all grammatical forms are listed in a single entry. Frequency of occurrence is noted in parentheses following the lemma. Cross-references link variant forms and spellings.

831. McGlynn, Patrick. **Lexicon Terentianum.** London: Blackie & Sons, 1963–1967. 2v. LCCN 67-006689.

While this work can also serve as an index to Terence, it does much more. It represents 40 years of toil. McGlynn's entries for each word are arranged by meaning and function, include full enumeration of instances, many with some context, and usually take note of variant readings. The entire work is written in Latin. It is a mine of information on Terentian language.

TIBULLUS

BIBLIOGRAPHIES

832. Harrauer, Hermann. **Bibliography to the Corpus Tibullianum.** Bibliography to the Augustan Poetry 1. Hildesheim: Gerstenberg, 1971. 90pp. ISBN 3–8067–0014–1. LCCN 73–884445.

"It is the aim of this bibliography to offer a complete list of the literature on the *Corpus Tibullianum* since the year 1900. Older literature has only been included as far as it proved to be of importance for further scientific work." The list consists of 1,111 works arranged in 21 topical chapters. Works are arranged chronologically within each chapter. Dates are inserted at intervals in the left margin as an aid to the reader. Entries for books include citations of reviews. There are no annotations. The subject arrangement is well thought out and logical. A full array of indexes is provided, including an unusually full *index locorum,* and subject and author indexes.

INDEXES AND CONCORDANCES

833. Nowosad, Adam, Dietmar Najock, and Hermann Morgenroth. **Concordantia in Corpus Tibullianum.** Alpha-Omega, Reihe A, 160. Hildesheim: Olms-Weidmann, 2002. 500pp. ISBN 3–487–11683–9.

The editors have based their concordance on the text of F. W. Lenz and G. K. Galinsky (3rd ed., Leiden: Brill, 1971). They have also consulted other editions, most notably those of Georg Luck (Stuttgart: Teubner, 1988 and 1998). Proper nouns are listed first, in a separate alphabetical sequence. Common nouns follow. All forms of a word are gathered into one entry, which is subarranged by line number. A full elegiac distich is supplied for each keyword, which is printed in bold. Textual variants are regularly noted in the concordance and are also marshalled in a line-by-line listing following it. The editors have also provided a full word frequency table, arranged alphabetically. This carefully differentiates the works of Tibullus and those of others (found in book 3 of the *Corpus*). There is also a second table of words in declining order of frequency (only words occurring 10 or more times). This is an extremely useful reference for anyone doing textual or stylistic studies of the *Corpus Tibullianum.*

834. O'Neil, Edward N. **Critical Concordance of the Tibullan Corpus.** Ithaca, NY: American Philological Association, 1963. 361pp. LCCN 63–23321

O'Neil covers the entire *Corpus Tibullianum* in this work, which is based on the edition of F. W. Lenz (Leiden: Brill, 1959). He includes variant readings from a variety of editions as well. For a few of the most common words (prepositions, conjunctions, etc.) O'Neil provides only citations; for the rest he provides a metrical line of context. Lemmata are in bold, and occurrences within each line italicized. This attractive and clearly printed work will still serve many needs. However, the work of Nowosad, Najock, and Morgenroth (entry 833) rests upon more recent editions and provides much more information on such matters as word frequency.

VARRO

BIBLIOGRAPHIES

835. Cardauns, Burkhart. **Stand und Aufgaben der Varroforschung mit einer Bibliographie der Jahre 1935–1980.** Akademie der Wissenschaften und der Literatur, Abhandlungen der Geistes- und Sozialwissenschaftlichen Klasse, Jahrg. 1982, Nr. 4. Wiesbaden: Franz Steiner, 1982. 46pp. ISBN 3–515–03709–8. LCCN 83–226042.

Cardauns, who has published extensively on Varro over many years, here offers a brief overview of the state of Varronian studies, followed by a bibliography covering 1935 to 1980. He provides 659 numbered entries, followed by eight reprints of earlier works and three addenda, all *sine numero*. The arrangement is not always clear. Cardauns begins with bibliographies and then turns to editions of Varro. He covers collected editions, followed by those of individual works. Then he covers congresses and *Festschriften*; at entry 29, without any heading, Cardauns launches a list of secondary studies by author that continues for the remainder of the bibliography. Cardauns notes reviews but otherwise does not annotate the entries. He does supply an index of passages discussed. For earlier work on Varro, see Riposati and Marastoni (entry 837).

836. Galimberti Biffino, Giovanna. **Rassegna di studi varroniana dal 1974 al 1980.** Pubblicazioni del Centro di Studi Varroniani 5. Rieti: Centro di Studi Varroniani, 1981. 67pp. LCCN 82–125973.

Galimberti continues the bibliography of Riposati and Marastoni (entry 837). She offers 282 numbered entries divided into editions and translations, bibliographical surveys, and studies. The lengthy studies section is subdivided further by subject. Within each, publications are arranged by date, then author. Galimberti provides brief descriptive annotations for many entries. There is an author index. Cardauns (entry 835) largely covers the same ground plus more retrospective coverage. Galimberti's format makes it easier to locate works on a particular work of Varro or subject.

837. Riposati, Benedetto, and Aldo Marastoni, eds. **Bibliografia varroniana.** Milano: Celuc, 1974. 255pp. LCCN 76–507325.

Riposati and Marastoni compiled this bibliography for the bimillenary of Varro in 1974. They include 1,305 numbered entries ranging in date from the earliest printed editions of 1471 to 1974. Arrangement is primarily chronological through the sixteenth century. The sections covering the eighteenth century and 1801 to 1974 are subdivided into editions, translations, and studies. Subarrangement remains chronological. Riposati and Marastoni occasionally supply very brief descriptive annotations. They also provide an index of names and a chronological index. For later coverage see Galimberti (entry 836) and Cardauns (entry 835). Galimberti has very little that is not in this work or Cardauns. Anyone seeking relatively complete coverage must consult both Riposati and Marastoni and Cardauns.

INDEXES AND CONCORDANCES

838. Briggs, Ward W., Jr., ed. **Concordantia in Varronis libros de re rustica.** Alpha-Omega, Reihe A, 65. Hildesheim: Georg Olms, 1983. 366pp. ISBN 3–487–07301–3. LCCN 83–220892.

Briggs has produced a keyword-in-context concordance to Varro's work on agriculture. There are no lemmata; words appear in strict alphabetical sequence with no effort to group inflected forms. Greek words are listed at the end. Briggs used the edition of H. Keil (Leipzig: Teubner, 1884) as the basis of his concordance. A few word frequency tables appear at the end. For other works by Varro see Salvadore (entry 839).

839. Salvadore, Marcello, ed. **Concordantia in M. Terenti Varronis libros de lingua Latina et in fragmenta ceterorum operum.** Alpha-Omega, Reihe A, 155. Hildesheim: Olms-Weidmann, 1995. 2v. ISBN 3–487–10049–5 (v. 1); 0–487–10050–9 (v. 2).

Salvadore provides a concordance for Varro's well-known work, *De lingua Latina,* and some of his other fragmentary works as well; for *De re rustica,* see Briggs (entry 838). His concordance is based upon a number of editions, which are listed following his introduction. He employs the keyword-in-context format, without lemmata. Salvadore lists all words and forms in alphabetical sequence. Latin words appear first, followed by Greek.

VERGIL

BIBLIOGRAPHIES

See also Sienkewicz (608).

840. Donlan, Walter, ed. **Classical World Bibliography of Vergil.** Garland Reference Library of the Humanities 96. New York: Garland, 1978. 176pp. ISBN 0–8240–9877–3. LCCN 76–52514.

This compilation includes three general bibliographical surveys on Vergil covering 1940–1973 and a "Bibliographical Handlist on Vergil's *Aeneid* for Teachers and Students in Secondary Schools." All of these originally appeared in *Classical World* (entry 95). The surveys are each arranged into broad subject divisions. Many of these are further subdivided. The compilers provide brief descriptions of the works cited. Although their primary emphasis is on English works, the surveys also cover many European-language publications. The "Handlist" is a general bibliography aimed at high school teachers. There are no indexes. While no longer up to date, this volume remains a useful entrée into the vast scholarly literature on Vergil. It can be supplemented by the annual bibliographical surveys on Vergil that appear in *Vergilius,* the journal of the Vergilian Society of America (see entry 854). Those seeking earlier works should consult Mambelli (entry 842).

841. Hardie, Philip. **Virgil.** New Surveys in the Classics 28. Oxford: Oxford University Press, 1998. 125pp. ISBN 0–19–922342–4.

As with other updates within this series, Hardie's *Virgil* complements rather than replaces Williams's earlier survey (entry 844). Hardie focuses primarily on work published subsequent to Williams but notes significant earlier works as well. His introduction provides an overview of recent trends in Vergilian scholarship; the four subsequent chapters cover the *Eclogues, Georgics,* and *Aeneid,* and style, language, and meter. Hardie's text provides a very readable survey of Vergilian scholarship of the last half century. He also offers an excellent working bibliography. Indexes provide access by subject and passage discussed.

842. Mambelli, Giuliano. **Gli studi virgilani nel secolo xx.** Guide bibliografiche dell'Istituto Nazionale di Cultura Fascista. Firenze: G. C. Sansone, 1940. 2v. LCCN 44–30789.

These two thick volumes cover work on Vergil between 1900 and 1939. Coverage is comprehensive through 1936, while that for subsequent years is less complete. Mambelli arranges his 3,952 entries by author; subarrangement is by date of publication. Some later items are found in the appendix rather than in the main list. Mambelli supplies descriptive annotations for most entries and notes reviews under entries for books. Indexes cover names, subjects, passages discussed, and journal titles. For works after 1939, see Morando Rando (entry 843), Donlan (entry 840), Williams (entry 844), and Hardie (entry 841).

843. Morando Rando, M. T. **Bibliografia virgiliana.** Passato e Presente 6. Genova: La Quercia Edizioni, 1987. 408pp. LCCN 89–177523.

This work continues Mambelli's bibliography (entry 842), covering the years 1937 to 1960 with some 2,133 numbered entries. The majority of these are in English, German, French, or Italian; a few works in other languages have been noted. Morando Rando arranges her entries in broad subject categories. The first section covers addenda to Mambelli, adding 203 works, most published during the 1920s and 1930s. Subsequent sections cover bibliography, biography, fundamental studies of Vergil's work as a whole, works on two of more of Vergil's writings, studies of particular works (subarranged by work), the *Appendix Vergiliana,* the thought of Vergil, the art of Vergil, and "Fortuna," which covers Vergil's influence, manuscripts, imitators, commentators, and translators. Two final sections present Vergilian iconography and a catchall "Varia." Most sections are extensively subdivided (users should consult the detailed table of contents, which appears at the end of the volume). Many entries include brief descriptive annotations; reviews are listed under book titles. The compiler provides indexes to authors, Vergilian passages, and subjects. The subject index is rather spotty, while the other two seem to be fairly complete.

844. Williams, R. D. **Virgil.** New Surveys in the Classics 1. Oxford: Clarendon Press, 1967. 44pp. LCCN 68–104147.

Williams, a noted Vergilian scholar, aims not to provide a general bibliographical survey of Vergil, but a synthesis of "recent important work of a critical kind." Williams focuses almost entirely on works of literary criticism. He discusses mainly works of the 1950s and 1960s, without entirely neglecting significant earlier works; the 1986 reprinting includes an addendum covering work published between 1968 and 1984. A brief appendix lists the most useful editions, translations, and commentaries. Hardie's later work (entry 841) in the same series complements and extends Williams's treatment. Donlan's compendium (entry 840) offers a much wider approach to Vergilian bibliography.

DICTIONARIES, ENCYCLOPEDIAS, AND HANDBOOKS

845. **Enciclopedia virgiliana.** Roma: Istituto della Enciclopedia italiana, 1984–1991. 5v. in 6. LCCN 87–127100.

Few authors rate a multivolume encyclopedia devoted solely to their works and influence; Vergil and Horace appear to be the only Latin authors thus far to have received this distinction. This work is modeled on the earlier *Enciclopedia dantesca* from the same publisher. In a single alphabetical sequence one finds articles on characters, places, expressions and words, objects, and topics found in Vergil's poems. There are also entries for earlier authors who influenced Vergil, later authors influenced by him, and noted Vergilian scholars. Virtually anything connected to Vergil, however tangentially, is likely to be found in the *Enciclopedia.* In some ways it forms a rather eccentric encyclopedia of classical and European culture. All articles are signed. The cast of contributors is international, although Italian scholars predominate. Many of the articles are quite extensive. Some are illustrated; all include bibliographies. The final volume includes the full text of Vergil's works (including minor and apocryphal writings) in the Latin original with a facing Italian translation. There is also a massive collection of *testimonia* pertaining to Vergil's life and works. These are drawn from writers dating from late antiquity through the fifteenth century. Indexes cover Latin words, illustrations, and contributors of articles.

846. Horsfall, Nicholas. **Companion to the Study of Virgil.** Leiden: Brill, 2000. 330pp. ISBN 90–04–11870–5. LCCN 00712668.

Unlike many of the companions found in this chapter, this one is primarily the work of a single author; Horsfall is responsible for five of eight chapters. Organization is straightforward: Vergil's life and times; the *Bucolics; Georgics; Aeneid;* style, language, and meter; Vergil's impact at Rome; his literary impact; and the transmission of his works. The final chapter on transmission is by M. Geymonat, a leading authority on the topic. Horsfall and his collaborators offer a lively and sensible guide to Vergil and his works, covering the basic facts and major scholarly issues. Bibliography is distributed throughout the chapters and footnotes; supplementary notes appear in the addenda to the 2000 edition (updating that of 1995). Horsfall provides a detailed index, which makes striking and effective use of shading to highlight major sections.

847. Martindale, Charles, ed.. **Cambridge Companion to Virgil.** Cambridge: Cambridge University Press, 1997. 370pp. ISBN 0–521–49539–3; 0–521–49885–6pa. LCCN 96–52447.

Martindale's *Companion* covers all aspects of Vergilian studies. His introduction sets Vergil in his wider role in European culture; not surprisingly, the first half-dozen essays address translations of Vergil and his reception from his own time to the twentieth century. The subsequent 15 essays cover the usual suspects: genre (pastoral, didactic, epic), the historical and cultural context of the poems, style, and poetics. Each is a solid introduction to its topic, with a brief reading list. Contributors include many of the today's leading Vergilian scholars. Several useful features appear at the end of the volume. Time lines cover key literary and historical events from the Trojan War to the death of Ovid and key events in the *Rezeptionsgeschichte* of Vergil from antiquity to the present. The general bibliography, while highly selective, offers an excellent guide to the literature. There is a detailed subject index.

848.   Wilson-Okamura, David. **Virgil.org.** URL: http://virgil.org.

This site covers all aspects of Vergilian studies and includes a biography, maps, and links to texts and other Web sites. Its most useful feature is a 95-page bibliography, "Virgil in Late Antiquity, the Middle Ages, and Renaissance," which is now in its sixth edition. *Virgil.org* is a convenient and reliable starting point for Vergilian research on the Web.

INDEXES AND CONCORDANCES

849.   Morgenroth, Hermann, and Dietmar Najock. **Concordantia in Appendicem Vergilianam.** Alpha-Omega, Reihe A, 68. Hildesheim: Olms, 1992. 541pp. ISBN 3–487–09592–0.

Morgenroth and Najock offer a very traditional concordance to the minor and apocryphal works of Vergil commonly called the *Appendix Vergiliana*. They used the Oxford Classical Text edition of Wendell Clausen *et alii* (1966); the "Poemata Ausoniana" have been omitted, and variant readings ignored. Lemmata are in bold, with all declined/ conjugated forms gathered in one entry. The full metrical line is cited for each. Detailed word frequency tables are included, which give numbers for each poem and totals. One table provides this in alphabetical sequence, another from highest to lowest frequency. Additional tables provide the frequency of various parts of speech.

850.   Wacht, Manfred. **Concordantia Vergiliana.** Hildesheim: Olms-Weidmann, 1996. 2v. ISBN 3–487–09848–2 (set); 3–487–09849–0 (v. 1); 3–487–09850–4 (v. 2).

This keyword-in-context concordance covers the *Eclogues, Georgics,* and *Aeneid.* It is based on R.A.B. Mynors's now standard Oxford Classical Text edition (Oxford: Oxford University Press, 1969). Wacht has employed lemmata and gathers all forms of a word in a single listing, with approximately two metrical lines of context for each. He does not note variant readings. Wacht includes word frequencies for each word (following the lemma). At the end of the second volume, he provides two word frequency lists: one from the most to least common, with number and percentage of occurrences, and one by part of speech, again in descending order of occurrence. Wacht's approach is more sophisticated and useful than that of the other Vergil concordances listed here, although all function well enough on a basic level. However, only Wetmore (entry 852) takes account of variant readings and includes the *Appendix Vergiliana* in the same work.

851.   Warwick, Henrietta Holm. **Vergil Concordance.** Minneapolis: University of Minnesota Press, 1975. 962pp. ISBN 0–8166–0737–0. LCCN 74–14138.

Warwick produced a keyword-in-context concordance to *Eclogues, Georgics,* and *Aeneid.* She does not include the minor works of dubious attribution in the *Appendix Vergiliana.* Warwick based the concordance on the standard modern edition of Vergil, the Oxford Classical Text edited by R.A.B. Mynors (Oxford: Oxford University Press, 1969). Variant readings are not indexed. She provides approximately three metrical lines of context, centered on each instance of a keyword. There are no lemmata, and the various forms of a word appear as they occur alphabetically.

852. Wetmore, Monroe Nichols. **Index Verborum Vergilianus.** New Haven, CT: Yale University Press, 1911; repr. Hildesheim: Georg Olms, 1961. 554pp. LCCN 11–2238.

Wetmore offers a complete word index to the *Eclogues, Georgics, Aeneid,* and the *Appendix Vergiliana.* He founds the index on the edition of Otto Ribbeck (Leipzig: Teubner, 1894–1895) but includes variants found in a number of other editions of the period, most notably Conington-Nettleship-Haverfield (London: Bell, 1883–1898), Thilo (Leipzig: Tauchnitz, 1886), and the edition of the *Appendix Vergiliana* by Robinson Ellis (Oxford: Clarendon Press, 1907). The second Yale printing (1930) and the Olms reprint both include two pages of errata and corrigenda, which should be duly consulted. Although based on older editions, the text of Vergil was already well established, and the index remains useful.

JOURNALS

853. *Vergilius.* Setauket, NY: Vergilian Society, 1938–1940, 1956– . Annual. ISSN 0506–7294. LCCN 81–644013. URL: www.vergil.clarku.edu/journal.htm.

The first four volumes of this slender annual appeared under the title *Vergilian Digest. Vergilius* offers articles and book reviews relating to Vergil, as well as news of the society and its activities. Its most noteworthy feature is an annual bibliography of Vergilian studies. The journal's Web site is rather spotty but includes a recent table of contents and bibliographies for several years. For more on the Vergilian Society see entry 854.

ASSOCIATIONS

854. **Vergilian Society of America.** c/o Holly Lorencz, John Burroughs School, 755 S. Price Rd., St. Louis, MO 63124, Tel.: (314) 993–4040 ext. 341. E-mail: vergilsoc@yahoo. com. URL: www.vergil.clarku.edu.

Organized in 1937, the Vergilian Society promotes the study of Latin literature and Roman history, with special emphasis on the life and writings of Vergil. Its members include primarily teachers and students of Latin from both high schools and colleges. The society maintains a study center in Italy and sponsors an annual summer school there. It publishes a newsletter and two journals, the *Augustan Age* and *Vergilius* (entry 853). The society also regularly meets at the annual conference of the American Philological Association (entry 1004).

17
Philosophy

This chapter includes bibliographies, dictionaries, encyclopedias, and handbooks dealing with ancient philosophy in general, or particular periods or schools. Works devoted to an individual ancient philosopher will be found in the chapters on "Greek Authors and Works" or "Latin Authors and Works" as follows: Aristotle (entries 650–658), Augustine (entries 748–760), Cicero (entries 766–773), Epictetus (entries 661–662), Heraclitus (entries 667–668), Lucretius (entries 788–790), Plato (entries 704–717), Plotinus (entries 718–721), Proclus (entry 727), Pythagoras (entry 729), Socrates (entries 730–731), and Xenophon (entries 739–743).

Greek philosophy subsumed many areas that have long since become separate disciplines. The early Greek philosophers, especially the Presocratics, were much concerned with scientific matters such as the origins of the world and the nature of matter. Politics, psychology, and medicine all fell into the purview of the ancient philosophers. Therefore anyone interested in the history of these fields will find material of interest here.

BIBLIOGRAPHIES

855. Bell, Albert A., Jr., and James B. Allis. **Resources in Ancient Philosophy: An Annotated Bibliography of Scholarship in English, 1965–1989.** Metuchen, NJ: Scarecrow Press, 1991. 799pp. ISBN 0–8108–2520–1. LCCN 91–39912.

This work is aimed primarily at college students and the reference librarians who work with them, although it will also be useful for teachers and scholars. Its more than 7,000 entries are arranged under 21 rubrics covering all the major philosophical schools and the most important individual philosophers of antiquity. Each of these is further subdivided into numerous sections. A particularly useful feature of the work is the provision of introductory notes for each chapter and section. These provide background information on the topic or individual covered and help orient nonspecialist users. The annotations provide brief summaries of works cited but rarely appraise them. Bell and Allis emphasize philosophical studies but also include a number of philological and historical items. This is an excellent single source on ancient philosophy for students and others who need primarily recent English-language works. For more detailed coverage and works in other languages, consult bibliographies listed under individual philosophers in chapter 6.

856. Donlan, Water, ed. **Classical World Bibliography of Philosophy, Religion, and Rhetoric.** Garland Reference Library of the Humanities 95. New York: Garland, 1978. 396pp. ISBN 0–8240–9878–1. LCCN 76–52512.

In this volume Donlan collects some 19 surveys by various hands that appeared in *Classical World* (entry 95) between 1954 and 1973. The philosophical component begins with two reviews of work on the Presocratics, which covers 1945–1966, and a survey of work on Plato (1945–1955). There are three essays on Aristotle: one general survey for

1945–1955, and one each on the *Psychology* (1954–1964) and the *Poetics* (1940–1954). Surveys of work on Epicureanism (1937–1954), Hellenistic philosophy (1937–1957), and Lucretius (1945–1972) complete the section. The single survey dealing with religion covers work on early Roman religion for the years 1945–1952. No fewer than five bibliographical essays deal with Cicero; two are general (1939–1965), and three focus on the rhetorical and philosophical works of Cicero (1939–1967). Two surveys on the prose works of the younger Seneca (1964–1957) and two general reviews of scholarship on ancient rhetoric (1939–1963) conclude the volume. As with other volumes in this series, all the surveys are arranged by subject and offer useful annotations or discussion of works noted. Most are selective in their coverage. As in Donlan's other compilations, an index is lacking.

857.   Gill, Christopher. **Greek Thought.** New Surveys in the Classics 25. Oxford: Oxford University Press for the Classical Association, 1995. 103pp. ISBN 0–19–922074–3. LCCN 96–127092.

Gill surveys recent work on Greek thought in four areas: psychology, ethics and values, politics, and nature as an ethical norm. He devotes a review essay to each, beginning with classic works from the middle of the twentieth century, such as those of Snell, Dodds, and Adkins, moving forward to important recent work. Extensive bibliographical notes accompany the readable narrative overviews. A final bibliographical note lists major editions and translations of the ancient philosophers, along with a few key works. There is an index of names, subjects, and passages cited.

858.   Navia, Luis E. **Philosophy of Cynicism: An Annotated Bibliography.** Bibliographies and Indexes in Philosophy 4. Westport, CT: Greenwood Press, 1995. 213pp. ISBN 0–313–29249–3. LCCN 95–16465.

This highly selective bibliography comprises 704 numbered entries. Navia includes many types of works, both popular and scholarly: books, journal articles, encyclopedia articles, plays, and works of fiction. These range in date from the nineteenth century to the 1990s. Most are in English, but French, German, Italian, and Spanish works are represented as well. Descriptive annotations accompany each entry. Sections cover general studies, Antisthenes, Diogenes, and Crates and other Cynics. Users seeking works in any of the categories should be sure to consult also the addendum. Navia provides indexes of authors and proper names, but not of subjects. While anyone interested in the Cynics will find much here, Navia appears to have no particular audience in mind and mingles the introductory, the advanced, and the banal.

859.   Navia, Luis E. **Presocratic Philosophers: An Annotated Bibliography.** Garland Reference Library of the Social Sciences 704. New York: Garland, 1993. 722pp. ISBN 0–8240–9776–9. LCCN 93–16207.

Navia has produced an extensive bibliography, including 2,683 numbered entries. His preface, which is strong on laments about the difficulty of his task and inaccurate generalizations about the Presocratics, provides too little information about his scope, chronological limits, and methods. The bulk of his citations are from the twentieth century (with approximate terminus of 1990), with a modest number from the nineteenth. Navia provides little coverage of lesser figures. He sometimes includes relatively trivial works, while missing others of importance. The organization is relatively straightforward. Navia covers bibliographical works, source collections, and general works in separate chapters at the beginning. Eleven chapters devoted to major individuals follow: Anaxagoras, Anaximander, Anaximenes, Democritus, Empedocles, Heraclitus, Parmenides, Pythagoras, Thales, Xenophanes, and Zeno. The chapter on Pythagoras is an update to Navia's earlier Pythagorean bibliography (entry 729) and must be used in conjunction with that work. Subarrangement within each chapter is by author. Annotations, which vary greatly in length and quality, are entirely descriptive. While there is an author index, detailed subject access is lacking. Students may find this an adequate resource, but scholars will need to consult the superior and more complete efforts of Paquet, Roussel, and Lafrance (entries 860–861). For a more detailed comparison of these, see Sylvia Berryman, Alexander D. P. Mourelatos, and Ravi K. Sharma, "Two Annotated Bibliographies on the Presocratics: A Critique and User's Guide," *Ancient Philosophy* 15 (2): 471–494.

860. Paquet, Léonce, and Yvon Lafrance. **Les Présocratiques: Bibliographie analytique (1450–1879): III Supplément.** Avec la collaboration d'Hélène Longpré. Collection Noêsis. Montréal: Bellarmine, 1995. 429pp. ISBN 2–89007–804–3. LCCN 95–940957.

This work, described as a supplement to the earlier bibliography of Paquet, Roussel, and Lafrance (entry 861), provides a relatively complete bibliography of the Presocratics from the beginning of printing through 1879. Its coverage for 1879 is partial, with additional works to be found in the earlier work, which begins with 1879. The compilers continue the same organizational scheme, although in a simpler form with fewer subdivisions: bibliographies, studies of more than one philosopher, studies of topics or terms, and studies of individual Presocratics or their schools. They provide descriptive annotations for each of the 788 entries and cite critical reviews under book titles. There are numerous cross-references. An extensive array of indexes of ancient authors, the Presocratics, modern authors, philosophical topics, and Greek words, as well as a chronological index, also facilitates access.

861. Paquet, L., M. Roussel, and Y. Lafrance. **Les Présocratiques: Bibliographie analytique (1879–1980).** Collection Noêsis. Montréal: Bellarmine; Collection d'études anciennes. Paris: Les Belles Lettres, 1988–1989. 2v. ISBN 2–890076–647–4 (v. 1); 2–89007–686–5 (v. 2). LCCN 89–208837.

This bibliography covers a century of work on the Presocratic philosophers, taking the publication of Hermann Diels's *Doxographi Graeci* (Berlin: G. Reimer, 1879) as its point of departure. Its major divisions include bibliographical works, general studies; studies of themes, ideas, and terms; and particular studies. Particular studies include individual schools, such as the Milesians, and individual philosophers, such as Heraclitus. The bibliography includes editions, books, and articles. Annotations offer summaries and, less often, critical comments. Some of the summaries have been reprinted from *L'Année philologique* (entry 44). Entries for books also list reviews. The 4,590 numbered entries provide comprehensive coverage of the modern scholarly literature on the Presocratics. An appendix lists nearly 200 doctoral dissertations; these are without annotation, although published reviews are noted. There is an index of modern authors. For earlier literature see the supplementary volume of Paquet and Lafrance (entry 860). Those desiring truly exhaustive coverage (or annotations in English) will also need to consult Navia (entry 859), especially since he extends coverage by a decade. However, this work and its supplement are clearly superior to Navia in most respects, including completeness and accuracy.

HISTORIES OF GREEK AND ROMAN PHILOSOPHY

862.   Algra, Keimpe, Jonathan Barnes, Jaap Mansfield, and Malcolm Schofield.
Cambridge History of Hellenistic Philosophy. Cambridge: Cambridge University Press,
1999. 916pp. ISBN 0–521–25028–5. LCCN 98–36033.

Hellenistic philosophy, like Hellenistic literature, was long relegated to the background of classical studies. This has changed in recent decades, and both now receive considerable attention. This handbook, the work of a group of distinguished scholars, finally
bridges the gap between Guthrie (entry 867) and Armstrong (entry 863). It focuses on
Greek philosophy from the last years of Aristotle (ca. 320 B.C.) to about 100 B.C. The substantial introduction covers sources, chronology, and the structure and organization of the
philosophical schools. The editors then turn to a topical approach, covering successively
logic and language, epistemology, physics and metaphysics, and ethics and politics. Each
section is subdivided into a number of chapters. Their extent of coverage is guided to some
extent by what has survived rather than relative importance. The contributors target students, graduate and undergraduate, rather than specialists. They try to avoid philosophical
jargon and largely restrict Latin and Greek to the notes. A chronology, guide to editions,
and extensive bibliography of secondary literature appear at the back of the volume. There
is an *index locorum* and a general index.

863.   Armstrong, A. H., ed. **Cambridge History of Later Greek and Early Medieval
Philosophy.** Cambridge: Cambridge University Press, 1967. 710pp. LC 66–12305.

This work was planned as a continuation of Guthrie's *History of Greek Philosophy*
(entry 867), although it has developed along somewhat different lines. Chronologically
it covers the period from the fourth century B.C. to the beginning of the twelfth century A.D.
Treatment of the earlier period (e.g., of Plato) aims at explaining the background of
Neoplatonism rather than giving a complete history of the period, for which one should
consult Guthrie. The work is divided into eight parts, each by a different scholar. These
cover Greek philosophy from Plato to Plotinus, Philo and the beginnings of Christian
thought, Plotinus, the later Neoplatonists, Marius Victorinus and Augustine, the Platonist
tradition from the Cappadocians to Maximus and Eriugena, Western Christian thought
from Boethius to Anselm, and early Islamic philosophy. A substantial bibliography and
several indexes (ancient and medieval works discussed, general, and Greek terms) round
out the volume. The work provides a good general survey of later Greek philosophy and its
influence, as well as early Christian and medieval thought. Those interested in the Hellenistic period should consult the more recent and extensive *Cambridge History of Hellenistic
Philosophy* (entry 862), which fills the gap between Guthrie and this volume.

864.   Flashar, Hellmut, ed. **Die Philosophie der Antike.** Voll. neubearb. Ausg.
Grundriss der Geschichte der Philosophie. Basel: Schwabe, 1983– . ISBN 3–7965–1036–1
(Bd. 2/1); 3–7965–0810–3 (Bd. 3); 3–7965–0930–4 (Bd. 4). LC 85–143004.

Flashar's *Die Philosophie der Antike* updates the venerable work of Friedrich
Ueberweg. To date, two volumes and part of a third have appeared. Volume 2/1 covers
the Sophists, Socrates, mathematical authors, and medical authors. Volume 3 encompasses
the Old Academy, Aristotle, and the Peripatetics to the beginning of the Roman Empire.
Volume 4 (in two parts) is devoted to Hellenistic philosophy including the Epicureans,

the Stoics, and the New Academy. Flashar and his collaborators provide brief biographies of the philosophers, overviews of their works, descriptions of the various schools of philosophy, and extensive bibliographies. Each volume has a detailed table of contents and an index of personal names. While most anglophones will prefer Guthrie's magisterial work (entry 867), this is an excellent handbook with more up-to-date bibliographies.

865. Friis Johansen, Karsten. **History of Ancient Philosophy: From the Beginnings to Augustine.** London: Routledge, 1998. 685pp. ISBN 0–415–12738–6. LCCN 97–45072.

This work first appeared in Danish in 1991. Friis Johansen's work is rooted in the primary texts and his own interpretations of them; secondary literature is largely relegated to the bibliography. He devotes the bulk of his work to Plato and Aristotle. Presocratics receive adequate, but not generous, attention. Friis Johansen gives short shrift to the major Hellenistic schools. He does give more play to Neoplatonism and early Christian thought than is typical in such works. While idiosyncratic, Friis Johansen provides the basic biographical and historical facts for the ancient philosophers, along with descriptions and discussions of their works. He often displays a better appreciation of the role of myth, mysticism, and poetry in ancient philosophy than some of his competitors. His substantial bibliography includes the usual suspects. The detailed table of contents and a general index make it easy to find treatments of specific philosophers and works. This is a useful work for students and general readers.

866. Furley, David. **From Aristotle to Augustine.** Routledge History of Philosophy 2. London: Routledge, 1999. 457pp. ISBN 0–415–06002–8. LC 98–8543.

Following C.C.W. Taylor's volume on Greek philosophy through Plato (entry 870), Furley brings the account down to late antiquity. Furley and his distinguished contributors offer a dozen essays in roughly chronological order. Aristotle (four essays on various aspects of his work) and St. Augustine frame the collection. Other essays address the various philosophical schools: the Peripatetics, Epicureanism, Stoicism, Skepticism, and Neoplatonism. Two survey Hellenistic sciences, with one primarily covering mathematics and astronomy, while the other examines biological science. Each essay provides a concise overview of its topic and a selective bibliography of texts, translations, and key secondary works. Supplementary material includes a chronology that sets philosophical developments in their historical and cultural context, a list of sources that identifies the individual philosophers discussed throughout the work, and a glossary of philosophical terms. Indexes provide access by name, subject, and cited passage. Furley offers a good introduction and reference for students and ambitious general readers.

867. Guthrie, W.K.C. **History of Greek Philosophy.** Cambridge: Cambridge University Press, 1962–1981. 6v. ISBN 0–521–05159–2 (v. 1); 0–521–29420–7 (v. 1, pbk.); 0–521–05160–6 (v. 2); 0–521–29421–5 (v. 2, pbk.); 0–521–07566–1 (v. 3); 0–521–09666–9 (v. 3, pt. 1, pbk.); 0–521–09667–7 (v. 3, pt. 2, pbk.); 0–521–20002–4 (v. 4); 0–521–31101–2 (v. 4, pbk.); 0–521–20003–2 (v. 5); 0–521–31102–0 (v. 5, pbk.); 0–521–23573–1 (v. 6); 0–521–38760–4 (v. 6, pbk.). LC 62–52735.

Long established as the standard work in the field, Guthrie surveys Greek philosophy from its beginnings through Aristotle. The first two volumes cover the Presocratics;

the third deals with the fifth-century Sophists and Socrates, the fourth and fifth volumes with Plato, and the final volume with Aristotle. Guthrie originally intended to extend the history through the Hellenistic period but was only able to reach Aristotle, who is himself treated on a more limited scale. While not neglecting the necessary biographical and historical background material, Guthrie focuses on the philosophical works and provides extensive discussion of these. The treatment is learned but remains accessible to the lay reader. Each volume includes an extensive bibliographical apparatus and full indexes. For the Hellenistic era see the *Cambridge History of Hellenistic Philosophy* (entry 862).

868. Kenny, Anthony. **Ancient Philosophy.** New History of Western Philosophy 1. Oxford: Clarendon Press, 2004. 341pp. ISBN 0–19–875273–3.

This is the first volume of a new history of philosophy from the Presocratics to Derrida. In it Sir Anthony Kenny, a distinguished British philosopher, covers philosophy from the Presocratics to St. Augustine. He gives a chronological survey of philosophers and their schools in the first two chapters. This provides basic biographical information and key ideas for each philosopher. Kenny then turns to a topical approach, covering successively logic, epistemology, physics, metaphysics, soul and mind, ethics, and God. Under each topic he examines the philosophical efforts from the Presocratics forward, providing numerous references to the ancient texts. Kenny writes for undergraduates and general readers. His prose is clear, and he generally explains technical terms. The very selective general bibliography will serve to orient the beginning student. A chronology and general index complete the work. Kenny is best used for a quick and reliable overview; those seeking more detail should consult Guthrie (entry 867) or the two-volume history edited by Taylor (entry 870) and Furley (entry 866).

869. Rowe, Christopher, and Malcolm Schofield, eds. **Cambridge History of Greek and Roman Political Thought.** Cambridge: Cambridge University Press, 1999. 745pp. ISBN 0–521–48136–8. LCCN 99–28162.

This work provides a history of Greek and Roman political thinking from the beginnings to about A.D. 350, which is where the *Cambridge History of Medieval Political Thought c.350 to c.1450* (Cambridge: Cambridge University Press, 1991) picks up. As is the case with most *Cambridge Histories*, it represents the work of a number of well-known scholars, most British, with a sprinkling of Americans and Europeans. It follows the usual chronological sequence, with a focus on individual authors and thinkers. Occasionally the editors have used genre and school for subdivisions. Socrates, Plato, and Aristotle receive much attention, as expected. There is reasonably strong coverage of the Hellenistic and Roman eras, with chapters devoted to the major schools, Cicero, Seneca and Pliny, Josephus, and the Jurists, among others. A final chapter looks at early Christianity, while an epilogue looks forward to the Middle Ages. A substantial bibliography and a detailed subject index round out the work.

870. Taylor, C.C.W., ed. **From the Beginning to Plato.** Routledge History of Philosophy 1. London: Routledge, 1997. 494pp. ISBN 0–415–06272–1. LC 96–21374.

This useful survey attempts to look at Greek thought both historically and philosophically. Its approach is chronological; an effort is made to present the Greek philosophers in their historical, social, and scientific contexts. A detailed chronology begins the work, which includes political, religious, artistic, and scientific events in addition to those relating primarily to philosophy. Then a list of sources identifies the ancient philosophers and works discussed in the text. A series of chapters, each by a distinguished authority, covers major philosophers and schools: the Ionians, Heraclitus, the Pythagoreans and Eleatics, Empedocles, Anaxagoras and the Atomists, the Sophists, mathematics from Thales to Plato, Socrates, and Plato (who receives three separate chapters). Each provides a solid overview, with many excerpts from the ancient works and well-chosen bibliographies. A glossary explains key philosophical terms. Indexes provide access by subject, passage cited, and proper name. While much less detailed than Guthrie's great work (entry 867), it provides a more manageable and up-to-date treatment for English readers. The next volume in the series, edited by David Furley (entry 866), extends coverage through Augustine.

DICTIONARIES, ENCYCLOPEDIAS, AND HANDBOOKS

871.   Brunschwig, Jacques, and Geoffrey E. R. Lloyd. **Le savoir grec: Dictionnaire critique.** Avec la collaboration de Pierre Pellegrin; preface de Michel Serres. Paris: Flammarion, 1996. 1089pp. ISBN 2–08–210370–6. LC 97–111213

872.   Brunschwig, Jacques, and Geoffrey E. R. Lloyd, eds. **Greek Thought: A Guide to Classical Knowledge.** With the collaboration of Pierre Pellegrin. Trans. under the direction of Catherine Porter. Cambridge, MA: Belknap Press of Harvard University, 2000. 1024pp. ISBN: 0–674–00261–X. LC 00–36032.

An extremely valuable work for all interested in Greek intellectual history, this handbook surveys primarily philosophy, but also science and religion, which the Greeks would not have viewed as separate categories. Five sections cover the emergence of philosophy, politics, the pursuit of knowledge (subdivided by fields, such as astronomy, cosmology, logic, etc.), major philosophers, and schools of philosophy. Each of these includes signed articles by leading scholars in the field. A bibliography of key editions and secondary works follows each article. Supplementary material includes a chronology, maps, and splendid color illustrations (the quality of these is much higher in the French edition). Frequent cross-references as well as name and subject indexes ease navigation of the work. Coverage is somewhat selective, but students will find readable and learned articles on most of the high points of Greek philosophy. Abridged versions of the English translation appeared in 2003 under the titles *A Guide to Greek Thought* (primarily the parts on philosophers and schools) and *The Greek Pursuit of Knowledge* (primarily the essays on the various fields of knowledge).

873.   Everson, Stephen, ed. **Epistemology.** Companions to Ancient Thought 1. Cambridge: Cambridge University Press, 1990. 288pp. ISBN 0–521–34161–2; 0–521–34969–9pa. LC 89–7116.

Everson has produced a series of companions to ancient philosophy aimed at students of philosophy rather than of classics. His approach is topical, rather than by period, philosopher, or school. This volume, for example, covers epistemology from the sixth century B.C. to the third century A.D. Everson's introductory overview is followed by 10 essays covering Greek epistemological thinking in roughly chronological order. The contributors are a distinguished lot, and their essays are generally accessible to undergraduates. Their discussions are firmly rooted in the ancient texts, with selective coverage of key secondary literature. The substantial bibliography is arranged to correspond to the chapters; it recommends both editions and secondary literature. One quirk, given the intended audience, is that readers are sometimes referred only to editions in Greek. There are indexes of names, passages discussed, and subjects.

874.   Everson, Stephen, ed. **Ethics.** Companions to Ancient Thought 4. Cambridge: Cambridge University Press, 1998. 300pp. ISBN 0–521–38161–4; 0–521–38832–5pa. LC 97–8899.

As with other volumes in this series, Everson intends his work primarily for students of philosophy rather than of classics. His introduction provides an overview of ethical thought from the beginnings of Greek philosophy through the Hellenistic period. The seven essays that follow cover major aspects in greater detail: Pre-Platonic ethics, Platonic ethics, Aristotle on nature and value, Aristotle's moral psychology, Epicurean ethics, Stoic ethics, Skeptic approaches to values and ethics, and moral responsibility in Aristotle and after. All are by leading scholars, such as Charles Kahn, Terence Irwin, and Julia Annas. The substantial bibliography, which lists nearly 1,000 editions and studies, is keyed to the individual essays. Indexes offer access by name, passage discussed, and subject.

875.   Everson, Stephen, ed. **Language.** Companions to Ancient Thought 3. Cambridge: Cambridge University Press, 1994. ISBN 0–521–35538–9; 0–521–35795–0pa. LC93–27234.

Following the pattern of other volumes in this series, Everson provides an introductory survey of philosophical treatments of language by the ancients. Ten essays by such scholars as Bernard Williams, Michael Frede, and David Blank cover specific topics and philosophers in more depth. While the usual suspects (Plato, Aristotle, the Epicureans, and the Stoics) receive due attention, this collection also includes studies of Apollonius Dyskolus, Galen, and Augustine. Everson and his contributors provide a good overview of ancient thinking about language; the extensive bibliography supplies ready assistance to those wishing to go further. Indexes provide access by name, passage discussed, and subject.

876.   Everson, Stephen, ed. **Psychology.** Companions to Ancient Thought 2. Cambridge: Cambridge University Press, 1991. 269pp. ISBN 0–521–35338–6; 0–521–35861–2pa. LC 90–40229.

This second volume in the *Companions to Ancient Thought* series examines *psyche,* which embraces the soul, the nature of mind, and the idea of self. As in the first volume (entry 873), Everson and his contributors move in a roughly chronological fashion, tracing their subject from Heraclitus through the Neoplatonists. There is also an essay on how Greek medical writers viewed the mind. Contributors are all leading specialists in their fields, such as Malcolm Schofield and A. A. Long. Students of philosophy and psychology will find this a reliable guide to ancient concepts of the mind and soul. The bibliography is arranged in sections corresponding to the essays. Each section directs the reader to the best editions and key secondary literature. Indexes to names, passages discussed, and subjects round out the work.

877. Inwood, Brad, ed.. **Cambridge Companion to the Stoics.** Cambridge: Cambridge University Press, 2003. 438pp. ISBN 0–521–77005–X; 0–521–77985–5pa. LC 2002031359.

Inwood and his contributors offer a guide to Stoicism as a whole. Beginning students will find it challenging but helpful; the intermediate and advanced will find it an invaluable resource. The first two essays cover the history of Stoicism in the Greek and Roman eras. Then eight essays survey such topics as epistemology, logic, natural philosophy, metaphysics, and ethics. Three essays cover the influence of Stoicism on ancient medicine, grammar, and astronomy. Finally, two essays discuss Stoicism in the modern philosophical tradition. All supply frequent references both to primary sources and to key scholarly writings, enabling students to pursue further study. An excellent bibliography, a general index, and an index of philosophical passages cited conclude the work.

878. Long, A.A., ed. **Cambridge Companion to Early Greek Philosophy.** Cambridge: Cambridge University Press, 1999. 427pp. ISBN 0–521–44122–6; 0–521–4467–8pa. LCCN 98–38077.

Long intends this volume as a guide for beginners and the Greekless, although the more advanced will also find it useful. The contributors include a number of distinguished classicists and philosophers from England, Europe, and America. It begins with several aids to the student: brief biographies of the philosophers (in alphabetical order), including citation of sources and a description of their works; a chronology; and a map. The first chapter provides an overview, while the second looks at sources. Subsequent chapters proceed in roughly chronological order to cover major figures and schools, along with a few topics. One of the book's strengths is the extensive quotation of the philosophical works in translation. The selective bibliography, which is arranged to correspond to the chapters, runs to some 553 items. The opening sections cover standard editions and translations, bibliographical works, and general surveys and histories. The first index covers passages, the second names and subjects.

879. Peters, F. E. **Greek Philosophical Terms: A Historical Lexicon.** New York: New York University Press, 1967. 234pp. LC 67–25043.

Aimed at the "intermediate student" of Greek philosophy, this is an alphabetical listing of terms used by the Greek philosophers. Peters defines each term and discusses its usage in the various philosophical writers; the discussions include numerous specific references. He supplies numerous cross-references and an English-Greek index, which provides access from English versions of the terms. This useful work allows students of philosophy who lack a good command of ancient Greek to get some idea of the actual meanings of Greek philosophical terms and to see some of the problems and uncertainties associated with the standard definitions.

880. Sedley, David. **Cambridge Companion to Greek and Roman Philosophy.** Cambridge: Cambridge University Press, 2003. 396pp. ISBN 0–521–77285–0; 0–521–77503–5pa. LC 2002035188.

Sedley and a team of leading scholars provide a guide for students of ancient philosophy. The introduction offers an overview of the field and the book. It also includes a brief discussion of the transmission of ancient texts (with examples and photographs of manuscripts), alien terrain to most. Eight essays offer a roughly chronological survey covering argument in ancient philosophy, the Presocratics, the Sophists and Socrates, Plato, Aristotle, Hellenistic philosophy, Roman philosophy, and late ancient philosophy. Three cover topics: philosophy and literature, philosophy and science, and philosophy and religion. A final essay discusses the *Nachleben* of classical philosophy, primarily in the Middle Ages and Renaissance. A substantial bibliography lists standard editions and translations along with a selection of key secondary works. A glossary of philosophical terms and an index complete the work. This book provides a solid and accessible introduction to the major philosophers, schools, and works of antiquity.

881.   Shields, Christopher, ed. **Blackwell Guide to Ancient Philosophy.** Blackwell Guides to Philosophy. Malden, MA: Blackwell, 2003. 333pp. ISBN 0–631–22214–6; 0–631–22215–4pa. LC 2002–6209.

This work is designed for undergraduate students of philosophy. Its six sections cover the standard chronological periods of Greek philosophy: philosophy before Socrates, Socrates, Plato, Aristotle, Hellenistic philosophy, and late antique philosophy (i.e., Neoplatonism). Each section has an introduction, which provides brief biographies of the major figures and basic background information, followed by one to four essays. The sections on Plato and Aristotle, for example, contain essays devoted to major topics, such as epistemology or ethics, while those on periods have essays covering the major schools, such as Epicureanism. Each chapter includes a bibliograpy of primary and secondary sources suitable for students. A general bibliography and index conclude the volume. Shields and his contributors have created an excellent handbook, which provides a solid survey of the major figures, schools, and ideas of Greek philosophy.

882.   Urmson, J. O. **Greek Philosophical Vocabulary.** London: Duckworth, 1990. 173pp. ISBN 0–7156–2335–4. LC 93–32407.

Urmson has produced an interesting and learned work but is unclear about his audience. He indicates in the introduction that his book "is designed to be an aid to students of ancient Greek philosophy who have some, but not necessarily a profound, knowledge of the Greek language." All Greek is transliterated, to the annoyance of those who can read it, but of little avail to those who cannot. Some of his comments are directed to beginners, while others require advanced knowledge. Urmson provides definitions and some discussion of usage, but the bulk of each entry consists of a series of sentences from the philosophers in transliterated Greek with translations, which, although accurate, tend to be rather free. He covers more than 500 terms found in philosophical writers between fifth century B.C. and the sixth century A.D. Those with substantial Greek will find valuable nuggets, but others will do better with Peters (entry 879).

883.   Zeyl, Donald J., Daniel T. Devereux, and Phillip T. Mitsis, eds. **Encyclopedia of Classical Philosophy.** Wesport, CT: Greenwood Press, 1997. 614pp. ISBN 0–313–28775–9. LC 96–2562.

This excellent encyclopedia will serve a wide range of inquirers, from college students and the curious to serious researchers. It covers Greek and Roman philosophy from the earliest philosopher-scientists of the sixth century B.C. to the demise of the Academy at Athens in the sixth century A.D. Ninety scholars, including some of the foremost in their fields, have contributed signed articles. The bulk of the articles are devoted to individual philosophers, both major and minor. Many writers on medicine and science, who would not be considered philosophers today but were in antiquity, also receive attention. Other articles are devoted to philosophical schools, such as the Academy. Still others address topics such as allegory, rhetoric, and Christianity. Articles range from a paragraph to several pages; each includes a bibliography of primary sources and key secondary works. The writing is admirably clear for the most part, although unexplained jargon sometimes occurs. Frequent cross-references and a general index assist navigation. The editors append a chronological outline and a rather spartan guide to bibliography, which will assist beginners.

18
Religion and Mythology

This chapter includes works on both mythology and religion, which are nearly inseparable subjects. It includes works on mythology in art and literature as well, although some relevant works will be found in other chapters (follow the cross-references in the entries below). The first part covers bibliographies. The second covers handbooks, dictionaries, and Web sites. The number of these is legion; comprehensiveness is neither possible nor desirable. However, all the major works and a selection of the more common secondary works appear below.

BIBLIOGRAPHIES

884. Accardi, Bernard, et al., comps. **Recent Studies in Myths and Literature, 1970–1990: An Annotated Bibliography.** Bibliographies and Indexes in World Literature 29. New York: Greenwood Press, 1991. 251pp. ISBN 0–313–27545–9. LCCN 91–18070.

While aimed primarily at students of British and American literature, this work is also of use to classicists. Its second chapter deals with myth in classical literature; others cover general works on myth and literature or specific periods of American or British literature. These chapters also include many studies on the use of classical myth in later literature. Some 1,081 works are cited; more than half discuss classical mythology in some way. Each entry includes a descriptive annotation. Many of these are fairly substantial, and a few include critical comments as well. Author and subject indexes are provided. Those interested in classical literature proper need only consult the second chapter, while readers concerned with the influence of classical myth in Anglo-American literature would do well to approach the work through the subject index. Users should also bear in mind that this bibliography is far from complete in its coverage.

885. Arlen, Shelley. **Cambridge Ritualists: An Annotated Bibliography of the Works by and about Jane Ellen Harrison, Gilbert Murray, Francis M. Cornford, and Arthur Bernard Cook.** Metuchen, NJ: Scarecrow Press, 1990. 414pp. ISBN 0–8108–2373–X. LCCN 90–47304.

Harrison, Murray, Cornford, and Cook were among the first to apply anthropological theories to the study of Greek literature, myth, and religion. Their works have had a lasting influence and continue to be read. Arlen, a reference librarian, has compiled an exhaustive bibliography both of their writings and of works about them. She lists 2,019 items in five major sections: one for works dealing with the "Cambridge Ritualists" in general, and separate sections for each of the four scholars. These sections each open with a portrait, a biographical sketch, and an overview of current research on the scholar. Works by the individual follow; these are subarranged by form: books, translations, articles, letters, and reviews. A bibliography of critical and biographical writings about the scholar closes each section. Descriptive annotations accompany many but not all entries. Entries for books include citations of reviews. Numerous cross-references link related entries. Arlen provides author, title, and subject indexes.

886.   Bremmer, Jan N. **Greek Religion.** New Surveys in the Classics 24. Oxford: Oxford University Press, 1994. 111pp. ISBN 019–922073–5.

Bremmer, who has himself published extensively in this area, surveys recent scholarship on Greek religion. He takes Walter Burkert's *Griechische Religion der archaischen und klassischen Epoche* (Stuttgart: Kohlhammer, 1977; see entry 900 for the English edition) as his point of departure and focuses on subsequent work, although he also discusses important earlier studies. Bremmer organizes his survey under eight rubrics: general characteristics, gods, sanctuaries, ritual, mythology, gender, transformations, and the genesis of Greek religion. His approach follows the familiar format of this series: each chapter consists of a critical discussion of recent trends and publications, with bibliographical details presented in notes at the end. Bremmer does depart from the series' normal practice of concentrating on English-language works and notes many valuable European-language publications. The index of names, subjects, and passages is very detailed and includes all authors mentioned in the notes. Those seeking more extensive retrospective coverage should also consult Motte (entries 887–888).

887.   Motte, André, Vinciane Pirenne-Delforge, and Paul Wathelet, eds. **Mentor: Guide bibliographique de la religion grecque [Bibliographical Survey of Greek Religion].** Kernos, supplement 2. Liège: Université de Liège, Centre d'Histoire des Religions, 1992. 781pp.

888.   Motte, André, Vinciane Pirenne-Delforge, and Paul Wathelet, eds. **Mentor 2: Guide bibliographique de la religion grecque [Bibliographical Survey of Greek Religion, 1986–1990].** Kernos, supplement 6. Liège: Université de Liège, Centre d'Histoire des Religions, 1998. 531pp.

The initial volume of this selective bibliography covers works on Greek religion published prior to 1985, with quinquennial supplements planned (one has appeared to date). The lengthy introduction provides a guide to the primary sources, including ancient texts (editions, commentaries, indexes, and concordances), epigraphical and papyrological works, iconographical sources, and numismatic materials. The introduction also notes relevant general bibliographical and reference sources. A listing of 2,060 books and articles comprises the main part of the volume. These are arranged by author. Substantial signed annotations accompany most entries; these both summarize and evaluate. Nearly all the annotations are in French. Although a rather odd and limited subject index appears at the end of the introduction, access by subject is generally inadequate. Otherwise, this work is a valuable guide to its subject. The supplement follows the pattern of the original volume and continues its numbering, adding 1,310 additional entries for the years 1986–1990. While the editors make no claim to completeness, scholars are unlikely to find as much in any other single source. Casual inquirers and those who read only English may find Bremmer's survey (entry 886) more helpful.

889.   Peradotto, John. **Classical Mythology: An Annotated Bibliographical Survey.** American Philological Association Bibliographical Guides. Urbana, IL: American Philological Association, 1973. 76pp.

Aimed at college-level teachers and students of classical myth, Peradotto's book has become a standard bibliographical reference for the subject. Although reprinted twice (most recently in 1981), it has never been revised and is now somewhat dated. However, it remains useful for its coverage of many valuable works published prior to 1973. This coverage is highly selective (only 212 items are listed) and limited to book-length works. Peradotto arranges his material in sections by form and topic. He begins with chapters on reference works and general surveys of myth. Then a series of topical chapters covers comparative mythology; myth in relation to such subjects as art, literature, psychology, anthropology, and religion; and the structural study of myth. At the end, Peradotto returns to form and treats general studies, specialized studies, and translations of the major ancient literary sources. In each section bibliographical citations are listed at the beginning. Peradotto follows this with critical discussions that give a clear description of the contents and merits of each work. Peradotto supplies numerous cross-references between sections. He also provides an author-title index and an index of publishers.

890.   Les religions dans le monde romain (200 av. J.C. à 200 ap. J.C.): Bibliographie analytique à partir des publications périodiques de 1962 à 1968 dépouillées par le Bulletin analytique d'histoire romaine. Strasbourg: Association pour l'Étude de la Civilisation Romaine, 1975. 247pp.

This bibliography consists of entries drawn from the volumes of the *Bulletin analytique d'histoire romaine* (entry 52) for 1962–1968. This material has been rearranged into two large sections: publications of source material subdivided by type (literary, papyrological, epigraphical, archaeological, and numismatic), and studies, which are subdivided into broad subject categories. The limitations of the parent publication apply to this volume: it lists only journal articles, and these from a somewhat restricted geographical area. It does, however, include citations from some European journals not indexed by more general sources, such as *L'Année philologique* (entry 44). There are a number of formal weaknesses in the bibliography. Entries retain their original numbers from the *Bulletin analytique*. This is confusing, since these have no relation to the present compilation. Also, there are no indexes. The abstracts, which are often substantial, are one of the few attractive features. This bibliography is of limited use and can only be recommended to specialists in Roman religion.

891.   Ruud, Inger Marie. Minoan Religion: A Bibliography. Studies in Mediterranean Archaeology and Literature. Pocket-Book 141. Jonserad: Paul Åström, 1996. 124pp. ISBN 91–7081–162–8.

Ruud, a Swedish librarian, lists 950 books, articles, book chapters, conference proceedings, and dissertations from 1900 through the early 1990s. After two sections covering bibliographies and general works, Ruud follows a topical schema: cult places, cult symbols and equipment, deities, epigraphic evidence, iconography/seals and sealings, priesthood and sacred kingship, relation to Greek and Mycenaean religion, relations to other religions, relation to Thera, sacred animals and demons, and tomb and burial customs. Entries provide basic bibliographical information; there are no annotations. There are indexes to subjects and authors. This is a convenient gathering of material, but those seeking wider or more comprehensive coverage should also consult *Mentor* (entries 887–888).

DICTIONARIES, ENCYCLOPEDIAS, AND HANDBOOKS

892. Adkins, Lesley, and Roy A. Adkins. **Dictionary of Roman Religion.** Oxford: Oxford University Press, 2000. 288pp. ISBN 0–19–514233–0. LCCN 00–44085.

Originally published by Facts on File in 1996, this work is an A-to-Z dictionary of all things relating to Roman religion. The more than 1,400 articles cover gods and goddesses, religious festivals, shrines, priests, oracles, religious terms, and objects. The Adkinses cover Judaism and early Christianity as well as the pagan religions of ancient Rome. Articles tend to be short and factual; many have one or two recommendations for further reading. The *Dictionary* includes numerous illustrations and plans. Some cross-references are provided, although more would have been useful. There is an index. This work is a good supplement to the mythological dictionaries listed here, such as Grimal (entry 906): it does a good job of covering the practice of Roman religion, which the dictionaries do not. For a more detailed narrative approach to Roman religion see Beard, North, and Price (entry 896). Those seeking broader treatment of ancient religion should consult Johnston (entry 912).

893. **Athena: Classical Mythology on CD-ROM.** Boston: G.K. Hall, 1994. 1 disk, accompanied by user's guide. ISBN 0–7838–2119–0 (single user); 0–7838–2120–4 (network).

Designed for students at all levels, *Athena* is a hypertext-based mythological-dictionary. It offers brief articles on the various mythological characters and stories. These are linked to both summaries and full-text translations of the major classical literary sources for the myths. Many entries are accompanied by illustrations, which are mostly drawn from ancient sources. These line drawings, which are rather uninspiring, are one of the weaker features of the database. A number of genealogical tables are also provided. The most attractive feature of *Athena* is the hypertext links, which enable one to move readily to the summaries or the actual texts of the primary sources and to articles on related myths. The straightforward search procedures permit both keyword access and browsing in the alphabetical list of headings. *Athena* is superior in both content and ease of use to most of the printed dictionaries of mythology, although researchers will still find Grimal (entry 906) somewhat better due to his extensive scholarly apparatus. The same disk contains DOS, Windows, and Macintosh versions; this rather antiquated disk may not run with more recent versions of these operating systems.

894. Avery, Catherine B., ed. **New Century Handbook of Greek Mythology and Legend.** New York: Appleton-Century-Crofts, 1972. 565pp. LCCN 75–183796.

This work is excerpted from the larger *New Century Classical Handbook* (entry 128). It takes the form of a dictionary. Most entries represent the characters of Greek mythology, although there are a few articles on places, events, and objects. These vary in length; most run to a paragraph or two, while a few extend to several pages. The articles provide clear identifications and summaries of the more important stories. A guide to pronunciation is also supplied. There are no bibliographical references. The *Handbook* compares favorably to other basic dictionaries of mythology, such as Schmidt (entry 929),

Stapleton (entry 930), and Zimmerman (entry 932), although it lacks some of the detail and the bibliographies found in the larger works of Tripp (entry 931) and Grimal (entry 906).

895.   Barthell, Edward E., Jr. **Gods and Goddesses of Ancient Greece.** Coral Gables, FL: University of Miami Press, 1971. 416pp. ISBN 0–87024–165–6. LCCN 72–129664.

For those who prefer a narrative approach to the myths, Barthell offers a good alternative to the mythological dictionaries described elsewhere in this section. He follows a "chronological" arrangement, which proceeds from the older gods through the Olympians and their descendants to the stories of the Trojan War and Odysseus. Barthell's quite readable text covers the stories in detail; his footnotes provide a good deal of background information and also discuss minor variants of the myths. He also includes a large number of detailed genealogical tables. His bibliography lists the primary sources (mainly in Loeb Classical Library editions) and a few general handbooks on Greek mythology. A thorough general index completes the work.

896.   Beard, Mary, John North, and Simon Price. **Religions of Rome: A History.** Cambridge: Cambridge University Press, 1998. 454pp. ISBN 0–521–30401–6; 0–521–31682–0pa. LCCN 97–21302.

This is the narrative part of a two-volume work; the second volume is a collection of sources (see entry 325). The authors survey more than 1,000 years of religion at Rome, from the local cults at its beginnings to the establishment of Christianity in the fourth and fifth centuries A.D. They do so in a series of broad topical chapters that proceed in a roughly chronological fashion: early Rome; imperial triumph and religious change; religion in the late republic; the place of religion; Rome in the early empire; the boundaries of Roman religion; the religions of imperial Rome; Roman religion and the Roman empire; and Roman religion and the Christian emperors. In addition to the traditional state cults of Rome, they cover the various Eastern religions that came to Rome: Judaism, Mithraism, Christianity, and others. The authors provide extensive references to both primary sources and the secondary literature, along with a substantial bibliography. Maps locate the various shrines of Rome. Many black-and-white illustrations accompany the text. The detailed index makes it easy to find discussions of specific topics.

897.   Bell, Robert E. **Dictionary of Classical Mythology: Symbols, Attributes, and Associations.** Santa Barbara, CA: ABC-Clio, 1982. 390pp. ISBN 0–87436–305–5; 0–87436–023–4pa. LCCN 81–19141.

Most dictionaries of mythology use the names of persons and places as access points. Bell's work uses a topical approach. There are entries for objects, animals, attributes of the various mythological characters, and topics. Under each the reader will find the mythical figures associated with the heading. Many of these are accompanied by brief notes that clarify the association, although Bell does not usually provide full identifications of characters or summaries of myths. There are also separate lists of "Surnames, Epithets, and Patronymics" of the characters of classical myth and of participants in various heroic expeditions (e.g., the voyage of the Argo). The final section, "Guide to Persona," functions as a name index. Bell provides an excellent companion work to any of the standard mythological dictionaries, such as Grimal (entry 906). Preston (entry 473), whose work is specifically intended for identifying representations of classical myth in art, is somewhat similar in form and content.

898. Bell, Robert E. **Women of Classical Mythology: A Biographical Dictionary.** Santa Barbara, CA: ABC-Clio 1991; repr., New York: Oxford University Press, 1993. 462pp. ISBN 0–87436–581–3. LCCN 91–26649.

Another of Bell's works on mythology (see also entries 397 and 897), this volume focuses on women in Greek and Roman mythology. Bell covers approximately 2,600 women who are mentioned in the classical myths. A few, such as Helen and Medea, are prominent, but the majority are minor figures. The entries clearly present what is known about each and supply references to the relevant ancient sources. Although the entries vary in length from a few lines to several pages, most are quite brief. In many cases, this is due to the obscurity of the character. Some of these characters will not be found at all in more general mythological dictionaries. Bell is particularly good for differentiating among characters of the same name and for identifying obscure epithets of the goddesses. He provides numerous cross-references. Bell also provides a list of "the men in their lives," which functions as an index based on the often better-known names of the male characters of classical myth.

899. Brumble, H. David. **Classical Myths and Legends in the Middle Ages and Renaisssance.** Westport, CT: Greenwood Press, 1998. 421pp. ISBN 0–313–29451–8. LCCN 96–53527.

This dictionary of classical mythology is designed to assist readers of medieval and Renaissance literature. Brumble covers a wide range of myths in his A-to-Z dictionary. Each entry summarizes the myth and provides references to relevant ancient sources. He is particularly strong in coverage of the late mythographers. Brumble then dicusses the use of the myth by medieval and Renaissance writers, with a special focus on its allegorical use. He supplies numerous references to literary works and extensive bibliographies. Brumble covers only those mythical figures who are used allegorically in later literature, so some otherwise important figures are omitted. Appendixes offer thematic coverage of music, bestialization, and animal envy. Brumble's lengthy annotated bibliography of primary sources offers a good guide to the medieval *Nachleben* of classical mythology. A bibliography of secondary scholarship and an index are also provided. Brumble is useful to anyone concerned with the reception of classical myth through the Renaissance.

900. Burkert, Walter. **Greek Religion.** Cambridge, MA: Harvard University Press, 1985. 493pp. ISBN 0–674–36280–2; 0–674–36281–0pa. LCCN 84–25209.

This translation of *Griechische Religion in der archaischen und klassischen Epoche* (Stuttgard: Kohlhammer, 1977) remains the standard work in English on Greek religion. Burkert updated bibliographical references for the translation. He begins with a brief survey of the most important scholarship from the eighteenth century to the present and a survey of sources. Major sections cover prehistory and the Minoan-Mycenaean age; ritual and sanctuary; the gods; the dead, heroes, and chthonic gods; polis and polytheism; mysteries and asceticism; and philosophical religion. The detailed table of contents facilitates finding sections on specific rituals, gods, festivals, etc. Those seeking a discussion of Greek gods and heroes as cult figures rather than just the myths will find Burkert an excellent source with much information and interpretation, accompanied by references to the sources and to noteworthy secondary literature. A selective bibliography, index of Greek words, and general index conclude the volume.

901.   Chiron Dictionary of Greek and Roman Mythology. Trans. Elizabeth Burr. Wilmette, IL: Chiron, 1994. 312pp. ISBN 0–933029–82–9. LCCN 93–43989.

Originally published in German as *Herder Lexikon: Griechische und römische Mythologie* (Freiburg im Breisgau: Herder, 1981), this dictionary provides good coverage of the basic characters, places, and events of classical mythology. Entries, which number more than 1,600, are concise and informative. An unusual feature is the material presented in the margins beside many entries. This consists of small illustrations, genealogical tables, or lists (e.g., the 12 labors of Herakles, the names of the 9 muses, and the events at the Olympic Games). The dictionary includes cross-references, but no bibliography or index. It is an attractive and convenient ready-reference tool for students and readers. Those who require fuller treatment should refer to Grimal (entry 906).

902.   Dixon-Kennedy, Mike. Encyclopedia of Greco-Roman Mythology. Santa Barbara, CA: ABC-Clio, 1998. 370pp. ISBN 1–57607–094–8; 1–57607–129–4pa. LCCN 98–40666.

This relatively recent offering provides A-to-Z coverage of Greek and Roman mythology. Its approximately 1,400 articles tend to be short and less sophisticated than those of Grimal (entry 906). Unlike most other such works, Dixon-Kennedy includes entries for many places as well as mythological figures, and also ancient authors (e.g., Aeschylus and Homer). The numerous cross-references and index make it easy to find needed information. Dixon-Kennedy also supplies brief chronologies of Greek and Roman history, a list of Roman emperors, and a fairly substantial bibliography. His work is a suitable ready-reference source for students.

903.   Encyclopedia Mythica. URL: www.pantheon.org/mythica.html.

This Web encyclopedia covers a broad range of world mythology, offering more than 6,800 articles. It is possible to search it as whole or to search or browse subsections devoted to Greek and Roman mythology. Articles are brief and usually include one or two references to the ancient sources. While generally accurate, they include a number of typos and eccentricities. For example, the entry on Agave cites Ovid, but not Euripides' *Bacchai,* among primary sources! As with many Web resources, it is difficult to ascertain the compilers' credentials. Lack of images is a major weakness. There are a few small genealogical tables. The site is useful for looking up basic information but is far inferior to most printed sources, such as Grimal (entry 906) or Hard (entry 909). Those who prefer using the Web would do well to use Parada's *Greek Mythology Link* (entry 918) instead.

904.   Gantz, Timothy. Early Greek Myth: A Guide to the Literary and Artistic Sources. Baltimore: Johns Hopkins University Press, 1993. 909pp. ISBN 0–8018–4410–X. LCCN 92–26010.

For anyone with a serious interest in early Greek literature, art, or mythology, this handbook will be an invaluable resource. Unlike most handbooks that offer composite versions of the myths, Gantz has attempted to determine and present the forms of the myths current in early Greek civilization down to the end of the Archaic period. His arrangement is the traditional one, with each cycle treated separately in what might be called the "chronological order" of the myths. In his discussion of each myth Gantz provides a very full discussion of the literary sources. His treatment of the artistic evidence is more selective; those in need of exhaustive coverage are referred to the *Lexicon Iconographicum Mythologiae Classicae* (entry 913). Gantz also supplies an extensive array of genealogical tables and a catalog of artistic representations. The catalog will be somewhat opaque to those without a solid grounding in Greek art. Notes (no longer a common feature in handbooks), a bibliography, and a reasonably full subject index complete the book. A two-volume paperback edition was issued in 1996.

905.   Grant, Michael, and John Hazel. **Who's Who in Classical Mythology.** London: Weidenfeld and Nicholson, 1973; repr., London: Routledge, 2002. 367pp. ISBN 0–415–26041–8.

One of the many productions of Michael Grant, this is a good basic dictionary of classical mythology. It includes entries for the characters (but not the places and events) of the myths. These range in length from a single sentence to several pages and serve to identify the characters and summarize their stories. For the most part there are no bibliographies, although Grant and Hazel occasionally supply general references to the ancient sources. The work lacks an index but does include many cross-references. In general this is a serviceable ready-reference tool, but not the equal of Tripp (entry 931) or Grimal (entry 906) even in his abridged edition.

906.   Grimal, Pierre. **Dictionary of Classical Mythology.** Trans. A. R. Maxwell-Hyslop. Oxford: Blackwell, 1986. 603pp. ISBN 0–631–13209–0. LCCN 85–7387.

907.   Grimal, Pierre. **Penguin Dictionary of Classical Mythology.** Ed. Stephen Kershaw from the translation of A. R. Mawell-Hyslop. New York: Penguin, 1991. 466pp. ISBN 0–14–051235–7.

Since it first appeared in 1951, Grimal's well-known *Dictionnaire de la mythologie grecque et romaine* has gone through numerous editions and been translated into several languages. Grimal's entries are chiefly for individual characters of the myths; topics and places are covered indirectly through these. The compact articles clearly identify each mythic figure and summarize what is known about him or her. Grimal provides full references to the ancient literary sources for each myth, although these must be sought from a separate section following the text. Amenities include maps of Greece and Italy, a selection of illustrations, and some 40 genealogical tables, which elucidate the often complicated family relationships of classical mythology. A comprehensive index rounds out the volume. Grimal provides more detailed accounts of the myths and fuller scholarly apparatus than any of the competing volumes. This excellent work is the best of the many general dictionaries of Greek and Roman mythology in English. The abridged version, which also appeared under the title *A Concise Dictionary of Classical Mythology,* lacks the many notes and bibliographical references of the full edition. The editor has also deleted material from some articles and greatly reduced the number of genealogical tables.

908.   Hansen, William. **Handbook of Classical Mythology.** Handbooks of World Mythology. Santa Barbara, CA: ABC-Clio, 2004. 393pp. ISBN 1–57607–226–6; 1–85109–634–5 (eBook). LCCN 2–004–00443–4.

Hansen, a well-known classicist specializing in myth and folklore, has produced an excellent guide to Greek mythology. Hansen's lengthy introduction focuses on myth as story, with extensive discussion of myth, legend, and folktale. It also discusses the places, characters, and nature of mythological narrative. The second part discusses mythology as a temporal construction, providing a chronological overview. The third and longest part covers deities, themes, and concepts in an alphabetical sequence. Hansen covers the key places, figures, and concepts in moderate detail. He also supplies current and well-chosen references for further reading. A general bibliography, glossary, and index complete the work. This is an excellent work for students and teachers of mythology.

909.   Hard, Robin. **Routledge Handbook of Greek Mythology.** London: Routledge, 2004. 753pp. ISBN 0–415–18636–6. LCCN 2003–46672.

Hard originally intended this to be a revision of Rose's *Handbook of Greek Mythology* (entry 928), but he has actually produced a new and different work, although partly based on Rose. Hard, like Rose, offers a connected narrative rather than dictionary entries, but in less formidable prose than his predecessor. The first chapter covers the literary sources for Greek mythology, including most of the minor ones. He then covers the creation myths, the gods, heroes, and local legends in the succeeding chapters. The sequence blends the imaginary chronology of the myths with genealogy. A final chapter covers Aeneas, Romulus, and early Rome. The myths appear in normal type, while historical, comparative, and interpretive material follow in smaller type. The stories carefully follow the primary sources, which are copiously documented in the notes. Hard also provides maps and 20 genealogical tables. His bibliographical note is highly selective but covers the essentials. The "main" index is actually an index of mythical figures; a special detailed index for the Olympian gods and a selective geographical index follow. This is an excellent compendium of the myths and a good guide to the sources.

910.   Hunger, Herbert. **Lexikon der griechischen und römischen Mythologie: Mit Hinweisen auf das Fortwirken antiker Stoffe und Motive in der bildenden Kunst, Literatur, und Musik der Abendlandes bis zur Gegenwart.** 8. erweiterte Aufl. Wien: Hollinek, 1988. 557pp. ISBN 3–85119–230–3. LCCN 89–116531.

Hunger's dictionary covers the full range of classical mythology. His short articles give the basic information and a synopsis of modern studies for each myth or character. Hunger then lists works of art, literature, and music featuring the myth. Articles conclude with an extensive bibliographical note. Those who are seeking only identifications or summaries of myths will be better off with Grimal (entry 906) or one of his competitors. Serious students of myth who have some German will find Hunger useful, particularly for his rich bibliographies. His lists of depictions of myth in art are also handy, although Reid's *Oxford Guide to Classical Mythology in the Arts* (entry 921) is much more comprehensive.

911.   James, Vanessa. **Genealogy of Greek Mythology: An Illustrated Family Tree of Greek Myth from the First Gods to the Founders of Rome.** New York: Gotham Books, 2003. 107pp. ISBN 1–592–40013–2. LCCN 2004–272120.

This 17-foot foldout accordion book provides genealogical tables for about 3,000 characters in Greek and Roman mythology. Gods are featured on one side of the chart, mortals on the other. Numerous sidebars provide short biographies of major figures. The whole is beautifully illustrated with ancient works of art. James bases her tables and stories on the ancient Greek sources. She also provides maps, a listing of the major gods with their consorts and offspring, and an index. James offers a bit less genealogical information than Parada (entry 917) or Newman (entry 915), but in a much more attractive and informative package. Her work is clearly the first choice for students and teachers of mythology. Scholars will sometimes need the greater detail of Newman's charts.

912.   Johnston, Sarah Iles, ed. **Religions of the Ancient World: A Guide.** Harvard University Press Reference Library. Cambridge, MA: Belknap Press of Harvard University Press, 2004. 697pp. ISBN 0–674–01517–7. LCCN 2004–54570.

This guide to religions of the ancient Mediterranean covers Egypt, Mesopotamia, Syria-Canaan, Israel, Anatolia, Iran, Greece, Eturia, and Rome. Chronologically, it ranges from the third millennium B.C. to the fourth century A.D. Johnston rejected a standard encyclopedic approach to offer short essays under three headings. The first, "Encountering Ancient Religions," includes broad topics: what is ancient religion?; monotheism and polytheism; ritual; myth; cosmology; pollution, sin, atonement, and salvation; law and ethics; mysteries; religions in contact; writing and religion; and magic. The second section offers historical surveys by region, with a final essay on early Christianity. The final section is devoted to key topics: sacred times and spaces; religious personnel; religious organizations and bodies; sacrifice, offerings, and votives; prayers, hymns, incantations, and curses; divination and prophecy; deities and demons; religious practices of the individual and family; rites of passage; illness and other crises; death and the afterlife; sin, pollution, and purity; ethics and law codes; theology, theodicy, and philosophy; religion and politics; controlling religion; myth and sacred narratives; visual representations; sacred texts and canonicity; and esotericism and mysticism. Treatment of each topic is subdivided by region, with Christianity usually tacked on at the end. An epilogue looks back and summarizes overall themes. About 140 scholars, including many of the foremost names in their fields, have contributed to this volume. The essays vary in approach but cover their topics well and provide short bibliographies for further study. Their approach to the whole Mediterranean as a region of interrelated cultures that were constantly interacting is a great strengh. The book may be read at length, as well as used to find information and bibliography on a specific topic. A detailed index facilitates finding discussion of specific individuals or topics.

913.   **Lexicon Iconographicum Mythologiae Classicae.** Zurich: Artemis, 1981–1999. 10v. in 18. ISBN 3–760–88751–1. LCCN 82–225552.

Commonly referred to as *LIMC,* this work "is designed to give an account of the present state of knowledge about the iconography of Greek, Etruscan, and Roman mythology from after the Mycenaean period down to the beginning of the early Christian." It is the most comprehensive source of information about the depiction of classical myths in ancient art. Since *LIMC* is a product of international collaboration, articles are written in English, French, German, or Italian according to the author's preference. Articles are arranged alphabetically by the name of the mythical character or event; preference is given to the Greek form if there is one. Each article is in four parts. The introduction gives a brief identification of the mythical character or subject and cites the chief literary sources. The second section is a bibliography. Third is a catalog of depictions of the myth in ancient art. This is exhaustive for early materials or in other cases where little is available; otherwise it is selective. All iconographical types and their variations are noted. Within each iconographical division, arrangement is by cultural area (Greek, Etruscan, Roman), then by medium, and then chronological. The fourth and final section is the iconographical commentary, which offers a brief scholarly study of the development of the iconographical types, chronological relations, and differences between the various types. Articles vary greatly in size, ranging from less than a full column to the length of a short monograph. The longer articles are often subdivided by theme; most of these supply a table of contents as a guide to the user. The illustrations, which consist of good-quality black-and-white plates, equal the text in bulk. This is by far the best source for locating and studying myths as they appear in ancient art. It is aimed chiefly at scholars and advanced students. The more casual seeker of images will probably prefer Rochelle (entry 478).

914. March, Jenny. **Cassell Dictionary of Classical Mythology.** Rev. ed. London: Cassell, 2001. 831pp. ISBN 0–304–35788–X. LCCN 2002–391108.

March has written an A-to-Z dictionary of classical mythology. She covers both major and minor figures, places, and events. While Greek mythology takes pride of place, March does cover Roman mythology as well. Her entries are concise, accurate, and informative; many include references to primary sources. March also provides maps, genealogical tables, a brief list of Greek and Latin authors with brief and sometimes idiosyncratic descriptions, and an excellent selective bibliography. This edition lacks the numerous attractive black-and-white illustrations of mythological scenes from ancient Greek art that appeared in the original edition (1998). There are numerous cross-references. Overall, this is a reliable guide for students and readers. It compares favorably with Grimal (entry 906) but is a bit more popular in nature. Those seeking a narrative treatment might prefer Hard (entry 909).

915. Newman, Harold, and Jon O. Newman. **Genealogical Chart of Greek Mythology: Comprising 3,673 Named Figures of Greek Mythology, All Related to Each Other within a Single Family of 20 Generations.** Chapel Hill: University of North Carolina Press, 2003. 263pp. ISBN 0–8078–2790–8. LCCN 2002–43574.

Chart is not exactly accurate: if one dismembered two copies, it would be possible to assemble a complete chart from 144 pages of genealogical tables. There is also a master chart, which presents only major figures and serves as a visual index to the main chart. The Newmans oversimplify relationships by attempting to fit all 3,673 mythical figures into a single family, often ignoring variants (which can be found in the index). The 95-page index is itself a valuable tool. It notes relationships, provides references to literary sources, and discusses variant family relationships ignored by the chart. For a more detailed discussion see Jenkins, *Bryn Mawr Classical Review* (2005.04.04) at http://ccat.sas.upenn. edu/bmcr/2005/2005–04–04.html. In general students will find James (entry 911) clearer and more helpful, while scholars will prefer this work.

916. North, J.A. **Roman Religion.** New Surveys in the Classics 30. Oxford: Oxford University Press for the Classical Association, 2000. 99pp. ISBN 019–922433–1.

Most works in this series have been bibliographical surveys of recent scholarly trends. North still does this in a sense but actually offers a compact survey of Roman religion itself. His chapters include "Stories of Early Rome"; "The Early Character of Roman Religion"; "The Religion of the Republic and the Empire"; "Gods, Goddesses, and Their

Temples"; "Rituals"; "Innovation and Its Accommodation"; "New Forms"; and "Reading Pagan Texts." Each provides an overview of the current state of scholarship, with references to key primary and secondary sources. North, who has published extensively on this topic, is both readable and reliable. One of the most useful features is the array of tables and charts that provide information on such topics as the major priestly colleges at Rome, the handling of omens and prodigies in the second century, major gods and goddesses, temple foundations, and major festivals. North focuses on the classical religions at Rome; Christianity enters the picture only incidentally. North supplies an excellent selective bibliography, which emphasizes important recent work in English. There is an index.

917. Parada, Carlos. **Genealogical Guide to Greek Mythology.** Studies in Mediterranean Archaeology 107. Jonserad: Paul Åström, 1993. 225pp. ISBN 91–7081–062–1. LCCN 93–248040.

The heart of this work is an alphabetical listing of figures of Greek mythology. Parada supplies the anglicized form of the name, the name in Greek, a brief identification, parents, consorts, children, and manner of death. He also includes extensive references to primary sources. Different mythological characters with the same name appear in roughly chronological order, each given a number to differentiate the entries. Parada uses a number of codes and symbols that will confuse the casual user. Supplementary lists cover divinities, personifications, constellations, objects, and places. Parada includes a very incomplete list of corresponding Greek and Latin words among these lists as well. A large array of genealogical tables and maps conclude the volume. The genealogical tables resemble flow charts rather than traditional genealogies; most will prefer the more straightforward charts in Newman (entry 915) and James (entry 911). Parada and Newman offer similar scope of coverage, although the visually oriented will prefer Newman. James's much smaller chart will best serve most students and readers.

918. Parada, Carlos. **Greek Mythology Link.** URL: http://homepage.mac.com/cparada/GML.

This Web-based reference source is based partly on Parada's *Genealogical Guide to Greek Mythology* (entry 917). Parada offers a great deal of information, mostly based on the ancient sources, although it is not always easy to find the thing wanted. He organizes material into several browsable categories: topics, biographies, groups, and people and places. Links to genealogical tables are found under biographies. Parada also offers A-to-Z dictionary lists for characters and places. In addition, he supplies a search engine. There are many hot links from the various articles, although the indexes do not have direct links. There is also a catalog of images. Parada provides bibliographies that cover the usual suspects plus a few out-of-the-way titles. Extensive primary source references, images, and genealogical information are the great strengths of this site; ease of use is not. It is relatively complete and reliable compared to other mythological resources on the Web.

919. Peterson, Amy T., and David J. Dunworth. **Mythology in Our Midst: A Guide to Cultural References.** Westport, CT: Greenwood, 2004. 234pp. ISBN 0–313–32192–2. LCCN 2004–40433.

This book covers mythologies from a number of cultures, although classical mythology receives the most attention. Peterson and Dunworth offer 50 A-to-Z entries focusing on major mythical characters and their stories, including such figures as Aphrodite, Cronus, Dionysus, Prometheus, and Romulus. Each begins with a brief retelling of the myth. This is followed by examples of the survival of the myth in modern culture: in art, movies, modern fiction, comics, and other media. The entries are superficial, although of some use to those interested in the influence of mythology in popular culture. Of more value are the lists found in the appendixes: mythology in nature, mythology in brand names, mythology in the solar system, and mythology in common words. The bibliography is weak rather than selective; there is an index.

920.   Price, Simon, and Emily Kearns, eds. **Oxford Dictionary of Classical Myth and Religion.** Oxford: Oxford University Press, 2003. 599pp. ISBN 0–19–280288–7.

Yet another of the recent derivatives from the third edition of the *Oxford Classical Dictionary* (entry 142), this volume gathers entries relevant to classical mythology and religion. Price and Kearns have edited the entries somewhat, removing the bibliographies of secondary literature but sometimes adding references to the primary sources. They cover a wide range of Greek and Roman mythology, along with Greek and Roman religion (including sacred places, rites, festivals, and sacred objects). They also offer good coverage of Judaism and early Christianity and selective coverage of Egyptian and other ancient Near Eastern religions. Price and Kearns provide a brief introduction, which includes an annotated bibliography of key works. A thematic index to articles follows. Maps and genealogical tables appear at the end of the volume. A useful volume, but redundant if one has the *OCD*[3].

921.   Reid, Jane Davidson. **The Oxford Guide to Classical Mythology in the Arts, 1300–1990s.** New York: Oxford University Press, 1993. 2v. ISBN 0–19–504998–5. LCCN 92–35374.

Of interest to literary scholars and art historians as well as classicists, Reid's work is an indispensable guide to mythological themes and influences in late medieval, Renaissance, and modern fine arts, music, dance, and literature. It contains more than 200 entries for mythological figures and themes. Each entry gives a brief account of its subject, provides references to the ancient literary sources, and notes any related entries. Works of art depicting the myth are then listed chronologically, with different formats interfiled. Listings include the name of the artist, title of the work, its date, its location or (for literary works) publication information, and a short bibliography. This very full work lists more than 30,000 works of art. Reid also provides an exhaustive index of artists. Those seeking depictions of myth in art predating 1300 will find useful references in Rochelle (entry 478).

922.   Room, Adrian. **NTC's Classical Dictionary: The Origins of the Names of Characters in Classical Mythology.** Lincolnwood, IL: National Textbook, 1992. 343 pp. ISBN 0–8442–5473–8.

Of interest to etymologists and students of myth, this dictionary lists more than 1,000 proper names from classical mythology. Each entry discusses the origin and meaning of the name. There are separate entries for Greek and Roman versions of the same character (e.g., Jupiter and Zeus), since the etymologies and meanings sometimes vary. Appendixes cover such topics as common elements in Greek names and their meanings (mainly prefixes and suffixes), bynames of the major gods and goddesses, and the corresponding names of characters (Greek and Roman equivalents). The content is interesting, if sometimes speculative. An earlier edition appeared under the title *Room's Classical Dictionary* (London: Routledge & Kegan Paul, 1983).

923.   Roscher, W. H., ed. **Ausführliches Lexikon der griechischen und römischen Mythologie.** Leipzig: Teubner, 1884–1937; repr., Hildesheim: Georg Olms, 1992–1993. 6v. in 9. LCCN 01–9584.

924.   Bruchmann, C.H.F. **Epitheta Deorum Quae apud Poetas Graecos Leguntur.** Leipzig: Teubner, 1893. 225pp. LCCN 1–15337.

925.   Carter, J. B. **Epitheta Deorum Quae apud Poetas Latinos Leguntur.** Leipzig: Teubner, 1902. 154pp.

926.   Berger, E. H. **Mythische Kosmographie der Griechen.** Teubner, 1904. 40pp. LCCN 5–15340.

927.   Gruppe, O. **Geschichte der klassischen Mythologie und Religionsgeschichte während des Mittelalters im Abendland und während der Neuzeit.** Leipzig: Teubner, 1921. 248pp. LCCN 21–12060.

Despite the passage of more than a century since the first volume appeared, Roscher's *Lexikon* remains a fundamental reference work for the study of classical mythology. Its many signed articles treat persons, places, peoples, and topics from mythology. It encompasses even the most obscure and minor figures of Greek and Roman myth. The articles, which vary considerably in length, recount what was known about each subject and include full references to the ancient sources and extensive citations of the modern scholarly literature up to the time of writing. No other dictionary of classical mythology is even remotely comparable in size or scope. Although interpretations have changed greatly and our knowledge of a number of myths has increased, most of the information in Roscher remains useful. Four supplementary volumes to the *Lexikon* have appeared as well. These are all monographs, which treat respectively the Greek and Latin epithets of the gods and goddesses, Greek cosmography, and the history of the study of classical myth and religion. These supplements are normally included in reprint editions.

928.   Rose, H. J. **Handbook of Greek Mythology, Including Its Extension to Rome.** 6th ed. London: Methuen, 1958; repr., London: Routledge, 1991. 363pp. LCCN 58–1932.

For those who prefer a more connected approach to myth, Rose is a good alternative to the mythological dictionaries. He covers Greek myth well, Roman myth merely adequately. The book is organized by the various cycles, in their "chronological" order: origins of the world, the children of Kronos, the queens of heaven, the younger gods, lesser and foreign deities, cycles of saga, Troy, legends of the Greek lands, *Märchen* in Greece and Italy, and Italian mythology. Rose does a good job of assenbling the basic stories and citing the primary sources. His style can be rather dry, while his interpretations are generally out-of-date and should be ignored. There are extensive notes and a bibliography. The work also has a good index. The *Routledge Handbook of Greek Mythology* (entry 909) was planned as an updated version of Rose but is really a different work.

929. Schmidt, Joël. **Larousse Greek and Roman Mythology.** Ed. Seth Benardete. New York: McGraw-Hill, 1980. 310pp. ISBN 07–055342–4. LCCN 80–15046.

Another of the many dictionaries of mythology, the *Larousse* provides fairly typical coverage of the characters, events, and places of the classical myths. Its entries tend to be a bit longer than those of Stapleton (entry 930) and Zimmermann (entry 932), but less full than those of Grimal (entry 906). The entries are readable and generally reliable; they do not include any bibliographical references. The work is well illustrated, chiefly with reproductions of ancient paintings and sculptures. Numerous genealogical tables are also provided. A brief listing of the major ancient literary sources for the myths and a detailed index conclude the volume.

930. Stapleton, Michael. **Dictionary of Greek and Roman Mythology.** London: Hamlyn, 1978; repr., New York: Wings Books, 1993. 224pp. ISBN 0–600–36291–4. LCCN 78–316936.

The various printings of this work sometimes include the epithets "concise" or "illustrated" in the title, but all have basically the same content. Stapleton offers brief, readable entries that identify the major characters, places, and events of classical mythology. Aside from occasional broad references to ancient sources, Stapleton provides no bibliographical citations within individual articles. There is a short general bibliography. Some illustrations accompany the text. There is a fairly extensive index of minor characters and place names. This dictionary provides the basic information and is adequate for ready reference; Grimal (entry 906) is a more substantial work.

931. Tripp, Edward. **Crowell's Handbook of Classical Mythology.** New York: Crowell, 1970. 629pp. LCCN 74–127614. Reprinted as *Meridian Handbook of Classical Mythology,* New York: New American Library, 1974, and *Collins Dictionary of Classical Mythology,* Glasgow: HarperCollins, 2002.

Presented in a dictionary format, Tripp's handbook is aimed at the general reader who needs help with mythological allusions in literature. He emphasizes the best-known version of each myth, although he does frequently include significant variants as well. Entries, which range from a few words to several pages, cover mostly characters and places. Topics and events are generally treated as aspects of these. Many entries include references to their major ancient sources. Tripp also supplies maps and a few genealogical tables. The "Pronouncing Index" is not an index as such but provides merely guidance in pronounciation. There are numerous cross-references. Tripp provides a very full and accurate account of the myths and is second only to Grimal (entry 906) for English readers. Grimal's superiority rests mainly upon his much more extensive scholarly apparatus.

932. Zimmerman, J. E. **Dictionary of Classical Mythology.** New York: Harper & Row, 1964; repr., New York: Bantam Books, 1985. 300pp. LCCN 63–20319.

This widely available dictionary of mythology contains approximately 2,100 entries covering people, places, events, and objects. The entries, which are generally quite brief, include a pronunciation guide, a concise identification of the subject, and, occasionally, some reference to the ancient sources. Zimmermann provides cross-references from variant forms, but no index. His dictionary is an adequate and reliable ready-reference tool for students and readers; those who want more detailed information should use Grimal's larger work (entry 906) instead or Tripp (entry 931).

19
Ancillary Disciplines

This chapter covers several important ancillary or subdisciplines of classics, most of which involve deciphering and interpreting primary sources materials. These include epigraphy (the study of inscriptions), numismatics (coins), palaeography (ancient and medieval manuscripts and writing), and papyrology (the study of documents written on papyrus). All of these are specialized and highly technical fields. The works noted below will provide information on the nature and use of such materials, as well as bibliographical guides to each field. The final area covered is the history of classical scholarship and the classical tradition, subjects that illumine not only the development of classical studies, but much of the cultural and intellectual history of the West.

EPIGRAPHY

BIBLIOGRAPHIES

933. Bérard, François, Denis Feissel, Pierre Petitmengin, and Michel Sève. **Guide de l'épigraphiste: Bibliographie choisie des épigraphies antiques et médiévales.** Guides et inventaires bibliographiques 6. 3ième ed. Paris: Editions Rue d'Ulm/Presses de l'École Normale Supérieure, 2000. 428pp. ISBN 2–7288–0254–8. LCCN 2001438185.

Allegedly aimed at beginning students of Greek and Latin epigraphy, this selective bibliography is more aptly described as a guide for advanced graduate students and scholars. The current edition lists 2,600 publications. While the compilers emphasize published editions of inscriptions, they also offer ample coverage of handbooks, bibliographies, and the more important secondary literature. Overall arrangement is by type of work, with subarrangement by place or subject as appropriate. The bibliography provides a good working guide to study of Latin inscriptions through the fall of the western empire (A.D. 476) and Greek inscriptions through the fall of Byzantium (A.D. 1453). The compilers also include a more limited selection of works on "peripheral epigraphies," by which they mean inscriptions in a variety of languages and dialects, such as Minoan, Myceneaean, Egyptian, Coptic, Persian, and Etruscan. Medieval Latin inscriptions of the ninth to fifteenth centuries are also treated under this rubric. Although relatively few entries are annotated, useful notes and comments are scattered throughout the volume. The three indexes cover authors, places, and subjects. A concordance of entry numbers from the second and third editions, and, more importantly, annual supplements can be found at www.antiquite.ens.fr/guide-epigraphiste.html. For a more detailed discussion of this important work, see the review by John Ma at http://ccat.sas.upenn.edu/bmcr/2001/2001–03–08.html.

DICTIONARIES, ENCYCLOPEDIAS, AND HANDBOOKS

934. Bodel, John, ed. **Epigraphic Evidence: Ancient History from Inscriptions.** Approaching the Ancient World. London: Routledge, 2001. 246pp. ISBN 0–415–11623–6; 0–415–11624–4pa. LCCN 00059202.

Bodel provides an excellent introduction to the use of inscriptional evidence for historians and classicists; rather than a discussion on how to do epipgraphy, it is a user's guide to work produced by epigraphers. Bodel himself contributes a broad overview of the field, "Epigraphy and the Ancient Historian," which surveys the nature of Latin and Greek inscriptions, the history of their study, and some of the problems in dealing with them. Other contributors, all accomplished scholars, cover more specific areas: local languages and native cultures, names and identities, family and society, civic and religious life (much more intertwined in ancient times), and inscribed *instrumentum* (tools, utensils, furniture, etc.). The book has a strong focus on the use of inscriptions for social and cultural approaches to history. It also offers guides to common bibliographical abbreviations, editing conventions, and standard publications in the field. Bodel also provides a substantial bibliography, an index of sources, and a general index.

935. Bodel, John, and Stephen Tracy. **Greek and Latin Inscriptions in the U.S.: A Checklist.** New York: American Academy in Rome, 1997. 249pp. ISBN 1–879549–05–0. LCCN 98–235084.

936. **U.S. Epigraphy Project.** URL: http://usepigraphy.rutgers.edu.

Bodel and Tracy offer a preliminary listing of inscriptions found in American collections; unfortunately, many collections failed to report holdings for the volume. Nevertheless, it is a useful tool, listing almost 2,300 inscriptions in 78 collections. As the work is somewhat complex, using the index is essential. Works are arranged by collection (alphabetically by state); codes are assigned to each collection and item. Entries provide basic descriptive information and bibliography. Indeed, the work is useful as a bibliographical tool as well as for locating inscriptions. For a full discussion of the virtues and vices of this work, see the review by Patricia Butz at http://ccat.sas.upenn.edu/bmcr/1998/1998–10–06.html. Bodel is director of the U.S. Epigraphy Project, of which the *Checklist* is a product. The project's Web site includes updates to the *Checklist* and many images of inscriptions in American collections.

937. Gordon, Arthur E. **Illustrated Introduction to Latin Epigraphy.** Berkeley and Los Angeles: University of California Press, 1983. 264pp. 64pp. of plates. ISBN 0–520–03898–3. LCCN 79–63546.

Gordon's work is really a chrestomathy aimed at students with a strong background in Latin and ancient history who need to acquire a working knowledge of Latin epigraphy. His substantial introduction covers such topics as the definition of epigraphy, the provenance of Latin inscriptions, sources and collections, technical matters (abbreviations, Roman names, copying inscriptions), the subject matter of inscriptions, and problems (chiefly palaeography and dating). It also includes an extensive bibliographical section, which describes the major corpora of Latin inscriptions and provides a basic working bibliography. The core of the book is a selection of 100 Latin inscriptions, presented in chronological order. Gordon provides introduction, text, and translation for each. The plate section that follows supplies illustrations for all the selections. The appendixes provide lists of archaic and unusual forms of words along with their classical equivalents and of abbreviations, a basic overview of the Roman calendar and dating systems, and an explanation of conventions used in printing epigraphical texts. There are two indexes, one covering subjects and ancient authors, the other modern authors. Gordon's manual offers a good working introduction to the field for advanced students and scholars. Keppie's informative but less demanding introduction (entry 938) will appeal to those who find Gordon too technical.

938.   Keppie, Lawrence. **Understanding Roman Inscriptions.** Baltimore: Johns Hopkins University Press, 1991. 158pp. ISBN 0–8018–4322–7; 0–8018–4352–9pa. LCCN 91–19853.

Aimed at the nonspecialist, Keppie's work offers an unusually readable introduction to a rather technical field. Several short chapters cover the basics: the ancient stonecutter, reading inscriptions (alphabet, abbreviations, Roman names, numerals, etc.), dating inscriptions, the survival of inscriptions, and their recording and publication (an overview of corpora of inscriptions, basic reference works, and bibliographical sources). Then Keppie uses a topical approach to survey selected inscriptions and demonstrate their uses as historical sources. Many illustrations accompany the text. Appendixes provide a chronological table of Roman emperors, a list of common abbreviations, an overview of the structure of the *Corpus Inscriptionum Latinarum,* and explanations of epigraphical conventions. A good working bibliography and a general index complete the volume. Although Keppie translates all Latin, some knowledge of the language is needed to get full value from his discussion. Those who need a more detailed and scholarly introduction should consult Gordon (entry 937).

939.   Woodhead, A. Geoffrey. **Study of Greek Inscriptions.** 2nd ed. Cambridge: Cambridge University Press, 1981; repr., Norman: University of Oklahoma Press, 1992. 150pp. ISBN 0–521–23188–4; 0–521–23188–4pa. LCCN 80–41198.

Aimed at both students of the classics and professional scholars who need an overview of Greek epigraphy, Woodhead is the standard introduction to the field for readers of English. He surveys all aspects of this highly technical subject in a clear and readable fashion. His chapters cover such topics as editorial conventions in printed editions of inscriptions, the Greek alphabet, the classification and dating of inscriptions, restorations, squeezes and photographs, inscriptions and the history of Greek art, epigraphical publications, and miscellaneous information (numbers, chronology, etc.). The chapter on epigraphical publications is especially useful; it provides an excellent guide to both sources of bibliography and the major corpora of published Greek inscriptions.

NUMISMATICS

BIBLIOGRAPHIES

940.   Christ, Karl. **Antike Numismatik: Einführung und Bibliographie.** Darmstadt: Wissenschaftliche Buchgesellschaft, 1967. 107pp. LCCN 68–080573.

A general survey of ancient numismatics by a noted ancient historian, this work could equally well be treated as a handbook or a bibliography. Its chapters cover general works, Greek numismatics, Hellenistic numismatics, Roman numismatics, and special studies. Various topical subdivisions appear under each. Brief narrative sections, which provide an overview of the various aspects of ancient numismatics, alternate with extensive bibliographical listings. There is a very selective subject index, but no index of authors cited. Although now rather dated, Christ remains an excellent guide to earlier work in the field. For more recent works, see Clain-Steffanelli (entry 941) and the *Survey of Numismatic Research* (entry 942).

941. Clain-Steffanelli, E. E. **Numismatic Bibliography.** München: Battenberg, 1985. 1,848pp. ISBN 3–87045–938–7. LCCN 85–138945.

Although a general bibliography of numismatics, this work offers the most comprehensive and up-to-date bibliographical treatment of Greek and Roman numismatics available in a single volume. Clain-Steffanelli lists 3,388 books, dissertations, articles, and catalogs dealing with the coinage of the classical world. Separate chapters cover Greece and Rome. Each begins with a section on general works and conludes with special topics (prices, coin types and iconongraphy, minting techniques, etc.). Aside from these, the Greek material is arranged geographically, and the Roman chronologically. Clain-Steffanelli occasionally adds a note to clarify content; otherwise, entries are not annotated. She also provides numerous cross-references. The extensive indexes cover authors, personal names, collectors, geographical terms, numismatic terms, and public collections. This bibliography is useful to those interested in economic history as well as ancient coinage. Those seeking more recent bibliography should also consult the *Survey of Numismatic Research* (entry 942).

942. **Survey of Numismatic Research.** Copenhagen: International Numismatic Commission, 1967– .

The *Survey* consists of bibliographies covering six-year intervals, beginning with 1960–1965. The most recent, published in 2003, covers 1996–2001. While these volumes cover numismatic research broadly, more than half of the space is usually devoted to ancient numismatics (Greece, Rome, and adjacent regions). A typical volume includes a number of bibliographical surveys, which offer both a narrative overview and a detailed bibliography. These cover regions, periods, and topics. Most surveys are in English, but some are in French or German. An index of authors is provided. Collectively, the *Survey* provides the most complete bibliography of ancient numismatic research for the last 40 years. Clain-Stefanelli (entry 941) is a more user-friendly work and offers more retrospective coverage but is not as up-to-date.

943. Vermeule, Cornelius C. **Bibliography of Applied Numismatics in the Fields of Greek and Roman Archaeology and the Fine Arts.** London: Spink, 1956. 172pp. LCCN 58–3889.

Vermeule is chiefly concerned with the use of coins in the study of Greek and Roman art, archaeology, and history. His 1,328 entries, which include both books and articles, are drawn from a wide range of publications in the fields of archaeology, history, and numismatics. He arranges these by author under several broad subject headings. Brief annotations accompany many of the entries. These useful notes are chiefly descriptive but occasionally criticize the work in question or provide hints as to its possible use. In the case of books, they also note important reviews. There is a selective index of subjects. This bibliography is especially helpful to students of antiquity who are not themselves numismatists but work in areas in which coins provide important source material.

DICTIONARIES, ENCYCLOPEDIAS, AND HANDBOOKS

944. Burnett, Andrew, Michel Amandry, and Pere Pau Ripollès. **Roman Provincial Coinage.** London: British Museum Press; Paris: Bibliothèque Nationale,1992– . ISBN 0–7141–0871–5 (set, BMP); 0–2–7177–1845–1 (set, BN), 0–7141–0894–4 (suppl. 1, BMP); 2717720499 (suppl. 1, BN). LCCN 99–183862.

So far only the first volume of this set, which covers 44 B.C. to A.D. 69, has been issued, along with a supplement. A revised reprint of the first volume appeared in 1998. The authors aim to remedy the somewhat narrow focus of *Roman Imperial Coinage* (entry 950) by offering coverage of provincial coinage (including that of many client kingdoms) produced under the empire, particularly in the eastern half. *RPC* is primarily based on 11 major collections in Europe and America, with some consideration given to others. The first volume includes a substantial introduction with chapters on authority and magistrates, the production and circulation of coins in the provinces, denominations, designs and legends, emperors and the imperial family, and emperors and the provincial coinage. The catalog is arranged geographically by province, moving roughly west to east. Each province is subdivided by city. After brief introductions, coins are listed chronologically. Entries include metal, measurements, weight, museum accession/inventory numbers, legends, and descriptions. Some 5,467 coins are listed for the late republic and the Julio-Claudian era. Numerous bibliographical references are provided throughout; indexes and plates may be found in the second part of the volume. Presumably future volumes will follow the same pattern as the first. When complete, this work and *Roman Imperial Coinage* (entry 950) will offer a very complete reference guide to all coinage under the Roman Empire for both historians and numismatists.

945. Cape, Robert W., Jr., ed. **Virtual Catalog of Roman Coins.** URL: http://artemis. austincollege.edu/acad/cml/rcape/vcrc/index.html.

This Web site includes many resources for the study of ancient coins. As the name indicates, this is an online catalog of Roman coins, with reasonably good-quality images and descriptions; this is arranged chronologically. While not as complete as the great printed catalogs, it is readily available. There are also many links to Internet resources on ancient numismatics, including academic sites, dealers, and the American Numismatic Society. Since the primary purpose of the site is educational, it also includes teaching materials and student projects. Overall it is a very useful starting point for those researching Roman coins on the Internet.

946. Carson, R.A.G. **Coins of the Roman Empire.** London: Routledge, 1990. 367pp. ISBN 0–415–01591–X. LCCN 89–6207.

Carson, a former keeper of coins and medals at the British Museum, provides an excellent account of Roman imperial coinage that is suitable for students and general readers as well as scholars. He covers gold, silver, and the principal bronze coins from

Augustus to Anastasius (A.D. 498). The first part of the book is a historical survey, which proceeds emperor by emperor. The second part deals with such topics as metals, coin production, mints, and forgeries. Carson focuses on the broader issues; those who want details on particular coins will probably need to consult Sear (entries 954–955) or the monumental *Roman Imperial Coinage* (entry 950). Carson's work includes an extensive section of plates, a substantial bibliography, and a detailed index.

947.   Crawford, Michael H. **Roman Republican Coinage.** Cambridge: Cambridge University Press, 1974. 2v. ISBN 0–521–07492–4. LCCN 77–164450.

Crawford is widely regarded as the standard handbook on coinage of the Roman Republic. His introduction provides a history of coinage at Rome from the beginnings through the first century B.C. The bulk of his first volume is a catalog of known Roman Republican coin types in chronological sequence. Entries give mint, date, description, legends (if any), and references to museum holdings and the secondary literature. Plates may be found in the second volume, which also includes studies of technique and technology, weight standards, moneyers, special issues, administration and control of coining, denominations, coinage and finance, types and legends, and art and coinage. Crawford also includes concordances between this work and other standard handbooks, a substantial bibliography, and an array of indexes covering types, legends, sources, persons, and subjects. Beginners may find Sear (entry 955), Vagi (entry 957), and Sutherland (entry 956) less daunting; scholars will find Crawford indispensable.

948.   Howgego, Christopher. **Ancient History from Coins.** Approaching the Ancient World. London: Routledge, 1995. 176pp. ISBN 0–415–08992–1; 0–415–08993–X. LCCN 95007596.

Howgego has written an introduction both to Greco-Roman numismatics and to the use of ancient coins as historical evidence. He covers the period from the earliest coinage (ca. 600 B.C.) to the reign of Diocletian. The first two chapters cover money and minting. The next two cover coins as political and imperial propaganda, while the final two cover coins as evidence for trade and economic history. Howgego provides numerous charts, maps, and illustrations. There is also a good bibliography and a general index.

949.   Jenkins, G. K. **Ancient Greek Coins.** 2nd ed. London: Seaby, 1990. 182pp. ISBN 1–85264–014–6. LCCN 91–148548.

Aimed at a general audience, this richly illustrated work offers a general account of Greek coins from the Archaic period to the time of the Roman conquest. Jenkins employs period divisions for his overall arrangement: Archaic, fifth century B.C., fourth century B.C., and Hellenistic. Within each of these he then organizes his material geographically. His narrative covers both technical and artistic developments and supplies much historical background as well. A glossary, a strong bibliography, and a general index complete the work. While this is a good introduction to the subject, those interested in identifying and studying individual coins will want to consult Sear's catalog (entry 953).

950.   Mattingly, Harold, E. A. Sydenham, C.H.V. Sutherland, and R.A.G. Carson. **Roman Imperial Coinage.** London: Spink, 1923–1981. 9v. in 12. LCCN 24–14275; rev. ed., London: Spink, 1984– . ISBN 0–907605–09–5.

The standard reference work on coins of the Roman Empire, this work was begun in 1923 and completed in 1981; Sutherland and Carson began a revised edition in 1984, of which only the first volume has appeared thus far. Unlike Sear (entry 955) and Vagi (entry 957), this work is aimed primarily at scholars, although serious collectors also find it of great value. The editors represent a who's who of twentieth-century British numismatists concerned with ancient coins. Mattingly and company cover Roman coins from Augustus (31 B.C.) to Theodosius I (A.D. 395). The vast work progresses chronologically emperor by emperor. Under each is introductory matter covering chronology, mints, types of coins, forgeries, and other topics as relevant, followed by a catalog of coins. The catalog is arranged by place, with extensive descriptive information and references. Plates appear at the end of each volume.

951. Melville Jones, John. **Dictionary of Ancient Greek Coins.** London: Seaby, 1986. 248pp. ISBN 0–900652–81–0. LCCN 87–37888.

Melville Jones, a respected authority on ancient numismatics, compiled this work with the needs of coin collectors and students of ancient history in mind, although scholars also will find it a handy reference work. He treats Greek coins issued under the Roman Empire, as well as the earlier issues. The dictionary covers people, places, and subjects found on coins; technical terms; metals and mining; and metrology and weight standards. In addition, there are a number of entries on coin collecting, which treat the history and terminology of the hobby and provide brief biographies of famous collectors. While individual entries do not include bibliographies, a brief list of the most important general works on Greek and Roman coins appears at the front of the dictionary. A companion volume covers Roman coins (entry 952).

952. Melville Jones, John. **Dictionary of Ancient Roman Coins.** London: Seaby, 1990. 329pp. ISBN 1–85264–026–X. LCCN 91–155684.

In this companion work to his *Dictionary of Ancient Greek Coins* (entry 951) Melville Jones treats Roman coinage from the earliest Republican issues to the beginning of the reign of Anastasius I (A.D. 491). As in the earlier work, entries cover coin types, technical terms, weights and measures, and mining and metals. Melville Jones also devotes some space to the history of collecting Roman coins. While aimed at a broad general audience, his concise and informative entries will also be of use to scholars. Melville Jones does not provide a bibliography; rather he refers the reader to the bibliographical note in his earlier *Dictionary*. A third volume on Byzantine coinage is projected.

953. Sear, David R. **Greek Coins and Their Values.** London: Seaby, 1978–1979. 2v. ISBN 0–900652–46–2 (v. 1); 0–900652–50–0 (v. 2). LCCN 79–309601.

Aimed at hobbyists, this work is also useful for those with a more serious interest in Greek coins or history. Sear covers Greek coinage from its beginnings down to the time of the Roman conquest. The first volume covers the Greek coins of Europe (the northern shore of the Mediterranean from Spain to Greece), while the second deals with the coinage of Greek cities in Asia and North Africa. Both volumes have essentially the same front matter: a brief history of Greek coins, a discussion of coin types, information on the principal deities found on Greek coins, weight standards and denominations, the dating of Greek coins, a bibliography, and a glossary. Sear arranges the actual catalogs geographically,

Under each city he makes entries for every distinct coin known to have been issued. These include a detailed description, dates, references to standard works on Greek coins, and an approximate value. The values, which are ephemeral, can be ignored. There are many illustrations. Each volume has a detailed index, which includes geographical names, rulers, and deities. Sear is useful for identifying coins and finding information about them. Those who seek a more connected history of Greek coins rather than a catalog should use Jenkins (entry 949) instead.

954.   Sear, David R. **Greek Imperial Coins and Their Values: The Local Coinages of the Roman Empire.** London: Seaby, 1982. 636pp. ISBN 0–900652–59–4. LCCN 82–145157.

In this work Sear lists and describes coins issued by the Greek cities of the eastern Roman Empire. His introductory material includes discussion of the types of coins and the inscriptions of Greek imperial coins, their denominations and marks of value, and their dating. There is also a short bibliography. Sear divides the catalog into three parts: the actual Greek imperial coinage (chronological by emperor from Augustus to Diocletian); the quasi-autonomous coinages of Greek cities (arranged geographically); and "contemporary coinage," the coins issued by independent kingdoms and client states of the empire. The 6,034 numbered entries include detailed descriptions of the coins, their dates of issue, references to the standard works on ancient Greek numismatics, and values. Many illustrations accompany the text. A list of Greek mints, several maps, and a very selective index conclude the work. Sear is a useful reference both for coin collectors and scholars.

955.   Sear, David R. **Roman Coins and Their Values.** Millennium edition. London: Spink, 2000– . 3v. ISBN 1–902040–35–X. LCCN 89–135362.

A standard work on Roman coins aimed primarily at collectors, Sear's catalog covers both the republican and imperial eras; the first volume covers the republic and the 12 Caesars (280 B.C.–A.D. 96), and the second Nerva through the Severans (A.D. 96–235). A projected third volume is to cover A.D. 235–491; until this appears one must still consult the old fourth edition (1988) for the later empire. The extensive introduction includes discussion of the denominations of Roman coins, reverse types, mints and mint marks, and the dating of coins. The catalog proper is organized chronologically. Entries include a full description, date, bibliographical references, and estimated value. Sear provides many illustrations and a bibliography. Each volume contains a selective index. For treatment of Greek coinage under the empire, one should consult his companion work (entry 954). Those who want a history of Roman coinage rather than a catalog of coins will prefer Sutherland (entry 956) or Carson (entry 946).

956.   Sutherland, C.H.V. **Roman Coins.** World of Numismatics. New York: Putnam, 1974. 311pp. ISBN 0–399–11239–1. LCCN 73–81400.

Sutherland, an eminent British numismatist, provides a general history of Roman coins from the earliest known issues of the republic through the reign of Romulus Augustulus (A.D. 476). The broad historical narrative gives attention both to technical and artistic developments in Roman coinage. Many illustrations accompany the text. The work is suitable for students and general readers as well as numismatists and historians.

It includes a brief bibliography, a glossary, and a general index. Although Sutherland offers the best overall account of Roman coins for nonspecialists, Carson (entry 946) supplies both a more recent and more detailed history of imperial coinage. Those who want information on specific coins might also consult Sear's work (entry 955). Specialists will prefer Crawford (entry 947) on republican coinage and *Roman Imperial Coinage* (entry 950) for the empire.

957.   Vagi, David L. **Coinage and History of the Roman Empire, c. 82 B.C.–A.D. 480.** Chicago: Fitzroy Dearborn, 2000. 2v. ISBN 1–57958–316–4.

This reference work on Roman coins is aimed at both historians and collectors. The first volume covers the history of Rome from the time of Sulla to the death of Julian Nepos. Vagi does this largely through biographies of the individuals portrayed on coins (emperors and their families from Augustus on). These are arranged in 13 chapters by period; the final two chapters (A.D. 364 and after) cover the eastern and western empires respectively. Vagi provides an historical overview for each chapter. Each biography gives the dates of the individual, family relationships, and a narrative of the individual's life; a brief numismatic note follows. A brief general bibliography and an index conclude the volume. The second volume includes a lengthy numismatic introduction covering the history of Roman coinage, typical inscriptions and portraits, denominations, dates, abbreviations, mints, coin production, and so on. The second and largest part of the volume is a catalog of Roman coins, arranged by individual portrayed (in chronological order). Vagi describes the various coins under each and provides approximate values as of 1999. He lists 3,845 coins, each numbered consecutively. There are numerous illustrations. Vagi also includes a concordance to the numbering of some other standard works on Roman coins, a bibliography, and an index.

PALAEOGRAPHY

BIBLIOGRAPHIES

958.   Boyle, Leonard E. **Medieval Latin Palaeography: A Bibliographical Introduction.** Toronto Medieval Bibliographies 8. Toronto: University of Toronto Press, 1984. 399pp. ISBN 0–8020–5612–1; 0–8020–6558–9pa. LCCN 85–157656.

Although primarily aimed at medievalists, this bibliography is of considerable value to anyone interested in the transmission of classical Latin literature and Latin palaeography. A leading scholar in the field (and a former prefect of the Vatican Library), Father Boyle modestly claims in the preface that the work is aimed only at beginners. This is not entirely true, since even specialists will find it a useful tool. Father Boyle has arranged his material in eight broad subject categories (with many subdivisions), which cover bibliographical and general works, the scripts, libraries, writing materials, scribes, the transmission and editing of texts, and research aids (general reference works). Many entries are accompanied by descriptive and evaluative annotations. In addition to a detailed general index, there is a special index of manuscripts.

959.   Braswell, Susan. **Western Manuscripts from Classical Antiquity to the Renaissance: A Handbook.** Garland Reference Library of the Humanities 139. New York: Garland, 1981. 382pp. ISBN 0–8240–9541–3. LCCN 79–7908.

The misleading subtitle of this book conceals a bibliography. Braswell covers all Western manuscripts, not just classical ones, through the Renaissance. She employs a topical arrangement, with chapters on such topics as bibliographical materials; libraries; microforms; incipits; special subjects; indexes, lists, catalogs, and *repertoria;* palaeography; diplomatics and archives; codicology; manuscripts and their contents; and textual criticism. Braswell provides descriptive annotations for most entries. Those interested in the history and transmission of classical texts will find much of interest in this volume. However, anyone with specific interests in Latin palaeography would do well to consult Father Boyle's more specialized (and more learned) bibliography (entry 958).

960. Kristeller, Paul Oskar. **Latin Manuscript Books Before 1600: A List of the Printed and Unpublished Inventories of Extant Collections.** Monumenta Germaniae Historica. Hilfsmittel 13. 4th ed., rev. and enl. by Sigrid Krämer. Munich: Monumenta Germaniae Historica, 1993. 941pp. ISBN 3–88612–113–5.

Now in its fourth edition, this well-known work is a fundamental resource for anyone interested in classical, medieval, or Renaissance manuscripts. This edition covers works published through the summer of 1992. Its first section notes general works that give bibliographical or statistical information about manuscript collections; this part does not, as a rule, contain manuscript catalogs. The second section lists manuscript catalogs that cover libraries in more than one city. Both of these sections are arranged alphabetically by author or title. Catalogs and inventories of individual libraries are found in the third section; these are arranged alphabetically by city. The final section lists directories and guides to libraries and archives. Brief annotations accompany some entries. The lack of indexes is inexplicable.

961. Richard, Marcel. **Répertoire des bibliothèques et des catalogues de manuscrits grecques.** Publications de l'Institut de recherche et d'histoire des textes 1. 2ième ed. Paris: Centre National de la Recherche Scientifique, 1958. 276pp. LCCN 68–33492.

962. Richard, Marcel. **Répertoire des bibliothèques et des catalogues de manuscrits grecques. Supplément I (1958–1963).** Documents, études, et répertoires publiées par l'Institut de recherche et d'histoire des textes 9. Paris: Centre National de la Recherche Scientifique, 1964. 76pp.

These two volumes comprise the standard bibliography of catalogs and inventories of Greek manuscripts. Richard divides each volume into four sections: bibliography, specialized catalogs, regional catalogs, and cities and other places. The bibliography sections include only a few general works, which are arranged chronologically. Specialized catalogs, which are organized by topic, include catalogs of manuscripts on specific subjects, such as alchemy or medicine. The other sections are arranged by place. Richard includes both books and articles. Many of the entries are annotated; some of these notes include additional information about the manuscript collections that various scholars and librarians supplied directly to Richard. Each volume concludes with a detailed index.

DICTIONARIES, ENCYCLOPEDIAS, AND HANDBOOKS

963. **Abbreviationes.** Version 2.3. URL: www.ruhr-uni-bochum.de/philosophy/projects/abbrev.htm.

Originally produced as a CD-ROM and still available in that format, this searchable database of Medieval Latin abbreviations is now also accessible through the Web. It includes far more abbreviations than the works of Cappelli (entry 965) and Pelzer (entry 966) more than 70,000 as of January 2005. *Abbreviationes* allows users to look up all the abbreviations for a given Latin word or to identify the meaning(s) of abbreviations found in manuscripts or early printed books. The database also provides information about when and where particular abbreviations were used. A valuable tool for anyone studying Latin manuscripts.

964. Bischoff, Bernhard. **Latin Palaeography: Antiquity and the Middle Ages.** Trans. Dáibhí O Cróinín and David Ganz. Cambridge: Cambridge University Press, 1990. 291pp. ISBN 0–521–36473–6; 0–521–36726–3pa. LCCN 88–34649.

Translated from the second edition of *Paläographie des romischen Altertums und des abendländischen Mittelalters* (Berlin: Erich Schmidt, 1986), this handbook is the product of one of the foremost Latin palaeographers of the twentieth century. Bischoff covers all aspects of his subject: writing materials and tools, codicology, writing and copying, the history of Latin scripts from the earliest surviving examples through the Renaissance, and the role of manuscripts in cultural history. The text is both readable and authoritative. Numerous illustrations and an extensive bibliography round out the work.

965. Cappelli, Adriano. **Lexicon Abbreviaturum: Dizionario di abbreviature latine ed italiane usate nelle carte e codici specialmente del medio-evo riprodotte con oltre 14000 segni incisi, con l'aggiunta du uno studio sulla brachigrafia medioevale, un prontuario di sigle epigrafiche, l'antica numerazione romana ed arabica ed i segni indicanti monete, pesi, misure, etc.** 6a ed., corr. Milano: Ulrico Hoepli, 1973. 531pp. ISBN 88–203–1100–3.966 Pelzer, Auguste. **Abréviations latines médiévales: Supplément au Dizionario di abbreviature latine ed italiane de Adriano Cappelli.** 2ième éd. Louvain: Publications Universitaires, 1966; repr., Bruxelles: Éditions Nauwelaerts, 1982. 86pp. LCCN 68–114011.

Cappelli is the standard dictionary of Latin abbreviations found in manuscripts. His work is sometimes useful for deciphering abbreviations in early printed books as well. The work begins with an introductory discussion of medieval shorthand and abbreviations. The dictionary of abbreviations proper follows. Entries consist of reproductions of the abbreviations in the original scripts, a printed transcription, and the resolution. Cappelli appends several additional lists to the dictionary. These include conventional signs, roman numerals, arabic numerals, and epigraphic abbreviations. The first three again include reproductions of the abbreviations in the original scripts. The epigraphic abbreviations are printed. A substantial bibliography closes the work. Although Cappelli has appeared in a number of editions, there is not much difference between them and, most will serve equally well. Pelzer's supplement notes a number of additional abbreviations.

967. Oikonomides, Al. N., comp. **Abbreviations in Greek Inscriptions, Papyri, Manuscripts, and Early Printed Books.** Chicago: Ares, 1974. 204pp. LCCN 75–302478.

In this volume Oikonomides reprints several valuable works on Greek abbreviations. These include M. Avi-Yonah's *Abbreviations in Greek Inscriptions* (Jerusalem: Government of Palestine, 1940), excerpts from Sir Frederic Kenyon's *Palaeography of*

Greek Papyri (London: Clarendon Press, 1899), T. W. Allen's *Notes on Abbreviations in Greek Manuscripts* (Oxford: Clarendon Press, 1889), and excerpts on abbreviations in early printed Greek books from the *Manual of Foreign Languages for the Use of Printers and Translators* (3rd ed., Washington, DC: U.S. Government Printing Office, 1936). Together these provide a good basic guide to Greek abbreviations for anyone working with inscriptions, manuscripts, or early printed materials.

968.   Thompson, Edward Maunde. **Handbook of Greek and Latin Palaeography.** International Scientific Series. 3rd ed. London: K. Paul, Trench, Trübner, 1906; repr., Chicago: Ares, 1980. 361pp. LCCN 11–513.

969.   Thompson, Edward Maunde. **Introduction to Greek and Latin Palaeography.** Oxford: Clarendon Press, 1912; repr., New York: Burt Franklin, 1973. 600pp. LCCN 13–9740.

These two works by Thompson, who was for many years director and principal librarian of the British Museum, have long been the standard manuals on the subject for English-speaking students. Though now rather dated, they remain useful. For Greek palaeography, Thompson is still the only general manual available in English. The *Handbook* is the earlier work. It first covers a number of general topics: the Greek and Latin alphabets, writing materials, the forms of books in antiquity, shorthand and cryptography, abbreviations, and numerals. Then a series of chapters surveys Greek and Latin scripts of antiquity and the Middle Ages. Thompson provides many examples of the various scripts. There is a bibliography and index. The *Introduction* is actually an expanded version of the *Handbook*. It generally follows the same plan as the earlier work but includes much more material. In particular, the *Introduction* has many more and better illustrations of the ancient scripts than does the *Handbook*. Its bibliography is also fuller. While Bischoff's authoritative treatment of Latin palaeography (entry 964) to some extent supersedes Thompson, there is no more-current manual available in English for Greek palaeography.

PAPYROLOGY

BIBLIOGRAPHIES

See also *Bibliographie papyrologique* (entry 48), *Electronic Bibliographie papyrologique* (entry 49), and *Subsidia Papryologica* (entry 50).

970.   Oates, John F., Roger S. Bagnall, Sarah J. Clackson, Alexandra A. O'Brien, Joshua A. Sosin, Terry G. Wilfong, and Klaas A. Worp. **Checklist of Editions of Greek, Latin, Demotic and Coptic Papyri, Ostraca, and Tablets.** BASP Supplements 9. 5th ed. Oakville, CT: American Society of Papyrologists, 2001. 121pp. ISBN 1–55540–782–X. LCCN 92–33810.

971.   Oates, John F., Roger S. Bagnall, Sarah J. Clackson, Alexandra A. O'Brien, Joshua A. Sosin, Terry G. Wilfong, and Klaas A. Worp. **Checklist of Editions of Greek,**

Latin, Demotic and Coptic Papyri, Ostraca, and Tablets. URL: http://scriptorium.lib. duke.edu/papyrus/texts/clist.html.

The purpose of this work is "to provide for scholars and librarians a ready bibliography of all monographic volumes, both current and out-of-print, of Greek, Latin, Demotic and Coptic documentary texts written on papyrus, parchment, ostraca, or wood tablets." Early editions covered primarily Greek and Latin texts; the fifth expands coverage to Coptic and Demotic texts as well. The focus is chiefly on documentary texts; literary texts are included, but there was no systematic effort to cover these exhaustively, since they can be found in Pack^2 (entry 972) and Mertens-Pack^3 (entry 973). The *Checklist* serves several additional purposes as well. It supplies a standard list of abbreviations for papyrological publications. It also serves as a canon of volumes containing documentary texts that have been or will be entered in the *Duke Databank of Documentary Papyri* (entry 976). As in earlier editions, the *Checklist* notes whether each volume is currently in print and provides information about publishers. Guides are also provided to corpora of texts, monographic series, periodicals (both current and ceased), and the proceedings of international congresses. An innovation with the fourth and following editions is a list of *instrumenta,* which is a guide to reference tools for papyrology. The Web edition is continually updated. While chiefly of interest to working papyrologists, the *Checklist* is an indispensable resource for anyone who must traverse this thicket of highly technical publications and arcane abbreviations.

972. Pack, Roger A. **Greek and Latin Literary Texts from Greco-Roman Egypt.** 2nd rev. and enl. ed. Ann Arbor: University of Michigan Press, 1965. 165pp. LCCN 65–10786.

973. Mertens, Paul, and Roger A. Pack. **La base de données expérimentale Mertens-Pack^3.** URL: http://promethee.philo.ulg.ac.be/cedopal.

Pack is a repertory of all Greek and Latin literary texts (defined broadly as all non-documentary texts) that have been preserved in Egypt. It includes texts preserved on papyrus, parchment, ostraca, and wooden tablets. Pack lists Greek texts first, then the Latin ones. Under each language, he divides texts into those identified by author (arranged A–Z) and *adespota* (arranged by genre). Pack also adds a separate category under Latin for legal texts. For works of known authorship Pack identifies the passage, cites the edition, and gives the date, provenance, and material of the manuscript. He also cites any additional scholarly literature. For *adespota* Pack characterizes the passage by form and subject matter; cites the original publication; gives the date, provenance, and material; and notes other relevant studies. Pack was long the standard bibliography of literary papyri; scholars often cite the texts by their Pack number. Paul Mertens has created an greatly expanded online database based on Pack. The printed edition of Pack^2 included 3,026 entries; Mertens-Pack^3 includes over 6,000 entries. It continues the numbering system of Pack and provides access by author and (to a limited extent) genre.

DICTIONARIES, ENCYCLOPEDIAS, AND HANDBOOKS

974. **APIS: Advanced Papyrological Information System.** URL: www.columbia. edu/cgi-bin/cul/resolve?ATK2059.

This Web site is a collaboration among most of the major papyrological collections in the United States, including Columbia, Duke, Princeton, the University of California at Berkeley, the University of Chicago, the University of Michigan, the University of Toronto, and Yale. It provides a searchable database of papyri from these institutions, including most published and some unpublished texts. It is possible to find descriptions, images, translations, and publication histories for the papyri. The site also includes links to numerous online resources for papyrology: the home pages of the various collections, bibliographies, journals, and so forth.

975. Bagnall, Roger S. **Reading Papyri, Writing Ancient History.** Approaches to the Ancient World. London: Routledge, 1995. 145pp. ISBN 0–415–09376–7; 0–415–09377–5pa. LCCN 95004136.

Bagnall has written a guide for ancient historians who need to use evidence from papyri. His first two chapters provide an overview of the physical nature of papyri, their geographic distribution, the nature of their contents, and the types of papyrus documents found in Greco-Roman Egypt. The following chapters offer a number of case studies in which papyri were used as historical evidence. Bagnall concludes by discussing the kinds of questions that historians can and should ask of papyri. He also provides an excellent working bibliography. Bagnall is the most useful of the works listed here for those seeking to use and understand papyri as historical documents. Those interested in more technical aspects should refer to the works of Turner (entries 980–981) and Pestman (entry 979).

976. **Duke Databank of Documentary Papyri.** URL: www.perseus.tufts.edu/cache/perscoll_DDBDP.html.

Begun by John F. Oates and the late William H. Willis at Duke University in 1982, this is a searchable database of documentary texts on papyri, ostraca, and wooden tablets. More than 500 volumes of published texts are now included. The texts are in Greek and Latin, and most are highly technical in nature, so this is a work for specialists. The database is freely available through the *Perseus* project (entry 137).

977. Gallo, Italo. **Greek and Latin Papyrology.** Classical Handbook 1. Trans. Maria Rosaria Falivene and Jennifer R. March. London: Institute of Classical Studies, University of London, 1986. 153pp. ISBN 0–900587–50–4. LCCN 90–159964.

Intended primarily for graduate students in classics, Gallo's handbook provides a concise overview of the major aspects of papyrology. A series of short chapters cover such topics as writing materials in antiquity, papyrology as an academic discipline, the Herculaneum papyri, literary papyri, documentary papryi, the dating and handwriting of papyri, and editorial conventions. Gallo also provides a reasonably good basic bibliography. His work will serve to provide a basic introduction to the field, although most will find Turner's classic work (entry 981) more readable and informative.

978. Montevecchi, Orsolina. **La Papirologia.** Rev. ed. Milano: Vita e Pensiero, 1988. 620, 184pp. ISBN 88–343–6910–6. LCCN 89–183062.

In spite of its title, Montevecchi's handbook deals exclusively with documentary papyri. She supplies information on the physical nature and history of papyri, the history of papyrology as a field, palaeography, chronology, metrology, and language. Montevecchi also covers the geography, history, and administration of Greco-Roman Egypt, types of papyrus documents, religions, schools, and culture. Lastly, she gives detailed lists of collections, periodicals and congresses, repertories of dated manuscripts, and abbreviations. An especially valuable feature is the large collection of plates at the end of the volume. Montevecchi is the most comprehensive single volume on documentary papyrology. Those who do not read Italian should consult Turner (entry 981), Gallo (entry 977), and Pestman (entry 979).

979.   Pestman, P. W. **New Papyrological Primer.** 2nd ed., rev. Leiden: Brill, 1994. 318pp. ISBN 90–04–10019–9.

This is the latest version of M. David and B. A. van Groningen's original *Papyrological Primer*, which first appeared in Dutch in 1940 and in English in 1946. It is an excellent handbook for any classicist who needs to learn the basics of papyrology. The lengthy introduction provides an overview of the history of the discipline, the history of Greco-Roman Egypt, methods of dating and calendars, forms of documents, money, measures, and so forth. The bulk of the work is a chrestomathy of 81 typical Ptolemaic and Roman documents on papyrus, with introductions and notes. These include such gems as a marriage contract; a letter to a wet nurse; and documents relating to the sale of a house, the circumcision of a priest's child, and an engagement of castanet dancers. Primarily of use to those with a good command of Greek.

980.   Turner, E. G. **Greek Manuscripts of the Ancient World.** Bulletin Supplement 46. 2nd ed., rev. and enl. Ed. P. J. Parsons. London: Institute of Classical Studies, University of London, 1987. 174pp. SBN 900587–48–2.

Originally published in 1971 as a companion to *Greek Papyri* (entry 981), this classic work was updated by Peter Parsons in 1987. The introduction discusses Greek palaeography as applied to papyri. The bulk of the work is a large collection of plates. Some illustrate scribes, writing implements, and the physical structure of papyrus. Most are papyri of famous literary texts. Each is accompanied by a commentary, including a partial transcription and a brief bibliography.

981.   Turner, E. G. **Greek Papyri: An Introduction.** Rev. ed. Oxford: Clarendon Press, 1980. 225pp. ISBN 0–19–914841–0. LCCN 80–40987.

Aimed at students of the classics and the interested lay reader, Turner's classic work provides an eminently readable overview of papyrology. He covers successively the nature of books and writing in antiquity, the history of papyrology as a discipline, the editing of papyri, and the importance of papyri both for social and cultural history and for the study of Greek literature. Several maps, an extensive bibliographical apparatus, and an index of names complete the book. In spite of Gallo's more recent handbook (entry 977), Turner remains the basic work for English readers. Pestman (entry 979) is a hands-on manual for those who want to learn to read and understand papyri in the original languages. Those who are interested primarily in documentary papyri and can read Italian might also consult with profit O. Montevecchi, *La Papirologia* (entry 978). Those seeking more information on the palaeography of Greek papyri and illustrations of papyri should also consult Turner's companion work, *Greek Manuscripts of the Ancient World* (entry 980).

TEXTUAL TRANSMISSION AND CRITICISM

982. Reynolds, L.D., and Nigel Wilson. **Scribes and Scholars: A Guide to the Transmision of Greek and Latin Literature.** 3rd ed. Oxford: Clarendon Press, 1991. 321pp. ISBN 0–19–872145–5; 0–19–872146–3pa. LCCN 90–41300.

Designed for beginning graduate students, this work is the only accessible introduction in English to the transmission of the classics from antiquity to the modern era. Reynolds and Wilson describe the nature of the ancient manuscript book and its copying, editing, and preservation from antiquity through the Renaissance. They also discuss the editing of printed editions of the classics during the Renaissance and later periods and introduce the reader to the rudiments of textual criticism. In the course of this they cover many of the high points in the history of classical scholarship. Their notes provide extensive references to the scholarly literature. Reynolds and Wilson offer an exceptionally lively and readable account of a subject too often considered dry and technical.

983. Reynolds, L.D., ed. **Texts and Transmission: A Survey of the Latin Classics.** Oxford: Clarendon Press, 1983. 509pp. ISBN 0–19–814456–3. LCCN 84–148890.

In this somewhat technical work, Reynolds and his collaborators present concise accounts of the transmissions of the texts of Latin authors from antiquity to the modern era. Reynolds covers all authors and texts from the beginnings of Latin literature down to Apuleius that had their own independent transmission. A selection of later authors is also included. The 134 entries are arranged alphabetically. These vary in character: some represent original research, while others summarize and update existing scholarship. In some cases the entries are rather slender because little is currently known about the transmission of the author in question. In general, each entry discusses the history and relationships of the more important manuscripts of the author, notes (and frequently summarizes) key studies, and gives some evaluation of major printed editions. A very full index of names concludes the volume. This handbook is especially useful for students and scholars who are not primarily interested in palaeography or textual criticism but need information on the transmission of a particular text. Those in need of a more general discussion of the transmission of the ancient classics should consult Reynolds's earlier work, *Scribes and Scholars* (entry 982).

984. West, Martin L. **Textual Criticism and Editorial Technique Applicable to Greek and Latin Texts.** Stuttgart: Teubner, 1973. 155pp. ISBN 3–519–07402–8; 3–519–07401–Xpa. LCCN 73–164029.

Those interested in how modern editions of the classics are constructed will find West's handbook enlightening. In it he provides effective guidance both to would-be editors and to readers of critical editions who wish to make use of the apparatus. The first part of the work, which is devoted to textual transmission, gives considerable attention to the common types of errors found in ancient and medieval manuscripts. West also discusses how relationships between manuscripts are established. The second part deals with the mechanics of editing a text: preparation for the task and the presentation of the edition (construction of the preface and critical apparatus). A final section provides sample editions of several passages with discussion of the problems involved. Reading West will give one a keen awareness of the basis and limitations of modern editions.

HISTORY OF CLASSICAL SCHOLARSHIP AND THE CLASSICAL TRADITION

BIBLIOGRAPHIES

985. Calder, William M., III, and Daniel J. Kramer. **Introductory Bibliography to the History of Classical Scholarship Chiefly in the XIXth and XXth Centuries.** Hildesheim: Georg Olms, 1992. 410pp. ISBN 3–487–09643–9. LCCN 93–150750.

986. Calder, William M., III, and R. Scott Smith. **Supplementary Bibliography to the History of Classical Scholarship Chiefly in the XIXth and XXth Centuries.** Paradosis 2. Bari: Dedalo, 2000. 222pp. ISBN 88–220–5802–X. LCCN 2001374542.

The *Introductory Bibliography* constitutes a catalog of books and reprints in the personal library of Professor Calder. Calder is one of the leading exponents of the study of the history of classical scholarship, and his library is large, although far from exhaustive. The bibliography is divided into sections for general works, works on institutions, and works on individuals. Calder goes far beyond the strict confines of classical scholarship and includes much on the general intellectual and academic history of the period covered. He has supplied annotations for many entries. These, which vary in length, are usually both informative and entertaining. They are also opinionated, and not everyone will find the opinions to their liking. Calder brings together many obscure and hard-to-find references, including quite a few from sources not familiar to the average classicist. In the preface to the supplement, Calder himself refers to his initial volume as now "standard" and cites a number of reviews, not all of which give this impression (e.g., J. B. Trapp, *Classical Review,* n.s., 44 [2]: 421–422). The supplement adds more than 1,000 new items, with numbers keyed to those in the original volume. It continues both the organizational structure and eccentricities of the earlier production. There are indexes of persons (as subjects) and of authors.

987. Kallendorf, Craig. **Latin Influences on English Literature from the Middle Ages to the Eighteenth Century: An Annotated Bibliography of the Scholarship, 1945–1979.** Garland Reference Library of the Humanities 345. New York: Garland, 1982. 141pp. ISBN 0–8240–9261–9. LCCN 82–9371.

Taking Gilbert Highet's *The Classical Tradition* (entry 993) as his point of departure, Kallendorf surveys 35 years of scholarly work on Latin influences in English literature. His initial chapters cover basic works on the classical tradition and works on rhetoric and prose style. Subsequent chapters cover the various periods in chronological order from the Middle Ages to the eighteenth century. Each is subdivided by topic. Kallendorf's 769 annotated entries include books, chapters in books, and journal articles. Most annotations consist of brief summaries; a few offer critical comment. The majority of the works cited are in English. While Kallendorf's coverage is not exhaustive, he does provide more than adequate material for students, and an excellent starting point for scholars.

988. Warburg Institute. **Kulturwissenschaftliche Bibliographie zum Nachleben der Antike [A Bibliography of the Survival of the Classics].** Leipzig: Teubner, 1934 (v. 1); London: Warburg Institute, 1938 (v. 2); repr., Nendeln: Kraus Reprint, 1968. 2v.

Despite the English title, virtually the entire text of this important bibliography is written in German. Although intended to be an ongoing project, the bibliography ceased publication after only two volumes, which cover the years 1931–1933. These list 2,490 books and articles on all aspects of the influence of the classics on Western European civilization. Entries are organized under a number of topical and period headings. Each is accompanied by a long, scholarly annotation. The two indexes provide access by author and by personal name and subject. This bibliography is a valuable resource for anyone interested in the classical tradition or the history of classical scholarship.

DICTIONARIES, ENCYCLOPEDIAS, AND HANDBOOKS

989.   Briggs, Ward W., Jr., ed. **Biographical Dictionary of North American Classicists.** Westport, CT: Greenwood Press, 1994. 800pp. ISBN 0–313–24560–6. LCCN 94–4785.

Briggs and his 170 contibutors (all classicists) provide biographical sketches of some 600 deceased classicists from the United States and Canada. Chronologically these range from the seventeenth century almost to the present; the most recent subject died in 1993. The chief criterion for inclusion, apart from geography and death, was that the individual should have made "some kind of significant contribution to the profession." This broad guideline has resulted in a work that includes all the household names along with a sizeable number of the now obscure. The work exhibits a tendency to keep skeletons in the closet; some biographies are less than candid. Often entries for classicists from the recent past are written by former colleagues and students, which allows for personal knowledge but does not promote objectivity. Aside from this, the *Dictionary* is a useful and accurate work. Entries offer an outline of the scholar's career, a short biographical note, and a bibliography. There are also two introductory essays in which William Calder and Alexander McKay review the history of classical scholarship in the United States and Canada respectively. Three indexes round out the volume; these provide access by date of birth, primary institutional affiliation, and the institution that granted each scholar his or her highest degree.

990.   Briggs, Ward W., Jr., and William M. Calder, III, eds. **Classical Scholarship: A Biographical Encyclopedia.** New York: Garland, 1990. 534pp. ISBN 0–8240–8448–9. LCCN 89–23294.

Not intended as a comprehensive biographical dictionary, this work aims at selective coverage of influential classicists. It presents accounts of the lives and work of some 50 scholars from C. G. Heyne (1729–1812) to Arnaldo Momigliano (1908–1987). Coverage is uneven, and the work is distinctly biased toward German scholars. French scholars, in particular, receive short shrift. All articles purportedly were written by scholars who are experts in their subject's own field, although this is not always obvious. Each includes a bibliography of works by and about its subject. There is some variation in length and content of the articles and also in the completeness of the bibliographies. Arrangement is alphabetical, although a chronological listing of entries is provided to facilitate an historical approach. There is also a subject index. While this work brings together much information that is difficult to find elsewhere, it is to be hoped a more comprehensive and balanced work will supersede it.

991.   Cosenza, Mario Emilio. **Biographical and Bibliographical Dictionary of the Italian Humanists and of the World of Classical Scholarship in Italy, 1300–1800.** 2nd ed. Boston: G. K. Hall, 1962–1967. 6v. LCCN 62–13227.

For those with a serious interest in the history of classical scholarship in Italy or in manuscripts and early printed editions of the classics, Cosenza's remarkable compilation is an invaluable source of information. Cosenza spent most of his scholarly life gathering the materials found in these volumes. He covers the Italian humanists and their patrons, other humanists who studied in Italy, copyists, owners and collectors of classical manuscripts, and users of classical texts (a broad classifcation, which includes, among others, astrologers). Entries include both Latin and vernacular forms of names, dates of birth and death, cities in which the subject resided, a brief biographical sketch, a bibliography of the subject's works, and a review of his interests in the classics. When appropriate, entries also include a list of the individual's teachers and students. While there are the inevitable lapses and omissions, this is generally a thorough and reliable work. Much of the biographical and bibliographical data supplied by Cosenza cannot be readily obtained from other reference sources.

Cosenza kept his material on index cards; these are photographically reproduced in the first four volumes of the dictionary. These handwritten entries are often cramped and difficult to read. In the fifth volume Cosenza provides summaries of the material in the earlier volumes. This synopsis is easier to use, since it is reproduced from typescript, but omits many of the entries and much of the information from main listings. This volume also includes a selected bibliography of works on Italian humanism and the history of classical scholarship. The sixth volume is a supplement, which includes additional entries in a second alphabetical sequence. While there is no index, Cosenza supplies numerous cross-references from variant forms of names.

992.   Eckstein, Friedrich August. **Nomenclator Philologorum.** Leipzig: Teubner, 1871; repr., Hildesheim: Georg Olms, 1966. 656pp. LCCN 01–17868.

Eckstein has compiled a biographical dictionary of European classicists from the Renaissance through the nineteenth century. It includes many obscure and minor scholars as well as the famous ones. The brief entries typically include dates, place of birth, education, and positions held. Some give citations of published biographical notices and obituaries. A short list of early printers and publishers of the classics is appended under the title *Nomenclator Typographorum*. A contemporary work by Pökel (entry 997) covers much the same ground as Eckstein. Pökel tends to give more information but lists fewer scholars. Since each work includes individuals and information not found in the other, one is well advised to consult both.

993.   Highet, Gilbert. **Classical Tradition: Greek and Roman Influences on Western Literature.** New York: Oxford University Press, 1949. 763pp. LCCN 49–11655.

A well-known and frequently reprinted book, the *Classical Tradition* provides a guide to the influence of the classics on subsequent Western literature from the early Middle Ages through the early twentieth century. Within a broad chronological framework, Highet devotes chapters to various periods, topics, genres, and, occasionally, important individual authors. His eminently readable narrative shows wide learning. While Highet covers most topics in summary fashion, his notes and bibliography furnish excellent leads for further study. This book is a good first choice for anyone seeking general information on the literary and cultural influence of the classics. The index is quite full and makes for interesting browsing in itself (some of the less probable entries include "corpses on stage," "skunkery," and "X, signing with").

994. Medwid, Linda M. **Makers of Classical Archaeology: A Reference Work.** Amherst, NY: Humanity Books, 2000. 352pp. ISBN 1–57392–826–7. LCCN 99–462362.

Medwid has compiled short biographies of notable classical archaeologists from the eighteenth century to the present. Only the dead are included. Medwid lists 119 archaeologists in an A-to-Z sequence. These include primarily Americans, British, Germans, Greeks, and Italians. She has missed nobody of great prominence, although coverage of secondary figures is selective. Entries give the dates of birth and death, along with the location, when known. Each has the following sections: education, appointments and awards, excavations, publications, a brief narrative account, and sources. For more recent archaeologists, Medwid draws heavily on obituaries. She provides a useful gathering of bibliographical and biographical data from often obscure and inaccessible sources.

995. Pfeiffer, Rudolf. **History of Classical Scholarship from the Beginnings to the End of the Hellenistic Age.** Oxford: Clarendon Press, 1968. 310pp. ISBN 0–19–814342–7. LCCN 68–112031.

996. Pfeiffer, Rudolf. **History of Classical Scholarship from 1300 to 1850.** Oxford: Clarendon Press, 1976. 213pp. ISBN 0–19–814354–8. LCCN 77–363045.

Pfeiffer, a distinguished Hellenist, is the first writer since Sandys (entry 998) to attempt a history of classical scholarship on such a scale. His first volume offers a magisterial treatment of the origins of classical scholarship among the ancient Greeks. While early chapters discuss the beginnings of literary criticism in classical Greece, the bulk of the work is devoted to the scholars of the Hellenistic age, especially those of third- and second-century B.C. Alexandria. Although Greek science is not entirely neglected, the central focus remains literary scholarship, especially the editing and interpreting of texts. Pfeiffer's work is indispensable for anyone interested in the history of Greek scholarship or the early transmission of Greek literature and largely supersedes Sandys's treatment of this period. The nonspecialist will find it slow going, since it is often rather technical and includes much untranslated Greek.

Pfeiffer skips over late antiquity and the Middle Ages to begin his second volume with the Renaissance. This volume, although no less scholarly, is much more accessible to the lay reader. In it Pfeiffer surveys the high points of classical scholarship from the time of Petrarch through 1850. He is highly selective and tends to focus on major figures, such as Lorenzo Valla, Richard Bentley, and F. A. Wolf. Here Pfeiffer serves to supplement and correct, rather than replace, Sandys. Both volumes include detailed general indexes.

997. Pökel, W. **Philologisches Schriftsteller-Lexikon.** Leipzig: Alfred Krüger, 1882; repr., Darmstadt: Wissenschaftliche Buchgesellschaft, 1966. 328pp. LCCN 07–20050.

Along with Eckstein's *Nomenclator Philologorum* (entry 992), this work is one of the basic biographical sources on European classical scholars of the modern era. Pökel's chronological limits run from the mid-fifteenth century to about 1880. His alphabetical listings give for each scholar dates, places of birth and residence, titles and institutions (for those with academic affiliations), and brief citations of major publications. Occasionally Pökel also furnishes references to published obituaries or biographies of his subjects. Pökel's entries generally offer more information than do those of Eckstein, although most users will need to consult both. Users of Pökel should also be sure to check the extensive additions and corrections found at the end of the volume.

998. Sandys, Sir John Edwin. **History of Classical Scholarship.** 3rd ed. (v. 1 only). Cambridge: Cambridge University Press, 1908–1921. 3v. LCCN 03–33012.

999. Sandys, Sir John Edwin. **Short History of Classical Scholarship from the Sixth Century B.C. to the Present Day.** Cambridge: Cambridge University Press, 1915. 455pp. LCCN 15–2366.

Sandys remains the standard comprehensive history of classical scholarship. His magisterial work covers the whole field from the sixth century B.C. to the end of the nineteenth century. Sandys covers virtually every aspect: scribes, editors, textual and literary critics, grammarians, historians, archaeologists, and antiquarians. The *History* is of value not only to classicists, but to anyone interested in European intellectual history and the history of manuscripts, books, and printing. The first volume, which covers antiquity and the Middle Ages, was twice revised by the author. The other volumes remain as they originally appeared in 1908. Each includes a detailed table of contents and an extensive index. Sandys's treatment of scholarship through the Alexandrian era has been largely superseded by Pfeiffer (entry 995). The rest of the work, although showing its age, is still without rival. The second volume of Pfeiffer (entry 996) and the brief history by Wilamowitz-Moellendorff (entry 1001) supplement it and correct some details but in no way challenge its preeminence. Sandys's *Short History,* while an abridgement of the larger work, also includes some updated material (primarily bibliographical) not found in that work.

1000. Todd, Robert B., ed. **Dictionary of British Classicists.** Bristol: Thoemmes Continuum, 2004. 3v. ISBN 1–85506–997–0 (set).

This biographical dictionary provides more than 700 entries for British classicists (very loosely defined) who flourished between 1500 and 1960. As is usual for such works, coverage is limited to the deceased. It includes the usual suspects, but also some obscure figures who will not be found in the new *Oxford Dictionary of National Biography* (Oxford: Oxford University Press, 2004). In addition to biographical information, entries offer bibliographies of works by and about their subject. The quality and reliability of entries varies widely.

1001. Wilamowitz-Moellendorff, Ulrich von. **Geschichte der Philologie.** 3. Aufl., mit einem Nachwort und Register von Albert Henrichs. Stuttgart: Teubner, 1998. 128pp. ISBN 3–519–07253–X.

1002. Wilamowitz-Moellendorff, Ulrich von. **History of Classical Scholarship.** Trans. Alan Harris. Ed. with introduction and notes by Hugh Lloyd-Jones. Baltimore: Johns Hopkins University Press, 1982. 189pp. ISBN 0-8018-2801–5. LCCN 81-48182.

Wilamowitz-Moellendorff, the preeminent Hellenist of the nineteenth and early twentieth centuries, published his *Geschichte der Philologie* in 1921. In it he covers the high points of the history of classical scholarship from antiquity to the early years of the twentieth century. Wilamowitz-Moellendorff covers less and offers less detail than Sandys's massive three-volume work. He does, however, take a more critical approach to the subject and does so with unique authority. The most recent German edition reprints the original text of 1921 but includes a valuable afterword by Albert Henrichs, along with a bibliographical appendix and an extremely detailed index. The English edition includes a substantial introduction and explanatory and bibliographical notes by Lloyd-Jones, himself a distinguished Greek scholar and former Regius professor at Oxford. An index of names is also provided.

20

Scholarly Associations and Societies

Listings in this chapter include national and international organizations whose primary concern is with some aspect of classical studies. National organizations are limited to those based in North America or the United Kingdom; for information on other national societies see the Web site of the Fédération Internationale des Associations d'Études Classiques (entry 1017). A few of the more important regional associations in the United States are also described below. Many of these organizations, especially the smaller ones, do not have permanent mailing or Web addresses. Often, the mailing address provided is that of the secretary of the association and is subject to change on a random basis. It is always wise to verify the address through the association's Web site or in the current edition of the *Encyclopedia of Associations,* the *World of Learning,* or a similar reference work. Associations devoted to individual authors may be found under the author's name in chapters 15 and 16.

1003. **American Classical League.** Miami University, Oxford, OH 45056. Tel.: (513) 529–7741. Fax: (513) 529–7742. E-mail: info@aclclassics.org. URL: www.aclclassics.org.

The primary purpose of the American Classical League, which was organized in 1919, is to promote the teaching of Latin and related subjects. Most of its members are high school and college Latin teachers. The ACL operates a placement service for Latin teachers and maintains a resource center, which supplies instructional materials for Latin and Greek. It also publishes a journal, *Classical Outlook* (entry 92), and holds annual meetings. Current information about the organization and its activities may be found on its Web site. The ACL also sponsors a second organization, the National Junior Classical League (entry 1021), for high school students.

1004. **American Philological Association.** 292 Logan Hall, University of Pennsylvania, 249 South 36th St., Philadelphia, PA 19104–6304. Tel.: (508) 793–2203. Fax: (508) 793–3428. URL: www.apaclassics.org.

Founded in 1869, the APA is one of the oldest professional associations in North America, and the principal one for classics. In its early period the association had a somewhat wider scope and included scholars working in a variety of languages and literatures. By 1919, however, the APA had come to focus exclusively on classical languages and literatures. Its membership now consists mainly of college and university professors of classics and related fields, although a number of secondary school teachers and independent scholars also belong to the association. The APA has an active publishing program, which produces a bimonthly newsletter, a directory of members (entries 1045–1046), and a semiannual journal, the *Transactions of the American Philological Association* (entry 126). It also publishes two monograph series (*Philological Monographs* and *American Classical Studies*) and a textbook series. In conjunction with the Archaeological Institute of America (entry 1007), the APA holds an annual conference, which always takes place

December 27–30. A number of other American classical organizations also hold annual meetings at this conference.

1005.   American Society of Greek and Latin Epigraphy. c/o Prof. Timothy Winters, Secretary/Treasurer, Dept. of Language and Literature, Austin Peay State University, P.O. Box 4487, Clarksville, TN 37044. E-mail: asgle@unc.edu. URL: http://asgle.classics.unc.edu.

This relatively new society, founded in 1996, is devoted to research and teaching of Greek and Latin epigraphy. The society meets annually in conjunction with the American Philological Association (entry 1004) and publishes a newsletter. Its Web site is ambitious, offering links to Web resources, bibliographical updates, and other resources. Unfortunately it appears to be updated sporadically at best.

1006.   American Society of Papyrologists. Dept. of Classics, ML 226, 410 Blegen Library, University of Cincinnati, Cincinnati, OH 45221–0226. E-mail: asp@papyrology. org. URL: www.papyrology.org.

This society, which was organized in 1961, promotes the study of ancient Greek and Latin papyri. Its membership is composed primarily of scholars working in the field. The ASP publishes a journal, the *Bulletin of the American Society of Papyrologists,* and a monograph series, *American Studies in Papyrology.* The society recently launched a new series, which reprints classics in the field. Its Web page offers detailed information about its programs and publications, as well as providing an index to the *Bulletin* and links to Web resources in papyrology. The society meets annually in conjunction with the American Philological Association's conference (see entry 1004).

1007.   Archaeological Institute of America. Boston University, 656 Beacon Street, 4th Floor, Boston, MA 02215–2006. Tel.: (617) 353–9361. Fax: (617) 353–6550. E-mail: aia@aia.bu.edu. URL: www.archaeological.org.

While the institute is concerned with archaeology in general, it also functions as the primary organization for those Americans interested in classical archaeology. Unlike many of the other societies listed in this chapter, the AIA blends both scholarly and popular activities. For professional archaeologists, the institute publishes the *American Journal of Archaeology* (entry 74), *Archaeological Fieldwork Opportunities,* and a monograph series. It also maintains close associations with a number of research centers in the Mediterranean region and Middle East. In conjunction with the American Philological Association (entry 1004), the institute holds an annual conference in December. For the interested nonspecialist, the institute publishes a popular magazine, *Archaeology* (entry 82), and, through its local branches, sponsors numerous public lectures on archaeological topics.

1008.   Association Internationale de Papyrologues. c/o Fondation Égyptologique Reine Élisabeth, Parc du Cinquantenaire 10, B-1040 Brussels, Belgium. Tel.: 32 2 7417364. E-mail: amartin@ulb.ac.be. URL: www.ulb.ac.be/assoc/aip.

An international society devoted to the study of papyri, this organization was formed in 1946. Its members include primarily working papyrologists and ancient historians. The AIP promotes international cooperation in papyrological research and sponsors a triennial international congress. The association's Web site includes the usual organizational information, grant information, and a membership directory. It also includes links to many Web resources of interest to papyrologists and a large collection of portraits of deceased papyrologists.

1009.   Association Internationale d'Epigraphie Grecque et Latine. c/o Pierre Ducrey, Treasurer, 52, Chemin de Caudoz CH-1009 Pully, Switzerland.

This international organization for researchers in Greek and Latin epigraphy was founded in 1972. Its membership consists chiefly of scholars working in the field. The association produces three annual publications: *L'Année epigraphique, Epigraphica,* and *Supplementum Epigraphicum.* It also sponsors a quinquennial congress. The association's Web site has been offline for some time.

1010.   Association of Ancient Historians. c/o Randall S. Howarth, Dept. of History, Mercyhurst College, 501 East 38th Street, Erie, PA 16546–0001. Tel.: (814) 824–2345. E-mail: rhowarth@merchyhurst.edu. URL: www.trentu.ca/ahc/aah/welcome.shtml.

This group, which is affiliated with the American Historical Association, promotes the study and teaching of ancient history. The majority of its members are university professors and graduate students. While much of its focus is on classical Greek and Roman history, the association also covers ancient Near Eastern studies and late antiquity. The association publishes a newsletter and a monographic series. It also holds an annual conference.

1011.   Classical Association. Senate House, Malet St., London WC1E 7HU, UK. Tel.: 44 (0)20 7862 8706. Fax: 44 (0)20 7255 2297. E-mail: office@classicalassociation.org. URL: www.classicalassociation.org.

The Classical Association, which dates to 1903, is the largest British organization devoted to classical studies. Its membership consists of classicists working in schools and universities. The association sponsors an annual conference. It publishes an annual *Proceedings* and, through Oxford University Press, three important periodicals: *Classical Review* (entry 67), *Classical Quarterly* (entry 94), and *Greece and Rome* (entry 99).

1012.   Classical Association of Canada. c/o Annabel Robinson, Treasurer, Classical Association of Canada, Dept. of Philosophy and Classics, University of Regina, 3737 Wascana Parkway, Regina, Saskatchewan S4S 0A2, Canada. E-mail: annabel. robinson@uregina.ca. URL: www.usask.ca/classics/cac/eindex.html.

Founded in 1947, the Classical Association of Canada is the major professsional organization for classical studies in Canada. It publishes two journals, *Phoenix* (entry 119) and *Mouseion* (entry 114). In addition, the CAC publishes an electronic newsletter and maintains a directory of Canadian classicists on its Web site. The association also sponsors an annual meeting.

1013.   Classical Association of the Atlantic States. Dept. of Humanities, University of the Sciences, 600 South 43rd Street, Philadelphia, PA 19104–4495 Tel.: (215) 596–8504. E-mail: classics@usip.edu. URL: www.caas-cw.org.

Founded in 1906, this group consists largely of high school and college teachers of classics from the mid-Atlantic states. Like the other regional classical associations, its interests include both scholarly and pedagogical matters. The association publishes *Classical World* (entry 95). It holds semiannual meetings.

1014. **Classical Association of New England.** URL: www.wellesley.edu/Classical-Studies/cane.

This organization for high school and college teachers of classics was founded in 1906. It publishes a quarterly journal, the *New England Classical Journal,* and holds an annual conference. The Web site has extensive information about the association's activities and numerous resources for teaching classics.

1015. **Classical Association of the Middle West and South.** c/o Anne H. Groton Secretary-Treasurer, CAMWS, Dept. of Classics, St. Olaf College, 1520 St. Olaf Ave., Northfield, MN 55057–1098. Tel.: (507) 646–3114. E-mail: newlands@stolaf.edu. URL: www.camws.org.

CAMWS is the largest and most active of the regional classical associations in the United States. Its territory covers most of the central and southern part of the nation. Members include a mix of high school and college faculty. The association focuses on both scholarly and pedagogical activities in classics. It publishes *Classical Journal* (entry 91) as well as a newsletter. CAMWS holds an annual conference. In the years when the main meeting is held in a northern venue, the southern section also generally holds a smaller second conference. Up-to-date information on the society and its activities can be found on its Web site, along with an e-mail directory and links to other classical associations and Internet resources of interest.

1016. **Egypt Exploration Society.** 3 Doughty Mews, London WC1N 2PG, UK. Tel.: 44 (0)20 7242 1880. Fax: 44 (0)20 7404 6118. URL: www.ees.ac.uk.

Founded in 1880 as the Egypt Exploration Fund, this is a society for those with scholarly interests in ancient Egypt. It has long supported excavations in Egypt (including those of W. M. Flinders Petrie and of B. P. Grenfell and A. S. Hunt.) and maintains an active publishing program. The society has been particularly active in promoting the study of Greco-Roman Egypt. Its publications include the *Journal of Egyptian Archaeology* and the *Graeco-Roman Memoirs* (an important series of papyrological publications).

1017. **Fédération Internationale des Associations d'Études Classiques.** Prof. Paul Schubert, Secrétaire général de la FIEC 7, rue des Beaux-Arts 2000 Neuchâtel, Switzerland. Tel.: 41 22 7742656. www.fiecnet.org.

The Fédération Internationale was founded in 1948 under the auspices of UNESCO to promote the study of classical antiquity. It is a society of societies: its membership includes some 65 societies in 38 countries, and 17 international groups. The chief role of the federation is to serve as a coordinating body for international efforts in classical studies. The federation sponsors a quinquennial congress. Its Web site is a good source of information about the many national societies not included in this chapter.

1018. **International Society for Neoplatonic Studies.** Contact: Prof. John Finamore. E-mail: john-finamore@uiowa.edu. URL: www.isns.us/index.htm.

This organization, formed in 1973, is devoted to the study of Neoplatonism from antiquity through the Renaissance. The society sponsors a journal, the *Journal of Neoplatonic Studies,* and a monograph series. It also sponsors meetings, usually in conjunction with the conferences of other societies, such as the American Philological Association (entry 1004).

1019.   International Society for the Classical Tradition. Boston University, 745 Commonwealth Ave., Suite B-3, Boston, MA 02215. Tel.: (617) 353–7370. Fax: (617) 353–7359. E-mail: isct@bu.edu. URL: www.bu.edu/ict/isct/index.html.

Established in 1991 and based at the Institute for the Classical Tradition (entry 1041) at Boston University, this organization promotes the study of the influence of the classics on other cultures in all time periods. The society publishes both a newsletter and a journal, the *International Journal of the Classical Tradition.* The society also sponsors periodic meetings and conferences.

1020.   National Committee for Latin and Greek. c/o Nancy McKee, Chair, 19 Donna Lynn Lane, Lawrenceville, NJ 08648. Tel.: (609) 896–1157. E-mail: mckeena@aol.com. URL: www.promotelatin.org.

The committee, whose membership consists of national and regional classical associations in the United States, was formed in 1978 to initiate and coordinate efforts to promote the study of Latin and Greek. The activities of the committee include various public relations initiatives, gathering statistics on enrollment in classical language courses and teacher supply and demand, and monitoring federal legislation affecting language study. The committee publishes a newsletter, *Pro Bono,* which features brief articles on the current state of and future outlook for classical studies.

1021.   National Junior Classical League. 422 Wells Mills Dr., Miami University, Oxford, OH 45056. Tel.: (513) 529–7741. Fax: (513) 529–7742. E-mail: administrator@njcl. org. URL: www.njcl.org.

Founded in 1936 by the American Classical League (entry 1003), the National Junior Classical League is an organization for high school Latin students. Its purpose is to promote classical studies at the secondary level. The league holds an annual convention.

1022.   Society for Ancient Greek Philosophy. c/o Prof. Anthony Preus, Dept. of Philosphy, Binghamton University, Binghamton, NY 13902–6000. Tel.: (607) 777–2886. Fax: (607) 777–2734. E-mail: apreus@binghamton.edu. URL: http://sagp.binghamton.edu.

Founded in 1953, this society is for both philosophers and classicists with interests in ancient philosophy. Its membership consists mainly of college and university professors. The society publishes a newsletter and holds meetings in conjuntion with the conferences of the American Philological Association (entry 1004) and the American Philosophical Association. It also publishes collections of essays on Greek philosophy on an occasional basis.

1023.   Society for Ancient Medicine. c/o Professor Lesley A. Dean-Jones, Dept. of Classics, University of Texas at Austin, 1 University Station C3400, Austin, TX 78712. E-mail: ldjones@mail.texas.edu. URL: www.medicinaantiqua.org.uk/mm_sam.html.

This group is interested in the study of all aspects of ancient medicine. It generally meets annually in conjunction with the American Philological Association's conference (see entry 1004). The society also issues a substantial annual publication, the *Society for Ancient Medicine Review.* Formerly called the *Newsletter,* this provides detailed information about conferences and recent publications.

1024.   Society for the Promotion of Hellenic Studies. Senate House, Malet St., London WC1E 7HU, UK. Tel.: 44 (0)20–7862–8730. Fax: 44 (0)20–7862–8731 E-mail: office@hellenicsociety.org.uk. URL: www.hellenicsociety.org.uk.

Founded in 1879 to advance the study of Greek language, literature, history, and art, the society has long shared quarters with its sister organization, the Society for the Promotion of Roman Studies (entry 1025). The two societies maintain a research library in association with the Institute of Classical Studies of the University of London (entry 1042). The Society for the Promotion of Hellenic Studies sponsors various lectures and publishes two periodicals: the *Journal of Hellenic Studies* (entry 109) and *Archaeological Reports.*

1025.   Society for the Promotion of Roman Studies. Senate House, Malet St., London WC1E 7HU, UK. Tel.: 44 (0)20–7862 8727. E-mail: office@romansociety.org. URL: www. romansociety.org.

This slightly younger counterpart to the Society for the Promotion of Hellenic Studies (entry 1024) was founded in 1910. The two organizations share quarters and, in association with the Institute of Classical Studies of the University of London (entry 1042), maintain a major research library for classical studies. The society's aim is to advance the study of Roman history, archaeology, literature, and art (from the beginnings down to about A.D. 700). To this end it sponsors public lectures and publishes two journals: the *Journal of Roman Studies* (entry 111) and *Britannia.*

1026.   Women's Classical Caucus. c/o Prof. Maryline Parca, Secretary-Treasurer, Dept. of the Classics, University of Illinois, 4080 FLB, 707 S. Mathews, Urbana, IL 61801. Tel.: (217) 333–1008. E-mail: mparca@uiuc.edu. URL: www.wccaucus.org.

This group, whose membership includes those working in all areas of classical studies, has two aims. The first is to support the professional status of women in classical studies. The second is to promote the study of women in antiquity. The caucus publishes a newsletter, *Cloelia,* and meets during the American Philological Association's annual conference (see entry 1004).

21
Research Centers

This chapter includes a number of special research centers for classical studies in both North America and Europe. Some are residential centers for scholars, while others primarily exist to maintain collections of resources. Centers that function mainly as graduate programs are generally omitted. The list is selective but includes those centers most likely to be of interest to North American students and scholars. While the directory information for research centers is less subject to change than that for associations (chapter 20), current addresses and telephone numbers can be verified in such annual reference works as *The World of Learning* or through the Web site of the center in question. Readers who are unfamiliar with international calling should note that all non-U.S. telephone numbers listed below include the applicable country and city codes for calls placed from North America.

1027. **American Academy in Rome.** Via Angelo Masina 5, 00153 Rome, Italy. Tel.: 39 06 58461. Fax: 39 06 5810788. U.S. Office: 7 East 60th St., New York, NY 10022. Tel.: (212) 751–7200. Fax: (212) 751–7220. URL: www.aarome.org.

Founded in 1894, the American Academy in Rome is a residential center for research in the fine arts, classical studies, art history, Italian studies, and archaeology. The academy offers a number of fellowships both for graduate students and established scholars. It also sponsors annual summer programs that are aimed primarily at high school Latin teachers and college students in classical studies. The academy maintains an outstanding research library, which now numbers over 130,000 volumes. Its monographic series, *Memoirs,* publishes works on Roman literature, history, and archaeology.

1028. **American Center of the International Photographic Archive of Papyri.** c/o Prof. Maryline Parca, Dept. of the Classics, 4080 FLB, University of Illinois, 707 South Mathews, Urbana, IL 61801. Tel.: (217) 333–1008.

This archive, which is the result of a project funded by the National Endowment for the Humanities, is a collection of photographs and negatives of papyri held in American collections. Although some of the largest and most important collections (e.g., those of the University of Michigan and Columbia University) are not part of the archive, it does include papyri from the majority of American collections. A partial listing of its holdings can be found in E.W. Wall, "Interim Report of IPAP," *Bulletin of the American Society of Papyrologists* 18 (3–4): 161–164. The archive is housed in the rare book room of the University of Illinois Library but is administered by the university's classics department. Materials are available for consultation on-site; and, in some cases, photographs can be supplied by mail. For papyri held by collections outside North America, see the International Photographic Archive of Papyri (entry 1043).

1029. **American School of Classical Studies at Athens.** Odos Souidas 54, GR-106 76 Athens, Greece. Tel.: 30 210–72–36–313. Fax: 30 210–72–50–584. E-mail: ascsa@ascsa edu.gr. U.S. Office: 6–8 Charlton St., Princeton, NJ 08540–5232. Tel.: (609) 683–0800. Fax: (609) 924–0578. E-mail: ascsa@ascsa.org. URL: www.ascsa.edu.gr.

Founded in 1881, the school is a research institute devoted to ancient Greek literature, history, and archaeology. It offers various fellowships for scholars and provides programs of study for graduate students during the academic year. The school also conducts summer sessions for advanced undergraduates, graduate students, and high school and college faculty. Two research libraries are maintained, the Blegen Library (80,000 volumes), which focuses on classical studies, and the Gennadius Library (over 100,000 volumes), which concentrates on Byzantine and modern Greek studies. Over the years, the school has sponsored or cosponsored important excavations in Greece (most notably Corinth and the Athenian Agora). In addition, it publishes a highly regarded journal, *Hesperia* (entry 105).

1030.   British School at Athens. Odos Souidias 52, 10676 Athens, Greece. Tel.: 30 2107210974. Fax: 30 2107236560. British Office: Senate House, Malet St., London, WC1E 7HU, UK. Tel.: 44 207) 862 8732. Fax: 44 207 862 8733. E-mail: bsa@bsa.ac.uk URL: www.bsa.gla.ac.uk.

Established in 1886, the school is a center for the study of Greek literature, history, and archaeology. It maintains a residential study center in Athens with a research library of more than 50,000 volumes and an archaeological laboratory. The school also operates a second residential field center at Knossos, on Crete. Among other activities, the British School sponsors archaeological excavations. It also publishes the *British School Annual* and *Archaeological Reports*.

1031.   British School at Rome. Via Gramsci 61, 00197 Rome, Italy. Tel.: 39 06 326 4939. Fax: 39 06 322 1201. E-mail:info@bsrome.it. British Office: British Academy, 10 Carlton House Terrace, London SW1Y 5AH, UK. Tel: 44 (0)20 7969 5202. Fax: 44 (0)20 7969 5401. E-mail: bsr@britac.ac.uk. URL: www.bsr.ac.uk.

The British School at Rome, which was founded in 1901, is a residential research center for British scholars working in classical studies, medieval and modern archaeology, history, art history, and the fine arts. Thus, while much of its focus is on classical studies, it is really a general institute for the study of Italian and Mediterranean history and culture. The school possesses a library of approximately 72,000 volumes; it also boasts an extensive photographic archive. In addition to sponsoring various research projects and excavations, the school publishes the *Papers of the British School at Rome* (see entry 117), a semiannual newsletter, and occasional monographs.

1032.   Canadian Archaeological Institute at Athens. Dionysiou Aiginitou 7, GR 115 28 Athens, Greece. Tel.: 30 210 722 3201. Fax: 30 210 725 7968. E-mail: caia@caia-icaa. gr. URL: www.caia-icaa.gr/en/index_en.html.

Founded in 1974, this institute is much smaller than its British and American counterparts. It is intended to be the main center for Canadian classical archaeologists working in Greece. Fostering cultural links between Canada and Greece is a central part of its mission as well.

1033.   Center for Epigraphical and Palaeographical Studies. Ohio State University, 190 Pressey Hall, 1070 Carmack Road, Columbus, OH 43210–1002. Tel.: (614) 292–3280.

Fax: (614) 688–4638. E-mail: watkins.72@osu.edu. URL: http://omega.cohums.ohio-state. edu/epigraphy.

The center was established in 1986 as a comprehensive research facility for the study of Greek and Latin inscriptions. In 1992, its scope was enlarged to embrace palaeography as well. The center maintains a working library and substantial collections of squeezes (paper impressions) and photographs of inscriptions. It offers both postdoctoral fellowships and short-term fellowships for established scholars.

1034.   Center for Hellenic Studies. 3100 Whitehaven St. NW, Washington, D.C. 20008. Tel.: (202) 745–4400. Fax: (202) 797–3745. URL: www.chs.harvard.edu.

Established in 1961, the Center for Hellenic Studies is administered by the trustees of Harvard University. It supports research on all aspects of ancient Greek civilization. The center maintains a substantial research library. It awards about 12 junior fellowships each year; fellows normally reside at the center during the academic year. In addition, the center has instituted summer seminars for graduate students. It also maintains an active publishing program, which has expanded in recent years to include electronic publishing.

1035.   Centre for the Study of Ancient Documents. The Old Boys' School, George St., Oxford, OX1 2RL, UK. Tel: 44 01865 288180. Fax: 44 01865 288262. E-mail: csad@classics. ox.ac.uk. URL: www.csad.ox.ac.uk/CSAD/index.html.

Founded in 1995 by the School of Literae Humaniores at Oxford University, this center focuses on epigraphy and papyrology. It possesses large collections of squeezes (paper impressions) and photographs of Greek and Latin inscriptions. The center sponsors digitization projects, seminars, and summer courses. The Web site includes links to digitized versions of the Vindolanda tablets and the Oxyrhynchus papyri.

1036.   Deutsches Archäologisches Institut, Abteilung Athen. Odos Fidiou 1, 106 78 Athens, Greece. Tel.: 30 210 33 07 400. Fax: 30 210 381 47 62. E-mail: allgref@athen. dainst.org. URL: www.dainst.org/abteilung.php?id = 264.

Founded in 1874, this branch of the Deutsche Archäologisches Institut is concerned with preclassical and classical Greek archaeology. It maintains a research library (currently 70,000 volumes) and sponsors excavations in Greece. The institute also publishes an annual journal, *Athenische Mitteilungen,* and a monographic series, the *Beihefte.*

1037.   Deutsches Archäologisches Institut, Abteilung Rom. Via Sardegna 79, 00187 Rome, Italy. Tel.: 39 06 4888141. Fax: 39 06 4884973. E-mail: dairsekr@vatlib.it. URL: www.dainst.org/abteilung.php?id = 263.

One of oldest foreign research institutes in Rome, the DAI was established in 1829. Its primary focus is on classical archaeology. The DAI is well known for its excellent library of more than 200,000 volumes; both a printed catalog of this and, for materials published since 1956, a computerized database (entry 53) are available. The institute also publishes the journal *Römische Mitteilungen.*

1038.   École Française d'Athènes. Odos Didotou 6, 106 80 Athens, Greece. Tel.: 30 210 36 79 900. Fax: 30 210 36 32 101. URL: www.efa.gr.

Established in 1846, the École Française supports historical and archaeological research on classical Greece. It has long sponsored important excavations, most notably that at Delphi. The school's library currently numbers more than 80,000 volumes. The École Française also carries out a major publishing effort, which includes both an annual journal, the *Bulletin de correspondance hellénique* (entry 86), and several monographic series.

1039. **École Française de Rome.** Piazza Farnese 67, 00186 Rome, Italy. Tel.: 39 06 68 60 11. Fax: 39 06 687 48 34. URL: www.ecole-francaise.it.

The École Française, which was founded in 1873, devotes its activities to Italian archaeology and history, with emphasis on the ancient and medieval periods. It provides a residential center for students and sponsors a number of excavations. The school maintains a research library, which now stands at more than 200,000 volumes. It also supports an active publication program, which produces a journal, the *Mélanges de l'École Française de Rome,* and several monographic series.

1040. **Institute for Antiquity and Christianity.** Claremont Graduate School. 831 North Dartmouth Ave., Claremont, CA 91711–6178. Tel.: (909) 621–8066. Fax: (909) 621–8390. E-mail: iac@cgu.edu. URL: http://iac.cgu.edu.

While focusing primarily on early Christianity, the Institute for Antiquity and Christianity also supports research on the ancient Near East and the classical world. Activities of particular interest to classicists include projects on Greek rhetoric, papyrology, and epigraphy. The institute maintains a small museum and various teaching collections of papyri and other antiquities. In addition, its facilities include a reference library of approximately 3,000 volumes. The institute offers both graduate courses (through the Claremont Graduate School) and continuing education programs open to the public. Its publications include a quarterly bulletin and a variety of monographs and project reports.

1041. **Institute for the Classical Tradition.** Boston University. 745 Commonwealth Ave., Suite B-3. Boston, MA 02215. Tel.: (617) 353–7370. Fax: (617) 353–7369. E-mail: isct@bu.edu. URL: www.bu.edu/ict.

This institute, which is closely associated with the International Society for the Classical Tradition (entry 1019), supports research on the later influence of the classics. Its facilities at Boston University include a growing library of books and offprints on topics relating to the classical tradition. The institute compiles an annual bibliography of work in the field, which previously appeared in *Classical and Modern Literature* (entry 88) and is expected to appear soon on the institute's Web site. The institute publishes a journal, the *International Journal of the Classical Tradition* (entry 108) and also hosts the editorial offices of the *Aufstieg und Niedergang der römischen Welt* (entry 315). In addition to its various publishing projects, the institute sponsors regular meetings.

1042. **Institute of Classical Studies.** Senate House, Malet St., London, WC1E 7HU, UK. Tel.: 44 020 7862 8700. Fax: 44 020 7862 8722. URL: www.sas.ac.uk/icls/institute.

Established in 1953, the Institute of Classical Studies is part of the University of London. Although it primarily functions as a graduate program in classical studies, the institute also sponsors a broad range of postdoctoral research programs. Major interests include ancient drama, philosophy, papyrology, epigraphy, and Mycenaean studies. In collaboration with the Societies for the Promotion of Hellenic Studies and Roman Studies (entries 1024–1025), the institute maintains a major research library for classical studies. The institute carries out an extensive publication program as well; it produces an important journal, the *Bulletin* (entry 87), and a monographic series (the *Bulletin Supplements*).

1043.   International Photographic Archive of Papyri. Fondation Égyptologique Reine Élisabeth, Parc du Cinquantenaire 10, B-1040 Brussels, Belgium. Contact: Prof. Adam Bülow-Jacobsen, 19, rue de la Tombe Issoire, F-75014 Paris, France. E-mail: bulow@hum. ku.dk. URL: www.igl.ku.dk/~bulow/aipdescr.html.

Founded by Ludwig Koenen and continued by Adam Bülow-Jacobsen and Revel Coles, the International Photographic Archive of Papyri holds negatives and photographs of papyri from a number of European and Egyptian collections. These include, among others, the Cairo Museum in Egypt, the Bodleian Library, and collections in Oslo, Lund, and Athens. Reports detailing the holdings of the archive are published on an irregular basis; the most recent is Adam Bülow-Jacobsen, "Report on the 1987 Mission for the International Photographic Archive of Greek Papyri," *Zeitschrift für Papyrologie und Epigraphik* 70 (1987): 63–64. While the primary repository is at the Fondation Égyptologique Reine Élisabeth in Brussels, a significant part of the collection resides in Copenhagen. A satellite archive, which includes either negatives or color slides of the entire collection, is located at the Institut für Altertumskunde at the University of Cologne. Inquiries about holdings or access to the archive should be directed to Professor Bülow-Jacobsen. For the American center in Urbana, Illinois, which holds photographs of papyri in U.S. and Canadian collections, see entry 1028.

1044.   Warburg Institute. University of London, Woburn Square, London WC1H 0AB, UK. Tel.: 44 020 7862 8949. Fax: 44 020 7862 8955. URL: www.sas.ac.uk/warburg.

Aby Warburg and his associate Fritz Saxl founded the Warburg Institute in Hamburg in 1921. Saxl moved the institute to England in 1934; it became part of the University of London in 1944. The institute supports interdisciplinary work on the classical tradition in European thought, art, and history. To this end it maintains a noted research library and sponsors a number of research fellowships. The institute also carries out an extensive publication program, which includes a monographic series, *Studies,* and the *Journal of the Warburg and Courtauld Institutes.*

22
Directories

This chapter includes a variety of directories that list either university departments of classics or individual classicists. Most are produced by professional associations; these are updated more or less regularly. Others appear as special issues of journals. In the last few years, many directories have migrated to the Internet; these tend to be much more up-to-date. Users should be aware that even recently published and online directories are likely to be out-of-date and incomplete. Additional directories may be found at www.trentu.ca/ahc/resources.html.

1045. American Philological Association. **Directory of Members.** Worcester, MA: American Philological Association, 1970–1997. ISSN 0044–779X. LCCN 74–644044.

1046. American Philological Association. **Directory of Members.** 1997– . URL: www. apaclassics.org/Administration/Membersonly.html#bw.

The American Philological Association (see entry 1004) traditionally published its directory biennially; publication of the print version ceased in 1997 when the directory was made available electronically. As of December 2004, access to the online directory is restricted to current members of the APA. The directory lists the names, addresses, institutional affiliations, and e-mail addresses of members of the association. Information is taken from the APA membership records. The membership of the APA includes most, but by no means all, classicists working in North American colleges and universities. It also includes a few overseas members. The current version of the directory is not really browsable but offers these search options: name, institution, city, state, and country. It is possible to browse large parts of the directory by searching by state or country only.

1047. **APA Guide to Graduate Programs in the Classics in the United States and Canada.** Worcester, MA: American Philological Association, 1992– . LCCN 99–34194.

Intended for those contemplating graduate study, this guide describes programs offering master's and doctoral degrees in classics, ancient history, and classical archaeology. There are two lists, one each for the United States and Canada. Within these, arrangement is alphabetical by institution. There are multiple entries for universities that offer more than one graduate program (e.g., separate programs in classics and in archaeology). Each entry includes mailing address, telephone and fax numbers, degrees offered, a brief description of facilities available, and a list of current faculty and their research interests. There is an index of faculty members. The *Guide* has appeared somewhat irregularly over the years, with the last (eighth) in 1999.

1048. Association Internationale de Papyrologues. **Liste des membres.** Bruxelles: Association Internationale de Papyrologues, 1993. 29 pp.

The association (entry 1008) produces printed directories of its members on an irregular basis; this is the first since 1987. A more current directory may be found on the AIP Web site at www.ulb.ac.be/assoc/aip. The AIP membership includes most of the working papyrologists in the world, along with some other classicists and ancient historians who have an interest in the field. Entries, which are arranged alphabetically, consist of name, address, telephone and fax numbers, and e-mail address. Frequently they include institution and title as well. The directory also provides a list of institutes and centers for papyrological study.

1049. Association of Ancient Historians. **Directory of Ancient Historians in the United States.** Claremont, CA: Association of Ancient Historians, 1992– . URL: www. trentu.ca/ahc/aahdir.html.

Two printed versions of this directory appeared before it migrated to the Web in 1999. The directory lists members of the Association of Ancient Historians (entry 1010), which includes primarily classical historians, but also some specializing in the ancient Near East. Organization is by state, then university and department. Entries include degrees, research interests, and contact information.

1050. Classical Association of South Africa. **CASA Directory of Classical Scholars and Research for Higher Degrees in sub-Saharan Africa.** Pretoria: Classical Association of South Africa, 1993.

1051. Classical Association of South Africa. **Classical Scholars in sub-Saharan Africa.** URL: www.classics.und.ac.za/casadirectory/default.htm.

The printed directory was intended to appear every two years but has since been superseded by a Web-based directory. It includes university faculty and graduate students in sub-Saharan Africa. The Web version offers access by name (alphabetical listing) or country. Entries include name, address, telephone and fax numbers, e-mail addresses, academic credentials, and research interests.

1052. Classical Studies in Canadian Universities. Peterborough, ON: Dept. of Classical Studies, Trent University, 1998– . ISSN 1486–8334. LCCN 99–470036. URL: www.trentu.ca/academic/ahc/cscu.html.

This directory appeared as a biannual print publication from 1987 through 1995. Early editions were called *Classics in Canadian Universities.* Since 1998 it has been available as a database on the Web, and print has been discontinued. The present version lists Canadian universities offering courses in classics and university-level teachers of classics (emeriti appear in an appendix; those with part-time appointments are excluded). Arrangement is alphabetical by university; the directory supplies the mailing address, telephone and fax numbers, and a brief description of programs offered in classical studies. Faculty with classical interests are then listed by department. Faculty subentries include academic degrees, rank, research interests, and contact information. Research centers and museums of interest to Canadian classicists are noted in an appendix. The site offers an index by university; individuals may be found by using a browser find command.

1053. **Classicists in British Universities.** Cambridge: Classical Association, 198?–. LCCN 96–32209. URL: www.classicalassociation.org/CLASSICI/index.htm.

Formerly called *Classics Departments in British Universities,* this directory is issued irregularly. The latest edition is the eleventh, which appeared in 2004. The former title was somewhat more accurate, since the directory actually covers classics departments in colleges and universities in the United Kingdom. Entries are arranged alphabetically by institution and include the college address and phone number, the department name, contact name, and a description of the department. They also provide e-mail addresses for individual faculty members, when available. The online version is much like the printed one: full information is listed only under university departments, with a name index that provides abbreviated information plus a link to the departmental entry.

1054. Gaichas, Lawrence E., ed. **Directory of College and University Classicists in the United States and Canada.** 3rd ed. Pittsburgh: Classical Association of the Atlantic States, 1992. *Classical World* 85 (5): 385–658.

Gaichas's volume, the most comprehensive directory of North American classicists, appeared as a special issue of *Classical World* (entry 95). Its scope is actually wider than the title suggests, since it includes academic administrators, librarians, secondary school teachers, and independent scholars as well as college teachers. Gaichas took great pains to find and list as many classicists as possible. The directory contains more than 1,800 entries in an alphabetical arrangement. Each includes name, title, institution, address, phone and fax numbers, e-mail address, degrees (with institution and date), home address and phone number, and up to three fields of specialization. All information was supplied by the individuals. Indexes provide access by specialization and geographical location. This now badly dated directory retains some historical value, but those seeking current information will want to look elsewhere.

1055. **International Directory of Aegean Prehistorians.** 1984– . URL: http://classics. uc.edu/nestor/IDAP/isearch.lasso.

This irregular publication last appeared in print in 1995 (3rd ed.). While new printed editions may appear in the future, most will prefer the more current searchable Web directory maintained on the *Nestor* Web site (entry 61). The directory includes primarily archaeologists and historians with interests in the Aegean Bronze Age. The printed directory is browsable, while the online version can only be searched by name.

Author-Title Index

This index covers modern authors and titles; for ancient authors and their works, see the subject index. Reference is to entry numbers, except where otherwise noted. Page references are provided to works mentioned in the chapter headnotes.

Abbott, Evelyn, 713, 716n
Abbott, Kenneth Morgan, 767, 769
Abbreviationes, 963
Abbreviations in Greek Inscriptions, 967n
Abbreviations in Greek Inscriptions, Papyri, Manuscripts, and Early Printed Books, 967
Abréviations latines médiévales, 966
Accardi, Bernard, 884
ABS International Guide to Classical Studies, 56
Adkins, Arthur W. H., 320
Adkins, Lesley, 290, 291, 892
Adkins, Roy A., 290, 291, 892
Aerial Atlas of Ancient Crete, 432
Aegean Bronze Age, 462
AEGEANET, 175
Aeschylus, 640
Âge de transition: De la littérature romaine a la littérature chrétienne de 117 a 284 apres J.-C., 592
Aland, Barbara, 501
Aland, Kurt, 501
Albrecht, Michael von, 584, 586n, 592n, 593n,
Alcock, Susan, 439n
Alexander the Great: A Bibliography, 250
Alexander the Great: Historical Texts in Translation, 343
Alexanderreich auf prosopographischer Grundlage, 193
Alföldy, Géza, 191
Algra, Keimpe, 862
Allen, James T., 664
Allen, Joseph H., 526, 535n
Allen, T. W., 688n, 967n

Allen, W. Sydney, 482, 483
Allen and Greenough's New Latin Grammar for Schools and Colleges, 526, 531n, 534n
Allis, James B., 855
Alltag im Alten Rom, 317
Alte Geschichte in Studium und Unterricht, 281, 282
Amandry, Michel, 944
American Academy in Rome, 1027
American Center of the International Photographic Archive of Papyri, 1028, 1043n
American Classical League, 93n, 1003, 1021n
American Classical Studies, 1004n
American Journal of Ancient History, 73, 1007n
American Journal of Archaeology, 59n, 74
American Journal of Philology, 75
American Numismatic Society, 945n
American Philological Association, 45n, 126n, 439n, 725n, 807n, 854n, 1004, 1005n, 1006n, 1007n, 1018n, 1022n, 1023n, 1026n, 1045, 1046, 1047
American Philological Association Newsletter, 35n, 36n, 1004n
American Philosophical Association, 1022n
American School of Classical Studies at Athens, 105n, 1029
American Society of Greek and Latin Epigraphy, 1005
American Society of Papyrologists, 49n, 1006

Biblographie zu Plautus, 1976–1989, 808
Bibliographie zur Antiken Bilderspache, 547
Bibliographie zur antiken Sklaverei, 280
Bibliographie zur archäologischen Denkmälerkunde, 448
Bibliographie zur römischen Agrargeschichte, 259
Bibliographies on Plato, 1912–1930, 707
Bibliographisches Lexicon der gesammten Literatur der Griechen, 17
Bibliography of American Doctoral Dissertations in Classical Studies and Related Fields, 36
Bibliography of Ancient Ephesus, 267
Bibliography of Applied Numismatics in the Fields of Greek and Roman Archaeology and the Fine Arts, 943
Bibliography of Dissertations in Classical Studies, 37
Bibliography of Editions, Translations, and Commentary on Xenophon's Socratic Writings, 1600–Present, 739
Bibliography of Etruscan Culture and Archaeology, 1498–1981, 446
Bibliography of Greek Education and Related Topics, 247
Bibliography of Homeric Scholarship. Preliminary Edition, 1930–1970, 679
Bibliography of Lucretius, 788
Bibliography of Pindar, 1513–1966, 702
Bibliography of Roman Agriculture, 284
Bibliography of Persius, 801
Bibliography of Petronius, 803
Bibliography of Scholarship on Plautus, 809
Bibliography of the Poetics of Aristotle, 650
Bibliography of the Survival of the Classics, 988
Bibliography on Plato's Laws, Revised and Completed with an additional Bibliography on the Epinomis, 708
Bibliography on the "Essay on the Sublime," 694
Bibliography to Catullus, 763
Bibliography to Propertius, 817

Bibliography to the Ancient Medical Authors, 219
Bibliography to the Corpus Tibullianum, 817n, 832
Bibliotheca Classica Orientalis, 51
Bibliotheca Classica Selecta, 15n, 24n, 26n, 27
Bibliotheca Graeca, 12n, 13, 29n
Bibliotheca Graeca et Latina, 24
Bibliotheca Latina, 12n, 14, 29n
Bibliotheca Scriptorum Classicorum, 12, 19n, 29n
Bibliotheca Scriptorum Classicorum et Graecorum et Latinorum, 12n, 19, 20n
Bibliotheca Teubneriana Latina on CD-ROM, 583
Bickermann, E. J., 293, 311n
Bieber, Margarete, 601
Biers, William R., 456, 457
Bildlexikon zur Topographie des antiken Attika, 417, 418n
Biographical and Bibliographical Dictionary of the Italian Humanists and of the World of Classical Scholarship in Italy, 1300–1800, 991
Biographical Dictionary of Ancient Greek and Roman Women, 223
Biographical Dictionary of North American Classicists, 989
Biraschi, A. M., 735
Birch, Cordelia Margaret, 761
Birley, Anthony R., 194, 813
Birt, Theodor, 774n
Blackman, D. R., 828
Bischoff, Bernhard, 964, 968n
Blackwell Guide to Ancient Philosophy, 881
Blass, Friedrich, 527, 532, 533, 660n
Blegen, Carl W., 685n
Boardman, John, 286, 287, 288, 458
Bodel, John, 934, 935
Boeckh, August, 125n
Boisacq, Emile, 502
Bolletino di studi latini, 65
Boned Colera, Pilar, 489
Bonitz, H., 657
Bonser, Wilfrid, 248

Subject Index

Reference is to entry number, unless otherwise noted. Page references are provided for material covered in the chapter head notes.

About the Author

FRED W. JENKINS holds a doctorate in classical philology and a master's degree in library science from the University of Illinois. He is currently the head of collection management at the University of Dayton Libraries, and also teaches classics and ancient history. He has published numerous articles and reviews in the areas of Latin literature, papyrology, and library science.